Qualities of Life

Qualities of Life

Critical Choices for Americans

Volume VII

Lexington Books
D.C. Heath and Company
Lexington, Massachusetts
Toronto   London

Library of Congress Cataloging in Publication Data

Main entry under title:
   Qualities of life.

   (Critical choices for Americans; v. 7)
   Papers prepared for the Commission on Critical Choices for Americans.
   Includes index.
      1. United States—Civilization—1945-   —Addresses, essays, lectures.
   2. United States—Social conditions—1945-   —Addresses, essays, lectures.
   I. Logue, Edward J., 1921-   II. Commission on Critical Choices for
   Americans. III. Series.
   E169.12.Q23   309.1'73'092   75-44725
   ISBN 0-669-00417-0
                                          9-19-79

Published simultaneously in Canada.

Printed in the United States of America.

International Standard Book Number: 0-669-00417-0

Library of Congress Catalog Card Number: 75-44725

Foreword

The Commission on Critical Choices for Americans, a nationally representative, bipartisan group of forty-two prominent Americans, was brought together on a voluntary basis by Nelson A. Rockefeller. After assuming the Vice Presidency of the United States, Mr. Rockefeller, the chairman of the Commission, became an ex officio member. The Commission's assignment was to develop information and insights which would bring about a better understanding of the problems confronting America. The Commission sought to identify the critical choices that must be made if these problems are to be met.

The Commission on Critical Choices grew out of a New York State study of the Role of a Modern State in a Changing World. This was initiated by Mr. Rockefeller, who was then Governor of New York, to review the major changes taking place in federal-state relationships. It became evident, however, that the problems confronting New York State went beyond state boundaries and had national and international implications.

In bringing the Commission on Critical Choices together, Mr. Rockefeller said:

As we approach the 200th Anniversary of the founding of our Nation, it has become clear that institutions and values which have accounted for our astounding progress during the past two centuries are straining to cope with the massive problems of the current era. The increase in the tempo of change and the vastness and complexity of the wholly new situations which are evolving with accelerated change, create a widespread sense that our political and social system has serious inadequacies.

We can no longer continue to operate on the basis of reacting to crises, counting on crash programs and the expenditure of huge sums of money to solve our problems. We have got to understand and project present trends, to take command of the forces that are emerging, to extend our freedom and wellbeing as citizens and the future of other nations and peoples in the world.

Because of the complexity and interdependence of issues facing America and the world today, the Commission has organized its work into six panels, which emphasize the interrelationships of critical choices rather than treating each one in isolation.

The six panels are:

Panel I: Energy and its Relationship to Ecology, Economics and World Stability;

Panel II: Food, Health, World Population and Quality of Life;

Panel III: Raw Materials, Industrial Development, Capital Formation, Employment and World Trade;

Panel IV: International Trade and Monetary Systems, Inflation and the Relationships Among Differing Economic Systems;

Panel V: Change, National Security and Peace;

Panel VI: Quality of Life of Individuals and Communities in the U.S.A.

The Commission assigned, in these areas, more than 100 authorities to prepare expert studies in their fields of special competence. The Commission's work has been financed by The Third Century Corporation, a New York not-for-profit organization. The corporation has received contributions from individuals and foundations to advance the Commission's activities. The Commission is grateful to the Vincent Astor Foundation particularly for its contributions to the work of our Panel VI, "Quality of Life of Individuals and Communities in the U.S.A."

The Commission is determined to make available to the public these background studies and the reports of those panels which have completed their deliberations. The background studies are the work of the authors and do not necessarily represent the views of the Commission or its members.

This volume is one of the series of volumes the Commission will publish in the belief that it will contribute to the basic thought and foresight America will need in the future.

WILLIAM J. RONAN
Acting Chairman
Commission on Critical Choices
for Americans

Members of the Commission

Ex-Officio Members

THE HONORABLE NELSON A. ROCKEFELLER
The Vice President of the United States
  (Chairman of the Commission until
  February 28, 1975)

THE HONORABLE HENRY A. KISSINGER
The Secretary of State

THE HONORABLE MIKE MANSFIELD
  Majority Leader
  United States Senate
  (Member of the Commission until
  March 6, 1975)

THE HONORABLE HUGH SCOTT
  Minority Leader
  United States Senate

THE HONORABLE THOMAS P. O'NEILL, JR.
  Majority Leader
  United States House of Representatives

LEO CHERNE
Executive Director, Research Institute
of America, Inc.

JOHN S. FOSTER, JR.
Vice President for Energy Research
and Development, TRW, Inc.

LUTHER H. FOSTER
President, Tuskegee Institute

NANCY HANKS
Chairman, National Endowment for the Arts

BELTON KLEBERG JOHNSON
Texas Rancher and Businessman

CLARENCE B. JONES
Former Editor and Publisher,
The New York Amsterdam News

JOSEPH LANE KIRKLAND
Secretary—Treasurer, AFL-CIO

JOHN H. KNOWLES, M.D.
President, Rockefeller Foundation

DAVID S. LANDES
Leroy B. Williams Professor of History
and Political Science, Harvard University

MARY WELLS LAWRENCE
Chairman and Chief Executive Officer,
Wells, Rich, Greene, Inc.

SOL M. LINOWITZ
Senior Partner of Coudert Brothers

EDWARD J. LOGUE
Former President and Chief Executive Officer,
New York State Urban Development Corporation

CLARE BOOTHE LUCE
  Author; former Ambassador
  and Member of Congress

PAUL WINSTON McCRACKEN
  Professor of Business Administration,
  University of Michigan

DANIEL PATRICK MOYNIHAN
  Professor of Government
  Harvard University

BESS MYERSON
  Former Commissioner of Consumer Affairs,
  City of New York

WILLIAM S. PALEY
  Chairman of the Board
  Columbia Broadcasting System

RUSSELL W. PETERSON
  Chairman, Council on Environmental
  Quality

WILSON RILES
  Superintendent of Public Instruction,
  State of California

LAURANCE S. ROCKEFELLER
  Environmentalist and Businessman

OSCAR M. RUEBHAUSEN
  Partner, Debevoise, Plimpton, Lyons
  and Gates, New York

GEORGE P. SHULTZ
  President
  Bechtel Corporation

JOSEPH C. SWIDLER
  Partner, Leva, Hawes, Symington, Martin
  & Oppenheimer
  Former Chairman, Federal Power Commission

EDWARD TELLER
    Senior Research Fellow, Hoover Institution
    on War, Revolution and Peace,
    Stanford University

ARTHUR K. WATSON*
    Former Ambassador to France

MARINA VON NEUMANN WHITMAN
    Distinguished Public Service Professor
    of Economics, University of Pittsburgh

CARROLL L. WILSON
    Professor, Alfred P. Sloan
    School of Management,
    Massachusetts Institute of Technology

GEORGE D. WOODS
    Former President, World Bank

Members of the Commission served on the panels. In addition, others assisted
the panels.

BERNARD BERELSON
Senior Fellow
President Emeritus
The Population Council

C. FRED BERGSTEN
Senior Fellow
The Brookings Institution

ORVILLE G. BRIM, JR.
President
Foundation for Child Development

LESTER BROWN
President
Worldwatch Institute

LLOYD A. FREE
President
Institute for International Social Research

*Deceased

J. GEORGE HARRAR
Former President
Rockefeller Foundation

WALTER LEVY
Economic Consultant

PETER G. PETERSON
Chairman of the Board
Lehman Brothers

ELSPETH ROSTOW
Dean, Division of General and Comparative Studies
University of Texas

WALT W. ROSTOW
Professor of Economics and History
University of Texas

SYLVESTER L. WEAVER
Communications Consultant

JOHN G. WINGER
Vice President
Energy Economics Division
Chase Manhattan Bank

Preface

Concern for the quality of life for all Americans has reached a new level of awareness in this country. The comfortable belief has all but disappeared that with enough legislation and enough money, quality could become a reality for everyone. Americans, and particularly young people, are looking beyond the "standard of living" as the measurement of quality—they are searching for new meaning, new self-realization, and new purpose in their lives.

There is no GNP for the quality of life, for individuals or for a society. Quality in one individual's life can be, and often is, meaningless in another's. While we can and do measure the objective areas of quality of life—per capita income, level of education, employment status, health care, housing—the subjective elements of quality of life—the values, the attitudes, the philosophies by which we perceive quality—are much more elusive. We pursue happiness in very different ways.

"Quality of Life of Individuals and Communities in the U.S.A." has been the concern of the Commission's Panel VI. To help focus on the critical choices in this area, the Panel asked the twenty contributors to this volume for their insights and ideas. Their essays cover both the philosophic perceptions so deeply infused with the quality of life and the more pragmatic elements which most of us recognize as being in some way related to quality in our lives—the arts, education, employment, health, care of our poor and our aged. The Commission believes these essays will stimulate a new thoughtfulness as we strive, as a nation, for quality in all of our lives.

W.J.R.

Contents

List of Figures

List of Tables

Introduction

"Quality of Life" is an awesomely sweeping concept, involving a whole array of subjective as well as objective factors. It encompasses both those concerns traditionally associated with "standard of living" and much more amorphous questions of attitude, value, meaning, and purpose. To define "quality" even for an individual, then, is most difficult; to define it for the life of a society, perhaps, impossible. Nevertheless, we can and must try, for until we understand the curious mixture of affluence and discontent that characterizes so much of modern America, we can do little to encourage the pursuit of happiness among our citizens.

The essays collected in this volume offer a wide range of past and present perspectives on the very many qualities of our lives, and they fall into two generalized categories. In the opening chapters, the authors address themselves primarily to the central questions of what constituted "quality" in life. Their approaches reflect a variety of academic disciplines—political philosophy, cultural anthropology, religion, sociology—on the one hand, and popular perceptions that have surfaced through media, public opinion polls, and all the myths and mechanisms of our daily lives, on the other.

The contributors ask: What *is* the quality of life? How do we perceive it—or enjoy it? What contributes to it? Can we measure it? Edward J. Logue says: "The idea of America is choice, freedom to make critical choices. Americans have believed, perhaps more strongly than any other people, that it is their right to be able to make critical choices about their lives and the communities they live in. A place to live. A job to earn one's keep. Education to prepare for life. Health to maintain. The institutional arrangements—private and public—through which all of this will or will not be achieved. The place of the family."

Werner J. Dannhauser examines the concept of "the good life" as understood in classical and modern political philosophy, and Edwin Scott Gaustad considers the role of religion. James P. Spradley presents an anthropological perspective as he suggests that "American culture is currently undergoing a process of revitalization." Peter L. Berger discusses some reasons for the current interest in the quality of life; William H. Overholt and Herman Kahn point out that quality of life means totally different things within different social strata; Angus Campbell and Robert L. Kahn attempt to apply some measurements to the quality of life.

The second group of authors deal more specifically with personal and policy choices in areas in which most people would agree have some effect on the quality of life. Although not all subjects are included, the essays presented suggest a theme: With so much attention being focused on America's current and impending economic constraints, it is well to remember that many things which contribute to a better life do not necessarily require very large sums of money or draw heavily on scarce resources. Public and private policies which effectively use available resources and individual initiative can and do help improve the quality of our communities.

Two authors, David Gardner and William E. Webster, look at our educational system today. The former asks if the established or traditional universities are able to accommodate the growing demands for flexibility in higher education; the latter urges that career and vocational education be made more responsive to the labor requirements of industries and communities. Robert Dubin examines the relationships between working and living.

Two authors look at a fundamental challenge facing America: that a nation as rich as ours should be able to provide adequately for its poor, its aged, and its disabled. Richard P. Nathan studies federal income-security policy questions, and Robert M. Ball reviews this country's social security system from its inception.

Gilbert S. Omenn addresses a variety of significant and troubling ethical issues in medicine and biology—questions moving ever more to the forefront of our lives as we learn more and more about our health. Bess Myerson considers consumer credit to be a blessing and a burden to millions. She vigorously attacks credit company abuses and proposes remedies. Paul H. Weaver's topic is the media. Wolf Von Eckardt emphasizes the importance of art and careful design in our everyday surroundings.

In a remarkable personal statement, Charles H. Malik of Lebanon, the distinguished diplomat, educator, and world citizen, contributes an informal glimpse of his own humane philosophy. In conclusion, Daniel Patrick Moynihan says there are two immediate critical choices affecting our lives in our Bicentennial Year and beyond. "The first is how much growth we want; the second is how much government we want."

The Idea of America Is Choice

Edward J. Logue

Active concerns about the quality of life for individuals and communities led to the settling of the thirteen colonies and to the founding of this nation, to its unparalleled attractions to immigrants, and to the relative prosperity it enjoys today.

Europeans began coming to these shores over three centuries ago, confident that they could make choices, critical to them, about the quality of their lives and of the communities they would live in that were difficult or impossible to make elsewhere. That immigration continues with much the same hope and the source is now worldwide.

In a very basic sense, the idea of American is choice, freedom to make critical choices. Americans have believed, perhaps more strongly than any other people, that it was their right to be able to make the critical choices about their lives.

Why then, in this Bicentennial Year, do we need a report on critical choices for quality of life in America today? Some reasons suggest themselves.

First, because a bicentennial is a time for renewal, it is most appropriate that we renew our long-held conviction that we as Americans have a right to make the critical choices. That in itself is a critical choice.

Second, with the problems of inflation and recession and uncertainty about our course as a nation, we seem to have become doubtful about our ability as a nation to make effective critical choices about the quality of life for individuals and for communities in the United States.

Third, and very critical, there is new but increasing awareness that we cannot afford to make all the critical choices that, absent money constraints, we might

1

like to make. This awareness should force us to reexamine well-established expenditure patterns to see if they really make sense in the light of today's priorities.

Fourth, we must recognize that there has never been an equal freedom of choice for all Americans. Far from it. However, it is encouraging that even the difficult and seemingly unending struggle of minorities in America is not for separate rights and separate places, but for the freedom and the opportunity to make the same kinds of choices that other Americans make. The separatism, the desire for apartness that seem to be the goal in many other lands, is not what is concerning America's minorities today. This may be our best hope of actually achieving what we swear allegiance to: "one nation, indivisible, with liberty and justice for all."

Our problem and our challenge is to attempt to focus on those critical choices which will significantly affect the quality of life for individuals and for communities—without drowning in the particular or reaching out for utopian systems of thought and values, whether spiritual or secular, which we too easily and nostalgically think were once typical of the American past, rather than of some minor if articulate portion of it.

In this spirit we pay attention first to the urban environment, to the physical world that most of us spend most of our lives in.

Next we consider the situation of the disadvantaged people who live in the slum and blighted sections of our environment and to the handicaps they face in joining fully in the main stream of American life today.

The great 'overwhelming problem in our domestic life as a people is the divisiveness and discord and evil occasioned by the barriers that race erects among us.

If we believed it were possible, would not all of us, well nearly all of us, like to end, once and for all, the troubles that racial distinctions have brought into our society? Easier said than done. Complex to be sure.

But is this not the greatest critical choice of all in this society?

This chapter will focus on basic needs and interests which concern everyone: a place to live, a job to earn one's keep, education to prepare for life; the institutional arrangements—public and private—by which all of this will be done or not done; and lastly, the place of family in our society in the years ahead. I have placed greatest emphasis on questions relating to employment, because of a deeply held conviction that this is, among important choices, perhaps the most important. I have ignored the question of health only because it is to be dealt with elsewhere in this series of volumes. For the same reason, critical choices concerning cultural matters have not been dealt with. Any statement less than encyclopedic is bound to be selective. Others will feel free to add other areas for concern.

Urban Growth and Community Development

There is currently much debate on the desirability of a "zero-growth" policy in the United States. Certainly the problems of population growth measured against projections of food supply raise questions of the gravest concern. However, we cannot ignore the fact that substantial population growth in the United States is inevitable for the rest of this century and probably beyond. One of the most important critical choices confronting Americans about the quality of life for individuals and communities is how we are going to provide for this growth.

Population Growth. In a very basic sense, the debate over growth-no growth is academic. The population of the United States will increase by almost 25 percent, or by more than fifty million persons by the end of this century. Despite a declining birthrate, America is adding to its numbers at the rate of a community the size of Philadelphia every year. Put another way, this is equivalent to adding to the Union by the year 2000 a population equal to the three states with the largest populations: California, New York, and Texas.

There is little if anything which can be done to alter this anticipated growth. Even if the birthrate continues to decline, the average life expectancy will continue to go up. For some time the birthrate will exceed the death rate, making increase inevitable.

If for the first time in our history we were to shut off immigration, growth would be significantly reduced. A critical choice is made by assuming that will not happen.

The real question is not how is this coming growth to be avoided but how it is to be accommodated. These fifty million additional Americans should have the opportunity to live in decent housing, to obtain a useful education, and to engage in productive, self-supporting employment. To make such opportunities available, there must be considerable economic growth and substantial community development. The alternative is for more to share less or for fewer workers to support more of their neighbors.

The form, shape, and nature of this growth will do much to determine the quality of life for individuals and communities in America for the rest of this century. The future shape of America is not foreordained.

Growth Patterns. Based on American experience to date, the anticipated population growth will be overwhelmingly urban in nature, following a trend established more than a century ago. Despite a recently reported decline in population in five out of eight of the nation's largest metropolitan areas, a continuation of urban growth overall is to be expected.

This growth can take many different forms. It can be guided by governmental action or evolve as it has to date as the haphazard consequence of the interaction of varied public and private forces.

At the present time, there is no considered national urban growth *policy*. There is, however, a national urban growth *pattern* which has been operating for thirty years at least.

The Megalopolis. Since the end of World War II, the all-but-universal pattern of urban growth has been incremental, on the periphery of already built-up urban areas. The pattern has of course varied in dimensions and intensity from one part of the country to another. The greatest surge of development has taken place in the four huge American megalopolises (Boston-Washington, Florida-Gulf Coast, California Coast, and the shores of the Great Lakes). The interior portions of the country have experienced relative declines which have been more pronounced in colder climes. The relatively greater growth in the warmer areas has become so pronounced as to give that portion of the country a new name, "The Sun Belt!"

Suburban Expansion in Numbers and Influence

Most cities were full up to their boundaries shortly after World War II. Most of them could not expand these boundaries, although some such as Houston could. Growth has thus taken place primarily in suburbs which were politically separate communities, a fact with profound consequences for patterns of development in housing, industry, commerce, and in the tax base.

Suburbanites now constitute the largest single geographically-based grouping in our population—a new fact of enormous political significance.

Thirty years ago when suburban totals were smaller, most of the population dwelt in cities and most of the remainder in rural areas. The layout of congressional and legislative district boundaries tended to give excessive legislative power to rural interest at the expense of city dwellers. City interests finally brought the question to the courts on constitutional grounds, and in a series of Supreme Court decisions on apportionment questions, the principle of "one man, one vote" was established and elaborated.

While this long drawn-out process was underway, many cities gradually lost population to the suburbs. This resulted in the locus of legislative power being shifted sharply, not to the cities but to the suburbs, where it is likely to remain for many years to come.

The largest single geographically-affiliated voting block in the country today is that of the suburbanites. It may soon become an absolute majority. This means that it will be difficult if not impossible to pass legislation for many worthy purposes if such legislation is regarded as hostile to suburban interests.

A consideration of that aspect of any proposed legislation has become essential.

Despite its evident and perhaps inevitable popularity, suburbia has its share of critics who complain about wasteful use of land, unnecessarily expensive infrastructure costs for roads, utilities, and other public services. Increasing concern is being expressed that suburbia is developing strong patterns of racial and economic segregation.

The suburban growth has been primarily of younger middle-income families, overwhelmingly white. Shopping centers and jobs have tended to follow them outside the city.

One troubling result, against a nearly worldwide trend in the opposite direction, has been loss of vitality and spreading decay in the central areas of too many of our older cities. Concern is also being heard about decreasing open space and lack of adequate park and recreation areas in expanding metropolitan areas.

Appeal of the Suburban Alternative. However, whatever its drawbacks may be, the way of life represented by suburban sprawl has many advantages and legions of supporters. In a huge diverse country, suburbanization appears, with a minimum of direct federal intervention, to have provided tens of millions of Americans with a way of life they find congenial. In physical and material terms, the quality of life in suburbia is very highly regarded by suburbanites. The single-family detached house on its own plot of land is the prevailing residential pattern. Safe, pleasant neighborhoods with most of the necessities and conveniences near at hand, are regarded as constituting the good life. Increasingly they are the dominant American way of life. The blandness of suburban life seems to worry social critics more than suburbanites. Jobs are following people to the suburbs. Local government seems closer and more responsive than the city halls left behind.

Forty percent of American whites and 16 percent of American blacks live in suburbs now. Undoubtedly, huge numbers of the inner city population would like to move to suburbia just as soon as they could. Although 16 percent of American blacks live in suburbs, the suburban population is still more than 95 percent white.

This dominant growth pattern has been largely unplanned and has given maximum scope to private enterprise. However, there has been a strong underpinning of federal support—FHA insured mortgages and federally-financed road building for example. Federal income tax credits for both mortgage interest payments and local property taxes have directly aided the suburban boom.

No critical choices can effectively be adopted and implemented if they are perceived to have a clearly adverse impact on the present suburban life style, in the absence of some overriding national crisis. This fact, all but instinctively understood by practicing politicians, often eludes more academic analysts.

Some Suburban Problems. Nevertheless, all is not well in suburbia. Its life style is threatened by:

1. Escalating local property taxes (voter rejection of initial school budgets has become almost commonplace in some areas).
2. Rising costs of maintaining the life style of the suburban household—two cars, energy, etc.
3. The rising costs of infrastructure caused by sprawl development are threatening to exceed the financial capacity of local governments. Once a certain scale of suburban development and population increase has passed, there is a need for a whole new wave of heavy capital investment. Water supply and sewage treatment plants, police and fire services, and traffic regulations are some major examples. Just as suburban communities needed major state financial assistance in school construction programs, they will need similar state aid particularly for pollution control and environmental protection.
4. Suburbia is particularly vulnerable to a recurrence of the energy crisis in terms of added cost or of shortages. Suburbanites consume more energy than city dwellers, and alternative energy consumption patterns may not be as readily available as they are for city dwellers.

A continuation of present suburban growth patterns is likely to present even greater difficulties. Increasing costs of land, labor, and materials are pricing an ever larger percentage of families out of the new housing market. In fact, there is evidence that the long preferred development pattern of a single-family house on its own, ever larger, lot is losing out in many suburban communities to apartments and mobile homes. Indeed, a full 20 percent of housing starts in the last five years in this country have been mobile homes.

Market forces are beginning to alter the suburban growth patterns of the last thirty years in the direction of less reliance on single-family housing, and more reliance on multifamily housing. It is still prudent to assume the single-family detached house is the *preferred* solution. However, there is increasing evidence that the inner suburbs are beginning to resemble more and more the outer city neighborhoods and to develop many of the same problems.

America's postwar growth patterns developed by something other than a rational public decision-making process. The pent-up housing demands created by the war and the depression were satisfied to a large degree by huge incremental expansions following established patterns.

As the cities filled up, growth went to the inner then the outer suburbs and finally into areas that in 1945 were almost entirely rural and agricultural. The growth pattern in a particular metropolitan area was channeled more by existing conditions, particularly geographical facts, than by planning considerations.

This rather spectacular urban growth phenomenon was accomplished by large numbers of local relatively small entrepreneurs (i.e., homebuilders) working with a very large number of suburban local governmental jurisdictions where they were usually personally known. That once effective alliance is in some disarray today. The extra impact inflation has had on housing has crippled the homebuilders. Increasing concern among suburban residents about rising costs of local government has led local officials to establish larger lot zoning and other restrictive practices which cut down homebuilding opportunities.

Consequences of Continuing the Incremental Growth Pattern

Given the momentum of the existing growth system and the political difficulties in securing approval of an alternate system, there are nonetheless sufficient concerns with it so that some questions need to be examined.

1. Is continued incremental growth economically feasible?
2. Is it environmentally desirable?
3. What is its impact on the quality of life for individuals and communities?

Economic Feasibility. There can be serious doubts about whether a continuation of present urban growth patterns is economically feasible. Particularly in the megalopolises, ever more complicated and expensive support systems seem to be required. Air and water pollution control measures for the largest urban concentrations have price tags that indicate serious diseconomies of scale. So do transportation and utility systems. Only to a degree are these costs offset by savings in the cost of energy attributable to greater urban densities.

Land costs also tend to be higher in denser areas. Not only does this lead to higher housing and other costs, but it creates difficulties in the financing of purchases of land intended for public use. Taken to extremes this can lead to the golf-net phenomenon which has proliferated in the Tokyo-Osaka megalopolis. Golf-nets are the Japanese version of driving ranges. They are in such abundance because they substitute for golf courses, which simply cannot multiply to meet demand because of land costs and the difficulties of assembling land.

The larger and more complex an urban society becomes, the more capital investment it is likely to require, the less its inhabitants can do for themselves and the more they have to have done for them. However, the data do not presently exist on which economic calculations can be made for a variety of urban growth alternatives. There is no technical obstacle blocking the way, just a lack of resources and commitment.

A basic critical choice involves the comparative cost of continuing as we were as against possible alternatives. Some priority should now be given to the economic research and cost analysis which would inform such choices. We just do not know enough.

Environmental Desirability. The question of the desirability of continuing present growth patterns from an environmental standpoint all but answers itself.

Almost every major effort to produce the added service capability that can handle increased growth is challenged in the courts on environmental grounds. Power plants are only the most large-scale example. Airports are another.

Without attempting to comment on individual environmental protests, it is clear that they have become a major factor to contend with and will have an impact on our existing policies all by themselves.

However, there can be little question that continuing growth will make it more difficult to preserve, let alone increase, environmental amenity in built-up urban areas. Open land, fresh air and water will be pushed further and further away from more and more of the urban population.

Impact on Quality of Life. It is hard to see how longer journeys to work, or continuing decline of the central city, increased pollution, much higher taxes to pay, less access to open space—all likely results of continuing incremental peripheral urban growth—are going to be offset by greater diversity, perhaps more job opportunities. Whether considered in terms of individuals or communities, it is likely that the pains and costs of continuing as we are will outweigh the pleasures and the savings.

It is important to acknowledge here, too, that hard data on these pleasures and pains, these costs and savings do not exist. However, there is more than enough doubt about continuing as we are doing so that it is timely to consider seriously a vigorously implemented national urban growth policy.

An awesome collection of public and private interests are deeply involved in carrying out an urban development pattern based on incremental growth on the periphery of settled areas. It seems unlikely that a positive political consensus for a rapid and sharp change in these patterns of such is likely in the remainder of this century.

This is not because these interests are committed consciously as a result of deliberate thought and consideration of alternatives. They cannot even be considered to be consciously associated groups. Rather they are interacting in what appears to them to be a perfectly natural way given the absence of a clearly defined and determined alternate growth policy.

Given the relative satisfaction of suburbanites with their way of life, and their political importance in the nation, a frontal assault on current urban growth patterns is unlikely to be effective, assuming it were desirable. Nonetheless, there is sufficient concern in the suburbs so that the subject is actively being discussed, with no clear result yet emerging.

Urban Growth

European Urban Growth Experience. We should take considerable interest in and comfort from the fact that other democracies, particularly the countries of northern and western Europe, have devised urban growth policies and programs which seem to have been quite effective. This fact is not well enough known, even among otherwise well informed Americans. As a result, there is too great a tendency, particularly among academicians, to view the urban problem as insoluble by public action.

Recognizing both this concern and this limitation, it is desirable to consider alternative urban growth and community development policies and land use control programs which can lessen the harmful impact of suburban sprawl. The respective roles of various levels of government and of the private sector need to be examined. Active effective citizen participation in urban growth and community development decisions is not only essential and desirable, it is also inevitable.

Critical Choices for Urban Growth. Since substantial population growth appears inevitable, should there be a national Urban Growth Policy supported by a strong congressional and Administration commitment? Or: Should America continue its present policy of no national Urban Growth Policy and rely on effective state, regional, metropolitan or municipal urban growth policy? Or: Should there be a conscious effort to rely on the private sector and individual initiative, while at the same time pursuing limited purpose policy goals, such as in transportation or in environmental protection, hopefully with some built-in systems for calculating their impact on urban growth.

Various Urban Growth Alternatives

Anticipated urban growth can be dealt with in a variety of ways and in a variety of combinations with heavy or light reliance on governmental participation and private sector involvement depending upon the policies and programs selected.

Expected urban growth could be accommodated by one or more of the following public policies, taken alone or in combination:

1. Incremental peripheral expansion on the edge of built-up urban areas.
2. Intensified use of existing urbanized land.
3. Free-standing new cities.
4. Satellite new towns.
5. Planned expansion of presently stagnant existing communities.
6. Stringent restrictions on growth of existing megalopolitan areas and "deep" subsidies for development of neglected or underdeveloped regions.
7. Active large-scale programs for the preservation of open land on the periphery of settled urban areas.
8. Active environmental protection policies which also have the side effects of (7) above of discouraging incremental peripheral growth.
9. Development of Metropolitan Transportation Policies, which are basically

guided by carefully articulated urban growth policies rather than mere extrapolations of present urban growth policy as is the usual practice.

Even a casual examination of these alternatives should convince one that no one choice is possible but that a combination is indeed possible. Put another way, there are no urban growth panaceas, no one magic solution. The question and the choice, therefore, is what should the mix be. However, it is useful to explore each of the alternatives.

1. Incremental Peripheral Expansion. Continued growth on the edge of already developed urban areas is the easy established way to accommodate expected and unavoidable growth. It is now established as the normal way for metropolitan growth to take place. Subject to the vagaries of individual suburban community land use and development controls, it creates relatively little political and social tension. It has been acceptable and, though less so now, has not been supplanted. Though wasteful of land and other scarce resources and eventually expensive for infrastructure, it requires the least commitment to a thoughtful concern for the future implications of routine decisions.

It encourages further deterioration of the central cities and perhaps most importantly it tends to promote racial and economic segregation between city and suburb, thereby sowing the seeds for future domestic strife.

This choice must be examined openly and objectively, recognizing its strengths and weaknesses and the possibility for adjustments rather than fundamental change.

The principal mechanism for controlling this growth pattern has been zoning, which has been getting more and more restrictive. Zoning can be an effective land-use and urban growth tool provided it is grounded in sound comprehensive physical planning which is too seldom the case.

Incremental peripheral growth is likely to remain our basic pattern, however shortsighted it may be. The opportunities for critical choices lie in the development of attractive alternatives which will act as modifiers to the basic pattern.

2. Intensified Use of Existing Urbanized Land. One way to diminish urban sprawl is to increase the density of already urbanized areas. Some of suburbia is already experiencing the development of apartments and town (row) houses. High-rise apartment construction in the cities and their "inner suburbs" is on the increase for nearly all income groups. There seems little reason to object to increased density in the suburbs, particularly if coordinated with transportation and shopping facilities. The present trends may be expected to continue and indeed to accelerate. However, serious questions have been raised about the desirability of high-rise apartment buildings, particularly for families with young children.

If increased density is taken simply to mean ever higher buildings with only a sterile relation to the land on which they are located, serious doubts arise. If on the other hand the effort is to devise greater density while preserving a human scale and a sense of community, the opportunities can be very great indeed. Mixed use development where housing is combined with schools, day care centers, stores, and factories could be particularly helpful in revitalizing central cities.

In our older cities it is quite common to find a thickening ring of slum and blighted neighborhoods around the central business district. Abandonment of property is rising. Often the land is clear but idle. Yet the area is served with utilities and public transit, which must be built from scratch on peripheral sites.

Making new development on such sites attractive to potential occupants and developers should become a high priority for all those who believe the good health and order of our society as a whole requires renewed vitality in our central cities. Many successful urban renewal projects show what can be achieved. Others reveal pitfalls which can be avoided. A more intense use of such land can do much to channel urban growth in desirable ways.

3. Free-Standing New Cities. The concept of creating an economically self-supporting new city (population 250,000 or more) in a previously undeveloped or underdeveloped area holds much interest for many urban development theorists.

The idea that a whole new city, making intensive use of the latest technology in building and maintaining public services, in industrial production, communication, and housing has much appeal at a time when there is so much despair about the future of established cities and when the latest technology is introduced with difficulty and incrementally rather than comprehensively.

However, it must be recognized that sites for such a city are hard to come by in the United States today and that it is difficult indeed to guarantee an economic base that will provide the core source of employment that will generate enough income to make the community and its inhabitants self-supporting. Perhaps the most likely economic basis would result from a comprehensive long-term commitment to increase dramatically domestic sources of energy. (Although not strong on urban design and amenity, the three wartime cities created by the Manhattan project are an example of the kind of economic base commitment a new city requires.)

It must be recognized that the "front end" investment (i.e., cash out before revenue in) is relatively high and that the period of negative cash flow is likely to be prolonged. It is unlikely to be financially viable without either a government equity contribution or government guaranteed financing.

The potential benefits *and* costs of a major city-creating program are so great it would probably be worth while to undertake the preparation of prototypical economic and physical development models. Such modeling should help determine whether this complex alternative should be pursued.

4. Satellite New Towns. A satellite new town is a community of from 25,000 to 100,000 population usually located just beyond the outer developed edge of a metropolitan area. While usually attempting to provide through industrial development a self-sustaining economic base, it relies on the central city for many services, as suburban communities usually do.

The appeal of the satellite new town is that it makes for less wasteful use of land and saves on infrastructure costs. It also makes it far easier to establish and maintain racially open but economically balanced housing patterns when that is proving continually difficult to do in established suburbs. Every resident is a volunteer. There are no existing occupancy patterns to change. The environmental impact should be quite positive.

On the negative side are heavy required front-end investment and a lengthy period of negative cash flow. In addition, the planning controls and red tape requirements are more cumbersome than private developers are accustomed to. The federal government has been cautious in its role in the United States New Towns Program. Most of the federally-funded new towns are in deep financial trouble. Unfortunately, the lead time and front-end investment requirements seem to mandate some active federal or perhaps state involvement. This is thoroughly understood in other nations following a new town approach.

There is considerable, quite successful experience with satellite new towns in many countries. The efforts in Scandinavia and the United Kingdom are particularly interesting.

Right after World War II the British launched a new town development program. Over twenty-five are substantially completed with well over one million residents and hundreds of thousands of new jobs. They have limited overspill from London, helped preserve the Green Belt, and provide well-developed sites for industry—which many American companies have found quite attractive.

Around the turn of the century, the Stockholm municipal corporation acquired most of the undeveloped land in a substantial area around the city. After World War II, a series of satellite new towns, primarily residential, were built on this land, surrounded by ample open space and connected to Stockholm by rapid rail transit.

Most Americans who have seen these new communities or others, such as the beautiful child-oriented new town of Tapiola outside Helsinki, come away convinced that America could profit greatly by following these examples.

Satellite new towns represent a clear alternative to incremental suburban growth. Particularly, they offer the opportunity to develop fair share housing programs, without the necessity of altering existing housing occupancy patterns, since all residents are volunteers.

Many experienced observers believe that the federal New Towns Program of 1968 has not been given a fair trial by the federal government. Authorized appropriations have not been sought and the program has had a low priority within the Department of Housing and Urban Development. Success elsewhere suggests this is a choice which should be pursued.

5. Planned Expansion of Presently Stagnant Existing Communities. Urban growth has taken place very unevenly in the United States and indeed in much of the rest of the world. This uneven pattern of growth has resulted in a declining population in much of the Northeast and Midwest outside the megalopolises. Hundreds of cities and towns in these states have schools, water, sewer, and other municipal services which are being used at far less than capacity. Furthermore, increases in the capacity of these services would cost far less than starting from scratch.

While the reasons for decline are varied and complex, there has been no massive effort to redress the balance as, for example, is being done in the United Kingdom with its "extended" towns programs, which grew out of a recognition of the problems of declining communities and of the opportunities, nonetheless, which they represented.

A critical choice confronting America today is whether urban growth policies should be adopted which would encourage revitalization and expansion of the older declining communities as one important means of dealing with anticipated population growth during the remainder of this century. There is every reason to believe this alternative could be quite popular.

However, it must be recognized that as with free-standing new cities and satellite new towns, the economic base is important. The European urban growth programs all have as a common element a requirement that governmental permission is necessary for a change in industrial location. Is that a critical choice we are prepared to make?

6. Stringent Restrictions on Growth of Existing Megalopolitan Areas. The simplest way to limit urban growth in overdeveloping areas is to impose a short- or long-range moratorium on new construction. Such a policy if effective would generate market pressures, not now present, in favor of other solutions, most likely the revitalization of presently declining areas. As a theoretical proposition, it probably should be carefully studied as a critical choice and it probably should be declined.

There are growing urban areas in South America and South and Southeast Asia where a ban on further growth is probably highly desirable. However, no nation except *perhaps* China has been able to control effectively population growth in its major urban centers. The Soviet Union has attempted for over fifty years to control the size of Moscow. In the process it has raised its growth limit targets from a population of three million to a population of eight million!

In America such a policy would be economically destructive and politically impossible. It would be regarded as overkill.

If, however, a total ban on incremental development is ruled out, it is important to understand that a critical choice has nonetheless been made. Alternative forms of accommodating urban growth will have to compete, at a disadvantage, with the established system. That strongly suggests that if the critical choice is made to attempt to alter and diversify existing urban growth systems, a system of incentives will be required.

7. Active Large-Scale Programs for the Preservation of Open Land. The constituency in America is limited for a British type of land use control which requires a planning permission before any significant change in land use. This is so despite the fact that it is probably the most effective way to channel metropolitan growth.

However, there is rapidly growing concern in the United States about the preservation of open land and increasing the size and nearness (accessibility) of land available for park and recreational use. Preservation of existing open land on the suburban fringes will reduce pollution and sprawl while promoting orderly and balanced growth. Open land can be preserved through public ownership for park and recreational uses. In addition, through agricultural zoning and federal income and estate tax incentives, as well as state and local ones, it is possible to preserve large tracts of land now in agricultural or other open land use. The use of this alternative is often popular and seems to be growing.

8. Active Environmental Protection Policies. The preservation of wetlands and estuaries, the protection of scenic vistas, the effective restriction of development in zones of air, water, or noise pollution, protection of slope lands, creation of wildlife sanctuaries, fly ways, and many more aspects of environmental protection undertaken primarily for environmental purposes could have massive impact on urban growth and development patterns. Given recent experience, it is entirely possible that the presentation and acceptance of such critical choices is more likely than direct efforts to establish urban growth patterns as such.

9. Development of Metropolitan Transportation Policies. Urban growth patterns have often been influenced decisively by transportation policies. Early commuter rail lines determined the first patterns of suburban development. The Paoli local on the mainline of the Pennsylvania Railroad west of Philadelphia is only the best known example. There are dozens of others.

In recent times, the emphasis has shifted to highways, and massive federal aid has flowed into highway building. A decision to provide increased federal and state aid for highways while denying such aid to mass transit leads to or assists in spread out car-oriented housing development, causes mass transit to suffer competitive and financial disadvantages, and over time decisively impacts metropolitan growth patterns. It also encourages free-standing suburban shopping centers with free parking, at considerable cost to downtown development. It encourages a car-oriented journey to work by factory workers.

In the last few years, there has been the beginning of a reversal of this pattern, but it is too early for it to have had any significant impact on growth and development patterns. This is unlike Tokyo, where a deliberate concentration of rapid transit, bus, and rail stops has led to strikingly visible urban development concentrations within Tokyo but away from the traditional center of the city.

With the tremendous increase in the cost of energy and the need to reduce excessive dependence on energy imports, there are now additional incentives to promote energy-saving transportation policies which can have a decided impact on the direction of urban growth policies, hopefully an impact which has been considered carefully and actively sought rather than accidentally achieved.

There appears to be increasing support for mass transit, but no agreement on the optimum level of technology to be applied. Financing systems for both capital and operating expense of mass transit are in disarray. Successful efforts would alter growth patterns by promoting clustered, denser development as an alternative to suburban sprawl.

Urban Growth—A Summing Up

We have examined critical choices concerning the ways we as a nation shall accommodate inevitable urban growth.

Incremental growth on the periphery though increasingly challenged will continue. However, its momentum will slow under the combined pressures of increased costs, the opposition of suburban residents, and increased environmental concerns. These indirect, localized methods of limiting peripheral growth are likely to expand in scale. It is not unlikely that they will, by blunting the established pattern, encourage alternative patterns and the public support required for their implementation.

In addition, it is likely that we shall greatly increase support for the preservation of peripheral open land. State governments are showing increasing interest in property and estate tax incentives to limit the development of private land without putting it in public ownership. Local governments are showing increasing sophistication about making use of these state provided tools. In making such choices, state and local governments have opted against the long-held conviction that growth was the critical measure of community progress.

We may take some comfort, perhaps, in the fact that existing growth patterns will be altered. But not too much! The trends under way will only make suburban housing more costly and therefore economically more segregated. There is also no real evidence of a deep concern about present urban-suburban patterns of racial segregation in housing.

Larger open space programs and a shifting of transportation priorities to mass transit over individual transit will be useful in providing more balanced and more orderly urban growth. However, in and of themselves, they will do little to open housing opportunities or to provide incentives for more positive and direct alternative forms of urban growth.

Therefore, we return to consideration of programs promoting free-standing new cities, satellite new towns, or expanded existing towns, singly or in combination. Free-standing new cities have limited applicability to the American contemporary scene. Except for new locations for extraction, processing or manufacturing industries, they have limited potential and limited appeal. Satellite new towns, on the other hand, do represent a tested, attractive *partial* alternative to urban sprawl. Potential, feasible sites exist on the outer edges of almost every metropolitan area (and a few more exist within cities in undeveloped or underdeveloped sites). Perhaps even more important are programs which build on an established if stagnant urban base. This approach could have wide political appeal.

For any of the three positive efforts to encourage new growth patterns directly, government assistance will be required. Assistance can take the form of mandatory allocations of industrial location, which we probably will not do; or local, state, and federal tax incentives, which we have done but never in an orderly way; or pure promotional efforts which rarely work. It is at the incentive level that more work must be done to identify what it takes to encourage the development of an economic base for better balanced urban growth.

We have considerable experience in America of direct federal intervention for domestic policy objectives and also experience with purely state or local or private initiative and responsibility. Since urban growth policy today is made by all these sources, it is perhaps a prudent choice to continue to utilize such a mix but with a clearer perception of what our policy objectives are.

Perhaps most importantly we need to establish urban growth policy guidelines at the national, state, and local level, to report annually our successes and failures in reaching those goals, and to establish systems for evaluating particular, significant public and private actions as to their impact on urban growth objectives. We do that now in a variety of areas of public concern. Perhaps it is time we made ourselves more aware of the consequences of our decisions on this land of ours.

Our basic focus thus far has been on growth outside cities. We now turn our attention to the urban core.

Central Cities

The years since World War II have not been kind to America's central cities. Federal housing policies and the popularity and easy availability of suburban housing drained older city neighborhoods of much of their vitality. Central business districts, particularly their shopping areas, lost out heavily to suburban shopping centers with free parking. The increasing use of the car for commuting and the increased difficulties of entering the city have led to ever increasing development of suburban office parks. The role of the city as the location of the factory has been seriously eroded by modern production technology which puts a very heavy premium on the availability of highly flexible one-story manufacturing space, surrounded by parking lots for the employees. Even the role of port cities has been changed as the shift to containerization required large back-up space usually not available in older port areas.

Finally, and perhaps most seriously, the central city has been adversely affected by dramatic changes in the nature of the population. Quietly, without much warning, millions of middle- and lower-middle-income young white families with children began leaving the city in ever larger numbers shortly after World War II. These changes have taken place on a dramatic scale with incredible swiftness. As the whites removed to the suburbs, their places were taken in large part by low-income disadvantaged minority families, who had little preparation for contemporary city life, and had few of the skills necessary to earn enough to provide them with a decent standard of living.

The unskilled broad back jobs which supported earlier generations of immigrants were disappearing. Many were unprepared for the jobs which were available. As consumers they had too little income to support the central city shopping areas.

The cities began to suffer an erosion of their economic base, accompanied by spreading slums and blight. Yet they were also faced with increased demands for municipal services by a population less and less able to pay for them.

Central city school systems once prided themselves on their ability both to educate the middle class and to prepare newly immigrant children for life in America. Gradually, then swiftly, in the central cities of much of the country, the middle class abandoned the city schools for the suburbs. Gradually and then more quickly their places were taken by minority children, many of them from poor families, often ill-prepared for city life.

The experience of change in the composition of the pupil population was not a new experience for most central city school systems. Most had had considerable experience with such change and prided themselves on their success in educating each new wave of immigrants. This time, however, the experience was different. The children and perhaps more importantly their parents were less prepared. Perhaps most importantly the prospects of successful entry into the mainstream seemed much less likely. The increasing break up of the family and increased welfare dependency only made matters worse. The schools were finding themselves unable to reach satisfactory levels of achievement in the basic learning skills. Lack of discipline and safety became major concerns. Hopelessness and alienation seemed too close to becoming the order of the day in the schools in the slums.

In the sixties, a variety of governmental programs, mostly federal, were created to assist the schools, their pupils and the parents in coping with the problems of acquiring the basic learning skills. There is little agreement that these efforts have been successful. There is even less about what are the root causes of the problem and what would be effective remedies.

However, there does seem to be a spreading view that before the child's progress in school can be improved, the problem of poverty, dependency, and alienation in the home must be dealt with first. It is necessary immediately to say there is no consensus, even among those subscribing to that view, about what program or combination of programs could alter the home condition.

It would seem critically important that through research and pilot experiment this matter be pursued at all levels of government and of the educational system.

Federal Aid for Slum Clearance and Urban Renewal

With rare and insignificant exception, local government made no serious and successful effort to cope with municipal slums and blight. Municipal efforts were more effective at raising standards to prevent recurrence. Finally, a bipartisan coalition in the Congress passed legislation creating a national program.

Beginning in 1949, the federal government accepted a certain responsibility for the physical renewal of central cities through the urban renewal program. There is considerable controversy about whether those programs were effective. One significant indication of merit is that requests for federal renewal funds kept increasing both in number of communities and projects as well as dollars sought. In any event, it is clear that with few exceptions, federal funds were seldom available in sufficient quantities to be applied comprehensively for the renewal of central cities. There were unending and widespread complaints about federal red tape. Federally-aided urban renewal had a dominant impact in only a handful of communities. The investment and disinvestment decisions that had such an impact on central cities were predominantly private.

In 1974 a whole new approach to federal assistance for community development was adopted. Called the "block grant" program it mandated local decision-making and purported to minimize red tape. Serious doubts were expressed about the adequacy of federal funding: $12.75 per capita per year does not seem like enough to do a meaningful community development effort in New York City.

On the basis of present trends and levels of federal aid, there is little reason to believe that troubled central cities will be able to reverse their present period of decline. That raises some important questions.

Critical Choices for Central Cities

Are America's urban centers important to its way of life? Should policies be adopted and programs carried out which will endeavor to restore the central cities to economic health? Inevitably this will mean that any such choice will channel investment, public and private, into the central cities on a preferential basis. Before such a choice is made, the country will have to be persuaded that cities are worth saving, that they have a contribution to make to life in America—a contribution which is as important to suburbanites as to central city residents.

If a basic decision in favor of strengthening central cities were to be made, a whole series of other critical choices would have to follow concerning the role of various levels of government and of the private sector.

Most, though by no means all, recent experiences in the revitalization of central cities have shown the process to be cumbersome and ineffective. There are of course many striking exceptions and there is no agreement on where the responsibility lies for the failure to achieve better results on the whole. It should, however, be clear that the normal operations of private enterprise cannot be relied on to do the job without public sector policy guidance and heavy financial incentives of one sort or another. These financial incentives can be direct or indirect and can involve any or all levels of government.

One critical choice already taken in the Twin Cities area is to metropolitanize the property tax base so that suburban development tax income is shared by the central city. This has apparently had a salutary effect on both development pressures and city revenues.

The central city is composed of many parts. The central business districts in their decline and the ghettos in their expansion seem typical. Another major area of concern is the flight of industry with its jobs and taxes from the city.

Central Business Districts

The centers of cities tend to exemplify and symbolize the urban life style. City centers have been the place of exchange for goods and services and ideas, the seat of government, the center of culture. Until recently it was widely assumed that vital urban centers were synonomous with an advanced civilization. "Spread City" has made that assumption less certain.

For traditional reasons and because of the vast investment in them, most city central business districts have suffered serious economic erosion and loss of vitality because of the competition from suburban shopping centers and office parks catering to the needs of the more affluent population increasingly concentrated in the suburbs. The central business districts have been the victims of the incremental urban growth and automobile-oriented transportation policies we have been following since 1945.

A critical choice is whether to attempt to aid central business districts directly and without changing other impacting policies or whether to alter those other policies with the intention in part of revitalizing the central areas.

A critical choice about fostering the revitalization of central cities would be easier if we had confidence in what programs and policies could be relied on to accomplish it. There have been remarkable examples of center city revitalization. Federal urban renewal funds have had an important role, but other elements appear to have been more essential. The quality of political and civic leadership, staff competence, and development systems in use are clearly more important than federal money. In fact the evidence is clear that without local initiative and competence, federal money is unlikely to be used effectively. No successful center city rebuilding program in the United States has taken place as a result of primarily federal or state efforts. The initiative and the follow-through have come from local political and civic leadership. That leadership has been in short supply.

We have contrived to make it very easy to desert the central city and very difficult to stay with it. Corporations are wooed by other jurisdictions promising they can set up new quarters and leave the city's problems behind. In fact, there is a large measure of truth in such claims. No one wanted to achieve the central area decline which has occurred. It is time that we at least knew what critical choices are being made. The private sector investment and locational decisions are the critical ones for the survival or regeneration of city centers. In most societies those choices are made only with public sector approval. In our society it is entirely a private decision. Is that a liberty to be protected or a license to be cursed?

Center City Industry

Thirty years ago, industrial areas were located almost exclusively in cities or adjacent to raw materials or both. Since that time, manufacturing processes have become more sophisticated. They require great flexibility and adaptability plus sufficient land for one-story structures. This is difficult to find in cities and a massive move-out to the periphery has taken place. Industrial parks are one example. Other plants have set up in small towns seeking a change in labor conditions. The multistory or otherwise obsolete structures formerly occupied had become inefficient, inflexible, and costly. In-city alternatives were hard to find. The movement out was natural, but for the communities left behind it was disastrous.

Forcing industries back into the cities is likely to be an impractical, unworkable and indeed impossible critical choice. Nonetheless, it is important to explore ways in which cities can be encouraged to offer labor intensive industry an opportunity to locate and prosper in multistory (loft) buildings offering day care and other services, including security services and transportation savings. A program which would actually encourage job creation in the center city is worth more of a concentrated effort than it has had to date. Any urban growth policy must recognize the close tie-in between job availability and housing patterns.

Ghettos

A case can be made that minorities in America, particularly blacks who are the largest minority, have made enormous progress into the mainstream of American society in the last twenty years. Certainly on a comparative basis there is much to be said for that view. However, no parade of statistics can gainsay the fact that blacks and other racial minorities are at a serious disadvantage in the United States, and that the end of disadvantagement is not yet in sight.

Few who have focused on the subject deny its critical importance or the need to pay more attention. However we have yet to see the commitment to rid ourselves of slum and blight. That would turn out to be too much.

Evidence indicates that ghetto populations are still increasing and will continue to do so. Nearly all black population growth now occurs in central cities rather than in the suburbs or rural areas. The white population has ceased to grow at all in most central cities and in fact has steadily declined in very many.

The Kerner Commission reported in 1968 that Washington and Newark already had black majorities and estimated that by 1985 the following cities will be over 50 percent black:

Baltimore	New Orleans
Chicago	Oakland
Cleveland	Philadelphia
Detroit	Richmond
Gary	St. Louis
Jacksonville	

The proportion of non-whites in the public schools in every case runs far ahead of the proportion in the population as a whole, and make it increasingly impossible to promote racial integration in the central cities' public schools, a fact lost sight of in much of the current debate about busing and school desegregation. The same Commission reported that this is because the black population in central cities is much younger and because a much higher proportion of white children attended parochial or other private schools.

It estimated that in addition to all the cities listed above the following eleven would have black school majorities by 1985:

Atlanta	Indianapolis
Buffalo	Kansas City, Mo
Cincinnati	Louisville
Dallas	New Haven
Harrisburg	Pittsburgh
Hartford	

Those estimates have proven quite conservative. The list by now would be far larger.

During the peak periods of European immigration to the United States before World War I, the schools took on the job of teaching the children to read and write in English and otherwise to adapt to American ways. In those days a grammar school education was sufficient for the broad back unskilled laboring jobs which were the first step up the ladder.

Our more complex society puts greater educational demands on its children for more and more areas of the job market. School systems which educated generations of earlier immigrants in a way that appeared to fit them for the work then available now seem to be failing to accomplish that for a large number of the latest wave of urban newcomers.

There are not enough jobs for the unskilled around by which a man can support his family in even the simplest way. High ghetto unemployment brings despair, alienation, and worse into the ghetto classroom.

According to the *Statistical Abstract* for 1972, 81.1 percent of the growth of the black population took place in the central cities between 1960 and 1970, whereas for whites the comparable figure was *minus* 3.4 percent. The evidence is clear that the ghettos are increasing in size and decreasing in the quality of municipal services provided, particularly in the effectiveness of public education. Ghetto residents bear the heaviest burden of unemployment in good times as well as bad. It is usually at least double the rate for the general population. For ghetto young adults, the unemployment rate is even greater.

Critical Choices for the Ghetto. Is America to continue with its present policies which, deliberately or not, allow discrimination and segregation, and continue the existence of the ghetto while allowing a slowly increasing percentage of minority citizens to come into the mainstream of American life? Is that good enough or should we attempt to make the effort and the choices which can lead to an end to discrimination and segregation and all the blight they have cast upon our national life? Should we set a time goal? We missed the centennial of the Emancipation Proclamation and the bicentennial of the Revolution. How about the year 2000 and a twenty-five-year plan to eliminate ghetto conditions from American life?

If we take the second course, how do we proceed? By a dispersal of poor minorities into the population as a whole, with greatly improved housing, education, and working opportunities; or by a substantial enrichment which attempts to achieve the same objectives within the ghetto itself? Or in some combination?

What are the prospects for either of these alternatives receiving the indispensable political support of suburbanites? Can we develop a believable cost-benefit analysis of the price over time of keeping the ghetto as against an effort to assist its disadvantaged residents into the mainstream of American life? Is it impossible to assist lower-class people into the mainstream as some analysts insist or is it that we have not tried hard enough? Besides money, what else is effective in changing conditions in the ghetto—community control, job training, employment incentives? A high level of general prosperity?

And along the way should America have a commitment to promote racial integration in the neighborhood, in the school, and on the job? Reliance on action by the courts no longer seems to be as promising as it once seemed to be. Is integration coming anyway or does it need to be helped along? Can ways be devised to promote genuine integration without it being so threatening to whites that the enterprise is hopelessly mired in controversy? Or is it time to pause and consolidate the gains as some have advocated?

Is it possible that we have most to learn and can get the best policy guidance from the experience in recent years of those blacks and other minorities who have made it into the mainstream of American society?

With legal barriers down on segregation and equal opportunity programs increasingly accepted, should our society perhaps concentrate on providing productive employment opportunities for ghetto residents with some reason to believe that other ghetto problems would begin to be resolved by a population which is self-supporting. Such productive work would also add to the gross national product and spur the economy generally. Is it naive to assume that we can do this?

The alternative choice is there and should be faced—to continue to accept very high levels of unemployment in the ghetto, thereby guaranteeing a continuing need for subsidized housing, welfare assistance and probably assuring a high degree of alienation and the violent crime that goes with it.

In seeking answers to these and related problems, we turn now to housing, education, and employment.

Housing

Few things are more basic to the quality of life than decent housing in a suitable environment.

America's Housing Dilemma

The standard of housing accommodation provided for the average American may well be the highest in the world. Yet housing quality is dreadfully uneven. The housing market favors the well-to-do and those who stay in one place. It disfavors the transient, the old, the young, those of moderate and particularly low income. It has consistently and pervasively discriminated against racial minorities.

Despite thoughtful quantifications of needs written into federal law, the financing and subsidy requirements for housing have never become an established high priority in national monetary, fiscal or budget policy. Housing production, including rehabilitation, is a stepchild among our national commitments. Congressionally approved targets for total housing production are missed by 50 percent or more and those for low- and moderate-income families are ignored for all practical purposes. As a result, housing, one of the fastest of start-up industries, is fueling recession rather than recovery. "Social housing," that is housing for the most needy, is virtually at a standstill.

There are many reasons for this dilemma which should be explored to determine if there are politically practical and financially feasible ways and means for ending it.

Housing Needs. In 1968, Congress determined the ten-year national housing need to be twenty-six million units, six million to meet the need of low- and moderate-income families.

An initial burst of activity from 1969 to 1972 led to production averaging around two million units per year. Low- and moderate-income housing in the period equaled the production totals of the previous thirty years. Since then, thanks to an executive moratorium on subsidized housing and a deemphasis on housing production generally, starts have dropped to a level somewhat over one million units per year. Housing production for low- and moderate-income families all but disappeared.

This recent swing up and then down is typical of housing production in the United States over the last thirty years. As a result, except in areas of economic stagnation or rare overbuilding, there have been very few housing markets which have had a modest surplus of vacancy rate of 4 percent in standard accommodations in a broad range of prices. In fact, all sectors of the housing industry seem to shy away from achieving even a modest surplus condition. Consequently, we deal with housing as a commodity in short supply and with continually rising costs. This is one of the least noticed but most important and unique elements in our national and local housing markets. We have normally, no shortages across a broad price in food, clothing or in a broad range of consumer goods—from radios and television sets to new and second-hand cars. Why in housing do we shrink from surplus or at least a condition of nonshortage?

There has always been a gap between "felt need" and "effective demand" for housing. The gap is simply the difference between the total units needed to provide families and other persons with a decent unit at a price they can afford and the price at which such housing is being made available.

The Cost of Housing. High cost is the major factor in the continued existence of a "housing problem" in the United States. Both absolutely and relative to other family budget items, that cost has been continually rising.

Land Cost. The price of open land for housing sites on the periphery of built-up urban areas, aided by restrictive zoning, has been increasing at a very rapid rate. Few if any suggestions have been made for subsidizing such cost. The few scattered efforts to give state agencies the power to override local exclusionary zoning have had marginal success at the cost of heated political controversy. It can perhaps be concluded that no direct effort to reduce land cost for such sites has much prospect of political success given the size of the suburban constituency. At the same time, it should be noted that the consequences of higher land cost will be either more scattered settlements further out beyond the fringe or an opportunity for some alternative growth pattern to evolve such as satellite new towns, expansion of stagnant towns or growth along an extended rapid transit system.

Site Preparation. More and more suburban communities are requiring residential developers to bear the full costs of servicing new subdivisions with roads, utilities, and sometimes the capital costs of schools and other facilities. This adds to the cost of new housing, but the policy seems unlikely to change. It makes local sense.

Construction. Construction, the so-called bricks and mortar element of housing cost has also been rising steadily. Partly because of higher costs of labor and material, but even more because of more sophisticated fixturing, more elaborate room layouts and just plain larger size. In addition, so far as high-rise structures are concerned, there is the extra cost of elevators, waste disposal, and security services that are provided by the owner or tenant in individual homes or town house apartments.

The American experience with industrialized housing suggests it has limited prospects. Off-site prefabrication of panels, bathrooms, kitchens, etc., unquestionably has genuine potential for savings if local restrictive practices can be overcome. However, complete industrialization is unlikely to satisfy American tastes. The more complete the industrialization and the more money saved—seldom a substantial amount—the more uniform and monotonous the end product. Industrialization has its place, but it is interesting to note that in Europe and in the Soviet Union, where there has been the most extensive experience with industrialization, the so-called artisan-made housing accounts for half or better of current total production.

Money can be saved on bricks and mortar, but it will not loom large in the final monthly cost of the occupants of conventional housing. The cost of carrying the mortgage, particularly interest, is what really makes the difference. Attempting to control or regulate the cost of the unsubsidized dwelling is probably less effective than allowing market forces to operate. The mobile home industry has recently contributed 20 percent of recent annual housing starts. That is a response to the rising cost of conventional housing, rather dramatic evidence that cost is a real factor. However, in subsidized housing, every effort should be made to reduce construction costs or keep them to a minimum. Public support will be more likely if economy in construction is the hallmark. The standards of publicly-aided housing in America are already the highest in the world, even if design standards are among the lowest. It is in fixturing and in building type, and therefore in required services, that the most significant savings are to be made. Design need not be abandoned for dreariness. That was an unnecessary and costly mistake in federally-aided public housing.

The Cost of Money

As 1976 began, the average interest rate on a new residential mortgage was reported to be over 9 percent. Except for a few brief periods, this is an all-time record high. Few qualified observers believe that interest rates, without special incentives (tax exemption, credit allocation, insurance or guarantees to the lender, for example) are likely to get back down to a comfortable 6 percent and stay there.

For a thirty-year mortgage, this means that over 50 percent of monthly housing cost will be attributable to interest payments alone. Large numbers of middle- and lower-middle income potential owners and tenants are priced out of the market at a 9 percent rate who would be perfectly able to afford housing carrying a 6 percent interest cost.

Assuming, as is warranted, that the length of a fully amortizing mortgage will range from twenty to forty years and that construction costs at any given point in time in any given housing market will have a much narrower range, a rise or decline in the interest rate is the variable that is going to have the most significant impact on monthly housing cost. How should such an important figure be set?

On the supply side, there is every reason to believe that, except in unusual circimstances, enough mortgage money can be made to flow into housing if the price is right—if mortgages can carry whatever interest rate the market demands. The critical problem of *illiquidity* of long-term mortgage loans in a portfolio has been resolved by the congressional creation of two secondary market institutions, FNMA and GNMA.

However, the mortgage market is not as elastic as other markets, for example, the corporate bond market, not to mention such short-term paper as Treasury notes or the certificates of deposit of commercial banks. In addition, federal and state ceilings on the rate of interest which can be charged for residential mortgages also have helped to limit the effective availability of mortgage funds.

The question thus inevitably presents itself: Can and should the federal government take action to increase the supply of lower-cost mortgage money for housing, both subsidized and unsubsidized?

Several alternatives can be considered, singly or in combination, for obtaining mortgage money at lower rates. Each constitutes a form of disintermediation, i.e., a change in the prevailing ground rules, public and private, for the allocation of available investment dollars.

Companies Collecting Long-Term Savings. Pension funds, life insurance companies, and other enterprises which, in effect, collect the long-term savings of the average person, could be required by federal law to plow back a certain amount of their annual net capital inflow into residential mortgages instead of purchasing, selling, and repurchasing already existing securities. This would create a substantial continuing pool of mortgage funds. It would of course require new expertise in the departments of the twenty-five major large city banks which administer most pension funds today. Or better perhaps a reassignment of the function of investing residential mortgage funds to institutions with experience.

Opponents might say that such a disintermediation would penalize pension fund beneficiaries. However, studies indicate this is not the case. Supporters would reply that the beneficiaries as a group would in turn be major beneficiaries of the lowered housing costs and of the economic activity thus generated. They would also point out that in many other nations, social insurance funds were routinely invested in housing. The volatility of the stock market presents its own problems to fiduciaries.

Universal Federal Mortgage Insurance. Taking the risk of loss of mortgage loans away from the private lender and giving it to FHA in return for a premium charge has been established practice for a minor portion of the housing market for forty years.

For thirty of the last forty years, nearly all FHA insured housing was located in racially homogeneous subdivisions in the outer parts of the city or in suburbs beyond. Inner city housing was ignored and suffered for lack of readily available mortgage financing. Equally important, most housing was uninsured and financed conventionally.

For most of its existence, FHA operated conservatively and cautiously. It took few risks and accordingly it had an extremely low loss ratio.

However, slowly in the late fifties and sixties and with a rush from 1969 to 1972, FHA went into inner city neighborhoods to make rehabilitation loans. Inexperienced, it was cheated wholesale and suffered substantial losses. Mortgage money is once again almost impossible to get in inner city neighborhoods, thereby encouraging the spread of blight and abandonment.

FHA should not attempt to return to its prior low loss ratio experience. Rather its base of coverage should be broadened as is that for social security. The Social Security Administration expects people to retire. Fire insurance companies expect some houses to burn down. Life insurance companies expect some people to die and their policies to be paid over to beneficiaries.

We need a mortgage insurance in this country which is universal. Not only would it reduce interest rates, it would stabilize marginal neighborhoods and encourage private rebuilding.

Individual Retirement Savings. In the last few years, Congress has permitted self-employed persons and more recently individuals whose employers do not have retirement plans to invest limited funds in retirement-type accounts and deduct the expenditure from taxable income. These retirement savings may be used to purchase mutual fund shares or to put money away in a savings account.

Why not turn these individual retirement plans into a very large and stable source of mortgage funds by removing the limits on the amount an individual may put into his retirement savings account in any one year if the money is earmarked for investment in insured residential mortgages? Everybody agrees we need to improve the amount of saving we do, particularly longer term saving. This approach would yield a substantial flow of lower cost mortgage loans. The cost of mortgage money over the next twenty-five years is a most critical one for the quantity and quality of housing. It deserves more consideration and a higher priority than it has received.

Matching Down Payments

Another aspect of the cost of housing is the amount of equity or down payment an owner is required to invest. Incentives should be considered for the accumulation of that equity by prospective owners particularly in the lower income ranges. If potential home buyers, for example, knew that every dollar they saved for a down payment would be matched by a federal low-interest loan, the volume of savings for home ownership would increase.

Operating and Maintenance Expense

Once the dwelling unit is occupied, a major expense is operating and maintaining it. Depending on the type and location, this involves such diverse items as taxes, insurance, energy, security, special services, such as elevators, and of course the proper physical upkeep of the building. Each of these costs has been increasing, though none as spectacularly as the cost of energy.

Inflation per se and energy policy per se are not within the purview of this report. However, in a period of increasing leisure time, it is perhaps not unreasonable to suggest that special attention be paid to the selection of housing types, particularly for subsidized housing which minimize the use of energy and outside labor and maximize the use of tenant labor.

Low-rise units, particularly if owner-occupied, can transfer much of the cost (or burden) for maintenance, security, and energy consumption, for example, to the occupant rather than to the owner and its agent, a management concern.

There are many critical choices about the cost of housing which deserve more consideration than they are currently receiving. Carefully made, they can improve the quality and quantity of housing for millions of Americans without raising expenditures excessively.

Subsidized Housing for Families and Elderly Persons of Low and Moderate Income

One of the most important parts of the housing problem is what should be done about providing an adequate supply of decent housing for those who cannot afford such housing at the market price. This is a problem which is worldwide. In most of the developed nations, it has been accepted as a continuing and priority responsibility of the national government. That has never been the case in the United States. Even today there is a widespread failure to understand that decent housing is simply out of the financial reach of too many low- and moderate-income families and of the elderly, through no fault of theirs.

The Congress found in the Housing Act of 1968 that there was a need for six million units of low- and moderate-income housing by 1978. As of January 1, 1976, with seven out of the ten target years passed, only one million units or one-sixth of the total have been started. The need is there. It will not go away. It must be provided for. Otherwise, we should stop saying our goal is to provide a decent home in a suitable living environment for every American family.

Housing Allocation for Families and Elderly—Urban and Rural. By a very conservative estimate of need, ten million units of subsidized housing will be required for the next twenty-five years. Twenty to 25 percent of these should be designed for and made available to the elderly. Without attempting to allocate this need among regions of the country, it should be emphasized that a certain portion, perhaps 20 percent, should be set aside for so-called rural housing for both families and the elderly. Not only is rural housing proportionately worse, almost no new rural housing is being built. If we want to reverse the pull of the cities, something deeply desired by governments all over the world, more decent rural housing will surely help.

Housing for low-income families in the United States generally has been pretty low on most priority lists. Rural housing programs hardly exist. Yet the need is there. An effective rural housing program could not only meet genuine human needs at much less than urban costs—it could help to alter the urbanization process which now seems so irresistibly under way.

Fair Share Housing. The single most controversial question in housing today is:

Where should housing for the poor and those of modest income be located? Should it all be located in cleared portions of slum and blighted areas? All in the peripheral communities where so little is located today?

At the theoretical level, it is easy to endorse the concept of "fair sharing." At a practical level, it seems close to impossible to get political support to place a quantitatively significant amount of subsidized housing in the suburbs, no matter what assurances are given.

The statistics previously cited demonstrated the ever increasing racial polarity of city and suburb. The school busing issue has obscured the true nature of the problem. Busing to school has been a commonly accepted phenomenon of American public education in cities and suburbs for decades. It has, however, been used for convenience and not as an instrument for social change.

The real source of school segregation in much of the country is the city-suburb pattern of segregated housing occupancy and the all but unwillingness of the suburbs to do their fair share in resolving the issue. To require in Boston, for example, that integration in the public schools be achieved by mixing the children of low and lower middle income South Boston, Charlestown, and Roxbury while excluding the children of the intimately related suburban communities of Brookline, Milton, Newton, Watertown, and Dedham is to commit an unjust and disruptive act.

Are our courts really the way to re-plan our cities in a most basic social sense? There is little if any evidence that the courts, good at striking down barriers, changing outdated assumptions, are truly right for continuing governance for complicated social systems.

Fair-share housing if mishandled is potentially the most divisive domestic issue in America. If on the other hand, it somehow can be made a central part of a rational process by which we seek a coming together as a people on the most enduringly broadly divisive issue of our time, it can be a healing, wholesome thing.

Fair sharing where every suburban community feels threatened by unknowns is destructive and unachievable. Fair sharing where every suburban community knew that it must provide sites for housing for at least 5 percent low- and moderate-income families but need not provide more than 10 percent would solve the distribution problem. Is that too painful?

It is entirely possible that financial rewards could be given to suburban communities who achieve fair housing goals, rewards which over the long run are not likely to increase the cost of government at all.

Rehabilitation

The conservation and rehabilitation of the existing center city housing stock must be a high priority effort of any successful housing progrram. Yet there is only a handful of examples of successful programs. In too many cities, abandonment takes out of the housing supply far more than new construction adds. The problem is usually not the housing itself but a lack of confidence in the future of the neighborhood by lenders, insurers, merchants, and the providers of municipal services. Unfortunately, by the time the problem has progressed to the point of serious concern nearly all families who are fully self-supporting have left.

Systems for rehabilitation can make a real difference, but large-scale rehabilitation depends upon the economic base of the neighborhood, who has confidence in the program, whether or not an effective system has been established for code enforcement, loan processing, mortgage insurance, and required related improvements is decisive. Conceptually a "rehab" program is simple. Administratively, however, it is quite complex, which is why so few programs succeed. A simplified, expedited system of rehabilitation mortgage insurance is the indispensable element in any program to combat blight and abandonment. Without it, the phenomenon known as "red-lining" will only increase, no matter what legislative and regulatory bodies do.

Nature and Extent of Subsidies

Over the last forty years, the United States government has attempted to subsidize housing in a variety of ways. The original formula was the simplest and perhaps the best. A local housing authority would borrow money in the private market to build projects and then sell long-term bonds to cover the development cost. The federal government agreed to pay 100 percent of the debt service on such bonds, in other words a 100 percent Federal capital subsidy. The local authority bonds were thus tax exempt and federally guaranteed and enjoyed the lowest possible interest rate. The local authorities were obliged to charge and collect sufficient rent to pay for the operating and maintenance expense. Such a policy emphasized local initiative in developing and managing a housing program.

Despite its simplicity and cost effectiveness, the program had slowed down to a halt, lost most of its public support and finally was repealed in 1974. What went wrong?

The product, the public housing "project," had lost most of its appeal. More particularly, the projects occupied or to be occupied by families were increasingly viewed as undesirable neighbors. Housing which originally provided for a primarily white working class tenancy had come in the last years to serve primarily minority families, large numbers of whom were on welfare. Alienation became common and led to vandalism and violence, all exacerbated in those communities which had built stark, large-scale, multistory projects.

With the need as great as ever, it had become almost impossible to win approval to locate a public housing project for low-income families anywhere but in a slum or blighted area.

Over the years, various other subsidy efforts were made, primarily by the reduction of the interest rate through one form of federal subsidy or another. In effect, money came to be borrowed at market rates and then interest cost was reduced through a very expensive federal subsidy. The various subsidy systems lasted for a relatively few years and in turn were abandoned for another approach. The current leased housing system is the fairest and therefore the costliest to date. It is having the usual start up problems that seem to afflict new federally aided housing programs. It is, however, too soon to give up hope. It can be made to work.

One of the more serious problems with the public housing program was that it served exclusively low-income families. Those families who increased their incomes beyond a certain limit were supposed to move out. Recent efforts to mix low- and moderate-income families in the same housing development have had considerable success and acceptance while providing motivational models for the low-income families. The moderate-income families were in a substantial majority in each project.

For most of the last forty years, the emphasis in subsidized housing has been on stimulating housing production. Complaints about excessive costs and red tape in housing production programs led to a renewed interest in housing allowances, once known as rent certificates. This approach basically gives the tenant a commitment that the government will pay his private landlord the difference between the fair market rent for his dwelling unit and a specified portion of his income (15 percent to 25 percent). This approach should work well where there is at least a modest vacancy rate in standard accommodations across a broad price range. However, its effect is likely to be quite inflationary in areas where there are severe shortages of standard housing over a broad price range. There is little if any evidence that the allowance approach is at all effective in stimulating housing production in slum and blighted areas.

While recognizing the urgent need for a subsidized housing program for low- and moderate-income families, it is important that we learn from the difficulties of the past and attempt to design an optimum system.

Given the current and perhaps continuing uncertainty in the long-term capital markets, should not the financing system for subsidized housing be as risk free as possible? Federally guaranteed tax exempt bonds used for both construction and long-term financing will bring the lowest possible interest rate. Why fool around with anything more complicated? That approach will reduce monthly housing costs very substantially. It will not be enough to reach low- and some moderate-income families. For these families we should consider returning promptly to the annual contributions contract approach under which the federal government paid all development cost. There is no reason why this approach can be carried out with maximum reliance on the private enterprise system. Where necessary for very low income or very large families a section 8 program will bridge the gap.

Recognizing that an income mixture is socially and economically desirable, should not rents be tied to a percentage of income and economic integration encouraged? This will require a more flexible subsidy system than we have had to date.

If ownership is not only more economical but more stabilizing than tenancy, should not projects be designed to be readily convertible to individual home mortgages? And should not incentives be given to tax credits or matching funds to encourage tenants to build up funds for a substantial downpayment?

To sum up, one of our most critical choices is to put our commitment on the line to end housing shortages, get rid of substandard housing, profiting both from our past mistakes and good experience as well. Surely this is one of the most important contributions we can make to improving the quality of life both for individuals and for communities.

Transportation

In the postwar period, America has steadily implemented transportation policies which have favored the private car, the bus, the truck, and the airplane over the railroad and waterborne transportation. For both passengers and freight, new systems of movement have been created with public subsidies from all levels of government at great damage to the rail and water systems, which had been among the finest in the world.

While everyone now knows that the shift in transportation modes led to massive increases in per capita energy consumption for travel and to extraordinary allocations of public capital investment for road building and airports, it is sometimes overlooked that from the standpoint of the commuter, the housewife, the traveler, there were enormous improvements in personal convenience. From the viewpoint of the individual, the overall consequences were secondary, he was better served, waited less for others, was more in control of his own time.

As the years passed and the older systems deteriorated, the consumer of transportation services had fewer options in America. Yet in Western Europe, with priority still given to rail transportation; it is interesting that the lure of the private car has proved irresistible.

The shift in modes of transportation has had enormous impact on urban growth patterns. Freed of the need to be close to fixed rail lines, housing and industrial growth has scattered over the landscape in incremental patterns which will not easily be reversed.

The excesses of the highway builders, the realities of suburban sprawl, the decay of the cities, the newly aroused concern about the environment, and most recently the energy crisis have led to the creation of a whole movement favoring mass transportation. As often happens with causes that become ideological, facts get obscured. Highly advanced technology came to be presumed to be the correct solution although practical evidence in support of it was minimal. The clumsy efforts of elements of the aerospace industry to establish high technology solutions to urban mass transit were on the whole quite unsuccessful. But somehow the less glamorous but more practical solutions lacked appeal.

Too often the debate about future transportation policy has been cast in either/or terms. The private car and the individual truck are more convenient. The airplane is faster. That is unlikely to change. What must be realized is the importance of assisting in the achievement of a more balanced transportation system, not only because it will save on energy consumption and protect the environment, but also because the evidence is overwhelming that there is no other way to prevent massive overload of the highways and consequent inefficiencies and frustrations in the use of the private car, the truck and the airplane.

Our basic critical choice in transportation is not one, therefore, of proposing to change modes, but of promoting means for achieving balance.

Education

The United States spends more money on education than any other nation in the world. A higher proportion of the American population completes secondary, collegiate, graduate, and professional education than any other nation. In recent years, access to higher education has been opened up to a broader economic, social, racial, and religious spectrum than ever before. Opportunities for training in the sciences and the professions that were virtually closed to women and to minorities have been greatly broadened in the same period. Employment opportunities for these groups are also opening up, but most students of the subject would say there is a long way to go.

Commitment to Education. For generations now and with a fervor that has only increased with the passage of time, the American people have believed that the way for an individual to "make it," to "get ahead" in America was to get educated. When collected and analyzed, the statistical evidence seems to demonstrate the validity of that belief. At least in terms of dollars earned there appeared to be a direct correlation between years of education completed and lifetime earnings.

Evaluation. American education was innovative, changing, experimental. More than any other essential activity, public or private, it was subjected to constant evaluation and reevaluation. Every postwar president and countless governors and mayors, plus almost every foundation has created an educational study commission. When added to the output of the college and university faculties of education, one can say with confidence that the flow of choices on education presented to all, or to segments, of the Republic have been critical and unending.

Pluralism and the Capacity to Change. Choices have been made. Curricula, teaching methods, and admission and grading standards have changed. Yet surveying the broad field of American education, higher and lower, private and public, one can surely say that its dominant aspect is pluralism. Despite the sweep of fashion from time to time, there remains an unending variety.

Surely that is one of education's greatest strengths in America and one we would not choose to change. Many other nations of course have rigidly uniform systems of education which insure an identical program in every classroom.

Financing Education. The supporters of education, particularly public education, point with urgency to things yet undone and with alarm to recent trends in budget cutting. The dispute over how much money should be devoted to various levels and kinds of education, for what purposes and from what levels of government is also unending. A few things have become rather clear.

1. The amount of money that will be sought to be spent for education is all but limitless.
2. Yet the money likely to be available will not increase annually at the rate it has in the recent past. Instead, considering inflation, we may well experience cutbacks.
3. As education has consumed an ever larger proportion of the local property tax bill, it has generated a not inconsiderable taxpayer revolt, particularly in the suburbs.
4. Nonetheless, there is a broad and deep consensus in America that public education is one of our most important priorities.

Imbalance in Funding. The question of the adequacy of funding for all educational purposes will probably always be with us. Among the most serious problems appears to be over reliance on the local property tax base which leads to serious unevenness among school districts depending upon the relative wealth or poverty of the school district's tax base. To an extent, of course, the same kind of imbalance exists among the several states. Another serious problem is the severe financial pressure on much of education's private sector. At the higher level especially, competition from tax-supported public institutions is alleged to have exacerbated financial problems.

Performance

How well is our educational system performing? The average level of education continues to rise. There is from time to time imbalance among the various skills society needs. Sometimes shortages, sometimes an over-supply. There is some recent evidence that test scores for college admission are declining, but no certainty that is a long-term trend and none as to its causes. On the whole, when compared to the educational systems of most other nations, ours seems to do rather well. Pluralism and popular support may be its greatest strengths.

There is one basic area of perceived failure. The educational system appears not to work for too many ghetto children. In grade levels of reading and by other measures, there is substantial evidence that there is a record of poor achievement which, if not pervasive, is indeed widespread.

In the last fifteen years, a very large number of compensatory programs have been tried to improve this condition. There is no professional consensus that any one program or combination has made a significant difference. The problem, if anything, seems to be growing. The consequences are quite critical for the children who are disadvantaged. It is also critical for the society as a whole, which has trouble devising useful work for them as young adults.

There seems to be a spreading consensus that the first years of life are perhaps the most decisive, not only for the children of poverty but for all children.

Despite our uncertainties as to causes, we know the deprivation exists, we know low performance exists, and we believe they have a direct connection not only with difficulty in finding useful, satisfying work, but also with the alienation so many of these children feel as they mature into young adulthood.

In my judgment, a system is in operation for making critical choices for education for the majority. It has a high social priority and a high level of citizen involvement. It contains evaluative and corrective elements.

For the children of the poor, much more must be done not only for their sake, but in the interest of the larger society as well. More research, more experiment, a higher priority and much more concern. The rewards of success would be very great, for those children and for their families but equally important for all America and all Americans. In our own deepest interest, we must greatly raise the level of our commitment to more effective education for these children. Such a commitment may cost more money, but not necessarily. Significantly, the critical changes may not be in the classroom at all but rather in the home and in the community.

Racial Integration in the Public Schools

One educational topic looms larger in the public mind these days than any other. It is the subject of school busing to achieve racial integration.

Racial segregation was all but endemic in America's public school systems until relatively recently. In most of the South, the segregation was de jure—required by state statute. In the rest of the country, racial segregation seemed to exist whenever there was a large residential concentration of minority school children. Their schools tended to be racially imbalanced. Within the boundary limits of a given school district, the courts have held that such de facto segregation is unconstitutional and must be cured by busing if necessary. In many school districts there has been ample evidence that local school officials have been inventive in pushing racial segregation in the schools well beyond what might occur simply through residential concentration.

Efforts to substitute patterns of integration have had some genuine success but have also run into widespread local resistance. Mandated integration plans have been reluctant to deal with the reality of rapidly changing urban residential patterns. With judges seemingly limiting themselves to achieving integration within the limits of a given school district, ignoring the reality of movement to the suburbs, many well-intentioned integration efforts are doomed to failure.

A policy of attempting to achieve racial integration in the public schools, by cross-busing between white and black low- and moderate-income children within a given city, while the middle-income families opt out by living in the suburbs or using private schools, seems not only unwise and unsound. It is also manifestly unfair. To this observer, at least, it promises to be unsuccessful within the span of a few years.

Here we have a critical choice indeed. Can the white majority devise programs by which all parts of the majority contribute their share of participation in the integration effort? Is there in fact any enduring solution to the question of school integration that does not rest on an effective commitment to fair share housing. The alternative of continuing as we are is unappealing, divisive and perhaps disastrous.

Across most of the spectrum of educational questions, our society has adequate mechanisms for making critical choices. However, there is reason for deep concern that in two very critical areas, education's effectiveness for ghetto children and the development of fairer and more effective solutions to the problems of racial integration, the existing systems of choice are not working at all well. We need a genuine commitment to the concept of devising workable systems for achieving effective education for all and for integration.

Personal Security for Urban Dwellers and the Criminal Justice System

Few issues have consistently been regarded recently as more important by the urban public than the fear of crimes of personal violence. Few issues have been more wholeheartedly embraced by candidates for elective office, including offices with only the remotest connection with the administration of the criminal justice system. Urban Americans envision a past which was relatively much safer, with a friendly cop always on the corner. The advent of "them" to the vicinity has appeared to change all that. The fact that this is a view which has been held by established city dwellers about succeeding generations of immigrants of diverse origins is either not known or forgotten.

Efforts to deal with this problem of personal security (which is a quite real urban problem and one which statistics show is most real for residents of the ghetto) have led to an elaboration of programs, more varied, if anything, than those attempting to deal with educational malfunctions.

The most popular response was always to put more police on the streets, preferably on foot patrol. But studies went further. Disposition of arrests was examined. What about the bail system? The judicial system? Sentencing? Incarceration? Rehabilitation? Parole? Recidivism? Prisoners' rights?

Reforms came flooding in. Basically defendants accused of crimes of physical violence were brought nearer parity in treatment to those who were accused of other kinds of crime. In terms of fairness and equality of treatment, substantial advances were undoubtedly made. In terms of the incidence of physically violent crimes against previously unknown persons, reforms appeared to make no difference.

The gradual adoption of the rule of equal treatment under the law, too often ignored or violated in the past, is positive progress. However, the basic problem remains. Who commits these crimes and why? Police, the world over, know that one of the largest single sources of violent crime is the crime of passion, committed by one person against another person previously known to the perpetrator. Evidence indicates that such crimes are higher in inverse proportion to the income of the persons involved.

Who commits the crimes of personal violence against persons previously unknown, the kinds of crimes that our society is currently most in fear of? The evidence is, sadly, starkly, that these kinds of crimes are committed by those who have nothing better to do, by those who are either unemployed or irregularly employed, by those whose family life is disrupted or nonexistent, by those whose life experience demonstrates that the system neither cares about them nor works for them.

This suggests that perhaps the basic remedy for the violent crime problem does not lie in the criminal justice system (though reform should continue—it is certainly needed) but in the economic system. Widely available last-resort jobs and the opportunity to move from them to better paying, more meaningful work in a full employment society are far more likely to make a difference in the rate of violent crime than the remedies regularly propounded. Recognizing that full employment will not necessarily reform those already alienated, it remains in my judgment the best and surest way of making our streets safe and our homes secure.

Equality of Opportunity

Any serious discussion about quality of life critical choices must deal with the fact that for too many Americans there is serious unequality of opportunity to enjoy what is already available to the majority. This denial to a minority is because of its race, color or creed or previous condition of servitude. Although much improvement has been made, much more remains to be done.

As a matter of principle, equality of opportunity has long been both explicit in our Constitution and ignored. In recent years, court decisions and statutory enactments have given new substance and new hope.

The critical choice facing America today on the matter of equal opportunity is not commitment to the broad principle. That is widely accepted. Rather it is to day-to-day practical implementation in a far-ranging span of public and private actions. Hopefully this will be implementation in a way which will not only give heed to those to whom justice has so long been denied but also will show a concern for those whose habits and customs are to be changed. Without such a concern we achieve improvements in social justice at the price of avoidable social conflict.

The notable advances which have been made in recent years put the goal of full equality of opportunity within reach. A commitment to that achievement deserves our highest priority and marks one of our most critical choices. The benefits to those who presently lack such opportunity are perhaps obvious. Of possibly equal importance is the healthful, healing, strengthening impact such an effort would have on our whole society.

Full Employment and Guaranteed Minimum Income vs. Recession and the Welfare Mess

For many Americans, the critical choices about the quality of life are aesthetic, cultural, moral, spiritual, political, vocational—involving choices among life styles, ways of using leisure time, and career choices. These Americans, by and large, are in the mainstream of American society. Though not necessarily affluent, they have either sufficient knowledge and skills and perhaps resources to be able to make some important choices themselves about the quality of their own lives.

It is not the primary purpose of this report to suggest critical choices about the quality of their own lives to these people. They are well enough able to do that on their own. However, those in the mainstream, so to speak, do not live in a world entirely apart from their less fortunate countrymen. The quality of their lives is adversely affected in many ways by the poverty and alienation of those others. The decay of so many of our cities deprives them of much of the pleasures associated with vibrant city life. The burgeoning cost of welfare and of other poverty-related public services has forced cutbacks in desirable public services or raised taxes or both. We all have a stake in full employment for all.

There is said to be a national malaise about the country and its goals and its prospects of reaching them. Polls show lower levels of confidence in elected officials and in government generally. This should surprise no one. We have been through it before in the years of the Great Depression, for example.

We have had an unusual and hopefully a nonrecurring series of calamities: assassinations; a bitterly divisive war which alienated many of the educated young; political scandal; the forced retirement of a president and vice president. They are enough in themselves to sap the nation's morale. When one adds the unusual combination of serious inflation and protracted recession, ennui is the least we should expect. However, there is no reason to believe that the ship of state will not right itself.

Looking back, it is clear that the civil rights advances of recent years and particularly the disturbances that at times accompanied them engendered considerable resentment. At the same time, the rhetoric of governmental promises to the poor and the minorities far outran the ability to deliver.

But 1976 is a new political and presidential year. There seems to be no lack of candidates offering to lead us. The American people are resilient. We can rise to the challenges which confront us.

The Welfare Mess

There are few public programs held in more total disrespect than the welfare program, which provides welfare assistance to families, primarily female-headed with dependent children. Yet there are few public programs on which there is less agreement for reform. While there are other welfare programs, this is one critics focus on.

Virtually unique on the world scene, ADC, (AFDC), as it is popularly known, started out as a state financed, then federally assisted program originally called "Mother's Aid" to make it possible for mothers who were the sole support of their small children to stay home and care for them rather than be forced to work long hours at low pay to provide for the necessities of life. If perceived in that way, the concept still has very broad support in the land. However, once the program became federalized, though still requiring state and/or local 50 percent financing, its character began to evolve and to change.

First, it became bureaucratic, regulations abounded, some good and some bad, but primarily, as has so frequently happened to "do-good" programs, the primary objective became the serving of the interests of the bureaucracy itself first.

Office hours, office locations, waiting lines, atmosphere, all contributed to making the process of applying for aid degrading—not because that was deliberate policy but because that is the way the bureaucracy chose to operate. Even with permissive attitudes about eligibility, the atmosphere was still bad.

Most notorious of the regulations was the one which made it clearly in the interests of a destitute nuclear family that the man of the house abandon his family in their financial interest. How much damage this has done to family structure is impossible to calculate. There is widespread belief that it is enormous. The bureaucratic response egged on by congressional critics was to proclaim the so-called "man in the house" rule forbidding same and launching midnight raids on welfare mothers to catch them. Bizarre.

Second, the nature of the clientele changed. It started out in urbanized states of the North and aided primarily white working mothers. It had no significant racial tones. That has now changed.

Over the last twenty-five years, there has been a swelling tide of minority migration from the agricultural hinterlands of the American South, from Puerto Rico, the West Indies, and Mexico to the cities of the North and West. Advances in technology or other changes in agricultural patterns denied these landless laborers their rural homes and sources of employment. There was no rural alternative livelihood for many of them. With the same basic hopes and aspirations for a better life, they followed in the footsteps of generations of white European immigrants before them.

The broad back and other unskilled jobs which awaited the earlier generations had for the most part disappeared. The new immigrants clearly identifiable, for the most part, as racial minorities had a hard time. They encountered discrimination in many forms, perhaps the most malignant being that "they" were treated as just naturally inferior because they were minorities.

Despite overwhelming odds, large numbers hooked on to the lowest rungs of the ladder and began the climb of those who preceded them to the cities. However, many could not really make it and many others fell off due to the mishaps which befall us all, yet which for the marginal income families can be so financially devastating.

ADC was available for these families if the man in the house "got lost" (except in special circumstances and programs). It provided enough money for the bare essentials, food, shelter, and clothing, and not much more.

At first there seemed to be a correlation between the size of the welfare rolls and the rate of unemployment. But in the mid-sixties, during a period of relatively low unemployment, the rolls kept growing and the costs mounting. Two phenomena then occurred simultaneously. On the one hand, villains were necessary and there was much talk of "cheating" and "permissiveness." Undoubtedly true to some extent. On the other hand, welfare mothers were organized into militant groups around the proposition that welfare was a right and that the standards should be raised to the level prescribed by the Department of Labor as providing a decent minimum standard of living.

There were increasing demands that welfare recipients be required to work for their stipends. As the recession deepened and lengthened, the working, self-supporting part of the population, of all races, grew increasingly resentful of those on welfare. Hard pressed state and municipal chief executives faced with mandated federal programs for welfare had to cut back on park maintenance, libraries, police, fire and other nonfederally aided municipal services.

It was and is a mess, the welfare mess.

The dissatisfaction with the system is greatest in those states, mostly in the North and West, which make the highest ADC payments. In those states, mostly in the South, with the lowest payments, the controversy has been more muted.

Welfare reform has been a pressing national issue for years, but there has been no consensus on the kinds of reforms which should be sought or even the objectives of the effort. One soon discovers the enormous complexity of the problem. It is an area where expert knowledge is required. However, because the service provided and its apparent consequences seem so simple, effective dialogue among concerned persons has proven inordinately difficult.

Some of the principal alternatives which have been discussed are the following:

1. *Transfer of full funding and administrative responsibility from state and local government to the federal government.* Not surprisingly, this proposal has the enthusiastic support of the great majority of state and local elected officials and administrators. Alarmed at rising welfare costs, feeling helpless to control caseload levels, disturbed at seeing nonfederally aided expenditures cut, these officials believe that the causes of welfare dependency are national in origin, not state or local. Others support full federalization because they believe it will more quickly lead to uniform national standards and more adequate levels of assistance benefits.

The costs of such a take-over and of equalizing benefits have discouraged serious federal interest. In any event, in and of itself, it does nothing for the problems associated with welfare dependency. Should serious consideration be given to a federal take-over, it would probably be preceded by a wholesale evaluation of the ADC program by the Congress and the Executive. One should be hesitant to predict the outcome of that effort.

2. *Incremental reform.* Those whose basic concern is for larger, more adequate benefit levels for welfare recipients are concerned about the hazards of wholesale reform and the hurdles before federalization. They would like to see gradual improvements in the program without attacking its basic premises and therefore probably without curing its basic faults. There is much in the history of American social legislation to say that precedent and experience may prove them right. However, incrementalism will not alter the damage the welfare system is doing to family structure or to the way recipients perceive themselves and are perceived by the larger society.

3. *Abandonment or curtailment.* Inevitably there are those who believe that ADC is intrinsically bad, cannot be reformed, and should be cut back and restricted as much as possible. This viewpoint, however bluntly argued, usually in political forums, falls before the undoubted large-scale human misery it would create.

4. *Wholesale reform.* Proponents of wholesale reform have had three basic notions. First, simplify the system, cut down the bureaucracy and its steadily rising cost. Second, make a guaranteed minimum income a matter of statutory

right. Third, provide a work incentive system. This combined concept was saddled with the inept name "negative income tax," thereby assuring it would be much discussed in academic circles and totally confuse even the informed public who have enough trouble with the "positive" income tax. The confusion has not abated.

Nonetheless, the principles of simplification, assurance of a minimum family (or individual) income would do much to rid the nation of many of the evils of welfare dependency.

Existing welfare systems require a give-up of welfare payments equal in amount to income earned. This is not exactly an incentive system. This phenomenon has been described accurately but somewhat confusingly as a 100 percent income tax.

Interestingly, the sponsors of the negative income tax and therefore of a guaranteed annual income were conservative economists for the most part, not wild-eyed do-gooders. Public men who would have to carry that banner in the political process have shied away from what was inevitably described as an abandonment of the work ethic that presumably ruled the rest of the populace.

In 1969, the Administration then in office combined the negative income tax with a work requirement and proposed benefit levels which would benefit primarily the South, where most of the poor lived. The proposal was complex and extremely difficult to understand. Nonetheless, it was launched with strong presidential support and passed in the House. However, it foundered in the Senate, caught between those who felt it would do too much and those who thought it would do too little. It is not likely to rise in that form again.

Thus, a critical choice on a most basic issue was presented and was rejected. The problem remains and grows larger and more costly.

This critical choice about the provision of the necessities of life for our most needy fellow citizens, must be presented again. It has much to do with the quality of all our lives in all of our communities.

As we trace concerns and suggested choices about growth, cities, ghettos, housing, and education, a common theme emerges. *Unless the nation vigorously supports a goal of full employment for all who are of age and physically able to work, much else that we seek becomes difficult of achievement.*

For the society as a whole as well as for those who are unemployed, a critical choice is whether we will commit ourselves to the goal of full employment. Discussions about the quality of life for those unable to find work have a certain irrelevancy. Similar discussions limited to those gainfully employed have a certain indecency.

The Central Critical Role of Full Employment

As I trace concerns and suggested remedial choices about urban growth, the decay and decline of so many of our cities and particularly the ghettos, the need for more housing more people can afford, for more effective education, a central critical choice seems to me to present itself.

There are many things we can do about these problems. We have tried in the past, we will continue to in the future to cope with these problems.

Inevitably, however, one is driven to ask—is there not a central, critical choice we must make or not make about the future well being of our society. I believe there is. I have become convinced that we must break the chicken and egg syndrome and determine that one national priority above all must be established if we are to reach and achieve the social health and national unity which are within our grasp.

Despite all the progress we might make on all the fronts we have been discussing we will either fail or run into astronomical unaffordable costs unless we determine once and for all that:

1. Full employment for every able bodied American is a topmost national priority.
2. That where normal employment is not available, there will be public sector last resort jobs at the existing federal minimum wage level.
3. Where such employment is not provided, a guaranteed minimum individual or family income will be available as a substitute.
4. The ADC (AFDC) program will be abolished. Women and men will have equal rights and obligations except for mothers of very young children.

It is time that we began to pay attention to the political economic and social benefits that would flow to our *entire* society, not just those directly benefited. Greater GNP, greater tax revenues, more effective schools, less alienation, a lowered crime rate. Controlling inflation by other than wage and price controls is a worthy objective only if its costs in poverty and alienation has not been too great.

Such a policy would have to confront the reality that many in the labor force are ill-prepared for work of any kind. To remedy such disabilities in the past, training programs have been proposed. Their effectiveness is regarded as having been limited.

Would it not be preferable to recognize that there are labor-intensive jobs in the society which need doing but are neglected because they are too costly? Maintenance of public spaces and places. Maintenance of private spaces, local security, for example. Labor intensive service such as day care. Is it not better to have this work done and paid for by money which would otherwise go for minimum assistance payments?

There will be those who say that any work in the public sector, for example, that is worth doing at all is worth doing at more than the minimum wage. However that is not the real choice. The real alternative is that the work will not otherwise be done at all and the welfare recipients will continue to receive their allowances.

This sort of work should be regarded as work of last resort. By offering an assured minimum income and an assured place to work and therefore a regular connection to the system, it should provide the incentives to acquire the skills to do better. Trying to do better in a full employment society will not be seen as the hopeless task it seems to be to so many of the unskilled unemployed today. If everybody who can is working, the body politic is much more likely to approve more adequate levels of support for those who cannot.

Should there be equality of opportunity for female heads of household as well as male and a correspondingly equal obligation to take proferred employment at the minimum wage? Why not? If we want to end welfare dependency and stabilize family life, is it not necessary that female heads of household be given the same opportunities and held to the same standards as male heads of household? To be sure, the mothers of very young children should have the option of caring for them in the home. Beyond that early age, which I do not here attempt to specify, day care should be made available to all parents who seek it. All agree that welfare as now administered for female-headed households is socially destructive, increasingly expensive and personally degrading. We must have a better system in place and then we must get rid of the present one.

Cost calculations for a last resort job program are difficult and beyond the scope of this report. They depend on assumptions about the number of persons receiving the guaranteed minimum annual income assistance and the number working at public sector jobs of last resort. With the whole program fully in operation, the cost of family assistance benefits should be far less than present expenditures for ADC. The local or state share of the costs of public sector last resort jobs should be more than offset by money saved from ADC. Additional costs beyond welfare savings should be distributed among the federal government and those other public or private employers who receive the benefits of work done. Care must be taken that last resort employees do not replace those working at a higher scale.

The impact of such an effort on the unity and outlook of the country could be electrifying. The critical choice we have is to deal with the problem comprehensively or in bits and pieces. The country would be better off in every way if it made such a commitment.

Things of the Spirit

Freedom of Religious Choice

I have suggested that the idea of America is choice. Although this report thus far has emphasized the physical aspects of the quality of life, it is important that the nonmaterial elements be considered as well.

A more adequate sharing of the necessities of life and the opportunities of achieving them for oneself are basic to our consideration of critical choices representing the quality of life. However, things of the spirit are also of the highest importance.

On the subject of religion America has made its critical decision—that there shall be effective freedom of choice. Individual Americans are free, as free as human beings have ever been, to practice the religion of their choice, or if they choose, not to practice any religion at all. Increasingly, Americans have been able to make that choice without fear of its consequences to their opportunities to lead their lives, otherwise, as they choose.

It is my belief that in a matter as critical and as personal as one's own religious beliefs, America has made the right critical choice and I do not propose others.

Family Life

American society has been organized since its inception with the concept of family at its inner core. Although migration to the New World often meant breaking up existing family ties the family immediately became re-established on these shores as the basic societal unit.

America began as a rural country, colonies, then a nation. It remained that way until World War I. The family was not only the key social unit, it was the key economic unit. The American farming family, unlike its European counterpart, tended to own its own land and to live on the farm apart from its neighbors. In addition, as was not uncommon elsewhere, the family was often an extended family and the entire group was involved in the work of the farm. Then there is the sad and separate history of the black family long subject to the whims of slavery. The evidence is that the black community has aspirations about family life that are not dissimilar from the white majority, but in terms of poverty segregation, discrimination, and misguided welfare programs is suffering still from severe handicaps.

In urban settlements, work was a part of family life from a very early age for every member, and because the family was most often an extended one, the housewife/mother had little time outside the home. In a basic economic sense, all of that has changed. As housing, employment, and welfare assistance patterns have evolved, the extended family is close to extinction. Labor saving devices have vastly reduced the necessary drudgery of housework for the housewife. Changes in the structure of the economy have opened up huge numbers of office and other service jobs to women which simply did not exist before. Child labor laws and increasing the number of years of education kept children in the home longer but with less to do.

These and many other changes in technology, communications, and mobility have changed the necessary economic and social basis of family life dramatically. In addition, as family life has moved away from at least partial self-sufficiency to interdependence with the world outside, each family member came, more and more, to have his own independent relations with the world outside.

In my view, America has not deliberately downgraded the central importance of the family in the life of our society. Few of us would choose to return to the older system with its labor-bound limitations for wife and children. Not to mention the six-day week, twelve-hour day for the breadwinner. There is no more reason for nostalgia about the old ways than there is for a return to the drudgery and higher mortality rates that also used to be the rule.

What has happened here and has happened elsewhere in developed countries is that the family relationship has shifted from a necessary association to a much freer association, particularly when children reach a certain level of maturity.

Despite changes in life style and habit patterns the nuclear family remains as the core unit of our society. I am confident that this should and will continue to be the case, despite the fact that there are competing life styles which receive more attention and therefore perhaps are considered more significant than their numbers would warrant.

We do, however, need continually, as we consider various other choices, welfare systems, full employment policies, housing programs, changes in the tax laws, and the like, to ask ourselves: Will this help or hurt the natural inclination of a nuclear family to stay together? The mess we have made of the family life of the poor under the welfare laws suggests how important such scrutiny can and should be.

Women's Liberation. It is hard to look back today and realize that less than sixty years ago, women did not even have the right to vote. Since that successful campaign of the suffragettes, there have been continuing efforts, usually led by women, often helped by national emergencies, to increase the equality of opportunity for women in education, in employment, and in a myriad other ways.

Recently, that effort has taken on another and rather different dimension. Recognizing that the role of women in our modern society was in fact largely a role assigned to them not by nature but by men, the women liberationists and their supporters have fought for a measure of equality never before sought or attained. While undoubtedly controversial, as are all efforts to make sweeping changes, however just, in established habit patterns, it is but a logical outcome of the fundamental change in the family from a necessary to a much freer association.

We cannot expect to encourage higher education for women, including access to top professional schools, without expecting to assure access to career opportunities which will put that training to full use. No more can we expect to change the nature of our economy away from a labor-intensive society, including the household, to a capital-intensive, service-oriented economy and not expect women to insist on free and equal access to all the opportunities which become available.

It was never necessary to the solidarity of the American family of a century ago that the housewife be a drudge and the young be engaged in child labor. It is not fatal to the vitality of the family unit as the core of our society today that women want equality in the broadest terms.

The Role of Public and Private Institutions
and of Individuals: Who Does What?

The structure of the American society is probably more pluralistic than that of any other nation. In this Bicentennial Year this may be America's greatest source of strength and resilience.

Whether it be government at whatever level, or the church or labor unions or private business or the incredibly varied panoply of voluntary associations, these entities can develop their own agendas and priorities, interact with one another, be influenced and attempt to exert influence. The vitality of American society is traceable at least in part to the extent to which individuals and organizations are free "to do their own thing."

We are and we should be deeply committed to the proposition that this vital pluralism be preserved. There is a role for government and for independent private associations of all kinds. Continuing renewal is the basic requirement for any society which expects to remain healthy and that our best hope of continuing to achieve that renewal is our pluralism. We should be wary of overweening concentrations of economic power.

Of all the basic organizing and acting forces in our society, government is the one that has the greatest continuing need for renewal. Its very power to exempt itself from the survival tests of so many other elements of society makes it most prone to stagnancy. Continuing reexamination of the efficacy of government and a strong two-party system are the most proven means of keeping government vital. Our healthy skepticism should be encouraged not decried.

For forty years our society has acted out the proposition that the public sector, and therefore the public purse were the best approach to solving basic public problems, particularly basic social problems. With the passage of time, the tendency to look to the federal government increased and the nation's elected leadership not only encouraged that reliance but spoke of its potential in the most positive terms. The confidence in both the wisdom and the effectiveness of this approach led to excesses in commitments, or more precisely, rhetorical commitments.

For a time the rhetoric from Washington appeared to bespeak a serious national commitment to social problem-solving for the least advantaged of our citizens and our communities. Unfortunately, the dollar resources and the administrative follow-through never caught up with that rhetoric. It has made too many of us skeptical about where federal action can be effective.

We tend to overlook the fact that in many advanced Western societies, the Scandinavian countries, for example, the critical choice has been made and the basic responsibility for eliminating poverty, providing social security and full employment has been successfully assigned to the national government while maintaining a very healthy private sector.

However, in our broad diverse land, certain diseconomies of scale arise. As the federal government moves away from routine, repetitive tasks in the local service delivery area it is frequently clumsy and ineffective.

There are some policies and some problems, however, which require a major national commitment. If it is determined that decent housing is to be made available at a reasonable cost to those who need it, the dollar cost of that subsidy must be picked up by the federal government. There is no financial alternative. The programs to implement such a policy, on the other hand, need not be federally administered at all.

If there is to be an effective national commitment to full employment, including a jobs of last resort program and an assured minimum annual income, that commitment can only come from the federal government. Again, carrying out the effort can be done by a combination of other levels of government and of business, labor, and voluntary associations.

On the other hand, in education and in cultural affairs, grateful for support and financial assistance though we might be, most of us would shrink from either federal control or federal guidelines.

Government should be limited in the functions and services it attempts to perform. Where feasible it is preferable to have state or local government in charge of day-to-day policy-making and of administration.

We are entering a period, perhaps prolonged, of serious public budget stringency. It is therefore appropriate that we embrace the difficult but important concept of zero-base budgeting on a regular and recurring basis. We all know of long-obsolete programs which are funded from year to year because "it's always been done that way." We need to reevaluate all of our customary commitments and see whether they fit today's priorities.

We have begun the painful process of acknowledging that we cannot afford to have government do all the things people would like it to do. We must develop understandable systems for making the critical choices for governmental resource allocations which a scarcity of funds require.

Having said all of that, it is important that we never forget that government is the sole legitimate representative of all the people, that it has the ultimate responsibility not only for national security and for keeping the domestic peace, but also that it is the ultimate vehicle for meeting the legitimate needs of the people if they cannot be met in any other way. Social justice, equal opportunity, and public safety cannot be left to other elements of society and abandoned by government.

Whenever and wherever possible, government should serve as the instigator, the incentive-creator, the catalyst rather than the actual doer. Our free enterprise system, for example, is extraordinarily responsive to changes in the internal revenue code. We should consider carefully how many of our societal goals could be met by tax incentives rather than by direct administrative actions or appropriations.

Our creative, productive business enterprise system should have the basic responsiblity for the development and management of our economy. With all its impediments and limitations, the profit system is the most effective system for managing the economy. We must be concerned about the damage which results from administered prices and from undue concentrations of business power. Not only do they tend to lessen competition, they tend to dilute a sense of corporate responsibility for the community in which the business, particularly an absorbed business, is located.

In a world economy of increasing state direction or ownership of enterprise, we should remain deeply committed to the preservation of a competitive free enterprise system. But we should be alert to the tendencies of that system to reduce or eliminate competition.

Among the critical choices facing the nation is the dual one of preserving our economic system from overregulation and control by government, on the one hand, and protecting it from the seemingly inevitable corporate tendency of combination, on the other.

The association of workers into labor unions to represent their economic interests is one of the hallmarks of a free society. A free and independent labor movement is the best means yet devised for seeing that workers have an effective opportunity to protect themselves. All of us are concerned about the abuses which from time to time have been found, and we believe that rooting them out is in the best interests of a strong and free union movement.

When it comes to churches, universities, and other voluntary associations in all their variety, our society has an opportunity, a self-interest, and an obligation to encourage as much strength, independence, and vitality as possible.

Looking over the landscape of Bicentennial America, the thing which may be most impressive about our nation is its deep and abiding commitment to pluralism. In this lies our strength, and one of our great critical choices is to keep that pluralism alive and healthy. Our society indeed can be strengthened not weakened by extending the boundaries of freedom in this way.

This is a critical choice America seems to be making. It is a healthy one.

National Morale. Finally, we need to consider our basic attitude about ourselves. It is fashionable today to cite national morale as being in a parlous state. Given what our country has been through in recent years, there may be cause for wonder that it is not said to be much worse. Would we be happier, given our recent past, if the body politic were uncritically confident that all was well in the best of all possible political worlds?

It is the function of the media in a free society and has always been to tell us what is wrong much more emphatically than what is right.

In our history there have been times when we have rallied together in a great thrust of unity and purpose to achieve certain agreed upon national objectives. Those have been heady times in the memory of those who have experienced them. Unfortunately, they have also usually been times of war.

Is it likely that we shall find in peacetime some soaring inspiration that will bring us together, leadership which will inspire us, work that will unite us?

Possibly. However, I suggest that the more important business of America is not to seek out that millennial answer but to get on with the day-to-day resolution of the problems that confront us and to press for answers.

What Constitutes "Quality" in Life?

Werner J. Dannhauser

By Way of Introduction

I begin with a silly scenario in order to make a point that is far from silly. Let us image a group of men, all of them learned and a few of them almost wise, gathered at the behest of a distinguished commission to ponder the question of what constitutes quality in life. Suddenly a member of the group divests himself of the following remarks:

Why are we pretending to be grappling with a difficult question when we are really dealing with a very simple one? Life may at times be well-nigh undefinable but for practical purposes—and we are practical men—it is almost unmistakable. We need go no further than to think of it as animate existence, in fact we don't even have to go that far. So much for one of the "big" words in the question. The term "quality" should give us no more trouble. It means a characteristic or a property or an attribute; for example hardness is one of the qualities of iron. Now all life has certain attributes or traits. The worker's life frequently has the quality of being boring; seediness is the outstanding quality of the bum's life. We have been overlooking the obvious fact that all the constituents of life compose its quality. In short, absolutely everything in life constitutes quality. And that's that. I propose we adjourn.

What would be the reaction to such a speech? Nobody would be shocked, for in our time the learned are not easy to shock, though some might doubt the

The author wishes to thank his colleague and friend Professor Myron Rush for his valuable comments on this chapter.

speaker's sanity. Yet, there is no self-evident madness in the speech, so someone in the group would have to discover what it is that makes the above remarks slightly puzzling and self-evidently beside the point. Sooner or later somebody would come up with an appropriate reply:

We agree with you that there is no need to ponder what constitutes life; human life is indeed readily recognizable for all practical purposes. But you misunderstand very badly our concern for "quality." We are not interested in all the traits and characteristics of life, but only with the *good* ones. If you will think twice about the word quality you will realize that it implies excellence. Thus if you ask for quality merchandise you expect good merchandise, and if you refer to someone as a man of quality you suggest he is a good man. We are only interested in the good qualities of life, wishing to know whether and/or how they might be enhanced.

That ought to satisfy our imaginary troublemaker, but let us, in the interest of furthering the argument, let him have the last word in this silly scenario:

I see. We say we are talking about the quality of life but we mean we are talking about the good quality of life. Fine. But the moment we make reference to goodness we might as well cease to refer to "quality." Let us face it, ladies and gentlemen; we are really asking a very ancient question: "What is the good life?" I do not for a moment doubt the urgency of that question, but at the moment a prior question demands attention. Why haven't we just come out and said what we mean?

Why indeed? In part, it is because the social sciences are seemingly unable to develop any immunity to fashionable jargon and to the tendency to make things sound as complicated as possible. Another reason seems to be at work here, however. By talking about quality, we are able to steer away from the word goodness, a word we assume to be hopelessly slippery, a word pointing to "values" and "value judgments." The word "quality" somehow makes the question sound more scientific. It is well known that social science is charmed by the evident competence of natural science and seeks to attain its precision, though it may thereby be seeking more precision than its subject matter permits.[1]

In any event, our hesitation in thinking of the good life *as* the good life betrays a certain anxiety concerning questions about the good life. That anxiety may be impossible to dispel—it may even constitute a reasonable dread—but it ought to be susceptible of articulation. Let us, then, try to articulate it.

We ask a simple question: What is the good life? The moment we ask it, however, we begin to discover that we are swimming, or diving, or perhaps even sinking, in very deep waters. In our search for an answer, we stumble on various difficulties. The list of difficulties here discussed is meant to be representative, not exhaustive.

1. One might argue that what constitutes the good life is known, but not a fit

subject for rational inquiry. "It hath been told thee, O man, what is good, and what the Lord doth require of thee: Only to do justly, to love mercy, and to walk humbly with thy God."[2] The good life has been revealed to man by God, and the thing most needful is not to discuss it but to live it; the thing most needful is obedience to the word of God. As Americans, indeed as human beings, only one critical choice confronts us: whether or not to obey the word of God. Such a point of view clearly deprecates our attempt to reason about the good life, but as reasonable men we must admit that such a deprecation of reason may be rational. It *may* be. We do not and we can not know that by the light of our reason, at least not until we have stretched our reason to its utmost limits. And those of us to whom God has not spoken or who have not understood Him clearly, have no other or better choice than to use our reason to try to understand the nature of the good life, though we should never preclude the possibility that our search may prove futile or unnecessary because it may end by merely repeating what the prophet Micah knew all along.

2. One may argue that there is not *the* good life but various kinds of good life. Now there may indeed be a number of goals to which men devote themselves, and we may be unable to decide which goal is the highest. For example, it is not at first sight completely obvious whether and in what sense a life devoted to public service is better than a life devoted to private learning. Suffice it at this point to say that the difficulty just described does not make rational inquiry either superfluous or obviously fruitless. Reason can attempt to describe the various kinds of good life. One suspects that it would have a hard time proving that the good life led by Abraham Lincoln is plainly superior or inferior to the good life led by William Shakespeare, but one also suspects that reason might well show that (at least for practical purposes) there is not an infinite variety of lives that can lay serious claim to being considered a form of the good life. Thus one would be hard-put to mount a successful case before the bar of reason for passionate bottlecap collecting as something noble; and reason probably could show that the life of the saint is clearly superior to the life of the drunkard. The achievement of such distinctions would be no mean thing and would amply justify an inquiry into the good life even though the latter fell short of finding *the* good life.

3. One might, however, argue that any rational inquiry into the good life is senseless because the question, What constitutes the good life?, is a senseless question. It is senseless because there is no objective meaning to "good." To say "this is good" is to say no more than, though also no less than, "I like this." To say that X is 6 feet tall is to state something that is subject to measurement, and therefore to verification or falsification. To say that X is a good man is merely to voice a preference for X, something that can never enjoy greater prestige, greater accuracy, than an expressed aversion for X. The size of X is an objective fact about X and inheres in X, but the goodness of X, or his beauty, is in the eye of the beholder. This is the type of argument that elaborates on the well-known

profundity that one man's meat is another man's poison, though one should note that the latter is, strictly speaking, factually incorrect. It does no more than point to the fact that different people prefer different diets, or that not every diet is equally suitable to every physical constitution. That argument hardly had to await the development of modern philosophy or science: It is already used in Plato's *Republic*.[3]

I am forced to deal with this argument at greater length than with the previous two contentions because of its enormous and continuing influence and popularity. It is an argument especially potent among the young, possibly because their elders have made its advocacy almost equivalent to learning itself. Thus one is considered educated once one comes to realize that one can't dispute about taste, that all values are in principle equal—in short, that "everything is relative." By holding such "truths" to be self-evident, one is presumably lifted above the ignorance of the many and the superstitions of a horrible past. One thereby escapes the bog of subjective evaluations and stands firmly on "scientific fact."

Let me first consider the consequences of a line of thought holding values to have no cognitive status, even though "values" are hardly ever defined by those denying them validity. If we cannot rationally decide as to the merits of various notions of the good life, then talk of the good life becomes a kind of chatter, potentially amusing but certainly useless. Now the adherence to this belief—let us call it radical relativism—almost inevitably constitutes an invitation to slothful thinking. A single example must suffice. A and B go to see a movie. Afterwards A asks B, "How did you like it?" B says, "I thought it stank." A replies, "Oh really? I thought it was great." After a bit of banter B good-naturedly says, "Well, there is no arguing about taste." A agrees and the subject is changed. What happened here? What happened is that a dogmatic belief in relativism caused thinking to stop just at the point where it should have started. The two might, after all, have pondered *what* it is that makes for a good movie. In that case, they might have ended by concluding that there is ultimately no such thing as an objectively good movie and still, in the process of benevolent controversy, learned a good deal about movies. But radical relativism, aborting discussions even about what constitutes goodness in movies, certainly tends to abort serious inquiry into what constitutes goodness in life.

Secondly, the belief that there is no such thing as an objectively good life, or that all evaluations are subjective and thus equally defensible (or indefensible) before the bar of reason, takes it for granted that all *subjects* are equal and thus precludes the possibility of establishing a possibly objective hierarchy of subjects. Again, one example must suffice. Suppose one man thinks of *Valley of the Dolls* as the greatest of all novels, while another thinks that distinction belongs to *War and Peace*. By focusing all attention on the alleged impossibility of objective judgments of books, relativists ignore the possibility of an objective judgment of the judges of books. But does it not make a difference that one of the evaluators is an inveterate and passionate student of literature, while the other reads books only when he is unable to gratify passions much dearer to him?

Finally, and most seriously, the inevitable consequence of our inability objectively to say what constitutes the good life is nihilism. If we are unable to distinguish between good and bad, then it would seem not to matter what kind of life we choose. That is precisely what nihilism asserts, according to Nietzsche, the greatest modern analyst of nihilism: If nothing is true, everything is permitted. In other words, nothing matters and anything goes. A life devoted to lechery, a life devoted to the murder of the Jews, a life devoted to the relief of man's estate—there is no self-evident hierarchy among these because it makes no difference what we do, and only some obscure drives or hesitations would lead us to prefer decency to indecency, assuming that such terms retain any meaning. Some nihilists go further and maintain that since no action is intrinsically worth doing, the only rational act is to destroy: It is, according to some Nietzschean nihilists, better to will nothingness than not to will.

Today, as Americans and as human beings, all of us know more about nihilism than we would like to know; we have it, as it were, in our bones. We have seen its effects in recent history, for there was a good deal of perspicuity at work in labeling Nazism the revolution of nihilism. And we experience it inwardly as a sense of loss of purpose. Nothing seems worthwhile to us. It is not that we are evil, it is that we do not know what is good and, if we do know, we do not know why it should command the full measure of our devotion. "The good life" has become an empty phrase for many of us, for too many of us.

What, then, is to be done? Nihilism is easier to describe than to refute. I have pointed to some of the dreadful consequences of nihilism, but one has not refuted a doctrine by pointing to its dreadful consequences. We may really be living in an utterly meaningless world about which we have previously been deluding ourselves by inventing delusions like standards for living the good life. Ours may be the time for which a capricious fate has reserved the discovery of the truth, the most fundamental truth being that the truth is dreadful. In that case, we have no way of escaping nihilism, for naïveté and innocence would seem to be beyond recovery once they are lost.

But does nihilism really render an adequate account of reality? Dreadful consequences do not, to be sure, refute nihilism, but neither do they prove it true. Our time seems to have a propensity for identifying the true with the terrible, but that is not obviously more sensible than the propensity, found at other times, to identify the true with the pleasant.[4] And while the terrible *may* be true, our terror certainly constitutes a legitimate motive for questioning the truth of nihilism and for seeking to refute, transcend, and overcome nihilism, of which many things might be said, but not that it makes us happy.

Our search, it ought not to need saying, should be as open-minded as possible. Now an open-minded approach to the way men look and have looked at the world discloses a tradition of thought which holds that the good life is more than a subjective delusion, but rather an objective standard that imposes penalties for its disregard. Nothing is clearer than that we are in need of help, and we may be able to find it in what the wisest of men have said and thought in the past.

In this respect, the history of political philosophy ceases to be merely an antiquarian academic exercise and becomes a possible source of guidance for modern man. It has been, and continues to be (contrary to reports of its death) the guardian of that part of our tradition stemming from Athens, the part maintaining that there *is* such a thing as the good life and that it is within the competence of reason to discern it.

I turn first to the articulation of the good life in the political philosophies of Plato and Aristotle.

The Good Life According to Classical Political Philosophy

Modern man, I have tried to show, is reluctant to refer to the good life *as* the good life and somehow afraid to ask the question, "What is the good life?" That reluctance and that fear, however, are aspects of his plight, making it urgent that he *do* confront the question of the good life. Haunted by the specter of nihilism, modern man is in danger of losing his bearings. More than forty years ago, Freud began his analysis of modern man's plight by writing: "It is impossible to escape the impression that people commonly use false standards of measurement—that they seek power, success and wealth for themselves and admire them in others, and that they underestimate what is of true value in life."[5] The passage retains its relevance today; modern man needs help.

Needing help, we should not succumb to the pride that insists that sources more ancient than Freud and the twentieth century have lost their ability to speak to us meaningfully because their wisdom, such as it was, has been superseded. It is safer to assume that the great books of the wisest men of old remain available and accessible to us precisely because they *are* able to help us, if only we admit our need for help, and remain open to the possibility that what makes a classic a classic is that it contains some reflection of the truth.

When we turn to classical political philosophy for help, in the spirit I have just described, we nevertheless find two obstacles threatening to bar our access and thus demanding at least cursory attention. I have referred above to Plato and Aristotle, certainly *the* two giants of the branch of our tradition stemming from Athens. In the interests of brevity and of obtaining an overview, I will almost completely overlook the admitted and considerable differences between Plato and Aristotle, differences that led Coleridge to proclaim that all men were *either* Platonists *or* Aristotelians. With all due respect to the eminent poet, it suffices for present purposes to mention that Aristotle was a student of Plato, thought that bad men did not have the right even to praise Plato, and that both men inhabit the same universe of discourse, the universe we call classical political philosophy. Moreover, what separates both Plato and Aristotle from modern political philosophy is of incomparably greater magnitude than what separates them from each other. Most of the principles I will be expounding have textual support in both Plato and Aristotle, though I will be relying a bit more on the latter than on the former. The reason is that Plato wrote elusive and shimmering dialogues, while Aristotle wrote treatises; the meaning of the latter is easier to establish than the meaning of the former.

A consideration of the second obstacle is tantamount to an introduction to the substance of the question under consideration. It is legitimate and even necessary to ask why, in seeking enlightenment about the good life, we should turn to *political* philosophy? What is the good life?—is that really a political question? Do we not rather want to know how to structure our own soul, deal with its most private sectors and dark nights? The answer, it would appear, must be sought in psychology (the study of the soul) or moral philosophy. Such reservations lose their force once one realizes the breadth of classical political philosophy and the fact that it antedates modern divisions of knowledge. Francis Bacon—and not the ancients—is the father or grandfather of the modern college catalogue. In Plato and Aristotle, no precise distinction among morality, politics, and psychology can be made. Thus Plato's *Republic* can be and is studied in courses in politics as well as ethics, and also contains an elaboration of the structure of the soul. Thus too, Aristotle's *Politics* is a continuation of his *Ethics*, and one book illuminates the other. As to the breadth of classical political philosophy: One does not exaggerate when one understands its theme to be the way man lives and ought to live on this earth. If one states that the single most important question guiding its endeavors is "What is the best political order?", one must add at once that this question tends to become indistinguishable from the question, "What is the best way for a man to live?" or "What is the good life?"

The reason for the convergence of the two questions emerges from the consideration of a single famous dictum by Aristotle, a dictum also leading eventually to the classical answer to the question. It reads ". . . it is evident that the polis belongs to the class of things that exist by nature, and that man is by nature an animal intended to live in a polis."[6]

That statement asserts many things. To begin with, it asserts that man has a nature. According to classical political philosophy, man is constituted by an essence that can be molded in various ways but is in the most decisive respects permanent and unchangeable. The good life, it will turn out, consists of living according to nature, in actualizing nature's potentialities to the fullest possible extent. Since man has a permanent nature, since human nature is an objective datum, the good life understood as the life according to nature is also in principle something objective. It scarcely needs to be said that modern thought frequently denies either or both the goodness or permanence of human nature. It denies nature as a standard. We will return to these points later; now we are concerned with learning more about what Aristotle meant by nature.

Nature, according to Aristotle, intends—or even impels—man to live in a polis; the statement now being explicated is sometimes rendered as follows: Man is by nature a political animal. (The word "polis," from which the word "political" stems, is difficult to translate. It is frequently rendered as city, or city-state, or state. Its closest equivalent is probably "country" as when we say "My country, right or wrong"—except, of course, that nobody says that any more.) Man is so constituted that he belongs in a social or political community. If this is true, it might follow that the good life presupposes a political order, that government is in most cases the cause and in all cases the precondition for the good life, that good political societies are more conducive to the good life than bad political orders, and so on. But is it true? What of the man who finds his fulfillment in solitude, and what about the way of life recommended by Thoreau in *Walden*?

The experience and even the happiness of solitary men do not refute the assertion that sociality is a basic and enduring characteristic of man. If the "loner" is more than a savage brute, he connects the good life he imagines himself to be leading with his contempt for and superiority to political communities; his contentedness presumes the existence of political orders he can despise or avoid. Or consider the case of Thoreau. His existence at Walden, admittedly attractive in many respects, was unthinkable without the close proximity of a civilized political community within walking distance. Moreover, Thoreau was an educated man, the beneficiary of the kind of schooling only organized political societies can provide. Finally, he wrote and published books, which is to say he desired a reading audience of the kind which once again presupposes political society.

Man's sociality is so obvious a datum that it needs little documentation. It is in part, but only in part, biologically determined: The human infant, unlike the animals preceding him on what is called the evolutionary scale, is born extraordinarily helpless. He can not even walk before he is one year old, and he will perish unless he receives continuous and even loving social care for an extended period.

Thus men come together into political communities because of their needs.[7] The most basic form of association, according to Aristotle, is between males and females for the sake of the reproduction of the species. Next there is an association of those naturally ruling and those naturally ruled. Neither is as yet a specifically human form of association, since animals copulate, and beehives have masters and slaves. As a form of association, the family comes closer to being specifically human and the village closer yet. Both satisfy either the daily or the regularly recurring needs of human beings. But the daily and regularly recurring needs of men are not necessarily the highest needs of man or his specifically human needs. Only an association meeting the latter can properly speaking be called a political association. Hence Aristotle writes:

When we come to the final and perfect association formed from a number of villages, we have already reached the polis—an association which may be said to have reached the height of full self-sufficiency; or rather [to speak more exactly] we may say that while it *grows* for the sake of mere life [and is so far and at that stage still short of full self-sufficiency] it *exists* [when once it is fully grown] for the sake of the good life [and is therefore fully self-sufficient].[8]

Since it makes explicit reference to the good life, the above passage deserves some explication. First of all, Aristotle suggests that the good life is in some way connected with self-sufficiency. But since the latter is in turn connected with political or social life, it can scarcely mean what modern man often takes it to mean. Today one frequently imagines a man self-sufficient if he has a minimum amount of contact and desire for contact with his fellowman. For Aristotle, by contrast, self-sufficiency implies a fulfillment of a human nature that is social. Thus friendship is a crucial part of the fulfilled life; indeed, Aristotle's political philosophy might be said to culminate in its advocacy and articulation of friendship.[9]

Secondly, Aristotle makes an absolutely essential distinction between mere life and the good life. One suspects that much of what current politics and politicians would classify as inescapable components of the good life would be held by Aristotle to be aspects of mere life. (Consider, for example, those portions of the programs of both major political parties concerned with the perpetuation and enlargement of the welfare state.) Roughly speaking, one can say that all those aspects of life man shares with other animals belong to the sphere of mere life, and that those aspects of life that are unique to human beings belong to the sphere of the good life. (I shall return to this distinction below.)

Which does not mean that Aristotle is insensitive to the requirements of mere life. Unless the latter are met, talk of the good life must remain mere talk. Hungry men will not be concerned with virtue, and they may be driven to steal regardless of what is decreed by positive, natural, or even divine law. Men who are unable to clothe themselves or their children must not be expected to have much regard for truth or beauty or goodness, and men living in hovels will not listen carefully to exhortations about the proper care of the soul. The requirements of mere life thus have a priority in time over the requirements of the good life. Aristotle and Plato realized as much, and recent history confirms our thesis. Talk about the good life—in the form of talk about the quality of life—became prominent only after giant strides had been made toward the amelioration of poverty. The good life becomes a matter of national concern after the birth and growth of what Galbraith called the affluent society. The concern follows the realization that adequate food, shelter, and clothing do not necessarily, or even frequently, make men happy or good. It ought to go without saying, but it probably does not, that such a realization does not constitute an argument—either for Aristotle or any other rational man—against insisting that one's fellow citizens be adequately clothed, fed, and sheltered.

According to Aristotle, the polis exists *for the sake* of the good life. The relationship between mere life and the good life resembles the relationship between means and ends. The requirements of mere life may have priority in time, but the good life has the priority of importance; it is the end or final purpose of life. On the one hand, therefore, classical political philosophy manifests a kind of severity and harshness: The idea of the infinite preciousness of life *as* life—as mere life—stems from Jerusalem rather than Athens. On the other hand, Plato and Aristotle do not for a moment underestimate the necessity of providing for the needs of mere life, or even the continuing and close connections between mere life and the good life. The good life is the life of virtue, but Aristotle realizes full well that virtue needs equipment.[10] Thus generosity with money is a virtue, but in order to exercise that virtue one needs money. Thus, too, a virtuous political order entails measures against excessive poverty—and wealth. The other side of the severity and harshness of classical political philosophy is its freedom from sentimentality. It can be said to teach morality without succumbing to the temptation of being moralistic.

The same lack of moralism comes very much to the forefront when we now seek more information about the substance or content of the good life according to classical political philosophy. The good life aims to secure the highest good. Now what is the "highest of all goods"? A verbal agreement about it exists, "for both the general run of men and people of superior refinement say that it is happiness, and identify living well and doing well with being happy. . . ."[11] By making happiness the end or final purpose of human actions and yearnings, classical political philosophy recognizes that when one is told to be moral, it is only natural to ask, "Why?" or "What's in it for me?"[12] The answer, crudely put, is "only the good life will make you happy (if anything will)." The pursuit of other goods is not nearly so self-evident. Thus the father who admonishes his son to go into business must expect the question, "Why should I want to devote myself to making money?" If the perplexed parent answers, "Because money is power," the perplexed son may wonder why he should desire power, and an infinite regress threatens to arise. It stops, however, when the answer becomes "It provides your best chance for happiness." People are so constituted that they do not ask "Why should I be happy?" If goodness is equated with happiness, the gulf between the "is" and the "ought," so agonizing to many honorable men, disappears. Men not only *ought* to be devoted to happiness; they *are* devoted to happiness.

The hard-headedness evident in the above considerations also manifests itself in classical political philosophy's refusal to grant absolute assurance that the good man will necessarily be happy. The good man may, after all, be subject to the slings and arrows of outrageous fortune, and calamity may exact an exorbitant fee from him. If misfortune strikes him—a crippling disease, the death of somebody beloved, and so on—he can scarcely be expected to feel happy. But Plato and Aristotle would insist that even in cases of extreme adversity it is better to be a virtuous man than a vicious man, for the simple reason that the virtuous excel the vicious in bearing adversity; they display more equanimity. Furthermore, while it is possible for the virtuous to be unhappy, it is impossible for the vicious to be happy. Their souls are in a state of disarray; they are unable to function well and thus to profit from good fortune; one is tempted to say that everything turns to wormwood for them. Men are forever asking why the wicked prosper. According to classical political philosophy the question has a very simple answer: They don't. Virtue may command insufficient reward but vice carries with it its own punishment; it makes those infested with it unhappy, at least in the long run.

At this point somebody might object that when one says that happiness is the greatest good, one has not said very much unless one goes on to state the ingredients of happiness. Of what exactly does happiness consist? That Aristotle is aware of the cogency of this objection appears from the fact that he states that one secures only verbal agreement by identifying living and doing well with being happy.[13] Furthermore, Aristotle identifies happiness as the chief and final good in the *first* book of the *Ethics*, leaving himself more than nine books to inquire into the nature of human happiness. He knows that some men find, or rather think they find, their happiness in sensual pleasure, some in wealth, some in honor. Others—a few—seek a life of contemplation. One should note, however, that Aristotle does not think there is an *infinite* number of possible ends that are identifiable with happiness. Also, men may think they are happy without being happy. Happiness is a kind of contentedness but it is an enviable kind of contentedness. The man in the insane asylum who thinks he is Napoleon may think himself blessed, but who would like to be like him? Happiness is not a subjective phenomenon; there are objective criteria for deciding who is happy.

All well and good, but what are these criteria? At this point we must have recourse once more to the classical concept of human nature, to a human nature that, according to Aristotle, "makes nothing in vain" and "always aims at bringing about the best."[14] The good life is the life according to nature. Nature points the way to the kind of life that makes man good and maximizes the chances of making him happy. Man can choose to ignore that way, to be sure, for unlike other animals he is capable of more than one way, of acting unnaturally, but by so doing he is going "against the grain," he violates the way he was meant to be and to act.

By stating that nature makes nothing in vain, Aristotle suggests that things, including men, are so made that they have a certain function or end, and that they are good when they perform their function well, or when they do their work well. Different beings have different functions, and the specific function of a being defines both its nature and its excellence or virtue. Thus it belongs to the nature of rivers to flow and of flowers to blossom.

What about the nature of man? We have already seen that, according to Aristotle, man is by nature a social or political animal, and that his sociality is in part, but only in part, biologically determined. Human society is specifically *human* society to the extent it differs from a beehive or a colony of ants, to the extent men differ from bees and ants. We have already pointed to an absolutely essential difference by observing that man can exercise free choice. An ant is so made that it can do nothing but try to be as good an ant as possible, and it is a member of a society governed by what we today would call instinctual behavior. Man, by contrast, can choose to act against the good of his society; he can even choose to leave it or seek to destroy it. And in that society a large measure of instinct is replaced by reason. One says as much when one attributes the capacity of choice to man, for true choice entails the ability to reason. What makes man unique, according to classical political philosophy, is his reason, his *logos*, a word also translatable as speech. Man is the only animal possessing language. That ancient dictum is most decidedly not refuted by the modern research indicating that many animals, especially dolphins, communicate by sound. For what can a dolphin "say"? At best he can "say" to a second dolphin, "Follow me." The second dolphin is unable to ask "Why?" And if he were able to ask that, the first dolphin could offer him no compelling *reason*; truly to speak is to reason together. Modern research has gone very little beyond what Aristotle knew when he asserted that by making sounds animals can signify their perceptions of pleasure and pain to each other, but that true speech serves to declare "what is advantageous and what is the reverse," and therefore, also, "what is just and what is unjust." Man's ability and need to speak makes him social to a much higher degree than ants or bees.[15]

Man is the only animal endowed with speech or reason. Since nature makes nothing in vain, man's specific fulfillment must have something to do with the highest possible development of his reason. Man's reason is meant to be sovereign over his passions. Common speech indicates as much. We are said to suffer our passions and to suffer from them, which is to say we are not identical with our passions. When man yields to a desire he is likely to say "I don't know what got into me," or "I was beside myself." When a man is unable to control his passions, he is said to be a slave to his passions, but when his reason is sovereign he is not said to be a slave to his reason.[16]

To lead a good life, then, means to lead a life of reasoning. It seems men always qualify the notion of being good by changing it to "good at." For example, in martial societies to be good tends to mean to be good at making war, and according to those influenced by modern psychological notions to be good tends to mean to be good at making love. Now to classical political philosophy to be good means to be good at thinking. The best life involves the unceasing and intransigent quest for wisdom; the best life is the life of the philosopher; *the* model of the good life is that of Socrates. That may be why Plato's political philosophy is not articulated in treatises but in a series of exquisitely etched portraits of Socrates.[17]

To sum up: According to the authoritative understanding of classical political philosophy developed by Leo Strauss,

> . . . the proper work of man consists in living thoughtfully, in understanding, and in thoughtful action. The good life is the life that is in accordance with the natural order of man's being, the life that flows from a well-ordered or healthy soul. The good life simply is the life in which the requirements of man's natural inclinations are fulfilled in the proper order to the highest possible degree, the life of a man who is awake to the highest possible degree, the life of a man in whose soul nothing lies waste. The good life is the perfection of man's nature. It is the life according to nature.[18]

Such an understanding of the good life obviously has many and decisively important consequences for man's political life. First of all, classical political philosophy is essentially inegalitarian. It holds that ultimately there is nothing more needful, or lofty, than man's quest for wisdom. But men, who may be equal in many respects, differ radically in their ability to think or to philosophize. Since the man who can and does philosophize is a better man than the common man, he deserves more than the common man. The classical conception of the good life leads to a conception of the good political order as an hierarchical political order. Such an order is more in accordance with nature than an egalitarian political order, for wherever one looks in nature, one finds that some creatures rule while others are being ruled.

Second, the best political order is necessarily of a very limited size. Man is social, but his sociality has limits. He must love his fellow-citizens, but there is such a phenomenon as spreading one's love too thin. He must understand the political order of which he is a part, but human understanding has natural limits. Thus a classical political philosopher might well say that the United States is simply too large to be either lovable or comprehensible. The optimum size of a polis is such that every citizen is at least acquainted with an acquaintance of every other citizen. The best polis, to understate the case, would have a population considerably less than that of New York City.

Third, life in the best political order partakes of the austere and the severe. The political order has the purpose of promoting the good life and the conditions most conducive to it. The best political order will therefore exercise censorship without hesitation; it will not tolerate atheism or religious freedom; it will employ capital punishment when necessary. It takes its bearings by nature, but it assumes that constraint and compulsion are fully as natural as permissiveness—indeed, more so. Nature endows us not only with unruly passions but with the brains to see that those passions must be ruled, and with the ability to devise ways of keeping them in check.

Fourth, the best political order is a closed political society. For most men the good life necessarily entails a good deal of public-spiritedness, and public-spiritedness entails distinction between "us" fellow citizens and "them," the foreigners. Cosmopolitanism, the doctrine of those who say "The world is my city," is not considered a viable political orientation by classical political philosophy. As can be seen from a study of Plato's *Republic*, the best political order is one occasionally engaged in war, though it is beyond doubt that in classical thought peace is superior to war.

Finally, political life is to some extent at least devoted to and justified by a transpolitical end. The good life for most men consists in the fullest possible development of their public-spiritedness and involves the fullest possible devotion to the common good. However, the good life of the best men is the life of the philosopher, and in the last analysis one may wonder whether the philosopher is not more loyal to the truth than to his fatherland. Philosophy is an essentially private activity. Classical philosophy culminates, then, in the recognition of the problem that the good life of the very best men may be in tension with the good of any and all political orders. Nothing illustrates this problem more profoundly than the life-and death—of Socrates.

One might, then, say that classical political philosophy never fully solved the problems connected with the good life. Before one condemns it for its failure, however, one would have to be sure that a solution exists. The best part of human wisdom may be the recognition that the problem of how men ought to live on this earth is not susceptible to any elegant solution. In that case we are all indebted to classical political philosophy, for it can be characterized on the one hand by its noble simplicity and serene grandeur, and on the other hand by its faithfulness to the complexity of reality.

The Limited Applicability of the Classical
Conception of the Good Life

Only a bigoted dogmatist would simply accept the teachings of Plato and Aristotle as unquestionably true, and if he did his advocacy of classical political philosophy would be perpetrated in a spirit completely alien to classical political philosophy. A benevolent skepticism, understood as a permanent will to open horizons, would seem to be an incomparably more intelligent orientation to bring to the teachings of Plato and Aristotle, an orientation close to the spirit animating them. It suffices in this respect to mention the repeated professions by Socrates of his own ignorance[19] and Aristotle's great emphasis on prudence or practical wisdom.[20]

The good life consists in doing and acting well under given circumstances, and prudence dictates that one be forever mindful of the circumstances providing the matrix for a given action. The radical relativist denies that any action can ever be objectively good; the doctrinaire dogmatist insists that certain rules always apply, regardless of the circumstances. Classical political philosophy takes the middle road; certain actions are objectively good, but the circumstances must be taken into consideration.

Because it is aware that circumstances change, classical political philosophy does not issue in any equivalent of the ten commandments. Aristotle was far from a moral relativist, but he went so far as to state that "there is something that is just even by nature, yet all of it is changeable. . . ."[21] One looks in vain for universally applicable maxims of behavior in classical political philosophy (which is why the full development of natural law doctrines had to await the emergence of Christianity). Plato and Aristotle might be said to teach that the good life is the life led by the best men. That statement only *appears* to be tautological. First of all, we all find it easier to know what a good man is than what, in any given case, a good action is; that is why, incidentally, the American electorate can be said to be both abysmally ignorant of specific issues and generally (by no means always) quite competent in electing "the better man" to office. In trying to live a good life, one can do far worse than trying to imitate Socrates, or the magnanimous man described by Aristotle.

Secondly, a good man at times—when necessity dictates—will perform actions that are *almost* always bad or even evil. A single example must suffice. It is wrong to kill, but a good man might well have chosen to kill Hitler had he been given the opportunity. To repeat: Classical political philosophy teaches us to take circumstances, and especially changing circumstances into consideration, which is precisely why classical political philosophy is of limited applicability today. I mention three enormous changes of circumstances since the days of Plato and Aristotle, circumstances demanding to be taken into consideration.

The first is the unforseeable emergence of Christianity out of Jerusalem. Rome, in some measure the heir of Athens, began by persecuting Christianity, but by 395 AD laid down its arms before the new faith. Today we think that the teachings stemming from Athens have much in common with the teachings stemming from Jerusalem. They may indeed have more in common with each other than either does with most modern conceptions of the good life, but we should understand that originally a great gulf separated Athens from Jerusalem. St. Paul knew whereof he spoke when he said that the new teaching was "foolishness" to the Greeks,[22] and so did St. Augustine when he maintained that from the standpoint of Jerusalem the virtues of the pagans were but splendid vices.[23]

The most massive difference between the two conceptions of the good life has already been alluded to above: According to Athens, the good life consists preeminently in living by the dictates of human reason, and according to Jerusalem, the good life is the life of loving obedience to God. The man of faith, as exemplified by Abraham, does not hesitate to take his only son, whom he loves, to sacrifice him if commanded by a mysterious God who gives absolutely no reason for His orders.[24] In the same situation the man of reason, as exemplified by Socrates, would, to say the very least, hesitate. One can, to be sure, attempt to produce a synthesis between the two conceptions of the good life, but even the imposing example of St. Thomas permits one to wonder whether a perfect synthesis is feasible. Be that as it may, the life which emphasizes the priority of revelation over reason presents a new problem to classical political philosophy. The latter apparently has to admit that reason can ultimately do no more than admit the possibility of revelation. Moreover, the problems confronting modernity, at least in the West, seem more closely tied to the alleged or real exhaustion of Christianity than to the alleged or real refutation of the classical concept of the good life. We admit as much when we equate the crisis of our time with the "death of God," the latter surely being a post-Christian phenomenon. In short, problems that could scarcely have been anticipated by Plato and Aristotle seem to have arisen.

The second of the many changed circumstances that should be mentioned is the amazing development, since the days of antiquity, of science, and technology. The ramifications of such a development are too numerous to enumerate completely, but some deserve special mention. To begin with, the new science tends to view the world mechanistically. To the extent, therefore, that classical conceptions of the good life are tied to an understanding of the universe as teleological or purposive, they are radically cast into doubt. Secondly, science allied with technology make it seem far from inevitable, and finally far from desirable, that man live according to nature, for they raise the serious possibility that nature might be subdued. According to the ancients, nature limits man. At times it even cuts him down: There are natural cataclysms such as earthquakes which can be understood, if they can be understood at all, only as the hidden beneficence of nature, her way of keeping man from excessive pride. According to the moderns, nature can be conquered "for the relief of man's estate."

According to classical political philosophy, man's good life must be lived in the context of certain limitations imposed by nature. Thus the classical conception of the good life assumes the existence of natural scarcity. If some men are to have the leisure to produce the high civilization to which human potentiality points, other men must labor long and hard. Some measure of poverty is unavoidable, and since full political participation demands leisure, it is beyond the reach of many, perhaps most. But if scarcity can be abolished, is there any remaining explanation for limiting political participation except mean-spiritedness?

The third and final changed circumstance I will mention is the disappearance of the polis. We live in an era of super-states. The ancients held that in political societies larger than the polis, good government—and hence the good life—was gravely threatened. This argument was still taken seriously enough by the Founding Fathers of the United States for them to expend a good deal of energy arguing against it.[25] Today we take large republics for granted, but we should realize that we thereby also take a number of other political "realities" for granted. A war between one polis and another might be undesirable and tragic, but it would hardly endanger the survival of the human species and might thus be considered an alternative of which one might avail oneself, there being things worse than war. A war between two nuclear superpowers, by contrast, might well endanger the survival of the human species, and war thus becomes "unthinkable."

In other words, and to coin a phrase, times have changed. It would be completely contrary to the spirit of the ancients to attempt to go back to ancient ways in order to enhance our chances of leading a good life. Such an attempt would be preposterous, because it would involve the demolition of the liberal democracy to which we are heir, and that demolition would entail upheavals calculated to make decent life impossible. Plato and Aristotle would almost certainly agree with a radically modern philosopher, Nietzsche, when he "whispers to conservatives" that, "today there are still parties whose dream it is that all things might walk backwards like crabs. But no one is free to be a crab. Nothing avails: one must go forward. ..."[26] The same Aristotle who counsels that the best regime ought ever to be the object of our wishes and prayers, teaches us the soundness, and even the nobility of saying, "Sparta has fallen to our lot; let us adorn it."

The United States of America has fallen to our lot; let us adorn it. It is in this spirit that we turn to modern conceptions of the good life.

The Conception of the Good Life in Modern Political Philosophy

We turn to this, our penultimate topic, in a sober and proper spirit, but we are at once confronted with an imposing difficulty. Is there enough homogeneity present in modernity and modern political philosophy to permit meaningful discourse and meaningful generalizations? Modernity, after all, includes not only liberal democracy but also fascism, communism, and a host of other "isms." Life-saving drugs, concentration camps, universal suffrage, ecological dangers, the approach of universal literacy, the decline of universally accepted norms, increased prosperity, decreased stability—all these are modern phenomena. And modern political philosophy emerges at first sight as a fierce contest among incompatible views: Locke takes Hobbes to task; Hegel corrects Kant; Burke detests Rousseau; and Marx and Nietzsche seem to agree only about the failure of all previous political philosophy.

I will attempt to circumvent this difficulty in various ways. First of all, I am primarily concerned with the philosophy informing and animating the conception of the good life in liberal democracies. Our first concern must be for the good life here and now, in these United States. That does not imply mere selfishness; we may have the duty to foster the good life everywhere on earth, but only by knowing what it is and living it ourselves do we become truly effective advocates of it. Secondly, I will restrict myself to predominant trends in modern political philosophy, readily admitting that such a procedure involves a certain injustice to certain thinkers. Finally, and most importantly, this chapter will concentrate on what may indeed be the most common feature of all or nearly all of modern political philosophy: its rejection of classical political philosophy. One is tempted to say that modern political philosophy *defines itself* by its opposition to past thought, and I will not attempt to resist that temptation. The strategy of elaborating a series of contrasts has an additional advantage. It permits frequent reference to what has been elaborated in earlier parts of this chapter, and thus it encourages greater brevity than I have hitherto attained.

Perhaps the most obvious difference between ancient and modern political philosophy, as seen from the perspective of the latter, is that classical thought is Utopian while modern thought understands itself as more realistic. Both Plato and Aristotle expend a good deal of energy on describing the best regime, even while conceding that such a regime is most likely to exist in speech rather than in deed. Its actualization is not absolutely impossible for it does not depend on an alteration of human nature, but one understates the case when one describes its actualization as highly unlikely. The best regime can come into being only when power and wisdom coincide, which is to say its actualization depends on coincidence or chance. Neither Plato nor Aristotle can point to any regime that has ever existed as even an approximation of the simply best regime.[27] But the best regime, it will be remembered, is always the precondition and almost always the cause of the best life. The classical conception of the good life can also be understood as utopian in its own right. According to both Plato and Aristotle, the simply good life is the life of contemplation, the life of the philosopher. But almost all men lack the natural equipment or good fortune needed to become philosophers, and all other varieties of life, though possibly not devoid of merit or dignity, pale by comparison to the philosophic life.

Classical political philosophy can, then, be accused of dreaming an impossible dream. In order to have the power to inspire and move men, the concept of the good life must lie within the reach of all or nearly all men. By being too idealistic, classical political philosophy is useless. It may even be worse than useless because the disappointment necessarily engendered by the pursuit of unreachable goals may make men worse than they already are.

Such considerations first come to the fore in the thought of Machiavelli, who has the distinction of being the first modern political philosopher, and to whom modern thought owes more than it is at times willing to acknowledge. According to Machiavelli,

Many have imagined republics and principalities which have never been seen or known to exist in reality; for how we live is so far removed from how we ought to live, that he who abandons what is done for what ought to be done, will rather learn to bring about his own ruin than his preservation. A man who wishes to make a profession of goodness in everything must necessarily come to grief among so many who are not good.[28]

Here, then, modern "realism" enters the scene. Machiavelli can be said to advocate a deliberate lowering of goals or standards in the interest of enhancing the possibility of actualizing the good life for man on this earth. Actualization need not be deterred by capricious fortune, for chance can be conquered,[29] or by the limitations said to be imposed by nature, for men are more changeable than the ancients had supposed.

If the good life is to be actualized, it must be based on foundations more firm than those erected by the ancients, and the counsel as to its achievement must be couched in terms less harsh and severe than the latter had employed. The ancients talked ever of duty and emphasized that the good life is that austere life in which a man dedicates himself to doing what he ought to do. In modern times the emphasis shifts from duties to rights, and the good life consists of exercising one's rights to the fullest possible extent. In this respect modernity opposes *both* Athens and Jerusalem. Whatever political ingenuity the Athenians may have possessed, they knew nothing of a Bill of Rights, and from Jerusalem one hears not of ten amendments but of ten commandments.

The shift of emphasis from duties to rights involves much more than a shift of terminology. One occasionally hears it argued that rights and duties are inseparable and ultimately indistinguishable, for a man's duty to treat his neighbor well is, in the last analysis, the same as that neighbor's right to be treated well. Such an argument is not so much wrong as insufficient. It completely abstracts from the question of priorities, and in matters political and practical, questions of priorities are always crucial. Ancient thought makes duties prior to rights; modern man puts rights above duties. He does so in part because he thinks that while men are prone to shirk their duties, they are eager to exercise their rights. In other words, the edifice grounded on rights has a better chance of arising and standing than the edifice grounded on duties. That it will be a substantially different edifice can be seen from the Aristotelian view that what the laws do not permit they forbid, as contrasted with Hobbes' view that what the laws do not forbid they permit.[30]

The differences between the two conceptions of the good life can be seen from another but similar angle by reviewing briefly Aristotle's understanding of happiness, virtue, and reason, and then stating the modern critique of that understanding. According to Aristotle, the good life aims at happiness. As the "chief good, happiness is evidently something final." It is "always desirable in itself and never for the sake of something else." Only the good life (if anything) leads to happiness, which can be defined as "activity of the soul in accordance with virtue." In turn, virtue is defined as a "state of character concerned with choice, lying in a mean, i.e., the mean relative to us, this being determined by a *rational principle*, and by that principle by which the man of practical wisdom would determine it" (emphasis added).[31]

Nietzsche, whose ferocious and sweeping but eloquent generalizations both conceal and reveal a profound understanding of classical political philosophy, refers to a bizarre Socratic equation according to which happiness = virtue = reason.[32] (There is no question but that Nietzsche would consider Aristotle a Socratic.) It remains now to be seen how modern thought changed either the terms of the equation or the meaning of the terms so as to transform it into something less than bizarre.

Happiness. First, happiness loses both the character of objectivity, and its traditional association with a state of repose rather than motion. Modern thought appreciates the varieties of notions men entertain as to what constitutes happiness—once more we encounter the "profound" assertion that one man's meat is another man's poison—while not being disposed to advocate a political order that would train or even compel men to distinguish between meat and poison. Moreover, it tends to hold that happiness is not to be associated with a state of rest, but rather understands it as "a continual progress of the desire from one object to another."[33] One must quickly add, however, that modern thought offers one solution for both of the problems it discerns in the traditional concept of happiness. One man's idea of happiness may differ from another man's, but all men share some of the same requirements for attaining happiness. For happiness, modern man substitutes "the pursuit of happiness" and thus thinks he escapes both the subjectivist morass allegedly produced by incompatible views of happiness, and the bad repute in which rest is held by frenetic modernity; after all, it is unlikely that the pursuit will cease in this life. We should note that our own Declaration of Independence speaks of "the pursuit of happiness" rather than of happiness. Nor should we forget that the objective requirements for that pursuit are usually thought to be life and liberty and a modicum of material goods: Modern thought tends to blur the Aristotelian distinction between mere life and the good life.

Virtue. Second, virtue is no longer considered the chief end which government is to cultivate, and its intimate ties with the good life are, to say the least, weakened. The modern critique of virtue may be summarized without caricaturizing it overly much as follows: The ancients had thought that morality was somehow a force in human life, but in thinking this they proved themselves naive rather than wise. Modern sophistication knows that the dictates of virtue are honored much more in the breach than in the observance. Moreover, the virtuous is not to be simply identified with the good; it makes more sense—it is more self-evident—that the good be identified with the pleasant, but the performance of one's duties frequently involves pain.

By raising doubts about virtue, modern thought did not, of course, advocate vice. Instead, it searched for acceptable substitutes for morality; it sought effective ways of making men good. Thus Machiavelli held that the desire for glory makes bad men do good things for bad reasons. Many men, however, do not desire glory and are not capable of attaining it. Their aims are and must be more modest. Glory is therefore replaced by acquisitiveness, the desire for gain. Men desire to preserve themselves in comfort, or, to put it more crudely, men are actually or potentially greedy. But greed is like glory in that it can cause selfish men to work for the public good. The man who mutters, "the public be damned" may well be the same man who constructs a railroad system of inestimable benefit to the public.

But modern thought does more than replace a concern for virtue with material concerns. One does it far less than justice unless one realizes that it espouses principles that, while not equivalent to virtue, resemble virtue in that dedication to them can be understood as noble and edifying. Those principles are above all freedom and equality. They seem to enjoy an obvious advantage over virtue because while men must be forced to be virtuous they *want* to be free and equal.

Freedom and equality are brothers who tend to quarrel. It is beyond the scope of our inquiry as to which has priority. Suffice it to say one can argue that it is because men are naturally free that they are in the decisive respect equal, or that it is because men are naturally equal that they are in the decisive respect free, no man being good enough to rule another without the other's consent. For our purposes, four observations are in order.

1. Both freedom and equality are abstract and formalistic notions. Thus one must at once distinguish between "freedom from" and "freedom for" and then ask "freedom for what." Modern man tends to prefer "freedom from" because "freedom for" implies that freedom is for the sake of something higher than freedom, which limits freedom even as it hallows it; "freedom for" tends to introduce a distinction between true freedom and a license that can legitimately be forbidden. Similarly, one must at once ask equality in what? Thus Tocqueville distinguishes between a noble equality of free men and the despicable equality of slaves.[34]

2. Both freedom and equality resemble virtue. It is *good* to experience freedom, though one may argue whether freedom tends to make one virtuous or virtue tends to make one free. And it is surely *good* to appreciate the kinship existing among men and to respect the dignity of one's fellow man. Freedom and equality are not the opposite of virtue though dedication to them may mean that instead of devoting oneself to the whole of virtue one dedicates oneself to parts of it.

3. Both freedom and equality are goals tending to recede as one pursues them, a matter of some importance if one understands them as the content of the good life, a content substituted for virtue because it was thought to be more

attainable. Human life seems so constituted that there seems always one more freedom to secure; if freedom is interpreted to mean the right to be left alone, then the demands of a necessarily social human life would seem to preclude anyone's being left absolutely alone. Equality turns out to be equally elusive. Nor will it do to settle for "mere" equality of opportunity. Since the smart have greater opportunities than the stupid, even the pursuit of equality of opportunity implies a eugenics program. In general, one can say, that the quest for equality runs into the recalcitrance of nature. The conquest of nature begins because nature is stingy but soon turns into a war prompted by her injustice in distributing human endowments so unequally.

Freedom and equality not only entail each other but contradict each other; they must be understood, to repeat, as quarreling brothers. At some indeterminate point, the maximization of freedom is bound to interfere with the maximization of equality. In many areas of American life we have passed that point. For example, the right of equal access of a black man to a hotel in a small town interferes with the freedom of the local hotel owner to keep black men out of his hotel. In such a case it is relatively clear that a decision for equality over freedom is warranted, but the clarity is due to our having picked a rigged example. In radical thought the quarrel has escalated to the insoluble tension between the demands of "doing one's own thing" and the demands of an egalitarian community. It seems, then, that the replacement of virtue by freedom and equality may have solved some problems in regard to the good life, but it has also produced a host of new ones.

Reason. Third, reason is no longer understood as man's highest faculty, and its claim to be able to articulate and define or discern the good life is denied. To a considerable extent the story of modernity is also the story of the deprecation of reason or the growth of irrationalism. From the perspective of antiquity even modern rationalism, as exemplified by Descartes, is already irrationalism. That is because true rationalism assumes not only a certain power of reason but a certain rationality in the objects which reason attempts to know. Modern rationalism, by denying purpose and intelligibility to nature, begins by emancipating itself from nature and assuming a spurious kind of sovereignty, but it ends by undercutting and denuding itself. It becomes little more than calculation; it becomes instrumental, a mere means that points the most efficient way to arbitrary ends.

Finally, it ceases to be master in its own house. Classically understood as the legitimate ruler of man's passions, it becomes in a whole line of thinkers from Hobbes to Freud but the servant (or at best guide) of the passions. But in that case the claim that the good life consists in rational contemplation must sooner or later be challenged, and challenged it is. The good life becomes the life of passions realized, and to the extent that it is not attained, it becomes not so much the object of dispassionate inquiry as the name of one's ruling desire.

At this point we are forced to realize that the modern understanding of the good life is as little free of difficulty as is the ancient conception. For modern man, man is no longer a social animal, and the individual is prior to the state.[35] One must then say that modern man's concept of the good life must somehow be closely connected with the development of the individual. That is true, but we must at once realize that the most obvious seat of our individuality is not our soul but our bodies. We are unique entities because we are discrete physical entities. It is in understanding an equation that we are all alike—and such understanding can be peacefully shared. It is in suffering pains that we differ radically—and nobody can share our toothaches with us. Individualism claims to be lofty but it is closely tied to materialism.

What is more, individualism seems to imply a limited state, and that means a state limited in its ability to foster the good life. According to the ancients, the greatest guarantor of even a tolerable approach to the good life is education, understood in the broad sense of character formation. But the modern liberal state does not see character formation as part of its legitimate agenda, and it relies not so much on the goodness of its citizens as on the soundness of its institutions. The result, even judged by the modern liberal state's own standards, are most charitably described as mixed.

All this assumes that we still know what the good life is, and that there is such a thing. But do we? Nature as a positive standard has disappeared; history as a substitute standard has proved untenable. Reason has been exposed as incompetent and the passions as a treacherous guide. We are thus brought back to the situation discussed in the introductory section, a situation that can be described as the crisis of our time. Modern man knows nothing more certainly than that he is not happy and that things are in a mess.

By Way of a Conclusion: Can Anything Be Done?

What, then, is to be done?

That question constitutes the title of a number of Left-wing pamphlets written during the past century. The question conceals and reveals the Marxist and optimistic assumption that mankind sets itself only such problems as it can solve. According to doctrinaire Marxism we can and do know what the good life is. Moreover, we can achieve it, live it; in fact, history guarantees its realization.

But history seems to have played a trick on Marxist optimism and to have gone so far as to make the Marxist solution part of our problem. The states having undertaken or undergone revolutions in Marx's name have not made men either happy or good. Our modern experience suggests, contrary to the grain of Leftist thought, that mankind sets itself *only* such problems as it is unable to solve, that *no* human problem is soluble on the human level.

Strange to say, the most modern experience thus enables us to recover an insight developed in all the richness of its ramifications both by the strand of our tradition originating in Athens and the strand of our tradition originating in Jerusalem. Ancient man, whatever the limitations of his accomplishments, possessed a sober awareness of human limits. He knew that the human things were not the highest things, whether what was higher was God or Nature. He thus learned to live with moderate expectations of human life. Indeed, an immense amount of ancient thought is devoted to the praise and articulation of moderation.

One begins to understand the modern project if one views it as a revolt against what really were or at least were thought to be the limitations of human existence on this earth. Modernity prides itself, and often with justification, on immeasurably increasing man's power. For example, the achievements of modern science would have to be described as miraculous if the authority of modern science did not forbid recourse to the notion of miracles.

The modern project includes a whole series of campaigns and conquests against external restrictions on man. Its progress can be seen when one compares Machiavelli's likening of chance to a woman who can be conquered to Nietzsche's supposition that truth is a woman who might be conquered.[36] The predominant strand of modern thought and, indeed, modern action, can be described as humanism, if by humanism one implies the sovereignty of man and the assertion that human things *are* the highest things. The modern project consists not only in a lowering of goals to ensure actualization of one's goals, but in a tendency to deny that anything higher than the lowered goals exists.

A simple but haunting question brings into focus that crisis of our times we not only read about in newspapers but feel in our bones: Is humanism enough? It is hardly a new question, appearing almost as soon as humanism itself emerged; it is implicit in many of the fragments of Pascal's *Pensées.* But it was a question easy enough to ignore while the world was seduced by the idea of progress and seemed to be heading into new eras of wild happiness.

Today the question demands attention, if only because men who either consciously or unconsciously subscribe to the tenets of humanism, are increasingly faced with the experience of meaninglessness. How can there be an objectively good life if all the standards of measurement have disappeared? Neither nature nor history provides standards, to repeat, and reason has declared itself to be incompetent. We no longer have anything to which to look up, but the consequence has not been a heady feeling of autonomy but a sense, first, of the loss of objects worthy of our reverence, and then a decline of our capacity to feel reverence. Our souls have become impoverished as life seems to lose all intrinsic meaning.

We may dispose quickly of those who suggest as a solution that we create our own meaning. We are so constituted that a meaning "means" something beyond our capacity to create it. One example will have to suffice. We can, of course, "posit" a god, create one, will ourselves to believe in him to the extent of erecting churches and even attending them. But such a god will bear little resemblance to the God of Abraham, Isaac, and Jacob, Who created *us*. Who can *really pray* to a god he has "posited"?

We began by asking: What is to be done? That question, by implying that we can solve all our problems, threatens to increase our problems by deluding us. But it hardly follows from the fact that we are unable to discover a "final solution" that *nothing* can be done. We therefore conclude by asking, "Can anything be done?" That question implies a sober expectation that *something* can be accomplished. Here, then, are some modest suggestions.

First of all, we can take stock of our situation; we can attempt to understand it. Understanding must precede action, lest our actions be so mindless as to deepen the crisis in which we find ourselves.

By taking stock, I mean that we seek not only to understand the world but also ourselves. Now such an endeavor will, in all likelihood, bring us some recovery of ancient wisdom. Men have thought about the good life for thousands of years, and it would be remarkable if they had not discovered some of its ingredients or at least absolute preconditions. By taking stock, we discover how much can be *recovered*; we learn that as moderns we have much to learn of the ancients. In practice we must be modern, but we can be radical enough, in our thought, to realize that ancient principles in many respects have never been refuted; they have only been rejected and they can still offer guidance if only we permit ourselves to be guided.

A second step seems possible. If we find that the passionate study of the best thought of the past *does* provide us with nonarbitrary guidelines for leading a good life, we can pursue excellence *privately*. One hears many complaints that our government does not foster excellence. One does not hear enough appreciation of the fact that it permits excellence. We may be living in corrupt times but corruption remains to an appreciable extent voluntary, and nothing but our sloth prevents us from becoming better than we are. The freedom that replaced virtue as a goal has become a precious good in a world not lacking in examples of governments dedicated to suffocating excellence.

The private pursuit of excellence, of the good life, must necessarily today be hesitant, various, and tentative. Yet certain topics seem to preoccupy all of us, no matter what our station in life. Let me boldly assert that in all cases today the good life entails a meditation on love, God, and death. We are unable to live well without loving, for all of us are creatures who need, and love begins in need. We are, all of us, unable to live well without wondering whether that deep and perhaps deepest stratum of our soul, the longing for eternity, can ever attain to any completion. We must ponder whether our deepest longings can be satisfied by a living God or are doomed to remain unrequited. And we are, all of us, unable to live well if we give no thought to dying well, if we do not recognize death as an ineluctable necessity. And therewith we reach the third and final point of our inquiry.

Government, as I have already indicated, can help negatively, by letting us alone, by zealously guarding the freedom that enables us to engage in our quest. It can do more. Whatever the good life is, it seems to entail reverence, and thus to be connected in one way or another with the religious life. A limited state such as ours ought not to establish religion, but nothing in the First Amendment prevents government from encouraging religion. Furthermore, the good life, whatever it is, involves the appreciation of the beautiful, and even a limited state can make beautiful things for men to appreciate. Then, too, we must know what the good life is, and knowledge requires education. The kind of education that addresses itself to questions of the good life is liberal education. It is a false economy to neglect liberal education on no better grounds than that we are not falling behind the Russians in philosophy. Finally, a good government is in itself an incentive to the good life, and good leadership teaches us as much by example as by precepts.

I have not attempted to propose grand schemes, because I do not know of any. We no longer quite know what the good life is, and therefore we no longer even know quite how to search for it. We search for it badly. But what Chesterton is reputed to have said remains true: If something is worth doing, it is not only worth doing well, but doing badly. Certainly the search is worthwhile, and it will not be futile, even if we fail to reach the goal (a most likely outcome), for the chances are that along the way we will be sustained by glimmers of truths that are meaningful because they are beyond our power of making.

Notes

1. Aristotle, *Nichomachean Ethics*, 1094b 10-15.
2. Mic. 6:8.
3. Plato, *Republic*, 338 c-d.
4. Leo Strauss, *Spinoza's Critique of Religion* (New York: Schozken Books, 1965), p. 11. Whatever there may be of worth in this essay owes far more than I can indicate by specific citation to the late Leo Strauss, my teacher. Only my sense of its inadequacy prevents me from dedicating this chapter to his beloved memory.
5. Sigmund Freud, *Civilization and its Discontents* (New York: Norton, 1962), p. 11.
6. Aristotle, *Politics*, 1253a. Barker translation.
7. Plato, *Republic*, 369b-d.
8. Aristotle, *Politics*, 1252b25-30.
9. See Aristotle, *Ethics*, Books 8 and 9.
10. See ibid., 1099a30-1099b5.
11. Ibid., 1095a15-25.
12. Consider the speeches of Glaucon and Adeimantus in Plato's *Republic*, 357a-367e.

13. Aristotle, *Ethics*, 1095a10-30.

14. Aristotle, *Politics*, 1252b5-10, 30-1253a10.

15. Ibid., 1253a5-20.

16. Consider Shakespeare, *Hamlet*, Act III, Scene 2, 11. 72ff.

17. In addition to above cited sources see especially Plato, *Apology of Socrates*, and *Gorgias*, 499e6-500a3.

18. Leo Strauss, *Natural Right and History* (Chicago: University of Chicago Press, 1953), p. 127.

19. See especially Plato, *Apology of Socrates*, 20d-23c.

20. Consider Aristotle, *Ethics*, Book VI.

21. Ibid., 1134b25-30.

22. Corinthians 1:23.

23. St. Augustine, *City of God* V, 12.

24. Gen. 22.

25. See especially *The Federalist Papers*, Numbers 10 and 14.

26. Friedrich Nietzsche, *Twilight of the Idols* IX:43. Translation by Walter Kaufmann.

27. Plato, *Republic*, 473d; Aristotle, *Politics*, Book II.

28. Machiavelli, *The Prince*, Ch. 15, beginning.

29. See ibid., Ch. 25.

30. In Aristotle's *Ethics*, one reads that "the law does not expressly permit suicide, and what the law does not expressly permit it forbids" (1138a5-10). This remarkable statement is to be contrasted with the position articulated by Thomas Hobbes in his *Leviathan*, especially Chapters 14 and 15 of Part I and Chapter 26 of Part II.

31. Aristotle, *Ethics*, 1097a25-30; 1098a15-20; 1107a1-5.

32. Nietzsche, *Will to Power*, fragment 432; *Twilight of the Idols*, II:10.

33. Hobbes, *Leviathan*, Part I: Chapter 11.

34. Tocqueville, *Democracy in America* Vol. I, Introduction, Part I: Chapters 4, 7, Conclusion; Vol. II, Preface, Part 2, Chapter 1.

35. See The Declaration of Independence, beginning.

36. Compare Machiavelli's *Prince*, Chapter 25, with Nietzsche's *Beyond Good and Evil*, Preface.

 Religious
Dimensions in
American Life

Edwin Scott Gaustad

In facing their critical choices in the years ahead, Americans act most responsibly as they reflect upon their past in order to understand their present. In Lincoln's words, so often and so fondly quoted by Sidney E. Mead, "If we could first know where we are, and whither we are tending, we could better judge what to do, and how to do it." Lincoln's choices in 1858 could hardly have been more crucial, America's agony hardly more acute than in that decade of slavery, secession, "this terrible war," emancipation, and exhaustion. It was a time for retrospection and introspection so that men and women "could better judge what to do."[1]

No parallels need be drawn between the degree or nature of crisis then and now. One only observes that the 1970s—bicentennial deliberations and celebrations quite aside—raise momentous questions about the direction, wholeness, vitality, and nerve of the nation collectively and of its citizens individually. This chapter approaches some of these questions with particular attention to the place of religion in American life.

I

To declare the obvious, religion has played a major part in this country's founding and in its shaping. Taking some comfort in Justice Holmes' observation that few things are more rewarding than a reexamination of the obvious, we shall glance briefly backward. Broad-gauged scholars such as Louis B. Wright and

Howard Mumford Jones help situate the white man's discovery and exploration of the North American continent in the context of the European renaissance. The dozen or more centuries of complex interweaving of Empire and Church, the intricate reciprocity of altar and throne, insured that any Europe-invaded shores would receive some mixture, some confusion, of the temporal and the spiritual estates. So the state-financed navigational adventure of Columbus could be justified, at least in part, because it "could prove of so great service to God and the exaltation of his Church." The Spanish conquerors who followed debouched soldier and friar together on Florida's inhospitable sands; together they died. Cabeza de Vaca's incredible survival of one such abortive effort seemed sufficient warrant for even greater sacrifices, though de Vaca himself clung to few illusions. Spain made further reconnaissances into Texas, Arizona, and New Mexico; later this leading Catholic power moved from Baja, California up into the remarkably receptive bays of San Diego, Monterey, and San Francisco. It was indeed a New World, the discovery and exploration of which shared fully the excitement and optimism in discovering those other Renaissance new worlds: in art, literature, language, manners and morals.[2]

So also France strung its mission beads along a line extending from the rock of Quebec up the St. Lawrence and down the Mississippi to the delta of New Orleans. The civil interests of defense and of trade comingled with the religious concerns of Jesuit martyrs like Brébeuf and Jogues. When, by a treaty of peace in 1763 and by a territorial sale in 1803, France withdrew politically from interior America, she left both a religious imprint in missions and schools and a hagiography on the face of the land. Since Gallic colonization was never a sustained policy, the total number of French Catholics between, say, New Orleans and Sault Ste. Marie was not large. The European thrust, however, had penetrated into the nation's heartland, carrying with it assumptions—and problems—concerning religion's role in the political and social evolution of a wide wilderness.[3]

England's freight was, ultimately, both weightier and more diverse. Initially, however, England appeared to lag well behind both France and Spain in voyages of discovery and exploration. (John Cabot was later called upon to carry a heavy historical and legal burden.) However casual the early cruising and marauding of England, this nation's colonization proved to be persistent and extensive. Richard Hakluyt, cleric-geographer-promoter, fidgeted uneasily as others seemed to outdistance and outmaneuver England in terms of both her spiritual and her national interests. The kings and queens of England, he observed in 1584, have been named "Defenders of the Faith." But they do so little, they delay so long, they lose so much. Are they, by such a title, "not only charged to maintain and patronize the faith of Christ, but also to enlarge and advance the same"? When England did move, however, she moved—as Hakluyt himself had urged—with families and settlers, with parishes and farms, to tame so much of that "gift outright."[4]

Thus thousands poured into Virginia, then New England and Maryland, later into New York, New Jersey, Pennsylvania, and the Carolinas, and ultimately into Georgia. The several understandings of religion's role in national affairs that Englishmen brought with them account for a large part of the readily observable variety in cultural patterns and life styles. Did the church serve culture, transform culture, coexist independent of culture—or what? To all this English variety, one must add the diversity of Swiss Mennonites, Sephardic Jews, French Huguenots, and Palatinate refugees. Within so mixed a medley, room could be found for many an accommodation, many a hostility, many an honest misunderstanding. Under the auspices of English Catholics, Maryland opened its doors to non-Catholics—who soon took over the colony. Massachusetts experimented in creating a true Church of England—from which members of the existing Church of England were paradoxically excluded. Pennsylvania as a Quaker colony became a haven of religious dissent—and of political manipulation that turned the Quakers out of power. New York (as New Amsterdam) needed settlers—but certainly not indigent Jews from Brazil.

William and Mary's Declaration of Religious Toleration took effect in the colonies—more or less, here and there. Virginia's official patronage of Anglicanism brought to that denomination sweet success—more or less, here and there. Neither pluralism nor the complexities of church and state were invented in the twentieth century. Religion played a role, and a vital one at that, in colonization, in the founding of colleges and the ordering of towns, in moving people across furious oceans and in sustaining them once transplanted. But it was never a simple role, never a single mold, nor were the majority of colonists ever at any time members of some church. The colonial period acquires an idyllic simplicity and pervasive piety only as it recedes in time.[5]

A generation before the Revolution a wave of religious excitement swept across Britain's North American colonies. For a moment, denominational lines were overridden (some, not all); Calvinism was embraced (broadly, not everywhere); intercolonial rivalries were minimized (though border disputes never died); and mankind generally seemed to be asking, "What must I do to be saved?" (in modern terms "What *is* the good life?"). This Great Awakening enhanced a sense of community, a community of—could it possibly be?—not Virginians or New Englanders but Americans. The movement also fed even as it fed upon an optimism concerning God's purposes, perhaps His millennial purposes, in the world at large but also in the America at hand. And the religious fervor created a "post-Awakening morality" which, by contrast, made the luxury and vice of England reprehensivel and a sign of her sure decline.[6]

This sweeping intensity of faith, passion, proposition, and hope helped prepare for that other popular intensity of the 1770s. Likewise helping to prepare the way was the evangelical resistance to England's encroachments upon colonial religious freedoms, even if those encroachments were more imagined than real. The "threat" of an Anglican episcopate in the colonies plus the "danger" of a Catholic establishment in Canada aggravated the anxieties of all those Americans for whom religious persecution was a recent and vivid experience or an ever refreshed and equally vivid memory. Just as civil and ecclesiastical tyranny had gone hand in hand in Europe, so civil and ecclesiastical freedom must be fought for as one in America.[7]

The most immediate effect of that Revolution for the churches was to guarantee their freedom from government interference and to set them all—some most reluctantly—on the path toward disestablishment. "Free exercise," it was immediately apparent, was more than a clause; the churches were, in Lyman Beecher's words, thrown "wholly on their own resources and on God." So the voluntary principle became a distinctive of American religious life. With a continent to conquer, a society to reform, and a gospel to proclaim, voluntary agencies and boards moved with confidence both at home and abroad. The government, for its part, was freed from the meddling of competing sects but not necessarily freed from the guidance or the restraints of religion. Most Americans would readily agree with the sentiments which Washington expressed in his Farewell Address: namely, that "reason and experience both forbid us to expect that national morality can prevail in exclusion of religious principle."[8]

The confidence of statesmen and churchmen withered in the dark shadows of Civil War. Clerical voices were either mute or raised in unbecoming discord. Major denominations broke along geographical lines, as institutional leadership stumbled, faltered, fell. The mantle of spiritual leadership then fell upon the stooped shoulders of Abraham Lincoln. Slavery, said Lincoln in 1854, "is founded on the selfishness of man's nature—opposition to it in his love of justice." If slavery is a good, it is "strikingly peculiar in this, that it is the only good which no man ever seeks for himself." Yet, the clear immorality of slavery did not make the North righteous and the South wicked. Men's motives and men's deeds have too much mixture, Lincoln observed, too much ambiguity to ever excuse the identification of our purposes with God's. Between those two sets of purposes, a difference ever exists; to ignore or obscure that difference, Lincoln wrote in 1865, "is to deny that there is a God governing the world."

To the burdens of Reconstruction, unevenly borne, were added the challenges of a rural, farming America becoming an urban manufacturing America. Pieties shared around the family hearth seemed drowned in or irrelevant to the factory's din and the ghetto's cry. Religion belonged more and more to the have's, with less and less to say to, or even on behalf of, the have-not's. Mass immigration only aggravated the social and economic problems while it disrupted the dreams of an assured national destiny for "Our Country." The "Righteous Empire" was swiftly passing; claims regarding a "Christian Nation" acquired an anachronistic ring. As revivalists grew more desperate, advocates of an applied Christianity grew more daring. But the problems of poverty and profit, of labor and capital, of assimilation and enclave, of justice and race continued to swell like science fiction monsters.[9]

In a flush of idealism, World War I came and went. The entry into, the conduct during, the settlement after that war still drew from those earlier dreams of destiny. The dreams were not selfish ones, perhaps not even dangerous ones. But they were dreams into which so much of religious hope and zeal had been invested that their shattering severely weakened the moral authority and self-confidence of much religious leadership. In the late 1920s, Walter Lippmann and Joseph Wood Krutch spoke of gods that had been toppled, of old certitudes that had vanished, of the readiness of citizens to trade "a majestic faith for a trivial illusion." Nonetheless, church membership grew, imposing church structures arose, and activity—were it only a more reliable index of health—increased.[10]

The economic collapse of the 1930s suggested that disease lurked nearby. Perhaps capitalism itself was the cancerous core; perhaps faithlessness or smugness infected the people. Religion was challenged to prove its relevance, if it had any, to the quality of life and to the survival of society. Was it not time to think of salvation, not in personal terms, but in corporate and structural terms? Was it not past time to undertake some "reconstructing of the social order," as the 1931 encyclical of Pope Pius XI suggested? Or was it time to follow the prophet Marx, casting overboard the religious ballast, bit by bit? In the midst of questions so sharp and economic woes so severe, America's worldwide missionary enterprise sagged. "Evangelization of the world in this generation" had been an earlier rallying cry; by the end of that generation, however, the world had not been evangelized but plunged into war once more.

If the idealism that took America into World War II was not as intense as that which was operative in World War I, the eventual disillusionment after the war was probably greater. The dismay over the endemic inhumanity of mankind found its most haunting symbols in the furnaces and graves of Dachau and Buchenwald. But there were other ghosts as well that would not let consciences sleep: from Dresden and the Ukraine, from Hiroshima and Siberia. "The fate of mankind," wrote Abraham Heschel, "depends upon the realization that the distinction between good and evil, right and wrong, is superior to all other distinctions." In a world where annihilation became routine and horror a soporific, Heschel could hardly be heard: "The true foundation upon which our cities stand is a handful of spiritual ideas."[11]

After World War II, good health for a time appeared to have returned both to the nation and to institutional religion. The Marshall Plan put a better foot forward as did the Church World Service, the Catholic Relief Service, the United Jewish Appeal, and a host of other agencies dedicated to relief and rehabilitation. The formation of the United Nations in 1945 had its counterpart in the creation of the World Council of Churches in 1948, the latter being an effort to transcend "race and nation, class and culture," working "together in faith, service and understanding." Here at home, the "revival of religion" received wide public comment as church membership grew larger, sanctuaries more stately, and income more abundant. The nation was equally self-assured as the domination of the dollar and the monopoly of the bomb made for a strength that could not be denied. The leadership of "the free world" was ours; perhaps, we were worthy of it.[1][2]

From the mid-sixties to the mid-seventies, however, the mood in both national and ecclesiastical affairs shifted sharply from confidence to uncertainty, then to anxiety and on occasion toward despair. All expectations were cast aside, all predictions found wanting. A society, suddenly afflicted, became sullen and introspective; it even came close to asking, "What must I do to be saved?"

II

Looking more closely at the present, one can distinguish at least five elements on the national scene that have clear implications for the quality of American life. The implications are clear not merely or even primarily to the "expert" but to the vast majority of the American people.

1. Though the development has been gradual, the years since World War II have accentuated the gigantification of structures that mold and invade our lives. Artisanship gives way to mass bargaining, entrepreneurship to cartel and conglomerate, social services to the bureaucratic buck-pass, creativity to joyless technology, personal identity to Orwellian data banks. This is an age where machines, not people, are described as compatible, where conversation is a series of inputs (or transcripts), and where the most intimate of human concerns are addressed to "occupant." A decade ago only the students begged not to be folded, spindled or mutilated. Now a general public shrinks from a blurred, unseeing, unhearing, unfeeling giant that may be tagged, indifferently, "business," "labor," "government," "they." An afflicted Job in desperation asked why there was no umpire to rule between him and God. A jaded American asks of his society if not of the cosmos: who listens? who notices? who cares?

2. Racism and sexism were supposed to have conquered long ago, the latter "at last" by a constitutional amendment, the former by the actions in 1776 or was it 1789 or was it 1861 or "at last" in 1954. In the 1960s and 70s the evasions grew more obvious, the protests more noisy, the irritations more general. Some progress could be pointed to, especially in the economic realm, but psychological stresses remained keen as many came to suspect that raising the quality of *your* life sooner or later lowers or endangers the quality of *mine*. As ethnic blocs solidified and liberation movements flourished, confrontation became a way of life. And where adversary relationships constituted the most familiar if not the only kind of relationships which many Americans knew, the quality of life and certainly of language did appear threatened. "Sex" and "soul" no longer suggested unification and commonality, but barrier and exploitation, separation and misunderstanding. The human race was falling apart, its dissolution being scandalously palpable in pluralistic America.

3. As president, John Kennedy had managed to arouse a flagging idealism, to suggest that sacrifice was an appropriate action, to rally young people into a willingness to serve the world. But his "let us begin" had only begun by November 22, 1963. That shock had not worn off before other bullets ended noble lives and encouraged cynicism. A decade of domestic madness could lead only to a despair over the quality of national life and, more often than not, a despair over the quality of one's own life. The former led to extremes of irrationality in politics or to an utter contempt for politics. The latter, more private despair led to an escapism, a hedonism, an unprincipled manipulation of structures and persons, a deliberate if demeaning exploitation of the "system" and its "benefits." Each time men and women were galvanized into the support of a cause, they found themselves frustrated, or defeated, or betrayed. People feared to follow, to believe, to be vulnerable once more.

4. Vietnam and all its attendant violence, Southeast Asia with all its deceptions and delusions—these weigh upon the present like some unwritten, unspoken elegy. The rhetoric of Manifest Destiny, of free world responsibility, and of national security has never soured so completely, so pervasively. The nature of the war, its duration, its purpose, its proximity (via the television), its cost, and above all its end all became matters of intense national debate. That debate, at first restricted and official, spread ultimately to every corner of the land. The daily diet of violence abroad soon had its counterpart at home: on campuses and in cities, at conventions and concerts, in marches and parades. "Bloodbath," at first an unthinkable possibility abroad, became a plausible alternative at home. With the fabric of society threatening to come apart, "law and order" sounded like the right critical choice. But "law and order" was a slogan turned into travesty, enticing a nation to lose its soul while trying so desperately to save it.

5. "They almost stole America." It is yet too soon to tell, for on top of Vietnam and mass violence came Watergate and mass betrayal. Too many words have been, are being, and for years shall be written on this seismic shake to permit any assessment in perspective here. The nation itself is on trial, with the obvious opportunity for ransoming even this dark hour. Probably at no time since the 1850s has a people been more self-consciously, even urgently ready for "critical choices." An ache, a void, a rudderless floundering all strongly suggest that the quality of life is suffering from a neglect that is no longer benign, if indeed it ever was. If death makes philosophers of us all, disease makes diagnosticians of us all. With the unhealthy state of the nation so starkly revealed, we all inquire into the condition of society: its institutions, its aims, its resources, its chances for recovery.

At such a time, one would like to be able to turn from national plagues and fevers to the bouncing good health of the ecclesiastical world. But the physicians of the soul are not all that fit either. Statistics, which for decades and even centuries have been the most convenient and convincing evidence of American religion's good health, now offer a different prognosis. Church membership in

proportion to the population has increased steadily from the colonial period to
the present; it does so no longer. Some denominations barely keep pace with
population growth, while others do not manage even that. For years, more than
a half of all Americans attended church in any given week; now, fewer than fifty
percent do so. More serious than these externals is the loss of a sense of mission,
the decline in observable influence, the abandonment of or failure to enter upon
religious vocations. Taunts of "cultural captivity" and the "noise of solemn
assemblies" were hurled at the religious establishment. True, newer and more
ecstatic religious communities flourished, but none could be certain that its
momentum too was more than a fleeting burst. Meanwhile, the more familiar
Protestant, Catholic, and Jewish "ways of being an American" each manifest
special problems.

One of their common problems could relate to Spenglerian decline: perhaps
the blight was more Western than American, a senescence on its way to senility.
For, to be sure, some of the psychic trauma and dispirited melancholia
experienced by Americans had its counterpart (if not its classic exposition) in
France or Denmark, in Italy or Britain. But apart from this broad cultural
malaise, or perhaps on top of it, religion in America labored under additional
stresses.

Protestantism was still adjusting to a post-Protestant America, to what Robert
Handy calls the second disestablishment. Finding themselves out in the cold,
many Protestants sought warmth in the company and heartiness of others. The
ecumenical movement, softly humming "the more we get together the happier
we'll be," promised a more powerful Protestantism in and for America, one
which would overcome the scandalous divisiveness, one that could at crucial
times speak with a single and more certain voice. By the mid-1970s the blush of
that optimism had faded as pluralism, even within Protestantism, was accepted
as a reality if not heralded as an ideal.

Catholicism, reveling in the charisma of its two Johns in the early 60s,
shuddered and cracked in the storms that followed Vatican II. Change,
long-postponed, came too swiftly and in waves not easily ridden. Liturgy was
tinkered with too often and theology was adjusted too readily. "Alternative life
styles" suggested more options than the faithful had easily imagined possible.
Bishops willing to change seemed headed for a shore fearful and unknown; those
unwilling to change seemed stuck with a ship unworthy of heavy seas. The
helmsman's orders were unclear; the discipline of the crew was unsure; the move
to abandon ship had begun. The rock that was Peter could prevail against the
gates of hell, but the contest with aggiornamento, pluralism, democratization,
and post-Christian scenarios was yet to be decided.

Judaism in America, though enjoying something of the third generation's
remembering what the second generation wanted to forget, suffered some of the
factionalism that afflicted Protestants. Reform, Orthodox, Conservative, Zionist,
Hasidic, Reconstructionist—each had special centers of influence and interest. In

the last decade, moreover, all groups within America have fastened their attention on the fortunes and fate of the State of Israel. Since 1967 the ancient question of "the land" has been the all-consuming contemporary question for so many American Jews, with the "role of religion in American life" being often reduced to a single question of the American stance vis-à-vis the foreign policy or predicament of Israel. The memory and meaning of the holocaust is, of course, not a separable issue from the security and survival of Israel; these two issues together constitute the special burden of Judaism's current effort in self-understanding and renewal.

Apart from the familiar trinity of Jew, Protestant, and Catholic (and the last term should be comprehensively understood to include the Eastern Orthodox), new religious phenomena reveal rapid acceleration. A kind of neo-fundamentalism is seen in the Jesus movement, the Children of God, and other such groups. Many communes orient themselves around religious understandings, sometimes traditional (East or West), sometimes novel and idiosyncratic. Eastern religions, notably Hinduism and Buddhism, had their public debut as far back as the World Parliament of Religions in 1893, but American interest has risen sharply in recent years. The occult and the mystical have also widened their appeal as many Americans, especially the young, have turned from a technocratic rationalism and scientized society to what John Wesley Powell scornfully called "the hashish of mystery." Finally, religion as therapy—as mental peace, physical health, material security—has continued to multiply in new sects and ephemeral one-man or one-woman stands. In all of these newer and smaller communities of faith, the quality of personal life receives a great deal of explicit attention, though the quality of national life tends to be ignored.

In a dimension distinct from that of membership counting, institutional waxing and waning, new religions and charismatic founders, there stands another aspect of religion in American life. This realm is usually called civil religion or the religion of the Republic. Such public religion can be seen (and often has been) as a thin veneer of pious platitudes covering the rawest bids for national power and the most unrestrained jingoism: "American Shinto," as Robert Bellah notes. It is possible to understand any interaction between religion and government as being at the expense of the former's integrity—religion as utensil, ecclesiastical institutions fawning and servile, all prophets transmuted into agents of the state. In this view, religion betrays its transcendent orientation, forgets its supramundane loyalties, and sells its birthright for a mess of politics.[13]

On the other hand, it is possible to conceive of other ways in which religion can relate to a community, a nation, a culture. Paul Tillich's familiar formula, "religion is the substance of culture, culture is the form of religion," can have application to the American scene. As Sidney E. Mead points out, the religion of the Republic holds before a people "the ideals and aspirations which define their sense of destiny and purpose." Such a religious orientation commits a people not to the nation as it is but to the nation as it ought to be. Beyond the specific sectarian doctrines stands a general understanding of a judgment and a providence over mortal men and prideful nations. William Penn argued for liberty of conscience not on the grounds of natural human rights but on the grounds that men must not "directly invade the divine prerogative, and divest the Almighty of a due, proper to none besides himself." God's "incommunicable right of government over conscience" is a major tenet of the religion of the Republic—even before there was a Republic.

In 1777 the Second Continental Congress spoke of the "indispensable duty of all men to adore the superintending Providence of Almighty God . . ." and a dozen years later George Washington acclaimed "that great and glorious Being who is the beneficent Author of all the good that was, that is, or that will be." Madison spoke of "the duty which we owe to our creator" and John Adams of religion and morality as the only path to "principles upon which freedom can securely stand." Lincoln acknowledged that "the Almighty has His own purposes" of which this or any nation is always an imperfect agent. And the Supreme Court has repeatedly implied a religion of the Republic, not so much through explicit reference to the religious heritage as through emphatic argument for a limited state.

In 1943, for example, in the midst of war with its potential claims of "national security," Justice Jackson spoke for the Court: "If there is any fixed star in our constitutional constellation, it is that no official, high or petty, can prescribe what shall be orthodox in politics, nationalism, religion, or other matters of opinion or force citizens to confess by word or act their faith therein." Three years later, the Court declared that "The victory for freedom of thought recorded in our Bill of Rights recognizes that in the domain of conscience there is a moral power higher than the State. Throughout the ages men have suffered death rather than subordinate their allegiance to God to the authority of the State."

The constant thread of the religion of the Republic, writes Sidney Mead, "has been the assertion of the primacy of God over all human institutions." The religion of the Republic proclaims something beyond the Republic. Or, as Thornton Wilder's Stage Manager says in *Our Town*: "I don't care what they say with their mouths—everybody knows that *something* is eternal. And it ain't houses and it ain't names, and it ain't earth, and it ain't even the stars . . ."[14]

All of this is clearly different from a baptism of the status quo, from a sanctification of American foreign policy, from what William Miller once called piety along the Potomac and God-in-the-last-paragraph religion. Civil religion can be prophetic, critical, bringing judgment and insight to a government limited not by the autonomy of men but by the prerogatives of God. And it is in this sense that the decisions and duties of religious citizens become at the same time critical choices—not merely for Catholics, Protestants, and Jews—but for *Americans*.

III

Americans, as has been pointed out ad nauseum, are a pragmatic people. But pragmatism, as one critic noted, is not so much a philosophy as it is a method of doing without one. While such a characterization is not fair to the genius of Peirce, James, and Dewey, it probably does fit the popular rejection of anything that looks like an ideology or even like a firm conviction. Thus, as a people, we live in the midst of game plans and scenarios; thus our commitment to novelty (called innovation) and to more (called growth). Plato, said Aristotle with reference to the former's Republic, makes love watery; we have managed a similar dilution for virtue and for truth. That the quality of life suffers can therefore occasion little surprise.

Choices that are critical, one must assume, are choices that affect life profoundly. They cannot be superficial options or disposable throwaways. "If we cannot . . . discover the real purpose and direction of our existence," Adlai Stevenson wrote in 1959, "we shall not be free, our society will not be free." Choice, not instruments or hardware, is decisive. And if choices of that magnitude are urgent, then one should give some attention to that cultural force with the greatest experience in the "choice business." For twenty-five or more centuries, the message of religion in the Western world has been: "Choose you this day whom you will serve." Such life choices are not normally the functions of education or urban planning, of budget outlays or systems analyses. They are more primitive, more elusive, more defiant of program and prediction. For the nation as a whole no single moment of choice presents itself; rather, one sees a series of options, a succession of forked-road situations. Many of these may be gathered into four ganglia of decision-making.[15]

1. *Sensuality or sacrifice.* Americans manifest a paradoxical attachment to both hedonism and duty, but one may define the ages of the nation's past by the dominance of one or the other. Rarely are the oxen evenly yoked, nor do they appear to be so now. For at least a generation, the major moral goal of American civilization has been to divest itself of all inhibitions, quaintly called "Puritan hang ups." The operating assumption has been that once that gayest of liberations was accomplished, life would be free, full, and abundant. These great expectations had a short fall. T.S. Eliot, who saw it coming, said that modern man imagines himself emancipated when in fact he is only unbuttoned. Inhibition, we tardily recognize, may be another word for civilization. And the ultimate criterion of moral worth, we may also have recognized, is not that consenting adults have consented. Today's society, says Philip Rieff, confronts the unhappy options presented by "two apparently opposing cadres: (1) rationalizers of technological reason; (2) orgiasts of revolutionary sensuality . . ." For both groups, "nothing remains true" and both "are hostile to culture in any form . . ."[16]

For the sensualist, any suggestion of sacrifice or call to duty falls on stony ground. Categorical joys are not worthy to be compared with doubtful moral imperatives. If one chooses to live in a world where all interest is self-interest and all noble action merely a disguised egocentricity, then one only plays the game as cleverly and as successfully as possible. Writing in the hedonistic 1920s, Walter Lippmann tried to stem that powerful tide by calling for a mature and rational asceticism, by declaring that "one of the conditions of happiness is to renounce some of the satisfactions which men normally crave." His humanism did not widely persuade, and it must be conceded that traditional religion did very little better.

From the religious perspective there is a greater glory than the glands. One moves beyond the idols fashioned and fondled by one's own hands, even as one moves beyond the egocentric island of the infant crib. We are bound in a bundle of life, said an ancient Hebrew writer. Being so bound is a religious notion, while discipline and deprivation on behalf of that bundle is a religious obligation. Or, in Berdyaev's words, bread for myself is a material problem, but bread for my neighbor is a spiritual problem. A terrible choice, and for the most part a private choice, is that between mindless tomorrows and a civilization of restraints, between limits and obligations. Kant could not perceive a culture in which that great question, "What ought I to do?", was never asked—a land perhaps, but not a culture.

2. *Alienation or community.* The pursuit of sensuality is connected with loneliness just as a sense of duty implies relationships. Modern Americans find themselves isolated and insulated, individually wrapped in sterile packages guaranteed to be untouched by human hands. The reasons for this alienation are both public and private. Privately, contemporary citizens pursue the goal of "making it" with a single-mindedness that narrows the circle of human concern. Despite the authoritative warning that seeking to save one's soul is a fairly sure way of losing it, such seeking becomes a national pastime. In the public domain, a faceless and monstrous bureaucracy calls to no unifying purposes, inspires a citizenry to no common goals. All that is common are the frustrations, and these lead not to community but to aggravated alienation. The fatal combination, privatization of life-purposes and computerization of life-needs, causes few Americans to ask or care for whom the bell tolls.

Such searches for community as do occur rarely rally around national symbols or tasks. The now discredited melting pot left not only the ethnics unmelted but much else of accidental heritage and casual custom. No national church existed to carry on a gradual and subtle program of assimilation or acculturation. As a result the nation attempted to be the church, occasionally functioning as such in earlier days. According to John E. Smylie, the nation has at one time or another "emerged as the primary agent of God's meaningful activity in history" or has been the "primary society in terms of which individual Americans discovered personal and group identity" or has even been understood as "the community of righteousness." The opportunity for as well as the tendency to community-creating of this churchly sort seems severely restricted at the present time.[17]

It would be most convenient if institutional religion were proving itself capable of creating broadly based communities upon which some national sense of community could build. But of most of the larger religious families, this is no longer true. In any major denomination, one can make few assumptions about how its members vote, what aesthetic or moral principles they honor, what they eat or drink or wear, or indeed what they truly and deeply believe about the nature of the universe in which they live. The sect-types (in Troeltsch's terms) do far better in creating and intensifying a sense of community, but by their very nature the extent of the communities is small. The result is that for most religious Americans, as for their nonreligious fellows, community is more likely to be found in ethnic ties and genealogical searches, in service clubs and sensitivity groups, in alumni association and business conventions, in bowling leagues and baseball stadiums. Men and women turn to the latter to erase or numb the estrangement and angst of modern alienated life in America.

On an individual basis, then, some of the separateness and division is overcome, though little contribution to national community is made. One careful student of pietism in America, William McLoughlin, believes that the critical turning points in the nation's history have coincided with religious awakenings of broad impact. Whether a kind of revivalistic enthusiasm is part of the nation's adolescence, now outgrown, or whether this fervor can yet appear in new garment and guise, it is impossible to say. It is easier to say that a sense of national community that binds at life's profoundest levels is conspicuously absent from the current scene. If the nation is in any sense a spiritual entity, the perception of such an entity is blurred. G.K. Chesterton once called America the "nation with the soul of a church." Two generations after Chesterton, such language sounds hopelessly, almost unintelligibly anachronistic.

3. *Self-approbation or judgment.* The signal contribution of religion, with its transcendent loyalties, is to confront and combat the pride of both men and nations. Greatest loyalty to the nation lies not in a worship of the state but in an ability to guide and bring judgment to that state. Perspectives of times and of space are wider and longer than the here and the now. The tragedy (not to say the banality) of judging all in terms of immediate relevance is that it so foreshortens and narrows one's view that all basis for judgment is gone. The highest standard we know is ourselves; the richest experience we acknowledge is our own; the keenest discrimination we experience is that of approving peers; the ultimate in taste is what we had this morning for breakfast. Truth, *c'est moi.*

"To leave the great past unremembered," writes Philip Rieff, "is to be lost in the howling present . . ." At least the perspective of history must be preserved if that of religion cannot be. "Barbarians are people without historical memory," Rieff also observes; "released from all authoritative pasts, we progress towards barbarism, not away from it." Rieff's observation excuses the structure of this chapter: a nation makes its most civilized choices by recalling its history, not by suppressing or ignoring it.

In his *Letter to the Soviet Leaders*, Solzhenitsyn calls for a disavowal of the "rubbishy ideology" that has led to hypocrisy, cynicism, and mass extermination, urging a return to the Russian past, to ancient values, to native inner strengths. He also sees religion as neither opiate nor escape, but as critical judgment and succor. In remembering the past, there is fidelity to the future. The philosophies of the Enlightenment sought escape from the stifling trap of self-approbation by appealing to posterity, for the immediate past seemed unworthy and infamous. But they too recognized that some standard beyond oneself and one's own time was a necessity of wisdom and of restraint. If not religion's beyond time, then the past; if not the past, then the future. For if one does not choose to be under judgment, then his pretension and his myopia prove fatal. The ancient tragedies play on.[18]

4. *Cynicism or faith.* Like cynicism, faith is a choice: first, concerning the kind of world in which one chooses to live; and, second, concerning how one wishes to live in that world. Faith replaces moral vertigo with moral courage. To a great many citizens, the choosing of faith is equivalent to the choosing of emotional sickness and intellectual surrender. Any national "return to religion" is seen as socially and politically disastrous, inviting a frightening extremism and the grossest irrationality. Against this sincere sentiment, Montaigne held that men are never so fanatical as when they have begun to disbelieve. And Rieff holds that totalitarians "are anything but men of deep and settled convictions . . ." Because they disbelieve, "they can be the more easily functionalized in our understandings, and made false to the terror of their acts . . ." Quoting Hannah Arendt, he adds: "The aim of totalitarian education has never been to instill convictions, but to destroy the capacity to form any."[19]

In the vacuum of faith, fear is only the beginning of what we have to fear. But "faith" like "tradition" needs a content. What faith does one choose? On a personal level, the question is impertinent; on a national level, it is virtually imponderable. Yet if religion is the substance of culture, it is difficult to see how the nation can opt for anything except that which is embedded, enmeshed, intermixt in its own historic past.

This, however, raises a final critical point: Who chooses the choosers? If culture-shaping choices are to be made in the realm of religion, who is to make them? Given both the nature of religion and the nature of our history, it does not seem appropriate that government make them. Religion, as distinct from magic, is not a means to an end, not utilitarian, but is an end in itself. Religion is not an instrument in the cold war, said John Kennedy, though the temptation to make it such has been virtually irresistible. The history of America, moreover, is rich with eloquent condemnation of governmental intrusion into sacred domains. What an "impious presumption of legislators and rulers," Jefferson noted, to assume "dominion over the faith of others, setting up their own opinions and modes of thinking as the only true and infallible . . ."[20]

If not government as choice-maker, then what of the major religious spokesmen and denominational leaders? No church-state line is overstepped, though Jefferson, in the comment above, explicitly included ecclesiastical as well as civil "rulers" as capable of "impious presumption." In addition to the question of propriety, however, is the question of authority. The leadership of "establishment religion" suffers too much uncertainty to be effective choice-makers for a people. This problem is not new to America. An eighteenth-century New England divine said of his own establishment: ". . . we know not how to speak living Sense into Souls . . . Our words die in our Mouths, or drop and die between you and us . . . long-experienced Unsuccessfulness makes us despond: We speak not as Persons that hope to prevail."[21]

If not government and if not hierarchy, then must it be left to the scholars, experts, and commissions to choose on behalf of the people. Not really, for these life-choices, like the jury's verdicts of guilt or innocence, are best reserved for the people themselves. Irresponsibility is one of the prices paid for the culture's insistence that decisions be left to the experts. Another price paid, of course, has been foolish decisions, this cost being now so great that there is some chance that choice-making will become a more widely resumed responsibility. Trivial choices can be surrendered to the experts, but profound choices are the province of the simple. "Thou hast hidden these things from the wise and understanding and revealed them to babes . . ."[22]

The four critical choices outlined briefly above are, in a sense, false choices. That is to say, the alternatives are loaded so that one option is noticeably more attractive. This is not the point, however, since the naked options are rarely presented. The point, rather, is to know in which direction we are moving, to "know where we are and whither we are tending." The remaining task is for the people. Two centuries after a declaration of independence that was also a declaration of faith, we must decide whether we hold "these truths," some truths, or no truths. If truths are perceived, the appropriate dedication now as then is one of lives, fortunes, and honor.

Notes

1. Lincoln's "House Divided" Speech, delivered in Springfield, Illinois, June 16, 1858. For Sidney E. Mead's assessment of Lincoln, whom he calls the spiritual center of American history, see his collection of essays, *The Lively Experiment* (New York: Harper and Row, 1963).

2. Louis B. Wright's *Gold, Glory and the Gospel* (New York: Atheneum Press, 1970), and H.M. Jones's *O Strange New World* (New York: Viking Press, 1967) skillfully keep all of Europe in mind in writing about early America. On

Spanish Catholicism in the New World, see Michael V. Gannon, *The Cross in the Sand* (Gainesville: University of Florida Press, 1965) as well as the many older works of Herbert E. Bolton.

3. More than one hundred years ago Francis Parkman introduced to a largely non-Catholic audience *The Jesuits of North America* (Boston: Little, Brown & Co., 1867). To this early effort, the names of many other editors and authors can be added: Reuben Gold Thwaites, Thomas Hughes, G.J. Garraghan, C.E. O'Neill, and more.

4. Hakluyt's words are from *A Discourse on Western Planting*. Louis B. Wright's early work, *Religion and Empire* (Chapel Hill: University of North Carolina Press, 1943), is still very useful for seeing the religious motivations in England's imperial adventures.

5. On the principal ways in which religion may interact with culture, see H. Richard Niebuhr, *Christ and Culture* (New York: Harper and Brothers, 1951); for the general large question with which this chapter deals, see also his *Radical Monotheism and Western Culture* (New York: Harper and Brothers, 1960).

6. For the relationships between religion and the Revolution, see Alan Heimert, *Religion and the American Mind* (Cambridge, Mass.: Harvard University Press, 1966); and Edmund S. Morgan, "The Puritan Ethic and the American Revolution," *William and Mary Quarterly* 24 (1967).

7. Carl Bridenbaugh, *Mitre and Sceptre* (New York: Oxford University Press, 1962) and Charles H. Metzger, *Catholics and the American Revolution* (Chicago: Loyola University Press, 1962) treat the Angelican "threat" and Catholic "danger," respectively.

8. William McLoughlin presents a most suggestive essay regarding the effect of the Revolution on religion in America: "The Role of Religion in the Revolution, Liberty of Conscience and Cultural Cohesion in the New Nation," in S.G. Kurtz and J.H. Hutson, *Essays on the American Revolution* (Chapel Hill: University of North Carolina Press, 1973).

9. The fading hopes of a Protestant hegemony are analyzed in Martin E. Marty, *Righteous Empire: The Protestant Experience in America* (New York: Dial Press, 1970); and, in Robert T. Handy, *A Christian America: Protestant Hopes and Historical Realities* (New York: Oxford University Press, 1971).

10. Lippmann's *Preface to Morals* (New York: Macmillan Co., 1929) and Krutch's *Modern Temper* (New York: Harcourt, Brace and Co., 1929) were early efforts at stiffening America's moral resolve.

11. See among Heschel's many moving works, *Man Is Not Alone* (New York: Farrar, Straus & Young, 1951).

12. The most recent and by far most comprehensive general survey of religion in America is Sydney E. Ahlstrom, *A Religious History of the American People* (New Haven: Yale University Press, 1972). What is only sketched in briefest fashion in this chapter is fully explicated in Ahlstrom's book.

13. Civil religion has enjoyed a full discussion and exploration of the issues in

the last decade. Much of the seminal material is included in Elwyn A. Smith (ed.), *The Religion of the Republic* (Philadelphia: Fortress Press, 1971). A decade before, the Center for the Study of Democratic Institutions gave intelligent attention to the role of religion in American life. The concern then, however, was less with defining "the ideals and aspirations" of a people than it was with helping to determine how pluralism could work. See particularly these booklets: *Religion and American Society, A Statement of Principles* (Santa Barbara, 1961); and, *Religion and the Free Society* (New York, 1958), both published by the Center for the Study of Democratic Institutions.

14. This long paragraph has drawn heavily from Sidney E. Mead's remarkable article, "The 'Nation with the Soul of a Church'," *Church History* 36, 3 (1967). See also his latest volume of essays, *The Nation with the Soul of a Church* (New York: Harper & Row, 1975). Relevant Supreme Court decisions are conveniently assembled in Joseph Tussman (ed.), *The Supreme Court on Church & State* (New York: Oxford University Press, 1962).

15. The Stevenson quotation is from an article of his in *Saturday Review*, February 7, 1959, p. 13.

16. All quotations from Philip Rieff are taken from his newest volume, *Fellow Teachers* (New York: Harper & Row, 1973), a dialogue of sorts with colleagues and students, but more of a confessional monologue that is provocative and wide ranging. See p. 19f. for material cited here.

17. Smylie as quoted in the Mead article noted above, #14. Smylie's article, "National Ethos and the Church," is in *Theology Today* 10 (1963).

18. Rieff, *Fellow Teachers*, p. 48, p. 39.

19. Ibid., p. 210.

20. Jefferson's words are from his "Bill for Establishing Religious Freedom," presented to the Virginia Assembly in 1779.

21. William Cooper, quoting the "late Reverend & learned Mr. How," in the preface to Jonathan Edwards, *The Distinguishing Marks of a Work of the Spirit of God* (Boston, 1741).

22. Matthew 11:25; cf. Luke 10:21. For an elaboration of some of the concerns hinted at in this chapter, see Robert N. Bellah, *The Broken Covenant* (New York: Seabury Press, 1975) and Robert S. Michaelson, *The American Search for Soul* (New York: Louisiana State University Press, 1975).

IV The Revitalization of American Culture: An Anthropological Perspective

James P. Spradley

In recent years a common concern has emerged among many Americans about our "quality of life." For some it involves the destruction of environmental resources and widespread chemical pollution. Others feel threatened by the loss of individual rights in a mass society or the increasing complexity of a technological culture. Still others point to the invasion of privacy, rapid social change, breakdown of family life, and the isolation of elderly persons. Everyone wants to improve the "quality of life," a theme that has become a slogan for politicians of every persuasion. Private foundations, large corporations, and a variety of other institutions all seek to project an image that their role is to safeguard our quality of life. Any discussion of this broad subject runs a serious risk of equating quality of life with some narrow, partisan point of view.

A Cross-Cultural Perspective

My aim in this chapter is to broaden the frame of reference for critically examining "quality of life," the elements that constitute this condition, and the forces that nourish and diminish it. A productive analysis of these complex issues must have many points of view. It requires the informed experience of diverse individuals within our own society. It demands the insights drawn from our collective experience as a nation. It must also draw on the total sweep of Western culture, including projections into the future, as a baseline for enriching the discussion. But these perspectives alone are insufficient. They will give an appearance of breadth while placing limits and distortions on our understanding. *It is imperative that we employ a frame of reference that encompasses all humankind.* More than 3,000 cultures have existed in time and space, each with its own distinct way of life. Within our own society there are dozens of subcultures that lie partially outside the mainstream of American culture. Anthropologists seek to investigate this total spectrum of human experience in order to broaden our culture-bound ideas about humankind. Their goal is more than a search for strange customs or exotic life styles. To the anthropologist, all cultures are natural laboratories for studying the mystery of human nature and the meaning of cultural adaptation. Each provides a natural experiment that reveals something of those conditions that sustain human life and happiness or foster fear, conflict, and apathy.

In this chapter I want to examine "quality of life" from this larger, cross-cultural perspective. What is the nature of this concept? Is it limited to certain cultures or does everyone learn to recognize and strive for some quality of life? Are the differences among cultures mere surface customs or do they go deep into the core of each culture? What forces nourish or diminish the quality of life? Can it be improved by human intervention? Does an improvement in the quality of life for all Americans require basic changes in our values or merely minor readjustment within our present culture? What choices can we make to alter our quality of life in some widely desirable way? Cross-cultural data can help answer some of these questions, clarifying our assumptions and providing directions for specific inquiry about our own culture. I also hope to show that the cross-cultural perspective can illuminate concrete choices that will face Americans in the coming years.

Quality of Life: A Universal Concept

In the broadest sense, "quality of life" refers to *an overall state of affairs in a particular society that people evaluate positively.* From the earliest band of human hunters to the present, every culture has been centrally concerned with quality of life. The Eskimo in the far north share a cluster of ideas about what constitutes this condition. So do the Dani of New Guinea, the Bhils of tribal India, the Kwakiutl Indians of British Columbia, and Americans from Maine to California. People everywhere learn a set of concepts with regard to the quality of their lives, the basic elements that make up quality, and the things that cause it to fluctuate. Such ideas may be vague and often on the edge of consciousness but they profoundly influence how people feel about their life situation. This overall state of affairs that people judge to be good is never present or absent in absolute terms: it is always a matter of degree. Given a certain minimum, most members of a society express feelings of confidence and well-being. When the quality of life deteriorates it arouses anxiety, concern, fear, and even a sense of panic. These emotions may lead to concerted efforts to change the quality of life or people may withdraw in apathy.

What are the basic elements of this universal concept? Every culture contains three interrelated components that make up a kind of "quality control system" for personal and community well-being. I shall refer to these as *cultural means, cultural goals,* and *value orientations.* The "good life" in every society is always defined in terms of these three components. Whenever any one element is threatened, the others are involved and the quality of life deteriorates. Although they must be discussed as separate elements, they form an interlocking system that together make up what we call "meaning in life."

1. *Cultural Goals.* Every culture and subculture defines the ends of human action, prescribed aspirations that people strive for. Not everyone in a society seeks the same ends, nor are all goals of equal salience, but people share a set of goals deemed appropriate. During the eighteenth century, the Seneca Indians of New York had developed their culture around three major goals for men: the good hunter, the forest statesman, and the brave warrior. Like our own goals, such as successful businessman, well-known politician, or erudite professor, their achievement for the Seneca was a measure of masculine success.[1]

No culture involves only a single goal nor does any allow unlimited choice. Each offers a number of related goals. The Nootka Indians, for example, on Vancouver Island, aimed to acquire power and assistance from a guardian spirit. A young man also hoped to acquire many items of nonmaterial wealth such as names and songs. Another major goal was to give away large amounts of material wealth on ceremonial occasions called "potlatches." These goals were learned early in life and expectations of their achievement became the basis for what every Nootka Indian considered "quality" in life.[2]

2. *Cultural Means.* Every culture also defines appropriate ways to achieve its goals. These modes of reaching out for cherished values make up many of the customs and mores of life. The skills, technology, and knowledge of hunting were the means to become a good Seneca hunter; political acumen and negotiating skills were necessary to become a forest statesman; a knowledge of warfare strategies and the ability to execute them were required to become a brave warrior. A Nootka Indian learned that some strategies for acquiring a guardian spirit were acceptable, such as fasting and repeated bathing in cold streams, while others were not. Songs and names had to be acquired in the proper way, through inheritance or marriage.

The things people do to achieve culturally prescribed goals come to have symbolic value in and of themselves. They provide a sense of security, symbolizing that the meaning of life is still intact, even when goals are not immediately achieved. The possession of a spear or an automobile become more than tools for hunting or transportation. They become symbols of status, masculinity, and achievement.

3. *Value Orientations.* All conceptions of "the good life," whether held by an

American senator, an Eskimo hunter, a European psychiatrist, a Yanomamo women in the jungles of Venezuela, or anyone else, involve fundamental assumptions about the nature of human existence. Cultural goals and the means for their achievement are always backed up by deeply held values and premises of this sort. They are usually taken for granted as inherent features of human nature. They often lie outside the awareness of the very individuals whose actions are based on such premises. These tacit assumptions that we make about life are called *value orientations.*[3] They refer to *broad concepts of what a people hold to be desirable*. Value orientations help resolve conflicts among goals by specifying some priority order. They also influence the selection of new goals and means. These broad conceptions of desirable conditions are also resistant to change for they provide the primary security base for members of a society.

Underlying the Seneca goals of good hunter, brave warrior, and forest statesman, was a deeply held value orientation of "the absolutely free and autonomous individual, unconstrained by and indifferent to his own and alien others' pain and hardship."[4] This value orientation gave meaning to the goals that Seneca men strove for and the means they used. Like all cultures, our own contains a complex set of goals, means, and value orientations. Although there is considerable variation, especially among our major subcultures, the variation is quite limited when we consider the cross-cultural record.

The system of means, ends, and value orientations that constitutes each society's definition of "quality" is a *moral order*. Human plasticity sets the stage for this characteristic of human social life. For most animal species the range of adaptive behavior is relatively narrow, fixed by heredity. What a bee, a dolphin, or a gibbon *must do* to survive and what each of these creatures *can do* are quite similar when compared with human capacities for an enormous range of behavior. Take language, for example. Each of us has the capacity to learn any one of at least 3,000 languages created by our species. But adaptation and survival always occur within a particular society, requiring restrictions on what people do. In order to communicate, a necessary condition for survival, the members of each culture learn a single language, or several at the most. And so it is with each aspect of culture. As Clifford Geertz has said, "One of the most significant facts about us may finally be that we all begin with the natural equipment to live a thousand kinds of life but end in the end having lived only one."[5]

How is this human plasticity molded within the limits necessary for social life? Every culture teaches people to cherish certain means, goals, and value orientations and to reject others. Every culture selects from the range of possibilities—for mating, making a living, rearing children, communicating, etc.—and defines the actions selected as part of the good life. Unlike other species which live out their lives conditioned only by the natural order, humankind can only survive by creating, learning, changing, and coming to terms with this *moral order*. Indeed, the ability to conceive some "quality of life" and aspire to achieve it, is unique to humankind, rooted in the moral and ethical dimensions of our nature.

As we analyze our own quality of life and identify the choices that face Americans, it is crucial to recognize that our complex system of means, goals, and value orientations is a moral and ethical system. Our own value orientations of rationality, objectivity, efficiency, and dominance over nature implicitly deny this premise, especially with regards to the *means* for achieving our cultural goals. That which is rational, efficient, objective or scientific does not *appear* to involve arbitrary values. When we ask whether "quality" in life is *partially* made up of moral values, in addition to standard of living and material things, for instance, it implies that some choices are not moral ones.

The starting point for improving our quality of life is to *create a new awareness of the value orientations in American culture*. This must include those held by our diverse ethnic and minority groups as well as more widely held mainstream values. The value orientations that underlie science, education, government, and large corporations must be identified, clarified, and their consequences examined. Any analysis of "quality" in American life that fails to go beyond the means and goals to understand our value orientations will be inadequate.[6]

Cross-Cultural Variation

Although the general concept of "quality in life" is universal, that which constitutes this condition *differs significantly* from one society to another. Cross-cultural studies overwhelmingly demonstrate that human beings equate an enormous range of different conditions with quality of life. That which contributes to the good life in one society detracts from it in another.[7] These differences not only involve distinct means, goals, and value orientations, but profound differences in the arrangement of these elements into a kind of "quality control system." Consider the following brief examples.

To a Mae Enga in the highlands of New Guinea, the number of pigs a person controls largely determines the quality of life.[8] Men talk of pigs constantly, sacrificing them often to the ancestral ghosts, but with great reluctance. Women live in the same houses with pigs and a woman will think nothing of nursing an orphaned piglet at her own breast to insure its growth. Most Americans would be repulsed by this interest in pigs and the constant, close association with such animals. But to the Mae Enga, pigs are supremely important. They are symbols of social worth and their significance has become interwoven with every facet of Mae Enga life. Furthermore, pigs are not primarily valued for food. They are usually only killed and eaten on ceremonial occasions. Without pigs the Mae Enga quality of life would suffer appreciably, for as the Mae Enga say, "Pigs are our hearts."

Or take the matter of having children, a universal feature of human societies. Many young American couples employ chemical, mechanical, and surgical means to achieve the goal of limiting family size and, it is believed, thereby improving the quality of their lives. A small number of children, it is believed, will increase each member's share in both the emotional and material resources of the family. Also in America, aging family members with their problems become unwanted burdens who often live out their last years isolated from families in special institutions for the elderly.[9]

In many cultures the reverse is true. The people of rural India, for instance, remember the gods faithfully to insure the birth of many healthy offspring. A large family may increase productive capacity in some societies, but large numbers of children are frequently valued for other reasons. People also want aging kinsmen nearby, perhaps living in the same household, for they are seen as an asset, contributing to the quality of life. As a Pomo Indian once said to an anthropologist, "What is a man? A man is nothing. Without his family he is of less importance than that bug crossing the trail, of less importance than spittle or turds."[10] Underlying our attitudes about family life is a value orientation that stresses the importance of individualism; many cultures place a contrasting emphasis on the importance of the larger kinship group.

But the varying cultural definitions of the good life do not only affect important symbols of social worth or our ideas about family and kin. What is considered as *essential* to the quality of life shows wide variation and includes the amount and kind of food we eat, the pace of life, health, definitions of manliness and womanliness, forms of play, relations with other societies, and expectations about the future. For most people, quality of life even becomes linked to the way we express the rational and emotional aspects of personality. The intellectual, problem-solving approach to experience, for example, is a major criterion to many Americans for a high quality of life. It is based on widely held value orientations of rationality and objectivity. We feel threatened in the face of seemingly uncontrolled emotional states, but these are frequently considered quite desirable in other cultures. The Balinese, for example, define highly emotional trance states as important for every adult.

The Balinese fall into extreme dissociated states in which they perform all sorts of spectacular activities—biting off the heads of live chickens, stabbing themselves with daggers, throwing themselves wildly about, speaking with tongues, performing miraculous feats of equilibration, mimicking sexual intercourse, eating feces, and so on—rather more easily and much more suddenly than most of us fall asleep. Trance states are a crucial part of every ceremony. In some, fifty or sixty people may fall, one after the other ("like a string of firecrackers going off," as one observer puts it), emerging anywhere from five minutes to several hours later, totally unaware of what they have been doing and convinced, despite the amnesia, that they have had the most extraordinary and deeply satisfying experience a man can have.[11]

Examples of significant differences could be multiplied from around the world and within our own multicultural society. This diversity must inform our plans for social change. Any choices aimed at improving the quality of life for Americans runs the risk portrayed in a fable of Southeast Asia. It happened that a monkey and a fish were both caught up in a great flood. The monkey, wise, agile and experienced, observed the situation. He calculated carefully the rate at which the water was rising and scrambled up a tree to safety. For the moment he had achieved a higher quality of life. As the swirling flood waters rose higher and higher, he looked down and saw a fish that appeared to be struggling valiantly against the swift current. Filled with a humanitarian desire to improve the quality of life for his less fortunate fellow, he reached down, and scooped the fish from the water. To the monkey's surprise the fish was not very grateful for his aid.[12]

Efforts to improve the quality of life, whether in other parts of the world or in our own pluralistic society, can easily fall prey to such ethnocentrism. Implicit in our definitions of "underdeveloped" countries, "culturally deprived" minority groups, or "primitive" societies is the belief that our own way of life is superior to others and really best for everyone. Ethnocentrism can also become inverted, holding that our way of life is *entirely corrupt* and that the "noble savage" or some other alternative has a more natural and authentic quality of life. In either case this attitude is rooted in the human tendency to become overcommitted to one set of values to the exclusion of all others. Quality of life discussions and programs are especially vulnerable to this ethnocentric bias.

Essential Features of "Quality"

It is clear that what people define as "quality" in life has been perceived differently from one culture to another. But, beneath the surface of each culture, are there not basic needs that must be met for a satisfactory life, no matter how that is defined? Are we purely and simply what culture makes of us? An extreme relativistic approach cannot be entirely supported from cross-cultural evidence. For one thing, individuals may leave one sociocultural system, opting for a different set of values they find more satisfying. Furthermore, entire cultures have been changed, sometimes quite radically, in a massive effort to create a qualitatively better way of life. Sometimes the quality of life deteriorates to such an extent that members of a society as well as outside observers conclude that conditions are extremely poor. At the end of the eighteenth century, for example, the Seneca Indians sold their last hunting grounds and became confined to reservations. Game was scarce and the good hunter hardly dared to leave the reservation because of hostile white men. The forest statesman and the brave warrior, likewise, could not enact these traditional roles. The fear of witches increased, drunkenness and apathy ensued, tribal factions developed, and the sense of community well-being declined seriously. In 1799 a religious movement developed advocating radically new goals and values, and as Wallace has documented, within a few years "A group of sober, devout, partly literate, and technologically up-to-date farming communities suddenly replaced the demoralized slums in the wilderness."[13]

Can we identify a set of *essential conditions for quality in life*? The answer appears to be a tentative yes, but it is not without problems. Various lists of basic needs and functional requirements have been proposed, but we shall only examine one here.[14] Alexander Leighton's work on mental illness in various cultures has been the basis for the following list of "essential striving sentiments." According to Leighton, the process of striving for cultural goals is a universal human experience even though the number and diversity of goals is quite large. Mental illness tends to occur when striving for certain categories of goals is blocked. These categories correspond to basic human needs. A sense of well-being and quality in life for any culture requires that these basic needs are met. The following tentative list is proposed by Leighton as a means for relating social and cultural systems to individual human needs:[15]

1. Physical security
2. Sexual satisfaction
3. The expression of hostility
4. The expression of love
5. The security of love
6. The securing of recognition
7. The expression of spontaneity (called variously positive force, creativity, volition).
8. Orientation in terms of one's place in society and the places of others.
9. The securing and maintaining of membership in a definite human group.
10. A sense of belonging to a moral order and being right in what one does (being in and of a system of values).

The major difficulty with these essential conditions for quality is their generality. How are we to know, for example, whether the matrilineal clans of the Trobriand Islanders provide a better sense of membership in a definite human group than the American nuclear family or the Elks Club? Is recognition secured in some "better" way through acquiring pigs, college degrees, or guardian spirits? In extreme cases of mental illness or social disorganization, comparative evaluation in terms of these essential conditions does seem possible. In most situations, however, they only provide general guidelines, not specific criteria for determining quality.

Another problem stems from the fact that there is never a one-to-one relationship between any cultural goal or institution and a single basic need. The family, for instance, which takes many forms cross-culturally, helps to meet a number of human needs. In most families love is expressed and secured; sexual satisfaction is provided for some members; belonging to a family means membership in a definite group. But other institutions also serve these basic needs making it extremely difficult to conclusively evaluate most cultural practices or the overall quality of life.

Quality of life—both as perceived in particular cultures and as a panhuman characteristic—appears to be extremely complex.[a] Again and again the anthropologist comes back to the fact that every culture, from the smallest tribal band to our own complex nation, involves complex patterns that are interwoven in a network of needs and solutions. If we isolate cultural goals such as physical health or peaceful relations with other societies, it appears relatively simple to make judgments about conditions that are "better" for everyone. But, negative cultural practices and beliefs that apparently detract from the quality of life cannot be so easily isolated without affecting other things that contribute to the essential conditions listed above. The means, goals, and value orientations of a culture are linked in systematic ways that makes isolated change difficult. The basic needs of humankind are so interwoven with the goals and values of specific cultures that improving the quality of life may be perceived as destroying it and may actually lower it. To take an extreme case, consider the headhunting Konyak Nagas of India and what happened after the British "raised" the quality of their lives by bringing peace to the region:

Konyaks were firmly convinced that the capturing of heads was essential for the well-being of a village and that a community which failed over a period of years to bring in a head would suffer a decline in prosperity. The men of Wakching and other villages of administered territory where Pax Britannica had brought raiding to an end often complained that their inability to capture human heads had resulted in a deterioration of health and general well-being. Their observation was probably accurate, for not only had life lost much of its zest, but increased contacts with the people of the plains had facilitated the spread of epidemics. In the days of headhunting Naga villages had been very isolated, and as there was little traffic, epidemics seldom affected more than a limited area. With the ban on feuding, however, travel between villages became safer, epidemics spread more widely, and the toll of death from small pox, dysentery, and cholera was much heavier than the losses sustained in the past as the result of sporadic head-hunting raids.[16]

The variability in ideas about quality of life and the lack of clear, universal criteria for its improvement does not mean there are no solutions to the current problems faced by Americans. The cross-cultural record does provide other avenues that can help in clarifying our choices. For example, on the basis of the

---

[a]It is important to point out that the distinction between "perceived quality of life" and "actual quality of life" is somewhat spurious. The "actual quality of life" turns out to be what some Western scholar perceives as universal or widely necessary for human happiness. Underlying the list of panhuman requirements for quality in life are the assumptions and values of psychological theory that is peculiarly Western in nature.

values in a single culture it may be possible to improve the quality of life for that culture. We might help the Mae Enga raise healthier pigs or show them ways to increase the size of herds. Our own efforts to raise the standard of living for all Americans by utilizing new energy sources is a similar approach. But such solutions do require acceptance of current value orientations. Another approach is offered by studies of cultures that have attempted to radically improve their quality of life. There are widespread reports of attempts at "revitalizing" a culture, some of which have been successful. They reveal the forces that foster quality of life in any society and provide some guidelines for the choices that face Americans. In the remainder of this chapter I want to discuss the nature of revitalization processes, especially as they apply to American culture.

Revitalization and Improving the Quality of Life

Implicit in the preceding discussion is the premise that quality of life is not a static phenomenon. It fluctuates, at some times resulting in an improved sense of well-being, at other times deteriorating. If the quality of life in human societies does change from time to time, then it should be possible to study the forces behind such fluctuations, perhaps to gain some control over them, and thereby influence the course of change. Anthropologists have studied culture change in the context of numerous small societies and certain change events known as *revitalization processes*, are especially important for our present discussion.[17]

Cross-cultural research has revealed numerous and widespread attempts to dramatically improve the quality of life in human societies.[18] The Ghost Dance, for example, was a nativistic movement that occurred among the Indians of Nevada and California in the 1870s. It promised an earthly paradise, one inhabited by the living and the resurrected dead, and required an immediate revival of native customs.[19] The Peyote Cult was another widely accepted social movement among American Indians aimed at restoration of the quality of life.[20] In New Guinea and the islands of Melanesia there have been dozens of "cargo cults" reported whose goal is to import parts of foreign cultures in order to improve the quality of life.[21] One of the earliest, the German Wislin cult of 1913, occurred on an island in the Torres Straits. A prophet announced that the spirits of the dead would return in a large steamer with all kinds of manufactured goods. They would kill the whites and bring prosperity to all who obeyed the prophet. Some cargo cults require the destruction of native customs, the imitation of Western practices like raising flags or marching as soldiers with wooden guns, and the refusal to work for Europeans as they waited the arrival of cargo. In recent years, one cargo cult in the New Hebrides Islands came to be known as the Lyndon B. Johnson cult. Its followers believed that Johnson would come to their aid, radically changing their quality of life and distributing large amounts of money to everyone. Throughout history there have been many social movements aimed at improving the quality of life including early Christianity, Mohammedanism, the Boxer Rebellion in China, and many contemporary revolutions.

Revitalization Movements

These efforts have usually involved fundamental changes in a culture and represent forms of revitalization. A revitalization movement refers to "deliberate, organized attempts by some members of a society to construct a more satisfying culture by rapid acceptance of a pattern of multiple innovations."[22] Some revitalization movements are abortive and unsuccessful, while others bring a new way of life and higher level of satisfaction. For example, in 1799, the Seneca Forest statesman, Handsome Lake, received a supernatural vision and proclaimed a message of cultural reform that resulted in a successful revitalization movement.

Anthony Wallace has reviewed the evidence on revitalization movements and sees a common underlying series of stages in successful movements. These overlapping stages include: (1) *a steady state* in which culture change occurs but most needs continue to be satisfied by current means and goals. (2) A *period of individual stress*, during which an "increasingly large number of individuals are placed under what is to them an intolerable stress by failure of the system to accommodate the satisfaction of their needs. Anomie and disillusionment become widespread, as the culture is perceived to be disorganized and inadequate; crime and illness increase sharply in frequency as individualistic asocial responses."[23] This is followed by (3) *a period of cultural distortion*, during which internal contradictions develop and the culture becomes increasingly disorganized. Individual crimes and deviance become institutionalized. Efforts to change the culture are poorly coordinated with the net result that they are quite ineffectual. (4) *The period of revitalization* involves the organized attempt to restore the culture pattern to a higher level of quality by creating new utopian patterns, returning to old ways, or importing some foreign cultural elements. If revitalization is successful, the last stage is achieved, (5) *a new steady state* with at least some new goals, means and value orientations.

I should like to suggest that American culture is currently undergoing a process of revitalization. Rather than a rapid, religiously based phenomenon, it has secular roots that go back for at least two or three decades and perhaps longer. Due to the scale and complexity of our society, there is considerable unevenness in the stages of this process, but the general features can be discerned in various groups. For some, the experience of individual stress is the primary one; for others, it is a time of cultural distortion. But more and more people are now working on specific programs of revitalization, designing new cultural goals and the means for their achievement. It is unlikely that revitalization will occur in the same rapid, revolutionary manner that is characteristic of the movements reported by anthropologists although that always remains a possibility.

It may seem spurious to compare our cultural condition with the ones experienced by the small tribal societies under the impact of the West, but it must be kept in mind that neither quality of life nor deprivation are absolute. David Aberle has emphasized that the impetus for revitalization is always based on *relative* deprivation:

> Relative deprivation is defined as a negative discrepancy between legitimate expectation and actuality. Where an individual or a group has a particular expectation and furthermore where this expectation is considered to be a proper state of affairs, and where something less than that expectation is fulfilled, we may speak of relative deprivation. It is important to stress that deprivation *is* relative and not absolute. To a hunting and gathering group with an expectation of going hungry one out of four days, failure to find game is not a relative deprivation, although it may produce marked discomfort. It is a truism that for a multi-millionaire to lose all but his last million in a stockmarket crash *is* a major deprivation.[24]

Rising expectations among all groups of our society have created widespread feelings of deprivation. Our own ideals of equality and the eradication of poverty have added to the sense of deprivation for many who are poor or experience discrimination. Furthermore, the communications media has provided nearly everyone with new standards for evaluating their relative deprivation.

Most analyses of American culture tend to emphasize factors that have led to increasing individual stress or cultural distortion. In the remainder of this chapter I want to focus instead on the period of revitalization as it appears to be developing in American society. In particular I want to examine three requirements for the successful revitalization of any culture as a basis for concrete suggestions to improve our quality of life. It must be kept in mind throughout the discussion that controlling the course of culture change, especially the process of revitalization, may well be an illusory goal. Perhaps the best that can be done is to understand the process and, in some small ways, help to facilitate those forces that nourish the quality of life for Americans.

Requirements for Successful Revitalization

1. *Successful revitalization requires the formulation of new goals.* One indicator of revitalization is the growing agreement on a limited number of *alternative goals* for American culture. (Revitalization may also involve a new emphasis on traditional goals that have not been achieved.) Many revitalization movements stumble at this major hurdle to creating a more satisfying culture. Some fail because they seek to revive inadequate goals of a past culture as a basis for

solving the current problems. Others offer such utopian objectives that their attainment is impossible. For purposes of discussion I would suggest that the following major goals, some more radical than others, are becoming widely recognized as candidates for a revitalized American culture. The list is not exhaustive. They have been articulated in one form or another by many different persons, and with increasing frequency during the past twenty years.

1. A health care system that provides adequate care for all members of the society.
2. The provision of economic resources for all people sufficient to eliminate poverty and provided in a way that does not destroy the privacy and dignity of any recipient.
3. Equal rights and opportunities for all classes of citizens, including women, blacks native Americans, Chicanos, the elderly, children, and others.
4. Public institutions, such as schools, courts, and governments that are designed for a multicultural constituency.
5. Socially responsible corporations that operate in the public interest as well as private interest.
6. Zero population growth.
7. An ecologically balanced economy based on recycling and responsible for the protection of natural resources.
8. Education for all people, at every stage of life, that equips them to cope with the complexity of choice in our rapidly changing society.
9. Work roles and environments that contribute directly to the workers sense of meaning and purpose in life.
10. Opportunity for alternative career patterns and more flexible life cycle sequencing with multiple occupational careers and meaningful involvement for youth, retired persons, and the elderly.

But a knowledge of goals such as these, and even formulating specific means to achieve them, will not inevitably lead to revitalization. The greater challenge is to gain acceptance of these goals and to translate them into action at every level of society. This demands that we shift attention to the *value orientations* on which these goals are based.

2. *Successful revitalization requires a marked increase in the salience of value orientations on which the new quality of life is based*. This may involve renewed commitment to traditional values as well as the necessary changes for clarifying and accepting new value orientations. Most revitalization movements begin with dramatic events that command people's attention. A revelation comes to a prophet, a leader dies and comes to life again, a miracle is performed, or some other supernatural event takes place. Leaders in revitalization movements often develop charismatic power and their words and deeds acquire a kind of mythical character. Individual conversions occur as people express their commitment to

the new goals. These kinds of events increase the salience of underlying value orientations for the people involved. As myths and symbols develop around a revitalization movement, they serve to remind the people of the important new values, reinforcing their significance, and providing a strong motivational force.

The bent of our own culture is towards the *means* for achieving goals rather than the *value orientation* on which they rest. Traditionally we idealize technological changes, all of which are defined as means to cherished ends. We often discount myths, rituals, and symbols as trivial. We have "think tanks" and government sponsored commissions to search for new *means* to implement national goals, but the value orientations go unquestioned and the ceremonial occasions for reinforcing these dwindle in number. One of the most neglected areas of research in our culture has to do with these "value reinforcing mechanisms." As pointed out earlier, no culture exists without values, yet social planners sometimes operate as if values did not exist.

But how do value orientations become more salient for a particular population? We might begin with a rational, explicit identification of the values that underly alternative goals, but this is only a first step. We must work to *identify incipient myths, symbols, and even ceremonies that serve to reinforce the alternative values required for revitalization*. These are already developing and some are gaining wide support. One of the most critical choices facing all Americans is whether we will support and foster the development of the myths and symbols that, in turn, increase the salience of values or let them die by neglect. We need to understand a great deal more about the nature and function of "myth-making" in our kind of culture, but an example may help to clarify some possible courses of action.

For several centuries, if not longer, Western culture has given allegiance to the supreme value of understanding and controlling the natural world. Scientific technology is essentially good in the American view because it serves this value. It can be used as a tool to adapt nature to human purposes, to increase the standard of living, and to raise the quality of life. Scientists and astronauts become symbols of this value and we laud new discoveries and ceremonialize the days our space ships leave earth on scientific missions. But our endless pursuit of science has run into a limited supply of resources as well as the destructive consequences of harnessing nature without regard for her well-being. There is a new voice heard now calling for different goals with regard to nature and the scientific exploitation of nature. Ecology, recycling, and conservation have become popular words, but these are only the means for achieving goals and can serve the old ones as well as the new. A significant change in our quality of life must involve a profound change in value orientations.

We can contrast our values with those of the Navaho, who deeply believe that *nature is more powerful than man*. Clyde Kluckhohn wrote, "Navahos accept nature and adapt themselves to her demands as best they can, but they are not utterly passive, not completely the pawns of nature. They do a great many things that are designed to control nature physically and to repair damage caused by the elements. But they do not even hope to master nature."[2][5] We spend our energies adapting nature to our purposes, instead of adapting to the demands of nature. But how will a shift in this basic attitude come about? How can this value orientation be symbolized? What myths are developing to support the acceptance of this value and to increase its salience for Americans? Myths need not be based on supernatural events. For example, Earth Day began as a kind of incipient symbol for this new value. It may have appeared to some as detracting from the hard job of preserving our natural resources, but it was an effort to dramatically symbolize a profoundly different value system. Significant court cases such as a recent decision in Minnesota to stop Reserve Mining Company from dumping its wastes into Lake Superior take on the character of mythical events, reinforcing the new value orientation. Some individuals may become models of new values, providing opportunities for a kind of symbolic affirmation of them. In the same way that the astronauts became folk heroes of an outmoded value system new types are needed who can symbolize the emergent values.

I suggest, then, a basic strategy for improving our quality of life, based on this second requirement for successful revitalization movements. (1) Clarify revitalization goals (e.g., provision of economic resources for all people). (2) Identify the underlying value orientation (e.g., social institutions should serve the needs of individuals, community welfare includes humanitarian care for all). (3) Locate incipient myths and symbols that reinforce this value orientation (e.g., the family as a model for society, government supports institutions, why not individuals, etc.). (4) Support the further development of myths and symbols that enhance these values (e.g., social science research, court cases, voluntary efforts, etc.). These steps will create a climate of change and acceptance of values which will make debates over the means (e.g., foods stamps, welfare checks, negative income tax) much less significant. As new value orientations become part of the fabric of our culture we can expect numerous innovations to emerge—some social, some technological—in the service of new goals.

3. *Successful revitalization requires adaptation to altered environmental conditions.* The vast array of cross-cultural differences about what constitutes "quality" in life is partially a response to different habitats. For several million years humankind had successfully adapted to a variety of terrestrial environments. From the frozen tundra to the steaming jungle, humans have built their homes, reared their children, performed their rituals, and buried their dead. In recent years we have escaped the thin layer of atmosphere surrounding the earth to live, if only for a few weeks, in outer space and beneath the ocean. All these achievements have been possible because of our capacity for culture. Science has been a most effective instrument in this process of adaptation. As a culture becomes more equipped to live in a particular environment, and if that environment remains unchanged, the quality of life usually become better or at least remains stable.

But stable environments lack permanence and the greatest problems for every animal species arise when there is a significant change in the environment. Genetic mutations that served hundreds of generations of a species in adapting to one habitat become barriers to survival with a change such as the ice age. In a similar fashion, cultural values and goals that were effective tools for adaptation to one environment become outmoded when it changes. Unless new cultural responses develop, the quality of life will suffer. Both animal species and human cultures have become extinct because of the inability to develop new adaptive strategies in an altered environment.

Now we come to a most significant observation: *the physical, social, and cultural environments can change in significant ways that go unrecognized.* Water supplies become chemically polluted without human knowledge. Urban crowding creates a new social environment that is not perceived as such until considerable damage results. Cultures come into intimate and prolonged contact resulting in subtle changes that are outside our awareness. When the Seneca could no longer hunt, revitalization required adaptation to this alteration in their environment. Not only was game less plentiful but the presence of white men prevented the Seneca from hunting. Farming offered at least one successful adaptation to these changes, but a difficult one that was only adopted in the context of the revitalization movement led by Handsome Lake.

Americans face a number of significant changes in their physical, social, and cultural environments. Our quality of life has deteriorated, in part, because we are using a system of cultural adaptation that was developed for an environment that no longer exists. I speak not so much of our natural resources but the social and cultural environments that have significantly changed in ways that often go unrecognized. Let us look at two such changes and ask what will be necessary for successful adaption to these altered conditions.

Culture Conflict. There was a time in our society when many youth learned a coherent system of values and made life choices in terms of these values. Differences were present but we smoothed them over in the belief that all groups would quickly assimilate into the mainstream. The apparent unity among values gave meaning and purpose to life. Divergent value systems were recognized but somehow they did not impinge on daily experience. Increased communication and travel, expanding population, the growth of urban centers, and unmasking the fiction that America was a great "melting pot" for different cultures, all worked to create a new condition—culture conflict.

Culture conflict is the result of a curious twist of fate. In a sense, our greatest resource for adapting to different environments—the capacity to create *different* cultural value systems—has become the source of one of our greatest problems. Diversity of cultures was required for survival in the ecological niches of earth, but it can be destructive when all humankind suddenly finds itself in the same niche. Diversity of cultures has provided humans with the capacity to meet fluctuating conditions of the physical environment in ways far superior to other animals. But now we are faced with a radically altered *social and cultural environment*. Isolation has disappeared. Successful adaptation will now require changes that fly in the face of millions of years of cultural specialization. Human ingenuity has been used to develop thousands of distinct value systems, but thus far we have failed to develop satisfactory patterns and rules for articulating these differences. Moreover we have not learned how to socialize our children to handle a cultural environment where conflict is pervasive. Can we survive in a world where our neighbors and even our children have different ideas about "quality" in life? Can we adapt to the close, intimate fellowship of a spaceship like earth when each group of passengers lives by different values?

The most difficult situations of culture conflict have been experienced by American Indians and other non-Western cultures dominated by some Western society. With the acceleration of culture change today, more and more people are facing this situation. Margaret Mead has suggested that all Americans may soon find themselves in the situation of those immigrants to America who watched their children grow up speaking a different language and learning a foreign culture.

What is the nature of this changed cultural environment we call "culture conflict?" A contrast may help illuminate this condition. During the 1960s many educators began to identify children in various minority groups as "culturally deprived." They suggested that these children did poorly in school because they had been deprived of important cultural values and experiences. Today we know that this is merely an ethnocentric fiction, for rather than being deprived, they are "culturally overwhelmed."

Cultural deprivation suggests that people have had a very restricted cultural diet, when, in truth, the diet has been too complex. Rather than having to learn a single, limited, cultural orientation, they have faced the extremely difficult task of learning two or more *conflicting cultural value systems*. This means far more than an awareness that other people have a different culture. It is, rather, the experience of being socialized into a world where the significant others in a person's life—teachers, peers, parents, friends, grandparents, cultural heroes— represent very different sets of value-orientations. Rewards and punishments from these different reference groups are doled out for contradictory reasons. The symbols of prestige in one situation become symbols of depravity in another. The actions valued in one group are considered crimes in another. The Navaho child goes to school where the educational experience revolves around science and the value of dominating nature; the conflict with Navaho values, while not articulated, is deeply felt. In this kind of situation the individual fights a losing battle to maintain personal integrity and a sense of self-worth as a human being.

Many individuals in culture conflict situations experience a lack of meaning and their response is *passive withdrawal*. They cannot totally reject the cultural heritage of parents because it involves important aspects of their self-identity. Neither can they reject the dominant culture because it is held by those in positions of status, power, and prestige. They have come to believe that the active pursuit of the goals of one culture involve the repudiation of the other. Caught between two ways of life, they withdraw to escape the conflict. Apathy, lack of achievement motivation, excessive drinking, and similar behavior traits appear to be the symptoms of those suspended between two or more incompatible cultural value systems. The essential *meaning in life* has been lost in the conflict between two cultures, for although humankind is able, as a species, to live any one of a thousand kinds of lives, each individual must live one kind of life to survive psychologically.

Successful adaptation to culture conflict does not lie in returning to a simpler, homogeneous value system. Rather, we must work to reshape our institutions to serve a *multicultural constituency*. Again, one set of choices open to Americans will involve supporting the incipient myths and symbols that reinforce the value of a multicultural society. The historical traditions of our minorities must be taught to all students and events such as "Black History Week" take on added meaning when seen as reinforcing the broader value of pluralism with dignity. Public and private schools must be adapted to this new environment, becoming bilingual in many cases and teaching a range of value orientations. Our legal system must also become multicultural. Although supposedly based on "equal treatment for all under the law," it functions on a single set of value orientations, distributing justice unequally.[26]

One form of adapting to cultural conflict involves developing a multicultural style of life. My own study of a Kwakiutl Indian who has dealt successfully with the problems of culture conflict revealed this kind of adaptation, one that involves commitments to seemingly contradictory values.[27] As Bohannon has pointed out,

Such is the nature of the successful answer to the impact situation and to detribalization. People learn, at whatever cost and with whatever personal problems, to be bicultural. . . . Response to the impact situation has led to the development of exceptional human beings: people with an extraordinarily wide range of cultural capability. It is a remarkable achievement that an African can one day participate with full commitment in a ritual, the next day step into a helicopter and go campaigning for votes, the next day board a plane to London or Paris and hold a successful conference there with representatives from many countries and cultures, and the next day fly to New York to manipulate international tensions in an appearance at the United Nations. All with the ease and assurance that come with knowledge.[28]

We need additional studies to understand this type of adaptation to culture conflict for such a condition is destined to grow more pervasive in the coming years. Principles for bicultural and multicultural living could be built into our educational programs, giving people a greater capacity to adapt to one of the major characteristics of American culture.

Cultural Complexity. The second environmental change that we must adapt to has to do with the number of *choices* confronting everyone. Although related to culture conflict, it is somewhat different. Take the matter of occupations. The Department of Labor lists nearly 25,000 different occupations and theoretically the total range is open to any citizen who meets the necessary requirements. But how can responsible choices be made when the individual has only a smattering of knowledge about less than 100 of these occupations? One of the major themes of Toffler's *Future Shock* has to do with the nature of this increasing complexity and how we can cope with it.

The shift is a significant one. The very culture we created to improve our quality of life has become a problem. We must now create ways to adapt to its inherent complexity. Two developments have already begun that hold promise of revitalizing our capacity to gain some control over cultural complexity. First, within the educational establishment there is a developing program called "Career Education." For some, this movement means earlier preparation of our youth for the occupations necessary to maintain a technological society. It appears that next year Career Education Programs administered out of the U.S. Office of Education will have a budget of $10 million, $20 million the year after that. As this program begins to affect school districts in every state, community colleges, and universities, a significant choice faces us: *Will Career Education be designed to train people for jobs or to educate people to cope with cultural complexity?*

As I have suggested elsewhere, the goal of Career Education should be "*to enable every person to make informed choices as he develops his own career. The objective is to give each person a greater command over his own life.* While this is often stated as a part of Career Education, I am suggesting that it be elevated to the status of its primary goal."[29] Career Education must involve a revised curriculum to infuse schools at all levels with information about the world of work. This must include information about the culture, value orientations, and the life style of occupations, not merely entry requirements and skills. Education must also focus more specifically on the decision-making process and the importance of values in this process. In our rapidly changing society, some predict that career patterns may require new occupations for many people every few years. If we equip students with a wide range of information and decision-making skills, they will be able to move in and out of various occupations more easily.

A second development that I see as part of the revitalization process involves new definitions of the life cycle. Every culture defines the stages of life for its members, making certain activities appropriate to the various ages. In our own culture we have had a restricted set of sequences from childhood to retirement and old age. Single career patterns have been the norm for most people with retirement frequently occurring long before productive capacities have declined. New value-orientations are emerging that place emphasis on a variety of career patterns. Recent legal decisions making mandatory retirement illegal will also influence this new direction in our culture. In part, the vast range of possibilities in our culture has raised the expectations for multiple careers, but our structure often prevents that. This new value orientation, if supported and reinforced, will have many ramifications and consequences. Career Education, for example, can become part of the means for bringing people of all ages back into colleges for new vocations and avocations. Learning itself could become a major avocation for the elderly, bringing the young and old together in the classroom.

The Growth of Powerful and Irresponsible Corporations. This is the third significant environmental change faced by Americans. Corporations are institutions that have a life of their own, growing in size and power over the years while the individuals in the corporation come and go. Originally created as cultural instruments to produce and distribute the goods and services of our culture, and thereby improve the quality of life, many corporations are no longer servants of the public interest. Every corporation is based on a set of values about self-perpetuation, growth, and profit. Individuals who work within the corporate structure nearly always live by a different set of *personal* values although these do include loyalty to the corporation as an institution. As *individuals*, those who are part of the corporation generally live in a responsible fashion. But the values, goals and size of large corporations *transform the responsible behavior of hundreds of individuals into irresponsible corporate actions*. It is this change in our cultural environment that often goes unrecognized. By artificially separating the values that guide personal conduct from those that guide corporate conduct our culture has created enormously powerful institutions that have no social conscience.

Revitalizing American culture will require new and effective ways to control the antisocial behavior of corporations. It will also mean new value orientations that define corporations as social institutions required to serve the public interest. The most significant crime today in the United States, in terms of number of arrests and convictions, is committed by individuals who appear drunk in public. Somehow our culture can still punish these individuals for irresponsible conduct of such an inconsequential nature while ignoring irresponsible corporate conduct that profoundly affects our quality of life. Our value orientations of individualism have made us blind to corporate behavior. During the past decade a variety of myths and symbols have developed around the theme of controlling the corporate giants to serve the public good. Perhaps the most critical choice facing Americans is to support the wide range of efforts to adapt to this feature of the culture we have created.

Conclusion

In this chapter I have discussed some of the basic issues related to the quality of life in American society from the perspective of anthropology. The cross-cultural evidence shows enormous variation in what human beings consider as "quality" in life. The value orientations that give meaning to each particular way of life also support different cultural goals and means for their achievement. Some general requirements have been suggested for a minimal quality of life in all societies.

The universal strivings of humankind provide an impetus in every society to improve the quality of life, to revitalize cultures. I have argued that our own culture is presently experiencing widespread and diverse revitalization processes. Three requirements for a successful revitalization movement were discussed in the context of American culture: (1) the formulation of new goals, (2) a marked increase in the salience of value orientations on which the new quality of life is based, and (3) adaptation to altered environmental conditions.

I believe that our new social and cultural environment presents the greatest challenge facing Americans. It is a new frontier that could become the focus of our national life. Coping with the destructive elements in this new environment must become as challenging as living in the hostile environments of space. This will mean a shift in the way our resources are expended from the physical sciences to the social and behavioral sciences. Only as we regain control of our cultural creations, pervasive culture conflict, rapidly increasing complexity, and corporations bereft of any social conscience—only then will the revitalization of American culture come to fruition.

Notes

1. See Anthony Wallace, *The Death and Rebirth of the Seneca* (New York: Knopf, (1970), and *Culture and Personality* (New York: Random House, 1961, 1970).

2. The best source on the Nootka is Philip Drucker, *The Northern and Central Nootkan Tribes*, Bureau of American Ethnology, Bulletin 144, Washington, D.C., 1951.

3. For a clear analysis of the nature of value orientations and their role in human action see Clyde Kluckhohn, "Values and Value-Orientations in the Theory of Action: An Exploration in Definition and Classification," in Talcott Parsons and Edward Shils (eds.), *Toward a General Theory of Action* (Cambridge: Harvard University Press, 1951).

4. Anthony Wallace, *Culture and Personality* (New York: Random House, 1970), p. 189.

5. Clifford Geertz, "The Impact of the Concept of Culture on the Concept of Man," in John R. Platt, Editor, *New Views of Man*, © 1965 by the University of Chicago. Reprinted in Yehudi A. Cohen, ed., *Man in Adaptation*, (Chicago: Aldine, 1968), p. 24.

6. See Robin M. Williams, Jr., *American Society* (New York: Knopf, 1960), for an extensive examination of American cultural values.

7. For a discussion of the good life for that class of societies referred to as peasantry, see Robert Redfield, *Peasant Society and Culture* (Chicago: University of Chicago Press, 1956).

8. See Mervyn Meggitt, "Pigs Are Our Hearts," *Oceania* (in press) for a discussion of Mae Enga values.

9. For a review of anthropological studies of the aged see Margaret Clark, "Contributions of Cultural Anthropology to the Study of the Aged," in Laura Nader and Thomas W. Maretzki (eds.), *Cultural Illness and Health* (Washington, D.C.: The American Anthropological Association, 1973).

10. Yehudi A. Cohen (ed.), *Man in Adaptation: The Cultural Present* (Chicago: Aldine, 1968), p. 17.

11. Geertz, "Impact of the Concept," p. 19.

12. Drawn from George M. Foster, *Traditional Cultures: and the Impact of Technological Change* (New York: Harper and Row, 1962).

13. Wallace, *Death and Rebirth*, p. 199.

14. See John Honigmann, *Personality in Culture* (New York: Harper and Row, 1967), pp. 73-75, for a discussion of basic needs and sources on additional authors who have proposed lists of such needs.

15. Alexander H. Leighton, "Psychiatric Disorder and Social Environment," in Bernard Bergen and C.S. Thomas (eds.), *Issues and Problems in Social Psychiatry* (Springfield: Charles C. Thomas, 1966), p. 168.

16. Christoph von Furer-Haimendorf, *The Konyak Nagas: An Indian Frontier Tribe* (New York: Holt, Rinehart and Winston, 1969), p. 99.

17. Wallace, *Death and Rebirth* is the major source for the following analysis of revitalization movements.

18. There is a large literature on revitalization movements, some of which has been reprinted in William A. Lessa and Evon Z. Vogt (eds.), *Reader in Comparative Religion: An Anthropological Approach*, Third Edition (New York: Harper, 1972).

19. See W.W. Hill, "The Navaho Indians and the Ghost Dance of 1890," in Lessa and Vogt, *Reader in Comparative Religion*.

20. See Weston LaBarre, *The Peyote Cult* (New Haven: Yale University Press, 1938).

21. For a review of cargo cults in the South Pacific see Cyril S. Belshaw, "The Significance of Modern Cults in Melanesian Development," in Lessa and Vogt, *Reader in Comparative Religion*.

22. Wallace, *Death and Rebirth* p. 188.

23. Ibid., p. 191.

24. David Aberle, "A Note on Relative Deprivation Theory as Applied to Millenarian and Other Cult Movements," *Comparative Studies in Society and History*, Supplement II, © 1962 The Society for the Comparative Study of Society and History, by permission of Cambridge University Press.

25. Clyde Kluckhohn and Dorothea Leighton, *The Navaho*, (Garden City, New York: Natural History Press, 1962), p. 308.

26. For one analysis of the way one group of men suffer in our system of criminal justice because of their different value orientation see James P. Spradley, *You Owe Yourself a Drunk: An Ethnography of Urban Nomads* (Boston: Little, Brown and Co., 1970).

27. James P. Spradley, *Guests Never Leave Hungry: The Autobiography of James Sewid, a Kwakiutl Indian* (New Haven: Yale University Press, 1969).

28. Paul Bohannan, *Social Anthropology* (New York: Holt, Rinehart and Winston, 1963), p. 395, 397.

29. James P. Spradley, "Career Education in Cultural Perspective," in Larry McClure and Carolyn Buan (eds.), *Essays on Career Education* (Washington, D.C., U.S. Government Printing Office, 1973), pp. 10-11. This book offers an orientation to Career Education from many different perspectives.

Public Policy and the
"Quality of Life"

Peter L. Berger

During the last few years it has become commonplace to say that something is wrong about the "quality of life" in American society. It has also been suggested that this alleged fact should be a concern for public policy.

The phrase has a Madison Avenue flavor about it. Indeed, it evokes the very "consumerism" routinely deplored by those who want to improve the quality of life. It is as if Naderism had gone metaphysical: Americans, it seems are entitled to government-certified quality control in their lives as well as their automobiles. Anyone with residual affection for the English language will be tempted to dismiss the whole matter out of hand and to relegate the phrase to the same terminological garbage can that already contains (or should contain) cognate phrases such as "life style," "quality education," "sexual orientation," or "religious preference." And anyone with some moral sensitivity to the agonies of contemporary humanity is unlikely to give a high priority to the problem designated by the phrase: In a world of mass starvation, genocide, rampant despotism, and the threat of nuclear annihilation, Americans complaining about the quality of their lives inevitably recall Hans Christian Andersen's princess who could not sleep because there was a pea under her mattress.

Perhaps unfortunately, social analysts and policymakers cannot afford certain luxuries of English professors or moralists. People who employ barbaric language may, nevertheless, express real problems. And these problems are not less real

Since the present essay was written, the author has begun a larger exploration of the place of intermediate structures in public policy. This project is being undertaken in collaboration with Richard Neuhaus and is funded by the American Enterprise Institute.

because other people, in other countries, have problems that are much worse. In other words, it is necessary to go beyond one's distaste for the phrase "quality of life" and to inquire into the significance of its current appeal.

What, then, does the phrase signify? It is unclear just who first coined it, but the phrase gained widespread currency with the appearance of the ecology movement in the late 1960s and early 1970s. Invariably, it seems the phrase has been used in a negative context: Nobody celebrated the quality of life in America; everybody deplored its absence or degraded condition. In the immediate ambience of the ecology movement, the meaning of this negative perspective has been fairly clear: What good is the much-vaunted American standard of living, it is asked, if it comes at the price of polluted air and water, depleted natural resources, and the massive destruction of the physical environment? If the standard of living has commonly been expressed in *quantitative* terms (income per capita, refrigerators per household, gross national product, and the like), it would seem logical to raise questions of a *qualitative* kind: Given the ecological costs of American technological civilization, is living in this society really as wonderful as the various statistical indicators seem to suggest? Put differently: With all this junk we have, are we really happier for it?

The phrase quality of life, however, has had a certain sponge-like character in soaking in other concerns that are quite unrelated to the ecological issues. American life, it has been said, is qualitatively defective not only because of the mess it has brought about in the physical environment but because of a wide array of social problems. Urban congestion, crime, racial conflict, poverty, sexual discontents, and even the aesthetic deficiencies of the culture have been cited as evidence for the unsatisfactory quality of life in America.

The connection between these social ills and the ecological issues has not always been clearly defined, though a number of ideological formulations have been attempted (notably by New Left intellectuals interested in forging alliances with the counterculture and the ecology movement). For those who remain unpersuaded by the basic ideological proposition that it is capitalism that must be blamed for every conceivable problem in the contemporary world, from the finite amount of petroleum deposits to the scarcity of great musical compositions, a different explanatory procedure might recommend itself. It has an analogy in medical diagnosis: If a patient has multiple complaints of a kind that cannot be plausibly related to each other, the suspicion arises that there is an underlying condition of which he is not complaining, probably because he is unaware of it.

In this case, then, it makes sense to put aside for a moment the multiplicity of complaints about the quality of American life and to ask whether there might not be an underlying condition that predisposes Americans to have all these complaints in the first place. It should be noted that asking this question in no way presupposes that the complaints are in themselves unreal or invalid. Asking the question, however, does suggest that there was a predisposition to complain before any specific complaints were formulated. Put differently: It is suggested that there exists today an underlying malaise about life in this society, and that specific grievances (running across the whole spectrum of current social criticism) may be understood as legitimations rather than as causes of this malaise. Put differently once again: The individual who is predisposed to look upon American society as an uncomfortable or even intolerable place, will find in each new societal problem of which he becomes aware an additional justification for his original feelings.

If there is an underlying malaise, which may serve to explain the multiplicity of complaints triggered by the phrase quality of life, what could be its character?

At least a hypothetical answer may be induced from the complaints themselves. Every one of them may finally be translated into an expression of doubt about the meaning of social existence, a variant of the New Testament exclamation about the man who had gained the whole world but lost his soul in the process: "What good will it do ... ?" The "goodness" of a society, empirically speaking, resides in the credibility of its values. If people believe in the values embodied in their social institutions, then the latter are meaningful—even if there are many reasons to complain. On the other hand, if people come to doubt these values, society takes on a quality of meaninglessness—even if an outside observer might conclude that the particular society is doing very well indeed.

Thus there have been many human societies plagued by ecological and social problems of cataclysmic proportions, yet no one in these societies thought of blaming these problems on the quality of life somehow endemic to the institutional order. On the contrary, the common response to processing problems is very much the opposite from the one observed here: The values of the institutional order are called upon as resources to confront the challenge of the various problems. In such cases, the very presence of grave challenges enhances social solidarity and fortifies the credibility of the society's values. But if there has taken place a radical weakening in people's adherence to the received body of values, then even minor problems are experienced as potent threats to the meaningfulness of social life; major problems are seen as posing the threat of overall catastrophe.

The following hypothesis emerges from these considerations: *Current complaints about the quality of life of American society are to be understood as results, and not as causes, of an underlying value crisis.* Put differently: People do not question the quality of life in this society because of the aforementioned catalogue of environmental and social problems, but they experience these problems as validations of a preexisting feeling that the society lacks "quality"—that is, lacks the specific qualities of meaningfulness and value. If this hypothesis is allowed, then the question of public policy and the quality of life may be put in quite different terms: *What can or should be public policy with respect to the underlying value crisis in American society?*

Before this question is taken up, one predictable objection may be anticipated and one widespread fallacy pinpointed. It will be objected that the
preceding argument expresses a conservative ideology that seeks to obfuscate the
real problems of this society by relegating them to a politically inaccessible
realm of value conflicts and other spiritual miseries. *Stipulation:* Of course this
society has real problems; of course not all of these, or even most of these, can
be ascribed to the aforementioned value crisis; and of course many of these
problems ought properly to be the concern of politics. The position taken here
denies neither the reality nor the political accessibility of specific problems of
the society; the position, however, is that adding up the existing problems of the
society will not serve as an explanation of the widespread feeling that there is
something wrong with America's quality of life. *Case:* Industry is causing a lot of
air pollution. This is bad, but has nothing to do with some underlying value crisis
(certainly not of capitalism, by the way—industry in Socialist countries is
polluting the air just as cheerfully). Clearly, air pollution must be a concern of
public policy, on various levels of government. However, very few people, it is
posited here, came to the conclusion that the quality of life is bad because they
became aware of air pollution. On the contrary, people who already felt that the
society was in bad shape were confirmed in that view by all the news about
pollution.

This leads directly to the fallacy that underlies much liberal thinking about
social problems in this country. It is the belief that the people who now feel that
the society is qualitatively bad will feel differently if their specific grievances are
taken care of. Of some this may well be true; of most it is a fallacious
expectation. Empirically, the sense of grievance usually *increases* as the overall
condition of the aggrieved improves (this, incidentally, is a basic psychological
fact about prerevolutionary situations). It will decrease as that overall condition
is valued in a different way. *Case:* An aggrieved population may rebel, despite
great improvements in its standard of living or its political rights, because it no
longer believes in the legitimacy of the institutional order (the prototype for this
was the French Revolution of 1789). There may be no further improvement
whatever following the successful rebellion; indeed there may be deterioration.
But the new order set up by the rebels will provide new values and thus new
legitimations for whatever unsatisfactory circumstances persist: These, say, are
now perceived as necessary sacrifices on the road toward some great historic
goal. It may then happen that *the same* deprivations that were previously
perceived as intolerable grievances are now understood as steps in the march
toward utopia. Conversely, in the present case: By all means let public policy
seek to do away with air pollution. It is indubitably bad for people to breathe
noxious air. At the same time, it is very naive to expect that the people who now
feel that American society is rotten to the core, and who cite air pollution as one
of their arguments, will change their mind if the air is no longer noxious. Rather,
they will find other reasons for their underlying feeling. The human condition
being what it is, we need not worry that they will run out of arguments.

Quite obviously this cannot be the place for an extended treatment of the character and the causes of the underlying value crisis in contemporary society. The author of the present chapter, in collaboration with Brigitte Berger and Hansfried Kellner, has made an attempt at such a treatment in a recent book.[1] All that can be done here is to provide a summary of some propositions emerging from this treatment that are directly relevant to the present topic.

The first point that ought to be stressed is that the underlying value crisis is by no means peculiar to America. It is present in every society of comparable economic and technological development. In other words, it is the common property of all so-called advanced industrial societies. It is for this reason that every American complaint over the last few years has quickly found an echo in western Europe—including, needless to add, the complaint about the quality of life. There is good reason to think that the same would be true in the advanced industrial societies of eastern Europe, including the Soviet Union, if there existed greater opportunities for free expression. (The situation in the so-called Third World is quite different and cannot concern us here.) The most that can be said is that America constitutes the most modernized large society in the contemporary world, with the result that American social criticism tends to have a certain avant-garde character. It is commonly American social critics who define the grievances first—the Europeans start taking up the particular complaint after the interval required for translation of texts. One irony of this is that most contemporary radicalism has an unmistakably American flavor—including radical anti-Americanism.

The value crisis is by no means very recent, although it has undergone a certain acceleration in recent years. Indeed, the value crisis is endemic to the process of modernization. While it is rooted in exceedingly complex historical developments, it can be described rather simply in terms of its major impact. Modernity has tended to undermine most of the structures of meaning and value by which human beings have lived before its advent. This fact has, indeed, been one of the major themes of sociological thought since its inception, although different sociological theorists have put different emphasis on the various elements that make up the process of modernization and have used different terminologies in describing the resultant difficulties. Thus Marxists put exclusive emphasis on the effects of capitalism, while those influenced by Max Weber have stressed the impact of bureaucracy and those walking in the footsteps of Emile Durkheim (for instance, Talcott Parsons and other "structural-functionalists" in this country) have blamed a more general institutional differentiation for the crisis. Thus Marx spoke of "alienation," Weber of "rationalization," Durkheim of "anomie" in describing the way in which modernity has shaken traditional certainties.

However one comes out in choosing between these (and other) theories of modern society, it is possible to make some statements with a degree of confidence. Throughout most of history, most human beings lived under social arrangements that provided them with comprehensive and certain values for the business of everyday living. Very importantly, these arrangements typically covered fairly small numbers of people, who moved neither physically nor socially throughout their lives. Put differently: Most human beings lived in communities that provided a sense of belonging and an order of values in an uncomplicated, direct and generally taken-for-granted manner. It is precisely such communities that are made to reel under the impact of modern institutions—of the market economy, the bureaucratic state, the large city, the growing network of large bureaucratic organizations besides the state, the various media of mass communication (to mention but some of the most important ones). As these institutions take over a society, most of the structures that previously "sheltered" the individual are greatly shaken, in some instances annihilated—such as the structures of the extended family, of clan and tribe, of the village economy, of small-scale political units. In consequence, the modern situation tends to confront isolated, "atomized," individuals, only weakly supported by communities that are "within reach," with huge and abstract institutions over which the individual has no control and which much of the time he cannot even comprehend. The phenomenon known as secularization (that is, the weakening in people's minds of traditional religious and moral certainties) is closely related to this disintegration of what could be called human communities of value.

It is probably a very deeply rooted need of human beings to live in communities that provide "shelter" in terms of meaningfulness and values. It is, therefore, plausible that the aforementioned effects of modernization have been experienced as deprivations. This does not mean that *all* of modernity has been so experienced. The process of modernization has also brought with it changes that have been generally perceived as benefits, not only in the enormous increase in the material standard of living, but also in the freeing of the individual from many traditional constraints and oppressions. The discontents of modernity, therefore, are generally experienced in an ambivalent relation to modernity's blessings. The individual lives longer, but he suffers from moral insecurity; he has a greater sense of personal freedom, but he lacks groups that provide feelings of belonging; and so forth. Different groups in society come out differently in such a "costs/benefits" accounting, not just in the perspective of an outside observer but in people's own minds. In any case, from the beginning of the era of modernization, there have been resistances to modernity and outrightly counter-modernizing movements.

While modern society has produced a crisis on the level of human meanings and values, it has also produced a kind of solution: This has been the emergence of what we have come to call private life. There is really no equivalent to this in pre-modern times. The private sphere is a sort of interstitial area between the vast institutions of modernity, an area in which the individual is allowed considerable freedom to shape his own life and to construct his own values. One of the great (and historically quite novel) ideas in modern society has been that the individual has a right, within increasingly broad limits, to be left alone in this special area. He can worship any way he chooses (or no way at all), he can marry whom he will, he can raise his children more or less by his own lights, he can choose his associates freely (one by one, or in organized groups)—and, in the course of all this, he can construct that part of his life in accordance with values that he himself chooses.

The private sphere has been a solution to the modern problem of "alienation" in that it provides a refuge from the abstractions and the powerful pressures of the large institutions—that is, from the megastructures of the public sphere, among which the state occupies a central position. In other words, there takes place a trade-off: As the individual confronts the megastructures, he inevitably feels the discontents of anonymity, powerlessness, lack of comprehensibility. By way of compensation, however, he can go "home," to his private life, where he is free to engage in almost any meanings, values, and solidarities that make sense to him.

For many people this solution has worked quite well. It has, however, produced discontents of its own. For one thing, precisely because private life is "left alone" by the powerful institutions, it only offers weak supports for the individual's efforts to construct meanings and values. Put differently: A considerable burden is imposed upon the individual by the demand that he concoct his own private values. Also, there continues to be among many people the yearning for communities of value that are more powerful and more comprehensive than the "little worlds" of private life. This yearning has been one of the strongest psychological impulses behind modern totalitarian ideologies, which invariably have promised to reintegrate the individual in all-embracing solidarities and thus to deliver him from the "alienations" of modernity. But even for many who do not desire to be saved from the discontents of modernity by this or that totalitarian utopia, there is a strong need for bridges between the value-deprived megastructures and the little "value workshops" of private life. At best, then, the solution of private life is only a limited response to the underlying value crisis.

If this were the entire story, the question of what public policy might do about the value crisis of contemporary society could only be answered in rigorously narrow alternatives. One alternative would be the effort to transform the megastructures, particularly the state, into value-generating agencies comparable to the tightly knit communities of traditional society. Inevitably this would mean transgressing against the immunity of the private sphere; that is, it would mean that private life would be reintegrated into the meanings and values of public life. As indicated before, this has been the thrust of all modern totalitarian movements, no matter whether they occur on the "right" or "left" side of the political spectrum. There is good reason to doubt whether such efforts can be successful for very long in advanced industrial societies. Except for brief periods of revolutionary fervor, it seems to be impossible to endow a modern nation-state with the psychological accoutrements of a traditional society. Short of totalitarianism also, such efforts are likely to have an unreal quality about them, except perhaps in periods of war or other society-wide calamities. Thus it would appear to be an unpromising project to overcome the "alienations" of contemporary Americans by having the federal government launch a great campaign to foster allegiance to what Gunnar Myrdal has called the "American creed."

The modern nation-state is simply too vast and too abstract an entity to serve as the primary source for the values of everyday social life. Patriotism, however noble and desirable a sentiment it is, simply cannot carry that kind of burden. The other alternative, of course, would be for public policy to limit itself to the defense and protection of the value autonomy of the private sphere. This, by and large, has been the liberal penchant. It would seem that, increasingly, it fails to meet the demands of the situation, proving helpless in the face of ever-new waves of strident dissatisfaction.

Fortunately, this is *not* the whole story. There continue to exist *intermediate structures* in modern society—intermediate, that is, between the megastructures of public life and the precarious "little worlds" of private life. It is very important that the character of these intermediate structures be adequately understood. Such understanding opens up new and much more promising options for public policy. In the context of the present discussion: *There are intermediate possibilities between the option of letting individuals work out the quality of life all by themselves in their respective private spheres and the option of the government going into the business of improving or perhaps even generating a satisfactory quality of life for the society.*

What are the intermediate structures that provide meaning and value in contemporary society? Some intermediate structures are old institutions, which antedate the advent of modernity, although they have been greatly modified in the course of modernization. The most important of these are the family and the church. What sociologists have (unattractively, alas) called the "nuclear conjugal family," the isolated unit of a married couple and their children, is of course a peculiarly modern innovation and it is located squarely in the private sphere. It cannot be called an intermediate structure. Recent data, however, indicate that sociologists have exaggerated the degree to which this family type has swallowed up the older forms of extended family. In broad segments of the population (and by no means only in rural regions) there continues to be a strong feeling for wider kinship ties, and this feeling expresses itself in a variety of activities.

Contrary to expectations, there has been an *increase* in the incidence of three-generation households, that is, of one or more grandparents living with their children and grandchildren under one roof. It is very likely that this trend will continue as the proportion of relatively healthy old people in the population goes up, as more married women enter the labor force—it is hard to beat most grandparents as babysitters—and as rentals and nursing-home costs go on rising. It is likely, therefore, that the demise of the extended family has been proclaimed prematurely.

The church, in its various denominational forms, continues to serve as a primary source of meaning and values in the lives of millions of Americans. The church, like the family, has been greatly affected by the forces of modernization. It has been pushed out of large sectors of the public sphere (one need only mention the separation of church and state and the secularization of education), and for many people it is simply one of the furnishings of their private lives (for them, by the way, the term "religious preference" is quite apt). But this is by no means the general case. Large numbers of people continue to look to the church to provide the values of both public and private life, and for many the church continues to be the principal organizing focus of their social existence. It is likely too, then, that the "privatization" of institutional religion has been exaggerated. Politicians, incidentally, seem to have understood this much better than sociologists—no wonder, since very few sociologists are dependent for their jobs on the votes of church-goers.

Other intermediate structures are newer arrivals on the social scene, and some of them can actually be best understood as responses to the discontents of modernity. Particularly in America, the place of voluntary associations should be emphasized in this connection. Some of these, to be sure, are themselves megastructures of sorts, large bureaucratic organizations in which the individual is "lost" in an anonymous mass. Others, however, fulfill the criteria of intermediate structures very fully. They stand between the abstract entities of modern political and economic life on the one hand and the tenuous constructions of private life on the other, providing meaningful "homes away from home" for the individual. This function can be fulfilled by voluntary associations of just about any content—from hobby clubs to the American Legion, from literary circles to professional groupings, and so forth. It is salutary to recall here the degree to which the vitality of the democratic process in America has depended on voluntary associations—and by no means only on those formed for expressedly political purposes.

Finally, though certainly not least, are groups, often informally organized or not organized at all, that coalesce spontaneously around specific solidarities and values. These are the structures of neighborhood, of ethnicity, of friendship in places of work or recreation. Often they are almost "invisible" sociologically, because of their lack of formal organization. All the same, they constitute primary foci of meaning for very large numbers of people in the society. There are moments in which such groupings dramatically reveal themselves as powerful social forces. Once more, these are phenomena of considerable political significance.

With this we have arrived at the final thesis of this chapter. *It should be public policy to protect and actively to foster the intermediate structures that generate values in American society.* And it should not only do this on the basis of a doctrine of tolerance or civil liberties ("these people have a right to do their thing"), but because it is in everyone's interest, in the public interest, that the intermediate structures continue to function. The society as a whole suffers from the deepening value crisis; the society as a whole would gain from a revitalization of values in its many constituent segments.

At the same time, our thesis does not suggest that government, on any level, should go into the "values business." The thesis, in other words, moves within the parameters of the classical liberal doctrine of pluralism: Apart from the very broad propositions of the "American creed" (if you will, the American "civil religion"), the state continues to be neutral with respect to the variety of *Weltanschauungen* in the society, protecting them and guaranteeing them free expression. The neutrality, however, is of the positive kind. For it can be argued that the very megastructures of the society, especially the state in its Western democratic form, cannot finally survive unless they are "nourished" by the value-generating communities that we have called intermediate structures. In protecting and fostering the intermediate structures, therefore, the state is actually husbanding the soil in which its own roots are planted.

Perhaps these considerations have seemed excessively theoretical. It is all the more important to see their very practical policy applications. Let us draw these out by applying the preceding thesis to the concrete cases enumerated before.

It should be public policy to protect and foster the family. Case: Increasingly the welfare (if you will, the "charitable") activities in the society are monopolized by state-run or state-controlled bureaucracies. In some instances, of course, this is unavoidable; in others, though, it is very avoidable indeed. There should be policies to "devolve" these activities from the bureaucratized "helping institutions" to the family. Instead of the government operating networks of day-care centers, it should provide subsidies or tax incentives for elderly relatives to take care of the children of working parents. Instead of pouring vast sums of money into chronically ineffective mental hospitals and nursing homes, there should be government subsidies or tax incentives to encourage families to take care of their afflicted and incapacitated members at home. There is enormous, even exhilarating scope here for innovation and experimentation—"surrogate grandparents," training parents to become "lay therapists," fostering alliances or even residential communities of families for purposes of taking care of the physically or mentally disabled. Yet all of these radical experiments can take place in the context of the family, the oldest and most traditional of human institutions.

It should be public policy to protect and foster the church. Case: On all levels of education, it is government (increasingly federal government) that has been taking over. If present trends continue, American education from kindergarten to graduate school will be as monopolistically run from Washington as the French education system is run from Paris. This is anti-pluralistic, anti-democratic, and profoundly destructive of the very genius of American society. Public policy, and public funds, should foster the greatest possible plurality of schools and educational subsystems, including those operating under religious auspices. The translation of the doctrine of the separation of church and state into a narrowly sectarian and secularist doctrine that denies public assistance to religious schools has been one of the greater follies of recent legal history. It must be stopped, indeed reversed. Tax funds should go to all schools (within very broad limits of safety standards and moral acceptability), including parochial schools—*not* only because "Catholics have a right to have their schools," but because it is *in the public interest* that they continue to have them, that they be *Catholic* schools, and that they be *good* schools. And if present law precludes the full realization of these propositions, then the law must be changed.

It should be public policy to protect and foster voluntary associations. Case: In recent years the trend has been to threaten the tax-exempt status of private foundations, thus further increasing the monopoly of public agencies in the welfare and educational sectors of society. Some of the legislation to control foundations may well have been necessary. All the same, the trend is thoroughly pernicious and should be speedily reversed. Public policy should encourage, not inhibit, a multiplicity of private initiatives in every conceivable area of social and cultural activity. There should be more foundations, not fewer, and particularly there should be many smaller foundations that are directly linked to voluntary associations.

It should be public policy to protect and foster the neighborhood. Two cases, this time: It has been one of the sublime ironies of recent years that the people supporting busing of school children for purposes of racial integration have also supported the "devolution" of municipal government functions (schools, police, and so on) to local community control, and that the people opposing the former have also opposed the latter. The irony of this is a good measure of the ideological confusion of the times. It is very important to understand that public policy should *oppose* busing for precisely the same reasons it should *promote* community control (and not only in the black areas of the cities). It appears that black political leadership is coming around to this insight rather rapidly now. Its white liberal supporters, blinded, incidentally, by an abstract doctrine of racial equality very similar in character to the abstract doctrine of the separation of church and state, still tend to considerable blindness on this point. Public policy should free itself of these absurd abstractions, should ignore the nonsense that anything deviating from the latter is "racism," and actively foster a flourishing and autonomous black community life—not segregated from the larger society, but part and parcel of its vital and enormously valuable plurality.

It should be public policy to protect and foster ethnicity. Case: In a number of American cities with large Spanish-speaking populations the question has been raised as to whether Spanish should be recognized as a second official language. Political groups speaking for the Spanish population (Chicano, Puerto Rican or Cuban, as the case may be) have generally been in favor, the educational and cultural establishments have generally been opposed. Once again, the opposition (whether using the rhetoric of American nationalism or that of the liberal public school ideology) has been based on an abstract, homogenizing vision of the society. The opposition is thoroughly misguided. It should be public policy to encourage, and to recognize officially, every significant expression of ethnic variety—again, not just because "Chicanos have a right to use their own language in court," say, but much more importantly because the society as a whole, including the vitality of its democratic political order, benefits from the vitality and the values represented by the Chicano community.

Hopefully the preceding subtheses have made clear that what is being proposed in this chapter is not just an arid theoretical exercise, but rather that it has very direct and very practical policy applicabilities. There is another point about the above paragraphs, however, that ought to be stressed: *The proposed policy options cut diagonally across the existing ideological lines.* Some of the policies proposed are currently considered "on the left," others "on the right." It is precisely in this fact that we would see a major political relevance of the viewpoint propounded here. There is a widespread feeling, in all the ideological camps, that the old rhetorics have gone stale and that, somehow, one ought to begin afresh. An understanding of the role of intermediate structures in American society and a rethinking of public policies in light of this understanding could offer a welcome opportunity for such a fresh start, in a sizable number of domestic policy issues.

Note

1. Peter L. Berger, Brigitte Berger, and Hansfried Kellner, *The Homeless Mind: Modernization and Consciousness* (New York: Vintage Books, 1974).

VI

Perceptions of Quality of Life: Some Effects of Social Strata and Social Change; The Erosion of Social Levers

William J. Overholt and **Herman Kahn**

Some important methodological and definitional perspectives and pitfalls should be highlighted to aid the reader in thinking about "quality of life," as that phrase is currently used.

1. The residual nature of the concept and the things it takes for granted;
2. The polemical nature of the concept as a reaction against its heavily economic and moral predecessors;
3. The degree to which the concept is frequently an expression of the narrow interests of particular social strata;
4. The extent to which quality of life problems should be viewed as what we call "failures of success"; and
5. The extent to which quality of life issues can be ordered and kept in perspective by viewing them as consequences of either (a) short-run attitudes or more importantly (b) major social trends connected with the rise of industrial, super-industrial, and post-industrial society.

Quality of Life as a Concept

The phrase "quality of life" reflects simultaneous concerns with particular issues of individual human happiness and with the direction in which American civilization is moving. In its broadest sense this phrase encompasses all those concerns which can affect the happiness of different individuals: humanization

135

of workshop or bureaucracy, friendship and human contact, landscape, esthetics, good neighbors, a good tennis companion, a stimulating intellectual environment, or the availability every night of a cold beer and a series of mindless television programs which facilitate rest for a tired mind. Far more importantly, however, the current discussion of quality of life is a reaction against the older concept of "standard of living," with its almost exclusively economic emphasis, and the concept of "a good life" or "a good place to raise children," with their almost exclusively moral emphasis.

Those who discuss quality of life typically regard an emphasis on "standard of living" as either crude and materialistic or as passé, because the high economic standard of living can presumably now be taken for granted. Similarly, most discussions of quality of life would regard the "good life" or the "good place to raise children" as bland, mindless, moralistic, and prone to babbitry. Quality of life is above all a heavily secular concept. Thus quality of life represents, to some extent, an evolution from these earlier concepts, but also a strong rejection of them. Very frequently it carries connotations of a rejection of further economic growth.

Discussions of the deterioration of quality of life usually refer to very different issues from positive discussions of quality of life. When one hears that quality of life in New York City is deteriorating, typically the reference is to lack of safety on the streets, inadequate housing, poverty problems, and so forth, which are problems whose solution is often heavily linked to economic growth and to adequate performance of traditional governmental functions. These things are precisely what positive discussions of quality of life usually take for granted. Positive discussions tend to emphasize leisure, recreation, the arts, the humanities, ecology, and so forth.

In discussing quality of life as a concept and an issue we find it useful to break up our discussion into six very different areas. And in doing so we believe we can take this relatively elusive concept and clarify much of the current discussion, by distinguishing the serious and frivolous issues that get raised, and by categorizing the former. One can sketch out in very broad fashion those conditions which influence human happiness and human satisfaction and then indicate which of these are of greatest concern to people discussing quality of life. The influences that we will consider can be divided up into six areas, four which are present in even the most unchanging societies:

A. Societal or governmental provision of key amenities such as parks, leisure, recreational opportunities, culture, appropriate land use, appropriate environmental and demographic land use, etc.
B. Political, economic, governmental, and private decisions about who gets what—when there is conflict in the distribution of services or goods.
C. Relatively short-term events and trends which affect greatly people's morale, attitudes, and general temperamental outlook. These include confidence in

government, attitudes toward various political regimes, short-term economic trends, and so forth.

D. Differences among various social classes, social strata, ideological groups, and personality types.

We believe that these four would be the main focus of attention in any community which had been stable for a long time, and which had more or less settled all the major strains of social change—although of course few such communities have ever existed. What makes discussion of quality of life terribly complicated is that these four issues are set in context of change, and this context may dominate the discussion. These influences are as follows:

E. Broad historical trends in the nation and society.

F. Traditional governmental functions such as law and order, economic welfare, and education.

The latter two are terribly important and may dominate the discussion in periods of change because different groups' views of quality of life depend on whether they are going up or down in society. They accordingly feel either frustration or fulfillment. Changes either favor them or hurt them whether they try to exploit the changes or not. In a stable situation the distinctions among social classes, social strata, ideological groups and personality types are taken for granted; they are conditions, not problems. But in a changing situation these differences create an extraordinarily large number of problems. These broad historical trends of society force enormous changes: People become richer or poorer, more prestigious or less, and more influential or less. Society becomes safer or more dangerous, more egalitarian or less, and more cohesive or less. Society goes from traditional to industrial, then from industrial to super-industrial and post-industrial. These latter changes alter basic social conditions and goals, so that one must focus attention on these changes rather than on some unchanging form of the four original criteria. How the original four criteria are modified by these changes becomes at least as important as the criteria themselves.

Finally, and most important, very often the traditional governmental functions fail in various ways during periods of broad social change, and this of course affects quality of life more than such amenities as parks, recreation, concerts, and so forth. If an enemy is invading, the quality of life deteriorates enormously; if it is unsafe to walk the streets, that can dominate perception of all other aspects of the quality of life. We will argue that this country is experiencing exactly this kind of change and that probably the most important issues will focus around E and F as a practical matter in the mid-seventies. Nevertheless, A, B, C, and D are still very important, especially in the long run, and deserve discussion. Most discussions of quality of life emphasize the latter almost exclusively; we shall deliberately resist this, and place our emphasis on E and F.

Whose Quality of Life?

A. One of the points upon which we would put great stress is the huge range of variations in what *different historical, cultural, and social groups* would regard as necessary to good quality of life. In other papers we have indicated some of the historical variations in what Americans considered crucial to quality of life.[1] One can also note Huizinga's description of medieval life to provide some sense of medieval standards for quality of life:

To the world when it was half a thousand years younger, the outlines of all things seemed more clearly marked than to us. The contrast between suffering and joy, between adversity and happiness, appeared more striking. All experience had yet to the minds of men the directness and absoluteness of the pleasure and pain of child-life. Every event, every action, was still embodied in expressive and solemn forms, which raised them to the dignity of a ritual.

Calamities and indigence were more afflicting than at present; it was more difficult to guard against them, and to find solace. Illness and health presented a more striking contrast; the cold and darkness of winter were more real evils. Honours and riches were relished with greater avidity and contrasted more vividly with surrounding misery. We, at the present day, can hardly understand the keenness with which a fur coat, a good fire on the hearth, a soft bed, a glass of wine, were formerly enjoyed.

Then again, all things in life were of a proud or cruel publicity. Lepers sounded their rattles and went about in processions, beggars exhibited their deformity and their misery in churches. Every order and estate, every rank and profession, was distinguished by its costume.[2]

Excerpts from the writings of Oliver Wendell Holmes and William James indicate the depth and seriousness with which outstanding Americans and others have regarded the importance of the martial virtues despite current low regard for such values:

To ride boldly at what is in front of you, be it fence or enemy; to pray, not for comfort, but for combat; to remember that duty is not to be proved in the evil day, but then to be obeyed unquestioning; to love glory more than the temptations of wallowing ease.[3]

What we now need to discover in the social realm is the moral equivalent of war: something heroic that will speak to men as universally as war does, and yet will be as compatible with their spiritual selves as war has proved itself to be incompatible.[4]

It is easy to demonstrate these great variations among cultures and during different periods of American history, but projecting them into the future is no simple matter. It is worth noting, however, that persistently throughout recent centuries the greatest men of the West would have despised many characteristics of their own society a century hence. The Founding Fathers would have been shocked at the disappearance of republican virtues, the Civil War generation would have been shocked at the decline of patriotism, and so forth. Perhaps the most useful comment we can make here is simply that a generation's standards for quality of life are determined principally by its own experience and knowledge rather than by the standards of other generations. In the days of westward expansion, many Americans supposedly moved on if they could see the smoke of another settler's cabin from their own home. Today such a criterion would be viewed as silly: contemporary Americans do not particularly miss the rigors and distances of the frontier. New Yorkers typically cannot understand why former midwesterners are so unhappy about the decline in fishing and hunting, and influential elements of our society regard these sports as peverse. In future generations one can expect such feelings to intensify, so that—even though we of contemporary America might find it difficult to live in the more heavily developed, more heavily populated America of a century hence—most men and women of future generations will not necessarily miss what we would miss or envy us our lower standard of living.

B. While crucial *class differences* in approach to the nature of quality of life, and to the correct resolution of quality of life issues, crop up everywhere, most of the discussion of quality of life takes place within an upper middle class which is not conscious of the full extent to which it is articulating class values rather than universal values. With regard to many and perhaps most of the issues discussed under the heading "Quality of Life," it is barely an exaggeration to define quality of life as that which deteriorates when five lower middle class cabins appear at the edge of a lake which had previously provided an unobstructed view for a single upper middle class family. Much of the indignation over crowding of park areas, suburban sprawl, "ticky-tacky" housing, and other esthetic and environmental issues represents principally an attempt by the upper middle class to preserve its traditional perquisites by excluding increasingly prosperous lower middle class groups from enjoying the same benefits. From the viewpoint of the upper middle class family with an isolated cottage on a lake, the appearance of lower middle class cottages constitutes deterioration of the quality of life, whereas for the lower middle class families such cottages represent a dramatic improvement in quality of life. Nevertheless, much of the environmentalist and quality of life literature would unselfconsciously label such a development an unequivocal deterioration in the quality of life.

Likewise, many other issues reflect the frequently unconscious imposition of upper middle class values on the rest of society. For instance, the prevalent concept of education as stultifying if it emphasizes discipline, mastery of information, and citizenship, rather than freedom, creativity, and critical judgment, frequently provides exactly what the highly motivated, independent, relatively well-disciplined upper middle class child needs, while depriving the ghetto youth of tutoring in the basic skills which he needs for economic survival and mobility. Restrictive zoning laws, gun control laws, freedom of abortion, and sex education represent improving quality of life for some groups and declining quality of life for others.

In saying these things we do not wish to denigrate the sincerity and frequent real importance of discussions of quality of life issues, and we would heartily concur that, despite the intensity of these class differences, very real and universal quality of life issues frequently arise. Among such issues are some kinds of food quality, reckless pollution of waterways, and the more senseless forms of strip-mining. However, it is wise to enter any discussion of these issues with a healthy skepticism for the selfless and self-righteous masks which so frequently obscure the assertion of class interests. The alacrity with which some of the most educated and normally most skeptical segments of American society swallowed the baldest and least defensible forms of the limits-to-growth thesis revealed the strength of class interest, and of intellectuals' traditional anticommercialism. The result was transformation of a scientific question into an ideological answer.

Frequently, too, differing perceptions which need not lead to conflict can lead to deprivation of one social group if other social groups are ignorant of or insensitive to its values. The New Yorker gives up almost nothing in order to concede to people from Wisconsin their desire to hunt and fish, but if the New Yorker fails to comprehend the values of Wisconsin hunters and fishermen, he may seek to pass unnecessarily restrictive national laws which harm many other people without any substantial advantage to himself. Liberal educationalists who are unaware of ghetto families' desire for discipline and for acquisition of certain key skills, even if these require learning by rote, may deprive the ghetto child of many of the prerequisites for a decent life while believing they have done the ghetto children a favor. The existence of even a few such situations is adequate justification for very careful scrutiny of differing groups' needs and perceptions of quality of life.

C. Related, but far from identical to, these class differences over the nature of quality of life are *differences among key social strata.* In particular, strata that are declining in numbers, influence, or status tend to be hypercritical of public policies, almost regardless of their substance. In contrast, rising strata will—again regardless of public policy—either evaluate quality of life as very high if their ascent is relatively unimpeded, or else regard quality of life as very low if there are key impediments to their ascent. Among declining strata whose dissent is predictable are: professors, who are becoming a mass profession and whose status and influence as individuals are therefore bound to decline; blue-collar workers, whose declining numbers and declining power threaten them; middle level businessmen; and in the future, possibly lawyers. Among the key rising strata in contemporary American society are: men in their thirties and forties, key professional and technical elites; and senior governmental and business bureaucrats.

In addition to these rising and declining strata, certain chronic critics of American society will evaluate the quality of life as despicable and public policies as inadequate almost regardless of content.[5] These groups include:

a. religious fundamentalists
b. exploited minorities
c. displaced elites
d. aesthetes
e. Europophiles
f. Socialists
g. fierce individualists
h. "noble savages"
i. atheists, skeptics, cynics, iconoclasts
j. bottom of society.

D. Finally there are key *interest conflicts* which are created or exacerbated by current socioeconomic trends. In order to avoid an exceedingly long discussion, we simply list the principal conflicts here:

1. The few vs. the many
2. Self-fulfillment vs. vocational vs. societal needs
3. Generalists vs. specialists (e.g., value-oriented and practical people vs. experts)
4. International vs. national goals; federal vs. state vs. community vs. individuals and groups
5. Growth vs. stability
6. Growth vs. environment
7. Growth vs. current consumption
8. Priorities for near essentials and important amenities, e.g., poverty of affluence
9. Public regulation and accountability vs. professional self-regulation and self-accountability vs. individual independence and self-responsibility
10. Vested interests vs. change and growth or vs. new interests
11. Participation vs. representation vs. expert authority vs. bureaucratic authority
12. Specialized issues such as various:
    a. conflicts among age groups
    b. city vs. suburbs vs. rural areas
    c. business vs. other interests
    d. organized labor vs. other interests
    e. media vs. other interests
    f. racial, ethnic and minority issues and conflicts.

It may be that the most intensely debated issues of the next generation will be those we have lumped under the title "The Few Versus The Many." Thus the interests of a whole state might benefit from siting a new nuclear power plant within the state, but every community within the state may well refuse to allow the plant to be built within its community borders. Towns such as Aspen, Colorado, have decided that they have grown enough and would prefer no outsiders to move in. Some of these conflicts are solvable through gimmickry. There is a story about a town which could not get any neighborhood to accept a fire department because of the noise of the fire engines and the intrusive architecture; the problem was solved by building a magnificent fire station, whose architecture contributed to local land values, and by instituting a rule that the fire engines could not use their sirens within several blocks of the fire station. However, many of these conflicts run so deep that such gimmicks are correspondingly harder to invent.

Amenities

So long as traditional governmental functions are performed adequately, discussion of the quality of life takes on its characteristic form of discussing the grand social trends of Western civilization (outlined below) and particular current issues. The latter may be referred to as amenities; although this characterization is not intended to denote insignificance, it does provide a sharp reminder that these issues are of great concern only when the more basic governmental functions can be taken for granted. Such amenities include: leisure, recreation, governmental provision of support for the arts and humanities, concern for the lifestyle of the elderly, controversy over the range of government responsibilities in society, and debate over the degree to which government is centralized or decentralized. Even concern for identifying national goals and critical choices is part of this category, since these concerns tend to be solved by definition whenever some important breakdown occurs in the performance of traditional governmental functions. Faced with war or famine or depression, identification of national goals becomes unnecessary.

Traditional Government Administrative Functions

As mentioned above, the concept of quality of life tends to take economic prosperity and adequate performance of traditional government functions for granted, but traditional governmental functions are so crucial to the way people live that, as soon as performance on any of these functions break down, perceptions of quality of life rapidly become focused upon, and dominated by, the consequences of breakdown. For instance, the government is responsible for maintaining law and order and, as long as it does so successfully, discussions of quality of life ignore the problem, even if the murder rate rises somewhat or if white collar crime becomes prevalent. Discussions of quality of life will tend to ignore these trends because they either affect very small or uninfluential groups of people or exercise very little influence over the general character of affected lives. By contrast, a rising prevalence of pornography, drug abuse, marital instability, or "mugging" does strongly affect the lives of vast numbers of individuals. It therefore tends to enter into discussions of the quality of life.

Likewise, quality of life discussions tend to take prosperity and sometimes growth for granted, but in times of difficulty, such issues as inflation, unemployment, inadequate housing, breakdown of the transportation system, and so forth, can come to dominate the quality of life and discussion of the quality of life. After this chapter was originally written, the tone of discussions of quality of life changed character because of the 1974-1975 stagflation. Most education, labor, and health issues also fall into this category where solutions are taken for granted so long as no trouble occurs, but which dominate the quality of life as soon as some breakdown happens.

In large part because American society is undergoing rapid change, some traditional governmental functions have partially broken down. Robbery has become so prevalent that vast numbers of people fear to walk the streets alone at night. Inflation threatens to deprive many people of the fruits of the economic growth and general prosperity which were taken for granted so recently. Polls show enormously widespread doubt among American citizens regarding the ability of America's most basic governmental and private institutions to perform their traditional functions. Much of America finds basic moral values outraged by the spread of previously banned forms of pornography. In such a situation, most of the society—but not necessarily the articulate upper middle class—focuses on these basic issues as the key to quality of life, rather than on the amenities mentioned above. George Wallace, for example, regardless of his views on racial issues, articulates "quality of life" issues for the less articulate strata who are more dependent upon adequate performance of traditional governmental functions.

Short-Term Influences on Morale and Attitudes

Although we shall very strongly emphasize the importance of basic social trends, such as the transition to a post-industrial society, as sources of quality of life issues, it is also important to acknowledge the existence of short-term fads and trends in morale which, although basically ephemeral, can prove very important for a few years; they can have more enduring influence by affecting decisions with long-range implications. The 1950s were a period of exuberant optimism and patriotism when basic challenges to American ideals came from the political right. In the early and mid-1960s a gradual descent into national self-doubt and despair took place; fundamental political challenges came from the "New Left." The early 1970s were marked by a profound malaise which was the cumulative psychological residue of civil rights movement frustrations, Vietnam, the assassinations of the two Kennedys and of Martin Luther King, Watergate, various other investigations and exposes, the oil crisis, and stagflation. But the seeds of a new spirit seem to be generating in renewed economic growth, in the slow return to university standards, in some renewed confidence in American judicial institutions, in renewed emphasis on responsible financial standards, and in a few other bright spots.

Trends in attitudes and morale tend to follow cycles of four to ten years, often striking rapidly with great intensity and disappearing with equal rapidity. Between 1963 and 1964 the civil rights movement suddenly died as an object of constant public attention and Vietnam replaced it. Ecology then replaced Vietnam. To point out the faddishness of such movements is not to deny that they frequently address important issues and cause useful long-range changes. But any enduring contribution to analysis of quality of life issues should rise above current fads and attain some larger perspective. Social and political leaders should try to choose policies and stances which are countercyclical in the sense that they attempt to damp down the cycle of fads and moods, and to restore a sensible balance among quality of life objectives. For instance, attempts to rally public opinion around celebration of the Bicentennial, or around reinvigoration of key long-term values, or around the achievement of one or more major national goals, might be appropriate in combatting the current malaise.

Basic Societal Trends

To a surprising degree the principal quality of life issues cluster around certain macro-societal trends which are part of the common legacy and destiny of Western civilization, especially (A) the transition from pre-industrial to industrial society, (B) the rise of a super-industrial economy, and (C) the concomitant rise of a post-industrial economy.

Industrial Society Trends

The transition from pre-industrial to industrial society and resulting discontentment have given the great sociologists of the nineteenth and twentieth centuries their principal subject matter—a subject matter which goes to the heart of today's quality of life discussion. In particular, the transition to industrial society implied:

1. The shift of population from rural areas to urban areas, and the resultant loss of a sense of community and continuity.
2. The development of a class of industrial workers whose *alienation* gave Marx a main theme.
3. The *bureaucratization* of much of society, with resultant constriction of individual freedom and demands for tailoring one's personality to the requirements of bureaucratic role; these led Max Weber to emphasize bureaucracy as the greatest threat to personal liberty and bureaucrats as an exploited social group.
4. Large increases in social mobility, which tears people from their social roots and thereby disorients them; this led Durkheim to emphasize *anomie* (loss of consensus on social norms) as the characteristic discontent of industrial society.
5. The *fragmentation* of society into specialized groups and of knowledge into specialized compartments which leads (a) to the pervasion of society by group conflicts and (b) to a universal loss of the sense of society as unified and as possessing some common meaning and purpose.

Post-Industrial Society Trends

Ironically, the problems of transition to industrial society are overlaid by the problems associated with the transition from industrial society to post-industrial society. Post-industrial society modifies and sometimes exacerbates those problems, but at least for a long period of transition does not eliminate them.

Post-industrial society involves a shift toward predominance of white-collar work in the economy, toward scholarship and codified knowledge as the basis of economic dynamism and guidance of social trends, and toward what has been called adhocracy rather than classical bureaucracy. In this amorphous, rapidly shifting society, anomie is exacerbated; at best the group conflicts and loss of meaning and purpose that characterize industrial society are not ameliorated.

In the transition to post-industrial society, a vast group of intellectuals is created, as needs for expertise increase. This group suffers from the most intense anomie of all social groups, but at the same time is quite self-conscious as a stratum and considers itself deserving of social power; in becoming a mass profession that professoriat becomes more visible and thus engenders more antagonism with other social groups than in the past, and also opens itself to sharper criticism as a group because in becoming a mass profession its average standards necessarily decline. As its internal standards and social status decline and its numbers rise, this group becomes organizable both as a union pressing for greater economic returns and as an agency of government or other social institutions. Thus a key new form of social conflict becomes institutionalized.

At the same time, society faces a momentous political and social choice regarding the degree to which scholarship will be either fragmented and autonomous, or unified and harnessed to the tasks of other institutions.

The ultimate degree of fragmentation and autonomy possible in post-industrial society is now being approached. If one imagines acceptance of zero economic growth thesis put forward by some groups today, together with a willingness to organize and harness scholarship, one can imagine a trend over several centuries toward an essentially Confucian social order dominated by an elite corps of university-trained mandarins.

The other key social trend of post-industrial society is the rise of white-collar service occupations and the numerical decline of blue-collar unskilled labor occupations. As this trend continues, unskilled workers become more and more dissatisfied because, even though their pay tends to rise quickly, they find themselves with relatively low social status compared with relatives and neighbors who have moved into white-collar occupations. This is less true of highly skilled blue-collar groups. Unions find their membership declining and union leaders react like cornered bobcats in largely successful drives to improve the pay and working conditions of their members. Each union is discontented if other unions achieve better pay, and the better-paid become discontented if others begin to catch up. Thus blue-collar organizations continue to struggle, using the same tactics and rhetoric as their predecessors, but in an entirely changed situation which renders traditional tactics and rhetoric irrelevant. White-collar workers become discontented because so many blue-collar workers are better paid; a New York garbage collector draws a higher salary than a Harvard assistant professor, and the professor is *very* conscious of this.

Post-industrial society and late industrial society tend to emphasize such values as scholarship, peaceful cooperation, and orderly adjustment, which facilitate achievement of the basic role requirements of the society. War becomes anathema, because of the destructiveness of industrial and super-industrial technology, and because of the cosmopolitanism inherent in an emerging post-industrial society. But certain values which are suppressed in such a society keep reappearing in peculiar fashion. Anomie leaves society vulnerable to movements and fads which seem to offer unity, structure, meaning, and purpose. The rightist movements of the 1950s, the leftist movements of the 1960s, the scurrying of much of the population into relatively fundamentalist religions, the rise of the Jesus freaks, the attractiveness of the Marines to certain social groups, the intensity of the ecological movement, and other vast social phenomena, all reflect, in part, a yearning for feudal structure, unity, meaning, and purpose. Likewise, the absence of the martial virtues of comradeship, heroism, and discipline so admired by Oliver Wendell Holmes and so eloquently discussed by William James, creates a vacuum in industrial and post-industrial culture, and these values keep popping up in such incongruous places as the intense sense of comradeship felt by the 1960s by civil rights workers and Vietnam protesters.

Finally, it may be worthwhile to note that, just as the auspicious trends carrying us from feudal to industrial to post-industrial society have generated these enormous problems, so some of the possible projected auspicious trends of post-industrial society will certainly generate their own forms of dissatisfaction. For instance, some writers believe that a leisure revolution is likely to occur in the United States. Professionals and managerial workers have good reason to be skeptical about the booming leisure of post-industrial society, but it is at least imaginable that substantial proportions of the population will eventually work a three-day week and not "moonlight" during their four off-days. If so, the intense boredom which afflicted the aristocracy of eighteenth and nineteenth century Europe could return with a vengeance as a mass phenomenon—not necessarily for all men, or for the average man, but possibly for major social groups. The result would be intense seeking for amusement and excitement on a scale far greater than today.

Super-Industrial Society

Just as incongruous as the coexistence of the problems of post-industrial society with those of industrial society is the rise of problems of *super*-industrial society in an era which we now refer to as being emerging post-industrial. When we use the phrase *post*-industrial, we refer to the fact that the characteristic forms of organization, dominant economic groups, and leading sectors of contemporary society are different from those of industrial society in its classical form, and we refer to the decline of production workers as a numerically dominant sector of the economy. However, in this post-industrial society the *scale* of industry expands to the point where the Tennessee Valley Authority seems like a middle-sized project, and the *scope* of industrial society expands to include most of the world. This phenomenon of industry with huge scale and scope is summarized in the phrase "super-industrial society."

The super-industrial society creates fundamental threats to environmental stability, to recreational uses of the environment, and to short-run availability of certain key resources and of adequate supplies of energy. Some particularly dangerous possible side effects of such technology are listed in the accompanying Tables VI-1 and VI-2. These side effects of the huge scale and scope of modern industry are of course exacerbated by rising population and affluence. This rising population is actually a hangover from the period of transition between pre-industrial and industrial society; it tends to become a less severe problem as countries go through the demographic transition. This makes it a relatively less severe long-run problem than is commonly supposed, but for the present it can cause severe difficulties in certain parts of the world such as India and China.

On the basis of considerable study done at Hudson Institute, we do not

Table VI-1
The Increasing Disillusionment with Progress

Ambivalent Nature of Progress

1 SOME MIXED BLESSINGS OF PROGRESS	2 SOME ASPECTS OF PRIVACY
1. Defunctionalization—partial (but increasing) loss of meaning of many traditional activities through the development of short-cuts to gratification: erosion of "traditional societal levers"	I. Right to idiosyncratic A. Thoughts B. Utterances C. Values D. Way of life E. Style and manners F. Methods of self-expression
2. Accumulation, augmentation, and proliferation of weapons of mass destruction	II. Isolation or protection from: A. Selected aspects of the physical environment B. Selected aspects of the social environment C. Many pressures and/or other intrusions by individuals, organized private groups and businesses, and political and governmental organizations
3. Loss of privacy and solitude	
4. Increase of governmental and/or private power over individuals	III. Right to: A. Withhold information B. Make many family and personal decisions C. *Be oneself*
5. Loss of human scale and perspective	
6. Dehumanization of social life or even of the psycho-biological self	IV. Enough elbow room: A. To be unobserved occasionally B. For aesthetic purposes C. To get things done D. *As a value in its own right*
7. Growth of dangerously vulnerable, deceptive or degradable centralization of administrative or technological systems	
8. Creation of other new capabilities so inherently dangerous as to risk disastrous abuse	
9. Acceleration of changes that are too rapid or cataclysmic to permit successful adjustment	
10. Posing of choices that are too large, complex, important, uncertain, or comprehensive to be safely left to fallible humans.	

3 A DYSTOPIAN SEQUENCE	4 OTHER WAYS TO GO WRONG
1. A series of relatively small changes is proposed	1. Criteria too narrow

2. In each case the changed situation is thought to be preferable (by, say, a vote of the *relevant* decision-makers or community) to the old situation.
3. The changes are cumulative.
4. Only after the series of changes has been made do people think of the new situation as undesirable or disastrous (or the situation becomes one that those who initiated the process would judge undesirable).
5. Yet it is now impossible to reverse the sequence because of irrevocable changes, too great an investment or changed values.

2. Decisions at inappropriate point in the structure (for the end in view)
3. Inadequate thought
4. Bad luck: unknown issues
5. Bad luck: unlikely events
6. Changes in actors
7. Inappropriate models
8. Inappropriate values
9. Over- or under-discounting of uncertainty or of the future
10. The best may be the enemy of the good (and sometimes vice versa)

Table VI-2
1985 Technological Crises

BY 1985 THE FOLLOWING AREAS ARE LIKELY
TO GIVE RISE TO SPECIAL TECHNOLOGICAL DANGERS

I.   Intrinsically dangerous technology
II. Gradual worldwide and or national contamination or de-
     gradation of the environment
III. Spectacular and or multinational contamination or degra-
     dation of the environment
IV. Dangerous internal political issues
V.   Upsetting international consequences
VI. Dangerous personal choices
VII. Bizarre issues

I. INTRINSICALLY DANGEROUS TECHNOLOGY

A. Modern means of mass destruction
B. Nuclear reactors—fission or fusion
C. Nuclear explosives, high-speed gas centrifuges, etc.
D. Research missiles, satellite launchers, commercial aircraft,
   etc.
E. Biological and chemical "progress"
F. Molecular biology and genetics
G. "Mind control"
H. New techniques for insurgency, crime, terror or ordinary
   violence
I. New techniques for counterinsurgency or imposition of
   order
J. New "serendipities" and synergisms

II. GRADUAL WORLDWIDE AND/OR NATIONAL CONTAM-
INATION OR DEGRADATION OF THE ENVIRONMENT

A. Radioactive debris from various peaceful nuclear uses
B. Possible greenhouse or other effects from increased CO_2
   in the atmosphere, or new ice age because of dust in
   stratosphere, etc.

IV. DANGEROUS INTERNAL POLITICAL ISSUES

A. Computerized records
B. Other computerized surveillance
C. Other advanced techniques for surveillance
D. Excessively degradable (or unreliably reassuring) centralized
   capabilities
E. Improved knowledge of (and techniques for) agit-prop and
   other methods of creating disturbances and disruption
F. Improved knowledge of and techniques for preventing dis-
   turbances
G. Complex or critical governmental issues leading to either "tech-
   nocracy" or "caesarism"
H. Nuclear weapons affecting internal politics
I. Excessively illusioned attitudes
J. Other dangerous attitudes

V. UPSETTING INTERNATIONAL CONSEQUENCES

A. Both new and "traditional" demonstration effects
B. Technological obsolescence of "unskilled" labor
C. New synthetics or processes, e.g., coffee, oil from shale, etc.
D. Forced modernization

C. Other special dangerous wastes—methyl mercury, DDT, NTA, phosphates
D. Insecticides, fertilizers, growth "chemicals," food additives, plastic containers, etc.
E. Other less dangerous but environment degrading wastes such as debris and garbage
F. Waste Heat
G. Noise, ugliness and other annoying byproducts of many modern activities
H. Excessive urbanization
I. Excessive overcrowding
J. Excessive tourism

III. SPECTACULAR AND/OR MULTINATIONAL CONTAMINATION OR DEGRADATION OF THE ENVIRONMENT

A. Nuclear war
B. Nuclear testing
C. Bacteriological and chemical war or accident
D. Artificial moons
E. Projects West Ford, Storm Fury, etc.
F. Supersonic transportation (shock waves, "greenhouse" particulates)
G. Weather control
H. Big "geomorphological" projects
I. Million-ton tankers (Torry Canyon was only 111,825 to and million-pound planes
J. Other enterprises or mechanisms of "excessive" size

E. Growing guilt feelings by many in wealthy nations—particularly among the alienated or young
F. Inexpensive and widely available "realistic" communications and physical travel
G. Accelerated "brain drains"
H. Cheap (synthetic?) food
I. Cheap education
J. Control and exploitation of the oceans, space, moon

VI. DANGEROUS PERSONAL CHOICES

A. Sex determination
B. Other genetic engineering
C. Psychedelic and mood-affecting drugs
D. Electronic stimulation of pleasure centers
E. Other methods of sensual satisfaction
F. Excessive permissiveness and indulgence
G. Dropping out and other alienation
H. Excessive narcissim or other self-regard
I. Super-cosmetology
J. Lengthy hibernation

VII. BIZARRE ISSUES

A. Generational changes: e.g. extended longevity
B. Mechanically dependent humans: e.g. pacemakers
C. Life and death for an individual: e.g., artificial kidneys, etc.
D. New forms of humanity: e.g. "live" computers
E. "Compulsory" birth control for "impossible" groups
F. Other external controls or influence on what should be personal or even institutionally private choices
G. Life and death sanctions or other control of "outlaw" societies which have not yet committed any traditional crime
H. Even the continuation of the nation-state system
I. Controlling and limiting change and innovation
J. Radical ecological changes on a planetary scale
K. Interplanetary contamination

believe the world in general or the United States in particular will suffer from long-term shortages of energy or resources, or that continued super-industrial development is inconsistent with a clean environment.[7] Nor does population growth in the United States mean overcrowding in any strong sense. However, super-industrial society does imply difficult transitions to new sources of energy and other resources, the necessity of new regulations and vast new expenditures to maintain a clean environment, almost complete disappearance of unprotected wilderness areas in the United States, and overuse of many existing recreational facilities to the point where the continued existence of some of them is occasionally endangered.

The Failures of Success

It is crucial to call attention to the extent to which many problems of modern society, and particularly those problems which affect quality of life, derive not from major social failures but from major social successes. Thus, the most pervasive and deeply rooted problems are caused by the successful transition from pre-industrial to post-industrial and super-industrial society. Discussion of quality of life therefore takes for granted the successful performance of traditional governmental functions and takes for granted the maintenance of high per capita income. Quality of life refers to a set of problems which are overwhelmingly the consequences of success: anomie resulting from successful promotion of social mobility; blue-collar blues resulting from successful transition away from the class structure and struggles of early industrial society; pollution resulting from successful rapid growth; perverse outbreaks of the martial spirit as a result of a generally peaceful world and the imposition of peaceful values; and intense concern with recreation and leisure issues because many people have nothing more important to be intensely concerned about. Other failures of success are listed in Table VI-3.

The concept of the failures of success deserves special mention because social morale would be utterly different if today's problems were viewed as resulting from extraordinary and multiple successes in attaining the goals which mankind has for centuries cherished most, rather than as the culmination of centuries of human failure and rapaciousness.

Summary

Quality of life as currently used generally refers to all influences on human happiness except for basic governmental and economic functions, which are taken for granted, and religious or moral concerns, which are ignored. It is

Table VI-3
Some Failures of Success

We Have	But We Also Have
1. Affluence	1. No need to wait for possessions that we desire, hence no need for self-discipline. As a result, people are overly concerned with satisfying their material wants, and are at the same time satiated, bored and petulant when they do not receive what they want.
2. Continuous Economic Growth, Technological Improvements	2. Impossible demands made on the government: steady growth uninterrupted by business cycles is required as a matter of course; unrealistically high growth rates are demanded; all groups in society must grow economically at the same rate so that no one is left behind. Improvements in technology encourage unrealistic expectations elsewhere.
3. Mass Consumption	3. Aesthetic and commercial standards are determined by the tastes of the masses.
4. Economic Security, Little Real Poverty	4. Emphasis on relative poverty, hence a desire for radical egalitarianism.
5. Physical Safety, Good Health, Longevity	5. A neurotic concern with avoiding pain and death. Alternatively, the lack of genuine danger and risks leads to the creation of artificial and often meaningless risks for the sake of thrills.
6. Government "For the People"	6. No realization that there are goals higher than the welfare of the people, e.g., the glory of God, national honor.
7. The Belief that Human Life Is Sacred, Hence that Each Individual Is as Important as the Next	7. The belief that nothing is more important than human life, hence that nothing is worth dying (or killing) for. Loss of aristocratic ideals and the idea that superior men should rule over inferior men.
8. Rationalism and the Elimination of Superstition	8. The loss of tradition, patriotism, faith: everything which cannot be justified by reason.
9. Meritocracy	9. No sudden rises to power. Everyone must show his worth by working his way up. By the time they get to the top, people have lost much spirit. Hence fewer, young, idiosyncratic hotheads, at the top to shake things up. Also, no respect for experience which does not constantly prove its worth.
10. An Open, Classless Society	10. No sense of one's proper place in society. In traditional societies, if you are born an aristocrat, you die an aristocrat. Now, when you rise upward, you don't know when to stop striving. Thus, you have ceaseless struggles for more money and power.

common, therefore, to treat the concept of quality of life as a residual concept. Doing so, however, renders quality of life virtually useless as an analytical tool. However, discussion of most quality of life issues can be structured if it is understood that they usually derive from the most fundamental trends of Western social history, particularly those associated with the rise of industrialism, the transition to a post-industrial and super-industrial society, and several congeries of "failures of success." By positioning one's analysis astride these great trends, one can assure that adequate attention is devoted to those issues which are fundamental, while some sense of the interrelationships of diverse particular issues is retained.

The basis for healthy, constructive discussion, as opposed to thoughtless complaints, is a constant awareness that most of our current problems derive from the success with which American society has attacked more fundamental and more difficult problems in the past. And finally, we have argued that quality of life discussions, like all other discussions of social issues, benefit greatly from tempered skepticism and frequent reiteration of the query, "quality of life for whom?"

The Erosion of Social Levers

One can best understand the problems that American society has created for itself by recalling Freud's position on human nature and civilization. He said three things. First, civilization is repression. Freud was probably the greatest Augustinian of the twentieth century, and it was terribly clear to him that there were dark and destructive tendencies within the human soul that had to be subdued if men were going to be anything but savages. His second point followed naturally from this vision: you must socialize the child at any cost. You will give him neuroses, ulcers, and complexes, but you must socialize the child. Babies are not sweet innocent creatures. They are selfish, grasping, and destructive. If they could, they would destroy the world in a fit of pique. They are monsters, and if you do not restrain them they will wreck your civilization. But then Freud makes a third point. Socialize the child at any cost, but reduce that cost as much as possible. Americans only heard, or at least only understood, the last half of the last point, and gaily set about liberating their children, acting directly contrary to Freud's counsels.

By socialization Freud meant that you needed levers with which to control people's behavior. In certain cases, rational arguments and practical necessity will serve as prods and guides to individuals. In other cases, emotional and supra-rational levers will be needed to control the irrational aspects of men. We regard such things as tabus, totems and tradition as barbarities best left behind us, but that is an almost totally incorrect view of the world. Tabus cannot be eliminated because they alone provide controls strong enough to withstand the passions. Some Pacific Islanders have eliminated all tabus with regard to sex, but this does not disprove the point. In place of sex tabus, they have developed elaborate rituals and socials patterns with regard to food. One eats in private and, in effect, one tells food jokes. You need tabus in order to establish a category of behavior by likening them to the tabu acts.

You cannot simply set out a list of rules of behavior, discuss them rationally, and still expect people to obey them. As an example, the American government used to have a firm and fast rule: balance the budget. If you ran a deficit, you were immoral and irresponsible. You could not argue with the rule. Then Keynes came along and pointed out, quite correctly, that it was sometimes good to balance the budget, sometimes good to run a surplus, and sometimes good to run a deficit. Unfortunately, governments have an inherent tendency to run deficits: it makes it easier to satisfy everyone's demands, it frees you from the necessity of tax increases, it enables you to defer decisions and problems. If you set down an inflexible, irrational *moral* precept that deficit spending is evil, you can check the tendency. If you permit argument about whether or not a particular situation requires a deficit, you will always have deficit spending. In fact this has been the case. No American government has achieved an intentionally deflationary policy with a budget surplus since the war. Keynes would remind us that as many situations demand a government surplus as demand a deficit, but his rational argument lacks the power to check men's appetites that the old, irrational rule had.

The problem the United States has is that we have consciously attacked all of the irrational techniques of social control, the societal levers, and have in some measure destroyed them. At the same time, we have become so rich and powerful that the old restraints set by physical reality have largely disappeared. It should not be surprising therefore to find that we have difficulty restraining or disciplining ourselves.

It will be useful to examine the levers which middle class America previously relied upon to direct individuals. If one objects to these levers on the grounds that they are repressive, we can only agree, and refer the reader back to Freud's original comments. If one mourns the passing of these levers, we sympathize, but we are forced to note that these levers are gone forever. You cannot restore myths and traditions once you have debunked them, as will be seen when we examine the levers individually.

To begin with, there is (or was) respect for authority and tradition. One obeyed a command, not because the person giving it was smarter than one—that is persuasion. Nor did one obey because he was stronger than one—that is coercion. One obeyed the command because a certain man was author of that command, and that was that. This is entirely rational. Consider two football teams. In one team, an individual is chosen, totally arbitrarily, and given a red arm band. From then on, he is obeyed simply because he has that arm band. The other team is left alone. The team with the leader will win, just because there is a leader.

Now any leader can be viewed as arbitrarily chosen if you are hostile to him. Why should we obey someone simply because he or she bores us, is older, or got more votes? In order to get people to consent to a leader, it is necessary to have a supra-rational belief in the wisdom of age, tradition or the majority. With the possible exception of the last, we are no longer willing to recognize authority, because we have destroyed the basis on which it rests.

Nor can we rely on more substantial factors to control people. Traditionally, you could not do certain things, simply because you would wind up dead or maimed if you did. Biology and physics presented iron laws which no one could violate with impunity. If you did not cooperate with the community, you starved or froze to death. We have now raised a generation of people who have never been too hot or cold, have never been hungry or thirsty, and who regard comfort as normal, rather than something which has been dearly bought. Taking comfort for granted inevitably causes people to present further demands on society, which by itself is totally acceptable. But a subtler damage has been done. When it was not uncommon for children to die young and for disasters to wipe out communities, people were not psychically destroyed by catastrophe and suffering. We are today psychologically unprepared for catastrophe. Our reactions to the idea of thermonuclear war are typical. If someone says that twenty million Americans will die and two-thirds of our industry will be wiped out, we cannot imagine rebuilding. Yet that is roughly the magnitude of the casualties taken by the Soviet Union during World War II. Note that we are not saying that such an event would not be a disaster. But one advantage of experiencing disasters is that you learn that you can survive them. We tend to despair when confronted by catastrophe or real suffering. Such a tendency is a weakness.

Nor have we ever had the problem of barbarians across the border. When you have such enemies, you realize that you must repress yourself and adapt to the ways of the community or see your wife and daughters raped, and your sons killed. Fear of alien enemies is a terribly effective tool for socializing children, and reinforcing such socialization in adults. Americans have never experienced this kind of fear. If you lived on the Central European Plain you did not talk about the sacred rights of the individual; you talked about getting good generals. Of course we received tremendous benefits as a result of our security: if you are building a free, democratic society it helps to have the English Channel or the Atlantic Ocean between you and your enemies. But at the same time we lost contact with one aspect of reality: that there are dangerous people in the world, and you need to get along with your neighbors if you are to survive.

The world today is generally a safe place to live, and all people will have to find reasons for achieving social cohesion other than the need for a common defense. The Israelis know this, and know that the Arabs are the primary factor keeping their tremendously fragmented society together. Most Westerners will agree that Israel should have the chance to see if it can survive as a nation, without frightening enemies. Everyone should also realize that the problem will be very difficult of resolution.

Similarly, one could appeal in the past to nationalism in order to create a sense of community. The nation-state happens to be perhaps the most successful form of social organization in the history of man, and pride in one's country is a terribly useful social force. Associated with patriotism were other ideal types and goals which helped channel and restrain individuals. Heroism, duty, and honor were virtues which required incredible amounts of self-discipline and self-denial. If the soldier is your ideal, it is possible to teach children the value of courage, glory, and the national honor. Oliver Wendell Holmes extolled the virtues of war precisely because it brought out these qualities, as did William James. When you are teaching a child the need for self-discipline, it is extremely useful to have some such ideal to inspire him and hold his attention while he is maturing. Duty, honor, and country were such ideals.

World War I destroyed all of that. It was not then uncommon for one wave of troops to be sent into battle and be totally wiped out. The second wave of troops would watch this and then they would be sent out to their death. The third wave would watch the first two and then they would die. After four years of this it was not surprising that there was a total disillusionment with many old values. If the nation-state produced World War I, then to hell with it. If war was like this, then to hell with it. If generals were too stupid to avoid this kind of atrocity, then to hell with soldiers. Consequently, the use of the martial values as tools for socialization is now totally unimaginable among many groups.

More prosaically, society can survive if it can insure that its day-to-day economic activity is taken so seriously that men suppress their passions for its sake. At one level this could mean disciplining oneself sufficiently to provide for the necessities of life. However, we have long since stopped worrying about such matters. The Chinese Communist communes guarantee their people five things: adequate food, clothing, shelter, medical care, and funeral expenses. By adequate they mean adequate by Chinese standards. If we take this level as the minimum standard of living, it is clear that no American has to work much—or compromise much—in order to survive.

Alternatively, if Americans believed that getting rich was an unqualifiedly good thing, or that economic activity was God's work, we would have a powerful social lever. This, obviously, was what actually motivated Americans in the nineteenth and early twentieth century. Herbert Spencer, Charles Sumner, and most Americans believed that capitalism was good because it made men rich and, equally important, because it forced the morally good man to the top of society and forced the feckless individual down. If you believed this, it made consummately good sense to deny yourself sex, family, material indulgences, and leisure in order to save, work, and succeed. The man who got an ulcer by knocking himself out in business used to be a hero. Now, he is considered a compulsive, greedy, and fundamentally sick individual.

We are now too rich for this mindless devotion to business to be reasonable, but we cannot yet dispense with the bourgeois character. Even if we had reached the point where material scarcity no longer existed, we would still hope that people would discipline themselves and defer gratification: Unlimited self-indulgence is simply wrong. But we have not yet reached the phase of super-abundance. With Lord Keynes we must remind ourselves that although Utopia is in sight, we must still work as if it were infinitely far off. For example, we believe it is just not possible to run a capitalist economy without recessions. But Americans have been conditioned to expect continuous, uninterrupted economic growth. In the recent past people were familiar with a phenomenon known as Hard Times. During these times, you tightened your belt and put off certain expenditures. Sometimes your career was interrupted or terminated. That was bad luck, but it was a fact of nature, and nature was not known for its fairness. Now we can manage our economy, which is good, but we cannot assure perfect performance, which is what is demanded. People will not accept the fact that they will not always get what they want, when they want it.

This is sometimes referred to as the poverty of affluence. Suppose one has a list of fifteen desirable projects: hospitals, schools, roads, etc. If the country is poor, you can say to people "We just can't do any of these things. We're poor, you'll have to wait." But now imagine the country is rich. You say to people "All fifteen of these projects will be completed within ten or twenty years, but we can't do them all at once. Some projects will have to wait." At this point, the people who have to wait get incredibly angry. You are "poor" because your expectations greatly exceed your performance. Bourgeois morality can be extremely helpful in dealing with such problems. It is not perfect, but it does preach the virtue of self-denial. When we destroyed that morality, we lost a useful social lever, and we also created enormous problems for ourselves.

Lastly, we no longer have the ability to use sex in order to restrain individuals. If you taught someone that premarital sex was a mortal sin, you repressed his instincts and probably made him incurably neurotic. But you also developed within him considerable self-discipline. You taught him that he could control his most powerful passion, and this was good. At the same time, you gave the institution of marriage a firm foundation. Marriage was the only way people could have sex without guilt, fear, or insecurity. This meant that one was extremely attached to one's wife (husband) as the first person with whom you had sex without having to worry about going to hell. This state of affairs is long since past, and as in the other cases, it cannot be restored.

Our discussion thus far has been somewhat overstated. It is primarily the upper middle class which has experienced the erosion of these traditional societal levers: perhaps three-fourths of the country still believes in "square" values. We believe, however, that this erosion may eventually affect the rest of society. More importantly, we do not believe that America can survive if the children of the upper classes remain unsocialized: too much productive capacity will be lost, and too much damage will be done by those children. But if we are correct, and traditional values cannot be restored, then we will have to import, invent, and inculcate new values. To believe that we can do so is optimistic. Values are not ordinarily created *ex nihilo*, but are formed, like nations, by blood and history. To the extent that we can do so, however, we should encourage the evolution of American values in certain directions. Moreover, we saw in the early 1960s the emergence of certain of these new values. While they disappeared during the middle and late 1960s, we believe that they can be revived.

First among them is the graceful acceptance of affluence. We are going to be enormously wealthy and we had better learn how to spend our wealth without becoming satiated or antimaterialistic. In this respect we have a lot to learn from the European upper classes, which is not surprising since they have lived with the problem of affluence for approximately five hundred years. The solution to the problem is best explained by giving an example. Greek food is the best food in the world if you eat it once a year. It is fresh seafood with butter and lemon, or olive oil and garlic. If you eat it once a week or every day however, it becomes boring. French food is infinitely complex. Each meal is a contest between the chef, who is trying to cook better than the gourmet can appreciate, and the gourmet, who is trying to develop a taste more refined than the chef can satisfy. There is no way to get bored by eating, no matter how affluent one is. We have to learn to take certain everyday affairs seriously (without becoming obsessed by them) in order to avoid boredom, and to compensate for the fact that we no longer have life and death struggles to engage our emotions. We have to hearn how to be gentlemen, who pass their time doing difficult things well.

If one objects that such a lifestyle sounds unbearably petty, we may reply that this is so but that is the result of not having to fear barbarians, Nazis, or famines any more. Such conflicts may have added flavor to our lives, but we have always claimed that we would rather not have to fight for survival every day. In any event, such things are largely behind us. In their absence, we must be like the Athenians who loved gymnastics. If there was a war, they did gymnastics to stay fit in order to fight. If there was peace, it was even better: they had more time for gymnastics. Unfortunately, Americans tend to be like the Spartans who got in shape to fight wars, but who tended towards sloth in peacetime.

If we miss the thrill which comes from dangerous activities we can regain it by doing such things as skydiving and deepsea diving. Such activities do much to reintroduce the reality testing which our (overly) safe world has eliminated, and thereby help to restore the need for self-discipline: If you are skin diving at 300 feet, there is no room for self-indulgence. And in fact, the early 1960s did see the growth of such sports at the American prestige universities.

We must learn the virtues of family life and conversing with our friends. Epicurean values will be vital if we are to spend our leisure time at home without killing everyone in sight out of overfamiliarity.

The primary problem will lie with our government. If the world does become safe and affluent, governing will be a very uncharismatic, low morale profession. But it will be just as necessary as it is now to recruit intelligent, competent people into government service. There will be no great projects which will attract people. We will be a mature nation at last, and will have taken the democratic ideal as far as it is practical to go. Externally, we may choose to go on crusades, but more likely we will be satisfied to sit back and watch everyone become as prosperous as we are.

If government is to continue in such an environment, a class of people will have to be developed who serve because they know it is necessary to serve. Their model will be the English civil service, their goal will be maintenance, and their motto will be the epigram of William, Prince of Orange: "It is not necessary to hope in order to act, nor succeed in order to persevere." Such men will most resemble the stoics who ran the Roman Empire for hundreds of years out of a sense of duty, while the rest of the populace pursued their private interests. There is a class of men in the United States who already have these characteristics: military officers. In talking to them one often hears the question, "We are expected to separate ourselves from our families, risk our lives and do menial tasks in peacetime. Do you mean to say that we will have to do this while being ignored or spat upon by the rest of the country?" When one answers, "Yes," they accept their duty like the good soldiers they are.

Most importantly, we must learn not to constantly question the myths which are the foundation of our society. It is the essence of cynicism to treat myths as ordinary propositions to be either proved or disproved. So treated, they lose the emotional force which alone makes them valuable. The people may or may not be wise enough to rule themselves successfully, but the belief that they are is part of the cement which holds the United States together. As Edmund Burke realized, it is the tragedy rather than the glory of our times that the fundamental nature of our society is being constantly examined. Once the United States is treated as just another social organization, more or less successful, men will stop dying for it. We must become neo-cynics, who see that our myths are myths and not truths, but refrain from publicly acknowledging this. In particular, we must take care not to disillusion those who still believe in the myths.

The price of not doing so is high. If people no longer believe the myths about our government, they will have no reason to moderate the demands on the government. If the state is nothing special, in fact just the organization with the most guns, it deserves no one's respect. If we further fail to teach people self-discipline, there will be no reason for them to deny any of their passions, material, sexual or political. Nihilism and anarchy will inevitably follow. Because they understood this, our Founding Fathers believed that a democracy was impossible where the people lacked republican virtue, by which they meant moderation, self-discipline, and modesty. We have attempted to suggest how that virtue may be regained.

Notes

1. Cf. B. Bruce-Briggs, "Changing Values and Attitudes in U.S. History," HI-2006-CC, and Herman Kahn, "Notes on the U.S. Political/Values/Morale Milieu in the 1970's," HI-1755/5-CC.

2. J. Huizinga, *The Waning of the Middle Ages* (Garden City, N.Y.: Doubleday Anchor, 1954), p. 9.

3. Oliver Wendell Holmes, Jr., "The Soldier's Faith," Speech, Harvard University, May 30, 1895.

4. William James, *The Varieties of Religious Experience* (New York: Colier Books, 1961).

5. This list is adapted from B. Bruce-Briggs, "Changing Values and Attitudes in U.S. History," HI-2006-CC.

6. These issues, and associated changes in the social concept of changes, are the subject of current work at Hudson Institute by A.J. Wiener.

7. Cf. Herman Kahn, William Brown, and Leon Martel, *The Next 200 Years* (New York: William Morrow and Co., 1976).

VII Measuring the Quality of Life

Angus Campbell and **Robert L. Kahn**

Defining national goals exclusively or primarily in terms of economic welfare was more suited to a past stage of American life than to the present or the future. True, millions of Americans are still "ill-housed, ill-clad, and ill-nourished"; their needs are apparent and urgent. But a larger proportion of the population now take almost for granted the fulfillment of their basic needs for food, clothing, and shelter. These people are concerned increasingly with "higher order" needs—for social recognition, community identification, achievement in work, self-actualization, and the like. A nation long fixated on goals which are basically economic is changing to include goals which are essentially psychological—changing from a concentration on being merely well-off to a concern with well-being.

Economic affluence in itself has not proved the touchstone to utopian levels of social harmony and personal fulfillment. Instead, the "revolution of rising expectations," without abating the national appetite for material things, has brought a growing demand for gratification of the needs of the "spirit," for a larger and more satisfying life experience.

We do not belittle the objective conditions of life, nor the statistics that describe them, but the quality of life cannot be adequately accounted for in these terms. Happiness and contentment are psychological experiences, and it is the experience of life which gives it its quality. That experience begins with objective conditions, past and present, but goes beyond them; it involves the feelings of individuals toward people and things and activities in their life-space.

The life experience is too complex to describe or understand as a single

163

whole, nor need we attempt that. Life is experienced in many domains. Some of these domains involve intimate and personal experiences (marriage, family life, friendship, etc.); others are more external and public (job, community, nation, etc.). Generally speaking, the external domains are more directly influenced by public policy, but they in turn expand or restrict the more private experiences.

To enhance the quality of life of the American people, it is necessary first to ascertain their experience in the major domains of life, as the people themselves perceive and evaluate that experience. It is necessary then to identify the objective conditions that change such perceptions favorably or unfavorably. Social scientists have already studied the American experience in some such life domains, and their findings provide the subject matter of this paper. We present them in the hope that they may contribute to the wisdom of critical and inevitable choices.

National Morale

Every citizen has a picture in his mind of the country in which he lives. This image may be simple or complex, unquestioningly positive or bitterly negative. It is not constant; it is influenced by passing events and may change for the better or worse as the individual watches and encounters the world around him.

There are many indications in the daily press that the morale of the American people has been declining throughout the last decade. From the grim days of November 1963 to the present time, this country has witnessed a parade of events that reflect contempt for traditional values, rejection of established authority, disregard for life and property, and the betrayal of public trust. It would be remarkable indeed if Americans had come through this period without some loss of confidence and trust in their society and its institutions, public and private.

To interpret the public mind from the headlines is always hazardous; it is the unusual events that attract the media and such events are by definition unrepresentative of the population as a whole. There is ample evidence, however, from national surveys conducted during the last few years, that disillusionment and unease are now widespread among the American people.

A comprehensive national study by the Institute for Social Research in 1971 found that the number of people who believed "Life in the United States" to be getting worse (36 percent) was twice as large as the number who thought it was getting better (17 percent). Aspects of life which respondents regarded as changing "for the worse" covered a wide range, and included morals, values, use of drugs, crime, students, and hippies, as well as inflation, high prices, taxes, racial protests, and ecological pollution. No one of these specific complaints dominated the public sense of life getting worse, but only 13 percent of the sample failed to mention some way in which American life had worsened when asked the question. In contrast, nearly two out of five of this same sample could think of no way in which life in this country has been getting better. Most of those who saw improvement spoke of technological or scientific advances, changes in economic conditions, improvements in education and medical care; few mentioned positive changes in human relationships.

Those people who feel that on balance the changes in American life are predominantly for the worse do not come from any single alienated segment of the population. They are not found any more commonly among youth than among the elderly, or among blacks than whites. People at high income and eduational levels are more inclined to see things changing for the better than are people of less affluent status, a reflection perhaps of their own advantaged circumstances. The one element of the population which is most negative in its assessment of trends in American life consists of that 10 percent who live in the metropolitan centers. As we will see in the following pages, these people have many grievances.

We must not assume that all the people who feel that this country is changing for the worse are in any serious way disaffected from it. Disaffection is a difficult concept to define, but we can approximate the proportion of the population who might be described as disaffected by counting the number of people who say they would leave the United States if they could do so. Setting aside those who would leave for such benign reasons as wanting to travel, to see new things, to be near relatives, or to start life over again, the 1971 ISR survey found between 5 and 10 percent of the national population who said they wanted to leave for reasons of "escape." They dislike American society or its form of government and they want to get away from it. No doubt every country has an alienated minority of this kind and the American proportion may even be comparatively small. It is important, however, to see where these disaffected people are concentrated. They are found in disproportionate numbers among young unmarried people, people of advanced education, people who live in the metropolitan centers, and black people. The study identifies the circumstances of life which are most productive of disaffection as being black and living in the metropolitan centers, with being young and college-educated as additional contributory factors.

Two national surveys conducted in 1971 and 1972 by Potomac Associates provide supplementary information on national morale. Utilizing different methods than those employed in the ISR study, they conclude that "the people's assessment of the state of the nation in 1971 was unquestionably the most pessimistic recorded since the introduction of public opinion polling . . . in the midst of the great depression of the 1930's." The public assessment of the current state of the nation in the 1972 survey was almost identical with that of 1971. The data from these two studies are not directly comparable to those we have presented earlier from the ISR study, but their general conclusions seem entirely compatible—national morale in the early 1970s, at a time of unprecedented economic affluence, was in a depressed state. The national malaise was not only in the headlines and the media commentary; it was in the minds of the people.

These studies dealt with the public image of the "state of the nation" without specific reference to government and politics. They were completed immediately prior to the Watergate period and were thus not influenced by it. When we examine trends in public attitudes toward government during the last ten years, we find a parallel picture and in some respects an even more disquieting one.

The Institute for Social Research began in 1958 a series of measurements of "trust in government," based on a set of questions asking whether the respondent saw "the government in Washington" as honest, trustworthy, knowing what it was doing, and run for the benefit of all the people, or whether it was seen as having the opposite characteristics. We see in Figure VII-1 that during the latter years of the Eisenhower period nearly two-thirds of our national sample were classified on this scale as expressing "high trust" in government. At that time there was no difference in the views of blacks and whites. This high proportion held up through the first Johnson Administration, even rising among blacks, but in 1968 it dropped perceptibly. In 1970 the white curve continued to decline and the black curve broke off precipitously. White trust in government recovered slightly in 1972 but then dropped to a very low level in 1973 after the Watergate disclosures. Black trust remained at rock bottom throughout the Nixon years.

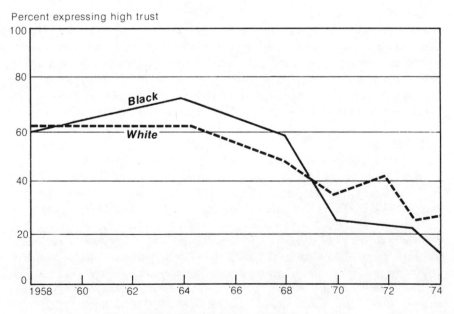

Percent expressing high trust

Figure VII-1. Trends in Trust in Government.

This continuing deterioration in confidence in government derives from many different sources; the Vietnam War was an early contributor, the personalities and behavior of leading political figures were important, and in the latter years the mounting economic problems became significant. It may be that the recent change in leadership in Washington has lifted some of the pall which the Watergate affair spread over the land but it is not likely in itself to bring the country back to the Eisenhower levels. The public has come through a long experience of deceitful, corrupt, and ineffective government and it is doubtful that it will soon forget it.

The most disturbing aspect of the sharp decline in the public's trust in government during the last few years is that it seems to have become part of a larger picture of public disillusionment. An ISR Index of Trust in People (expressing the individual's belief that other people can be trusted, that they usually try to be helpful, and that they will be fair in their personal dealings), which remained stable from 1964 to 1968, showed a sharp drop in 1972. Louis Harris found in a poll in 1973 that there had been a decline in public confidence in virtually all forms of leadership between 1966 and 1973. This included not only the various branches of government, but leaders of business and labor as well, and those professional men who have traditionally been held in high respect, doctors and scientists. Americans seem to be in a phase of disenchantment, their faith in their leaders and institutions badly compromised.

It is hardly necessary to extend this research documentation of the depressed state of public morale. The question is whether the nation must suffer slowly through this "crisis of confidence," or whether there are choices that can promote recovery. Without presuming to offer the solution to this problem, we can at least identify its major dimensions:

Public Corruption. A great many Americans were shocked and disillusioned at the revelations of illegal acts committed by members of the Nixon Administration, many of them involving the exchange of large sums of money. Whether or not such activities have been commonplace in previous administrations, they have never before been so thoroughly and convincingly displayed to the public. Legislation is now needed as it has never been needed before to reduce the opportunities for corruption in government and to convince a suspicious public that elections are not being bought and sold, that legislation is not being influenced by secret payoffs, and that their elected representatives are indeed as clean as they profess to be.

Crime. One of the most obvious and oppressive contributors to the decline in the quality of American life, especially in the cities, is the threat of crime. A society which lives in fear of assault is not living the good life. The causes of crime undoubtedly lie deep and must be treated, but we cannot wait until these causes are cured; we must treat the symptoms as well. Up to now we are not succeeding.

The Economy. Even though some economists still argue that our current inflation is not hurting the country seriously, the ordinary man and woman are convinced that they are being seriously hurt. The ISR's economic studies make clear that people regard their increases in pay as the just reward of their efforts, but they consider rising prices an unfair and unwarranted attack on their standard of living. The sense of economic inequity has risen sharply in the last years, largely as the result of price inflation, and it will remain high until some convincing level of price stability is achieved.

Racial Discrimination. We have seen in Figure VII-1 how alienated the black population of this country was by the Nixon Administration. Black achievements and rewards have risen substantially in the past decade but so have black aspirations. Black leadership does not expect to see discrimination wiped out by federal decree but it wants to see progress. A concerned government should be able to find ways to demonstrate to the black population that this country is still on the road to racial equality.

Community Membership

Despite the great mobility of the American people and the great distances covered by some, most Americans live their daily lives within rather narrow areal boundaries; within an hour's drive of their homes. They are realistically associated with restricted geographical communities, and these communities have significant meaning for the quality of their lives.

One of the major structural changes in our society since the turn of the century is the increasing urbanization of the population. A nation which was 60 percent rural in 1900 is now nearly 75 percent urban, and with the growth in total population the urban centers are greatly enlarged. The iniquities of urban life have been a favorite theme of social moralists for generations but the increasing urbanization of the population, the flight of the middle class to the suburbs, and the resulting creation of black ghettoes in the inner cities give the problem an unprecedented urgency.

There is now clear evidence that residents of the urban centers do not find their lives as satisfying and pleasant as people who live in smaller places. The 1971 ISR Study of Quality of Life found the following proportions of people scoring high in its Index of Sense of Well-being:

Metropolitan center	18%
Other cities over 100,000	24%
Suburbs	25%
Towns, small cities	32%
Rural	34%

When the study asked specifically how satisfied people were with the city or county in which they lived, a similar array of scores was found. The following proportions described themselves as completely satisfied with their community:

Metro center	20%
Other cities over 100,000	29%
Suburbs	36%
Towns, small cities	40%
Rural	48%

This generalized dissatisfaction reflects dissatisfaction with specific aspects of community life. People in the metropolitan centers are more often dissatisfied than people in smaller communities with their schools, their police protection, police-community relations, parks and playgrounds, garbage collection, and street repair. They are also of course far more likely to express fear of walking the streets at night. Forty-three percent of metropolitan residents say it is safe to walk outside at night as compared to 86 percent of the residents in rural areas. We do not have evidence from earlier years, which might document changes in these attitudes toward community over time, but it is apparent that at the moment the perceived quality of life in the metropolitan centers is very negative when compared to the rest of the country.

Satisfaction with the larger community is related to satisfaction with the neighborhood, although there is more dissatisfaction with the former than with the latter. Satisfaction with the neighborhood derives from a variety of factors, depending less on the physical characteristics of the surrounding area than on the way the residents perceive their neighbors and the upkeep of their neighbors' property. Residents of large cities are less satisfied with their neighborhoods on the average than residents of smaller places, and people who live in neighborhoods composed entirely of their own race tend to be more satisfied than residents of racially mixed neighborhoods. Blacks are substantially less satisfied with their neighborhoods than whites.

A succession of studies have shown that the social setting is a major determiner of the way people evaluate their neighborhoods. Areas which would be regarded as ugly and monotonous by professional architects and planners may be regarded as very satisfying by the people who live there. Satisfaction is associated with strong attachments to friends and family living in the neighborhood. Circumstances which enhance these social relationships may be expected to strengthen identification and satisfaction with neighborhood.

The flight to the suburbs which is taking place all over the country aggravates the problems naturally inherent in the crowded metropolitan situation. The metropolitan centers have an overrepresentation of young people under thirty and older people over sixty. The former group is the major source of crime, violence, and alienated behavior in any community, and the older people have serious financial problems growing out of their restricted income and rising taxes and costs of living. The continuing increase in the black proportion of the metropolitan populations is also creating new conditions in these large cities.

The trend of black-white relationships throughout the country is very difficult to plot. The civil rights laws of the 1960s have brought about obvious changes in the external aspects of racial contact and have opened opportunities for black people previously denied them. There is also evidence that substantial changes are taking place in the attitudes white people hold on racial issues. Although the question of busing has revealed strong resistance among white parents sending their children to schools which are heavily black, this appears to be based at least as heavily on considerations of social class as of race. Other indicators, based on ISR national surveys from 1964 to 1974, show a progressive shift away from traditional segregationist attitudes, especially among younger and better educated white people. A single comparison will indicate the character of the change; in 1964, 81 percent of an ISR national sample of white people reported that they had no black friends, in 1974 this figure had fallen to 53 percent.

The mood of black people is more difficult to assess. Interracial contact has clearly increased and there is very little separatist sentiment expressed by national samples of black people. On the other hand, black people are more dissatisfied than white people with many aspects of their lives, are more likely to feel themselves unfairly treated by public officials and less free to live the "kind of life they want to." As we have seen, the core of this dissatisfaction is located among young black men living in the metropolitan centers.

Many more blacks see a "lot of improvement" in the position of black people in the last few years than see "not much at all." But achievement is inevitably followed by rising aspirations and in many important respects blacks and whites appear to aspire to the same standards of achievement.

Accordingly, the dissatisfactions of blacks are greatest in those domains of life in which they most obviously fall below the national averages—standard of living, level of education, neighborhood quality, and housing. It is important to recognize, however, that black dissatisfactions are not entirely the result of their economic disadvantages; even when these are statistically removed, sizable discrepancies between black and white satisfaction levels remain. It is not likely that black dissatisfactions can be erased in this country by equating their material conditions of life to those of whites, as long as blacks feel themselves psychologically "put down" by the majority white population.

It is a safe prediction that the problems of the nation's communities will move forward on the national agenda during the next decade. The quality of life of the individual citizen is certainly influenced by what happens in Washington, but it is directly dependent on circumstances in the immediate environment and these appear to be deteriorating. There are at least four areas of critical choice:

1. Life in the metropolitan centers has become a national disgrace. Even though the residents may adapt to their beleaguered lives as they do to polluted air, the trauma of the cities demeans the entire nation. The metropolis is becoming a sociological disaster area; it deserves a higher priority than it is receiving.
2. Racial segregation in the urban communities is a leftover remnant of a culture of racial apartheid of which this country has largely freed itself. The aggravated question of school segregation is largely a problem of neighborhood segregation. This pattern is in part an economic problem, but it is maintained by a complex system of regulations, covert business practices, and various forms of white resistance; it is stubbornly resistant to change but it must be overcome. Black people cannot be expected to view themselves as free citizens unless they arc free to live where their means and their preferences take them.
3. The country needs some new ideas on ways to enhance the psychological quality of the neighborhoods. We are not likely to create a small town atmosphere in the large cities, but an effort should be made to offset the anonymity which develops in the urban situation. Greater decentralization of important community services—the police, for example, could reduce their impersonality and remoteness. The psychological gains in the quality of urban life could be far greater than the economic costs.
4. The nation is beginning to think seriously about the development of planned communities and there is evidence that the best of the new towns, such as Columbia and Reston, are very pleasing to their residents. As an alternative to the unappetizing prospect of confounding the metropolitan problems by additional growth, the possibilities of diverting a larger part of the population into smaller communities need to be seriously examined.

Living Standards

By simple objective standards, Americans probably have, on the average, the highest levels of housing in the world. But there is very great variation in the quality of housing in this country, ranging down into urban slums whose squalor exceeds almost anything to be seen in Northwestern Europe. Many Americans express some dissatisfaction about their residences and a sizable minority (28 percent) say they would like to move.

Satisfaction with housing is not a simple function of social status, reasonable as it might seem that higher status people would be more content with their more palatial quarters. The actual relationship between income or educational level and satisfaction with housing is very weak, being confounded by the counteractive effect of age. Young people are particularly critical of their housing, especially young parents with preschool children. They are in an upward-mobile stage of life, with aspirations their incomes may not be large enough to fulfill. Older people are generally content with their residences, although those who are retired may have very restricted incomes.

Two out of three American families live in detached, single-family houses and these people are more satisfied with their dwelling units than are people who live in other types of structures. Least satisfied by a considerable margin are those who live in multiple-unit apartment houses. Generally speaking, satisfaction is highest among those who have the most space per person; 40 percent of the people with less than one room per person are dissatisfied with their housing; of those with more than three rooms per person only 12 percent are discontent. This latter group includes older people whose children have grown, leaving them in a house which is larger than they need.

It has proved difficult to ascertain what the impact of housing is on the lives of the residents. People who express satisfaction with their housing also tend to be satisfied with their neighborhood and their community but it is not clear which of these domains of an individual's experience is preeminent. One's house or apartment can undoubtedly serve as a source of pleasure and gratification or it may contribute little. As students of this subject conclude, "People have shown themselves to be remarkably flexible in adapting to their housing environments."

As we have seen, people of very modest circumstances express surprisingly high levels of satisfaction with housing which is physically substandard and it has become clear that many well-intentioned forms of "urban renewal" are not panaceas for the ills they seek to cure.

The experience of Pruitt-Igoe, ending with the demolition of newly constructed public housing in St. Louis, illustrates the problems involved in attempting to upgrade the housing of urban slum dwellers without anticipation of the sociological side effects. The destruction of established neighborhoods and the transfer of the population to high-rise apartments may improve their housing amenities without improving the quality of their lives. Both improvements are needed.

The housing of black people presents a special problem. Over the last fifty years, blacks, like the rest of the population, have been moving out of the rural areas into the cities. There, partly as the result of racial discrimination and partly because of other economic considerations, they have inherited the most deteriorated areas. Not surprisingly we now find black people considerably more dissatisfied with their housing than white—even when income is held constant— and more anxious to move to different quarters (43 percent of blacks and 25 percent of whites).

The development of the black middle class has far-reaching implications, including the question of where these people will live. Those black families with adequate means show the same impulse to move out of the slum areas as earlier waves of prospering whites have shown. Relatively few middle class black people prefer to live in all-black neighborhoods; their problem is to find housing which is appropriate to their economic status, and this problem will increase as education and occupational levels among black people continue to rise. As we have noted earlier, white society has traditionally utilized a variety of maneuvers to keep these people within the confines of the ghetto and, despite various forms of open housing legislation, these practices have been very effective. High income blacks are clearly less satisfied with their housing than whites of equivalent income level, a discrepancy which must derive from the fact that black people are not really free to live where they wish.

This chapter cannot deal with the complexities of a national housing program. The housing industry is currently in a depressed condition, partly the result of reductions in federal support of new housing starts and partly a reflection of larger economic problems. It cannot be said that housing is the nation's highest priority problem; inflation and unemployment are certainly more pressing. Nevertheless, decisions regarding housing policies at both the federal and community level must be made and they will have important implications for the quality of life of the population.

1. It is not likely that the American ideal of a single-family house on a separate lot is going to be universally achieved in this country, despite the determined efforts of millions of city dwellers to find a home in the suburbs. Apartment living appears to be an inevitable attribute of urban life, despite the fact that apartments are the least popular form of dwelling unit in this country. We need multifamily dwellings that do not incorporate the characteristic disadvantages of conventional high-rise apartment complexes. It has become apparent that providing such dwellings is more than just an architectural and economic problem. Housing programs of the future need to be evaluated as to whether they will enhance or diminish the psychological quality of the community where they are located.

2. Housing may turn out to be the most intractable aspect of the racial problem in this country. Although the number of white people who say they would object to having black neighbors has declined substantially over the last twenty years, there is no doubt that much resistance remains. The problem for the next decade is to move away from housing policies which tend to maintain racial segregation and all its related consequences toward a policy which makes housing a positive contributor to improvement in the relations between the races.

Education

One of the most commonly cited indicators of the quality of national life is the level of attained education. We appear to assume that the higher the proportion of young people completing high school and college, the greater the national sense of fulfillment and well-being. Whether or not this assumption is justified, this country appears to be committed to (some would say obsessed with) education. We put far more money into formal education than any other country, and the bill continues to rise. Whether because of the strong orientation toward upward mobility in our culture, or a belief that education is a great democratic equalizer, or that it is the ultimate key to the good life, we seem intent on making every child a college graduate.

Earlier in this century the main burden of public education was contained between the ages of six and sixteen. Now we are concerned with compensatory training for the preschool children of disadvantaged parents, we send 80 percent of the eighteen-year cohort through high school, half of these go on to college, and we are just beginning to sense the ultimate demand for continuing education of some sort for people formerly considered beyond school age.

This extensive program has not been achieved without controversy, and there is an increasing demand for a demonstration of the value which society derives from these immense investments. There is, for example, an intense discussion going on at the present time as to whether the much-publicized Head Start program is achieving the goals it was intended to attain. Assessment studies have not produced consistent results and they raise questions about the age at which public education should begin and the procedures that are most effective. There is a rising call for "accountability," but in this area it is not yet clear what should be counted.

At the high school level national attention has been focused on the "dropouts." Much well-intentioned propaganda has been circulated implying dire consequences for any boy or girl who does not complete high school. It is not sufficiently recognized that dropping out is not a casual act; it customarily follows difficulties the child has had with authority figures, either because of delinquent or other disapproved behavior or because of academic failures. Many students who drop out of high school experience the change as a relief from persistent failure and a gain in self-esteem. Moreover, a certain proportion of dropouts eventually return to school and get their high school diplomas. It is not clear that a campaign to capture the rest of them would be socially profitable or desirable, unless it also solved the problems which caused them to leave.

Ten years ago a national survey showed that some 90 percent of the population felt a boy who had graduated from high school should certainly go to college if he had the chance and most of these felt the same way about a girl. Why is a college education so highly valued in this country? Largely, it is clear, because most people believe that it will lead to a better job. This rationale is particularly important among people who do not themselves have college training; those who have are more likely to emphasize other values. Despite occasional fulminations from and about college students in recent years, it is not likely that popular convictions about the value of college are less now than they were in 1964.

There is no reason why they should be. It is perfectly apparent that all the high-prestige professions are closed to people without college degrees. It is less obvious but nonetheless true that a college education is a very profitable investment. Of course income is not the only return from a college degree; there is also social status. Certainly one of the major appurtenances of social class in this country is level of education. More problematical is the effect of college education on other aspects of the quality of life—cultural, esthetic, familial, and community-oriented. These are researchable issues, but they have not been sufficiently investigated.

In short, it is not easy to assess the total value accruing to the nation from its support of higher education. National rates of economic growth are correlated with national educational levels and it may well be that our highly technical economy requires our present levels of educational achievement. On the other hand, our high investment in education has not produced a uniquely high level of social harmony and it would be hard to argue that the psychological quality of American life surpasses that of all other industrialized nations. College-educated people are better informed than other people and more likely to participate in community affairs, but it is not clear that their values or ethics were favorably influenced by their college experience. The nation has recently had a convincing demonstration of self-serving corruption by people of high education.

The reports of the Carnegie Commission on Higher Education have dealt extensively with the questions of who should go to college and who should pay. The Commission was concerned with the problem of access and the barriers which reduce the probability of young people's entering college. The proportion of high-test-score children who go on to college has increased substantially in recent years and it can be said that for visibly gifted children the barriers of income, race, and so on have been largely removed. This is not true, however, of children in the middle range of ability. The current spectacular inflation in tuition and other college costs aggravates this problem and is very probably responsible in large part for the tapering off in college enrollments which is now occurring.

The typical college student (or his parents) pays about one-half of the costs of his education; the federal government pays for a fifth and the rest comes from state and local sources. There is mounting evidence that these latter institutions are finding it hard to meet the demands which rising costs are putting on them. The resistance of state legislatures and city councils to increased budgets tends to shift the burden to the individual student or the federal government. It also raises questions as to the "productivity" of the colleges and universities, and stimulates the search for alternatives to the expensive campus style of higher education.

The critical choices the nation must deal with in the field of education are numerous; we mention only those which seem to us most important.

1. The most far-reaching problem is that of equal opportunity. There is no

doubt that our educational system has discriminated against the children of poor families and racial minorities, not only in the blatant manifestations associated with the "separate but equal" doctrine in the South, but throughout the country. On the average these children have less chance of realizing their educational potential than does a child of equal talent from a middle class white home. The concept of an "equal chance" is implicit in the democratic ethic in this country and the educational system ought to be a major instrument in achieving it.

2. Changing values and aspirations are leading many people to seek new ways of self-fulfillment and they look to further education for assistance. This is especially true of women, an increasing proportion of whom look beyond their commitment to marriage and childbearing, and think in terms of sustained involvement in or return to the work force. The educational establishment, oriented toward full-time young students, needs to find ways to accommodate women who want "second careers" along with other older people who wish to enhance their lives with intellectual stimulation. We need a system of higher education that allows and encourages adults to move in and out of it as their life circumstances and aspirations move them. It is ridiculous that "continuing education" should be defined as second class; it implies that the opposite—discontinued education—is somehow desirable. The initiative for changing our present rules and norms about higher education will not come primarily from within the institutions of higher education themselves. National aims and programs must be urged independently.

3. There is a great unresolved problem as to what the schools should teach. There are continuing complaints that the schools do not prepare students to make a living, always met by the argument that the schools have a more broadly educational obligation. The teaching of values is increasingly the subject of debate as the deterioration of public morality appears to grow. Our schools and colleges are basically very conservative institutions, frequently so apprehensive of public disapproval that they resist innovations and avoid asking unpopular questions. They need help.

4. It is doubtful if the current system of financing the educational investment can continue. There are substantial differences between the standards met by the different states and by communities within the states, largely resulting from differing local abilities to pay the school bill. The property tax as a major source of support of local school systems is under attack in the courts. The private schools are suffering from rising costs and their problems appear to be increasing. The need for alternatives to the current methods of meeting these costs becomes more pressing as time passes.

Delivery of Services

The Gross National Product is a summation of agricultural outputs, manufactured goods, and services. It was for many years a rapidly growing product, although that has been less true since the middle of the last decade. It has also been a product characterized by component changes, especially by a steady increase in the service component. Increasing affluence has meant not only a reduction in the proportion of income spent on food; it means an increase in the proportion of income that goes to buy services, directly for fees and indirectly through taxes.

The implications of these facts for the nature and quality of individual lives are profound. They remind us that, in spite of "do-it-yourself" slogans, we are less and less a do-it-yourself society. Furthermore, services that used to be performed within families or among friends are increasingly likely to be rendered for pay, directly or indirectly. And an increasing proportion of those increasing services are delivered through agencies of government—federal, state, and local.

Imagine, for example, a person who needs help—in finding a job or getting training for a better one, getting compensation for an injury or because of unemployment, getting medical care or hospitalization, obtaining money for the necessities of life, or getting old-age payments. These varied needs are likely to be expressed, and fulfilled or frustrated, by means of procedures that have become familiar to all of us—a kind of encounter between an individual and an organization.

On one side of the desk sits the applicant for service, with all the needs, experiences, and idiosyncratic characteristics that have combined to bring him there. On the other side of the desk sits a person whose function it is to determine the validity of the presenting request, the goodness of fit between it and the franchise of the agency, and thus the entitlement of the person to service. It is likely to be a brief conversation, although the preliminaries may be long. It ends with a decision that may satisfy or frustrate the presenting request. It may also end the person's contact with the agency, although there may of course be other contacts.

To the extent that the individual's access to needed services is granted or denied on the basis of such transactions, they do much to determine the quality of individual life. Yet there has been a conspicuous neglect of systematic assessment of the quality and efficiency with which public services are delivered by public agencies. The phrase *evaluation research* has become popular but little evaluation has been done. Moreover, the small fraction of evaluated programs is by no means representative, the research is sporadic, the criteria are often superficial, and the results are not geared to the improvement of agency functioning.

These facts would be less important if the usual mechanisms of consumer choice were operative, the usual range of alternative sources of supply available, and if the usual significant though imperfect competition existed among suppliers. For most government services none of these conditions exists; rather, a unique source of service subject only to remote and indirect kinds of control confronts a citizen in need of the service purveyed.

Admittedly, the problems of assessing the quality of government services are substantial. There are no uniform standards in terms of which assessment can be made, no agreed-upon measures of quality or efficiency. Moreover, the "product" is frustratingly intangible. Once given, it cannot be "recalled" like a defective automobile. The transaction cannot be directly inspected after the fact, and sometimes the only evidence of good treatment or bad is the recollection of the client and staff member.

The difficulty of evaluation, however, is outweighed by its importance. The summation of such service-seeking experiences for any individual says a great deal about the quality of his or her life. The summation of such experiences for a particular group or category—say, blacks or women, elderly people or adolescents—can tell us to what extent services are adequate and to what extent, adequate or not, they are allocated with equity. The summation of such service transactions for a particular agency, would provide a basis for evaluating its performance in relation to its mission and in comparison with other agencies.

A recent nationwide study by the Survey Research Center has provided the beginnings of such data for government services in the sectors of employment service, job training, worker's compensation, unemployment compensation, public assistance, hospital and medical care, and retirement benefits. It tells us that knowledge, utilization, and evaluation of these services vary a great deal.

To begin with, utilization is widespread; the majority of adults report contact with government agencies in at least one of these service sectors. Employment services and unemployment compensation are most widely used, with about one-fourth of all adults having used each of these services. The low utilization of some other services, however, does not signify a lack of need. For example, of the many people who reported needing job training at some time (30 percent of all adults), relatively few (9 percent) actually received training through a government agency. The main reason for failure to utilize a needed service is lack of knowledge; difficulty in getting to the service agency is the next most serious obstacle. There is a clear indication for better communication regarding the availability of some services—especially those in the employment sector. Many more people report a need for job-finding services than for public assistance.

Client evaluation of the services received was more positive than negative; about two-thirds of all people who had dealt with some government service agency reported themselves satisfied, at least "fairly satisfied." There were, however, substantial differences among agencies in this respect. Retired persons, dealing with offices of the Social Security Administration, were most favorable about almost all aspects of the agency—ease of finding the right person to deal with, fairness of treatment, efficiency, etc. Welfare and health services were generally at the bottom of the list on all attributes.

Finally, the Survey Research Center study revealed certain paradoxes in American attitudes toward government and its agencies. One such paradox involves the relationship between specific and general evaluations of government, or in other words, the relationship between experience and stereotypes. People's specific experiences are consistently more positive than their general attitudes.

For example, 80 percent of clients interviewed said that they had received fair treatment in their contact with government agencies, but only 42 percent rated government offices in general as being fair.

Another paradox has to do with public perceptions of private versus public service agencies. Among people who see a difference between the two, private enterprise is favored on all counts asked about—taking care of problems, giving considerate treatment, giving fair treatment, avoiding mistakes, correcting mistakes, and giving prompt service. Nevertheless, when people are asked how a long list of major social tasks should be dealt with, they express a preference for government rather than business, and for state and federal agencies rather than local units.

Among the questions which confront us are the following:

1. Shall there be established a general policy of monitoring the performance of public service agencies? If so, a number of lesser but very difficult issues arise—for example, the establishment of criteria of performance that go beyond merely counting papers or people, the organization of the assessment effort so that it is appropriately independent in its conclusions, and the creation of arrangements that will assure the utilization of such evaluative data for the improvement of service.

2. Shall there be a serious effort to inform people of the services that are available to them? This could be opposed on the grounds of increasing citizen dependence on government, overloading agencies already overloaded, or the ever controversial increasing tax burden. Nevertheless, the facts are that many people in need are unaware of sources of help.

3. Are we prepared to take on the sensitive and politically difficult task of simplifying complex and overlapping service functions, clarifying oversophisticated and ambiguous criteria of entitlement and otherwise bringing other service sectors at least to the level of satisfactoriness reported for the retirement sector?

4. Most difficult of all, perhaps, are the choices implied by the expressed paradox of demand for, dependence on, and distrust of, government sources of service. People seem not to relate their own specific experiences to the remote policymakers and programs on which they depend. In place of a conception of public programs and policies, people turn to a personal image of "politicians in Washington." This is a stance that is all too vulnerable to demagogy and populist oversimplifications. The need is to involve people in policy formulation and thus to enhance their understanding. Many attempts have been made, within and outside government; more effort and more creativity are needed. Citizen understanding and involvement remains a survival problem for democracy.

Domain of Work

A sort of national gossip seems to have developed with respect to work. The gist of it is that the work ethic has deteriorated almost beyond recognition, that most workers' behavior on the job ranges from apathy to insubordination, and that there is a special alienation from work on the part of the young. Along with these statements about bad going to worse there is a common assertion that people work less time than they used to at some unspecified moment in the past—fewer hours per day, days per week, weeks per year, and years per lifetime. Like most gossip this is a fascinating mix of truth, distortion, and outright error. Data are available to provide correction in some respects and counter-opinions can be offered in others.

With respect to time spent at work, the record is well documented. Hours of work dropped steadily during the early half of the century—from an average of almost sixty hours per week in 1900 to thirty-eight hours in 1940. Since that time, however, working hours have been quite stable. Irregularities seem to reflect the availability of work rather than voluntary absences of an extended sort. The trend to annual paid vacations and regularized retirement (usually at age sixty-five) persists, although millions of workers have yet to receive either benefit.

The greatest continuing trend in the labor force, of course, is its growth, in part a reflection of population growth. But the labor force has grown also because of the steady increase in the proportion of women who work outside their homes. The 1870 Census reported women workers as only one out of seven; the 1970 Census showed them to be about one in three, and the trend continues. Meanwhile, the proportion of white-collar workers has more than tripled, the percentage of manual laborers has reduced almost correspondingly, and the percentage of farmers and farm workers has dropped even more steeply.

Data on job satisfaction and motivation are not available for times long past, nor were they available on a national basis until very recently. Since 1935, however, more than 2,000 studies of job satisfaction have been published and many more have gone deservedly unpublished. Despite differences in coverage and methods of measurement, there is a certain consistency in the response patterns: few people call themselves extremely satisfied with their jobs, but fewer still report extreme dissatisfaction. The modal response is on the positive side of neutrality—"pretty satisfied," and there is no evidence of significant change.

This stability is well established for recent years. In 1969 the Department of Labor commissioned the first nationwide survey of the quality of working conditions and satisfaction with work as reported by workers; a similar study, under the same sponsorship, was done in 1973. (Both studies were done by the Survey Research Center.) When the results of the two studies are compared, very few significant changes appear, either in overall job satisfaction or its major facets—comfort, challenge, financial rewards, relations with coworkers, and adequacy of materials and resources for getting the work done.

There is, however, some evidence of decrease in work involvement, as measured by asking employed people whether they would continue working even if they "were to get enough money to live as comfortably as you'd like for the rest of your life." Almost two-thirds of all workers say that they would continue to work under these improbable circumstances, a statement that hardly suggests deep-seated alienation. On the other hand, the figure was insignificantly higher than that in 1969, and in 1958 (when the question was first asked) 80 percent of the respondents (all men) said they would go on working. Moreover, young people are *more* likely than the middle-aged or elderly to say they would prefer to go on working irrespective of economic need. We conclude that there may well be some tendency toward reduced commitment to work, but that the majority continues to be work-oriented.

Such overall generalizations must be qualified by the considerable differences that exist and persist among subgroups. People in different occupational groups differ in reported quality of working conditions, with professional and technical employees at the top, machine operators and laborers at the bottom, and craftworkers and white-collar workers between. Young people report lesser quality of working conditions than those older, blacks lesser quality of working conditions than whites, grade school graduates less than college graduates. Such differences, however, appear to be stable rather than changing.

Changes have occurred during the past few years in a few respects. In 1973 more union members reported problems with "how democratically their unions were run" than had done so in 1969, and more reported problems with "how well their unions were managed." More women reported discrimination than had done so in 1969, although the proportion remains small—8 percent in 1969 and 13 percent in 1973. Both figures are almost certainly underestimates of the actual amount of discrimination. A comparison of employed women with men of the same occupation, education, hours worked per week, supervisory responsibility, and seniority on the job and with the employer shows that the women earned $3,241 less than the men, on the average, in 1973. A similar difference had been computed in 1969.

Blacks, on the other hand, report no more experience of discrimination at work in 1973 than they had reported in 1969. The percentage of black workers who said that they felt "in *any* way discriminated against because of race" was 17.4 in 1969 and 14.9 in 1973. A difference that small could have occurred by chance, but it may show the beginning of a trend. Moreover, among blacks who reported discrimination, few called it a "great problem." These findings certainly show no increase in experienced racial discrimination, and they may well show some progress. Nevertheless, they show also the persistence of discrimination in the face of legal and organizational efforts to eliminate it.

Past stability in people's attitudes toward work may be reassuring, but it offers no guarantees for the future. Moreover, a concern for the quality of life leads one to ask whether acceptance and faintly positive responses to work could not become enthusiasm, thoroughgoing satisfaction, and self-actualization. Much is known about the job characteristics that evoke strong positive feelings: status, variety, "whole" rather than fractionated tasks, autonomy and control with respect to pace and method, considerate supervision, involvement in decisions, opportunity for informal interaction with peers, adequate pay, and opportunity for promotion.

Not every job can have these properties, but research suggests that most jobs can be redesigned to incorporate some of them, and that the quality of working would be improved by such changes. Such welcome experimentation is going on, as a few managements try programs of job enrichment, job enlargement, various forms of participative decision-making, and other kinds of "organization development."

But the efforts are sporadic, underfinanced, and little-measured, and there is corresponding danger that they will come and go as fads rather than contribute anything enduring to organizational knowledge and practice. It is ironic that America must turn to the activities of other countries—the much-publicized modification of the assembly line at Volvo, for example—to see what can be learned from experiments to improve the quality of the work experience.

Many such experiments—pilot plants in the organization of work—are needed to determine how far we can go in building into all jobs the qualities that enhance much professional, managerial, and scientific work. The nature of such changes, and their costs and benefits are well within the capabilities of existing research, but the research has not been done.

Among the choices and questions that confront us in the domain of work are the following:

1. Discrimination against blacks, women, and certain minority groups persists in the work situation. Will we act further to eliminate it, and assess continually our progress toward that goal?
2. Things counted and measured tend to be acted upon; those uncounted are often neglected in other ways as well. Will we institute continuing national measures of the quality of the work experience, so that its improvement becomes a national goal—like the reduction of unemployment or air pollution?
3. Will we launch a series of major experiments and demonstration projects on the quality of job content? The work *experience* is as much an outcome of the job as the work product, and it may have equally important implications for the national well-being.
4. Finally, what national policy shall we evolve with respect to work and its tangible products? To what extent shall technological advances be translated into increased volume of consumer goods, to what extent reduced hours or years of work, to what extent improvement in the public environment, etc.?

Leisure and Recreation

Leisure has been less researched than work, and it is less understood. Even the definition of leisure is uncertain, although the evidence of leisure activities is all around us. Skiing, with its ramifying requirements and embellishments, is on the way to becoming a sizable industry; many roads are clogged with recreation vehicles; campgrounds require reservations; and tennis clubs, indoors and out, are springing up in growing numbers.

These developments are typical of others in the emerging "leisure industry," and they reflect an availability of time and money in combinations not previously available.

In 1972 there were published the results of an international study of time use, which included estimates of time spent each day in each of thirty-seven major activities. Adult Americans reported about two hours per day spent on all leisure activities exclusive of the mass media, and about an equal amount in media-oriented leisure, the bulk of it watching television. Indeed, no leisure activity comes close to equalling the hour-and-one-half or so that television claims among adult Americans. And that counts only the time for which watching was the primary activity. By comparison, study averages five to ten minutes, religion about the same, and organizational activities no more.

These data remind us of the two broad hypotheses that have been advanced by students of leisure to explain and predict its patterns in American life. The hypotheses, basically incompatible but each yet to be proved or disproved, are as follows:

1. The *compensatory hypothesis* states that leisure activities are chosen in a way that balances or compensates for the required activity pattern of work. Thus, the sedentary worker seeks physical outlets during leisure hours; the person who must engage in meaningless and repetitive work finds leisure activities that are varied and meaningful, and thus maintains a tolerable sense of self.

2. The consistency or *spillover hypothesis* proposes that we seek consistency or perhaps that we become what we are required to do. Thus, the worker in an automated plant goes from watching dials to watching television; the craftsman from his trade to tinkering with his car; the business executive to some business-like leisure venture—raising and selling horses or leading community organizations.

A plausible possibility is that both these predictions apply, and that the research task will be to discover the circumstances and the people for which each applies and the consequences for person, family, and community. Some research has been done on factors that facilitate various uses of leisure time. In addition to the obvious requirements of time and money, accessibility plays a substantial role. A comparative study of planned and unplanned residential environments showed that many outdoor recreational activities are engaged in according to the distance from home that must be transversed. Hence the frequency of swimming, boating, tennis, walking, and cycling in such communities as Reston and Columbia.

Among the problems and choices before us with respect to leisure are the following:

1. How much of time and resources shall we invest as a nation in the encouragement of various recreational forms and in providing facilities for recreation? It is perhaps ironic that present methods of computing Gross National Product still neglect or underestimate such investment.
2. To what extent are we prepared to initiate the changes in policies and institutional arrangements that would make the allocation of leisure more equitable and more satisfying? Some people have too much and some too little, depending not only on the amount and source of their incomes but also on their time of life.
3. We must choose also how much of leisure facilities shall be marketed according to private choices and discretionary income (like ski holidays and indoor tennis).
4. Even more difficult, perhaps, is the choice with respect to active versus passive forms of leisure. Can we be comfortable about a democracy in which the average number of minutes per day spent watching television is twenty times the number spent in all voluntary organizational activities?

Standard of Living

Much is known about our national economic life—the amount of Gross National Product, the allocation of personal income, the nature of savings and expenditures, reported intentions to purchase or save, perceptions of economic well-being, and optimism or pessimism about the future. At present the long-range upward trends in such indicators are obscured if not obliterated for many people by the effects of increasing inflation and unemployment, and by the fear that the increase will continue. These trends, short-range and long, were well summarized in the recent testimony of F. Thomas Juster before the Joint Economic Committee of the Congress and in a recent article of his, titled "Inflation and Consumer Saving Behavior."

Professor Juster points out that real disposable income in the United States has expanded rapidly and consistently for several decades, slowing down briefly during periods of recession and expanding more rapidly during periods of recovery. About these facts there is general agreement. Since the recession of 1969-70, however, the data are more ambiguous or at least the agreement is less. From 1969 to 1973 money income increased at an annual rate of 8.6 percent. Conventional adjustments for the effects of inflation reduce this to 4.8 percent as the growth rate of real income; And if this is in turn adjusted to take account of population growth and the number of new households, the annual per household increase in real income amounts to only 1.4 percent. This performance is of course much worse if one examines the period from 1969-70 to the present, since the worst post-World War II recession began in late 1973.

Economists are not agreed on the preferred manner of making such adjustments, but the current attitudes of consumers are consistent with the more pessimistic adjustment procedure. Consumers state that their experienced growth in real income has been unsatisfactorily low since the end of the 1960s. They state in increasing numbers that they are worse off, or at least no better off than they were in the past; they are increasingly pessimistic about the short-term future and even about the longer term. Charts on which economist George Katona and his colleagues have been mapping such consumer sentiments over the years must now be redrawn; the data have literally dropped off the conventional lower line.

The reasons for the slow growth of real income as measured are not all clear, but some factors stand out, among them the sluggish behavior of productivity (in spite of an annual growth rate of more than 2 percent in the size of the labor force). The reasons for slow productivity are also arguable. Many managements cite restrictive behavior and lack of effort by the work force, and counteraccusations come from labor. An additional factor is the diversion of some investment to uses that are socially important but nonproductive as production is usually defined. Installing equipment to retain fly-ash, neutralize air-borne toxic materials, or recapture dangerous particles in industrial waste may add to the quality of life and the prospects for it. As things are now counted, however, they add to industrial costs without adding to productivity.

Such problems increase the inflationary tendency of the economy, which is certainly one of the chief problems of the moment. Data from the consumer surveys of the Survey Research Center suggest that it is also a problem much misunderstood, at least in terms of traditional economic predictions. Traditional economic logic argues that the expectation of inflation causes a movement from money into goods, that consumers reduce savings and increase spending in order to avoid still higher prices at a later date. American consumers have at times acted in ways consistent with this view, but they are not now doing so.

As Professor Juster puts it: This analysis leads to the conclusion that high or uncertain rates of price inflation will tend to be positively associated with the rate of personal saving, basically because inflation produces uncertainty about real income and thus induces conservative consumption planning.

When people experience inflation, they thus report that this is a "bad time to buy." They expect more inflation, but the expectation is accompanied by pessimistic expectations about their own prospective well-being and about the outlook for the economy as a whole. That pessimism has become controlling, and it leads people to guard against possible economic adversity in the future by holding down expenditures and maximizing savings now. Table VII-1 summarizes some of the data on which these interpretations are based.

All these findings argue that inflation and the expectation of more inflation are primarily responsible for people's pessimism about the economy and about their own economic prospects. This in turn leads to the restriction of expenditures, as consumers decide that the advantages of "buying now" are outweighed by uncertainty about their own future incomes.

Table VII-1
Recent Trends in Selected Consumer Survey Measures* (Survey Research Center, The University of Michigan)

Survey Measure	5/72	8/72	11/72	2/73	5/73	8/73	11/73	2/74	5/74	8/74	10/74	2/75	5/75	8/75
Personal Financial Situation														
Compared to year ago														
Better	45%	34%	37%	34%	33%	29%	37%	29%	33%	27%	27%	25%	26%	29%
Worse	19	18	22	28	30	36	31	41	34	42	44	44	39	36
Expected in next year														
Better	38	33	31	31	28	25	30	22	29	24	24	22	30	25
Worse	6	7	9	13	17	19	14	22	18	22	25	19	12	16
Expectations about General Business														
Next 12 months														
Optimistic	44	54	46	35	30	26	26	13	26	20	12	15	34	36
Pessimistic	26	15	22	35	47	48	47	68	51	57	67	70	43	39
Next 5 years														
Optimistic	26	32	28	17	18	17	17	10	16	14	10	8	13	18
Pessimistic	37	26	35	45	49	50	49	64	51	54	57	61	48	43
Expected Price Change														
Less than 5%	28	34	34	26	19	10	13	15	13	14	10	11	12	20
10% or more	4	5	5	13	12	21	14	28	25	25	32	16	8	19

*Proportion of all households in survey.

Among the difficult choices in the present economic situation are the following:

1. We must assess the relative risks of sluggish growth and recession as compared to accelerating demand and demand-induced inflation. Professor Juster argues that policies which induce further retrenchment in the consumer sector run a serious risk of producing a deeper recession.
2. We must arrive at a series of priorities with respect to consumer goods and such "public goods" as cleaner air, purer water, and a more tenable environment.
3. We must make those political moves that will reestablish the believability of the national government in economic affairs. It is not merely that people doubt the economic omniscience of their national leaders; little blame attaches to that. But people do not believe that the government will do the things it announces it will do—whether the announcement is the control of prices or wages. That skepticism has been born of sad experience, and only a new experience of truthfulness will replace it with trust.

Conclusion

The people of this country have come to the end of an age of innocence. For generations we have assumed without much question that the American way of life is not only the most affluent but also the most advanced, the most open, the most peace-loving, the most moral of any on earth. The experience of the last decade has made it increasingly difficult to maintain this naive image and we are now asking ourselves questions we would not have thought to ask as recently as twenty-five years ago. What is the real quality of American life and how is it changing? This will not be an easy question to answer but we believe it is the fundamental question of our time.

VIII

An Analysis of Forces for Change in American Higher Education and Nontraditional Responses to Them by Colleges and Universities

David Pierpont Gardner

Universities and colleges in the United States are confronted with an array of fiscal, educational, social, and political problems as unrelenting as they are seemingly unresolvable within the context of established educational conventions.

The higher learning in America, for example, is expected to cope with the diverse wants and needs of a student body and faculty more heterogeneous and less patient with the settled form of learning than before, with shifting governmental and social priorities which tend both to spread and diminish resources available to colleges and universities, with costs which are rising at a rate faster than that of the nation's production of goods and services as a whole, with the rise of public interest in higher education and the consequent intervention of various governmental agencies into the internal affairs of such institutions, and with the unmet educational needs of adults and unequal educational opportunities for the poor, among others. Thus, single-valued forecasts and perspectives which tended to dominate academic planning and expansion in the 1960s ought not to limit the present range of policy options nor compromise promising alternative educational strategies, for it seems quite likely that the uncritical expansion of our institutions of higher education along established and familiar lines is, for the most part, a thing of the past. "Hardly anywhere," as Roy Niblett has observed, "is it generally believed that the recipe for meeting the next twenty years is to continue to do, only better, what has been done in the last twenty."[1] The more likely prospect is that higher education in this decade and the next can be expected to assimilate or at least accomodate a variety of alternative, experimental, and unconventional educational forms and structures. This will be so for a number of reasons.

1. *The impact on the educational system by the drive for greater access to higher education and more equal educational opportunity.* Enrollments in America's colleges and universities doubled during every decade to a decade-and-a-half for the past century and doubled again during the 1960s. Roughly 4 percent of college-age youth were enrolled in America's institutions of higher learning in 1900; today, more than 40 percent are enrolled; and estimates are that nearly two out of three of the age group will be enrolled as this century closes. The pressure to expand has been and will remain relentless although the rate of increase will drop and the pattern of formal enrollments will shift somewhat within the established learning system, away from the senior colleges and universities and towards the community colleges and post-secondary vocational and technical schools and institutes. The nation is moving from mass to universal-access higher education, or perhaps more accurately, to universal post-secondary education.

The most evident and consistent pressure for expansion in recent years has come from the poor, the educationally disadvantaged, and the ethnic minorities, primarily black, brown, and American Indian, for whom higher education until now has not been a real option; and from the federal government, politically attuned to the demand and generally supportive of such educational aspirations and stirrings. The proportion of such college-age youth enrolling in America's colleges and universities has steadily risen in recent years owing to (a) the maturing of the comprehensive secondary school system; (b) the growth and development of the community college system with its "open door" policy of admissions; and (c) the huge student aid program which so dramatically increased since the close of World War II, both in scope of program and scale of assistance.

The demand for higher education, especially in recent years, as Cerych and Furth have suggested, "has led not only to massive expansion of enrollments but also to a change in the clientele of higher education, i.e., to a considerably increased variety and greater heterogeneity of aptitudes, abilities, motivations and expectations of students with regard to their future education, professional career and life in general."[2]

As recently as a decade ago, it was assumed that the extension of educational opportunities to the poor, the educationally disadvantaged, and the ethnic minorities could be accomplished merely by availing such new students of the same programs, resources, and academic conventions as had been extended in earlier years to the upwardly mobile middle class. The assumption proved to be false not only because a conflict ensued between the new students and the forms and practices of established institutions but also because of the unanticipated rejection of conventional academic values by significant numbers of middle class students, what Trow calls the "involuntary student" and what Ashby describes as the "semi-drafted student"—students, in short, who feel compelled to attend college for educationally irrelevant reasons.

Thus, America's universities and colleges found themselves fighting on two fronts in the 1960s; and they are still skirmishing today. The turmoil carries very real implications for the life pattern of the educational system itself and long-accepted values of academic life: "patient inquiry, the sequential development of ideas, the emphasis on reasoned discussion and criticism, the continual reference to evidence, and the special attention to negative evidence . . ." as Martin Trow describes it.[3]

The academic environment can no longer be regarded "as the sole preserve of the faculty and administration," Clark Kerr has observed,[4] for students will take a more active interest than in the past in the quality of teaching, the form and substance of the curriculum, the supporting counseling and advisory services, and the costs to them of pursuing their studies.[5]

2. *An inability to fund higher education in the future as in the past.* Higher education is facing more than a financial crisis about which much has already been written. It is faced instead with the gloomy prospect that if the system merely grows and spends money consistent with established forms and patterns, it will almost certainly soon fall well short of what is needed merely to survive. The Carnegie Commission has reported that expenditures by the nation's colleges and universities approximated one percent of the GNP in 1960, two percent in 1970 and, if present trends persist, would equal roughly 3.3 percent in 1980, even though not more than 2.7 percent is expected to be forthcoming from the various funding agencies or parties by that time. Budgets will be harder to come by; enrollments will be relatively stable (at least in conventional academic institutions), competition for resources by other social agencies and service institutions will become more intense, costs will rise more rapidly than the GNP owing to the labor intensive nature of educational institutions generally and, as Clark Kerr has suggested, "the lack of productivity increase will become a widely discussed naked fact instead of a harsh reality hidden behind the cloak of expanding numbers."[6]

Colleges and universities have generally responded to existing fiscal pressures not by reconsidering goals or by altering the educational process, but instead by across-the-board cost-cutting by delaying expenditures that would otherwise have been made on ordinary administrative support services, and the development of academic programs, e.g., deferred maintenance, postponed capital projects; postponed expansion of existing academic programs, or introduction of new ones. Such economies are only marginal and temporary, however, as Virginia Smith of the Carnegie Commission has pointed out, for these measures avoid the problem of productivity in the teaching and learning process itself.[7] This is not to say that such economies bear no relationship to the effective performance of an institution's educational mission and to its momentum. They do, but in less visible and immediate ways. Real increases in productivity will occur only if the educational process itself is changed, that is only if the time and spread of curriculum, the form and methods of institutions, and the relationship of the student to the institution are somehow modified.

There is no doubting the fiscal crisis afflicting the higher learning in America. It is real, omnipresent and foreboding.[8] The reasons are many and complex: (a) a prolonged and costly war in Southeast Asia; (b) student unrest in the 1960s and early 1970s; (c) inflation; (d) competing social programs, especially in government-sponsored welfare and health services; (e) disenchantment with research; and (f) a startling loss of public confidence in the entire enterprise. "Taxpayers, legislators and private donors," as Lord Ashby has reported, "want universities to demonstrate (i) that they can govern themselves in reasonable tranquility; (ii) that they are being run efficiently . . .; and (iii) that they can restore a consensus about 'a unifying set of purposes—purposes that the supporting public can understand and defer to'."[9]

These pressures arising out of these problems have translated into institutional budgets inadequate to maintain, much less to strengthen, existing programs and practices or to permit growth within the conventional context. It should be evident that any significant expansion of the system along familiar lines must anticipate some wearing away of standards and capability.

3. *A marked increase of interest and involvement in the internal affairs of higher education by government at all levels.* "The greatest change in governance now going on is not the rise of student power or faculty power but the rise of public power," Clark Kerr noted not long ago in his David D. Henry Lecture at the University of Illinois.[10]

Public control of America's colleges and universities is steadily increasing. The involvement by state budget experts, governors, legislative committees, federal agencies, and the courts in the internal affairs of our institutions of higher education is unquestionably increasing and in the most fundamental of ways. Formerly independent institutions of higher learning are now "coordinated" if not actually merged, as state government especially undertakes to subject them to essentially the same bureaucratic controls, measures, expectations, and efficiencies as apply to any other "state agency," and massive bureaucracies within statewide systems are rising up to do the job.

Regulation of the sort now characterizing some state systems of higher education is giving rise to standardized course offerings for lower division work; a standard academic calendar; a mandated uniform teaching load; a common salary schedule for faculty; and a standard formula for space utilization and the acquisition of books for the library—often as though there were no distinctions between institutions in the quality of their work, in their respective missions, in their learning environment, in the desires and abilities of their student bodies, in their basic character, in their inner selves.

It is equally true, of course, that the rise in public power and the corresponding diminution of institutional autonomy have created conditions favorable to the creation of new or affiliated institutions with unconventional approaches to teaching and learning which, in earlier years and times, would not have been encouraged, much less tolerated by the "educational establishment," such new ventures, for example, as the Empire State College in New York, the Extended University in California, the State University of Nebraska and Minnesota Metropolitan State College, among several others. The nontraditional programs fostered by these institutions, as might be expected, are perceived by some as a boon both to higher education and to those it serves for they promise to break the time, space, and age constraints which have always bound conventional learning patterns; and they are seen by others as debasing the essential nature of the university itself together with its standards and further dispersing scarce educational resources.

Whatever the view, the fact remains that a heightened public interest in the affairs of our colleges and universities tends, over time, to make them more alike and to enlarge the scope of their service, the breadth of their programs, and the number and nature of persons deserving of their talents, time, resources, and programs.

4. *The preference of some full-time students to mix part-time study with work and the growing desire of the fully employed to combine work on the job or at home with periodic full-time or part-time study.* Pressure on the higher learning system to expand and accommodate the educational needs of adult students wishing to study part time and the desire of some full-time students of college age to opt for part-time study is a relatively new phenomenon but one quite likely, in the long run, to effect significant changes in the form and structure of American higher education.

Adults, because of work schedules, family or home responsibilities, financial constraints, and cultural or geographical isolation cannot now effectively enroll in most degree programs offered by America's colleges and universities; and this is especially true of the more prestigious universities. The impediments are both philosophical and procedural and are deeply rooted in institutional prejudice and practice. Adult students seeking further educational opportunity do so for a variety of reasons: (a) to conclude degree programs started but unfinished in earlier years; (b) to shift careers at midpoint; (c) to improve competencies in established career patterns; (d) to enhance intellectual, social, cultural, political, and environmental understanding and awareness; and (e) to initiate studies in later life because the opportunity or motivation was lacking earlier.

A recent report of the Carnegie Commission on Higher Education, in a general discussion of the flow of students into and through the formal structure of higher education, suggested educationally and socially relevant reasons for encouraging the enrollment of adults:

Society would gain if work and study were mixed throughout a lifetime, thus reducing the sense of sharply compartmentalized roles of isolated students v.

workers and of youth v. isolated age. The sense of isolation would be reduced if more students were also workers and if more workers could also be students; if the ages mixed on the job and in the classroom in a more structured type of community; if all the members of the community valued both study and work and had a better chance to understand the flow of life from youth to age. Society would be more integrated across the lines that now separate students and workers, youth and age.[11]

If American higher education should rid itself of barriers to adult part-time study, it would also provide options to the "involuntary" student of college age now attending full time: either deferred enrollment, of recurring periods of study, or continuous part-time study mixed with work; in short; it would have cleared away the assumption, as Ashby has put it, "that full-time education should be digested all in one gulp, from age five to age twenty-two."[12] It would also introduce highly motivated adults into the system and reduce the enrollments of "semi-drafted" students whose presence now tends to weaken the overall effectiveness of the learning process.

The changing nature of the job market itself may very well prove to be the most important single influence in bringing about the interweaving of work and study that the Carnegie Commission has favored. More jobs are requiring some basic skills and knowledge in order to begin work in the anticipation that such will be coupled later with recurring periods of study. Thus, the spacing of work and study may come to favor a pattern which reduces the period of time in early life for formal education, while increasing the periods of study available later on according to some schedule of alternating periods of study and work—or as some labor-management agreements in recent years have called for, a blending of part-time work with part-time study.

Gösta Rehn, director of Manpower and Social Affairs for the Organization for Economic Cooperation and Development anticipates that the established forms and patterns of the higher learning will be profoundly affected by already perceived trends in the more industrialized nations of the world, e.g., a progressive reduction in the hours of work per week, accompanied by a rising level of real income per hour, an expansion of the service sector of the economy with its more flexible working schedule, a rising rate of urbanization accompanied by changes in life styles and values which mitigate against rigid and intense working conditions and for a more varied and enriching pattern of life experiences.

5. *The influence of communication technology on the typical time, space and age requirements of the conventional learning process—what a recent Carnegie Commission Report calls the "first great technological revolution in five centuries."*[13] Of the revolutions taking place in our time, one of the most significant and exciting, from the viewpoint of educators, must surely be the one in telecommunications and educational technology. The impact of scientific and technological breakthroughs in this area will, in very major ways, affect the

entire educational establishment, and perhaps higher education even more than the lower grades.

The new electronics has already impacted research and administrative methods in higher education and is now moving to transform the library and the teaching process itself. The instructional uses of such devices as cable television, cable and television technology in general, microwave, videophone, microfiche, digitalization and switching, long-range facsimile, communication satellites, and the computer, among others, may offer "the greatest single opportunity for academic change on and off campus," the Carnegie Commission has suggested, and wil make it possible for education to be brought

... to the sick, the handicapped, the aged, the prisoners, the members of the armed forces, persons in remote areas, and to many adults who could attend classes on campus but who will find instruction at home more convenient. It can create new uses for leisure time, can facilitate job to job movement through new training, and can improve community participation by imparting greater skill and knowledge to citizens.[14]

As the multi-channel, closed circuit education TV systems develop and cable television expands its network, satellites will tend to diminish the now dominant position of the networks, or at least will very likely diversify them. As the use of satellites increases, there will be an obvious trend toward the internationality of learning as such barriers of distance, geography, race nationality, language, and religion are modified— a matter posing both immense problems and immensely exciting possibilities, especially for educators.

Within the context of domestic educational change, these forms of technology will most surely be converted into uses implicating virtually every aspect of our educational institutions. They will influence our time and places of instruction, our methods of teaching and our curricula, and indeed, after a period of careful and systematic experimentation with such forms of education, they may well prove to be desired modes of instruction for large numbers of students and prospectively more cost-effective as well.

Educational technology, however, has not been fully and effectively employed by higher education for a variety of reasons: (a) hesitant acceptance by faculty and student alike; (b) compartmentalization of the technological resources from the educational process itself; (c) absence of comprehensive cost data in the instructional use of such technology and standardized patterns of utilization; and (d) reluctance to expect or require faculty knowledge of and proficiency in the use of technology for educational purposes. "The overriding imperative of technology is system," as Bernard Trotter reminds us, and "any discussion of educational technology must therefore be about the systematization of the educational process. Systemization of a new and different kind."[15]

Thus, the effective and economical use of educational technology by colleges and universities can be anticipated only if new, collaborative arrangements (intrainstitutional and interinstitutional) and a systems approach to the educational process are successfully pursued. The benefits that such technologies can provide, of course, are substantial:

1. duplication of high-quality instruction at low cost for convenient and repeated access by students in-residence and off-campus;
2. individualization of instruction;
3. collaborative arrangements among institutions having common academic interests, unencumbered by geographical considerations;
4. improved opportunities for independent study and a richer mix of course-work and methods of instruction for students;
5. fewer routine teaching duties for faculty members, especially at the more elementary level; and
6. opportunities for research and increased understanding of basic learning processes.[16]

The Carnegie Commission has predicted that by the year 2000, "a significant portion of instruction in higher education on campus may be carried on through informational technology—perhaps in a range of 10 to 20 percent. It certainly will penetrate much further than this into off-campus instruction at levels beyond the secondary school—in fact, it may become dominant there at a level of 80 percent or more."[17]

Should the Carnegie Commission prediction be realized, future generations of students will surely be less bound by a campus than have been those of the past, while at the same time the campus itself will become an even more central link between the present condition of society and the future. By the turn of the century, technology in various forms may well have transformed the campus from a center of learning into a learning center—one which houses a highly mobile population of students and scholars, a small resident population for study primarily at the most advanced levels, a panoply of laboratories for residential research and an integrated network of libraries, computers, television, and other teaching resources designed as much for residential as for off-campus study and research; in short, a network of associations, arrangements, and resources that will permit the student to have the university or college with him at home, at work, and at his leisure throughout his lifetime.

Responses

The educational response to these and related pressures by institutions of higher learning in the United States has been as unassured as it has been uneven.

In general, such educational initiatives as there have been divide into either

(1) new and often student-initiated and sometimes student-designed academic programs developed and offered mostly within conventional settings, or (2) what has come to be called nontraditional studies, efforts largely intended to offer new student constituencies newly designed or already established academic programs in novel ways and at times and places convenient to the learner.

The development of student-initiated programs results mostly from the generational revolt of the 1960s and from the demand for curricular options matching the heterogeneity of the American student body. Self-designed programs "range from rather small informal programs involving four students to programs available to the entire student body."[18] While it is generally assumed that students will consult with faculty members in planning their academic program, they are ordinarily expected to arrange an interdisciplinary course of study responsive to their special learning interests and style by drawing on any combination of courses, tutorials, and independent study options available within the host university or college. Better known institutions with developed programs such as these include Princeton, Cornell College, Ithaca College, and Chatham College, among others.

As part of the trend, learning contracts entered into between a university or college and a student—sometimes formally written—have been gaining favor in recent years. Evergreen State College, in the state of Washington, has drawn considerable interest and much applause for its program of "contracted studies." The pertinent reference in the college's *Bulletin* reads:

For a substantial part of your career at Evergreen, you may work in contracted studies. Using this pattern, you as an individual or as a member of a small group sharing your interests can sign up with a faculty member or other staff member to earn credit by doing a specific project, carrying out a specific investigation, mastering a specific skill, or dealing with a specific body of subject matter . . . We call this arrangement a "contract" for learning to emphasize that it is an agreement to do a piece of work and that it implies direct, mutual responsibility between you and the experienced person whom you have asked to help you.[19]

Variations on the same theme are to be found in the curricular options of an increasing number of institutions, among them New College at the University of Alabama, New College in Florida, Simpson College in Iowa, Whittier College in California, and Ottawa College in Kansas.[20]

To the extent that nontraditional programs have been undertaken at all in recent years, and that alternative educational strategies have been planned, they are more or less embodied in the typology suggested by John Valley of the Educational Testing Service:

1. Nontraditional programs that extend existing curricula through new means to new students.
2. Nontraditional programs that not only offer conventional education in

unconventional ways to new students, but also offer new curricula, learning experiences, and degrees to both new and traditional student bodies.

3. Nontraditional programs that seek to compress or accelerate the post-secondary learning experience, whether new or conventional, by such means as advanced placement, achievement tests, competency exams, year-round operations, and more compact curricula.

4. Nontraditional programs that are designed to certify competence but offer no instruction.

Some Examples

Nontraditional study plans and programs have received widespread and generally favorable publicity in the United States. This has been true since Alan Pifer of the Carnegie Corporation made known his support for such unconventional post-secondary educational initiatives in 1970, and when the chancellor of the University of the State of New York in the same year announced the creation of a new Regents' External Degree Program (degrees by examination).

1. The following year the Board of Trustees of the State University of New York authorized the creation of *Empire State College* as an autonomous college within that vast system of higher education. The college, having its own degree-granting capability (A.A., A.S., B.A., B.S.) and committed to a learning contract approach, has a dual purpose: to increase accessibility to students of any age wishing to study in nontraditional ways and to "test most thoroughly a model of nonresidential learning . . . exploring . . . new approaches [which] will redefine the meaning of the college environment and the role of the residential experience."[21] The college enables students to earn nonresidential credit throughout the state of New York, relying on several modes of instruction, learning centers on the Open University model, and the resources of the residential campuses of the university, other colleges and universities, public libraries, museums, galleries, and other learning resources where their students reside.

Student learning options divide into six general modes, as described by Cyril Houle:

(1) *Formal courses* offered by any kind of institution, not merely by colleges or universities . . . (2) *Cooperative Studies*, in which several students with similar interests work collaboratively. (3) *Tutorial* in which a teacher guides an individual student studying a particular area of knowledge or competence. (4) *Organized self-instructional programs*, such as correspondence courses, programmed learning, or televised instruction. (5) *Direct experience*, which may be supervised or unsupervised, but permits self-examination and reflection by the student. (6) *Independent study* by reading, writing, travel, or other means.[22]

The organizing framework for the degree, arranged between the student and his mentor on the learning-contract model, may be "vocational/professional, disciplinary/interdisciplinary, problem oriented, or holistic/thematic.[23] Degrees are awarded when

the student completes a program of study which the faculty supports, at a level of competence which meets college standards. In general, formal credit study undertaken at accredited colleges will be completely transferable. Expectations for a typical high school graduate normally call for eighteen months of full-time study or its equivalent for the associate degree, and thirty-six months of full-time study for the baccalaureate degree. Every student will complete a minimum program of study with Empire State of not less than three months' duration for the associate degree and six months for the baccalaureate degree.[24]

It should be noted that prescribed amounts of time of study in the college are requisite for the degree to be awarded, even though the program in every other respect is nontraditional by nearly anyone's definition.

2. *Minnesota Metropolitan State College* is another new institution which has attracted national attention for the unconventional nature of its academic program. The college, which serves undergraduate students at the upper-division level and also offers a professional post-baccalaureate at the master's level, was organized to serve an urban student body in an urban setting with curricula designed to teach students "how to make cities work." The learning contract is at the academic heart of the program and is drawn up expressly to engage the support and resources of the surrounding metropolitan area in the development of "life-related curricula," that is, a program designed to assure the immersion of the student in real urban problems within a goal-oriented and educational context.

Members of the faculty are for the most part persons employed full-time elsewhere, usually as practicing professionals in the Twin Cities area, and only part-time at the college. Students, who are rather independently expected to initiate and carry their programs forward, prepare their contract under the general supervision of an advisor and a special student-faculty committee to be approved later by a Contract Review Committee. The learning contract, or pact as it is more generally called, is designed to develop "competency areas," including (1) *Basic learning skills* (communication, method, handling of data); (2) *Civic skills* (social and community-related skills); (3) *Cultural-recreational competencies* (the heritage); (4) *Vocational competencies* (marketable skills); (5) *Personal and social awareness* (the individual in society).[25]

A Final Assessment Examination is requested by the student when he believes he is prepared to take it. Should he fail, he is encouraged to prepare further and read again for the examination at a later date, the purpose being to provide a continuing incentive for the student to demonstrate the skills and competencies appropriate to his educational objectives.

3. The Union for Experimenting Colleges and Universities' *University Without Walls* is another alternative form of higher education, and the best known example of a consortium of several institutions of higher learning joining hands (since 1964) to extend individualized traditional and nontraditional educational opportunities off the campus and throughout the country to students of whatever age.

There is no single curricular model for instruction in the University Without Walls. UWW programs can, theoretically, be established anywhere, and the forms of learning and assessment of the learning process are limited only by the ingenuity of the participants. The curriculum is said to place a heavy emphasis on independent study tailored to the interests and objectives of the individual student. The role of the teacher is intended to be that of a facilitator and coparticipant in the learning experience; and the learning experiences overall are meant to build a new dialogue and trust between younger and older persons.

The emphasis is upon the right of the student actively to participate in the formulation of his "course of study," to go wherever he is most likely to find what he needs, to mix traditional with unconventional learning experiences, to mix study and work simultaneously or to do one or the other intermittently as part of an overall educational plan and to determine the curricula and to prepare the examinations consistent with the individualized needs and objectives of each student. One of the more crucial purposes of the UWW experiment is to discover unconventional means of measuring academic progress and growth, cognitive and affective.

Students who feel themselves ready to read for the degree present their work to an evaluation team composed of faculty, students, and others with whom they have been working.

Since the range of experiments embraced by this model is so broad, and the geographical locations so dispersed, questions of quality control and assessment of the experiments themselves become paramount. To this end, the UWW has undertaken a program of evaluation, but its precise content is not clear at this point in time.

4. Nebraska's new open-learning system—called The State University of Nebraska (S.U.N.)—warrants the close attention of those interested in new ways of offering instruction and in new audiences for higher education. Funded by the National Institutes of Education, S.U.N. plans to use television as a major means of delivering courses to adults for whom the traditional forms of higher education are either unresponsive to their needs or the institutions inaccessible.

The course development teams resemble in form those responsible for preparing and producing the curricula for the British Open University, i.e., teams of faculty members and media and instructional design experts working together, the former being responsible for.course goals, content, and concepts, and the latter for solution of the most appropriate media and the most effective means of delivery. The Nebraska Educational Television Network, which has channels covering the entire state and parts of six others, will play an instrumental role, as will the Omaha World-Herald, which will publish the coursework once each week.

The university plans to develop "resource centers" throughout the state so as to make counselors, testing, and supplemental course materials readily available to students.

Current plans call for S.U.N. to have some forty courses in their catalog by 1980, with roughly 75 percent of them given over to general education and 25 percent to specialized professional, paraprofessional continuing education. It is anticipated that an A.A. degree could be earned through enrollment in courses offered by S.U.N., although no permanent decision has yet been made as to whether such credit ought to be granted by S.U.N. directly or channeled through other cooperating institutions of higher learning.

Nebraska's initiative has given rise to a regional system or consortium of five institutions in four states that are cooperating to form the University of Mid-America for the purposes of discovering whether the concept can be regionalized as well.[a]

5. The University of California's *Extended University* offers degree programs to upper-division and graduate students (masters level only) qualified to engage in university studies but effectively denied access because of work obligations, finances, location, home responsibilities, and other impediments to full-time residential study. The program is in a pilot phase (1972-1975) and experiments with modifications in the time, space, and age characteristics of the present pattern of higher education. Nearly 800 full-time equivalent students were enrolled in nineteen degree-producing programs during the 1973-74 academic year.

Nearly two years of study, planning, and negotiation were required before the decision was finally made in 1971 to reject the creation of a new and separate academic structure such as those just discussed, in favor of developing degree programs for adult, part-time students as an inseparable part of, and as a fully integrated effort within, the university's campuses and established schools and colleges. The decision was crucial on several counts:

a. It meant that the university's regular faculty would not only create, review, approve, and monitor the programs, but that they would also be responsible for the teaching of them;
b. It meant that the university would attempt to meet the educational needs of persons throughout their lifetime, and not just during what has come to be regarded as the "college years";
c. It meant that the university intended to mix older with younger students in its established academic programs;

---

[a]The cooperating institutions are the University of Nebraska, the University of Missouri, Kansas State University, the University of Kansas, and Iowa State University.

d. It meant that the university, not wishing to discriminate against older, part-time students or to mount the program as an extramural effort, would seek state funding for the program on essentially the same basis as its established offerings are funded;

e. It meant that innovations in curricula and methods of instruction would quite deliberately be fostered throughout the full range of the university's academic programs; and

f. It meant that responsibility for the maintenance of quality would rest with the same faculty committees and university procedures as govern all other degree programs offered by the university.

In short, the university intended to build on its existing strength, to assure academic rigor and standards appropriate to the University of California, and to use the Extended University as a way of effecting significant changes in the university itself over a period of time.

During the pilot phase of the program, varied admissions procedures especially appropriate to selecting adult students are to be carefully developed, tested, and evaluated for their effectiveness in predicting student success. Off-campus learning centers are planned as an inseparable part of most of these programs, not as mini-campuses but as unconventional learning environments. Services to be provided by such centers are expected to include, for example, information concerning educational programs available in the community, counseling and guidance, library and reference sources, seminar and classroom facilities, audio and video tape equipment, terminals for computer-assisted instruction, and related self-directed learning facilities. Actual locations are expected to include Agricultural Extension and Field Station facilities, community colleges, high schools, municipal and county government offices, libraries, museums, and places of employment.

New curricula are also expected to be developed in ways responsive to the kinds of experiences, motivations, and goals of the part-time student, almost all of whom are beyond normal college age. Experience will also be sought with advanced academic placement practices, credit by examination, and the certification of relevant work experience and self-education.

The already well-established University Extension and Summer Sessions programs of the university will articulate with and support the overall nontraditional effort while continuing to serve the adult population of California by meeting their nondegree related continuing education and retraining needs.

In addition to the initiation of pilot programs on the campuses, a new administrative unit—the University of California Consortium for the Extended University—was established by the president of the university on July 1, 1972 in his office in order to coordinate systemwide activities of the Extended University, as follows:

1. To advise the president on university-wide policy affecting extended degree programs.

2. To facilitate the exchange of information throughout the university on extended degree programs offered in California and elsewhere.
3. To plan, develop, and coordinate the use of various educational technology and media in the university's extended degree programs.
4. To engage in a continuous program of research on the university's extended degree programs, extended degree programs elsewhere, nontraditional study, and the educational use of technology and media as they relate to extended degree programs.
5. To act as a university-wide contact for professional organizations, government agencies, regional and national associations, foundations, and other parties interested in these programs.
6. To recommend to the president the establishment of off-campus learning centers.
7. To encourage the campuses to develop extended degree programs, to coordinate multi-campus programs, and to encourage and authorize campuses to offer campus-based programs on a statewide basis.
8. To design and develop degree programs for part-time students in cooperation with the campuses (a) when such programs promise greater cost effectiveness when offered by one or more campuses; (b) when part-time students are unable because of distance or similar geographic constraints to enroll in a campus-based program; and (c) when programs are not otherwise offered by the campuses.

Scores of other nontraditional programs undertaken by colleges and universities singly or through consortia have also been started in recent years, such as New Jersey's Thomas A. Edison College, Lincoln State University in Illinois, the Florida International University's External Degree Program, the California State Universities and Colleges External Degree Program, or are in the planning and early developmental stages, such as the Central New York Consortium for nontraditional secondary and higher education, the University of Hawaii's new off-campus degree plans, the University of Maine's new Bachelor's of Liberal Studies for Adults, or the Wisconsin study now underway based upon the European principle of "education permanente."[26] The trial use in several American colleges and universities of some of the British Open University materials also bears review and monitoring as the evaluation of these experiments is prepared and reported.

Discussion

The common purpose shared by such nontraditional programs as those mentioned and others like them is that they are intended to be less bound by conventional concepts of time, space, and age than now typifies the established learning process. Universities and colleges in the United States have ordinarily limited instruction in degree programs to a prearranged, scheduled sequence of courses to those of college age studying full-time in residence on campus. It is true, of course, that the community colleges and urban universities and colleges have been more accommodating of part-time, commuting, and working students than have been the major public and private universities and prestigious liberal arts colleges, whether or not in urban or rural settings. Nevertheless, the academic values implicit in the prevailing conventions have tended to discourage experimentation with fundamentally new educational concepts in much of the higher learning.

Most nontraditional programs as are in place or anticipated in the United States take relatively little account of their prospective impact on the established learning system. Interaction between the nontraditional and the conventional is, seemingly, to be more inadvertent than intended. Thus, new colleges, schools, divisions, institutions, structures, and administrative procedures and processes are everywhere emerging, mostly as autonomous and self-generating units. Each is striving to establish itself before organized resistance to its unconventional academic program assumes form and direction.

The most likely impediments will be introduced by the dominant institutions of higher learning, usually out of fear for a further scattering of scarce educational resources, and from government mostly out of a desire to couple such politically attractive programs with the less academic, more vocationally-oriented and paraprofessional ones comprising so much of the new demand for post-secondary education. Either move, if successful, would blunt whatever momentum had at the time been achieved and, in the end, would probably compromise nontraditional *academic* programs whatever the positive effects in other parts of the post-secondary educational system.

There is, of course, much to be said for mounting such bold new initiatives within the nurturing environment of an entirely new institution whose present and future welfare depends upon the successful achievement of nontraditional educational objectives. Those responsible in such settings, among other things, (1) can settle upon their own administrative and admission procedures rather than confront the task of revising those already in force; (2) can devise and design new curricula unencumbered by the constraints of others already in place; (3) can recruit and appoint a faculty committed to the purposes for which the new college or school is dedicated; and (4) can pursue resources and support with little regard to who may be hurt by a shift in the pattern of funding for higher education. In short, the range of discretion is greater and the constraints are fewer, however demanding and difficult may be the task of giving life to a new institution.

New institutions, of course, are as vulnerable as they are administratively attractive to persons determined to achieve major gains within a short span of time: (1) they can be blocked by more powerful interests without doing damage to or implicating an established enterprise; (2) they can be captured by competing interests for different but related purposes; (3) they can be embraced by influential interests whose purpose is not to nurture but to smother; (4) they can become too closely associated with the fortunes of one charismatic personality whose ill-timed departure would compromise the effort; and, (5) in the instance of educational institutions, they can be badly hurt by a hostile or indifferent higher education community should it collectively choose to boycott the entire effort by refusing to acknowledge the essential worth and academic integrity of nontraditional study and the transferability of credit earned in such programs.

Whether or not such nontraditional programs as are now underway in this country, or are being planned, will have a significant impact on American higher education is really quite uncertain. Each is encumbered by the negative influence of conventional academic biases or by inadequate funding or by hostile administrative interests, by unfavorable structural arrangements, by disjunction between their goals and those of their potential clients, or by all or some combination of these and similar impediments.

The educational quality of such nontraditional study programs is also an issue of major concern both to traditional academics as well as to academics who are supportive of these unconventional educational initiatives. The several regional accrediting associations are only now beginning to grapple with the issue as are other state and national study commissions interested in the movement. Samuel Gould, for example, chairman of the Commission on Non-Traditional Study, whose final report was submitted in 1973, has identified some of the dangers:

1. There is the danger of deterioration of standards:
2. There is the danger of the external degree being used too much as a political instrument and too little as an educational instrument;
3. There is the danger of curriculum content vagueness;
4. There is the danger that in the excitement of developing new ways of delivering instruction and credentialling [sic] people, the important and needed debate over what constitutes an educated person will continue to be postponed.[27]

The competence and motivation of the students; the adequacy of funding; the sufficiency of supporting library, laboratory, and counseling services; the knowledge, skill, and dedication of the faculty; the rigor of the program—these and related considerations bear upon the essential worth and integrity of any coherent academic program *leading to a degree*. Nontraditional study programs should be scrutinized no less in this regard than are established offerings (but surely not with greater zeal nor bias than would normally attend a review of new programs proposed along familiar lines).[28]

Research and evaluation associated with the development of nontraditional and student-initiated programs, if carefully planned, amply funded and meaningfully articulated with program development can measurably contribute to the academic quality of new programs. It can also broaden our overall understanding of the learning process, the nature of maturation and motivation, and the adequacy of existing forms and processes of the established learning system.

It is far from clear that such research and evaluation has been undertaken as innovative programs have developed in recent years. Most nontraditional programs have emerged during times of fiscal stringency. Under such circumstances, the allocation of scarce resources to research and evaluation at the expense of program funding is too often seen as shortsighted and extravagant. Thus, few of these new programs have been consciously structured to include systematic corrective mechanisms which would assure a thorough evaluation and provide evidence of desired academic quality.

These difficulties notwithstanding, much can be learned from systematic studies of potential student populations. Market research could well be aimed at revealing (among other things):

1. The current level of felt need for university or college level degree programs among the adult population.
2. The perceived functions of such education (certification; vocational training, retraining, or upgrading; general cultural interests; etc.)
3. The perceived barriers to full-time study at the university or college level among the adult population.
4. The perceived barriers to such part-time opportunities which presently exist.
5. The educational needs within specific occupational groups.
6. The extent to which students enrolled in full-time programs of study would opt for part-time alternatives, were the latter available.

In the absence of extensive sampling and verifiable evidence, one can only suspect that the two major sources of positive attraction to nontraditional degree programs will prove to be (1) a desire for greater time and space flexibility in gaining access to higher education, which arises out of objective familial and financial impediments to easy full-time residential enrollment, and (2) a negative view of established forms and modes of higher education, whether this negative valence be due to personal experience or to a contrary ideological view of traditional higher education.

In order to respond to both of these needs, American higher education would find it necessary, on the one hand, (1) to create flexible time-space arrangements and thereby facilitate access, but without basically changing the internal structure of curricula or the basic values which underly them and, on the other hand, (2) to create new programs and new modes of learning which are responsive to the values and educational ideologies of individual students, which may or may not be located in space and time such as to make them more accessible than are existing traditional academic programs. No single response or model is likely to serve each group equally well.[29]

Controversy can be expected to surround the development and evolution of nontraditional programs as criticism continues to be heard about the concept and emergence of mass higher education in Europe and universal post-secondary education in America. Lord Ashby's insightful observations about this phenomenon are pertinent and deserving of an alert and attentive concern:

So, within the system of mass higher education, there must be opportunities for the intellect to be stretched to its capacity (the critical faculty sharpened to the point where it can change ideas), by close contact with men who are intellectual masters. Not many students are fit for this austere discipline or are willing to submit to it but those who are must be able to find it, or the thin clear stream of excellence on which society depends for innovation and for statesmanship will dry up. Personally I am not in favour of herding such talented students into special institutions. Talent and mediocrity can share the same central heating plant and cafeteria, and they should, for talent has to learn to operate in a world of mediocrity.[30]

There are many factors, of course, which will influence the direction of both traditional and unconventional forms of post-secondary education in the United States. The more crucial of them have been thoroughly discussed in reports issued by the Carnegie Commission on Higher Education:[31] (1) The social environment for learning including both facilitating and impeding characteristics and opportunities; (2) the relative competitive attractiveness of learning as against other available options for the use of time; (3) the inclination to and adeptness at learning; (4) the reinforcement and rewards associated with learning, monetary and nonmonetary; (5) the efficaciousness of and accessibility to educational and learning programs and institutions; and (6) methods of financing post-secondary education.

"The movement toward recurrent lifetime education with adequate provision to offset personal income loss," the Carnegie Commission has suggested, "appears to be a logical step for the last quarter of the Twentieth Century. Particularly in the United States where universal access to collegiate education is now nearly assured to all youth," the Commission notes, "the next step in the evolution of our educational system would seem to be the assurance that lifetime educational opportunities be within the reach of all motivated adults."

Whatever the outcome of present efforts to innovate and breathe change into the nation's institutions of higher learning, the very questioning of so many of the assumptions about *who* will partake of their programs, and *how, when,* and *where* they will do so assures continuing efforts to deal unconventionally with the established forms and patterns of higher education in America.

Notes

1. W. Roy Niblett, "Issues and Choices," in W.R. Niblett and R.F. Butts (eds.), *Universities Facing the Future* (San Francisco: Jossey-Boss, Inc., 1972), p. 3.

2. L. Cerych and D. Furth, "On The Threshold of Mass Higher Education," in W.R. Niblett and R.F. Butts (eds.), *Universities Facing the Future*, p. 19.

3. Martin Trow, "The Expansion and Transformation of Higher Education," *International Review of Education* 18,1 (The Hague, 1972): 71.

4. Clark Kerr, *The Administration of Higher Education in an Era of Change and Conflict* (First David D. Henry Lecture, University of Illinois at Urbana-Champaign, 1972), p. 21-22; published as "Administration in an Era of Change and Conflict," in *Educational Record* 54, No. 1 (Winter, 1973), pp. 38-46.

5. "These demands do not mean that students are widely dissatisfied with their colleges. The situation is quite to the contrary. Only one in eight undergraduates is 'dissatisfied' or 'very dissatisfied,' and the level of satisfaction is highest in the great research universities ... but within this high level of satisfaction with college in general, and the research university in particular, do exist the specific dissatisfactions noted above. They deserve special consideration because they do not reflect an all-pervasive disenchantment but, rather, specific grievances. Students want more to say about certain aspects of their educational experience, and they are increasingly (and I think fortunately) being placed on committees where their voices can be heard and their votes counted." Ibid., pp. 21-22.

6. Ibid., p. 19.

7. "Substantial increases in productivity will likely be achieved only through changes in the educational process itself. Certainly, the significant advances in productivity in industry have involved the processes of production rather than support functions. In higher education, such changes can occur only with experimentation and innovation in academic programs, in instructional techniques, and in the relationship of the student to the institution." Virginia Smith, "More for Less: A New Priority," in American Council on Education *Universal Higher Education*, Logan Wilson and Olive Mills (eds.) (Background Papers for participants in the Fifty-fourth Annual Meeting of the ACE, Washington, D.C., 1971), p. 127; published by the American Council on Education (Washington, D.C., 1972).

8. See Earl F. Cheit, *The New Depression in Higher Education: A Study of Financial Conditions at 41 Colleges and Universities*, (New York: McGraw-Hill, 1971).

9. Eric Ashby, "The Great Reappraisal," in Niblett and Butts (eds.), *Universities Facing the Future*, p. 36.

10. Kerr, *Administration . . . in an Era of Change and Conflict*, p. 21.

11. The Carnegie Commission on Higher Education, *Less Time More Options: Education in the High School* (New York: McGraw-Hill, 1971), pp. 1-2.

12. Eric Ashby, *Any Person, Any Study* (New York: McGraw-Hill, 1971), p. 99.

13. The Carnegie Commission on Higher Education, *The Fourth Revolution: Instructional Technology in Higher Education* (New York: McGraw-Hill, 1972), p. 1.

14. Ibid., pp. 1-2.

15. Bernard Trotter, *Television and Technology in University Teaching: A Report to the Committee on University Affairs, and the Committee of Presidents of Universities of Ontario* (Toronto, Canada: Council of Ontario Universities, 1970), p. 50.

16. For an elaboration of these benefits and a thorough detailing of the educational implications of the new technology, see The Carnegie Commission's *The Fourth Revolution*, especially pp. 4-7.

17. Ibid., p. 1.

18. Paul R. Givens, "Student-Designed Curricula," *Research Currents* (Washington, D.C.: ERIC Clearinghouse on Higher Education, May 15, 1972), p. 3.

19. The Evergreen State College *Bulletin*, Olympia, Washington, 1971-72, p. 89.

20. For a more complete list of learning contract colleges and universities and of student-designed programs see Givens "Student-Designed Curricula," pp. 5-6.

21. Empire State College, *The Non-Residential College of the State University of New York* (Bulletin of the State University of New York, 1971-72).

22. Cyril O. Houle, *The External Degree* (San Francisco, Jossey-Boss, Inc., 1973), p. 98.

23. Ibid., p. 99.

24. *Interim Report*, 1971-72 (H.P.: Empire State College, n.d.).

25. For a fuller description, see Houle, *The External Degree*, p. 103.

26. For a comprehensive inventory and summary description of recent developments in nontraditional study, see John R. Valley, *Increasing the Options* (Princeton, New Jersey: Educational Testing Service, September 1972), 56 pp.

27. John Valentine, "The Bold Vision and the Hard Road," *College Board Review*, No. 85 (Fall 1972), p. 8.

28. For a brief summary of how some nontraditional programs are coping with the quality issue, see Carol H. Shulman, "A Look at External Degrees," *College & University Bulletin* 25, 3 (November 1972): 4-6.

29. See Joseph Zelon and David P. Gardner, "Alternatives in Higher Education—Who Wants What?" in *Higher Education*, 4 (1975), pp. 317-33.

30. Eric Ashby, *Adapting Universities to a Technological Society* (San Francisco: Jossey-Boss, Inc., 1974), p. 143.

31. See esp. *Toward a Learning Society* (New York: McGraw-Hill, 1973).

IX Education for Careers: Yesterday, Today, and Tomorrow

William E. Webster

Each year thousands of young people in America successfully leave high school and enter the job market or go on to higher education. Too many young Americans, however, graduate from high school neither prepared to enter college nor to become gainfully employed. Furthermore, many potentially productive young people leave school prior to graduation to be labeled "dropouts."

This systemic bankruptcy leaves many of America's youths with a personal sense of failure and frustration that becomes a lifetime burden for them when they are unable to take a useful place in society. These young people, however, do not pay the cost of their predicament alone. Society joins them by paying for the variety of social and welfare programs that its rejects always need.

We have known for decades the inadequacies of the educational system, particularly that of secondary education. However, with the dramatic technological changes confronting society today, it would appear that the shortcomings will only become more serious unless we take very determined steps to reform

The writer is indebted to the following people in the California State Department of Education who assisted in the original development of this document: Sam Barrett, State Director of Vocational Education; Paul Peters, Manager, Career Education Task Force; Dr. Ramiro Reyes, Chief, Office of Program Planning and Development; Patrick Weagraff, Education Project Specialist, Vocational Education (now Director of Vocational Education, Massachusetts State Department of Education); Fred Wolff, Office of the Deputy Superintendent for Programs.

Particular thanks go to Dr. Vernon Broussard, Director, Office of Secondary School Planning. His contribution on the disadvantaged minority youth made that section possible.

all of secondary education, but most particularly that segment of it which historically has been known as "vocational education."[a]

Several recent studies have been quite critical of vocational education as it has been made available to students. The study prepared by the Department of Health, Education, and Welfare entitled *Work in America*[1] clearly states that many people feel that vocational education has failed to teach students useful skills or place them in satisfying jobs. A report from the Panel on Youth of the President's Science Advisory Committee, *Youth: Transition to Adulthood,*[2] explores the contention that today's vocational programs are often used as dumping places for students not doing well academically or lacking interest. Other studies emphasize the unmet needs of minorities, particularly blacks, Indians, people with Spanish surnames, and women.

A new concept called "career education" is now broadening the province of vocational education to include career guidance and preparation for life-long career development. Since career education and vocational education are interrelated, one cannot be discussed without consideration of the other. In this chapter, therefore, they are discussed together under the heading career/vocational education.

The specific purpose of this chapter is to examine some major issues in career/vocational education, place them in their historical context, cite some hopeful developments, and suggest possible courses of action for the future. However, in a document of this kind only the barest outline of the issues can be drawn and further in-depth study, analysis, and planning will be necessary in order for substantive progress to be made. Although the recommended reform steps focus primarily on career/vocational education, it is important to reemphasize that all of secondary education needs extensive reform to meet the needs of America's youth.

To set the stage for a discussion of career/vocational education the first section gives the historical background of vocational education in the United States. This section is followed by a discussion of the present status of vocational education, indicating the increased number of students involved in this segment of education and emphasizing positive steps that are being taken in California.

The third section deals with the recently emerging career education movement, stressing broadening the province of vocational education beyond that of simple skill development, career guidance, and the introduction of career education at early elementary levels.

---

[a]Awareness of this need for total reform prompted California State Superintendent of Public Instruction Wilson Riles to call together a representative group in July, 1974. His charge to this group was to bring him recommendations that would establish the foundation for secondary school reform in California. The group reported to Dr. Riles in May, 1975, and the California State Department of Education with the support of the State Board of Education is in the process of submitting legislation to the State Legislature. If enacted and signed by the Governor, this legislation will initiate the first steps for comprehensive reform of California secondary schools in September, 1977.

The fourth section discusses one of the major failures of the schools and vocational education programs to prepare the disadvantaged groups adequately for productive roles in the working world. This section calls for reform by all of education, society, industry, and government, but stresses the important and constructive role career/vocational education can have in helping to educate and prepare the disadvantaged minority youth for more successful employment.

An integral part of the career education effort and its vocational subunit is the increasing attention being given to attitudes of the worker and the growing realization that the very nature of work is changing as we move, as Peter Drucker says, from the "manual workers" to the "knowledge workers."[3] Another section, therefore, attempts to capture very briefly some of the major new ideas being developed concerning the nature of work and the worker and its implications for vocational education.

The concluding section looks at the future projections of career/vocational education as it will help youth to fit into the futurists' views of what our world will look like in several decades. By matching future trends with present problems and hopeful developments, the chapter closes with some recommendations for action.

Brief History of Vocational Education in America

As the United States moved from an agrarian to an industrial society, the development of vocational education was inevitable. No longer did the father train his own son in his own career nor apprentice him to a craftsman to learn another trade. As industrial America dramatically developed, a larger trained labor force than could be supplied through the master-apprentice relationship became an economic necessity.

The Philadelphia Centennial Exposition of 1876 emphasized the relationship between national progress and education, arousing criticism of the secondary schools by many businessmen in the larger cities. The businessmen wanted schools to provide training in manual skills for boys and pure intellectual training de-emphasized.

During the thirty years that followed, many schools of manual training were started, originally at the college level and later at the secondary level. At first they were mostly private, being sponsored by businessmen. Their purpose was to replace the long apprenticeship training of industry, and they provided very little intellectual education.

While industry was calling for manual training schools for urban youngsters, farmers, using the National Grange as their spokesman, were calling for agricultural schools to train their sons. During the 1880s and 1890s the farmers became organized to obtain legislation which provided federal funds for rural colleges and Experiment Stations. They eventually were successful in adding agricultural studies to the secondary and elementary school curricula.

In 1910 the labor unions, which had been very hostile toward vocational training, formally endorsed vocational education through the AFL Committee on Education, and these programs became an accepted part of American education, at which time twenty-nine states were providing some form of industrial training.

The landmark date for vocational education usually cited is 1917 with the passage of the Smith-Hughes Act by which the federal government provided the states with a $7 million annual appropriation for certain vocational education programs. Within three years of the passage of this Act enrollment in federally-subsidized programs doubled, and total program expenditures, including state and local funds, quadrupled. The passage of compulsory school attendance laws by each of the states by 1923 also brought larger and larger numbers of students into skilled labor and agricultural programs.

Lawrence Cremin, in his book *The Transformation of the School*,[4] feels that the Smith-Hughes Act served to speed up the vocational education process and standardize it along certain lines, confirming vocational education rather than innovating it. He further adds that technology advanced so rapidly with World War I and its aftermath that the equipment in the schools quickly became outdated and the teachers remained isolated from industrial advances. This is a situation which continues to inhibit vocational education.

War again stimulated interest in vocational education in the 1940s. Congress put more than $100 million into a program called "Vocational Education for National Defense" (VEND), which between 1940 and 1945 gave seven million war production workers preemployment and supplementary training.

Following World War II, Congress enacted the George-Barden Act (1946), authorizing funds in the amount of $29 million for agriculture, home economics, trades and industry, and distributive occupations. In 1956 practical nursing and fisher trades were added to the Act.

Under Title VIII of the National Defense Education Act of 1958 federal funds were made available ". . . for the training of individuals designed to fit them for useful employment as highly skilled technicians in recognized occupations requiring scientific knowledge . . . in fields necessary for the national defense." The implementation of this Act was to be through "area vocational education programs" conducted by high school and post-high school institutions of "less than college grade" serving more than one school district.

There was a resurgence in the expansion of vocational education in the '60s with the passage in 1963 of a new federal-state cooperative program and its amendments in 1968. These new pieces of legislation included more students and more skills under vocational education appropriations.

Further broadening the scope of vocational education is a new concept in the schools which has been labeled "career education." This concept encompasses the study of careers, personal interests and abilities, and special career counseling, which many feel has the potential of making vocational education more meaningful and practical.

Although the career/vocational education programs are now including more students than ever before, they are still geared toward a small segment of the population. Some educators are looking at this new movement positively, however, as a vehicle to integrate many aspects of a child's education.

Vocational Education in America Today

In viewing vocational education in America today there are some clear indications in its patterns of growth. Enrollments have continued to climb; new occupational training programs are being introduced at all levels—secondary, post-secondary, and adult; financial support at the federal, state, and local levels has been substantially increased; involvement of business, industry, and labor has expanded significantly; and legislative support at both the national and state levels has been strong.

These trends are evidenced by a national enrollment in vocational education for 1972-73 of 11,602,144, distributed by educational level as follows:

Total	11,602,144 (100%)
Secondary	7,231,648 (62.3%)
Post-Secondary	1,304,092 (11.2%)
Adult	3,066,404 (26.4%)

Another measure of the change in vocational education is the dramatic impact the program has upon the total population as shown by the substantial increased enrollment per 1,000 total population:

	Total Enrollment in Voc. Ed.	Enrollment in Voc. Ed. per 1,000 Total Population
1960-61	3,785,773	21.1
1965-66	6,070,059	31.3
1970-71	10,495,411	51.6
1971-72	11,602,144	56.3

Vocational education traditionally has represented a partnership between the states and the federal government. Federal funding has served as a stimulus to the growth of vocational education. Increases in federal dollars have always resulted in more state and local dollars being expended for the program. At the present time on a national basis for every $1 of federal money spent for vocational education approximately $6 of state and local funds are expended. This ratio varies among the states, reaching high values, for example, of 1 to 8 in Maryland and 1 to 9 in California.

Reflecting the national trend, the growth of the vocational education program in California has been steady and widespread:

Total Vocational Education Enrollment (all levels)

1963	462,687
1968	1,036,086
1972	1,233,920

The nine-year growth was 165 percent; projected enrollments by 1977 are 1,679,115, an increase of nearly 300 percent since 1963.

The growth and characteristics of vocational education in California, as is true in any state, have been influenced significantly by the state it serves and by the organization of the public school system through which it functions.

California's high schools, community colleges, and adult schools are structured to be comprehensive by nature and in composition. Furthermore, long-prevailing policy and philosophy indicate that these schools shall enroll and serve the needs of all youth. The degree of comprehensiveness of each institution varies in relation to its size, finances, and commitment to the various disciplines. No specialized "trade" or "vocational" schools exist in California, with only minor exceptions. Instead, vocational education is offered in all of California's 763 public high schools, 96 community colleges, and 193 adult schools to some extent. In addition, specialized vocational education programs are offered in the 60 Regional Occupational Centers and Regional Occupational Programs, expanding components of California's vocational education effort.

Vocational education in California is in a period of rapid change. The program, initially established as employment-bound education, is moving from the philosophy of strict concentration on labor market needs toward an emphasis on human needs. While sound vocational education programs must still relate to labor market opportunities, the emerging philosophy is attempting to consider the individual's life-long career needs in light of the ever-changing world of work. The concept of the "new" vocational education is captured in the following suggested "Declaration of Purpose" developed by the American Vocational Association for inclusion in new federal vocational education legislation:

It is the purpose of this Act to authorize Federal grants to States to assist them to maintain, extend, and improve existing programs of vocational education, to develop new programs of vocational education, and to provide part-time employment for youths who need the earnings from such employment to continue their vocational training on a full-time basis, *to provide stipends and loans to out-of-school youth, young adults, and adults who are improperly employed and who need such education to adjust their employment to their abilities,* so that persons of all ages in all communities of the State—*those in elementary schools and junior high schools who must develop an awareness and orientation about the world of work and must have an opportunity to explore occupational areas of their choice with the assistance of competent vocational guidance and counseling,* those in high *school who must prepare for the world of work,* those who have completed or discontinued their formal education and are preparing to enter the labor market, those who have already entered the labor market but need to upgrade their skills or learn new ones, those with special educational handicaps, and those in postsecondary schools—will have ready access to vocational training or retraining which is of high quality, which is realistic in the light of actual or anticipated opportunities for gainful employment, and which is suited to their needs, interests, and ability to benefit from such training.

Although still not meeting the needs of all students it should serve, the vocational education effort has been developing new ideas and programs which are attempting to meet the needs of a greater number of young Americans.

Among the developments in California are the Regional Occupational Programs and Regional Occupational Centers (ROPs/ROCs). The basic intent of ROPs and ROCs is to provide a means whereby vocational, technical, and occupational educational opportunities can be extended through a wider variety of specialized courses to serve a larger number of students than can be provided adequately, efficiently, and economically by a single school district. By using existing facilities in schools and local industries, the ROP/ROC concept determines that funds, both federal and state, go for programs rather than for bricks and mortar.

ROPs and ROCs are established by a joint effort between and among two or more high schools, county offices of education, and/or community colleges. This new approach to providing vocational education is now available in all but nine of the state's 58 counties. Both high school and adult students, in about equal numbers, are enrolled in these special arrangements. Yearly enrollment increases have averaged 35 percent over the past three years to a total enrollment of approximately 85,000. Rapid expansion of the program seems to be a result of a combination of short, high-intensity training; open entry/exit scheduling; small classes; job-site training experience; day, evening, weekend, and year-round classes; and special funding incentives.

Another example of California's expanding vocational education opportunities is the strong program of work experience education. More than 100,000 youth and adults are enrolled in California's three types of work experience education programs—exploratory, general, and vocational—which constitute integral parts of the total vocational education system. Each type involves an organized, systematic relationship between the school curriculum and real-life job experience in the community; and each type is an essential component of career education.

Occupational and technical education in California's 96 community colleges is the most extensive post-secondary education program in the nation. Occupational education in the community colleges has been planned to provide the knowledge and skills needed by a student to obtain a job and to advance. This objective is carried out through short-term certificate programs, apprenticeship education, two-year occupational programs leading to an associate of arts degree, and courses designed to upgrade skills and to lead to job advancement. More than 50 percent of the total day and evening enrollments in California's community colleges is made up of occupational course enrollments.

Although statistics indicate more students are becoming involved in vocational education, the basic philosophy for vocational education is changing, and new programs and ideas are being developed, there is still evidence that there are many more young people who should be served by these programs. Statistics of unemployment and underemployment of young people indicate that schools are not preparing all youngsters adequately for the world of work.

The Concept of Career Education

Recognizing that vocational education has been inadequate, educators have attempted to expand the province of the traditional program. The broadened concept, already mentioned in this chapter and generally referred to as "career education," is felt by many to have the potential to bring increased relevance and purpose to education and open up new options for all students.

It had its beginnings nationwide in 1970 when the late commissioner of education, James E. Allen, advocated a recasting of the entire educational system to education centered on the career development theme. However, the term "career education" is usually credited to former commissioner of education, Sidney P. Marland, who in 1971 in his famous "Career Education Now" speech, proposed that every high school graduate should be prepared to enter useful and rewarding employment and that there should be a sound and systematized relationship between education and work.

The need for a systematic career development and preparation process was recognized in California in 1969 when the California State Board of Education adopted a policy statement calling for education to prepare each student for a career consistent with his desires, abilities, and realistic expectations.

Career education is essentially preparation for life. When the concept is fully implemented, instructional strategies are used that integrate academic, vocational, and general studies and guidance along with the individualization of instruction. A reconstruction of educational curriculum is designed to parallel the sequence of developmental tasks from the pre-kindergarten through adult age span, emphasizing the relatedness of self, education, work, and leisure. Career education concepts are infused into all courses and disciplines, not added on as a new subject to be taught.

The elements of career education are accomplished through the meeting of the goals of self; occupational, educational, and economic awareness; attitude development; consumer competency; and career orientation, exploration, and preparation. To enable all students to reach these goals, school personnel utilize the resources of the community in ways that enhance interests, values, aptitudes, and aspirations of students. Implicit in this is the active involvement of representatives from business, industry, and labor with school activities.

Research and development efforts in California's school-based model of career education have demonstrated that there are implications for instruction, management, professional development, and guidance and counseling.

Career education implies modification of curriculum content in all disciplines at all grade levels. Adding occupational information and career-oriented experiences to the present curriculum represents a minimal modification. A more substantial modification occurs when the entire curriculum uses the organizing theme of life career development, and these concepts are infused into every course that is offered.

Career education also implies changes in the instructional process such as the following:

1. A greater use of community resources as instructional agents and instructional settings with direct student involvement in real-life settings.
2. A wider variety of instructional information to accomplish instructional objectives. Multimedia materials and multisensory experiences occur in traditional classroom settings and in learning centers on and off campus, and vicarious experiences gained through gaming, simulation, and role playing.
3. Individualized instruction in which instruction is designed to serve students based upon their needs, interests, and abilities, and which facilitates open-entry, open-exit access to educational opportunities.
4. Teacher-managed instruction in which the teacher diagnoses and prescribes educational experiences and supervises the use of various instructional information in keeping with the needs of the students.
5. Interdisciplinary approaches to instruction by teams of instructors who plan and implement instructional programs in learning centers and facilitate an understanding of interrelationships that exist in the structure of the educational program.
6. Supervised work experience for each student that expands the present exploratory, general, and vocational work experiences to internships in the community.
7. A change from time and unit accomplishment to competencies acquired by students, with the curriculum designed to lead to proficiency and accomplishment measured by predetermined logical criteria and a broad liberal education without gaps. For example, "took three years, or 15 units of French" is replaced by a measurable degree of fluency in that language.
8. School organization modifications, such as differentiated staffing, team

teaching, alternatives in scheduling patterns, and in-service training during the school day for professional growth.

To make career education a reality requires a profound rethinking of priorities and restructuring of the curriculum within American educational systems. State legislators, members of business, industry, and labor groups, and the general public need to be involved in making these decisions. There are elements of career education that educators have used for many years, yet the gap between the fully developed and implemented career education concept and the current state of educational practice at all grade levels in most educational settings points to the necessity for restructuring our educational system.

Writers on career/vocational education see a fully implemented program as reaching more students than at present, especially the disadvantaged groups; being better integrated with the academic program; attempting to give greater understanding of the world of work and the students' options; including both sexes in all programs; having provision for continuous retraining; having more training take place outside the school building with people other than official teachers; having student participation in the decision-making processes; and involving the community more.

Career/Vocational Education for the Disadvantaged

In the previous sections we dealt with the success and dynamic growth of career/vocational education, with emphasis on California's programs. However, many thoughtful educators are disturbed by an awareness that many youths are still not affected by these efforts, particularly those generally categorized as disadvantaged.

A review of the literature and interviews with persons familiar with the field of vocational education and related areas of job opportunities make quite clear that the problem of forced idleness among these youth is far from new. Its roots lie deep in the nation's past. True, some significant steps have been taken, particularly after the explosion of a "Watts" or "Newark" or "Washington," and yet the action of the past decade has been inadequate. Perhaps the most acute symptoms have been treated and, for a time at least, checked, but the responses have given rise too often to an unjustified sense of accomplishment and complacency.

The ghetto, the barrio, the reservation, and Appalachia appear as a "no man's land" for many Americans, who fail to recognize that the lack of opportunity for disadvantaged youth is a condition that continues to be with us. Disadvantaged youth, particularly the black, are too often the victimized, invisible poor whose plight was publicized in Michael Harrington's *The Other America*.[5] Although opportunities have opened up for some, many know only the drudgery of dead-end jobs or are condemned to the bleakness of a permanent place on the welfare rolls; others have no official existence except, of course, in the grim statistics of police dockets and city morgues.

Available research questions the belief once widely held that achievement of full employment will benefit all Americans. However, when full employment is reached, a substantial proportion of disadvantaged minority youth, including women, is unable to find jobs, and when unemployment is well above the accepted figure, as it is now, the rate of joblessness among young disadvantaged men and women becomes even higher. Present methods of reducing unemployment, including a stimulated economy, as yet have failed to deal with the high rates of minority youth unemployment. There are many who feel that broad and concerted programs must be implemented to avoid a series of crises which could possibly involve violence.

While the research concerning vocational education and disadvantaged youth does not paint a picture of optimism, it appears there is still time to defuse the situation, provided that policymakers at federal, state, and local level are permitted to make firm resource and program commitments. Such commitments are critical since too many minority youth feel that the fundamental American dedication to equal rights with equal opportunities is only a mockery where they are concerned.

A decade has passed since James B. Conant first warned of the "social dynamite" planted in our cities by the enforced idleness and empty expectations of great numbers of young people.[6] As late as January, 1976, this problem was still being referred to as the greatest concern in the labor market with black teenage unemployment running double and triple the high unemployment for white youths.

At the height of this country's economic boom in 1969, more than 25 percent of nonwhite male and female teenagers in the central cities of our twenty largest metropolitan areas were unemployed. This constituted about seventeen times the unemployment rate of 1.5 percent for white males in the entire country.

Since 1969, the softening economy has led to a serious deterioration in the overall employment situation, but its effect on disadvantaged youth, particularly black youth, has continued. There are about 1.2 million black teenagers and 1.3 million blacks between the ages of twenty and twenty-four in metropolitan areas with populations of 250,000 or more. As against a white adult unemployment rate of 4.6 percent during the second quarter of 1971, the overall black teenage unemployment rate was 34.9 percent, or more than seven times greater; in the poverty areas, it was 39.1 percent. For black adults between the ages of twenty and twenty-four, the unemployment rate was 19 percent. Statistics are based on those who look for jobs and a conservative estimate is that 200,000 young disadvantaged people have given up hope and stopped looking for jobs.

A step above the unemployed and the dropouts from the labor market are those who have found jobs that are menial and dead-end. Their jobs provide fewer hours of work than those of whites, less pay, low permanence, and fewer prospects for advancement.

Compounding the hardships of slack in the job market and the handicap of race and ethnicity is the sex disadvantage with which disadvantaged women, particularly black women, must contend. They are held back by multiple layers of discrimination. The highest unemployment rates of any group are those for black female teenagers in low income areas of central cities. Their unemployment rate has seldom been below 33 percent and often as high as 50 percent.

A growing minority of disadvantaged youth now have the preparation to enter and complete junior or senior college or to acquire a manual or technical skill that can aid them in a job search. However, they, too, continue to face major discrimination in the world of work, which takes its toll by forcing them to accept jobs at lower incomes and with less opportunity for advancement than the jobs for which they are qualified.

We have specifically talked about black youth since their problem is a nationwide issue and statistics are available for every part of the country. However, the American Indians, the Puerto Ricans of New York City, and the Mexican-Americans of the West and Southwest suffer the same kinds of deprivations. The problems are often more severe among this group because of the language barrier.

After Conant's warning, two factors decelerated but did not negate the growth of unemployment among disadvantaged youth. One was the economic expansion of 1961-1969, the longest in our history, which generated an average of 1.5 million new jobs each year. The other was expansion of the armed services, which drew more than two million additional men, many disadvantaged minorities, out of the labor force. The moderating influence of these factors, however, no longer exists, and now opposite trends are at work.

Now we are faced with economic recession and inflation coupled with a high national unemployment rate, 8.2 percent as of October 1975. This high level of unemployment further diminishes the opportunities for disadvantaged minority youth whose hardships were crippling even while the boom was in full swing. Great numbers of veterans are moving into the labor market, leading to an intensified competition for those jobs available.

The urgent problems of race and ethnicity in a tight labor market continue to be with us. More young disadvantaged minority people will enter the job market in the decade ahead, representing a higher proportion of all new entrants than in previous years. Teenagers among disadvantaged minority groups will increase from about 2.1 million in 1970 to 2.6 million in 1980. Among young adult blacks aged from twenty to twenty-four, the projections show an increase from under 2.2 million to about 3 million.

There is little doubt that there is need for constructive action as these youths become aware of the widening gap between their expectations and reality. This group of young people must receive great attention in the reformation efforts of career/vocational education to make sure they are included in the plans. They must be a concern when educators talk with business to attempt to enlarge the job market and assimilate them in productive ways.

Work and the Worker

Historically, the belief that work is grim, that work is uninteresting, and that workers should be blindly obedient has been accepted. The authoritarian, hierarchical nature of work has been the law, and the average worker has had little to say about what he did, how he did it, or when he did it.

Such conditions of work were given quasi-scientific validity through the efforts of the time and motion people early in this century. This group studied manual work and reduced it to a series of the most efficient, precise movements by the worker. Inherent in their thinking was that the worker would do as he was told, that he had no thought or mind of his own.

There, of course, has been some amelioration of this primitive view, largely through the works of the human relations group mostly in the twenties and thirties. This group called attention to the social relationships of the workers in organizations, seeing interpersonal relationships as primary and work as secondary.

Alvin Toffler in his book *Future Shock*[7] suggests—and it is hard to disagree with him—that the routinized, mechanized, inhumane industrial world strongly influenced the development of the American secondary schools which have been designed until most recently to resemble factories both in appearance and in the lock-step manner in which the students are taught. Both the student and the worker are expected to obey without questioning.

In recent years there have been some serious doubts by many thoughtful people about these views of work and the schools. Furthermore, there have been some attempts to make environments more humane, and a look at some of the emerging ideas and trends in the world of work would be appropriate to any discussion of career/vocational education.

Several recent developments aroused considerable interest in the treatment of the worker on the job. One of the more publicized accounts has been the problems encountered by General Motors at the new Vega plant in Lordstown, Ohio. The claims by workers that they were being treated inhumanely in the new and most technologically advanced plant in the world, the highly publicized strategies of General Motors to deal with the problems, and the alleged sabotage by the workers, gave workers and management in other industries cause to examine their own practices.

The interesting element in the Lordstown issue is the very dramatic measures manual workers took to alleviate what they perceived as a hostile work situation.

They restructured the nature of work without the consent of either the corporation or the union.

While the Vega plant was receiving great attention, the Department of Health, Education, and Welfare released its study entitled *Work in America.*[8] The study evidences the negative consequences resulting from the way most offices and factories are organized for work. At about the same time, David Jenkins published his book entitled *Job Power: Blue and White Collar Democracy,*[9] supporting worker democracy and worker participation in decision-making. This book was followed by Studs Terkel's book *Working*[10] in which Mr. Terkel, using the same techniques that had brought him success in his earlier work *Hard Times*, taped the ideas of workers from almost every kind of working situation in the country. Terkel's book gives poignant evidence of the worker's need to be treated as a human being.

These publications, particularly the HEW work and the Jenkins book, strongly suggest that today's worker no longer accepts the inhumanity of industry with the resignation that "that is how it will be." Money is no longer the only gratification he seeks from his job. He wants to be significant and contributing. He wants respect as an individual. He wants to feel that his work is worthwhile, that he helps make decisions about that work, that he can be proud of his commitment. He wants to feel that he controls his own destiny in ways that fulfill his own desires.

It is further suggested that very few companies organize work to meet these needs of today's workers. Most instances of worker unrest, both in America and in Europe, are marked by lack of humane treatment, both bodily and mentally, for the worker; lack of democracy in industry; and industry's feeling that higher wages and better fringe benefits will salve the worker's dissatisfaction. As in the Vega plant, workers in other industries have used sabotage tactics to try to convince companies that they seek to be occupied in the use of their higher capabilities. The "knowledge worker," too, can be affected and turn technology to his own benefit by slowing down production or producing an inferior product, affecting all of society: the consumers.

There is evidence, however, that conditions can be improved. There have been positive innovations where industries have taken a totally new approach to worker-management relations, worker satisfaction, and production methods. There are examples in industry where workers have been part of the decision-making process, boring jobs have been rotated including supervisory positions, or teams have worked together to produce one whole product. In industries where such innovations have been introduced, worker morale has improved, worker commitment has increased, and profits have not suffered, but rather, improved. There is evidence that when management listens to the worker his practical knowledge often leads to an innovation for production improvement rather than a slowdown. Too often, however, these innovations happen accidentally and are not structured into the organization.

At the present time, however, neither industry nor the schools are prepared to deal with the changing role of the worker and his newly expressed needs on a large scale. It is not new technology we need now, but a new way of looking at work and the worker and a methodology to apply this new knowledge.

Those who suggest that work can be more humane follow a long line of researchers in the area of organizations and human behavior. Too often, however, the findings of such writers as Chris Argyris and Abraham Maslow[11] have been centered on the white-collar/management-level worker. The research of both of these men can apply very well to the blue-collar worker as well as to his manager. Argyris argues strongly for constructive participation of the individual in the making of decisions. Maslow's famous hierarchy of needs starts with the most basic, leading to the highest needs of self-actualization.

In addition to the research pointing to the need for greater self-fulfillment on the job there are studies cited in *Work in America* which indicate that there is a clear class distinction between white- and blue-collar workers, the white-collar worker perceiving himself as the superior of the two groups. Research indicates that the blue-collar worker is rarely called upon to make decisions. This research is supported by the way work is arranged, as well as by the fact that the career ladder for the blue-collar worker is very short. Almost every major company in the country selects top-level managers primarily from groups of college-level trainees, who rarely, if ever, have had actual manual work experience.

The long-range implications for an American society with growing class differences and continued conflict are enormous. If one were to accept the fact that work should be more humane and, further, that dramatic class division in the factory is not desirable, then some definite measures should be taken by schools, industries, unions, and government to bring about reforms to help all individuals to lead significant and fulfilling lives while at the same time reducing the conflict between the two classes.

As Toffler indicates that schools reflect industry, one evidence of this is that academic and vocational students are two different groups. In other words, a teacher of advanced foreign language has contact with an entirely different group of students than one teaching auto mechanics or drafting. The system is set up so that academic students who might want to take vocational courses are not able to crowd them into an already full schedule geared to meet competitive requirements for college. What emerges in an allegedly comprehensive high school is a school that is divided by class lines with hewers of wood and carters of water separated from future white-collar managers as early as age fourteen in the ninth grade.

If, in fact, there is class consciousness, schools need not contribute to this. One solution is work experience providing for all students to work together. Attempts are needed within schools to discuss these very topics, and not only in academic classes. If colleges were prepared to give credit for work experience, as they do for fourth-year Latin or fourth-year French; more youngsters would be willing to get involved. Writings, research, and reports relative to work experience could be permitted to satisfy academic admissions. In addition, courses in school could be offered explaining how industry works, the real dynamism of the corporation, and/or the dynamics of promotion.

Vocational training becomes relevant when schools and industry cooperate. Then young people have authentic, planned working experiences and become trained to do actual work in the world of the new worker. Communication and dialogue between these two kinds of institutions are important for awareness of each other's current needs and resources.

An important aspect of reorientation in school and industry is the reforming of the stereotype of the "worker." Successful examples of industrial innovation should be studied and analyzed to determine the basis for worker attitudes. Schools must provide students in vocational education the same humane treatment that successful businesses are offering their workers. Classrooms must be examples through being democratic, providing student participation in decision making in matters affecting them.

One of the worker/student stereotypes to be overcome is sex. Certain jobs have traditionally been open only to men, perhaps for physical reasons or perhaps just because "that is the way it always has been." For the same reasons certain courses in school have been for boys and others for girls. Now equal opportunities for jobs are slowly breaking this barrier. Schools can participate in this industrial revolution by avoiding sex discrimination in courses (now prohibited by Title IX regulations) and offering a variety of work experiences for girls to provide for experimentation in different careers.

Another worker stereotype is in the teaching profession. The vocational education teachers are often considered inferior to their academic colleagues and therefore tend to form a separate group. This needs to be overcome so that vocational education teachers and academic teachers can work together to provide non-college-bound students with more than manual skills. The better educated future worker needs basic math and language skills and an understanding of the dynamics of the real working world. In addition, all students, college- or non-college-bound, should have some vocational training so that different groups will exchange ideas, learn together, and understand each other. The blue-collar/white-collar barrier can be broken down in the future through such efforts.

Industries' part in reforming work will be a major one since changes will affect them and will have to be considered in their long-range planning. Greater cross-industry communications will be needed as well as communication with schools and unions for studying mutual problems and goals and planning strategies of benefit to all. Opportunities could be provided for work experience and seminars where youngsters could talk with workers and managers. Attention could be given to setting up career ladders where workers would not be trapped in hopeless dead-end jobs.

The government always assumes a major role in reforms of this nature since it provides the legal structure. An example of its impact is the new Title IX regulations, already mentioned, which provides for nondiscrimination in schools on the basis of sex.

Unions would have an extremely important role in helping to restructure these institutions. Labor unions are envisioned as the voice of the worker and should help develop ideas and methods to improve work and worker relations. Workers should participate in the union's as well as in industry's decision-making, thereby minimizing hierarchy in unions. Labor unions could encourage companies to develop programs to involve young people and to build into contracts worker decision-making and career-ladder opportunities. Unions may have to change practices to allow for the systematic, organized working of students. Students should not be kept out of jobs because of union regulations and certainly could not be expected to pay dues. On the other hand, industry cannot exploit this part-time group as a means of cheap labor, thereby depriving union workers a decent living.

Since all systems interact with each other, all organizations involved with work and the worker will have to take part in the reforming of these institutions and the environments they create. Whether or not they all actively participate in reform, if one system changes, the others are automatically changing.

As with all change, the activities will have to start on a limited basis and in some area where success seems likely. It will take a long time to reach the ultimate goal of all workers leading productive, self-fulfilling lives. It is realistic to accept that this goal will not be reached for everyone, but planning and cooperation by these various institutions should make the world of work better for the vast majority.

The Future of Career/Vocational Education in America

We have now covered the history, status, and some of the key issues of career/vocational education. Before making recommendations for any reformations of career/vocational education, however, it is necessary to take a look at what the future may hold for workers. Taking into consideration where we are, present trends, and the mistakes and successes of the past, we can project to some extent the kind of world we should be preparing young people to face. In doing this we can foresee what career/vocational education programs might look like.

We are in the process of moving from an Industrial Age to a New Age where the knowledge worker is in demand. Making the transition to a New Age is of utmost importance if people are going to be productive, meet their own personal goals, and make choices that will make life more satisfying for more people in the future.

The transition to the New Age means that society must develop new institutions, values, goals, and programs. We have to question if society is to be based on a cooperative and less exploitative use of limited resources.

Futurists project certain trends that will affect the working world:

1. People will have longer retirement.
2. Fewer young people will be in schools and entering the labor market.
3. People will have many lifetime career changes necessitating constant re-training.
4. There will be more industrial automation.
5. There will be new kinds of technological opportunities.
6. More people will work in larger organizations.
7. There will be more retailing automation with less personal service.
8. There will be greater use of technological teaching systems.
9. More people will demand more from a day's work than a day's pay.

In this world of change, career/vocational education will have a viable role in preparing young people for the world of work and at the same time in continually retraining all workers. Many current career/vocational programs are in serious trouble because they are not responding to the dynamic changes needed and because of their failure to reach large numbers of youth who have no other source of assistance. Further, students question what we are doing in the adult world, their doubts being emphasized by the Vietnam War and Watergate.

If work is to become more humane and workers are going to be better prepared for productive, satisfying roles in society, there must be changes in education, and specifically career/vocational education, business and industry, government, and labor unions. All elements of these institutions must cooperate, study, plan, and act to improve the world of the worker and make it more self-fulfilling. One institution alone cannot achieve this. Vocational education cannot change to a more democratic, student-participating program without the cooperation of industry and the unions; otherwise, education will be accused of preparing students for an unreal world. If, on the other hand, students are not prepared for the kind of jobs that exist in industry and knowledgeable of negotiations and attitudes of workers, they are not being trained to fit into a world that exists.

On the basis of the problems and trends presented in this document some overall recommendations are proposed for consideration. There is no doubt such reforms as are being recommended here are necessary and timely. There is also no doubt that such reforms can be successfully implemented. It will take cooperation, communication, patience, and intelligent planning, but to prepare people to lead purposeful and satisfying lives is a goal all institutions should hold as a highest priority.

Recommendations

1. Every youngster should have a vocational experience while he is in school.

2. There should be structures and systems to assure cooperation and communication between schools, business and industry, labor unions, and government to plan and implement reform efforts for career/vocational education.

3. There should be community involvement in career/vocational education programs to assure that the specific needs and desires of all community groups are met.

4. Discussion and analysis of jobs and career guidance should be integral components of all curricula of all school systems.

5. Business and industry should participate actively in facilitating job placement.

6. There should be greater integration in the high school between vocational education and the academic programs, with both programs available to all students.

7. Schools, business, and industry should see as a top priority their making available to minority groups and women vocational training and jobs.

8. There should be arrangements with universities and colleges to give youngsters college credit for work experience.

9. There should be a reeducation of people involved in career/vocational education to understand the world of work, today's worker, and the important role career/vocational education will take in making the working environment better for everyone.

10. There should be student opportunity for decision making to teach them how to share in the decision-making process when they enter the labor market.

11. There should be determined efforts to avoid bureaucratic wrangling between important segments involved in career/vocational education, such as, the Department of Health, Education, and Welfare vs. the Department of Labor, career education vs. vocational education, junior college vs. high school.

12. All institutions involved in the reform should be aware that work should be a humane activity, and every organization should be such that each person has the opportunity to develop himself as a significant human being.

Notes

1. Report of a Special Task Force to the Secretary of Health, Education, and Welfare, *Work in America* (Cambridge, Mass.: The MIT Press, 1973), p. 134.

2. Report of the Panel on Youth of the President's Science Advisory Committee, *Youth: Transition to Adulthood* (Chicago: The University of Chicago Press, 1972), p. 86.

3. Drucker, Peter F., *The Age of Discontinuity* (New York and Evanston: Harper & Row, 1968), p. 264.

4. Cremin, Lawrence A., *The Transformation of the School* (Vintage Books, New York: Random House, 1961), pp. 56-57.

5. Harrington, Michael, *The Other America* (Baltimore, Md.: Penguin Books Inc., 1963).

6. Conant, James B., *Slums and Suburbs* (Signet Books, New York: The New American Library of World Literature, Inc., 1964), p. 10.

7. Toffler, Alvin, *Future Shock* (New York: Bantam Books, 1971), p. 400.

8. *Work in America*, p. 38, pp. 137-138.

9. Jenkins, David, *Job Power: Blue and White Collar Democracy* (Garden City, New York: Doubleday & Company, Inc.).

10. Terkel, Studs, *Working* (New York: Random House, 1972).

11. Argyris, Chris, *Integrating the Individual and the Organization* (New York: John Wiley and Sons, 1964), p. 31; Maslow, A.H., *Motivation and Personality* (New York: Harper and Row, 1954).

X
Working and Living: Their Relationships

Robert Dubin

The most distinctive feature of our system is not a system, but a quest, not a neat arrangement of men and institutions, but a flux.

—Boorstin, *Democracy and its Discontents: Reflections on Everyday America*

Is the nature of work itself, or the settings in which work is carried out the root of *blue-collar blues*? Are Americans really disenchanted with their work and work organizations? Does citizen discontent spill over from discontent with work into other institutions? Or, do the discomforts and problems of living generate a scapegoating of work and work organizations as convenient targets for the real and alleged ills of daily living?

We are concerned here with describing and analyzing the linkages between work time and nonwork, waking hours. In particular we ask: Do the quality of working life and the quality of life in general bear any relationship to each other? The result of the analysis is to suggest some critical choices facing Americans in the next several decades.

Quality is a subjective idea. In our technologically sophisticated society, quality has come to mean the absence of defects, or errors, not the presence of some desired characteristics. Indeed, we take our cue from quality control in industrial and commercial activities where the minimization of error is its meaning. How, then, is it possible to give meaning to the quality of working life or the quality of life in general? Does the lowering of the infant mortality rate, or the reduction in the amount of substandard housing, or the decline of the proportion of the citizens living below the poverty level of income constitute improvement of the quality of life? Each of these indicators measures the reduction of error or defect, yet none tells us anything about the future life of the saved infants, or the livability of the housing provided, or the uses to which the income is put.

In the end, quality as a set of positive attributes is defined by consensus—it is a value rather than a fact. All government policy, indeed, all social policy, whether grounded in special interest groups or institutions, turns on a group consensus with respect to values. The fundamental critical choices for Americans are choices among values and valued goals. It is not a matter of choosing among feasible or attractive means.

The burden of the discussion in this chapter is to set forth some general value choices that constitute options for Americans during the next several decades. Some underlying trends in the work institution, and other institutions, will be stated in order to indicate why these options are now open. This analysis is *not* focused on means, for it is believed we already have many more alternative means than are used at any given time, and that we can readily invent new means if the value choices require it.

Critical Issues—An Overview

I present seven basic issues that represent important social choices for Americans in the next several decades. The American social system is, indeed, in a state of flux. The choices we make will guide a course of change. Whether such change improves on the present, or worsens the affairs of state and the state of affairs, depends on the options selected in resolving the critical issues. Twenty years hence new critical issues and new options will have to be faced, and continually into the future. Therefore, the chosen options for action at any given time, even if found wrong in subsequent experience, do not necessarily do irrepairable damage to the society, for we can choose again when the mistakes are obvious. A far greater threat is drift—doing nothing—either from fear that all available options may be wrong, or because of social paralysis.

Issue #1: To Determine the Limits of Functions
to be Performed by the Productive Institution

It would seem simple to assert that the productive institution should produce goods and provide services—those are the commodities sold in the market place. But the productive institution is also burdened with additional functions as well.

For example, it is probably true that industry and commerce do as much schooling as the educational institution. In the office and factory the education

is called training; retraining; executive, supervisory, and organizational development; or apprenticeship (so-called for the manual learner, but also a functionally
apt designation for those "next in line" among the ranks of executives).

The productive institution provides important welfare functions for its
members and their families (health and welfare benefits, pensions). The extent
of this function is revealed by the fact that about 25-33 percent of the total
manpower costs of industry are costs of welfare services. The American
industrial system today warrants the designation of *welfare capitalism* much
more than the period of the late nineteenth and early twentieth century when
that term was applied to significant portions of industry. To be sure, American
welfare capitalism takes a different form than industrial welfarism in Japan or
Italy or West Germany. As ecological consciousness becomes more widespread,
industry and commerce are placed under further obligation actively to curb
industrial pollution and environmental degradation, as a positive contribution to
general social welfare.

There are expectations that innovation will be an important function of
business not only in the technology and products of each firm, but also in
solving large social problems like housing and traffic congestion and adequacy of
water resources. The research and development activities as innovative functions
of business firms draw upon the same intellectual resources as universities and to
the same ends of adding new knowledge and solving problems demanding
solution. Business firms are now also expected to provide organizational climates
in which each individual employee will have the opportunity to be creative on
his own job, a different but important aspect of the innovation function
expected of the work organization.

These examples should be enough to demonstrate that the productive
institution does carry a number of important societal functions besides those of
producing goods and services. The critical issue is whether the number and mix
of such functions should be expanded, maintained at the present level, or
reduced.

To expand will probably generate opposition from industrial leaders who
traditionally have resisted taking on new functions. Social critics may also resist
the moves to expand the functions of industry on grounds that it will only
enhance the power already in the hands of industrial leaders. Furthermore, there
are questions as to the directions in which such expansion might take place.
Functions to minimize abuse of the environment are already being added as
pressing welfare functions of productive organizations. Welfare activities might
also include psychological counseling and be enhanced to cover drug and alcohol
rehabilitation of addicted employees as part of company programs; and consumerism may be aided by increasing and supplementing consumer services to
employees, such as discount purchasing of goods and services beyond those
made or sold by the company. Considerable expansion of activities is possible in
the field of employee recreation as well as housing. Much expansion could also
be made into education beyond vocational areas now covered.

To contract the functions now performed in the productive institution would probably be strongly opposed by employees and their unions on grounds that this would be retrogressive, at least in the areas of personnel practices. Certainly, if there is any contraction of functions it would involve a transfer of those functions to other institutions, since functions are almost never eliminated, once instituted in a social system. Thus we would have to invent new institutions or expand other institutions to carry the functions shifted from the work arena.

If no positive action is taken we predict that there will be a continual drift toward loading more functions on the productive institution. As this happens the clarity of goals to produce goods and services becomes diluted with a probable loss of productive efficiency (this inspite of the usual claims that increased personnel functions in a wide range of areas will or can improve efficiency by raising motivational levels).

The resolution of the issue of the range of functions to be performed by the productive institution lies in two related steps: (1) to establish a rank order of desirability for those additional functions that *could* be loaded onto the institution; and (2) to determine what existing or new institutions might do as well or better in carrying out the functions.

Issue #2: To Organize Work Regimes so that the Quality of Working Life is Materially Improved

In the historical development of the man-machine relationship the emphasis has been on fitting man to the machine. So long as man was utilized as a machine operative, the major limits to the design of technology were the mental and physiological limits of man. It was assumed that man as worker was almost infinitely malleable, and with proper training of workers, and appropriate subdivision of work, the man-machine fit could be optimized. In the continuing analyses of human factors psychology some of the more esoteric aspects of human limits are still being explored.

One of the central features of the new industrial revolution is that it is now possible to conceptualize technology as being almost infinitely malleable. There are now many more degrees of freedom available in the design of technological systems than had ever before existed.

Perhaps one of the most important implications of the broadened options for machine design is that now the *needs* of man can be taken into account in the design of technology. It may no longer be necessary to push man to his limits of intellectual capabilities and physiological functioning to get the most out of technology. Many technical process and machine designs have alternatives that are equally productive, but that make very different demands on the human beings involved in utilizing them. It is now possible to set as a criterion of the selected design that it satisfy some human needs.

We have so little explored the possibilities of adapting machines to the needs of men that the field has unlimited possibilities. Among those actively pursuing this course are the social scientists who analyze socio-technical systems and a number of industrial firms in Scandanavia which are following leads developed by the Work Research Institute of Oslo. A number of American companies are also moving in this direction.

There is still much to be done to improve the creature comfort of work places as well as to reduce health hazards. The steps in this direction are well known. Action occurs when there is a will to do something about it, and a justification that the financial investment will produce returns in improved morale and the presumption that this, in turn, will positively affect quality and quantity of output. Most such improvements occur when new plants are built, or new equipment is installed.

Progress toward improving the quality of working life will be greatest in the reconceptualization of the man-machine relationship. This is probably as much an educational task as it is a subject for social policy and/or governmental action. There will undoubtedly be required considerable intellectual pressure from outside the arenas of engineering design since one of the fundamental precepts, or values, of engineers will have to be modified, namely, that the needs of social man can be ignored. This is very difficult for values are among the most stubborn of all human attributes in resisting change.

Issue #3: To Orient the Environments of Human Life
to Human Size, Both in Work Organizations and in
General Living Spaces

A little understood aspect of human life is the relationships between human reactions and environmental stimuli. We are especially ignorant of the human reactions to man-made features of environments within which man works and lives. Indeed, we now know more about the relations of subhuman living things to their environments than about man in his environments because of the outstanding work of ethologists and ecologists.

Is there some notion about size, or complexity, or distance, or numbers such that if certain limits are exceeded there are negative reactions by human beings? We now know something about *territoriality* among subhuman species and can understand that limited space can be claimed and defended for exclusive occupancy. At the human level there may be an additional idea that when upper limits of human acceptability are reached there may occur something we can call *environmental disorientation*. Is there a distance, or a size, or a level of complexity, or large numbers beyond which a person's linkage to the environment becomes confused or is viewed as meaningless or even threatened? Can a person's environment be perceived as too big, or too remote, or too full of stimuli to the point where he withdraws from an environment or rebels against it?

Of special interest here is that portion of the total environment that is man-made. The buildings that house offices, factories, and living spaces; the technical processes and equipment that produce goods and services; and the densely packed areas called cities may come to exceed a size or complexity that makes them repugnant to man's sense of environmental order. Do the boundaries of a city extend so far out that the idea of citizenship is no longer meaningful to its inhabitants? Can an airplane become too large or an ocean vessel too big for its passengers to feel safe and comfortable in them?

Reactions to natural environments may be of a different order since they are not the product of or controllable by man's efforts. A high mountain, a remarkable canyon or a powerful waterfall may elicit awe or esthetic responses because they are placed in a realm beyond man's doing. It is meaningless to say the mountain is too high, but the claim that the skyscraper is too tall may be a valid human reaction.

Increasingly in the future more attention will be turned to the man-environment relationships. This is just as important in the work organization, on the factory floor or the business office, as it is in the daily flow of traffic to and from work, and in the living and playing spaces of the community.

Many of the complaints of citizens about modern living can be traced, I suspect, to their very negative reactions to the environments man himself has created. If we do no more in the next twenty years than to find out what the limits are to human tolerance for the features of man-made environments, we will have contributed importantly to the knowledge base from which further critical choices can be made by Americans. This is essentially a research task and deserves the support of public and private agencies interested in human welfare.

Issue #4: To Encourage a Larger Number of
Legitimate Options for the Interrelationships
Between the Working Life and the Total Life
of the Individual, in Ways that Optimize the
Quality of the Individual's Life History

The central social issue is to ask whether or not the standard life cycle of schooling, followed by work, followed by retirement, with some minor variations on the work and nonwork balance during the working lifetime, is open to modification that would somehow or other improve the quality of the individual's life history. The available options in this area seem to be to consider if the time devoted to working and not working can be modified with respect to its scheduling during the individual's life.

The standard American life history for males consists of a first six years of childhood, twelve years of schooling, forty-five to forty-eight years of work, and the remainder of life being spent in retirement from work. An increasing proportion of the total younger population (now in excess of 40 percent of high school graduates) go on to continuing education beyond the twelve years. In the course of working lifetime, the length of vacations from work typically increases with tenure on the job. For females there is likely to be a more varied relationship between work and nonwork such that after formal schooling a short period of work ensues up to and through the first years of marriage, then leaving the labor force to rear a family, returning to the labor force as a second breadwinner, or head of household during the middle years, often continuing to work until normal retirement age is reached.

Some variations on these patterns of the relationships between work and nonwork periods may be introduced by such practices as a three- or four-day work week, or seasonality of employment, or "moonlighting," or in rarer cases, the return to further schooling in order to achieve a career change. There is, of course, a substantial number of individuals who are maintained through most of their lifetime as welfare recipients, and whose pattern of work and nonwork is different from that of the majority of citizens. A small portion of the total population seldom, if ever, enters the world of work at all, either because of physical or mental limitations or because their favorable financial condition makes remunerative work unnecessary.

The problem of scheduling work and nonwork periods divides into two major segments. One possibility of introducing variation in the work, nonwork balance, is to change the schedule of hours worked. The other major source of variation in this balance is to modify when, in the life history of the individual, work and nonwork will occur. We turn to examine these two major alternatives.

With respect to varying the hours of work over short time periods, standard practice in multishift industries is to have rotating shifts so that individuals will serve on different shifts in sequence, thereby changing their personal diurnal balance of work and nonwork. The so-called "gliding time," introduced in Europe and now being utilized in the United States, provides for a total expected work day with the individual being given some option as to the hours at which he reports for work and leaves the work place. The gliding time phenomenon was, of course, well institutionalized by so-called outside salesmen who have considerable autonomy in determining the hours and days of their own work. Even the balance between regular time and overtime work constitutes a short time variation in the work and nonwork relationship as it affects individuals.

It is notable that, in collective bargaining, there is a recent demand that the working out of overtime be made an optional decision of the individual rather than a matter of unilateral employer decision. In government service it is often possible to accumulate annual and sick leave so as to take a prolonged absence from work at the choice of the individual. It is also notable that at least at the blue-collar level there is a growing tendency to consider unemployment compensation to be an institutionalized feature of work and to manage to be made unemployed with compensation benefits so as to have nonworking time without total loss of income. In special industries, like air transportation, the legal limitation on total hours of continuous work, or over a given time period, leaves a substantial portion of time each month available for nonwork activities or a "moonlighting" job. In short, there already exist a wide variety of means for introducing short term variability in the work, nonwork balance.

Over the entire life cycle we have been much less imaginative in articulating the periods of work and nonwork. Practices have been institutionalized in some special areas that indicate the possible range of such options. In the field of education the work period is typically nine or ten months with the remaining months being unpaid time (but with salaries spread over twelve monthly payments). In higher education sabbatical leaves permit a much longer time period away from usual work routines. At executive levels in industry, and increasingly in government, there exist resident executive development programs that take the individual from his work setting to give him further education in the arts of executive leadership. Some such programs run as long as a year so that they amount to a work-oriented sabbatical.

Relatively little attention has been focused on where in the life cycle changes might be made in the work and nonwork balance. It is possible, for example, that sixteen continuous years of schooling to a college bachelors degree, or longer to a higher degree, might be broken at some point in the post-high school period with a spell of work. Military conscription serves this function in those societies that have compulsory military service. The argument could well be made that maturity that comes with a period of work is functional for future education, as the experience of military veterans in continuing their interrupted education seems to attest. Even more imaginative is the possibility that individuals may earn the opportunity to "retire" for a significant block of time in mid-course of a work career, to make up that time during a period when retirement would normally occur. Or, alternatively, to reduce the total length of working life, not by taking years off the end, but by inserting nonwork years within the total work span. It is not even too fanciful to consider that males may increasingly adopt the work and nonwork balance of contemporary American females, following Swedish examples of men as homemakers and women as breakwinners.

There is involved in this critical issue the notion that life style is intimately associated with the way in which individuals use their waking hours. Waking hours devoted to work are usually scheduled. Working behaviors are also typically routinized and standardized. Nonwork waking hours are considered residual—what is left over from the scheduled work hours, but the ways in which such time is used is much less structured. It is in this latter fact that the quality of the individual's life history might be significantly improved since the relative lack of structure in nonwork waking hours may provide one of the largest reservoirs of behavioral opportunities for individual choice and decision. If we truly believe that individual freedom is a valued attribute of American society, then providing these behavioral opportunities to express individual freedom may be an exceedingly important goal for the society.

*Issue #5: To Develop Institutions Outside of Work
that Fill and Fulfill the Nonwork Waking Hours of
Citizen's Lives*

There is a fundamental issue of whether or not a social system organized around work as its central institution now has sufficient institutional richness to fill the nonwork waking hours of citizens. It may very well be that the most important innovation in social structure over the next several decades will be the invention of new institutional forms and new institutional practices that provide richness in the living portion of individuals' life histories.

We have essentially two images of nonwork. Both derive from the activities of a small class of the idle rich. We have an image of the leisure class as either engaging in, or patronizing "culture," or utilizing their waking hours in hedonistic pursuits. Often the leisure class in history has urged the pursuit of culture on the working classes while following the hedonistic alternate itself. Planners in Socialist societies give great emphasis to culture for the masses as the preferred nonwork activities.

Our institutional practices have followed these two alternatives so that we cater to cultural through museums, the theater, mass media, and amateur artistic pursuits. Hedonistic pleasures of spectatorism, gambling (there are state lotteries even in Socialist countries), and various forms of institutionalized vice are characteristic opportunities for the masses. True recreation lies somewhere between hedonism and culture.

It is not easy to anticipate in which directions new institutions might be invented to supplement cultural and hedonistic activities. Two ideas do present themselves as viable possibilities.

From Eastern religion and philosophy we can learn the importance of developing the human psyche at an emotional level beyond presently realized stages. The more extreme forms of this, as in Yoga, are not too far removed from consciousness raising, or T-group, or various "therapies" that characterize contemporary American society. The point is that we may now be in the process of legitimating and institutionalizing the idea that the individual should somehow or other devote a significant portion of his waking lifetime to massaging, improving, or self-actualizing his psyche.

In the recent course of human history we can see the individual's political freedom being developed in the seventeenth and eighteenth century; followed by his economic freedom in the nineteenth century; his social freedom in the mid-twentieth century; and culminating in the possibility of attaining psychological freedom as a next stage of historical development. We now know that learning does not stop at early adulthood. Perhaps the greatest opportunity for lifetime learning may be to learn about one's own psyche, and developing it beyond its present stage.

Another great opportunity for expansion of institutions to fill the nonwork waking hours of citizens is in the development of greater skills in interpersonal relations. The battered child is but one evidence of the primitive level of present skills in handling person-to-person relations, even in that most basic of social units, the family. Sociability is a fundamental human need, and if it does not develop as a skill through the simple experiences of living, we may have to institutionalize the learning of social interaction skills and include this as part of the broad educational program of a society throughout the lifetime of citizens. Industrial practice has already institutionalized the learning of interpersonal skills in the form of group training and "team-building" systems designed to teach adult workers and executives how to develop more cooperative relations with working colleagues. It would be unfortunate if such efforts are limited only to business firms with the sole outcome in mind being to improve output and productivity. If training in improving interpersonal competence works in industry, it surely could work as well or better in the body politic as a whole.

Over the next several decades there is no reason to believe that the nonwork waking hours of citizens will be filled in optimum fashion. One can become addicted to the Big Eye to catch the early, regular, late, and late-late shows. The real issue for the immediate future is to determine if the institutions available to the nonwork hours of citizens also fulfill their human needs and develop their human potentials. We need a great deal of imagination to be directed at answering this question.

Issue #6: To Sustain Distributive Justice
(Legitimized Differential Rewards)
Along with Equality of Opportunity

Various important social movements and governmental programs have been operative in the society over the past several decades to encourage and enforce equality of opportunity among individuals. These efforts have been successful enough that administrative law is now employed to demand compliant actions from educational organizations and businesses to employ greater proportions of minority citizens and women at the middle and higher levels of occupations and professions. Over the past decade there have been absolute gains in enhancing equality of individual opportunity, and the institutional pressures will continue operative to produce further gains.

All solutions to problems in turn are likely to generate new problems. There is now emerging in capitalist societies, and has already appeared in Socialist societies, the fundamental issue of distributive justice. Distributive justice is the consensus that exists in any society with respect to unequal distribution of rewards among all citizens. Where a consensus about distributive justice prevails with respect to work there is agreement in the society that certain occupations and professions legitimately deserve to be rewarded more than others, depending on such criteria as length of training, responsibility, and physical or intellectual skills employed. Should a particular occupational group either exceed the accepted level of reward for that group, or fall significantly below the accepted level, then criticism and disaffection are produced. In Socialist economies, for example, where the range from lowest to highest paid jobs in industry usually does not exceed a multiple of three or four, there is considerable discontent among middle and high level executives, and professionals like engineers, because they feel their rewards are comparatively inadequate. In countries where recent changes have been made in repressive regimes, like Portugal, those receiving minimum rewards are now demanding a larger share of rewards for working in the society.

One of the possible consequences of an extreme emphasis on equality (often ignoring the full meaning—equality of opportunity) to encompass equality of reward, will be a significant change in the notions of distributive justice that prevail in the society. The special condition under which extreme emphasis on equality may have dysfunctional consequences would be the one in which seeking equality of rewards leads to a leveling downward of rewards across the entire system. Insofar as rewards are reinforcing of effort (including personal investment of energy, intelligence and knowledge), individuals and groups may react negatively if they feel their *relative* rewards are diminished. This comes about not necessarily because absolute rewards are reduced, but rather because relative payoffs are less than they formerly were. When lower level persons gain major pay increases that narrow the differential between their level of pay and that of higher paid people, the latter become disgruntled (persons at higher pay levels prefer general wage increases as a percentage increase rather than an equal cents-per-hour one applying to all jobs since the former maintains between-job relative differentials of reward, while the latter reduces the differentials).

We have been imaginative in maintaining reward systems for high level executives and managers and professionals. Organizations and professions have, for example, been inventive in developing ways to provide tax sheltered rewards to high level personnel in order to sustain or even improve their total consumable payoffs for working. The same has not been true for middle and low level employees. Clearly, we have been able to invent new incentive and reward systems for part of the working population. It should be of concern to the society that this skill in inventing social practices not be lost, and that it be applied throughout the full range of the occupational structure in the interests of sustaining or even enhancing consensus about the distributive justice of differential rewards as a companion goal to equality of opportunity.

Issue #7: To Raise the Level of Honesty
and Moral Behavior in the Workplace
and in the Society at Large

The central issue here is whether the moral standards of the society are made in the workplace, or elsewhere. A good argument can be presented that experiences in the workplace, based on what people actually do, are more compelling with respect to ideas about morality and honesty and truth than are the preached ideas coming from other institutions.

It is estimated that between $5 billion and $40 billion worth of goods are annually stolen from American business firms by their own employees. There have been enough spectacular court cases in recent years exposing embezzlement, deliberate mismanagement, bribery, and illegal plundering of the assets of firms by the highest levels of executives to establish public examples of dishonest behavior at the highest levels of business. The use of bribes in securing foreign business contracts has been widely publicized. At much more mundane levels cheating on the expense account, or nepotism, or falsification of production or inventory records, or restriction of output by rank-and-file workers are all evidences of daily practices in business firms that are knowingly engaged in even though they are dishonest, or even illegal. The dishonesty, of course, extends especially to relations with customers, ranging from sharp practices in pricing (including collusive pricing among alleged competitors) to outright deception in the description and advertisement of products. It is not necessary to push the examples any further.

One conclusion to draw is that the average citizen who works is just as likely to encounter dishonest behaviors as part of his experiences at work as he is to encounter morally and socially acceptable behavior. What, in the end, becomes the basis for his own moral judgments? The conclusion that "everyone does it" may become the most useful guide for personal behavior (especially if the evidence is that one will not readily get caught).

This is not an inconsiderable issue nor is it one that is limited to capitalist economies. There are no systems of productive operations that are beyond the immoral exploitation of them by individuals. There are even institutional imperatives (to get out production, for example, or to meet the plan) that will impel executives in Socialist as well as in capitalist economies to make the record "look good" regardless of the morality of the means employed.

Insofar as there are morals guiding behavior in the productive institution, they are more likely to be of a secular character and intimately tied to a manipulative view of managerial functions. Thus, the popular belief that minor changes in organizational structure and interpersonal relations ("organizational development") can provide opportunities for individuals to "self-actualize" in their work, has the very satisfying character of appearing to be moral concern for the individual's intellectual and psychic comfort. Behavioral scientists who push these techniques upon industrial and other organizations have become the lay moralists for the executives of the society. Social scientists usually justify their emphasis on using scientific knowledge to induce self-fulfillment on the job by contending that in the end it will also result in greater individual productivity and, therefore, total productivity. This outcome is yet to be proved. We may have here an instance of doing the right thing for the wrong reason. The development of the individual may, as indicated in the discussion of Issue #5, be an important goal for the society as a whole, but the contention that the individual will pay back this opportunity with greater productivity, may not be true.

In any event, the lay morality that characterizes much of industrial practice is a pragmatic, output-oriented one. It might be well, in the next several decades, to raise the question of whether honesty and truth are just as important outputs from business practice. The failure to consider this issue may lead to a further degradation of morality of social life generally.

Caveats

There are many more issues than have been examined above. Individual issues as discussed have varying degrees of empirical support. There is no ordering of the listed issues according to some hierarchy of criticalness. Nor is it even certain that the listed issues are readily addressed within the next two decades for they may persist as issues for a much longer time.

Caveats notwithstanding, I believe that at least some of these issues are now critical and are worthy of serious attention in evaluating critical choices for Americans.

XI

Alternatives for Federal Income-Security Policy

Richard P. Nathan

A rich nation such as the United States should be able to provide an adequate income for all who are in need.

A simple proposition, yes, but it involves many hard questions. What is "adequate"? What is "need"? What for that matter is "income"—cash transfers, food stamps, housing subsidies, health care benefits, scholarship assistance? How should these various programs work in order to be fair, to be efficient, to maintain incentives? Where are we now; how close are we to meeting this standard? How well or how poorly do current income-security programs operate?

The term *income security* is defined broadly for purposes of this chapter. It includes Social Security (OASDI),[a] veterans benefits, unemployment insurance, aid for families with dependent children (AFDC), and supplementary security income (SSI) for the aged, blind, and disabled established under the Social Security Administration January 1, 1974. It also includes *in-kind* assistance, such as food stamps, health care benefits, and housing subsidies. In the proposed federal budget for fiscal year 1975, cash benefits for income security alone were projected at $101 billion.[b] Combining them with in-kind benefits produces a total

---

Richard P. Nathan is a Senior Fellow at the Brookings Institution. The material presented in this chapter is his alone. It does not represent the views of the trustees, officers, or other staff members of the Brookings Institution.

[a]The letters OASDI refer to Old Age Survivors and Disability Insurance financed from the Social Security trust fund. There are currently thirteen million primary annuitants (aged and survivors) under OASDI and over fifty million persons in covered employment.

[b]This total also includes retirement benefits for federal employees, merchant marine, railroad workers, etc. (See Table XI-1).

of nearly $130 billion. The cash assistance figure standing by itself is over one-third of the federal budget (one-half of federal spending for civilian purposes). It exceeds total spending for defense and space by nearly $5 billion. Defense-space spending has almost doubled since 1960. Cash income maintenance spending has grown *fivefold*.[1]

Estimated federal outlays by program for fiscal year 1975 are shown in Table XI-1.

Table XI-1
Federal Income-Security Benefits, Fiscal Year 1975 Estimate
(In millions of dollars)

Federal outlays for cash benefits:	
Social Security (OASDI)	$ 62,919
Federal employee benefits	13,485
Veterans benefits	6,923
Public assistance	8,291
Unemployment insurance	6,193
Railroad retirement	2,972
Other programs	999
Subtotal, outlays, cash benefits	$101,454
Federal outlays for in-kind benefits:	
Food and nutrition	$ 5,768
Health care	20,048
Housing	2,245
Subtotal, outlays, in-kind benefits	$ 28,006
TOTAL BENEFITS	$129,459

Source: Special Analysis K, Fiscal Year 1975 Federal Budget.

Total benefits by target group are shown in Table XI-2. The most benefited group by far is the aged—accounting for *nearly 60 percent* of total payments.

Twelve percent of the nation's population was classified as below the official poverty income standard in 1972 ($4,275 for a family of four). The incidence of poverty was highest for families with a female head (37.9 percent); it was 18.6 percent for the aged.[2] These figures do not count in-kind benefits as income, thus they fail to take into account the dramatic expansion of the food stamp and medicaid programs in recent years, as discussed below.

Organization of Chapter

The chapter is organized around major policy alternatives for the future. It concentrates on three areas:

Table XI-2
Income Security Benefits by Target Group, Fiscal Year 1975 Estimate
(In millions of dollars)

Social Security retirement recipients	$ 38,135
Other aged	38,172
Disabled	20,370
Mothers and children	9,625
Unemployed	6,530
Other low-income	7,899
Other	8,728
Total	$129,459

Source: Special Analysis K, Fiscal Year 1975 Federal Budget.

Overall Welfare Policy Options. The second section considers major welfare policy options. Should we adopt a negative income tax or something like it? Should we stay where we are? Should we adopt what this chapter refers to as "incremental changes"?

The Guaranteed "Job" Approach. The third section briefly examines the idea of guaranteed "jobs" as an approach to assisting the employable poor of *working age*.

Social Security Options. The fourth section separately considers major social security issues and options. With the establishment of the SSI program in 1974, important questions of equity have been raised. Why should a person who has "earned" benefits (by having paid OASDI taxes) receive almost the same benefit as an aged, blind, or disabled person on SSI who never paid taxes into the OASDI trust fund? This subject leads into a series of broader questions of equity about the role of Social Security for the future and its financing.

Several additional points should be made in this introductory section. Although this chapter is organized around alternative choices for the future, I have in a number of places indicated my own preferences so that the reader can take them into account.

The figures presented above and later in this chapter do not include state and local welfare expenditures for income security (estimated at another $12-15 billion in fiscal year 1975). These state and local expenditures are mainly for: (1) matching under the AFDC and Medicaid programs; (2) state supplements to SSI; and (3) state and local general-relief spending, which in some states (New York, Michigan, Pennsylvania, Massachusetts) involves significant levels of cash assistance to poor and near-poor persons not covered under federally-financed programs.

At various points in the material presented, long footnotes on major points and facts are included. These are presented in order not to interrupt the discussion of the principal policy options, and at the same time to enable readers to take into account major issues of program design.

Overall Welfare Policy Options

This section considers three overall welfare policy options for the future. One is the adoption of a comprehensive reform to replace all or almost all existing income-security programs of the federal government for the poor and near-poor. The second is the "incremental reform" position, which says we should build needed improvements into the current program base, integrate and revise these programs, but not replace them. The third position, treated more briefly, holds that no legislative reforms should be advanced.

The Comprehensive-Reform Position

While there are several comprehensive reform options (children's allowance, tax credits, demogrants), they have similar characteristics. The most common is the negative income tax (NIT). The abbreviation NIT is used in the chapter as shorthand for the comprehensive-reform position. The NIT position has over the past decade had broad support from both conservatives (Milton Friedman) and liberals (James Tobin).[c] It proceeds from an analysis of the deficiencies of existing programs. NIT advocates frequently point out:

1. That existing programs, because of the way they overlap, in many cases produce untenably high marginal tax (or reduction) rates. This means that a family can only keep only a small amount, sometimes only five or ten cents, out of each additional dollar earned, because their welfare grant is reduced by ninety or ninety-five cents for each additional dollar in earnings. In some cases, they can face a *net loss* if they earn an additional dollar of income.[d]

---

[c]NIT plans are often referred to also as "guaranteed-income plans." I have not used this term as I find it confusing. Many programs today, e.g., food stamps, are income guarantees in that they assure a minimum income level to broad classes of the population. However, the food stamp program has a strong work requirement. It can be argued that if there is a work requirement, benefits are not guaranteed. This question of the role and significance of a work requirement emerges later on as an important difference between an NIT and the incremental position.

[d]For those who know the history of the Family Assistance Plan (FAP) this is the John Williams dilemma. Williams, a former Republican senator from Delaware effectively undercut FAP by pointing out how a combination of cash and in-kind assistance programs could produce such high cumulative tax (or reduction) rates as to undermine seriously the work incentives of recipients.

2. That existing programs are unfair. Some recipients receive quite high benefits, others no or very low ones.
3. That existing programs are so hopelessly fragmented they produce formidable administrative problems, which is both inefficient and demeaning to recipients.
4. That in-kind programs stigmatize recipients, e.g., when they have to use food stamps.
5. And that the only way to overcome these and other deficiencies politically is to build support for a fundamentally new approach.

Problems under current programs were summarized as follows in a recent paper on welfare reform issued by the staff of the Subcommittee on Fiscal Policy of the Joint Economic Committee of the Congress:

The growth in noncash Government programs for specific "needs" is a matter of significant policy concern. Noncash benefits are popular chiefly because they can be justified in terms of particular goods that avoid the need for choice. In-kind benefits escape debate over the difficult issues of income distribution that generally confront proposals for cash supplements to the poor: fairness, cost, work incentives. When noncash programs are scrutinized on these grounds, however, they fail. The existing array of such programs generally is unfair, costly, and damaging to work incentives. Moreover, there is a long laundry list of remaining "needs" that could be translated into still more Federal benefit programs targeted on the needy. Given recent history, the establishment of clothing vouchers or utility stamps or transportation coupons is not inconceivable.[3]

Milton Friedman, who has supported NIT for nearly twenty years, argues further that only with such a comprehensive reform bill will we be able to eliminate other programs. In his words,

The advantages of this arrangement [an NIT] are clear. It is directed specifically at the problem of poverty. It gives help in the form most useful to the individual, namely, cash. It is general and could be substituted for the host of special measures now in effect.[4]

President Nixon, in his 1974 State of the Union message and subsequent speeches by HEW Secretary Casper W. Weinberger suggest that the Nixon Administration was on the verge of proposing an NIT. President Nixon said, in his 1974 State of the Union:

In these final three years of my administration I urge the Congress to join me in mounting a major new effort to *replace* the discredited present welfare system with one that works, one that is fair to those who need help or cannot help themselves, fair to the community, and fair to the taxpayer—and let us have as our goal that there will be no government program which makes it more profitable to go on welfare than to go to work.[5]

In March 1972 HEW Secretary Casper W. Weinberger spoke to the Detroit Economic Club about Administration plans (in the president's words) "to replace the discredited, present welfare system." A news account said that, without specifically endorsing it, Weinberger made a case for the negative income tax on both economic and philosophical grounds.

However, three months later it was announced by Secretary Weinberger that such a plan would not be advanced in 1974 and that other options were under review.[6] (The basic paper produced by the HEW planning staff on which the Administration's plans were based has been published by the University of Wisconsin.[7])

Ideally, an NIT would have the following characteristics:

1. It would be smoothly integrated with the positive tax system.
2. It would be nationally administered, very likely by the Internal Revenue Service to put it on a firm, business-like basis.
3. It would treat all persons the same according to their needs, i.e., the aged, the disabled, employable family heads and their children, single persons, childless couples.
4. It would have a sufficiently low tax (or reduction) rate so as to preserve work incentives.[e]
5. It would provide an adequate minimal income, probably with an automatic cost-of-living escalator, such as we now have for Social Security.

One of the main underpinnings of the current case for an NIT is the results of the NIT experiment in New Jersey conducted from 1967 to 1972. Although some interpret the data differently, those involved in the experiment conclude from their data that providing a guaranteed minimum income did not "appreciably" reduce the work effort of recipients.[8]

The Incremental Reform Position

The second overall welfare policy alternative, which I personally favor, is the incremental reform position. It says, in effect, that we have moved so far in the past decade in terms of the development and growth of income-security programs that the NIT position has been passed over by events. The need now is to fill in gaps that remain and take steps—some quite important ones—to improve and rationalize existing programs, rather than replace them with a comprehensive new system.

The most important change since the mid-sixties involves food stamps. When the FAP program was first introduced in 1969, there was a significant gap in

---

[e]Milton Friedman says this reduction rate should be no higher than 50 percent.

welfare-program coverage. Intact families with a working head could be so large and have such a low income that they received significantly less in income than broken AFDC families. This group (the so-called "working poor") were aided in 1969 in some states if the family head was *unemployed*, defined generally as working thirty hours per week or less.[f] However, in states that did not choose to aid intact families under AFDC, the working poor were left out entirely. All of this was changed by the food stamp program.

A virtual pilot program assisting around two million persons in only a few states five years ago, the food stamp program today aids over thirteen million persons and is universally available. Moreover, the food stamp program today provides more aid to most working-poor families than they would have received had the Family Assistance Plan been enacted by the 92nd Congress in 1972. Food stamp benefits are adjusted automatically every six months to reflect increases in the price of food, which in the recent period has been rising much faster than other consumer purchases. Federal food stamp expenditures are now running at about $5 billion per year and according to one estimate could go as high as $10 billion by 1976.[9]

It is argued that food stamps are inefficient and demeaning—both good arguments. However, on the other side it needs to be noted that, while the political process would not accept FAP, the food stamp program (people have to eat!) was politically a much more acceptable way to provide benefits to families with working-age members. (This has always been the Achilles heel of welfare policy—aiding people of working age.)

Other welfare programs have also expanded greatly since the mid-sixties, notably AFDC and Medicaid. The idea of the incremental position is that several things need to be done which now can be achieved reasonably well (and in politics, this is a high standard) without starting all over again. They are:

1. Benefits for working poor families in some cases are too low relative to other income-security programs.[g] Various options exist to add *one more piece* to the existing system which would remedy this problem. For example:

a. a *housing allowance* is one possibility. (The Nixon Administration came close

---

[f]Twenty-three states currently provide federally-matched benefits for this group under what is called AFDC-UP, the "UP" standing for unemployed parent. Some of these states (about seven) also aid intact poor families *without* an employable adult entirely out of their own funds.

[g]This is actually a very complex statement. The tax (or reduction) rate for food stamps is low in comparison to other income security programs—about 30 percent. This is an important positive feature of the program. One effect it has is to make the bonus value of stamps relatively high, again compared to other programs, for families or persons who have *some* income—say $2,500 per year. However, food stamp recipients with no income or very little income receive low benefits compared to other programs. The latter group is really only a problem in the states that do not have AFDC-UP. In the twenty-three AFDC-UP states, if the family head is unemployed, he is eligible for AFDC benefits.

to accepting this idea in 1972 in the president's message on housing, September 19, 1973.)[h]

b. a *work bonus* is another.[i]

c. Still a third possibility, like the work bonus, would be to extend unemployment insurance (UI) at reduced rates for the long-term unemployed, new entrants, and other unemployed persons not now eligible for UI benefits. (The AFL-CIO and other groups interested in welfare policy are currently working on such an option.)

At the very most, some combination of three programs (including a program for medical care), all of which would be integrated conceptually and administratively, is envisioned. Four possible packages are:

Two programs—AFDC and a parallel program of work bonuses with food stamps cashed out for both groups, plus a medical-care program.

[h]Housing allowances have the added advantage of being relatively easily adjusted for cost-of-living differences between urban and rural areas.

The current policy of the Administration closely resembles a housing allowance. The Administration proposes in the housing area to rely almost entirely on the Section 23 (rental assistance) section of the Housing Act of 1937. This program, while operating like a housing allowance in many ways, differs from it in that it is available in limited quantity. (Approximately four hundred thousand commitments are planned for fiscal year 1975. This is a small fraction, less than 5 percent, of all families and persons that might be eligible under the income definitions used for this program.) To the extent Section 23 assistance is made available for *"existing"* housing units, the equity issue raised by its limited availability in relation to the universe of need is a serious one. This assumes that the Section 23 program functions reasonably efficiently as a means of stimulating *"new"* starts and thus can be justified on efficiency grounds, quite apart from welfare policy considerations. Even then, the current average costs projected—approximately $2,400 per unit per year—are *extremely* high.

On the whole, the incremental position assumes that existing housing subsidies should be minimized, even eliminated because they are so costly and unfair.

[i]Senator Russell B. Long, chairman of the Senate Finance Committee, has proposed a work-bonus plan which passed the Senate last year. It is in the form of a rebate to low-income workers of their Social Security taxes. Such a program, if it were changed to be unrelated to Social Security taxes, could add a piece to existing welfare benefits on a basis that would achieve most of the major advantages of an NIT—plus other important purposes. For example, it could: (1) create two tracks for welfare, one, which would be small and contracting, for those who cannot work (AFDC) and another for those who work or could work (the work bonus); (2) create conditions under which it would make sense to "cash-out" (convert to cash) food stamps, either universally or at state or individual option; and (3) retain the state as the administering agency of payments to working-age persons, assuming they administer the work bonus. The third point has important implications for American federalism. If one assumes that service-type functions (job placement, training, child care, supported work, *etc.*) should be state and locally administered, not administered by the federal government, then having the state pay both the work bonus and AFDC would be administratively sensible in that the same level of government that made payments would administer the services for the working-age poor to which these benefits would be linked. Presumably, this state agency would also administer the work requirement, assuming there is one. Many NIT plans would drop a work requirement. Even if they don't, it is hard to see how it could be effectively administered by the federal government under an NIT.

Three programs—AFDC and a work bonus with food stamps continued, plus a medical-care program.

Three programs—AFDC and unemployment insurance extended with food stamps continued, plus a medical care program.

Three programs—AFDC and a parallel program of work bonuses with food stamps cashed out *plus* a housing allowance and a medical care program.[j]

As an alternative to *an additional piece* as a gap-filler, the food stamp bonus could simply be increased and at the same time perhaps be expanded to cover other needs as a way of improving benefits for the working-age poor and their dependents.

2. Also as part of the incremental position, a national minimum benefit for AFDC probably should be adopted.

3. The incremental position could also include parallel administrative changes to rationalize and integrate existing programs, conform the application processes and the definitions of eligibility and benefit entitlement, and at the same time make the state (no longer counties) the responsible payment agents. Under such an arrangement, states could be required to use automated payment systems which many jurisdictions are now developing along with improved management techniques.[k] This would enable the states to tie assistance payments and the administration of the work requirement to manpower and other services for the poor of working age.

4. The incremental position with state administration makes sense for persons who believe that there should be a work requirement for the working-aged poor where suitable work and child care are available. National administration of NIT benefits to this group would make the administration of such a work requirement very difficult.

5. Finally, the incremental approach, adding or revising benefits and reorganizing program administration, would leave the SSI program in place.[l] This program is now beginning to take hold and be debugged. An NIT that converted this population to a new program could have two types of undesirable effects; (a) it

---

[j]The important point in relation to the NIT position is that in almost all cases, it envisions having *at least two programs*, that is, one for cash assistance and a separate additional program for medical care.

The incremental strategy could also include a deduction for child care for eligible working single parents, which could be set up in such a way as to minimize its effect on the tax (or reduction) rate. Again, the same issue has to be faced under an NIT.

[k]Currently some thirty states directly administer AFDC benefits and food stamps. In the other states, counties have this responsibility. One possible feature of incremental welfare reform legislation would, over an appropriate period of time, be to require state administration. Several major states with county administration are moving in this direction.

[l]The rationale for national administration for the aged, blind, and disabled as federalized under the Social Security Administration rests on the fact that they are no longer in the labor force and hence do not need work-related services provided by states and localities, and secondly, on the fact that three-quarters (and eventually more) in this group are already Social Security recipients.

would disrupt newly-established administrative relationships for these persons, and (b) it would probably cause some SSI recipients to lose income if the flat national minimum benefit was lower than SSI in order to be a reasonably priced total package.

Another aspect of the incremental position concerns health care. Assuming a major new health plan is enacted by the 93rd or 94th Congress, one of the most important beneficiary groups would be the working poor. Medicaid already aids the nonworking poor on AFDC, in some cases materially and in a way that is inequitable for blue-collar persons immediately above them on the income ladder. At the same time, many persons who are better off (middle income groups) have private health insurance that is reasonably adequate, or at least have some coverage. Thus, the big gainers would be the near-poor and working poor, which, in effect, makes health care reform a sensible and integral part of the incremental position on welfare reform.

The Politics of Choice. Thus far, the substantive and operational aspects of the NIT and incremental options have been discussed. There is also an important tactical and political dimension to the choice between the two positions. NIT advocates argue that unless a truly sweeping measure that proposes to do away with current welfare is advanced, it will not be possible to mobilize sufficient national opinion to achieve legislative action to bring about needed improvements in the condition of the poor. Incrementalists, on the other hand, contend that the overall price tag (gross of $40 billion to $50 billion) on an NIT would produce an emotional and divisive national debate, the net effect of which would not be to add in any appreciable way to the benefits of the poor. In fact, AFDC and SSI recipients in high payment states would be likely to be worse off unless the minimum benefit were set at what would seem to be an unrealistically high level in terms of winning support for an NIT. (In an interesting way, the politics of welfare may be changing with conservatives moving more towards an NIT as a way of stemming program growth and liberals moving away from an NIT for the reason just stated.) A third welfare policy option, treated below and at less length, is one which rests most heavily of all on these kinds of tactical and political considerations.

The Status Quo Option

Among the strongest advocates of better treatment and larger benefits for the poor, there is strong sentiment for a position which says, "keep your cotton-picking hands off." The reasoning is as follows: Because of the national animosity towards welfare generally, when legislation is advanced, the conservative provisions typically are adopted and the liberal provisions discarded. There is considerable evidence to suggest this is so. In the case of the Family Assistance

Plan, for example, the Congress separately enacted President Nixon's proposal for a strong work-requirement, but did not act on FAP benefit improvements. (The Talmadge Amendments enacted in 1972 considerably strengthened the work requirement in the law applying to AFDC beneficiaries.)[m]

The *status quo* liberal position further holds that at certain points in history (for example 1967 to 1970) it is possible to liberalize regulations under welfare programs—quietly and unobtrusively—and that this can have the effect of improving benefits materially, much more so than would be the case if the legislative route were taken. Frances Fox Piven and Richard A. Cloward are among the principal advocates of this position. Citing the rapid rise in welfare roles (notably AFDC) in the late sixties and early seventies, they conclude:

In the absence of fundamental economic reforms, therefore, *we take the position that the explosion of the rolls is the true relief reform*, that it should be defended, and expanded. Even now, hundreds of thousands of impoverished families remain who are eligible for assistance but who receive no aid at all.[10]

Gilbert Y. Steiner of Brookings puts it somewhat differently. He uses the food stamp program, in addition to the explosion of the AFDC rolls, to show that where welfare planners have failed, welfare programs, as far as the poor are concerned, have nevertheless succeeded.

The "discovery" of hunger in the 1960's have led to revival of the dormant, but previously used, program of food stamps. Slower than AFDC in its initial explosion, the food stamp program accelerated directly with the growth of social concern over hunger and malnutrition. The Department of Agriculture responded to its critics by mounting a massive food stamp campaign. Ultimately, stamps developed an independent constituency and an independent life. That separate relief system stands as an unplanned major barrier to welfare simplification.

Steiner concludes his discussion of welfare growth as follows:

The lesson is that reform follows reality. To the extent that welfare reform involved perfecting a mechanism that would simplify the system and minimize the costs of public charity, virtually all welfare-policy change since 1961 has been counterproductive. To the extent that welfare reform involved recognizing and relieving dependency, policies pursued in the 1960's effected that purpose. Paradoxically, the latter occurred in the face of persistent efforts to achieve the former. While the planners are frustrated, the welfare poor are better off.[11]

Welfare Reform and Income Redistribution. Although this chapter concentrates on programmatic considerations, other writers would start at a very different

---

[m]In effect, there is also a *status quo* conservative position which says we should stay where we are because benefits are already high enough or too high, and additional legislation is likely only to expand and increase them.

point, not with issues as to how to reform welfare, but rather questions of *how much?* That is, how much income should we redistribute as a nation to lower-income groups? In 1971, the lowest fifth of the population grouped by family income received 5.5 percent of aggregate income; the top fifth received 41.6 percent. (The highest five percent of families grouped by income in 1970 received 14.4 percent of aggregate income, nearly three times the amount received in that year by the lowest fifth.)

Several points should be made about these data:

1. Census data do not include in-kind benefits, i.e., food stamps and Medicaid.
2. With the food stamp program just now becoming universal and more widely known, it could in the next several years (the JEC forecasts such an outcome) shift substantial resources to the lower-income groups. Health care reform now in the works may have the same effect.
3. The earnings of lower-income persons are often not well-reported. While there are undoubtedly compensating errors, (*viz.* under-counting) there is good reason for raising a further question as to whether the income of the lower-income groups is accurately represented in Census data.

In any event, the choice for welfare policy is not really changed. It can be argued that any one of the three options discussed above would serve best as a device for income distribution.

For those who favor significant income redistribution, there is an additional important point: One cannot just look at welfare programs in this connection. In considering the larger question of income redistribution, tax policy issues far more comprehensive than the issues raised in this chapter need to be addressed.

Work-for-Welfare—The Guaranteed "Job" Approach

Still another school of thought about how best to assist the working-age poor has developed around the idea that "jobs," not "checks," are the solution, and that if this requires a policy of "government-as-employer-of-last-resort," then that is what we should do. Critical questions in this area are: (1) could we actually mount a program to achieve this goal; and (2) if we did, how large and expensive would it be?

If government, for example, provided jobs at the minimum wage for all persons who are employable, it is likely that there would be significant employment-displacement effects as a result. That is, workers in jobs currently paying at or below the minimum wage would leave their jobs in order to be "employed" in the public sector. Moreover, large numbers of persons above the minimum wage might also prefer government employment because the conditions and hours presumably would be better. The displacement effects of such a

Table XI-3
Percentage Share of Aggregate Income in 1971, Received by Each Fifth of Families

Income Rank	1971
Families	
Total	100.0
Lowest Fifth	5.5
Second Fifth	11.9
Third Fifth	17.4
Fourth Fifth	23.7
Highest Fifth	41.6

policy could be far-reaching. HEW is currently planning a saturation experiment of the public employment approach in Washington State, although no decision has been made yet on whether to proceed. (The design for the HEW experiment is such that even if undertaken it might not provide usable results as to the employment-displacement effects of the guaranteed "job" approach.)

Using reasonably conservative assumptions, available Census income data suggest that a national program of guaranteed "jobs" would require at least three million "jobs" at a *net* cost of $20 billion per annum. This is double the number of enrollment opportunities in all work and training programs administered by the Department of Labor in 1972, and about seven times the total cost of these programs.[12]

The significant point that emerges from such estimates is that unemployment and poverty are not necessarily linked. Millions of poor people work; any plan that relieves poverty by providing employment must therefore absorb large numbers of people who are already working, or have some connection with the labor force. This is why the cost and participation projections above are so large.

In sum, a guaranteed employment program, however packaged, would have profound labor-market effects. We need to approach this option with a healthy respect for the fact that even with the "best" of results and administrative systems such a fundamental policy reorientation is so far-reaching that it should not be undertaken without the most penetrating scrutiny.[13]

Social Security Options

Related to the welfare-policy issues dealt with so far, the nation is currently faced with difficult issues of Social Security financing not treated above. Public attention is just now beginning to be focused on this subject:[14]

A person retiring in July 1974 who worked long enough to qualify for minimum social security payments would receive about $95 a month. If he or she had no other income, the SSI program would pay about $71 a month, bringing total income to $166. Another person who never paid any social security taxes and who became eligible at the same time would qualify for $146 per month in SSI if there were no other source of income. Many people would question whether it is fair that only a $20 per month advantage accrues to the person who paid payroll taxes for many years.[15]

A Social Security Advisory Council—one is appointed by law every four years—is working on these and related issues. It is chaired by W. Allen Wallis, president of the University of Rochester.

Viewing the overall options, the more conservative position on current social security issues says that we should: (1) move more towards the insurance objective of wage replacement; (2) eliminate the minimums for Social Security benefits and use SSI instead for welfare purposes; and (3) steer clear of general-revenue financing of the Social Security system. On the liberal side, changes commonly urged are: (1) expand coverage of the poor under Social Security thus avoiding having to use means-tested programs; (2) rely more on general-revenue financing for this purpose (some urge complete general-revenue financing); and (3) broaden disability coverage. Other issues to be dealt with which are less polarized are:

1. whether there should be a tax credit to low-wage workers of their Social Security taxes.
2. whether the income test (limiting benefits for wage-earners who are between sixty-five and seventy-two) should be liberalized further or eliminated.
3. whether benefits for married women should be the same as for men.

Total estimated Social Security receipts in 1975 of $62.3 billion are nearly one-half of those projected for the individual income tax. They significantly exceed corporate income tax receipts estimated at $48 billion. Public finance experts have criticized the growth of the OASDI tax and its general regressivity (the extent of its regressivity being arguable). Again the arguments are both substantive and tactical. On the tactical side, one view is that the contributory concept built into Social Security has the effect of restraining its growth and that we should be mindful of this point in decisions about major OASDI tax policy changes. Wilbur Cohen, former HEW secretary and one of the architects of Social Security, contends that the payroll tax "makes the program fiscally conservative." In his words, "Since the benefits are paid out of payroll tax proceeds, the politicians who govern the system cannot wildly expand benefits without also increasing the tax to intolerable levels."[16] Others argue that the level of federal taxes *per se* is sensitive enough, and that the OASDI tax bite is big enough, so that we are now effectively in a position to give up, or move a long distance from, contributory financing.

Concluding Comment

Analysis of income maintenance issues has now become a quite active field, in part stimulated by the "industry" created around experiments, such as the New Jersey income maintenance experiment, the housing allowance experiments,[n] and HEW's health-insurance experiments. Knowledge of these issues and their dynamics has greatly increased. But one would be remiss not to emphasize in any policy paper in this field that "practitioners" (politicians, commission members, interested groups) proceed at their peril if they do not take into account the strong public attitudes that exist in this area. The Family Assistance Plan surely demonstrated this point. Social value considerations about work obligations, child care and its meaning in terms of the socialization process, the attractiveness of work-for-welfare and the notion of a contributory Social Security system have deep importance for the success of any attempted policy change in the areas discussed in this chapter. The power of the imagery of welfare issues has been demonstrated many times. Unless the Commission wants to embark (as perhaps it should) on a major educational campaign, there is wisdom in designing any plans in this field in a manner which takes public attitudes into account and builds upon them.

On a personal note, I would be very dubious about any plan which challenges the "work ethic." Properly qualified, this is a very serviceable social value. It is fundamental to the competitive enterprise character of our economic system. In a way, it is also a dignified approach for persons whose income is so low that a public subsidy in some form is regarded appropriate. For it says to the recipient, if what we are talking about is the application of a work requirement and attendant program elements, "You are just as good as the next man; you should be in the labor force."

Perhaps one of our critical choices for the future is to let some Americans opt for more leisure—for nonwork "life styles." This is hardly an empirical question. But for what it is worth, my own experience with welfare issues and welfare politics, and indeed my own preference in these matters, is that this is not a critical choice that our society as a whole is ready to make, wants to make, or should make.

Notes

1. Year-to-year comparisons from Barry M. Blechman, Edward M. Gramlich, and Robert W. Hartman, *Setting National Priorities: The 1975 Budget* (Brookings, 1974), Chapters 1-2. This book is referred to later in the paper as *SNP-1975*. Other expenditure and program data are from the federal budget for fiscal year 1975. See "Special Analysis K" on income-security programs.

n HUD's housing allowance experiments are especially large, projected at approximately $210 million over five years for three sets of concurrent experiments. This is over twenty times greater in cost than the New Jersey income-maintenance experiment.

2. *SNP-1975*, Chapter 7, p. 167.

3. Vee Burke and Alair A. Townsend, "Public Welfare and Work Incentives: Theory and Practice," U.S. Congress, Joint Economic Committee, Subcommittee on Fiscal Policy, Paper No. 14, April 15, 1974, p. 7. See also Alair A. Townsend, "Can We Have an Income Strategy?" The Urban Institute, Working Paper 786-2, March 1974, and Henry J. Aaron, "Why is Welfare So Hard to Reform?" Staff Paper, The Brookings Institution, 1974. The JEC Subcommittee on Fiscal Policy has published other useful materials on welfare policy options to which the reader may wish to refer. A number are quite technical papers. Staff Paper No. 14 (cited above) is a summary of major issues in nontechnical language.

4. Milton Friedman, *Capitalism and Freedom* (University of Chicago Press, 1962), p. 192.

5. State of the Union, January 30, 1974, U.S. Government Printing Office, House Document No. 93-206. Emphasis added.

6. Paul Delaney, "Nixon Abandons Income Aid Plan for Reform of Welfare System," *New York Times*, May 26, 1974. Another source, indicating my own views on this issue, is "Tax Aid to the Poor—Reconsidered," *Wall Street Journal*, April 24, 1974.

7. Michael C. Barth, George J. Carcagno, and John L. Palmer, *Toward an Effective Income Support System: Problems, Prospects, and Choices* (Madison: University of Wisconsin, 1974).

8. The New Jersey experiment did find that secondary earners in a family tended to reduce their work effort considerably more than the primary earner. The New Jersey experiment actually consisted of several plans with different payment levels, reduction rates and other characteristics. For a discussion of the results, see HEW, "Summary Report: New Jersey Graduated Work Incentive Experiment," December 1973, *Journal of Human Resources* (special issue on this subject), 9, 2 (Spring 1974), and the report from the Brookings Institution conference on the results from the New Jersey Experiment (April 28-30, 1974), Joseph A. Pechman and Michael Timpane, editors.

9. This estimate is by Representative Martha W. Griffiths, chairman of the Joint Economic Committee's Subcommittee on Fiscal Policy. Statement, April 15, 1974. An excellent assessment of the food stamp program is contained in an address by P. Royal Shipp, Assistant Deputy Administrator of the Food and Nutrition Service, U.S. Department of Agriculture, presented to the Welfare Staff Seminar, May 8, 1974. His title, an appropriate one, "Food Stamps—A Funny Thing Happened on the Way to Welfare Reform." (Processed)

10. Frances Fox Piven and Richard A. Cloward, *Regulating the Poor: The Functions of Public Welfare* (Vintage Books, 1972), p. 348.

11. Gilbert Y. Steiner, "Reform Follows Reality: The Growth of Welfare," *The Public Interest*, Number 34 (Winter 1974): 65.

12. *Manpower Report of the President*, March 1973. Table F-1, p. 227.

13. This approach is advocated by Arnold H. Packer, senior economist for the Committee for Economic Development, among others. See "Employment Guarantees Should Replace the Welfare System," *Challenge*, March-April 1974, pp. 21-27. It would have less far-reaching economic and labor-market effects if limited to family heads.

14. See, for example, Roger LeRoy Miller, "Social Security: The Cruelest Tax," *Harpers*, June 1974, pp. 22-27.

15. *SNP-1975*, p. 191.

16. Interview, *Milwaukee Journal*, June 21, 1974.

 Critical Choices
in the Federal
Social Security
Program
(Old-Age,
Survivors, and
Disability
Insurance)

Robert M. Ball

Introduction

History and Concept

In the latter part of the nineteenth and the beginning of the twentieth century many of the European states began to develop a new approach to the problem of economic insecurity. This new approach was "social insurance," a compulsory government plan designed to compensate for the loss of earning power. It was based on the simple idea that each covered worker would be required to pay a small portion of his earnings into an insurance fund, with the workers' payments supplemented by payments from employers and frequently by the government as well. The insurance fund paid benefits to contributors and their dependents when wages stopped or were greatly reduced because of sickness, accident, old-age, permanent disability or death, and later on because of unemployment.

Prior to this time, governments had frequently taken responsibility for directly relieving the poor by identifying them through a test of means and then giving them assistance, but the idea of preventing poverty by having workers and their employers participate in an insurance program to compensate for the loss of wages was a social invention of the nineteenth century. Although new in the nineteenth century as a compulsory, large-scale government-operated system, social insurance grows out of a long tradition of people getting together to help themselves.

The opinions expressed in this chapter are those of the author and not necessarily those of any organization with which he is connected.

Formal benefit plans, for example, were established by the guilds of the Middle Ages. We have many records of these plans which provided information on how much each member was expected to pay while working, and how much, in turn, he would receive should he become disabled, or what would be paid his family in the event of his death. Another forerunner of social insurance was the customary fund found in the mining districts of Austria and other central European countries, with some funds dating back to the sixteenth century. Later, of course, fraternal orders and friendly societies were organized by the hundreds with the central purpose of protecting their members against risks now covered by social insurance. Trade unions throughout the world developed protection plans for their membership, and commercial insurance covering some of the same risks of income loss became widely available.

The tradition of social insurance is clear. It grew out of the efforts of workers to protect themselves and their families against the risks that were likely to cause a loss of earnings. The approach is in sharp contrast to the method of relief and assistance. In relief and assistance the applicant demonstrates a lack and proves that he does not have enough to get along on. Applying for assistance is, therefore, essentially a negative and to some extent an humiliating experience. In insurance, one demonstrates past work and contributions; entitlement grows out of the demonstration of having done something one can be proud of. Modern social insurance follows the same basic principles as its precursors in the guilds, the customary funds, and in a variety of other insurance mechanisms. However, social insurance uses the instrument of government to administer the plan and to make it universal through legal compulsion.

The idea of an insurance against the loss of wages—"income insurance," is the apt phrase of Arthur Larson[1] —was a social invention with far-reaching effects on human lives. It spread across the world until today in every industrial country there are universal, or nearly universal systems, collecting contributions from workers and their employers and paying out benefits to partially make up for the loss of wages that accompanies old age, disability, illness, unemployment or death.

On the whole, the social insurance approach has worked well because in a wage economy it is the right prescription for a large part of the problem of economic insecurity. Most people are dependent on income from a job. If that work income is cut off or greatly reduced, poverty and insecurity result. Thus, income insurance prevents what would otherwise be widespread poverty and insecurity among older people, the disabled, orphans and widows, and the unemployed.

Developments in the United States

Until recently, our system of social insurance was considerably less effective than that of other major industrial countries. We were late to start—1935, some fifty years after Germany—and the retirement system features of social insurance, like any pension plan, mature slowly because those already retired when the system starts are not protected. Thus, even by 1950 in the United States, only about a fourth of all older people were protected by social security, and even by 1960 only about 70 percent. Now, however, the American system has reached practically full maturity with over 90 percent of older people protected.

Moreover, benefit levels have been greatly improved in recent years. Coverage is just about universal, and the federally-administered system covers income loss arising from extended total disability and death, as well as from old age, and state systems with federal participation cover the risk of unemployment. The federal system of old-age, survivors, and disability insurance is kept up to date automatically with the movement of wages and prices. Except for health insurance, which is not included in the subject of this chapter, the major part of the agenda of social security advocates has been carried out in the United States. The system is responsible for keeping some twelve million Americans out of poverty and is the most important single source of income for the great majority of beneficiaries.

Major Questions About the Soundness and Fairness
of the Program

Yet, at the very time social security has reached maturity and for the first time is doing well the job it was designed to do, probably more questions are being raised about it than at any time since the initial arguments over whether to adopt such a system at all. This seeming paradox may well grow out of the increased size of the program, the higher contributions required, and the larger number of people covered; it is now big enough to argue about.

It is argued that the program is unfair because it denies benefits to those who work after 65, and because it gives more in relation to contributions to low-wage earners than to average and above-average earners. It is argued that women are unfairly treated as compared to men, and working wives are compared to wives who are not in paid employment. It is said to cost too much compared to what a young worker would be able to buy in protection elsewhere, and that low-income workers and blacks are discriminated against because they start to work sooner and pay in longer, but on the average receive less in retirement benefits because they die sooner. The system is said to be bankrupt because it does not have reserves sufficient to pay the benefits promised in the absence of future contributions, and it is argued that the contribution rates in the law will be insufficient to pay benefits in the next century because of the relative increase in the number of older people as compared to those of working age. Social security financing is attacked for being regressive. And it is argued that social security is an inefficient approach to the problem of poverty and "wastes money" since there is no means test, and the program pays those who could take care of themselves as well as the poor.

In this chapter I will attempt to separate the valid criticisms from the invalid, and to point up the critical choices that should be made now that will affect the future effectiveness of the program and, therefore, its long-run contribution to the quality of American life.

It may be helpful, however, before dealing with criticisms, possible problems, and the evaluation of alternative responses to problems, to briefly describe the main features of the program under discussion—the federal social security system for the payment of old-age, survivors, and disability insurance benefits.

Social Security Today

In 1935 when the Social Security Act was passed, there were only about six million persons, less than 15 percent of those employed, who were in jobs covered by any sort of retirement system. About two million government employees were covered, plus around 200,000 nonprofit employees, such as clergymen, university and college teachers, and perhaps 3.7 million workers in business and industry, including railroad workers under the government system of railroad retirement.

In 1975, at any one time, over 90 percent of all jobs in the United States were covered by social security. In recent years, this nearly universal coverage of jobs has been effectively translated into the protection of the people who are at risk. In 1975, 91 percent of the people 65 and older were eligible for social security benefits, and 95 out of 100 young children and their mothers were protected by social security survivors insurance. Four out of five people in the age group 21 through 64 had protection under social security against loss of income due to severe disability. Thirty-two million people, one out of seven Americans, received a social security benefit each month.

Benefit Amounts

Since 1940, benefit amounts under social security have been related to average monthly earnings in covered employment. Benefit amounts originally paid were very low, averaging from $23 to $26 a month for retirement benefits from the first payments in 1940 up to the amendments of 1950. Even as late as 1968, the average was still under $100 a month. By 1976, as a result of a series of liberalizing amendments, and the maturing of the program—that is, the fact that large numbers of people now retiring have been under social security for a major part of their working lifetime—the average benefit amounts, though still quite low, are considerably higher. In 1975, the average retirement benefit was $205 a month. As will be discussed later, the amounts payable for those newly coming on the rolls will be substantially higher in the future.

In most cases today, the average monthly wage on which benefit amounts are computed is based on earnings from 1950, with the five years of lowest earnings being dropped from the computation. The earnings used in computing benefits include only earnings below the specified amount that was covered for contribution purposes in a particular year. The maximum amount was $3,000 in 1937, the year the program actually began operation, and has been increased many times as wage levels have risen over the years. In 1976, the maximum amount on which people pay, and the maximum amount credited toward benefits, was $15,300. This amount will increase automatically in relation to increases in average covered earnings.

While both benefits and contributions are related to earnings, they are related somewhat differently. The contribution rate is the same for each dollar of covered earnings in a year, currently for cash benefits 4.95 percent each for the employee and the employer. The benefit amounts, however, are a substantially higher percentage of the first $650 a month of average monthly earnings than they are of the remainder. Thus, a person with relatively low average earnings gets a benefit which replaces a higher proportion of his earnings than does the worker who has relatively high average earnings. This "weighting" in the benefit formula is an advantage both to the regular worker who earns low wages and to the person whose average covered earnings are low because he or she is not under the system full time. This provision is particularly advantageous to women who may leave the labor market for substantial periods in order to take care of young children. The minimum benefit for the worker who retires at 65 or later was $101.40 in 1975.

A worker may choose to receive retirement benefits as early as age 62, but the benefits are reduced if he takes them prior to 65. The amount of the reduction takes account of the longer period over which the benefits will be paid, and on the average is the equivalent in value of the higher benefit payable at 65 for a shorter period—a so-called "actuarial reduction."

Dependent's and survivor's benefits are related to what would be paid a retired worker starting at age 65, an amount referred to in the law as the "primary insurance amount." Thus, a wife's or husband's benefit is equal to one-half of the primary insurance amount, a widow or widower who begins to receive benefits at 65, or later, gets a benefit equal to the PIA (if he or she takes benefits earlier, or if the wage earner had an actuarially reduced benefit, the payment to the widow or widower will be less than the PIA). The benefit for a surviving child of an insured worker is three-fourths of the PIA, and the benefit for a child of a retired or disabled worker is one-half of the PIA. Other benefits payable to dependents and survivors are similarly related to the PIA. Total amounts payable on a single wage record are subject to maximums that range from 150 percent to 188 percent of the PIA, depending on the amount of the PIA.

A worker eligible for a benefit based on his or her own wage record always gets the full amount of that benefit, but if he or she is also entitled to a dependent's or survivor's benefit, the latter amount is reduced so that the combined payment does not exceed what the individual would have been entitled to simply as a dependent or survivor. The adjustment is made in this way rather than just paying whichever benefit is higher, since there are substantial advantages (described later) in being eligible for a benefit based on one's own earnings and contributions.

Benefit amounts payable in the future will be considerably higher than those presently payable for two reasons: First of all, as wages rise, the average earnings on which the benefits are based will be higher, and this will mean higher benefits. This is now true at the upper range of earnings, as well as at lower earnings levels, since the maximum amount credited for benefits will rise automatically as average wages rise in the future. Secondly, benefits will be higher in the future since the benefit table in the law which determines the benefit amount payable at a *particular* average earnings level will also be automatically revised each time the cost of living increases by 3 percent or more. Those already receiving benefits will have their benefit amount increased to keep up with the cost of living.

Table XII-1 indicates the extent to which benefit levels have recently been raised and how benefits will be kept up to date with rising wage levels and prices in the future. The table compares the benefits payable at various wage levels for people now retiring with what those people would have received under the benefit formula in effect prior to February 1968, just before the recent series of across-the-board benefit increases. The table also shows what individuals retiring at 65 in 1980 will be getting as a result of the automatic provisions now in the law. Because the adequacy of retirement benefits is best measured as a percentage of recent earnings, the figures are given both in dollar amounts and as a percentage of earnings in the year before retirement.

Even taking into account the fact that about half of all retired workers receive benefits that have been reduced because they apply for benefits before 65 (as much as a 20 percent reduction if they apply at 62, the earliest possible age), it is clear that for the first time benefits are reasonably adequate for many workers when measured against final earnings. Couples fare quite well in terms of the replacement of recent earnings at all wage levels below those earned by the median male worker. Even for those earning above the median earnings, the amounts for the first time provide, for couples at least, a reasonable base on which they can build retirement income. On the other hand, some improvement for single workers seems called for. Table XII-1 also illustrates the very substantial "weighting" for low earners in the benefit formula, as previously discussed.

Table XII-1
Benefit Amounts and the Percentage of Last Year's Earnings Before Retirement for Selected Earnings Levels and Selected Benefit Formulas

February 1968 Formula[1]

	Amount		Percentage of Last Year's Earnings	
	Single	Couple	Single	Couple
Worker Earning Federal Minimum Wage[4]	$93.20	$139.80	37.4%	56.1%
Worker Earning the Median Wage for Male Workers	$154.90	$232.40	25.9%	38.8%
Worker Earning the Maximum Covered Amount	$180.80	$271.20	20.1%	30.1%

June 1975 Formula[2]

	Amount		Percentage of Last Year's Earnings	
	Single	Couple	Single	Couple
Worker Earning Federal Minimum Wage[4]	$198.60	$297.90	61.5%	92.2%
Worker Earning the Median Wage for Male Workers	$288.20	$432.30	45.0%	67.5%
Worker Earning the Maximum Covered Amount	$341.70	$512.60	31.1%	46.6%

1980 Formula[3]

	Amount		Percentage of Last Year's Earnings	
	Single	Couple	Single	Couple
Worker Earning Federal Minimum Wage[4]	$295.80	$443.70	56.5%	84.7%
Worker Earning the Median Wage for Male Workers	$441.10	$661.70	46.3%	69.4%

Table XII-1 (cont.)

	1980 Formula[3]			
	Amount		Percentage of Last Year's Earnings	
	Single	Couple	Single	Couple
Worker Earning the Maximum Covered Amount	$566.80	$850.20	34.4%	51.5%

1. The amount and percentage of earnings in the year before retirement that would be payable to people retiring at sixty-five today if the February 1968 formula were in effect.

2. The amount and percentage of earnings in the year before retirement payable to people retiring at sixty-five under the formula in effect in June 1975.

3. The amount and percentage of earnings in the year before retirement payable to people retiring at sixty-five in 1980 under the formula then in effect, assuming: (1) benefit increase of 6.6% in 1976, 6.4% in 1977, 6.3% in 1978, 4.8% in 1979, and 4.0% in 1980, and (2) an increase in earnings of 6.2% in 1975, 9.0% in 1976, 11.0% in 1977, and 8.8% in 1978.

4. Assumes that the worker earns federal minimum wage each year after 1950 up to the year of retirement.

Eligibility for Benefits

Workers and their dependents and survivors are eligible for benefits only if a worker has been under the program for a minimum amount of time. To be "fully insured" the worker is required to have been under the program about one-fourth of the time from age 21, or 1950, (whichever is later), until he reaches retirement age, becomes disabled, or dies. Thus, for retirement benefits, a worker now young needs the maximum required for anyone—ten years out of approximately a forty-year working lifetime. But for older workers the requirement is on a sliding scale related to age. For example, the worker who becomes 62 in 1975 will need six years of coverage, technically twenty-four calendar quarters, (one-fourth the number from 1950 up to 1975), in which he is paid wages of at least $50. A worker who becomes 62 in 1976 will need twenty-five quarters of coverage, and so on. Most survivor's benefits are payable on the basis of a less stringent rule. Benefits to surviving children, for example, are payable upon the death of a wage earner if he or she has six quarters of coverage out of the thirteen quarter period ending with the quarter in which he died.

On the other hand, to be eligible for disability benefits, workers over age 30, in addition to being fully insured must have been covered under the program for five years out of the ten (twenty quarters out of forty) just preceding the onset of disability. There is a more liberal rule for those under 30.

In accord with the objective of partially replacing earnings that have been lost, benefits are not paid before age 72 to the worker or his dependents if he continues to earn substantial amounts. The rule in 1976 is that an individual earning $2,760 or less in a year receives full social security benefits without reduction and above this amount social security benefits are reduced $1 for each $2 earned. In addition, regardless of the amount of annual earnings, a worker gets benefits for any month in which his earnings do not exceed $230 and in which he does not perform "substantial services" in self-employment. The exempt amounts will increase automatically in the future to keep pace with increases in general levels of earnings. Benefits of dependents and survivors who have earnings of their own are also reduced or withheld under the same rules. This earnings test, however, does not apply to those receiving disability benefits. To be eligible for disability benefits one must be unable to engage in "any substantial gainful employment," defined generally in 1975 as being unable to earn more than $230 a month.

Contribution Rates for Cash Benefits

The contribution rate for the cash benefit program, as indicated earlier, is currently 4.95 percent each on the employer and employee, and under present law remains at this level until the year 2011, when it is increased by 1 percent each to 5.95 percent of covered earnings. The rate for the self-employed is now 7 percent and remains at that rate indefinitely.

The social security laws are both detailed and complicated and many points of considerable importance have had to be omitted in this brief summary. The purpose of the summary has been to review only those program provisions of major pertinence to the issues that will be discussed.

A Look at the Future

The social security system is a group insurance and retirement system covering just about the entire population. All figures connected with the program are, therefore, very large. In 1975, for example, 100 million workers paid in, together with employers, over $66 billion to social security, and some 32 million beneficiaries received benefits of an approximately equal amount. The $45 billion trust fund will earn interest of $2.5 billion, and administrative expenses will run a little over $1 billion.

All figures get bigger. By 1985, it is estimated that instead of 32 million beneficiaries, there will be nearly 38 million. By the year 2000, there will be 46 million beneficiaries; and by 2050, 68 million.

Under the automatic provisions, as already explained, the average benefit amount also goes up. In 1975, the average award for retirement benefits for individuals coming on the rolls was about $2,750. By 1985, the average is estimated to be $5,021 and by 2000, $15,206. A large part of this increase is in wages and prices—6 percent a year in wages, and 4 percent a year in prices from 1980 on, more between now and then—and does not represent anything like such an increase in the relative value of retirement benefits as compared with earnings in the future. Because of certain peculiarities in the way the automatic provisions now in the law work, however, it is true that by the year 2000 the average new-award benefit, under the assumptions stated, will be about 12-1/2 percent higher in relation to wages than it was in 1975. By the year 2050, the increase relative to wages would be about 50 percent higher under the assumptions. Automatic benefit increases that go so far beyond rising wages would, however, never be allowed to go into effect. As discussed in a later section, well before this result came about, the law would undoubtedly be changed to prevent large numbers of people receiving benefits on retirement greater than any wages they had ever earned.

It is, of course, not the absolute dollar figures but the relation of the dollar figures to payrolls in the future that measure the burden of future commitments. Thus, the system in 1975 cost roughly 10 percent of covered payrolls and the actuarial projections on which the present contribution schedule in the law is based showed that cost as a percentage of payroll would continue to average about 10 percent until the year 2010, when the average cost for the next thirty-five years was shown to rise to about 12 percent of covered payrolls. However, the latest trustees' report shows a very different picture.

What has happened? Why does the new report show the system substantially out of balance over the long run? There are two parts to the answer. The first part of the answer lies in new assumptions concerning the long-range fertility rates (live births to be expected per female of childbearing age) in the United States and the consequent shift in the age composition of the population in the next century. The second part of the answer lies in the assumption that under the automatic provision benefits would over the long run be allowed to greatly outpace the increase in wages.

Can We Finance What We Have Promised?[2]

Population Changes and Social Security

The fertility rate in the United States has been dropping steadily since 1957 (see Table XII-2).

In terms of the quality of life this is good news indeed. It appears now that instead of the U.S. population moving up from 220 million in 1974, to 312 million in the year 2000, and 515 million by 2050 as was thought likely a few years ago, estimates today are in the neighborhood of 264 million for the year 2000, and 308 million for 2050, with near zero population growth being reached at that time.

Table XII-2
Fertility Rate in the United States

Year	Rate	Year	Rate
1957	3.77	1966	2.74
1958	3.70	1967	2.57
1959	3.71	1968	2.48
1960	3.65	1969	2.46
1961	3.63	1970	2.48
1962	3.47	1971	2.28
1963	3.33	1972	2.02
1964	3.21	1973	1.90
1965	2.93	1974	1.90

Actually, fertility rates are already slightly below the level that would eventually produce zero population growth—1.9 live births per female of childbearing age in 1974, as compared to the ZPG rate of 2.11. But under any possible conditions, the population will continue to grow for the next 75 years or so. This is true because those now of childbearing age were born at a time when fertility rates were much higher than at present, and until this generation dies out, the total population will increase, even though over the long run births are only sufficient to balance the number of deaths expected in the future.

The most important result of the drop in the fertility rate, of course, is that it removes the threat of unbearable pressures on the environment, on living space, on power, water, and on other resources. But good as the drop in the fertility rates is in terms of the quality of life, the shift in the age composition of the population that results means that there will be relatively more older people to be supported out of the production of those of working age than is true today.

Here is what we may expect: As shown in Table XII-3, in 1940 there were 77 million persons in the 20-64 age group, and 9 million people over 65, a ratio of 11.7 aged persons for every 100 persons of working age. Comparable figures in 1974 were 18 million and 22 million, for a ratio of 18.6 aged for every 100 persons of working age. Projecting fertility rates that ultimately would produce ZPG, results in only minor fluctuations in this ratio between now and 2010, but at that time the growth in the age 20-64 population comes to a halt, while at the same time there is a very major increase between 2010 and 2030 in the number of people age 65 and over.

The ratio of people 65 and over to the working-age group moves up to 30 per 100 under this fertility rate assumption and then stabilizes at a little over 28 per 100. Thus, assuming a continuation of a fertility rate that will ultimately produce ZPG, the result is a population distribution beginning about 2010 that will require the active labor force to support a much larger retired group relative

Table XII-3
Actual Past and Projected Future Population of the United States by Broad Age Groups, and Dependency Ratio

Year	Population (in thousands)			
	Under 20	20-64	65 & Over	Total
				Actual[1]
1930	47,609	68,438	6,634	122,681
1940	45,306	77,344	9,019	131,669
1950	51,295	86,664	12,257	150,216
1960	73,116	98,687	17,146	188,949
1970	80,637	112,500	20,655	213,792
1973	79,665	117,956	21,916	219,538
				Projected[2]
1990	71,929	147,457	28,789	248,176
2000	76,333	157,038	30,214	263,585
2010	76,222	167,432	32,662	276,316
2020	78,561	167,873	42,061	288,494
2030	80,768	164,636	51,227	296,632
1040	81,989	169,501	50,806	302,296
2050	84,462	173,843	49,352	307,657

Year	Dependency Ratio[3]		
	Under 20	65 and Over	Total
1930	69.6	9.7	79.3
1940	58.5	11.7	70.2
1950	59.2	14.1	73.3
1960	74.1	17.4	91.5
1970	71.7	18.4	90.0
1973	67.5	18.6	86.1
1990	48.8	19.5	68.3
2000	48.6	19.2	67.8
2010	45.5	19.5	65.0
2020	46.8	25.1	71.9
2030	49.1	31.1	80.2
2040	48.4	30.0	78.4
2050	48.6	28.4	77.0

1. Figures for 1930, 1940, and 1950 are for the United States according to Census counts. Figures for 1960 and 1970 are according to Census counts and include adjustment for other areas covered by social security as well as for net undercount. Figures for 1973 are Census estimates for the United States including net undercount, plus an adjustment for other areas covered by social security.

2. Based on the population projections prepared by the Office of the Actuary for the 1975 long-range cost estimates.

3. Dependency ratio is here defined as the total number of persons aged under 20 and/or over 65 per hundred persons aged 20 to 64.

Source: Office of the Actuary, Social Security Administration.

to the size of the labor force than is true either today or between now and 2010. This is so, of course, quite aside from social security. If all the support for the retired aged were to come from private pensions, or a negative income tax, or from private savings and relief, the fundamental economic fact would still be that it would take a higher proportion of the goods and services produced by active workers to support older people in the next century than it will in this century, assuming a continuation of the same relative living standards between the two age groups.

Fortunately, the increasing demand on goods and services by the aged which would result from these new population projections will be more than offset by a decline in the number of younger dependents. As shown in Table XII-3, the number of nonworkers of all ages compared to the number of persons between 20 and 65 drops considerably.

If we look, then, not just at the aged, but at the combined number of people below 20 and over 65, and consider this combined group to be the number to be supported by active workers, we get a very different picture than from looking at the aged alone. In fact, the "dependency ratio" (the number of persons aged under 20 and over 65 per 100 persons aged 20 to 64) significantly improves between now and 1990 and continues to improve slowly up until 2020. The trend then reverses slightly and levels off at 77 per 100 persons of working age, which is considerably better than where we were in 1973 (86.1 per 100 persons of working age) or for that matter, better than at any time since before 1960. Even allowing a higher per person living cost for older people than for children, it still can be said with considerable confidence that the kind of population shift that is expected to occur does not represent any real overall economic burden on active workers, but rather an increased obligation to support older people, balanced by a lessening of the obligation to support children.

From the narrow point of view of the closed system of social security, however, there may well be a problem. Since about four-fifths of the cost of the system is for the payment of benefits to older people, the somewhat lower cost to the system for benefits to children is offsetting to only a minor degree. Looked at strictly from the standpoint of the social security system and financing in the next century, the issue could well become whether the "savings" from the lessened burden of dependent children can be translated into a willingness to pay higher contribution rates for retirement protection. The present social security law provides for roughly a 20 percent increase in contribution rates beginning in the year 2011 (5.95 percent of covered earnings compared to 4.95 percent). This was considered sufficient to approximately meet the additional cost to the system arising out of the increasing proportion of the aged in the population in the next century when the social security actuaries were using fertility rate assumptions significantly higher (2.5) than the rate they used in their most recent calculation (a drop to 1.7 by 1977 and a slow rise to 2.1 in 2005). Under their most recent assumptions, the system would be in balance over the next twenty-five years, if the income to the program were increased about 10 percent, but because of the way the automatic formula works and because of the population changes, much more than that may be needed later.

For the short run the main problem is the unprecedented economic situation—high rates of inflation combined with a general slowdown in economic activity. The high rate of inflation is resulting in substantial increases in benefit outgo under the automatic cost-of-living provisions at the same time that the income of the system is substantially below expected levels because of the high rate of unemployment. As a result, under the law in effect in 1976, it is expected that outgo will exceed contribution income by about $4 billion in fiscal year 1976 and by approximately an equal amount in 1977.

The fact that social security benefit payments will exceed contribution income for a short time would not, in itself, be a proper cause for concern. This is why social security has the reserves it does. They should be drawn on in a period of recession. For social security beneficiaries to get more money to spend than is being deducted from workers' earnings and paid by employers as social security contributions during a recession is good for the economy. The annual deficit cannot, of course, be allowed to continue, and it would unless additional financing is provided.

One way to solve the short-run problem—a way which would also improve the long-run actuarial balance—is to increase the maximum amount counted for the computation of benefits and for contributions. Contribution *rates* are already quite high (5.85 percent of earnings) and to increase these rates which apply to all covered workers above the level now scheduled would certainly meet considerable resistance unless accompanied by major additional benefit protection. Increasing the contribution and benefit base, on the other hand, would make the financing of the system more progressive and at the same time those who paid more in contributions would receive more in insurance protection.

Under the automatic provisions of present law, the maximum base rises as average earnings covered by social security increase. Thus under present law the maximum amount covered was $15,300 in 1976 and is estimated to be $16,500 in 1977. The financing problem for the next ten years or so could be solved by increasing the maximum base legislatively to about $22,000 in 1977. A significant contribution to a longer-run solution would be, in addition, to increase the wage base from year to year more than would be required by the automatic provisions in present law until gradually the program covered the full earnings of all but the very highest-paid earners, as was the case when the program started in 1937. At that time, the maximum earnings base of $3,000 covered the full earnings of about 97 percent of those in covered occupations. The present maximum earnings base ($15,300 in 1976) covers the full earnings of only about 85 percent of those in covered occupations. The 1 percent increase in the contribution rate now scheduled for the year 2011 could be moved up to the point—probably some time in the 1990s—when, after the changes already indicated, the outgo of the system would otherwise once again exceed income. These changes would fully finance the program into the next century.

In any event, the increase above that which would result from the automatic provisions of present law should not start until 1977 for reasons of economic policy. Starting the increase in 1977 would mean that the change would have no effect until the fall—a time when we should be well on our way to economic recovery—because it is not until fall that any significant number of workers would have earnings exceeding the base that would, in any event, be in effect for 1977 under the automatic provisions.

Adjustments to meet the financing problem into the next century are, therefore, easily manageable on an entirely self-financed basis, and this part of the problem should not be confused with whether or not the system is faced with major financial difficulties in the long run. (It should be noted that in this section and the sections that immediately follow we are dealing with the *adequacy* of social security financing under the traditional full financing by employer and employee contributions. Whether the method itself should be changed is discussed under the heading, "Should the Burden of Social Security Financing Be Redistributed?".)

Financing Social Security in the Next Century

As touched on before, one reason there could be a problem in financing social security in the next century, at least theoretically, is that under the present automatic provisions, under some wage and price assumptions, benefit protection rises proportionately more than wages rise. Nearly half of the predicted long-range deficit of 5.3 percent of payroll in the 1975 trustees' report arises because the wage and price assumptions used result some fifty years or so from now in the automatic formula producing benefits that, for a high proportion of people, are in excess of the highest wages they have ever earned. Quite obviously, this would never be allowed to happen. Such a result would be completely contrary to the purpose of the automatic provision, and Congress can be counted on to make a change in the law well before any such situation could develop.

But it is true that under the wage and price assumptions used, such a result is *theoretically* possible under present law. The automatic provisions should be changed so that it is not possible.

The problem with the present automatic provision is that while under some assumptions benefit protection rises proportionately as wages rise, under other assumptions, in the long run, the benefit protection may rise *less* than wages rise, or under other circumstances—as in the trustees' reports—*more* than wages rise, depending on the happenstance of how wages and prices move. The automatic benefit provision should be changed so that the relationship of benefits at the time of retirement to wages previously earned is stabilized. The desirable goal would be to have an automatic system which paid benefits in the future which at the time of retirement were the same proportion of past earnings as benefits are for those retiring today. This means that benefit protection for contributors would be kept up to date with increases in the level of living in the community generally, but not allowed to exceed such increases without specific legislative change. Once on the rolls, the purchasing power of the benefit would be guaranteed as under present law.

Such a change in the automatic provisions is desirable in any event, but because of the specific wage and price assumptions used in recent cost estimates, such a change would also have the effect of greatly reducing the long-range actuarial deficit shown in the estimates.

With the increase in the maximum earnings base and the changes previously discussed in the contribution schedule, a system which kept benefit protection up to date with wages but would not allow benefit protection to arise automatically above wages would still show an actuarial imbalance for the long run of about 2 percent of payroll under the assumptions used by the trustees in 1975. It is this 2 percent of payroll deficit, a deficit which occurs entirely after the year 2010, that we should be addressing. How serious is it, and what, if anything, should we be doing about it?

Perhaps the first point to be dealt with in considering whether the remaining 2 percent of payroll deficit constitutes a serious problem of financing is to consider the question of whether it is reasonable to expect, for the long run, a fertility rate that will approximate the rate needed for zero population growth. If we look not at the period just since 1957, but, say over the last seventy-five years, there have been many ups and downs in the fertility rate in the United States. It was high at the turn of the century, dropped sharply at the beginning of the depression of the 1930s, began to rise during World War II, and remained on the rise until 1957. If the fertility rate were to rise rapidly to the level of 2.5 experienced in the late 1960s, there would, of course, be no social security financing problem of the type now anticipated.

Population experts have, on the record, not been particularly successful at predicting United States fertility rates, and in that sense everyone can take his choice on the basis of past experience. Yet it would seem imprudent to count on there being a reversal of the long-extended decline in the fertility rate since 1957, and in this way dismiss any long-range social security financing problem.

The widespread knowledge about, and availability of, inexpensive (for the United States) methods of contraception, the tendency to prefer a higher level of living made possible by a smaller family, and the widely recognized major social reasons for ZPG, persuade me that it is reasonable to base projections of social security costs on a fertility rate ultimately producing ZPG as the social security actuaries have done. This does mean, then, that it is reasonable to assume there will be a larger number of those who will take out of the social security funds in the next century relative to those who will pay in, over what has previously been assumed to be the case. The wise and prudent course would seem to be to take the steps now that would hold down social security costs in the next century, particularly since this can be done in a way that is socially desirable and does not significantly reduce or undermine promises already made. After all, although unlikely, it is possible that fertility rates would stay below those needed for ZPG.

There is one decision in addition to the change in the automatic provisions that can be made now that will help hold down social security costs in the next century and which would not undermine commitments already made.

The Trend Toward Early Retirement

The most significant social trend causing higher than necessary social security costs in the next century is the trend toward earlier retirement. The Social Security actuaries have assumed a continuation of this trend that has been going on in the United States for a long time, and have estimated a further long-range reduction in labor force participation on the part of people over 60. If we could reverse the trend and have a greater labor force participation rate among older people than we have today there would be a significant saving for social security over what is currently estimated.

There may well be a question whether a policy of earlier and earlier retirement makes sense—either for the individual or for society—when one considers the probability of more older people living somewhat longer and with a high proportion of those in the younger part of the aged population being in reasonably good health. One quite possible and highly rational response to the change in the population distribution that will arise under the fertility assumptions leading to ZPG would be for society to employ more people over 60, rather than fewer. Here is one critical choice with long-range effects that is being made day by day in a variety of institutions. The choice will greatly affect what life is like in the next century.

The most fundamental determinant of the cost of pensions is the proportion of the aged group that is productively employed. This is true because private plans almost always require retirement from the particular employer or industry as a condition of drawing benefits, and social security reduces benefits in proportion to earnings for those who earn more than relatively low exempt amounts.

But, in any event, is retirement at an early age necessarily a desirable goal from the worker's viewpoint? Certainly the idea of an absolute right to a payment at an early age for the rest of one's life—or, even better, the chance to have a good pension *plus a new salary elsewhere*, a second career—has a lot of appeal, but I would stress that from an employee's point of view, early retirement is not a good thing unless it is a matter of his free choice, and what tends to happen is that the availability of full retirement benefits at earlier ages is followed by rules and customs that *force* people to retire whether they want to or not. Many employees want to continue to work even with an adequate pension, and almost all prefer work to compulsory retirement on incomes that require a drastic reduction in their level of living.

Retirement, even with an adequate pension, is for many people decidedly inferior to work in terms of personal satisfaction. For those with an adequate pension, if one is to believe the advertisements, between retirement and death lies holiday after holiday. Fishing, or painting, or gardening—whatever the form of recreation adopted—has charm for most people, however, largely as a change from a serious occupation. It is hard for an adult to be without a serious occupation, to be without responsibilities, not to be needed when he still feels power and strength. It is much harder than being a child, for there is no challenging future for the retired person, and he cannot, like a child, play at adulthood while he is waiting to meet that challenge.

The retired worker is faced with emotional problems equally as serious as the economic one of a greatly reduced level of living. Work means recognition in our society, and it is largely through work that one gets a sense of being a useful participating member of society. Our friendships, our social and recreational life, our place in the social order—all tend to be organized around our work. The fear of being unwanted and useless is hardly less of a threat to the security of the aged than the fear of poverty and economic dependency.

In terms of organizing life for the benefit of the individual it hardly seems reasonable to promote a complete concentration of leisure in the last twenty or twenty-five years of life. If we are to have more leisure to distribute as an economic good in our society, there is a lot to be said, on the contrary, for distributing it more evenly throughout the life cycle rather than having it all come in old age. A shorter work week, sabbaticals, etc., are another way of distributing the economic good of more leisure rather than further lowering the retirement age, particularly on a compulsory basis. It seems to me that we should resolutely resist lower compulsory retirement ages in American industry and government and also those actions which help bring about pressure for such a lowering in the compulsory retirement age. I believe, for example, that it is undesirable to pay full-rate social security retirement benefits below age 65. Not only would it add expense to the system, but it would tend to institutionalize the idea that normal retirement comes before 65, and such a change in social security would encourage employers to adopt a lower age for compulsory retirement. Given the large increase expected in the number of aged between 2010 and 2030, it seems unwise to adopt institutional policies that will greatly increase the proportion of older people who consume without currently producing.

Although success in preventing a further decline in labor force participation by older people would lessen the economic burden of supporting older people, and under conditions of full employment would increase total production, it would not lessen the specific cost of the social security system *unless we continue to make the payment of social security benefits contingent on substantial retirement.* For many years there has been a strong drive under way to pay social security benefits as an annuity without regard to whether the individual has continued substantial earnings or not. This issue will be discussed separately in the next section of this chapter. Suffice it to say at this point that dropping the test of retirement in social security would significantly increase the cost—about $5 billion a year in 1975, and obviously much more later as the population ages. Such a move would, of course, largely nullify the cost savings that would otherwise arise from a policy of increased labor force participation on the part of older people.

Extension of Coverage to Government Employees Not Now Under the Program

The Armed Forces of the United States and approximately three-fourths of the employees of state and local governments are covered by social security, but the civilian employees of the federal government are not. Generally speaking, policemen and firemen are not covered, and in many states a high proportion of employees of the state and local governments are not covered. Yet, a high proportion of government employees who do not contribute to social security over their working lifetime nevertheless pick up coverage either by "moonlighting," or by jobs under social security coverage that they work in while not employed by the government. This creates a very unfair situation. The career government employee who qualifies for social security coverage on the basis of a relatively few years of contribution (only a little over six years of social security coverage would be required for a person becoming 62 in 1976, for example) receives a benefit heavily weighted in his favor as compared with the contributions made. This is true because his "average monthly wage" figured from 1950 up to the year in which he becomes 62 is low because of the many blank years during which he was working for the government. As previously explained, there is a heavy weighting in the social security program for the low-wage earner. But the weighting is intended for people dependent on low earnings, not for those who have escaped lifetime contributions to the system by having most of their earnings under programs uncoordinated with social security. This failure to cover all government employees under social security costs the system, and thus other contributors to the program, nearly one-half of 1 percent of covered payroll. It should be decided now to correct this injustice and cover all government employees under social security with appropriate modifications in their own staff retirement systems.

Summary of the Adequacy of Social Security Financing

To summarize the results of the discussion of the adequacy of social security financing: The best solution of the short-run financing problem of the social security cash benefit program (the next twenty-five years), in my opinion, is to raise the maximum earnings base to about $22,000 in 1977, and, then increase the maximum more than enough to keep up with rising earnings until once again practically all workers have all of their earnings counted for social security, as was the case at the beginning of the program. Higher-paid people would pay more, and they would get more.

With the additional income from such a higher earnings base and speeding up—but not increasing—the present contribution schedule, the program would be adequately financed into the next century.

To reduce costs for the very long run, it would be highly desirable to take three steps. One step would be to increase the labor force participation rates for older people above today's rate. The second step would be to modify the automatic provision in present law so that in the next century benefit protection for current workers could not increase at a rate faster than the increase in the general level of wages. Third, all government employees should be covered under social security like everyone else.

With these changes (but without taking into account the possible reduction in costs from greater labor force participation by older people), under the assumptions in the 1975 trustees' report, there would still be a 1 and 1/2 percent of payroll long-range imbalance in the cash benefit program. This imbalance could, of course, be met by an immediate increase in the contribution rate of three-fourths of 1 percent on the employer and a like amount on the employee. However, the deficit projected occurs entirely in the next century and rests on such hard-to-predict factors as mortality rates, labor force participation rates of older people, and fertility rates. It seems to me we could take something of a wait-and-see attitude on the question of whether any additional financing would actually be needed in the long run. Should the projected imbalance develop in the next century, serious consideration should be given to the gradual introduction of a government contribution.

In most other countries, social security is supported in part by the direct contributions of workers, in part by the contributions of employers, and in part by a contribution from the government. Such a government contribution would be a recognition of the social objectives of the program and the fact that to carry out these objectives lower-paid workers and those with dependents to not fully pay their own way.

The Retirement Test

Is It "Fair" to Withhold Social Security Benefits from Those Who Work?

One of the most controversial provisions of the social security program is the provision which, prior to age 72, reduces benefits $1 for each $2 of earnings above an annual exempt amount ($2,760 in 1976). Many people feel that benefits ought to be paid without regard to how much an individual earns, and each year a large number of bills are introduced in Congress to abolish the so-called "retirement test" or to greatly liberalize it.

There are many criticisms of this provision. One relates to a question of fairness. It is argued that it is unfair for a worker who has been paying toward social security all his life to lose out because he has enough self-reliance to keep on working, while other people who stop working get the benefits. Actually, however, a contributor under social security is paying for protection against the *risk of a loss of earnings because of retirement* before age 72; the contribution rates are set for this risk; people are not paying for an annuity at 65. An annuity payable at 65, regardless of whether one works or not, is, of course, a more valuable form of protection than a retirement benefit payable only if one does not have substantial earnings, and the annuity costs more.

Among things that could be done to improve protection under social security, there is considerable question as to whether paying a straight annuity at 65 should have a very high priority. Looked at in terms of risk, the question is: What risks are most important to be protected against? It can well be argued that the important risk to be protected against in old age is loss of earned income because of retirement.

How desirable is it to have to pay a higher contribution rate (about one-quarter of a percent of payroll from the employee and a like amount from the employer) throughout one's working life in order to have one's income shoot up *after* 65 because an annuity is added to one's regular work income? It might be better protection to put the same amount of money into providing higher benefits payable after one had retired. Or, it might be better not to increase the contribution rates at all and have the money to spend when one is younger. In any event, there seems to be no question of *fairness*; it is a question of what the program objective is and what kind of protection one is paying for—a retirement benefit, or a straight annuity.

Is There Another Kind of Test that Would Be Less Controversial?

Little of the discussion about abolishing the retirement test focuses on the fact that as a result of abolishing the test benefits would go largely to those who continue to work just as they did at 50 or 55 in their regular full-time jobs, and who have not "retired" in any sense of the word. The discussion, rather, tends to focus on the way the test restricts the activity of people who have left their regular full-time jobs and are now concerned with second careers or part-time or irregular employment. If it were possible to devise a test that prevented the payment of benefits to people still working in their regular full-time jobs, while allowing those who had entered into something that was defined as "retirement" to do whatever work they wished without having it affect their social security payments, I believe we would meet the objections that most people have about the test.

The problem is that very serious inequities are introduced by the tests so far considered which would pay benefits without regard to earnings after one had retired from one's "regular job." Self-employed people, for example, as compared to the ordinary employee, might have a significant advantage in being able to meet the terms of any such test and still have substantial income from earnings. Also, such a test would hardly seem to be applicable to occupations where one normally changes employers frequently, such as in the construction industry, or in the case of longshoremen, migratory agricultural workers, etc. Although it is easy to tell when someone has retired from the U.S. Steel Corporation after working there for twenty years, it is frequently not easy to tell when one has retired from household employment. The inequities are very considerable even among those who have had the same regular job for a substantial period of time. Would it seem fair to pay full social security benefits to the salaried employee who had managed to obtain a second-career job at the same or larger salary but not pay benefits to a low paid wage earner who continued in the same job?

Should Income from Investments Be Included in the Test?

Another question about the retirement test that is frequently raised is whether or not the limit ought to apply to unearned incomes, such as dividends, interest, pensions, etc., or should it continue to be confined to income from current work. It is argued that the way the provision works now would seem to favor those who are better off and able to live on income from investments; that the provision penalizes the low-income person who has to go out and work in order to make both ends meet.

If social security were to be judged entirely in terms of its efficiency as a welfare program, then, in defining who is needy and how much a needy person should get, it would be important to count income from all sources in a definition of need. However, social security is not based primarily on welfare principles; the concept of need gets into the program only indirectly on the basis of certain broad presumptions—i.e., the low-income worker and those with dependents "need" a higher proportion of past earnings to live on than does the higher-paid single worker. The concept behind social security is one of insurance against the loss of earned income, and the function of the retirement test is to help define the risk against which people are insured. The payments go to those who suffer a loss of earned income because they are no longer earning substantial amounts. In most instances this means that payments go to those who otherwise would be needy since most people are largely dependent on work income. But the payments may also go to retired people who have other sources of income. Nevertheless, they are people who have suffered the specific loss insured against.

Under social security, the question of who should get paid, and how much is not determined directly by need, but first of all by whether there has been a loss of earnings and how much that loss has been. Then the amount paid is related both to the amount of the loss, with a weighting for low-wage earners, and with additional payments for dependents. In determining whether there has been a loss, one naturally takes into account only earned income. Income from capital investment exists independently of whether one is working or not, and is not properly part of a test of retirement; the individual had the income from capital before he retired and he has it afterwards. There is no loss of this income on retirement and no payment is made to make up for any such loss. But earned income does go down after retirement and a social security payment is made to partly compensate for that specific loss, a loss suffered by all those who retire whether or not they have income from other sources.

This is true, of course, not only of social security but of retirement programs generally. No private pension plan or retirement system set up for government employees ever reduces retirement benefits because of income from savings. The object in all cases is to pay a benefit as partial compensation for the loss of earnings growing out of retirement.

If we were to drop the concept of "income insurance" and redo the social security program following welfare principles, and relate eligibility and the amount of benefit to total family income, it would, of course, change the nature and function of social security in very basic ways, and also change people's attitudes toward the system. For example, the way the retirement test now operates allows social security payments to be used as a base on which people build other forms of retirement income. Any income from savings that people have is added to social security benefits. In the same way, all private pension plans in the country build on top of social security. In the design of the private plan there is an assumption that the worker will receive social security benefits, and thus the private pension can be made supplementary to it. If, instead, private pension payments served to reduce social security benefits because they were counted in an income test, there would be little or no incentive to set up such plans (except possibly for high-salaried employees) since private pension payments would result merely in reducing the government's liability for social security payments; the individual would be no better off. As it is now, social security supports the efforts of the individual to save on his own and the efforts of private industry and labor unions to build additional protection in the form of private pension plans.

Should Work Income Be Allowed as a Supplement to Low Benefits?

Some have argued that people ought to be allowed to get both social security and whatever they can earn because social security benefits are so low that people cannot live on them. The problem with this argument is that the overwhelming majority of social security beneficiaries either cannot work, or cannot get jobs, and abolishing the retirement test would, therefore, not help most of them. If the benefits are too low, that problem cannot be corrected by allowing the beneficiary to retain both benefits and substantial earnings; most people would continue to be dependent just on the benefits, in any event. As a matter of fact, abolishing the test would divert funds to people who have regular and substantial earnings, and make it less possible to have adequate social security benefits for the much larger number who have to rely more or less exclusively on social security.

The Retirement Test as a Barrier to Work

The objection to the retirement test that has the most validity is that withholding benefits because of work is a disincentive to work, even though the present test has been carefully designed so that the more one works and earns the greater total income one has from earnings plus any social security benefits. It is, nevertheless, true that older people are getting, in effect, only half pay for the work that they do above the exempt amount ($2,760 in 1976), until their earnings exceed twice their social security benefits plus the exempt amount. Undoubtedly, some would seek jobs at higher pay if this were not so. In this respect one needs to also keep in mind that social security benefits are not subject to taxation while any earnings that the individual has are taxed. As a consequence, depending on total income there may be less return from working than appears from looking at the retirement test provision alone. Also, the fact that the test is complicated tends to make people shy away from jobs that pay above the exempt amount. Many just do not realize that it is possible for an individual to have quite substantial earnings and still get some social security benefits. For example, if a couple in 1976 was getting social security benefits of $350 a month, $4,200 for the year, the wage earner in the family could earn $10,000 a year and the couple would still get $1,160 in social security benefits.

The issue to be determined in whether or not to abolish the test is whether we have been able to strike a reasonable balance between two desirable but conflicting goals. One goal is to preserve the funds of the social security system and keep down contribution rates by reserving payments for people who may be presumed to have suffered a loss of income. By not paying workers solely by reason of having attained a specified age, it is possible to have higher benefits for those who have suffered a loss. The other goal is to design the system so that it interferes as little as possible with the desire of people to perform useful work and the needs of the economy to have that useful work performed. The sort of test now in the law may well be about as good as we can do in balancing these objectives.

Considering the fact that stopping work is not a decision made voluntarily in most cases, it is easy to exaggerate the importance of the effect of employee incentives. In most cases, stopping work is the result of a company policy of compulsory retirement at a given age, or failing health, or a unilateral decision by the employer. Truly voluntary retirement probably does not account for more than 20 to 30 percent of the employment separations of older people. Given this basic situation, it is questionable whether abolishing the social security retirement test would have very much effect on the number of older people holding full-time regular jobs. It is more likely that a major cost would be incurred to pay benefits to those who would have full-time employment, in any event. However, it is likely that we would find more workers seeking temporary, or part-time employment and, to some extent, second careers if there were no retirement test under social security, even though, as discussed earlier, the present test does make it profitable, in terms of total income, for the individual to work and earn as much as possible.

Although the present approach in the retirement test may be about as good as we can do in balancing the conflicting objectives, there is, of course, nothing magical about the figure of $2,760 in the annual exemption, or for that matter, age 72 as the age at which the program becomes a straight annuity. Although liberalizing the retirement test, in my opinion, should have a low priority among improvements that can be made in social security, in principle there is no objection to raising the exempt amount to, say, $3,000 or reducing the age at which the benefit becomes a straight annuity to 70.

On the other hand, it would be particularly undesirable to offer to pay the actuarially reduced benefit to individuals aged 62 to 65 at the same time they are performing full-time work. Eliminating the test altogether, including between age 62 and 65, would set up a substantial temptation—particularly for relatively low-paid workers—to accept an actuarially-reduced benefit while working, with the consequence that when they stopped work they would have to try and live on a benefit that was only 80 percent of what they would have otherwise received. There is frequently such strong interest in getting a higher income right away that many people might be led to make a choice they would later regret.

There is one matter related to the retirement test that ought to be changed: There is little excuse for exempting all social security benefits from taxation. I would propose that three-fourths of the social security benefit be included in gross income for income tax purposes so that the treatment of social security benefits would be more like the treatment of private pensions. The rationale would be that the worker would pay income tax on that part of his social security benefits that exceeded what his own contributions would bring, roughly the rationale behind private pension plan taxation.[a] Including social security in gross income for income tax purposes would have two desirable results in addition to

[a]It will be many years before workers pay in more than one-fourth of the value of their benefits.

making for fairer treatment of people under the income tax laws. It would lessen the advantage that higher income people enjoy from the fact that social security benefits are not taxable, since, of course, to people in the higher brackets an exemption is more valuable than for those in lower brackets; and, secondly, inclusion of three-fourths of the social security benefits for income tax purposes would improve the incentives for beneficiaries to work by lessening the tax advantage one gets from receiving social security as compared to work income.

Conclusion

All in all, considering particularly the expected large increase in the aged population between 2010 and 2030 relative to those of working age, it would seem to me unwise to increase the cost of the program by shifting from a system designed to partly make up for the loss of earned income to a system that would pay benefits at a specified age, regardless of whether or not one continues to work regularly and full time. Hopefully, society will adjust to the population changes that are likely to occur by the employment of more older workers, and there is every reason to hope and plan for such a change being one way of reducing the cost of the social security system. This cannot occur unless some form of retirement test is maintained. At the same time, from the same perspective of expected population changes, obviously it is important that the design of the retirement test be one which interferes as little as possible with incentives to work.

Are Women Treated Fairly Under the Social Security Program?

History and Present Situation

When the first major amendments to the original Social Security Act were made in 1939 and benefits for survivors and dependents were added to the program, women workers did not constitute as high a proportion of the employed labor source as they do today (25.2 percent in 1940, and 38 percent in 1973). Moreover, work by married women was much less common than it is today. (In 1940, 14 percent of married women were working; in 1975 over 50 percent.)

Thus the fundamental framework of protection for women under the social security program was focused on: (1) protection for single women as workers, the same as for single men; (2) protection for women as dependents of retired husbands, or as survivors of deceased husbands, with provisions designed to prevent the payment of full worker's benefits and full dependent's or survivor's benefits to the same person. The situation of the married working woman did not, at that time, apparently receive a great deal of attention. Today, with women representing almost two-fifths of the work force, the issue of equal treatment between the sexes under social security is a major policy area. Some changes seem clearly to be called for—not because women workers are treated less generously in relation to their contributions than are male workers, because this is not the case, but because there are several situations in which sex determines specific benefit rights, and because married women who work do not, on the average, get additional protection equal to their additional contributions.

First of all, however, it is of some importance to dispose of the gross charge that women workers as a group fare badly under social security as compared to men workers. Actually, more by coincidence than by design, the cost arising from the average women worker's account is approximately the same as from the average male working's account. This is true because the longer life expectancy of women, the fact that fewer of them work beyond 65, and the fact that as a group they receive a greater advantage from the weighted benefit formula makes up for the fact that male worker accounts generate more secondary beneficiaries—that is, wife's and widow's benefits as compared with husband's and widower's benefits.

In other words, if one were to leave all the other provisions of the social security program exactly as they are now written, but set level contribution rates for the next seventy-five years to cover the cost of cash benefits derived from the records of female workers, and a separate contribution rate for the benefits derived from male workers, the rates would be approximately the same.

This obviously is not, however, the only criterion of fair treatment. First of all, it seems to me that the same legal rights in all respects should flow from a worker's wage record regardless of whether that worker is male or female. Making the changes necessary to bring this about would have relatively minor cost consequences. Second, there are changes that should be made to make the program fairer to the married woman who works, and more adequate for single retired women and widows.

Remaining Sex Discrimination in Social Security

Over the years, most of the provisions of the law which treat workers differently because of sex have been removed. Most importantly, the program today pays benefits to the surviving children of women workers under the same conditions as it does to the surviving children of male workers. This was not always the case. In 1939, when the social security law first provided for social security dependent's and survivor's benefits, benefits for a child of a married woman worker were not payable in the event of the mother's retirement or death if both the husband and the wife were working and more or less equally supporting the child, whereas the child's benefits based on the father's earnings were generally payable upon the father's retirement or death. It was not until the amendments of 1967 that the conditions were made exactly the same for the child of a married woman worker and a married male worker. Now, regardless of whether or not a woman worker is survived by her husband, a benefit is payable to the minor child the same as has always been the case for the surviving child of a male worker.

The conditions under which an aged widower, or an aged husband, can receive benefits, however, still differ significantly from the conditions under which an aged widow, or aged wife can receive benefits. In the case of women, the present law presumes that the wife or widow suffered an economic loss on the retirement or death of her husband and a benefit is paid automatically. In the case of a husband or widower, benefits under the law are paid only if he had been receiving at least one-half of his support from his wife. I believe that the proof of specific dependency for widowers and husbands should be removed. The cost of these changes are low because in most cases the widowers or husbands would either be working at wages sufficiently high so that no benefits would be payable, or they would be eligible for benefits based on their own wage records which were as high, or higher, than those derived from their wife's wage record so that, again, no additional benefits would be payable.

It should be noted, however, that the cost would be very large if the program were amended so that benefits based both on the wage record of the men themselves and also dependent's or survivor's benefits based on their wife's earnings were payable in full. This is the proposal that many women's groups have made in the case of wives and widows who are also entitled to benefits based on their own wage records. If this were to be done, and if equal treatment were to be given widowers and husbands, not only would the cost be very large but a substantial number of people would get benefits that exceeded their previous wages.

One significant discrimination was removed by a Supreme Court Decision, *Weinberger vs. Viesenfeld* no. 73-1892, March 19, 1975. As previously indicated, under the law children get benefits regardless of whether it is an insured father or an insured mother who dies, but until the provision was overturned by the Supreme Court, the widowed father got a benefit for himself only if he proved dependency on his wife at the time of his wife's death, whereas the widow gets a benefit automatically. Now the widower also becomes eligible for a benefit automatically. However, although important in principle, the actual effect of this change will probably be small because the overwhelming majority of widowed fathers with young children will undoubtedly choose to work regularly outside the home so that benefits would not ordinarily be payable to them under the terms of the earnings test discussed in the last section. However if, as has been advocated by some, the earnings test were to be abolished for young widows with entitled children and equal treatment were given to widowers with young children, the cost would be greatly increased.

One additional discrimination that remains is that benefits are provided to divorced former wives who have been married for twenty years or more. Benefits should be provided for divorced former husbands on the same basis.

Much more important in practical effect would be the completion of steps taken in the 1972 amendments toward equal treatment of male and female workers in determining insured status and in the computation of benefits. The 1972 amendments provided that the determination of insured status for men and the computation of benefits for men shall in the future be made on the more favorable basis that was applied to women in the past. That is, the quarters of coverage needed for insured status and the computation of average earnings on which benefits are based will in the future be determined for retirement benefits over the period from age 21 or 1950, if later, up to the year in which the individual becomes age 62, for both men and women, rather than up to 65, in the case of men, as has been true in the past. However, for men who were born prior to 1913 the discrimination still remains. It would be highly desirable to compute the benefits of these older men *and their dependents and survivors* on the same basis as everyone else. Typically, Congress has applied improvements in the program retroactively. It seems to me it should do so in this case.

About fourteen million people would get significantly higher benefits immediately as a result of this change and the first year costs would be large, approximately $1.9 billion (assuming a 1976 effective date). However, since the change to the more favorable basis has already been made for the future, the long-range cost of the program would not be large, approximately 0.07 percent of payroll or a contribution rate increase of only 0.035 percent.

Married Women Who Work in Paid Employment

A high proportion of married women who work feel that they have a grievance against the social security system. This comes about because married women who do not work, nevertheless, have protection based on their husbands' earnings, and the additional protection that working wives get from employment, while substantial, is not "worth" the additional contributions that the working wife pays.

It is important to recognize that the working wife does have additional protection as compared with the wife who is not in paid employment, even if the *rate* of benefit turns out to be the same because of the offset provisions previously described. The worker who is insured has certain rights that a dependent or survivor does not. For example, if one is insured in one's own right and one becomes disabled, a benefit is paid regardless of the situation of the spouse. Moreover, an insured worker can retire and get her own benefit without regard to the earnings of a spouse, whereas a wife's benefit is payable only on the retirement of the spouse. It is not at all unusual, for example, for a man to be working at 63 or 64, but for his wife to be retired at 62 and receiving a benefit based upon her own wage record. When he later retires she may be entitled to an additional amount as a wife. And, of course, as discussed earlier, survivor's and dependent's benefits are payable on the worker's own record, so that a child would get a benefit on the death of a working mother but not on the death of a mother who is not insured under the program in her own right. These are all valuable rights but taken together, on the average, they are not worth the extra contributions which the working wife must pay.

Attempts to get the working wife to view the program as one in which she is treated as a worker, exactly as a single woman worker, with the additional advantage of having residual protection based on her husband's wage record have been almost totally unsuccessful. She wants to know what additional protection she gets as a married woman by reason of the fact that she has gone to work and made contributions.

Nor is she apt to be impressed by the more elaborate official rationalization of the present benefit structure. The rationale for the present benefit structure is that if there is sufficient paid employment by the wife outside the home to produce a benefit greater than the dependent's or survivor's benefit based on the husband's record, then she is considered self-supporting and entitled solely on the basis of her own wage record rather than as a dependent or survivor. On the other hand, if she is entitled to a benefit on the basis of her own wage record, but to a larger benefit as a survivor or dependent, she gets the advantages that flow from being entitled in her own right, and as a dependent gets a supplement which brings her total benefit *rate* up to the amount payable to a dependent or survivor.

It is still true, however, that the more married women who go to work the more the system gains because they pay more in contributions than they get in additional protection.

Feelings on this point have increased as the contributions under social security have increased. It is my belief that something needs to be done if the married woman worker is to feel that she is being treated equitably under the program. There have been many proposals. A married woman worker could be given benefit rights both as a dependent and as a worker, adding the two together—a solution which is very expensive and in many instances would result in a very high benefit indeed.[b] Another possibility is to place a limit on the overall con-

[b]In considering this solution it should also be kept in mind that in all likelihood the benefit rights that flow from a man's record will, in the future, in all respects, also flow from a woman wage-earner's record. If either by legislation or court decision a husband becomes entitled to a benefit equal to one-half of his wife's benefit, *without any test of dependency*, then equal treatment would require that this benefit be added to his own benefit as a worker. The cost results would be astronomical and would result in benefits, in many instances, exceeding the level of wages previously earned. In fact, considering the situation after husbands' and widowers' benefits are payable without a test of dependency, throws a new light on this whole discussion. Perhaps men, too, will at that point consider that they are not getting full value for the contributions they make under social security because they could have stayed home and received benefits as a husband or widower without specific contributions!

tributions to be paid in any one year by a working couple. Under the latter proposal, deductions would be made from earnings on the same basis as they are at present, but a working couple could claim a refund for a part of the contribution at income tax time, much as workers who move from employer to employer and earn more than the maximum earnings base during the year may today claim a refund on their income tax for contributions paid on earnings above the yearly maximum. This seems to me to be preferable to adding benefits together. After all, dependent's or survivor's benefits should be sufficient in themselves for the purpose to be served and so should the worker's benefit. If they are added together for the same person the result is to pay benefits which by definition are higher than they need to be to serve the program purpose.

A limitation on the total amount of contributions paid by a working couple would also help with another situation. At present a working couple may be paid less in total retirement benefits than another couple with the same total earnings where only the husband works. In the extreme situation where only the husband works and has average monthly earnings of $650, the benefit payable according to the law in 1975 would be $396.90 for the husband, and $198.50 for the wife, a total of $595.40 a month. If the husband had average earnings of $500 and the wife had average earnings of $150—combined earnings of $650—his benefit would be $323.40 and hers would be $161.70, a total of $485.10—$110.30 less a month than the couple with the same total average wages when only the husband worked. However, the tax ceiling solution reduces the income to the program, and, of course, does not provide any benefit improvements.

It would also be possible, as has been proposed, to equalize the retirement benefits for the two couples described by combining the earnings of the couple where both worked and applying the same formula to the combined earnings as is applied to the earnings where only the husband works. The resulting benefit would then be divided equally between husband and wife. There are, however, several difficult technical problems in working out a restructuring of social security based upon combining the wage records of husbands and wives. For example: What about couples where several marriages are involved? Moreover, while producing a more equitable benefit structure in retirement, the combined wage record approach actually gives more total protection—for the reasons already explained—to the working couple who pay the same contributions as a couple with only one worker. The equity argument about benefit-contribution relationship then shifts and the couple with only one worker becomes the aggrieved party. After all, the two couples pay the same contributions but the wife who does no paid work does not have disability protection and the children do not get survivor's benefits if she dies, etc.

Dissatisfaction with the way married women are treated under the program has led to other proposals as well. For example, the equity question, but not the more important social question, would be solved by dropping the wife's benefits and the widow's benefits and having all rights flow entirely from employment covered under social security. This would result, of course, in a major loss of protection for many people. Widows particularly would suffer. Consequently, this proposal is not likely to be seriously considered, nor should it be.

Another proposal would replace wife's and widow's benefits by covering the wife who does not work in paid employment as a homemaker who received some hypothetical wage. This approach has the appeal of making the wife's protection independent of the continuation of a marriage, but, on the other hand, there seems to be no good way to fit such a proposal into the American social security system as it is now set up. Should the coverage be voluntary or compulsory? If compulsory, and contributory, it adds a significant cost to what people are now paying for protection. If voluntary, it gives an advantage to selected risks. How does one deal with the question of the amount of the wage credit in comparing one homemaker with another—say one with six children and one with none, or one who works and also keeps house, or when the husband does a lot of the housekeeping. There is also a major problem in comparing homemakers with those in paid employment.

Better than this, I would think, would be a system of granting free wage credits to wives based upon their husband's contributions to the system. The plan could be so designed that the maximum benefit derived from such credits to a wife would equal the present rate of one-half the husband's benefit, but at the same time if she were to leave her husband the credits would, of course, be hers irrevocably. Although such a proposal has some merit, it obviously does not help with the issue raised by the married woman in "paid employment." "What do I get for my specific contributions over and beyond what I would have received as a wife?"

I do not favor any of the above "solutions" although some are obviously preferable to others. The coverage of homemakers proposal, for example, has the fundamental defect that the homemaker after 65 just keeps on doing what she has been doing. When does she retire? What loss of earnings needs to be replaced?

What I would propose is that benefits for married couples where only one person works be held to the levels provided by present law and that benefit levels for the contributing worker, whether single or married, be increased. This approach would not only improve the benefits for all single workers, a group now particularly disadvantaged both from an equity standpoint and from the standpoint of actual need. The proposal would also increase benefits for elderly widows since, in general, they receive the same rate of payment as the retired worker. This result could be obtained specifically by increasing the retired worker's benefit by 12 1/2 percent and reducing the ratio of the spouse's benefit to the retired worker's benefit from 1/2 to 1/3. The proposal is expensive and for this reason might have to be approached gradually.[c]

[c]Assuming that the law is changed to stabilize the relationship of benefits in the long run to past wages, as it will need to be, the long-range cost of this proposal is about 1 1/2 percent of payroll, requiring an increase in the contribution rate of 3/4 of 1 percent.

What About the Question of Equal Treatment of Various Other Groups in the System?

The claim is sometimes made that judged in terms of the relationship of protection to contributions the program is unfair to various other groups. It has been argued that the program is unfair to the single worker, the low-income worker (particularly the black worker), higher-paid workers, young workers, etc.

As one considers these charges, one needs to keep in mind that the social security program is a very large-scale, group insurance and retirement system which averages costs and benefits for large and diverse groups of people. Within such a system it would always be possible to define a group that does not get as much protection per dollar as some other defined group, or as the average. This is inherent in a group plan, whether public or private. Contributory group life insurance, for example, must require the same contribution per thousand dollars of coverage per worker regardless of the age of the worker. Yet the protection is much more valuable for the older than for the younger worker. The employer makes up the difference. Any health insurance system that does not require examinations shifts costs from those who are relatively healthy to those less healthy, etc. It needs also to be kept in mind that calculations of equity under social security are extraordinarily complex since it covers so many risks and for such a variety of situations. At least one point should be clear. It can hardly be unfair to all the groups concerning whom the charge has been made—for example, both low-income and high-income workers.

Nevertheless, as contributions have risen, interest in the comparative treatment of various groups under the program has grown, and it is clearly impossible to avoid the comparison of how one group is treated in terms of benefit-protection relationship as compared with another.

The Worker Who Never Marries

Since a substantial part of social security contributions go for the protection of dependents and survivors, it is clear that the single worker, judging *retrospectively*, would conclude that he does not get as much for his social security contribution as other people. He may in fact have received as much protection as he could have bought elsewhere with his money, but it is clear that he would have had more protection than he did have if he married and had dependents. But is it reasonable to judge the equity of the system at the end of a working life? If one thinks of the system as providing protection for a variety of risks as one starts out to work at, say, age 20, then we have a different situation. At age 20, and for a long time thereafter, there is an unknown risk as to whether any particular person will later have dependents and survivors to protect. Relating the contribution to all the risks that may occur does not seem to do any violence to the fair treatment of individuals or to commonly accepted social goals. Individual voluntary insurance, of course, could not be set up on this basis. Under individual voluntary insurance each person seeks to change his protection to fit his individual circumstances at a given time.

The Low-Wage Earner

It has been argued that low-wage earners, as a group, tend to go to work at earlier ages than higher-wage earners, and thus the low-wage earner pays social security contributions over a longer period of time; yet, as a group, low-wage earners have shorter life expectancies and thus will receive retirement benefits for a shorter period of time. On the other hand, low-income workers have higher disability rates and higher mortality rates and thus derive more protection from the disability and survivorship features of the program. Most importantly, the social security benefit formula is very heavily weighted in favor of earnings averaging below the $7,800 a year level—the formula now being, in rounded percentages, 120 percent of the first $110 of the social security average wage, plus 44 percent of the next $200, plus 41 percent of the next $150, plus 48 percent of the next $100. After that level, the replacement of average social security earnings drops to 27 percent of the next $100, plus 22 percent of the next $250, with earnings above this figure being replaced at the rate of 20 percent.

Taking all of these factors into account, the system is substantially favorable to the low-wage earner but not as favorable as was expected by those who designed the weighted benefit formula. It is quite true that there would need to be weighting in the formula to give equitable treatment to the low-income earner even if one were designing a system built on the idea of closely relating lifetime protection and lifetime contributions.

A weighted benefit formula is also necessary to give fair treatment to woman workers as a group and to black workers. As indicated previously, the benefits derived from the accounts of women workers are just about equal in value today to the benefits derived from the accounts of men workers. This would not be true except for the weighted benefit formula.

For quite different reasons, the weighted benefit formula is necessary to give black workers as a group equal protection for the contributions that they make as compared with white workers. Black individuals, probably because they have lower average incomes, have shorter life expectancies on the average. According to calculations made by the Social Security actuaries, if only this factor were taken into account, whites on the average would have a 5 percent better benefit than blacks. However, if we take into account all the factors that affect protection under the program, such as the greater value of survivor benefits because of higher mortality rates, larger family size among blacks, higher disability incidence, earlier retirement, and particularly the weighted benefit formula, then the system, on the average, has a value to blacks in relation to their contributions about 3 percent higher than to whites.

The original idea behind the weighted benefit formula was not, of course, to promote equity by balancing a higher replacement of earnings rate against some ways in which the system treated low-wage earners, women workers, and blacks less favorably than the average. A weighted formula was established, rather, on the theory that if the program was to serve the function of preventing poverty among low-income earners it would be necessary to replace a high proportion of their earnings, whereas for those earning above the average the replacement rate could be lower and benefits still be above the poverty level. It was argued that there was just not room for substantial reduction in the earnings levels of low-wage earners in the event of retirement, disability, or the death of the main earner in the family. Without weighting in the formula, social security would either have had to pay high replacement of earnings rates to all workers, or large numbers of those earning low wages would need to get supplementary assistance even after having contributed to social security over a working lifetime. Without a weighted benefit formula the system would have served little purpose for low-wage earners.

There has been a significant theoretical argument in recent years over whether such a benefit design was appropriate for social security, or whether the system should replace the same percentage of earnings at all earnings levels, leaving to a means-tested program the task of providing adequate supplementation for those whose total incomes were inadequate. It now appears, however, that part of this argument is somewhat moot since a weighted benefit formula is necessary merely to provide equal protection per dollar contributed by lower-paid workers, women workers and blacks, as compared with average and above-average earners. If we were to change the system to relate benefits exactly to wage loss as some have advocated, the result would be to give the higher-paid person more value per dollar than the lower paid, and on the average more protection per dollar than women or blacks. The only legitimate current issue in this area is not whether there should be a weighted benefit formula, but whether it should be weighted still more or weighted less.

My own view is that the present weighting in the benefit formula provides a reasonable balance of equity and social purpose. Since, so far at least, social security financing has come almost entirely from the contributions of workers and their employers, it follows that any greater weighting in the benefit formula decreases the protection of the average and above-average earner. I do not think this would be a desirable result. To continue to be a success, contributory social insurance needs to be perceived as fair to the average and above-average earner, as well as to the low paid. Therefore, in my view, any additional weighting in the benefit formula, if such additional weighting is considered important, should be financed out of a government contribution.

Although there is a case for applying a weighted benefit formula somewhat higher up the wage scale than the present $7,800 a year if the additional cost is financed from general revenues, there is no legitimate case for a disproportionate increase in the social security minimum benefit as such. The big bargain in social security is for those who barely qualify for this minimum benefit ($101.40 in 1976) and, unfortunately, frequently those who qualify for the minimum amount are not necessarily low-wage earners, but rather individuals who spend the major part of their working lifetimes under other government systems, such as the federal civil service system, or those state and local systems not built on social security.

Disproportionate increases in the overall general minimum benefit of social security in the past have been the result of expecting contributory social insurance to do the whole job of abolishing poverty among the aged, whereas this is a job more appropriately done by a combination of contributory social insurance and an income-tested program of assistance. In the amendments of 1972 this issue was met head-on, and a special minimum benefit was provided for workers with long service under social security but earning relatively low wages. At the same time, a special federal income-tested program, paid for entirely out of general revenues, was established for those whose total incomes were insufficient. Thus the federal government made the decision that contributory social insurance would take the responsibility for being sure that long-term contributors to the program—even though low-wage earners—had social security benefits which in themselves were sufficient to keep most workers and their families out of poverty, but that short-term contributors—in and outers under the system—whose total incomes fell below specified amounts would be assisted directly on an income-tested basis.[d] This seems to be eminently sensible.

The Young Worker

It is clear that up until now social security protection has been a tremendous bargain. Contribution rates have been very low in relation to the protection furnished and most insured workers have paid even the low rates of the past for less than a full working lifetime. But what of the worker, say, 20 years old today, starting out his working lifetime, paying at the rates that are and will be required from now until 2020? Could he take the same amount of money and buy better protection elsewhere? Some have argued that he could.

On analysis, however, it is clear that the illustrations used to "prove" this point make one or more of the following major errors:

1. They focus on retirement benefits and either give no recognition, or inadequate recognition, to survivor's and disability protection.

---

[d]This decision may be somewhat eroded in the future because the "special minimum benefit" is not kept up to date automatically with rising prices and wages.

2. They fail to take into account that social security protection for current workers will automatically be kept up to date with rising wages, and for beneficiaries with the cost of living.
3. They propose alternative investment schemes that carry an element of risk greater than the government guarantee which underlies social security.

Private insurance actuaries do not make the claim that comparable protection could be furnished cheaper in the private sector. The advantage of low administrative costs (two cents on the dollar) which arise in part from a compulsory system of tremendous size, and the government guarantee of benefits makes it impossible to offer better protection for the same cost, if indeed any private company could conceivably underwrite the variety of protections offered by social security, including, for example keeping benefit protection up to date with rising wages.

The facts are that, on the average, the value of the protection furnished the young worker by social security over his lifetime is greater than he could purchase through any variety of plans using both his own contribution *and the contribution of his employer.*

As indicated earlier, special cases can be developed, after the fact, at the end of a working lifetime, of an individual who turned out never to have had dependents and always paid the maximum social security contribution and who might have been better off to have privately invested the combined contributions, or to have taken out private insurance that did not include the cost of protection for dependents. However, assuming no dependents and the highest possible contribution makes an unfair comparison with a group plan (social security) that includes the risk of having dependents and the possibility of earning less than maximum wages.

The expert actuarial conclusion is that social security protection cannot be provided by private insurance at a lower cost when the automatic provisions and the entire array of protection is taken into account, as it should be.

Supplemental Security Income and Contributory Social Insurance

The Supplemental Security Income program, while administered by the Social Security Administration, is a completely separate program—separate in concept and separately financed. It is not contributory social insurance but means-tested assistance paid for from general revenues. It makes sense for Social Security to administer both programs since in the future practically all elderly, blind, and disabled people who will need Supplemental Security Income will also, because of the universal coverage of social security, be individuals who are in touch with the Social Security Administration as a result of being entitled to social insurance benefits, even though those benefits are too low to meet all their needs. Thus it was practically inevitable that any federally-administered assistance program for the aged, blind, and disabled would, for reasons of economy and efficiency, be handled through Social Security's nationwide network of offices and personnel.

Unfortunately, the administration of these two programs by a single agency leads to some public confusion. Some people have thought that their social security contributions were being used to pay benefits to people who had not contributed to social security. This, of course, is not the case. Some have felt that a reasonably adequate income-tested program, which Supplemental Security Income could become, would fulfill the same objectives as social security and that both programs would not be needed. This line of reasoning leaves out of account that the social security program is designed not only to prevent poverty but to prevent economic insecurity, not just for the poor but for the average worker. Thus, contributory social insurance built on the idea of a partial replacement of earned income is a base on which everyone can build his own program of income maintenance. Social security is geared to the level of earnings that a person has had while working and may support a level of living considerably above poverty, as is true in private pensions and private group insurance plans. Assistance, by definition, is geared to a concept of minimum need and pays amounts sufficient to bring people up to a community-determined minimum, taking into account what other income the individual has. Thus the two programs have very different objectives, methods of benefit determination, and financial sources.

Supplemental Security Income is very much of a residual program. For a person with no other income the payments in 1976 were $157 for an individual and $236 for a couple. The first $20 a month of any kind of income, however, is disregarded in figuring the benefit, so that, for example, all individuals who get social security benefits have an assured level of total income of at least $177 for the single person, and $256 for the couple. All states had programs supplementary to the federal program. Twenty-six of the state programs are entirely federally administered and twenty-four are either wholly or partly state administered. Average supplementary payments in the federally-administered state programs in 1975 were $68 for the aged, and in the state-administered plans $38.

In 1975 some 2.3 million people over 65 were receiving Supplemental Security Income as compared with 20.4 million over 65 receiving social insurance benefits, and 1.9 million disabled persons receiving Supplemental Security Income, as compared with 2.9 million disabled persons receiving social insurance benefits. There are probably substantially more people eligible for some benefits under Supplemental Security Income who either do not know they are eligible or who are entitled to such low amounts that they are hesitant to go through the process of filing. In the long run, the proportion entitled to Supplemental Security Income among the aged and disabled should decline since social security benefit amounts for those coming on the rolls in the future will be more nearly adequate.

Supplemental Security Income with state supplementation has taken the place of the federal-state assistance program for the adult categories. It is a decided advance to have the federal government take responsibility for providing a minimum standard throughout the whole country as compared with having the federal government's contribution to assistance depend, as it previously did, on how much the states were willing or able to put up. Moreover, a federal needs-tested assistance program, operated by Social Security under conditions that are as objective and with as little stigma as possible should help prevent distortion of the contributory social insurance system. The system relieves some of the pressure to give social security benefits that are unreasonably high in relation to contribution to those people who barely qualify.

The most important reason for establishing a federal program of this kind was to improve the adequacy of care for older people, the blind, and the disabled. There were many states with general eligibility standards below those set by the new program. The Supplemental Security Income program is also an improvement over many of the old state systems because those systems contained provisions that kept many older people who would otherwise be eligible from applying for the payment. For example, many states had lien laws which allowed older people to continue living in their homes, but required that the home be signed over to the state so that the state on the recipient's death could recover the assistance it had paid to the individual during his lifetime. Many older people just would not take assistance under those circumstances since they wanted to leave whatever small property they had to their children. Also, many states examined not only the income and assets of the applicant, but the income and assets of legally responsible relatives before they made payments to older or disabled persons, and many individuals did not want to involve their relatives in a determination of need. The federal program does not have these restrictions.

Veteran's Pensions

Contributory social insurance also has an important interrelationship with the income-tested program of veteran's pensions. Veteran's pensions are paid to wartime veterans who are aged 65 or over or are permanently and totally disabled and meet a test of income and resources, and to the families of deceased wartime veterans. Veteran's "compensation" arises from service-connected disabilities, but the veteran's pension is not service-connected and constitutes merely a liberal assistance program for the aged and disabled with the eligibility confined to those who have served in the armed forces during periods which for the purpose of veteran's benefits are defined as "wartime."

In 1975 over a million elderly veterans were on the pension rolls. Of this total number, about half a million were veterans of World War I and the other half veterans of World War II. Since the program is based upon a test of need, the improvement in social security payments has resulted in recent declines in the veteran's pension rolls for the elderly despite the growth in the aged veterans' population.

If the veteran's pension program retains a means test, as it should, it will continue to decline as social security benefits for the newly retired become more adequate. On the other hand, if as was true prior to World War I, veteran's pensions were to be payable without regard to other income, the cost in the next century would become enormous.

Almost half of the twenty-nine million veterans in the United States at the end of 1974 were World War II veterans. Today this group is largely middle-aged with only about two million in the age 65 and over group. By 1985, however, the number of veterans over 65 will rise to close to five million, and by the year 2000 to almost ten million. Thus, it is of great importance to make the decision now to keep these pensions income-related if we are to avoid huge costs in addition to social security costs just at the time when the active labor force will be leveling off and the number of aged beginning to increase rapidly.

On the other hand, a good case can be made for establishing benefit eligibility levels for the veteran's pension program equal to the poverty level. If this were to be done and pension eligibility and the pension amounts kept up to date with the cost of living—while the income and resources test in the veteran's program was made somewhat more stringent, the veteran's pension program, to a large extent, would merely be a substitute for part of the Supplemental Security Income program and not represent a significant net additional cost.

Social Security and Private Pensions[3]

Everyone who is earning protection under a private pension plan, at the same time, from the same work, is earning protection under social security. Thus, private pension plans correctly take into account that social security benefits will be paid to all private pension plan recipients. Whether or not the pension plan includes any specific recognition of social security protection in its formula, the plan recognizes the level of protection to be provided by social security, and builds a layer of protection supplementary to the basic social security system. For those covered by both social security and the supplementary plan, the "retirement system" is, in fact, the combined protection furnished by both the basic and the supplementary protection. For the two-thirds of older people retiring today, and the 50 percent or more of current workers who can be expected to get only social security retirement benefits, the "system" consists only of this basic protection. Thus, social security needs to be reasonably adequate in itself for a very high proportion of the elderly and the case is even stronger for the totally disabled and the survivors of workers, since these risks are less adequately covered by private plans than is the risk of retirement.

Social Security and Private Pension Plans Compared

It is important, then, to maintain the adequacy of the social security benefit and the primacy of social security protection as a matter of basic social policy. It is not only inadequate coverage under private plans that makes this so, but the fact that there are several key features in the social security program that are not generally present in private plans and that from a social standpoint deserve to make social security the primary source of income protection. The recently passed federal regulation of private pension plans (P.L. #93-406, "Employee Retirement Income Security Act of 1974"), it is interesting to note, had the general objective of extending to private pension coverage—although in a quite limited way—some of the advantages that already exist under the social security program.

The major advantages of the social security approach are: first, its nearly universal coverage and the complete portability of its credits; second, the fact that the benefit rights the worker earns under social security are protected by the capacity of the entire economy to finance benefits rather than on the capacity of a single firm or industry; third, the scope of benefit protection under social security is broad, with benefits being paid not only on retirement but in the case of death or disability of the insured worker; and, fourth, a social insurance program can more readily be financed in a way that can keep the program up to date with increases in wages and the cost of living—it is not so dependent for income on the savings of the past.

Now that social security is beginning to do as good a job as it is for the low-wage earner and the average wage earner (see Table XII-1), the major question for the future relationship between social security and private pensions is whether social security ought to be made more nearly adequate for those earning average and above-average wages, thus making private pension plans less important for all workers. Given the advantages of the social security approach, a good case can be made for this position. A universal retirement system operated by the government is in many ways the most socially efficient way to get the major part of providing retirement income accomplished. Contrariwise, as evidenced by the outcome of the most recent legislative enactment concerning private pension plan regulation, it appears that private pension plans while improved in several respects, will continue to contain provisions that hold workers to old jobs when they may want to change jobs, and to penalize those who go into new or expanding enterprises. It is doubtful that private pension plans will do an adequate job of providing income for elderly widows supplementary to social security payments, and, of course, there remain problems of portability of protection. To some extent there are still problems in the area of security of benefit payments, and most important of all, perhaps, problems in keeping benefits up to date with rising wages and the cost of living.

Why Private Pension Plans Will Grow in Importance

Yet, in spite of these arguments for relying more and more on social security, I would guess that progress in that direction will be slow, if indeed there is progress at all, and that we will probably continue to look to private pension plans to supply an increasing amount of protection supplementary to social security, at least for workers earning above-average wages. I think in many respects this is unfortunate, particularly for the large body of wage earners who have no real opportunity to be covered under private plans, but, nevertheless, I think this conclusion is correct for the following reasons:

1. There is little understanding of who pays for private pension plans, whereas the burden of social security on the worker is visible and, therefore, politically more difficult to increase. This is both a question of wage earners directly experiencing a deduction from earnings labeled "social security" as compared with the common "employer paid-for pensions," and also a matter of the attention which tax economists pay to the incidence of social security financing as compared to the attention paid to the incidence of private pension financing. Because social security contributions are compelled by government and rest on the taxing power, they are fair game for tax analysis.

Widespread attention is given to the conclusion reached by most economists that workers pay not only the employee share of contributions but either all or a large part of the employer's contribution, with the employer contribution being paid in lieu of what would otherwise be higher wages. The additional objection is made that this heavy rate of tax is particularly burdensome for the low-wage earner, because the rate is the same at all wage levels and there are no exemptions for dependents. Since private pension plans are not required by government, but only subsidized by government, little, if any, objection has been expressed at the fact that, by the same line of reasoning, workers also pay for private pension plans, since the employer pays these labor costs also in lieu of higher wages. Thus the notion that the employer pays the full cost of private pension plans tends to be left undisturbed, whereas traditional social security financing now has very hard going indeed. It is increasingly more difficult for those who have to run for office, whether trade union officials or congressmen, to support increases in social security contributions, and it is no problem for them to go along with the idea that private pension plans are somehow paid for by employers.

2. Another reason it is difficult to increase substantially social security protection for workers earning wages at the middle and higher end of the wage

scale is that we have made an ideological virtue out of keeping social security to a "floor of protection" to allow room for private pension supplementation. We have attributed to private pensions—somewhat carelessly—the virtues of individual voluntary actions. No matter that coverage under a private plan is usually the automatic accompaniment of a job just as social security is, and no matter that the individual worker has as little or as much influence on the terms of a pension arrangement as he does in influencing social security provisions through his elected representatives—social security is "government compulsion" and private pensions are "voluntary action."

3. By now there are many people in organizations that have an important stake in having private pensions retain an important role in supplementing social security benefits. Obviously, this includes pension consultants, insurance companies, banks, tax consultants, certain employees of unions and businesses, and so on. In other words, there are many forces to give support to the ideological superiority of nongovernmental action.

4. It can be argued with some merit that private pension plans produce net savings that would not have taken place if more of the job of providing retirement income were done by social security. Whether or not the institutional saving merely takes the place of what would have been individual voluntary saving is hard to determine, but it appears, superficially, at least, that private pension funding results in capital formation and the essentially pay-as-you-go social security system does not. Once, however, a private pension plan reaches maturity it does not add "savings" under any line of reasoning; new income goes out immediately as benefits just as in social security.

5. Perhaps the most important reason of all is strategic. If practically all retirement protection were financed through direct earmarked social security contributions, it would *seem* like too much of a burden on workers, whether it was in fact any more of a burden on them than having part of the job done through private pensions.

Although I am not sure that there are good continuing reasons for the tax breaks that are used to encourage the development of private pension plans when compared, say, with giving the same amount of general revenue subsidy to the social security system for the benefit of all workers, not just those covered by private pensions, I, nevertheless, believe that it will be continued and that it would be a useless effort to try to make a change.

Summary

In summary, then, although I do not completely accept the theoretical desirability of having a strong supplementary role for private pension plans (primarily because of the virtual impossibility of covering more than half the workers with such plans, and because of the great difficulty of solving the problems of portability and financial security to the same extent as under social security), I think it is the part of wisdom to accept the three-layer approach that has been prevalent for a long time in the United States. There seems to be widespread agreement that there should be a universal, compulsory, contributory social insurance system providing benefits reasonably adequate in themselves for those earning average wages and below, with private pension plans providing important supplementation for higher-paid workers, and with a universal income-tested program, such as Supplemental Security Income, underlying the whole for those whose incomes are inadequate when all other sources are taken into account.

Should the Burden of Social Security Financing Be Redistributed?

The Importance of the Contributory Principle

As suggested in the introduction to this chapter, social security grew out of the efforts of people to help themselves. It is based on a long tradition of self-help. The main features of social insurance which distinguish it from "welfare" are: (1) those who get protection for themselves and their families pay specifically toward the support of the system; and (2) there is an absence of a means test. The proper financing principles for such a program—a government-operated, contributory, retirement and group insurance plan—are by no means the same as the financing principles one would want to follow in raising money for the support of general government. Social security financing should not be considered separately from social security benefits and approached solely as a tax issue. Flat rate deductions from earnings, with matching amounts paid by employers are regressive when viewed just as a tax. But when the weighted benefit formula is taken into account the system as a whole—contributions and benefits—is progressive.

It seems to me that proposals to finance social security entirely from general revenues or through some sort of income tax surcharge which would completely exempt low-wage earners are misguided and based upon a failure to understand the nature of the program.

If the financing principles of social security were to be changed so that large numbers of people are paid benefits without contributing, while large numbers of other people are charged much more than they would have to pay for obtaining the protection elsewhere, fundamental changes in the benefit side of the program are almost bound to follow. Without a tie between benefit rights and previous contributions, questions would undoubtedly arise about the basis for paying benefits to those who can support themselves without the benefits. If financing were related to ability to pay, it is very likely that benefits in time would be related to need. Thus, as a result of a change in financing, we could find that social security had been turned into a welfare or negative income tax program designed to help only the very poor, and that it no longer was a self-help program serving as a base for all Americans to use in building family security. The security of future benefit payments is greatly reinforced by the concept of a dedicated social security tax or contribution *paid by the people who will benefit under the system*. The moral obligation of the government to honor future social security claims is made much stronger by the fact that the covered workers and their families who will benefit from the program made a specific sacrifice in the anticipation of social security benefits in that they and their employers contributed to the cost of the social security system, and thus they have a *right* to expect a return in the way of social security protection.

This is true in social security, railroad retirement, civil service, and state and local retirement systems, even though there is not ordinarily in any of these programs—nor for that matter in private group insurance—an exact relationship between the amount of protection provided and the contributions made by the individual. Very importantly, the contributory nature of the system helps to make clear that it would be unfair to introduce eligibility conditions into the program, such as an income or needs test, that would deny benefits to people who have paid toward their protection.

It does not follow from this line of reasoning, however, that workers need to bear all of the costs of social security directly. The benefit principle of taxation requires that their right rest on a clearly earmarked, specific contribution related in part to the amount of protection received, but it seems to me it is not at all necessary that they pay the entire cost.

For example, it seems quite reasonable to have half the cost of the system met by contributions from employers as a recognition of their responsibility to provide for part of the cost of the retirement of those who work for them. Thus, employers match the contributions of workers in the American social security system, and in most systems around the world the employer pays as much or more than the workers do. In many countries there is also a recognition of the broad interests of society in social insurance by having part of the cost borne by direct government contributions.

Should the Low-Paid Worker Pay a Lower Rate?

While it seems very important to the preservation of the nature of the system that workers should "contribute," it does not settle the question of what proportion of the cost ought to be borne by workers and how the costs that they do not pay for should be borne.

There is a real dilemma, for example, as far as the low-wage earner is concerned. He may in fact be getting a "bargain" for his social security contributions—as he does—in terms of long-range retirement, disability, and survivorship protection but, nevertheless, questions can be raised about a social policy that forces him to substantially reduce an already low level of current living in order to provide this protection. A possible solution to this dilemma would be to make the refundable earned income credit in the 1974-1975 tax bill permanent and to have it apply to low-wage earners whether or not they have children. Under this provision, low-income people would get either an income tax credit, or if they do not have to pay an income tax they would get a positive payment offsetting a considerable part of what they are required to pay for social security. This seems to me preferable to singling out the low-income worker under social security and having him pay a lower contribution rate.

Is There a Good Substitute for Part of the Employer's Payroll Tax?

One idea that deserves further exploration is the possibility of changing part of the source of the employer's contribution. As mentioned previously many economists are of the opinion that the employer contribution is in large part shifted directly to employees in terms of lower wages. And all economists would agree that the employer tax is largely shifted in one way or another, either to workers in terms of lower wages or under some circumstances to consumers in terms of higher prices. In other words, capital does not, in fact, pay toward social security to any significant extent. Thus the cost of social security to workers realistically approaches twice the rate directly assigned to them.

Query: Is there some way of having the owners of industry pay a fairer share of social security costs? One possibility would be to assign part of the corporation income tax to social security. In all likelihood a major part of this tax does fall on the owners of capital. If part of the corporation income tax substituted for part of the employer payroll tax, the economic result would be to reduce the real burden on employees. If this were to be done it would then be necessary, of course, to find substitute sources of revenue for general purposes to take the place of the part of the corporation income tax assigned to social security. The only reasonable substitutes would be through tax reform and higher rates in the individual income tax. The combined effect of these changes would be highly progressive.

Under this proposal, social security, in the long run, including national health insurance, might ultimately be financed one-third by deductions from employees' wages (this is usually lumped in as part of a payroll tax, but, of course, since employees have no payrolls this is a misnomer), one-third from a combination of the employers payroll tax and the corporation income tax, and one-third from a progressive general revenue base largely derived from the federal income tax. Such a result would retain the best elements of contributory social insurance and greatly mitigate the present burden of social security financing on lower-paid people.

Should Social Security Protection Be Improved?

In this section I want to repeat proposals that have been made in other sections of the chapter and add some new ones.

Proposals Previously Discussed

1. Revise the automatic benefit provisions so that increases in the protection provided for current workers is kept up to date with rising wages but is not allowed to exceed such increases.
2. Include three-fourths of social security benefits in gross income for income tax purposes.
3. Increase the maximum earnings base to about $22,000 in 1977 and then gradually increase it somewhat more than enough to keep up with rising wages as under present law until just about all workers—say 95 percent—had all their earnings covered as was the case when the program started. In addition, move up the 2011 rate increase to that point in the 1990s where, otherwise, outgo under the system would begin to exceed income.
4. Provide for fully equal protection of the dependents and survivors of women workers with those of men workers.
5. Cover all government employees under social security with appropriate modifications in their own staff retirement systems.
6. Increase retirement benefits by 12.5 percent and reduce the rate of the spouses' benefit to the retirement benefit from one-half to one-third, thus retaining the same "replacement" rate for couples where only one person works, but increasing benefits for other couples, for single workers and for widows.
7. Apply the age 62 provision for the computation of benefits for men retroactively.
8. Increase the amounts payable for Supplemental Security Income and veteran's pensions to the official poverty level and keep the eligibility standards and benefit amounts up to date automatically for the veteran's programs in accordance with the cost of living, as is now done for the Supplemental Security Income program and social security.
9. Make permanent the refundable earned income credit contained in the 1974-1975 amendments to the income tax law, and apply the credit to workers without children as well as to those with children.
10. Consider earmarking part of the corporation income tax for social security

purposes and substitute an increase in the federal income tax to make up for
the loss of revenue to general funds, and, thus, making it possible to reduce
the employer payroll tax for social security.
11. Work toward a long-range schedule for social security plus national health
insurance that would be financed one-third by deductions from workers'
earnings, one-third by the earmarked corporation income tax and employer
payroll tax, and one-third from the general revenues of the federal government.

Provisions Under Attack That Should Be Retained

Below are some of the key policy points of present law that are under frequent
attack and that I feel should be retained:

1. A test of retirement in social security;
2. A resources and income test in the veteran's pension program;
3. A significant share of social security cost to be borne by the specific
earmarked contributions of workers, including low-income workers;
4. A weighting in the benefit formula so that a higher proportion of relatively
low social security average earnings are replaced than is true of higher average
earnings under social security, but the retention of the minimum benefit at
no more than the same relative level as today (certainly not increased
disproportionately to other benefits and possibly held at the present dollar
level);
5. The avoidance of any change (such as the lowering of the first age of
eligibility for full benefits) that would encourage the lowering of the
compulsory retirement age in American industry and government, and
contrariwise, the promotion of greater labor force participation rates at
higher ages.

Additional Changes Not Previously Discussed

Improvement of the disability program:
1. A major area in which the American social security system is deficient is in
its failure to protect against wage loss resulting from illnesses that last less than a
year. Practically all other major social security systems throughout the world
provide benefits to workers who are unable to perform their work for relatively
short periods of time. (There are five state programs—New York, New Jersey,
Rhode Island, California, and Hawaii—that do provide such protection, but, by
and large, American workers who are disabled for less than a full year have
inadequate protection.) I would propose that the waiting period in the disability
program, which is now five months, be reduced to a much shorter period, say,
two or three months, and that the requirement that the total disability be one

which is expected to last for at least one year before it is compensable at all be dropped.

2. The present definition of total disability under social security is unrealistic when applied to older workers. I would propose that at age 55 benefits be paid if an individual is unable to perform work for which he has demonstrated a capacity by previous training and experience, rather than payment of benefits only if he is unable to perform "*any* substantial gainful activity." The present definition seems a proper one for younger workers. In the case of the disability of middle-aged and younger workers the most important thing is to get the worker rehabilitated—trained for a different job, if necessary—and back in employment. However, above the age of 55 there is little realistic opportunity, in most cases, for the worker to become employed in an entirely different kind of work.

Such a change not only has merit in itself but would help the case for keeping the age of first eligibility for full retirement benefits at 65. The proposed change in the disability program meets that part of the case for lowering the retirement age that has the most merit—paying those who are realistically unable to get jobs because they cannot do the work that they previously could.

3. Disabled widows today can receive payments under social security at age 50 or later but the amount is reduced the earlier the benefit is claimed. At age 50 it is only 50 percent of the benefit amount that the widow's husband would have received had he survived to age 65 and retired. The present reduction in benefit amount was designed solely to save money; the logic of the provision is to pay full-rate benefits to totally disabled widows at any age and this should be done.

4. Initial disability determinations for the federal disability insurance program are now made by state vocational rehabilitation agencies. The state agencies perform under contract and get 100 percent reimbursement of their administrative costs from the Social Security Administration. Federal control over the disability program and the ability of the federal agency to get nationwide uniformity of decision-making is complicated by the need to work through these fifty different state agencies. The program would be more efficiently operated if the federal government performed the work directly as it does in the rest of the cash social security program. Such a change in administrative arrangements is particularly important in light of the fact that disability rates (and consequently the cost of the program) have been continually rising. The federal agency needs to be put in the best possible position to make proper and uniform decisions and to be held fully accountable for those decisions.

Separate Organization and Financing Outside the
General Budget

I believe it would help public understanding of the nature of social security as a government-operated, contributory, retirement and group insurance plan if it were operated by an independent government organization. The form of this organization does not seem to me to be as critical as that it be independent and nonpolitical. The Board organization provided for in the Church bill (S. 388) would seem to me to be satisfactory as would, also, organization in the form of a government corporation.

Whatever the form of organization, it is of considerable importance that social security financial transactions be kept separate from the rest of the federal budget. The social security system is a compact between the federal government and those who work in employment covered by the system. In return for paying social security contributions while earning, the worker and his family receive certain benefits under defined conditions when those earnings have ceased or may be presumed to have been reduced.

Unlike individual annuities under private insurance, social security does not, and indeed should not, build up reserves held to each worker's account sufficient to pay off accumulated rights. Such reserves are necessary under a voluntary insurance system since the insurer cannot count on selling new policies and must have the funds invested to cover the rights already established.

Under a government-operated compulsory system, resting on the taxing power, it is proper to assume the continued existence of the system and to balance future income against future obligations as they fall due. Thus, social insurance in this country and abroad is considered to be soundly financed if the contribution rates in the system, plus earnings on reserves, are estimated to be sufficient on into the future to meet the benefit obligations and administrative expenses *as they fall due*. It is quite correct that the social security system has created future obligations of very large amounts, but, at the same time, the system has established a method of meeting these obligations through future contributions and interest earnings on reserves. Those paying in are building rights under the system through the establishment of a wage record and through contributions. Social security is financed on a current-cost basis with nearly all contributions in a given year ordinarily being used in that year to meet benefit payments and administrative expenses. The funds to pay for current benefi-ciaries are advanced by current workers. This way of handling the obligations of the system need not be of concern to those paying in, as long as the government recognizes that paying in creates the right to be a payee later.

The social security trust funds are contingency reserves designed to avoid the need for sudden and disruptive contribution rate increases that otherwise might be required by a sudden drop in the nation's payrolls and consequently in social security income. The funds are not primarily an earnings reserve intended to supply a major part of the financing of future benefits.

Instead, as indicated above, future benefits are dependent primarily upon contribution income in the future. Precisely because of this fact—that the security of future payments rests on future income—it is important to public understanding that social security income and benefit payments be kept separate from other government income and expenditures. This would be similar to the way it used to be. Until the fiscal year 1969 budget, the financial transactions of the social security system were separate except, of course, for purposes of economic analysis. Today they are part of a unified budget which lumps together general revenue income expenditures and the separately-financed social security system. This is leading to confusion on just how separate from other government programs social security really is.

Putting social security funds in the general budget tends to make people forget that the security of future social security payments is underwritten by a separate, dedicated tax based on the benefit principle of taxation. In the interest of protecting social security's very long-term commitments, the separateness of social security financing should be made unmistakably clear.

Social security does not belong in the annual budget. The purpose of the annual budget is, on the one hand, to make choices among expenditures, giving preference in the budget period to one expenditure over another and, on the other hand, to determine who pays what and how much for the expenditures. Social security promises—stretching into the distant future, resting on past earnings and contributions, and with separate financing—are not a proper part of this essentially competitive process.

The inclusion of social security transactions in the unified budget is bad for other reasons as well. It leads to a distortion of the decision-making process as it relates to non-social security programs. Occasional excesses of income over outgo in social security operations in the short run tend to be used as an excuse for financing additional general revenue expenditures since social security income, although legally reserved for social security expenditures, is treated in the budget in the same way as general revenue income and shows up as if it were available money.

A separate organization—either a board like the old Social Security Board or a corporation—would also help to emphasize the trustee character of the social security operation. Whatever justification there might have been in 1939—when the old Social Security Board was moved into the Federal Security Agency, which later became the Department of Health, Education, and Welfare—for grouping social security with other programs, today a separate organization is fully justified on administrative grounds alone. Social Security now, with over 80,000 employees and some 1,300 district offices across the country, is one of the very largest direct-line operations of the federal government. It accounts for over 60 percent of the personnel of the Department of Health, Education, and Welfare, and pays out $1 for every $3 spent by all the rest of the federal government. It does not make sense administratively to have this huge program, which intimately touches the lives of just about every American family, operated as a subordinate part of another government agency. The management of social security could be made more responsive to the needs of its beneficiaries and contributors if it were freed from the frequent changes in the levels of service to the public which grow out of short-term decisions on employment ceilings and varying management value systems which follow the frequent changes of HEW Secretaries and their immediate staffs. The supervision of social security operations by essentially political hierarchies which come and go with great frequency is not in the best interests of the efficient management of this important program with its long-term commitments.

Conclusion

Social security is a program with more than one purpose. It is our largest antipoverty program, keeping some twelve million people above the poverty level who would otherwise, in the absence of social security, be below that level.

It is however, much more than a poverty program. It is a group insurance and retirement system for just about everyone in the United States. It serves as a base to which other income can be added to provide a level of living well above the poverty level.

In other words, the adequacy of the retirement protection and the group insurance protection can best be measured by the extent to which the program provides income that, together with other income, supports a level of living not too far below what the worker enjoyed in the years before retirement or disability, or which the family enjoyed before the death of an earner in the family, taking into account, of course, differences in taxes and the expenses of working.

By and large, the American social security system is beginning to fulfill these dual purposes admirably. The recent rash of scare stories and attacks on the system are clearly not justified. But, as suggested in this chapter, there are improvements to be made and steps that can be taken now to help control the long-run cost of the system, and steps that can be taken now to improve administration and public understanding.

Notes

Basic Sources. The data in this chapter come almost entirely from official sources.

Historical data have been taken largely from the *Annual Statistical Supplement*, 1973, *Social Security Bulletin*, published by the Social Security Administration, U.S. Department of Health, Education, and Welfare, DHEW Publication No. (SSA)76-11703.

Estimates of the future are largely from the *1973, 1974 and 1975 Annual Reports of The Board Of Trustees Of The Federal Old-Age And Survivors Insurance And Disability Insurance Trust Funds.*

Some of the current data are from the series, *Research and Statistics Notes*, from the Office of Research and Statistics, Social Security Administration.

1. Arthur Larson, *Know Your Social Security* (New York: Harper Brothers, 1959), p. 15.

2. Some of the material in this section appears in various testimony before the Congress and was condensed in an article in *Public Welfare* 33, 4 (Autumn 1975).

3. The material in this section is adapted from an article by the author "Social Security and Private Pension Plans," *National Tax Journal* 27, 3 (September 1974).

XIII

Critical Choices in the Area of Biomedical Ethics

Gilbert S. Omenn

The general public seems greatly interested in the exciting scientific developments and speculations about biology, genetics, and medicine which have been transmitted by the media. Fearful that new technologies may be loosed upon mankind without adequate understanding or control, physicians and biological scientists, sociologists and philosophers, theologians and lawyers have initiated efforts to evaluate the state of the art at present and to assess various conceivable future developments. The literature in this area called "bioethics" (Motulsky 1974; Hamilton 1972; Hilton et al. 1973) has grown very rapidly, mostly with a crescendo of opinion that science and technology are moving too fast. We should note at the start the complementary concerns that excessive caution in developing new biomedical discoveries may leave many patients untreated who otherwise might have benefited. The balance to be achieved between risks and benefits has always been a difficult matter; attempts now are being made to institutionalize the evaluation of the balance, rather than leaving the matter to the doctor/patient relationship or to the scientist/institution/ funding source relationship. The potential risks seem too grave and too diffused through society to rely upon individual decisions.

Some perspective may be gained by realizing that most of our worst fears were outlined in detail in Aldous Huxley's *Brave New World* in 1932 and George Orwell's *1984* published in 1949. In fact, J.B.S. Haldane provided much of the background for *Brave New World* in his 1923 monograph entitled *Daedalus, or Science and the Future*, part of a series of eighty small books called *Today and Tomorrow*. Haldane predicted that the center of science would pass from mathematical physics to biology, that medical progress would practically abolish infectious diseases (except for India), that discoveries in nitrogen fixation would multiply crop yields, and that "by 1951" children would be produced through artificial insemination and maintenance of ovaries in the laboratory. The present sense of urgency arises from the accelerating pace of laboratory achievements, with some writers claiming that Huxley's notions of producing human individuals according to design by cloning or artificial fertilization and of controlling and directing human behavior are now "potentially feasible."

In this chapter, I will bring together a variety of significant and troubling ethical issues in medicine and biology. Although we will consider the major futuristic possibilities, emphasis will be given also to those problems we face now or see rising into prominence soon. Among these current problems, some critical ethical choices must be made to serve both the individual and society for the present and the foreseeable future. The processes by which our society deals with the more immediate ethical concerns will surely determine how we might approach future issues when they require attention. I have categorized the various issues into ten categories and summarized some of the polar positions on these categories in two sets of "ten commandments" (Table XIII-1).

Health Care Delivery

The most important present issue to the largest number of Americans is access to quality health care. The term "health care" represents a significant revision from the term "medical care" for we recognize that many factors, other than the direct intervention of physicians and other health professionals in the medical setting, are crucial to health. These include income, nutrition, educational opportunities, employment, protection from toxic agents in the environment, and protection from discrimination. It is striking that consumer organization has been very weak in the health care arena, suggesting that most people still prefer to place their physical well-being in the hands of a trusted physician, if they can find such a person and establish such a relationship. The physician is not the only professional source of health care, of course. In fact, nurses and paraprofessionals in the hospital have much more contact with the patient and enormous influence on the patient's clinical improvement and sense of well-being. Everyone on the "health team" must recognize that illness is an alarming event in an individual's life, to be understood and dealt with in human terms, not just a scientific malfunction in the biological systems of the body. With more and more women who previously went into nursing gaining entrance to medical school, there is a great risk that nursing care will suffer. A concerted effort to erase sexism in nursing and attract men is overdue. Furthermore, with unionization of hospital personnel finally providing better wages and conditions for the workers, hospital positions have become more like jobs in other businesses, and there is a risk that "TLC" will be forgotten.

Table XIII-1
"Ten Commandments": A Summary of Views in Two Sets of Polar Statements

1. THOU SHALT NOT promise quality health care for all when most cannot afford it.
2. THOU SHALT NOT restrict the imagination of creative technologists because of other priorities.
3. THOU SHALT NOT direct basic scientists what to do and what not to do.
4. THOU SHALT NOT "play God" and decide when the lives of others should be terminated.
5. THOU SHALT NOT "commit murder" by doing abortions.
6. THOU SHALT NOT "do experiments" on fetuses or even fatal tissues without the consent of the fetus.
7. THOU SHALT NOT engage in unnatural means to conceive or bear children.
8. THOU SHALT NOT use technological advances to change the genes of man.
9. THOU SHALT NOT use drugs, surgery, or electrical methods to modify or control the behavior of others.
10. THOU SHALT NOT reveal confidential medical information under any circumstances.

1. THOU SHALT declare health care a right of all people and develop funding and practices to deliver such care.
2. THOU SHALT allocate resources to apply the fruits of medical research to the largest numbers of people.
3. THOU SHALT protect society and scientists themselves from potentially hazardous types of experiments.
4. THOU SHALT be compassionate to those who seek a quiet death rather than a depersonalized prolongation of life.
5. THOU SHALT perform abortions when abortion is decided by the parents to be in the best interests of all concerned.
6. THOU SHALT study tissues obtained from miscarried or aborted fetuses to learn how to prevent and treat disorders.
7. THOU SHALT develop means to assist infertile couples to have children of their own.
8. THOU SHALT use new technologies to correct specific genetic defects in humans.
9. THOU SHALT seek new methods to control impulsive or violent behavior.
10. THOU SHALT find ways to maintain privacy while using confidential medical data for evaluative purposes.

The landmark legislation which requires *assurance of quality* in medical care through Professional Standards Review Organizations (Public Law 92-603) has made hardly a ripple among laymen. Even the matter of national health insurance, which has become something of a political hot potato, has drawn far less public attention than was expected. I believe that medical care and physicians retain a remarkable mystique with most people, especially those who are not ill. However, when serious illness strikes and physicians are hard to find or their bills and the bills of the hospital are hard to pay, people begin to recognize the dilemma of health care delivery in the United States. We surely have the best of medical care in the world, yet for many it is either not accessible or not affordable. Furthermore, there is moral debasement in the fact that individuals who become ill, usually through no avoidable action of their own, suffer more financially, as well. For example, if complications set in after surgery, the patient faces a larger hospital bill at the same time the extended illness prevents him from returning to work to earn the necessary money to meet basic costs. Political momentum is moving inexorably to some system of prepaid health insurance. Most physicians will retain the right to fee-for-service, even though health maintenance organizations and other group practices are being encouraged.

Choice A. Leave present system intact, for fear of making things worse. Limit national health insurance to a mechanism for paying the bills of those who gain care, of whatever quality, in the present health scene. Allow the marketplace to function, presuming that care will be provided to poor people and all others, once funding is available to meet their bills.

Choice B. Recognize that quality health care should be a right of all in this country. Adopt and enforce policies to assess and improve the quality of care, to control unnecessary costs, to distribute physicians more evenly to be certain that disadvantaged persons gain access to care and are treated without discrimination. Nevertheless, recognize the dominant position of physicians and provide incentives to achieve these objectives.

Recommendation. Recognize the overriding need to assure protection against financial ruin from expenses associated with illness. Assess critically the private versus federal mechanisms for administration of a national health insurance scheme. Plans should be evaluated to determine whether the costs of administering complicated schedules of deductibles and coinsurance are justified by savings. If not, it might be wise to risk some "abuse of the system" without these disincentives. Try to establish the concept of standards of quality care and effective peer review, with or without consumer input. Evaluate outcomes of health care, not just the thoroughness of effort, so that procedures and treatments that add cost but not real benefit can be eliminated. Encourage young physicians, probably through a scholarship program, to commit themselves voluntarily to at least a two-year stint of paid service in an underserved area, especially since the doctor draft has been terminated. Review other social policies and the general public tenor in hopes of facilitating well-being for individuals, rather than reliance of individuals upon medical care for deficiencies in their lives; give more emphasis to moderate eating, moderate exercise, and the capacity of the body to heal itself.

Applying the Fruits of Medical Research

No matter how wealthy a nation is, choices must be made in allocating scarce resources—funds, institutional facilities, skilled and creative people. In biomedical research fields, basic scientific discoveries have provided the groundwork for important applications: vaccines against viruses have virtually eliminated previously devastating diseases; knowledge about essential vitamins and amino acids can lead to better selection of crops; design of diets; mechanical devices can simulate the function of kidneys or hearts; computer-assisted biofeedback devices may serve to control high blood pressure or violent impulsive behavior. The costs per unit of these fruits of research vary greatly and the number of people who might need them varies also.

Often there is great public fascination with initial reports of high technology developments in medicine. Too often the implementation of straightforward programs, such as those of mass vaccination, generates no such public interest and the needs become forgotten until headlines bring such news as the 25,000 deaths from smallpox in unvaccinated populations in central India. Far less attention has been paid to serious outbreaks of diphtheria in San Antonio and other cities, particularly among unvaccinated migrant families. Recent studies have demonstrated, furthermore, that some 40 percent of children entering first grade in school lack immunization against polio. Those of us old enough to recall the children's wards full of patients in artificial respirators as a result of polio must do more than simply deplore the situation; a renewed effort to immunize youngsters against polio would seem uncontroversial.

However, there are two problems. First, federal funds for immunization programs have been cut in recent years, with funding going to other projects and with the expectation that children will be taken to private physicians to be immunized. The fees involved constitute an important barrier to many families. Second, a recent court decision has dropped a veil over immunization programs and serves to highlight the issue of informed consent and liability for complications. The U.S. District Court for South Texas recently awarded the plaintiff $200,000 in a case where a young girl contracted polio two weeks after receiving the usual trivalent oral polio vaccine. Such a complication is thought to be a one in fifteen million chance, and both the drug company and the American Academy of Pediatrics amicus curiae brief argued that individualized warnings would impair the immunization programs by unduly alarming all parents.

The biomedical research effort in the United States presently amounts to some $4 billion per year, a fairly small figure in relation to the more than $100 billion per year spent on health care services. In this category of issues, the application of research knowledge, we face some of the most difficult ethical choices. Should large sums of public monies be spent on artificial hearts, for example, which will be utilized primarily by older people with limited lifespans, involving tremendous investments of other resources from surgeons to hospital space to nursing care, and helping probably only thousands of people per year, if successful? The Social Security Amendments of 1972 mandate extensive care, including dialysis with a kidney machine or transplantation, for all patients with severe kidney disease. The passage of these amendments as the omnibus bill was pushed through the Congress committed the federal government to heavy expenditures for Medicaid and Medicare patients with just one type of disease. Its passage reflected the effective lobbying of those concerned with kidney disease. Analogous efforts have been mounted for other major diseases, with the distinct possibility that the federal government may back into national health insurance on a disease-by-disease basis. Critics charge that the small change from such expenditures would suffice to support a vigorous immunization campaign against measles, polio, and other communicable diseases in children, for which millions of children can be helped for certain and with minimal requirements for other care. It is simply not the case that both or all good programs can be supported fully in the present budgets.

Technological advances have led to exaggerated claims of the value of multiphasic screening of normal people in the search for disease before it produces symptoms. Batteries of chemical tests on blood and urine plus X-rays and electrocardiograms can be done relatively cheaply on each individual, but the aggregate investment and profits become huge. The payoff in treatable diseases found earlier has been disappointing, however. Furthermore, except for certain surgical conditions and the Pap smear for uterine cancer, the patient may be just as well off if diagnosed properly when symptoms occur, as from diabetes or heart disease. The routine standbys of blood pressure measurement, blood hemoglobin level, and urine testing for protein and sugar pick up the most important abnormalities. It is almost heretical to oppose automated programs to enhance "prevention" and early detection, but critical review of the results of such programs is overdue.

Creative approaches to modify individual behavior or decrease the risks associated with certain behavior might be encouraged for the three major ravagers of young adults: accidents, cigarettes, and alcohol. It is one of the great ironies of medical research and its application to benefit the population that very well-documented research findings in these three areas have made little impact.

Accidents, particularly automobile accidents, produce more deaths for people in the age group 15-44 than any other category or causes. Only recently has the government taken an interest in such items as flammable clothing, dangerous toys, and automobile design. Most manufacturers have followed a policy of caveat emptor, partially on the basis of "leaving the choice to the individual" and partially on the assertion that people would not pay for safety.

Alcohol, of course, is a major factor in half of the fatal automobile accidents.

According to the National Council on Alcoholism, some 9.5 million Americans are alcoholics. A good many more occasionally drive after socially imbibing more than they can tolerate. Research knowledge on the biological and social effects of acute and chronic alcohol ingestion is extensive, yet application of that knowledge to deal with the widespread impact on individuals and their families and on society as a whole has been resisted.

Similarly, extensive research has demonstrated beyond challenge that cigarette smoking is associated with enhanced risks of lung cancer, earlier onset of heart disease, considerable morbidity from chronic bronchitis, and increased susceptibility to respiratory infections, stomach ulcers, and bladder cancer. Despite the massive publicity given the Surgeon General's Report on the Hazards of Cigarette Smoking ten years ago, the use of cigarettes has remained high. For several years the per capita consumption declined, but the population increase made up the difference for the producers. Now with a new surge of cigarette smoking among the very young, the per capita tobacco consumption is rising again. Dr. Jerome Jaffe, who was the first director of the Special Action Office on Drug Abuse in the Nixon Administration, wrote in *Science* magazine (1974) that the biggest drug problem is nicotine addiction and the vast influence of the tobacco industry. The $5.7 billion revenues in taxes on tobacco and the similar large tax revenues from alcohol make these habits almost indispensable sources of state and local support!

This discussion of accidents, alcoholism, and smoking may seem far afield from the polarized debate over whether to allow medical technologists to build artificial hearts when children are going unimmunized. However, these three giant killers illustrate better than any ordinary disease categories the incongruities between our knowledge gained from medical research and our capacity to mobilize political, social, and economic concensus to do something to enhance health and safety. In the development of biomedical technologies, increased emphasis must be placed upon informed consent of subjects and patients, confidentiality of patient data, and minimization of risks. Havighurst (1970) has criticized the procedures for human experimentation as limited to exercising care and obtaining informed consent signatures. He proposes mechanisms to provide financial compensation for those who suffer injuries from participation in experimental procedures. He also attaches importance to financial incentives for researchers and their institutions to minimize risks by requiring that the institutions, rather than the funding sources, pick up the costs of indemnification.

Choice A. Do not restrict the imagination of creative technologists to develop more sophisticated machinery for diagnostic and therapeutic purposes. Allow the marketplace or public opinion to determine how widely the techniques should be utilized.

Choice B. Devise a broad view of priorities in applying modern medical research knowledge. Insist that high priority be given to those techniques helping the largest number of people. Seek techniques which do not commit the patient and the system to enormous follow-up costs, thus favoring preventive and curative measures over palliative approaches. Perform cost-benefit analyses that assess the full life-span impact and the external impacts on society.

Recommendation. Given the public and professional fascination with spectacular technologies and dramatic improvement in patient condition, public support and corporate investment will tend to be greater than any cost-benefit analysis would allow for such things as artif cial hearts and automated multiphasic screening. A comprehensive national health policy in the area of applied research and development must, therefore, emphasize the more mundane, high-yield programs, such as immunizations, prenatal and perinatal care of mother and newborn, childhood and occupational safety, and control of alcoholism and cigarette addiction. The prowess of American technology should not be underestimated, of course; many techniques which seem far too expensive when introduced may prove so helpful that initial costs are tolerated and costs fall as economies of production scale are realized. As common needs are recognized, that technological prowess might be directed to attack some neglected problems, with similar or greater payoff. It is of interest, I believe, that twenty-eight of the sixty-four graduate students in the five engineering departments at the University of Washington recently chose to do their projects in the area of Bio-Engineering. The prize for the best project was for a wheelchair design! Much more could be done in design and production to improve care in hospital and out of hospital for chronically ill patients and for others.

Basic Research: Should Work With Biologically Hazardous Materials Be Restricted?

There is a long, glorious, sometimes tragic tradition of risk-taking in biomedical research. When research results are applied to patients, the potential benefits are often accompanied by risks taken by the patients. Usually preliminary trials can be performed in animals. In the basic research stage, however, the risks may be taken exclusively by the research workers and their assistants. Those who have studied all sorts of infectious organisms have occasionally become infected and even died. The risks are particularly high for organisms for which there is no treatment, still including all the viruses (Hellman et al. 1973). Those who studied X-ray and radioactivity incurred severe risks, especially the pioneers, such as the famed physiologist, Bradford Cannon. Cannon demonstrated the Barium swallow and "upper GI series" of X-rays on himself first and repeatedly, leading to his demise from cancer. Others have taken risks by performing research in hazardous natural environments.

This particular issue has been pushed to the forefront as a result of new developments in molecular biology and genetics. Several leaders in this field have sounded an alarm against utilizing available skills to produce new types of viruses or bacteria with special resistance to antibiotics, for fear that such virulent agents might "get loose" from the lab and become untreatable infectious agents in the general population. Laboratory tricks with DNA and enzymes that can hook together pieces of DNA from different sources now permit the creation of recombinant DNA from a variety of animal, bacterial, or viral sources. Experiments producing such molecules and hybrid organisms may lead to important understanding of basic biological questions, but their biological properties may not be predictable. Such a statement is usually a stimulus to research, in order to learn what cannot be predicted from present knowledge. Nevertheless, a highly prestigious committee of biochemists, under the banner of the National Academy of Sciences, has called upon their colleagues to voluntarily defer certain types of experiments (Berg et al. 1974). These experiments include introduction of genetic determinants for antibiotic resistance or toxin formation into bacteria that do not presently carry them and production of hybrid DNA from viruses that tend to cause cancer or infect humans. The group requested that the director of the National Institutes of Health establish an advisory committee to oversee an experimental program to evaluate these potential biological and ecological hazards of recombinant DNA molecules; to develop procedures to minimize the spread of such molecules within human and animal populations; and to devise guidelines to be followed by investigators working with these molecules.

In addition to scientific concensus of this sort, two other types of controls may be recognized. The first is provided by administrators and scientific review committees of the funding agencies, usually the National Institutes of Health, but also foundations. These agencies are capable of requiring explicit guarantees of safety and limitations of risks to workers and patients and the general population, as a condition for funding. The second review, a posteriori, comes from the editors and reviewers of scientific journals when the work is submitted for publication. There is, in fact, considerable debate about the ethics of editorial decision-making and about the responsibility of editorial boards to make judgments about the ethical propriety of work to be published (DeBakey 1974).

Choice A. Leave to the individual scientists the responsibility of deciding what work is scientifically promising, and what work is either unpromising or too hazardous. Recognize that much valuable research might never have been allowed by cautious administrators.

Choice B. Add to the criteria of scientific merit and promise for societal benefit the criterion of acceptable hazard when reviewing and sponsoring biomedical research proposals. In fact, go further and prohibit sufficiently hazardous work, even if not supported by federal or other governmental funds.

Recommendation. Since this issue has been raised by the leading researchers in the field, it is desirable to follow the proposed plan and attempt to rationally evaluate the hazards involved and the methods to be employed in any studies that are permitted. The precedent may be stultifying to other fields of research, as fear overtakes judgment. Important improvements in laboratory conditions where viruses are studied have been made in the last few years. Improvements in the disposal of organisms and chemicals are needed as well. Reasonable caution and open, informed discussion of these issues must be supported.

Prolongation of Life

The capability of physicians and hospitals to prolong life—or prolong dying—has been an active issue among laymen, as well as health professionals and health economists. Two common situations are encountered: the very premature or hopelessly malformed infant and the terminally ill older person. Most laymen carry a dreaded image of a slow death in a hospital, with multiple tubes inserted, remote from loved ones, suffering beyond what can be communicated in words. Williams (1973) has reported a survey in which physicians and laymen were asked: "With appropriate changes in the laws, with detailed consideration of the status of the patient and others by his physician and two or more additional professional hospital personnel, and with consent of the patient and/or appropriate relative, do you favor in certain carefully selected instances (a) negative euthanasia (planned omission of therapies that probably would prolong life)? (b) positive euthanasia (institution of therapy that it is hoped will promote death sooner than otherwise)?" About 80 percent of both physician and lay groups favored negative euthanasia and 80 percent of the physicians reported that they had practiced it in selected cases. Eighteen percent of physicians and 35 percent of laymen favored positive euthanasia.

The medical profession has been taught to prolong life as a primary goal almost without regard to other consequences. The Hippocratic Oath is interpreted as stressing both the relief of suffering and the protection and prolongation of life. Sometimes these objectives are in conflict. Physicians find themselves in the uncomfortable position of potentially facing prosecution for criminal negligence if they withhold therapy, yet knowing that prosecution is most unlikely. In several state legislatures, model statutes have been introduced to provide a legal framework within which families and health professionals can deal openly and honestly with this matter.

Duff and Campbell (1973) reviewed the experience in the special-care nursery at Yale-New Haven Hospital. Of 299 consecutive deaths, 43 (14 percent) were related to the withholding of treatment. In each case, parents and physicians in a group decision concluded that prognosis for meaningful life was extremely poor or hopeless. The nurses, parents, and physicians considered it cruel to continue, yet difficult to stop therapies. All were desperately attached to the child, whose life they had tried so hard to make worthwhile. Typically, the family endured extremely high expenses, strains to the marriage and to the relationships with siblings. Some parents were resentful that children might be kept alive "as teaching material," to learn more about the disease in the hope of helping others. Sometimes, particularly in children with open spine, the decision to stop treatment leads only slowly to death, making either treatment or nontreatment unsatisfactory, continuing dilemmas. In these cases, of course, the child is incapable of giving informed consent. As Fletcher (1966) has argued with the term "situation ethics," the decision by the parents in the interests of the child must be acceptable. Genetic disorders raise an additional element in this complicated equation—the chance the prolongation and improvement of life for the affected individual may make it possible to pass on the deleterious genes to subsequent generations.

Choice A. Maintain the sanctity of life and preserve the role of the physician as the protector and healer of life by eschewing measures that would shorten life expectancy or suddenly terminate existence. Provide care at the level of the state of the art, as if hopeful that the patient could make a miraculous recovery.

Choice B. Condone and legally allow the cautious and joint decision by family and professionals to terminate extraordinary measures that prolong life.

Choice C. Develop means to decide when lives consumed with pain or devoid of brain function should be actively terminated, even though no extraordinary measures are being used to support life.

Recommendation. Open discussion of Choice B may be most reasonable for the present, allowing the evolution of public opinion and the relaxation of medical zealousness to keep patients alive at all costs. Given the array of religious views and personal feelings, legislation that prescribes how to manage these situations will be very difficult to draft. As noted in the next section on abortion, the removal of proscription may allow the issue to be dealt with more openly with toleration for all views. Hopefully, experience will prove that families and health professionals can maintain compassion. In the Yale newborn study, repeated participation in these troubling discussions and events did not appear to reduce the worry of the staff about the awesome nature of the decisions.

Abortion

The debate over reform of abortion laws has been pitched at a high emotional level with reformers generally labeled as "murderers" by the "right-to-lifers."

Laws are clearly out of touch with the real fact that thousands of women and couples were seeking and obtaining abortions illegally or in other states or countries. Yet the argument raged that allowing abortion would undermine the sanctity of life and lead *pari passu* to infanticide.

The development of safe and reliable tests for certain genetic defects in fetuses, including most importantly mongolism, made the availability of elective abortion desirable even to many people who would oppose abortion on demand. However, it is certainly the case that the issue was fought over the broad matter of the right of a woman to control whether or not she would carry a baby to term. Furthermore, the abortion issue became embroiled in the tide of opinion concerned with rapid growth in population and, conversely, the desire to limit family size and space children through contraceptives and, if necessary, abortion. Public opinion surveys (Blake 1971) in the 1960s found little support for abortion done for economic or discretionary reasons, while abortion to preserve the mother's health or prevent child deformity was already well-tolerated. Laws making abortions easier to obtain were first passed in 1967 in California, Colorado, and North Carolina. In 1970, the legislature of the state of Washington still refused to vote on abortion reform, but allowed the electorate to decide via referendum. A surprisingly large plurality (55 percent in favor) voted for what was described as "abortion on demand" up to sixteen weeks of pregnancy.

In all, fifteen states had adopted similar laws by 1970 and during 1970 approximately 200,000 women in the United States obtained legal abortions. In 1971, the number increased to about 500,000, 35 percent of which were performed for nonresident women in states where abortion was legal. Sklar and Berkov (1974) conclude that legal abortions in 1971 data decreased overall fertility, but especially illegitimate fertility, by giving women an opportunity to terminate pregnancies when other means of birth control either had not been used or had failed. If legalized abortion had not been available, an estimated additional 39,000 illegitimate babies and 28,000 legitimate babies would have been born in 1971 in the United States. These numbers make up a small fraction of the 3.5 million total births, but the illegitimate births prevented represent 10 percent of out-of-wedlock children born in this country for that year. In addition to preventing these births, the legalization of abortion appears to have reduced the incidence of pregnancy-related marriages, perhaps thereby helping limit subsequent marital disruption. Finally, the data indicate that 65-75 percent of all legal abortions were replacements for what would have been illegal abortions.

Early in 1973 when the Supreme Court unanimously struck down statutory restrictions on abortion, the majority of the electorate was in support. Nevertheless, the issue has not died. Vigorous opposition groups are active in many parts of the country, and constitutional amendments and legislative bills have been introduced in the Congress to attempt to thwart the decision of the Supreme Court. In addition, foes of abortion reform have focused on the fetal research described in the next section. Perhaps most discriminatory of all is the action by many jurisdictions to prohibit use of public medical care funds for abortion services. This policy returns the situation to pre-1973 status for the poor, who cannot afford the abortions now legally available and who then are berated for adding children to the welfare rolls.

A potentially controversial application of amniocentesis and abortion is for choice of sex of the baby. There has long been interest in influencing the sex at the time of conception (Etzioni 1968). However, the examination of fetal chromosomes, as in testing for mongolism, in the amniotic fluid cells obtained during the second trimester of pregnancy, provides direct evidence of the sex of the fetus, XX for girls and XY for boys. At present this method is utilized only to detect and abort potentially affected males from mothers who are carriers for serious X-linked diseases such as hemophilia or the Duchenne type of muscular dystrophy. However, we have been approached in our Genetics Clinic in Seattle to arrange for such testing to assist couples to have a child of desired sex after they had had several children of one sex only.

At present, such requests seem a relatively frivolous indication for a still-experimental technique. However, if the couples are sufficiently perturbed about the birth of another child of undesired sex, they may seek abortion on the basis that there is a 50 percent risk of a condition they consider reason for abortion. As more and more couples seek to limit family size to two children, emphasis on the health of those two children and, in many cases, having one child of each sex, may stimulate interest in the procedure. The choice of one child of each sex would be desirable in that it would not shift the sex ratio in the population. Assuming that couples would accept the sex of the first child, such a scheme would require abortion of 50 percent of all second pregnancies and 6 percent of couples would require four abortions to attain their goal. If some better method, such as separation of X- and Y-bearing sperm, would become feasible, it is almost certain that the new method would be preferred.

Choice A. Try to reimpose the unworkable prohibitions on abortion that have been so recently removed.

Choice B. Maintain the new status quo by providing safe, well-supervised clinics for abortions and respecting both those who choose abortions and those who reject abortions for themselves and their families. Similarly, respect physicians and other health personnel who choose either to perform or not to perform abortions, so long as they do not obstruct the will of the patient.

Recommendation. Choice B.

Fetal Research

Research on the development of the embryo and fetus is central to efforts to learn more about birth defects and their prevention. Fetal tissues obtained from spontaneous or induced abortions are valuable for such studies and as medium for growth of viruses to make vaccines. Ordinarily there is not much objection to use of dead embryos in the tradition of medical autopsies. Major objections are raised, however, when embryos are removed for abortion and then kept "alive" for research purposes, assessing the effects of physical, chemical, infectious, and pharmacological agents. The mother may be willing to give informed consent, but some critics insist that only the fetus could give the desired consent. This position is an extension of the view that the fetus is already a living human being and that abortion is equivalent to murder.

A truly sensational case developed in Boston. A gynecologist at the Boston City Hospital was indicted for manslaughter in the "death" of a fetus in a legal abortion, and four colleagues were accused of violating an 1814 law against grave-robbing for using tissue from aborted fetuses for research. The colleagues were involved in a federally supported experiment to determine whether antibiotics taken by pregnant women crossed the placenta to act in the fetus for use in preventing congenital syphilis in babies. The study which triggered this chain of events had been approved in advance by the hospital's Human Studies Committee, carried out with reasonable precaution that the study would in no way prejudice the manner in which women received abortions for which they were admitted to the hospital, and published as valuable data in the prestigious *New England Journal of Medicine*.

The great bulk of fetal research is directed at understanding why an infant is born prematurely, subject to greatly enhanced risks of disability or death. Techniques used in intensive care units to try to rescue sickly preemies are themselves experimental and would be judged so by the courts if a research ban on living fetuses is enacted permanently into law. Attempts to understand and prevent congenital malformations require studies of fetuses since animals have not proved good indicators of what goes wrong in man. The procedure called amniocentesis, in which a needle is inserted through the pregnant woman's abdominal and uterine walls into the amniotic fluid sac around the fetus to obtain a small amount of fluid for tests, is now widely applied to check high-risk pregnancies for mongolism or Tay-Sachs disease or a growing list of other specific serious genetic disorders. Usually the fetus is found to be unaffected so that the couple is reassured and can face the rest of the pregnancy much more optimistic that they will have a healthy baby. Instruments are now being tested that allow visualization of the fetus and a search for certain recognizable birth defects. Demand for such still-experimental services is high, but the development of such tests could well be stymied by bans on fetal research.

Fetal tissues have been extremely valuable for other research. John Enders of Harvard won the Nobel Prize for learning how to grow polio virus in tissue from aborted fetuses, making possible the development of the Salk and Sabin vaccines. Similarly, a vaccine has been developed against German measles, protecting expectant mothers from the ravages of this virus on their babies. The relationship of the fetus to the mother also raises fascinating questions about the tolerance of a transplanted organ and the protection against growth of a cancer, since the fetus is genetically different from the mother (composed of tissues partially derived from the father's genes). If we could understand how the mother's body avoids rejection of the foreign material that is the fetus, we might have crucial clues to understand why the body tolerates rapidly dividing tumor cells instead of destroying them. The prevention of Rh disease, the avoidance of future thalidomide incidents, and many other specific medical problems of the pregnant woman and the growing fetus require imaginative research with fetal tissues and fetuses.

Nevertheless, the furor over the "rights of the fetus" has led already to passage of laws in several states, including California, Massachusetts, and Ohio, to curb or forbid research with fetuses; the indictments in Boston; and the passage by Congress of the "Protection of Human Subjects Act," which banned for six months any experimentation in which living human fetuses are used unless the research is to save the fetus' life. The moratorium applied even to procedures like electrocardiograms and ultrasound studies, which are used routinely in monitoring pregnancies. An eleven-member federal commission was formed to prepare a report on what to do after the moratorium is over. There is grave concern that political pressures, led by Representative Roncallo and Senator Buckley of New York, will make the ban permanent. The fear of such political and religious objections has already "dried up" sources of fetal tissues for laboratory research. Obstetricians and pathologists became reluctant to be involved in any way in such programs, even before the HEW ban took effect.

Those who oppose research on human fetuses base their case largely on the argument that one human being should not be used experimentally for the benefit of another without the consent of the first. Since the fetus is incapable of giving this consent, research on living fetuses should be outlawed, even if society may be deprived of important benefits as a result. This view of unobtainable consent is a spillover from other unfortunate incidents in which mentally retarded or mentally disturbed individuals or prisoners have been made part of experimental programs in which their informed consent is suspect. Some who attack fetal research charge that scientists are akin to Nazi concentration camp experimenters, a nasty charge indeed. The HEW ban and the preceding restrictive guidelines from the National Institutes of Health, which directly funds most of the research, may have the further unsavory effect of driving important research to other countries, just as women seeking a legal abortion went elsewhere for a time.

Choice A. Prohibit all experiments on fetuses and fetal tissues, since consent of the fetus is impossible.

Choice B. Require informed consent of the mother for all experiments to be performed on the fetus or fetal tissues.

Choice C. Require institutional review with guidelines from the National Institutes of Health on what sorts of experiment may be performed with fetuses or fetal tissues.

Recommendation. Choice C. The kinds of valuable experiments carried out with fetal tissues to make vaccines or understand the growth of cancer cells or test the effects of drugs are far afield from the concerns of the woman who legally seeks an abortion. Zealous efforts to inform her sufficiently to have truly informed consent may be a grossly unfair impingement upon her sensitivities at a difficult time in her life. To carry Choice A to its logical extreme will violate the "rights" of premature newborns to adequate medical care.

Reproductive Engineering

Interfering with the natural process of fertility and childbearing may be termed reproductive engineering. Methods include all types of contraception or family planning, abortion, sterilization, artificial insemination by husband or other donor, and *in vitro* fertilization. Each of these topics has manifold ethical ramifications. Abortion has been discussed briefly above. Sterilization remains a sensitive topic, since incidents continue to occur with minors or mentally retarded or prisoners. When sterilization or abortion is denied for lack of informed consent or adult status, serious consequences must be faced, as in the birth of children from matings in hospitals for mentally ill or mentally retarded. Artificial insemination with sperm from sperm banks raises complex emotional issues for the woman and her husband and also raises long overdue concern about the lack of regulation of such sperm banks.

The most popular issue in this category, however, is the matter of "test-tube babies." In July 1974, newspapers all around the world carried the story that a British gynecologist had disclosed in a casual remark at the British Medical Association Meeting the birth of three test-tube babies conceived in a laboratory and then implanted in their mothers' wombs. They were said to be one to two years of age and doing well, one in England and the other two in Europe. To protect the babies' privacy, the gynecologist steadfastly refused to disclose any information about them or their parents or the scientists involved. The most renowned team of researchers in this area, Edwards and Steptoe in Cambridge, England, immediately disavowed any involvement. Whatever the status of these purported cases, the approach pioneered by Edwards and Steptoe is of interest.

The patients involved deeply desire children, but are infertile for a highly specific reason: the wife's tubes are blocked. Otherwise, her normal ovaries and normal uterus and normal husband would allow conception. Her physicians face a dilemma: Should they deny her the "right" to have her own children, admittedly with a technological assist, in order to protect the child and society from conceivable but unproved risks in trying new procedures? The approach is rather straightforward. The ovaries are stimulated to ovulate by normal female hormones; an instrument is introduced through the abdominal wall, through which eggs can be "collected" from the visualized ovarian surface. Washed ejaculated sperm are capable of penetrating the membranes of the egg and achieving fertilization in quite simple culture medium in the laboratory. Then different culture conditions support successive divisions of the fertilized egg and development of the blastocyst to 100 or more cells. At this point comes the extremely delicate procedure of implanting the laboratory-reared blastocyst into the hormone-stimulated uterus of the (donor) woman. One can imagine, of course, implanting blastocysts derived from eggs from one woman, fertilized with sperm from one or more men, into many hormonally prepared women. The notion of growing the embryo to "full-term" in an artificial womb is a far more remote possibility, with a much higher risk that something might go wrong.

It is worth discussing this matter in more detail, for even a few cases of *in vitro* fertilization will challenge the imagination of the public and touch deeply rooted and strongly held beliefs and values. With changing views of marriage, procreation, kinship, and biological family ties, it is difficult to predict how people will react to future technological prospects. These procedures seem all the more ironic at a time when the emphasis on zero population growth has fostered more liberal attitudes about contraception, voluntary sterilization, and abortion.

Case 1: Fully intramarital case with egg from wife, sperm from husband, embryo transfer to wife for gestation and delivery, simply circumventing blocked tubes. Especially now that so few children are available for adoption, this method may offer a unique means for such couples to satisfy a long-frustrated desire to have a child. The parents must understand, of course, that the scientists cannot guarantee a "normal," much less a "superior" baby, any more than does normal reproduction. In the present state of the art, between five and ten laparoscopies on the woman to obtain ovulated eggs and possibly several attempts at implantation may be required before a viable child is produced. Of course, the matter of gaining informed consent from the "patient" produced is impossible to satisfy. A healthy child should have few special problems of identity, status, and self-image. However, these children may face intense scientific curiosity about their physical, mental, sexual, and emotional development. If substantial numbers of these procedures were ever to be contemplated, consideration of society's investment in financial and professional resources would be pertinent and the establishment and regulation of egg, sperm, and embryo "banks" might be desirable.

Case 2: The "adopted embryo." The egg would be from another woman, the sperm from either the husband or another man, and the prospective child would be genetically unrelated, as in other adoptions. Here the woman and her husband would have the experience of pregnancy and delivery. Women with infertility due to ovarian disease and fertile couples known to carry genes for serious inherited disorders would be candidates. If sperm and egg banks were so organized, there might be some interest in "selective mating." The recipient woman would be spared the laparoscopy to obtain ovulated eggs, but a donor woman would have to subject herself to the procedure without any further personal involvement. Considerable emotional problems and fantasies may occur, as in ordinary adoption or organ transplantation, especially when the parties are not anonymous. If the child's special origin should come to light, as in a dispute or divorce, there could be unfortunate consequences for the child and uncertainty about the rights of custody.

Case 3: The "surrogate womb." The embryo, grown *in vitro* from an egg of one woman fertilized by sperm from her husband, would be transferred to another woman to carry and deliver the child and return it to its genetic parents. Candidates would be women who are infertile because of disease or removal of the uterus and women who wish to avoid pregnancy for reasons of fear or convenience. It is unlikely that this scenario would be chosen commonly; it is likely that the cost of "renting" the use of another woman's womb for nine months would be substantial. Conflicts are to be expected: the bearer might decide to have an abortion, or to keep the child; the husband and wife might change their minds and try to force the pregnant woman to undergo an abortion; or they might reject a deformed or defective baby. There would be need for clear definition of the status and social identity of the child. There is the risk that poor women might be hired for such services, with degrading connotations.

Choice A. Prohibit the use of unnatural means to conceive or bear children.

Choice B. Allow people and their physicians freedom of choice to satisfy their desire to have children by any means they consider reasonable.

Recommendation. Develop guidelines for candidates for case 1 procedures, maintain the privacy of the couples involved, restrict support for such procedures to highly qualified scientist-physicians. Withhold support for cases of types 2 and 3 for the present.

Genetic Engineering and Cloning

Cloning is one of the most popular and, at the same time, most fanciful, worries of writers about biomedical ethics. Cloning of man would involve the creation of human beings who are genetically identical to the donor of somatic cell nuclei, from intestinal lining or skin, to be implanted into enucleated eggs. The basic experiments have been performed only in amphibians and only in certain species of tadpoles, in fact. However, Gurdon's nuclear transplantation experiments are of great significance for basic biological understanding, for they demonstrate that the nucleus of even a highly differentiated tissue cell still contains all the genetic information to program the development of an entire organism, if put back into the cytoplasm of a normal egg cell. The frog egg is deposited outside the mother and is large enough to be manipulated to remove its nucleus. Intestinal lining cell nuclei are isolated and inserted into the enucleated egg.

Although Huxley anticipated the procedures of cloning in *Brave New World* and modern molecular biologists have described its implications for man, cloning has not yet been performed with any mammals. Both technical and biological barriers may preclude its use in man. In addition, of course, even if cloning becomes feasible, there is no compelling reason to decide to allow its use. Scenarios have been painted of the creation of groups of clonee military scientists or brute soldiers in the service of a state bent to conquer the world. Simpler and well-tested ways of subjugating people will almost surely seem more attractive to any despots, who tend to be interested in the immediate future rather than a wait of at least a generation before the putative clonees would be available. Articles which claim that "a far more suitable technique for eugenic purposes will *soon be upon us*—namely, nuclear transplantation, or cloning" (Kass 1971) are unreasonably inflammatory in my opinion.

Before leaving the subject of cloning, I should emphasize that the image of unlimited numbers of identical human beings is exaggerated, as well. It is true that the clonees would be identical genetically, having started with nuclei from a single source. However, for the human traits of greatest interest, including personality, aggression, intelligence, and compliance, the direct actions of genes are modified through multiple experiences and through development. Although identical twins are much more similar to each other than other pairs of individuals are, there are still substantial differences. Among clonees there would likewise be significant variation.

Treatment of genetic diseases does not necessarily require genetic engineering (Omenn, in Williams 1973). An impressive number of genetic conditions can be treated by correcting biochemical abnormalities in the tissues or blood, even though there is no way to alter the abnormal gene itself. Treatment approaches include administration of products the body cannot make, dietary restriction of ingredients the body cannot metabolize, infusion of an enzyme which is deficient, use of drugs as inhibitors or inducers of enzymes and as chelators of toxic metals; other methods include surgical removal of organs (colon, spleen, lens); transplantation of kidney, bone marrow, or cornea; use of artificial aids ranging from hearing aids to kidney machines; and manipulation of the immune response, as in administration of Rhogam to prevent sensitization of the mother from her Rh-positive baby. With effective treatments, the situation calls for best medical care for the patient, far overwhelming any dysgenic effects to society of surviving and passing on deleterious genes. The fitness of the patient for survival should be maintained so long as the culture that permits his treatment is intact.

In many cases, treatment approaches are novel and raise anew the questions of human experimentation and truly informed consent.

Gene replacement with normal DNA: true "genetic engineering." Permanent genetic modification of human cells with DNA requires four successive steps: (1) preparation of the DNA containing the desired gene(s), either by direct isolation or by enzymatic synthesis of DNA from the messenger RNA; (2) efficient and selective insertion of the DNA into the cells of the recipient, probably carried by a virus with specificity for the type of recipient cell; (3) stabilization of the exogenous DNA by insertion into a chromosome in the recipient cell; and (4) expression of the new gene in the cell, with synthesis of the needed protein product in the normal amounts. (See Figure XIII-1.) Each of these steps is fraught with massive technical difficulties. However, before even embarking upon such maneuvers it is essential to know just which gene or genes account for the disorder under investigation for treatment. It is not sufficient to know simply that the disease is inherited. Also it is essential that the defect causes production of an abnormal protein, which can be replaced by the action of the normally functioning gene which is inserted. If the defect were in the regulation of synthesis of a structurally normal protein, the insertion of a gene coding for that protein structure would have no benefit.

The list of conditions for which specific enzyme deficiency is known will continue to grow, so that the potential applications will be more numerous. Unfortunately, our knowledge is greatest for the rarer disorders and most limited for the common diseases in which genetic factors are certainly involved but act through unspecific polygenic mechanisms. Thus coronary heart disease, high blood pressure, schizophrenia, depression, and diabetes all have significant genetic determinants, but the mechanisms are unknown. Thus, there are no clues as to which genes would need to be replaced. For the foreseeable future, genetic control of these common diseases will rest on genetic counseling and control of childbearing, rather than molecular intervention.

Even if technological advances were to allow the orderly construction of pseudoviral particles containing both a coat that will attach selectively to the cells that need gene replacement and the desired gene for an increasingly long list of specific genetic disorders, certain scientific and social issues remain to be considered. The safety of the treated individual must be guaranteed against the possibility that the carrier virus produces cancer or is contaminated with other, unwanted viruses. Such contamination occurred a few years ago in the preparation of one batch of Salk polio vaccine on monkey kidney cells in culture; fortunately, no untoward effects have been noted. The inserted DNA must function under normal control within the cell; otherwise, all sorts of metabolic imbalance might result, possibly damaging the tissue and patient even more than the original disease. Any such experiment must be limited to patients who will be seriously impaired if untreated and for whom no simpler and safer treatment is known. The natural history of the disease must be well established, so that the effect of the gene therapy can be evaluated as unequivocally as possible. It will

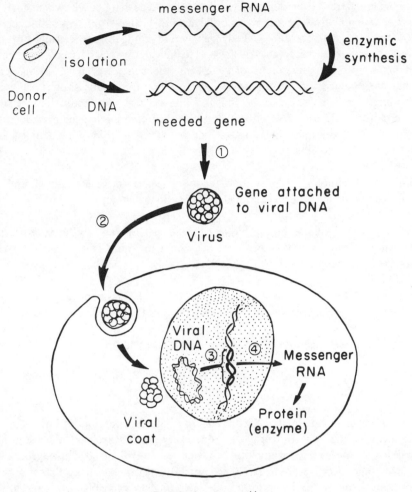

Figure XIII-1. Scheme for True Genetic Engineering by Replacement of a Faulty Gene. See text for details. (From Omenn, in Williams, 1973).

be desirable to start therapy before the disorder results in irreversible damage to tissues, possible during pregnancy, in which case prior informed consent from the treated individual would be impossible. Changes in the genes and chromosomes may result long-term in altered germ cell function that does not become manifest until children of the affected child are examined.

Finally, there is a matter of social priorities. Lederberg has drawn an analogy to the technological potential to build a land bridge from San Francisco to Honolulu; presumably other challenges would compete successfully for the energies and resources even if "merely technical obstacles" were overcome! Research into the functioning of genes and the control of gene action when genes are inserted into chromosomes will provide important knowledge about the functioning of human cells. But will society invest in applications of such research for a relatively few individuals with specific, rare inherited disorders? Or will priorities demand that applications be directed toward control of risk factors for common diseases?

Choice A. Technological prowess to modify genes in germ cells should be restrained for fear that unanticipated complications may arise.

Choice B. New technologies in biology should be directed to alleviate suffering in highly selected specific disorders for which no more convenient or better established therapy is available.

Choice C. There should be no restrictions on the development and application of new technologies (see above) "Applying the Fruits of Medical Research."

Recommendation. Choice B, with caution and discussion.

Behavior Control

Human achievement and behavior in general depends upon both genetic endowment and the nurturing of one's capacities through education and experience. Means to manipulate behavior of individuals or large groups of people come from several disciplines: psychological measures, political forces, neurophysiological and neurosurgical techniques, behavior-modifying drugs, electrical stimulation, and genetic engineering. Operant-conditioning techniques are widely used, particularly in schools and mental hospitals, with apparent success. Electrical and pharmacological stimulation of the brain can produce sensations of pleasure, control rage or anxiety, and modify sexual perversion. When electrodes are placed in certain discrete regions of their brains, animals repeatedly and indefatigably press levers to stimulate their own brains, with resultant enjoyment. Even starving animals prefer stimulating these "pleasure centers" over eating, and analogous experiments have been performed with humans (Delgado 1969). Leaving wires inside a thinking brain may seem dangerous or unpleasant, but many patients have undergone the experience without expressing concern about the presence of the wires or discomfort. These experiments call to mind the dramatic novel by Michael Crichton, *The Terminal Man*.

It is certainly true that neurophysiological and psychopharmacological manipulation of man is in its infancy, with crude, imprecise, and somewhat unpredictable techniques, compared to those which might flow from the blossoming field of neurobiology. Nevertheless, fears of what might happen may be exaggerated, if only because biomedical technologies would add very little to our highly developed arsenal for mischief, destruction, and stultification in society (Kass 1971).

As in the examples of abortion for mongolism and gene therapy for specific disorders, behavior modification of individual patients to enable them to function more nearly normally seems an acceptable and ethical objective. When proponents project the capability to enhance intelligence, imagination, memory, or other higher functions, to improve man or control people, then our antennae recognize danger signals. A particular controversy has swirled around neurosurgeons Sweet and Mark of Boston since they presented a number of cases in which temporal lobe resections had terminated violent impulsive, criminal behavior associated with temporal-lobe seizures. Soon such "psychosurgery" was being proposed for large numbers of "criminals," even though the original experience was fairly carefully limited to those with seizure foci. Public suspicion identified this refined operation with the crude lobotomies carried out in most mental hospitals thirty years ago.

Emotions run so high on discussions about crime and criminals that rational applications are difficult. Those who acknowledge the role of disrupted urban life, poverty, unemployment, lack of education, and poor health are termed permissive, while those who try to protect the ordinary members of society from personal attack or property loss are termed repressive. It is undeniably true that our present system of arrest, eventual trial, occasional imprisonment, and repeating cycles of the same has been unsatisfactory for society in general and for the incarcerated individual as well. For specific individuals whose criminal behavior is significantly determined by remediable or compensatable biological abnormalities, such as temporal-lobe seizures, careful medical documentation and then therapy with drugs or with surgery seems highly justifiable and desirable from all points of view. The patient must be followed for both untoward consequences of the treatment and recurrence of the undesired behavior.

Narcotics addiction treatment programs also have become highly politicized. The White House Special Action Office on Drug Abuse was given a very visible role in reducing rates of heroin addiction and associated crime. Middle class physicians and administrators have had particular difficulty in relating to these addicts and adjusting treatment protocols to lifestyles of the patients. Since the programs are run almost exclusively by whites and serve primarily blacks and Chicanos in many parts of the country, charges of politically-motivated behavioral control with psychoactive drugs are rampant.

A common behavioral problem with large-scale modification schemes is hyperactive behavior in children. It is estimated that some 5 to 10 percent of

schoolboys merit this diagnosis, with motor hyperactivity, impulsivity, distracti-
bility, and poor learning performance. Girls are affected less commonly. In
some, but clearly not all, of these children stimulant drugs like amphetamine and
Ritalin are effective in reducing the hyperactivity, increasing concentration span,
and improving school performance. At the same time, physical growth is
retarded and the children and others are accustomed to psychoactive medication. In some school districts, administration of these agents even without
medical evaluation has been advocated for unruly children. The potential for
undue restraint of curious and active children and children who do not get along
well with the teacher is obvious.

As discussed in the previous section, one of the most fanciful notions for the
manipulation of behavior would be the use of cloning to produce genetically-
identical individuals of prescribed specifications. We noted, however, that precise
behavioral specification would be difficult even with such genetically-identical
individuals.

Choice A. Prohibit use of drugs, surgery, or electrical stimulation to modify or
control behavior of others. For those whose untreated behavior is intolerable or
dangerous, simply incarcerate them.

Choice B. Seek new methods to control impulsive or violent behavior.

Choice C. Seek new methods to improve intelligence, memory, and other
normal functions.

Recommendation. With carefully developed and monitored programs, it should
be feasible to pursue Choice B. There can be little doubt, however, that a great
many individuals will pursue any hopes of Choice C. Often these discussions are
couched in terms of a malevolent dictator subjugating his people, even against
their will. On the contrary, the propensity of large numbers of people to take
potent medication to reduce anxiety, control diet, buoy spirits, and serve as
elixirs of youthfulness may provide all-too-fertile ground for a steady evolution
to a society on drugs.

Confidentiality and Privacy

One of President Nixon's last actions in office was to announce a top-level study
of the protection of privacy, headed by the Justice Department. Many senators
and increasing numbers of private citizens are outspoken about the dangers of
data banks. Given the special nature of the doctor/patient relationship and the
extremely private and emotional nature of many aspects of an individual's
physical and mental health status, confidentiality has been a cornerstone of

medical practice and of medical research. Patients and physicians alike are alert to breaches of confidentiality. Since the confidential relationship is prejudiced completely to protect the individual, there has grown a considerable tension with law-enforcement agencies over the need to gain information to protect society from dangerous individuals. The definition of danger, however, is laced with many social and cultural and political elements.

Problems of confidentiality have been recognized recently in large programs screening for particular genetic diseases. In several regions of the country, major screening programs for sickle-cell trait and sickle-cell anemia and for Tay-Sachs disease carriers have been initiated. The Massachusetts State Legislature approved an Act in 1971 "requiring the testing of blood for sickle trait or anemia as a prerequisite to school attendance." Even though this disorder in the United States is almost completely restricted to blacks, the statute requires that all children be tested in order to avoid charges of racial discrimination. Since screening programs acquire genetic information from large numbers of normal and asymptomatic individuals and families, often after only brief medical contact, their operation falls outside the usual patient-initiated doctor/patient relationship.

A group convened by the Hastings Institute of Society, Ethics and the Life Sciences published a proposal for dealing with ethical, social, and legal questions arising from genetic screening programs (Lappé et al. 1972). First of all, the goals and objectives of the program must be explicitly formulated and promulgated: providing genetic counseling services, early diagnosis, and information about therapy for the benefit of those screened; acquiring knowledge about the disease; reducing the frequency of apparently deleterious genes. The last of these objectives is of dubious merit, since heroic measures would be required to make a significant dent in the frequency of specific deleterious genes, involving abortion of carriers on a large scale or drastic changes in mating patterns. In the actual design and operation of the program, the Committee recommended pilot stage demonstration of the feasibility of attaining stated objectives; community participation from the outset; open and equal access to all interested in being tested; reliable testing methods; avoidance of compulsion or stigmatization, which requires extraordinary sensitivity; informed consent; protection of subjects; access to information for each individual; provision of counseling; education about current state of therapy.

Since most states do not have statutes that recognize the confidentiality of public-health information or are even minimally adequate to protect individual privacy, researchers were advised to take special measures to protect individual privacy. Results are to be given only to the person screened or, with his permission, a designated physician or medical facility; records are to be kept in code, with a prohibition on storage of noncoded information in data banks having telephone computer access; private and public access to data are to be limited to anonymous data used for statistical purposes.

A common example of the need for such care in these programs is the following: a child is found to have sickle-cell trait, and the genetic explanation states that the gene for sickle-cell trait had to come from one or the other of his parents; when the parents are tested, neither has the sickle-cell trait. In the vast majority of cases, the source of the gene must have been another man. Dealing with this common finding is a delicate matter; some counselors pass off the finding as a possible new mutation ("maybe the change in the gene to become sickle-type occurred in the egg or sperm that became you"), while other counselors try gingerly to talk confidentially with the mother to be sure she knows the situation. If she acknowledges that another man was the father of the one particular child and not of her others, she can clear up a potentially confusing testing result for the whole family. Her acknowledgment, of course, is no one else's business.

Data banks have become a hot issue in the narcotics addiction treatment programs. Detailed federal guidelines require that all personal information be coded; however, law-enforcement officers at every governmental level are permitted access to the code! Some treatment programs have discussed "laundering" their data in Canada, by depositing the code outside the reach of law-enforcement officials. Addicts are justifiably paranoid about breach of confidentiality. At the same time, law-enforcement officials are frustrated about the difficulties of gaining evidence. Somehow the medical profession must continue to maintain its neutral and professional status when working with criminals or addicts or the military. Many physicians objected to the placement of advertising in several AMA journals a few years ago by the FBI requesting assistance in identifying and capturing "wanted" alleged offenders.

One of the most serious elements of fear about data banks is the recognition that the individual does not know when information on him is being entered or used, what it includes, or whether it is accurate. Ralph Nader's Health Research Group has charged that the health insurance companies contribute supposedly confidential medical history data to a common data bank, to be certain that individuals do not go from company to company seeking a better deal with incomplete information.

In genetic counseling a family member is often diagnosed with a particular condition and then a decision must be made about whether or not to seek out multiple other members of the family who may be at risk for the same disease. It is most helpful if the patient volunteers to make these contacts. If he or she prefers that no one else in the family know about his disease, there are serious problems. More often, other members of the family prefer not to be bothered. It is our policy in the Genetics Counseling Clinic at the University of Washington to be more aggressive about contacting family members when we can offer effective therapy or prevent serious disease and to be less aggressive when we have little to offer. Examples are polyposis of the colon, in which multiple polyps line the large bowel and become cancerous over ten years or so. Removal of the bowel in those affected will prevent the certain development of cancer. At the other extreme is Huntington's disease in which a progressive deterioration of neurological and psychological function occurs in middle life, rendering the person helpless and demented. In the absence of really effective treatment, early diagnosis is valuable only from the point of view of family planning.

As patients come to rely more and more on specialist physicians and multi-doctor clinics, rather than an individual physician who knows them well, much more attention to the explicit maintenance of privacy and confidentiality will be demanded. Yet in doing family studies for inherited diseases, in pursuing leads about occupational exposures, and in following up venereal disease it is essential to have the cooperation of the patient and his relatives or contacts in order to serve the best interests of all of those at risk. For the purposes of some medical research, good statistical data suffice; however, anonymous data are of limited use when explanations are sought for statistically significant findings. The ability to break open a code and do further studies on particular informative individuals is very important in some cases.

Choice A. Keep confidential information confidential under all circumstances, making it available neither for law-enforcement nor for research purposes.

Choice B. Develop procedures to maintain privacy while using confidential medical information for bona fide evaluative and research purposes.

Choice C. Make confidential information available to law enforcement officers if a crime has been alleged.

Recommendation. Choice B.

Bibliography

Altman, L.K. "Auto-Experimentation and Unappreciated Tradition in Medical Science." *New Engl. J. Med.* 286 (1972): 346-352.

Beecher, H.K. "Ethics and Clinical Research." *New Engl. J. Med.* 274 (1966): 1354-1360. *Research and the Individual: Human Studies*. Boston: Little, Brown & Co., 1970.

Berg, P. et al. "Potential Biohazards of Recombinant DNA Molecules." *Science* 185 (1974): 303.

Blake, J. "Abortion and Public Opinion: The 1960-1970 Decade." *Science* 171 (1971): 540-549.

Crichton, M. *The Terminal Man*. New York: Knopf, 1972.

DeBakey, L. "Ethically Questionable Data: Publish or Reject?" *Clin. Research* 22 (1974): 113-121.

Delgado, J.M.R. *Physical Control of the Mind: Toward a Psychocivilized Society*. New York: Harper & Row, 1969.

Duff, R.S. and Campbell, A.G.M. "Moral and Ethical Dilemmas in the Special-Care Nursery." *New Engl. J. Med.* 289 (1973): 890-894.

Etzioni, A. "Sex Control, Science and Society." *Science* 161 (1968): 1107-1112.

Falconer, M.A. "Reversibility by Temporal Lobe Resection of the Behavioral Abnormalities of Temporal-Lobe Epilepsy." *New Engl. J. Med.* 289 (1973): 451-455.

Fletcher, J. "Ethical Aspects of Genetic Controls." *New Engl. J. Med.* 285 (1971): 776-783.

Fletcher, J.F. *Situation Ethics: The New Morality*. Philadelphia: Westminster Press, 1966.

Freund, P.A. "Ethical Problems in Human Experimentation." *New Engl. J. Med.* 273 (1965): 687-693.

Gurdon, J.B. "Transplanted Nuclei and Cell Differentiation." *Scientific American*, December 1968.

Haldane, J.B.S. *Daedelus, or Science and the Future*. London: K. Paul, 1923.

Hamilton, M. (ed.). *The New Genetics and the Future of Man*. Grand Rapids, Michigan: W.B. Eerdsmans Publ. Co., 1972.

Hastings Institute of Society, Ethics and Life Sciences. Reports.

Havighurst, C.C. "Compensating Persons Injured in Human Experimentation." *Science* 169 (1970): 153-157.

Hellman, A.; Oxman, M.N.; and Pollack, R. *Biohazards in Biological Research*. Cold Spring Harbor Laboratory, 1973.

Hilton, B.; Callahan, D.; Harris, M.; Condliffe, P.; and Berkley, B. (eds.) *Ethical Issues in Human Genetics*. New York: Plenum Press, 1973.

Huxley, A. *Brave New World*. New York: Harper and Row, Inc., 1932.

Jaffe, J.H. "Tobacco Addiction." *Science* 185 (1974): 1039-1040.

Kahn, H. and Wiener, A.J. *The Year 2000. A Framework for Speculation on the Next Thirty-Three Years*. London: Macmillan Co., 1967.

Kass, L.R. "The New Biology: What Price Relieving Man's Estate?" *Science* 174 (1971): 779-788.

Lappé, M. et al. "Ethical and Social Issues in Screening for Genetic Disease." *New Engl. J. Med.* 286 (1972): 1129-1132.

Marston, R.Q. "Research on Minors, Prisoners and the Mentally Ill." *New Engl. J. Med.* 288 (1973): 158-159.

Motulsky, A.G. "Brave New World? Ethical Issues in Prevention, Treatment and Research of Human Birth Defects." *Science* 185 (1974): 653-663.

Omenn, G.S. and Motulsky, A.G. Biochemical Genetics and the Evolution of Human Behavior." In L. Ehrman, G.S. Omenn, and E. Caspari (eds.), *Genetics, Environment, and Behavior: Implications for Educational Policy*. New York: Academic Press, (1972), pp. 131-178.

Orwell, G. *1984*. New York: Harcourt, 1949.

Ramsey, P. *Fabricated Man*. New Haven: Yale Univ. Press, 1970.

Skinner, B.F. *Beyond Freedom and Dignity*. New York: Knopf, 1971.

Sklar, J. and Berkov, B. "Abortion, Illegitimacy, and the American Birth Rate." *Science* 185 (1974): 909-915.

Torrey, E.F. (ed.) *Ethical Issues in Medicine*. Boston: Little, Brown & Co., 1968.

Williams, R.H. (ed.) *To Live and To Die: When, Why, and How*. New York: Springer-Verlag, 1973.

XIV

Consumer Credit and the Quality of Life

Bess Myerson

What Credit Means To Us

More than 200 million credit cards are in the hands of American consumers today. Ninety percent of American households are sustained by the use of installment credit. For most of us, credit is a necessity for the ordering and planning of better lives. For many, major financial commitments probably could not be made without credit—homes, automobiles, travel, education, raising a family.

Credit, as initiated and developed by the American marketplace, is an innovative purchasing tool that is an integral part of our national and individual growth. The opportunity to use it, and the knowledge and discipline to use it well, can be a great blessing. When it is denied, or misused by the consumer, or abused by the creditor, it can be a debilitating burden.

There are danger warnings of credit conditions that must be improved if our lives are to be improved. The arbitrary denial of credit; the 400 percent increase in outstanding consumer installment debt in the past twenty years; the unwritten and written credit laws and practices which create a double standard of justice for consumer and creditor; and the increasing invasion of our right to privacy by governmental and private interests through misuse of consumer credit data.

Trust and confidence and fair play are the keys to that improvement. Any credit practices which do not reflect those qualities are bad practices. Any credit laws which sustain those practices are bad laws. Ability and willingness to pay

347

must be the bedrock standard for credit availability. Mutual respect and equality before the law must be the bedrock standard of credit contracts. Wherever those standards are missing, in whole or in part, lives are less than they should or could be, and the critical choices we must make are imperative.

Credit Victims

To deny or diminish credit to individuals mainly on the basis of the social groups to which they belong is to deny and diminish individual rights—civil, consumer, and human. Occupation, place of residence, personal habits, age, race, and sex are existing criteria for many credit examiners today, beyond an individual applicant's own ability and willingness to meet financial obligations. This policy is defined and defended by the creditors as "the law of probability"—an unwritten law that confines too many of our people to a financial ghetto, with walls that are invisible but high.

Women have bumped into those walls. And blacks. And residents of poor neighborhoods. And consumers of all income levels whose credit history has been misjudged, too often because of reliance on irrelevant information, some of it obtained through practices which border on illegal invasion of privacy.

Credit worthiness must be based on financial considerations only. Prejudice, in credit opportunities or any aspect of our national life, is not a firm foundation on which to guarantee quality in our lives. Social labels or "the law of probability" is the convenient prop of prejudice. Decent people are harassed and hampered by it, from the simple effort to obtain a credit card at a local store to such major aspirations as obtaining a mortgage for the purchase of a new home.

On the local store level, those who are denied access to responsible credit facilities are doubly burdened by the need to seek—or, more often, be sought by—the questionable credit outlets which impose the harshest terms, and usually for the shoddiest of products or services.

On the mortgage level, the U.S. Commission on Civil Rights said this about minorities and women in its latest report, issued in July 1974:

For minorities and women, the mortgage finance system is a stacked deck—stacked sometimes inadvertently, often unthinkingly, but stacked nonetheless.

While discrimination against minorities is subtle, discrimination against women is blatant. Minority women suffer the double effect of both sex and race discrimination.[1]

"Traditional mortgage lending criteria" the report concluded, automatically consider women as suspect risks. This "tradition" particularly hurts minority families, where many women are heads of households, and young unmarried women, who are considered by many credit examiners as only marking time until they get married and quit the job from which they could make the payments to meet their credit commitments.

The 1972 Report of the National Commission on Consumer Finance[2] confirmed this, noting that employed single and married women have more trouble getting credit than their male counterparts. Their income is discounted, if not altogether ignored. Married women are made to apply in their husband's name and thus are denied the opportunity to develop their own credit history; this becomes particularly harmful upon separation, divorce or death of the husband.

Single or married, "the law of probability" is enforced. If a woman and her husband apply for a mortgage, some companies will not even consider it until she signs an affidavit that she will not have children during the period the mortgage is in effect, as if raising the mortgage payments and raising a family were mutually exclusive goals—and the quantity of payments has priority over the quality of parenthood.

If she continues to work after marriage, she may still be discriminated against by the credit examiners. Her salary is considered "secondary income," and rarely credited more than 50 percent, if at all, in determining the family's income and ability to pay. As already stated, the family's "credit history" is usually in the husband's name, which can prove detrimental to a woman's credit potential in future years when she may be widowed or divorced.

The recently enacted Equal Credit Opportunity Act aims at overcoming some of these discriminations by banning sex bias in any aspect of a credit transaction. Unfortunately, the Act does not live up to its name; it says nothing about ethnic, religions or age discrimination. And if recent experience with state laws banning sex discrimination is any guide, it will not be vigorously enforced.

The "law of probability" may be different for each group which is discriminated against—but the result is always the same: unfair roadblocks in the path of reasonable expectations and responsible participation in our economic system. Credit discrimination imposes a higher cost of living on the individual consumer against whom it is directed—but the highest cost will be paid by all of us, because the residue of that discrimination is a social atmosphere of anger and bitterness that defeats the unity and understanding that are needed by any society which seeks to better itself.

The artificial barriers to credit availability must be removed. The rights of those in the business of credit must be protected—every consumer must meet the standards of ability, responsibility, and willingness to pay—but to deny credit for discriminatory reasons beyond those basic standards of creditworthiness is a violation of the quality of life of those who depend upon credit as a practical bridge between the reality of today and the hope of tomorrow.

The Dark Side of Credit

Wider availability of credit, therefore, must be accompanied by credit laws fairly written and vigorously enforced.

One of the by-products of increased consumer credit has been increased consumer fraud. When transactions depended on cash, sellers had little incentive and opportunity to sell expensive merchandise to people who could not afford it. This restraint has weakened with the advent of consumer credit. Whether the consumer can afford the merchandise is now largely irrelevant, for once the creditor gets the buyer's signature on the contract, he knows he can depend upon the courts to enforce collection, no matter how lopsided the contract, or how harsh or harassing the pressure on the consumer. To consumers immobilized by fear, intimidation, and inadequate opportunities of legal defense, the courts have become the final harassment.

Lending institutions must be strongly encouraged and urged to self-regulate credit discrimination and other unfair credit practices out of their programs. Consumers must be informed of protections already established and what they must do to protect themselves. That information is a joint responsibility of the credit industry, government, community, and consumer organizations. Credit counseling groups should be expanded on a community level for those consumers whose lack of awareness or buying discipline has diminished the opportunities of their lives through the burden of serious debt.

To insure equality before credit law, court-supported harassment must not be part of any future law, and where it exists in present law it must be rooted out, because wherever it exists—in the letter or spirit of any law—it is a sneer at the quality of justice in our society, and a sneer at the quality of life for those who may be without special favor or influence.

The Law vs. the Consumer

Truth-in-Lending was signed into law in May 1968, as Title I of the Consumer Credit Protection Act, and became effective July 1, 1969. It belatedly corrected essentially one of the most abusive practices of the credit industry by requiring the disclosure of the cost of consumer credit. Prior to its enactment consumers more often than not were unaware of the additional, sometimes hidden, costs they were required to pay on the money they borrowed.

In the ensuing years, many additional credit protections have been proposed and some enacted, among them the anti-sex discrimination Equal Credit Opportunity Act, a Fair Credit Billing Act to force creditors to fairly respond to consumer complaints about billing errors, a Fair Credit Reporting Act to ensure that consumer credit reports will not be misused by creditors, and several Federal Trade Commission rules aimed at overcoming abusive sales and collection practices.

Some have become good laws; some have been compromised into bad laws; most have never found the strength and support to emerge from the legislative committees on federal, state, and municipal levels. This history of delay and diversion in credit protection is part of the lingering toleration of seller-bias in many credit protection laws, and in the courts' enforcement of them.

If unconscionable contracts and harsh collection practices were not legally sanctioned, irresponsible sellers would hesitate to inflict their frauds and deceptions on consumers. If it were not for this body of permissive law (permissive toward sellers), the success of a company would depend on the quality of its products or services, not on the weight of its legal department.

The built-in harassments of unfair credit protection laws could not function without the supportive role of the courts in the resolution of creditor-debtor conflicts.

The legal system compounds this injustice. Laws encourage creditors to start lawsuits whenever a consumer defaults by permitting them not only to recoup the debt balance but also late charges, court costs, attorney and sheriff fees, and interest, the total amount of which can result in a doubling of the principal debt. Thrown into this are collection laws that allow creditors everything from executions against income (called garnishments) to civil arrest and imprisonment.

All this, of course, leads to a glut of lawsuits—almost one quarter million in New York City's civil court in 1974 alone. Because the court filing fees that creditors (and ultimately consumer defendants) must pay are not enough to cover what it costs the court to process the suit, the difference in expense is taken up by tax revenues. In short, the taxpayer subsidizes the creditors collection efforts, thereby financing an overwhelming number of specious, unnecessary lawsuits.

Most of those consumers sued on credit transactions, according to the report of the National Commission on Consumer Finance,[3] defaulted on their debts because the merchandise they bought was defective or because of factors beyond their control—loss of employment, illness, family problems, overextension, but "not because they are deadbeats." To permit collection against people with these problems amounts to nothing less than legalized harassment. The problem, however, is conveniently ignored by creditor and court alike. This indifference invites suspicion and contempt and further weakens a judicial system already well into the crisis state.

David Caplovitz, in his perceptive study of the imbalances of our credit system, *The Poor Pay More*,[4] notes that about 25 percent of credit debtors have valid defenses—but that valid defense or not, many debtors never have the opportunity of their day in court, because almost all suits brought against them result in default judgments.

The reasons are many. They may be reluctant or unable to take time off from work. They may never receive the summons announcing the lawsuit—faulty service of process is quite common in many communities, so much so that a cynical term has evolved to describe it: "sewer service." They may not understand the summons if they do receive it—the language of the summons is not noted for its clarity. They may not know where to report—in New York City, for example, before the introduction of neighborhood courts, consumers were summoned to a location that was alien and not easily accessible to most. They may be afraid to appear because they wrongly think that a lawsuit based on a consumer debt involves possible criminal penalties or because they are just suspicious of courts. Fear and suspicion of the courts, especially among the poor and others not familiar with the legal processes, is a major cause of default.

The machinery of the law is predicated on assumptions that do not apply in many consumer-creditor disputes. It assumes that both sides to the dispute will be represented by legal counsel or equally knowledgeable of the ways of the law, and that 9 to 5 are ideal hours for everyone, even though it could mean loss of a day's pay to the consumer defendant.

If a consumer defendant does appear, he may appear without legal counsel, probably because the amount of money in dispute is often less than the cost of a lawyer, and legal aid is unavailable.

The creditor's lawyer is always there, familiar with the system and how to use it to his client's advantage. Within this system overburdened judges have little alternative except to rule against consumers who are unaware of possible defense, ignorant of courtroom jargon, and overwhelmed by procedures which allow no exceptions for the uninitiated. In those cases, the courts cannot and should not remain neutral or hide behind dubious standards of objectivity, which in the end makes them become mere collection agencies for the creditors.

Even those few debtors who are determined to have their day in court find that despite their persistence, including the loss of several days work (to file a defense to the lawsuit, to refile when the plaintiff protests the answer, to appear in court for the trial, and then to reappear when the trial is inevitably postponed), their day in court may still be denied.

Too often, the judge, concerned about his crowded calendar, urges the parties to settle the dispute themselves outside the courtroom. To the consumer, for whom the court and the law should be barriers against injustice, that is like advising a trusting sheep to go outside and settle his dispute with a legal wolf. Lawyers for irresponsible companies which profit from abuses are not known for their impartial justice or compassionate understanding.

Beyond the indifferent court personnel and attorneys exists a subculture of debt collectors almost always ignored by those who would cleanse the system. They are perhaps as much victims of the system as the people they so fervently pursue. More often than not they are transients between better paying, higher status jobs; or in the job because they lack skills to do anything else. How this affects their attitude can only be guessed. They play the role of policemen for their creditor-employer. Like policemen, every day they are exposed to the full panorama of problems that exist in our society, but unlike policemen they must close their eyes. They know that if compassion enters their decision process another creditor less compassionate may beat them to whatever assets the unfortunate debtors possess. If there are no competitors for the scarce assets, there is probably an employer demanding that collection quotas be met. Collection by harassment still exists.

The ultimate harassment, to our spirit and to our effort to improve the quality of our lives, is that its existence is endorsed by laws and court practices in many areas of our country. Those laws and court practices are an affront to our dignity, our self-respect, and our mutual respect—and the only protection they give is to the small minority of fraudulent merchants in the credit community, at the physical, financial, and emotional expense of those consumers who need the protection of fair treatment, and a fair hearing when they think they are being abused.

It is time to define the critical role which the courts can play in effective protection of consumer credit rights, and to review and revise those laws in which consumer harassment is the court-supported order of the day.

Holder-In-Due-Course

The holder-in-due-course law, more than any other, has underwritten consumer fraud.

It refers to the situation where a retailer sells to lending institutions (called the "holder") the contracts it takes from buyers who pay in installments. If the holder buys the contract in the "due course" of its business, without knowledge of any defense against it, the buyer will be forced to pay on it even if the underlying merchandise falls apart or is never delivered.

Since such contracts are usually sold immediately after the sale, the lender is rarely made aware of a defense. Several studies have shown that the holder-in-due-course doctrine is responsible for widespread fraud, costing consumers billions of dollars annually. The holder zealously pursues collection, but not the responsibility for the quality of the product or service. If payments are missed or withheld, the contract becomes a legal strength for the collector and a scrap of paper for the consumer. In court, it is a one-way street, always going against the consumers' interest.

In Great Britain, where the law began, holder-in-due-course has been abolished, the rationale being that a lender-holder should never be allowed to stand in a better position than the supplier. Several states have done the same, apparently without adverse effect on the supply of consumer credit. The Federal Trade Commission has issued a rule which is designed to end the practice—unfortunately, it is a design with loopholes. The rule requires all credit sales contracts to contain a clause which legalistically says the buyer can assert against a holder of the contract any defense it has against the seller. The FTC's goal is to get lending institutions to police the merchants with whom they deal to make sure that the products and services they sell are free of defects. Abolishing holder-in-due-course cannot guarantee this. Because of sheer size or intimidating tactics, irresponsible lenders will continue to hold the upper hand. They know that if they force the issue to the point of a lawsuit, most consumers will retreat. Our great national strength is that we are a nation of laws—but unfair laws sap that strength. A Federal law was enacted recently to correct the inequities of Holder-in-Due-Course, but it is too early to determine its effective application.

Deficiency Judgment

According to the law in most states, a creditor who repossesses merchandise is entitled to sue the debtor for the balance when the proceeds of the resale of the merchandise are deducted from the debt—(the "deficiency" of the debt). Presumably, an automobile, for example, is expected to be sufficient collateral for an automobile loan. After all, the function of a down payment is to assure a finance company that the money it is advancing is roughly equivalent to the value of the car. If a debtor makes a down payment of $500 on a $3,000 car, and then defaults on the very first payment, the finance company presumably should have little difficulty selling the repossessed car for $2,500, the amount the debtor owes. The car and the loan are intimately tied together; while the loan is being paid down, the auto is depreciating. However, the fact is that repossessed merchandise is almost never resold at an amount close to the unpaid balance, and debtors who have had their automobiles repossessed are confronted with deficiency judgments, sanctioned by the courts, for substantial sums of money.

In his classic study of this abuse, "Profit On Default: An Archival Study of Automobile Repossession and Resale,"[5] Professor Philip Shuchman, of the University of Connecticut Law School, documented the typical technique by which the consumer is legally handcuffed. Professor Shuchman revealed that cars repossessed by finance companies are usually sold back to the original dealer at what amounts to a "wholesale" price. The dealer then puts the car on his lot and resells it for a "retail" price which is close to the true value of the car. The debtor, however, is credited only for the "wholesale" price, and the finance company sues him—and is invariably sustained by the court—for a substantial "deficiency."

An interesting contrast is found in the case where a bank's trust department handles the liquidation of the assets of an estate. There the incentive to produce the highest possible price on tangible assets is great because the clients usually come from upper income groups who may withdraw profitable business if their interests are slighted.

On the other hand, the person who defaults on an auto loan usually lacks an equivalent leverage. The law says a repossession sale must be "commercially reasonable" (i.e., aimed at getting the best price) in all respects, yet this is a meaningless protection to a person who cannot pay his normal debts. It costs substantial time and money to enforce the protection. A more equitable solution has been proposed by the FTC. Under it, deficiency judgments will be eliminated. It is a long overdue proposal; many average consumers will continue to be abused before it becomes required practice.

Confession of Judgment

Consumer credit contracts in several states legally are allowed to include a confession of judgment clause whereby the consumer waives all defenses in the event of default and agrees judgment may be entered without a lawsuit, regardless of the reason for default. This is equivalent to pleading guilty in advance to charges of a crime you may never commit or even contemplate. It permits a creditor to employ immediately, at his discretion alone, legal remedies for collection. Often they are used by creditors to coerce payment by debtors who may have good reasons to explain their default.

These clauses generally are hidden in standard form contracts in small type and legalistic language and accepted by courts which presumably are sworn to defend the constitutional right that innocence is presumed until guilt is proven. The National Commission on Consumer Finance and the FTC have called for their complete abolition.

Aside from the fact that it is a circumvention of the spirit of law, it is a further fact that a high percentage of debtors forced to pay under the "confession of judgment" clause have cases they could win if permitted to be heard in court. In his book, *Consumers in Trouble: A Study of Debtors in Default*,[6] Professor David Caplovitz documented that as many as 30 percent of the debtors trapped in the "confession of judgment" abuse had valid defenses that were never allowed to be made. Until this collection abuse is removed from all contracts, the courts which sustain it must be judged guilty of malfeasance until proven innocent.

Wage Assignments

A wage assignment is a transfer by a debtor to a creditor of the debtor's right to collect all or a given part of his wages. It is generally given as security in a consumer credit transaction and its operation is contingent on default without first having to go to court to obtain a court judgment. Most consumers who "assign" their wages usually are not aware that they did until a default occurs, the reason being that the assignment language in most loan agreements is hidden in small print and unreadable legalistic terminology. Because they often lead to abuse, wage assignments have been severely limited in many states.

A recent landmark decision of the United States Supreme Court (*Family Finance Corp.* v. *Sniadach*), which found a Wisconsin prejudgment wage garnishment law unconstitutional, placed particular emphasis on the nature of wages, stating that wages are "a specialized type of property presenting distinct problems in our economic system," the taking of which may impose "tremendous hardship" and may as a practical matter drive a wage earning family to the wall."

Since most consumers, according to the National Commission on Consumer Finance, default because of circumstances beyond their control, getting a consumer to commit himself in advance that, notwithstanding his future problems, a part of his income may be applied to pay off a debt is unfair to say the least. In short, imposition of a wage assignment during a time of misfortune can wreak havoc on the borrower and his family. The practice has been severely limited in many states and municipalities, but wherever it exists, and to whatever extent, it is a harsh and insensitive "solution" of a credit dispute, and a denial of a consumer's "day in court." It is important to our way of life that debts be paid, but it is equally important to our way of life that due process of law be fairly and fully observed. The Uniform Consumer Credit Code, already adopted by several states, and a proposed FTC rule would end this oppressiveness by outlawing wage assignments.

Garnishment

Like a wage assignment, a garnishment also involves attaching the wages of a debtor, but a garnishment order is issued only after a court judgment has been obtained. It provides a day in court, but remains a disruptive and cruelly damaging blow to the lives of families on any economic level, especially to those of low and middle income. Also, the day in court may be one more in name than fact, because of the ignorance or fear of the legal process among many consumers.

Garnishment can result in loss of a job, although this is illegal under the Truth-in-Lending Act. Despite the law, firings or "voluntary" quittings continue because it is difficult to prove the garnishment is the ultimate reason for severance.

Even where jobs are not lost, garnishment causes hardships to the average wage earner. Truth-in-Lending limits the percentage of garnishment to 25 percent of gross income, but to families which have difficulty making their full weekly salary match their needs, it is really the quality of their lives that is attached.

Professor Caplovitz's study[7] showed that for those who keep their jobs, a garnishment nevertheless can result in denial of promotions and raises and severe restrictions on the debtor's ability to provide for his family. While the creditor gets paid, food spending and necessary medical and dental care are curtailed.

The challenge of garnishment is plain. Creditors must collect what is rightfully due, and consumers must meet their obligations, but we must find better ways to develop the disciplines which will avoid default situations. The vast majority of consumers and business persons bring to their transactions with each other a sense of responsibility and fairness. We can find those ways to present and pay our bills with dignity. We do not have to lose our individual dignity or national character while we collect from each other.

Seizure of Property

Whenever possible creditors attempt to secure their contracts with consumers by requiring the promise to pay to be backed with some kind of collateral. Usually the collateral is the merchandise purchased with the credit, but more often that now-familiar legalistic, small-printed standard form contract also included collateral yet-to-be-purchased. The contract may even say the consumer's home, automobile, furniture are all collateral for the loan. If and when the debtor defaults, the creditor then may seize and sell such property without first going to court. Too often the seizure practice lends itself to excessive abuse.

The recent report by the National Commission on Consumer Finance[8] revealed a high percentage of seizures of consumers' personal and real property to satisfy debts. Seventy-four percent of the banks and 51 percent of the finance companies surveyed reported that they attach personal property to collect on personal loans.

In many states, consumers with credit debts risk losing their homes. Homes have been sold at auction for defaults on a $300 or $400 product. Recent news stories indicate similar practices in many states. To add insult to financial injury to the consumer, too often the "auction" is a sham that raises only enough money to pay off the minor debt, although its value is considerably more to the eventual purchaser. The kind of creditors who engage in this practice usually overwhelm the isolated consumer with a battery of lawyers and a maze of legal complications. Those who write our laws and those who administer them should not be overwhelmed by this mockery of what we think our laws should be.

Body Attachment

Body attachment is the ghoulish term applied by the National Commission on Consumer Finance to the practice of imprisonment of debtors for failure to meet their obligation. Most people think debtors' prisons no longer exist—they are wrong. Today's "debtors' prisons" contain many who are there not simply because they owe money, but also because they may have failed to appear in court to answer questions about their assets. Whatever their reasons for nonappearance—and the fault is not always theirs—they are judged in contempt of court, arrested, and placed in jail. It is difficult to understand how placing a person in jail can generate income that will liquidate a debt. Legal assistance is often minimal, and sometimes not even sought.

According to the NCCF report,[9] up to 62 percent of the banks surveyed admitted the use of "body attachment" in default situations for certain types of credit. The percentage of finance companies using "body attachment" in defaults of certain types of credit, ranged up to 65 percent in "some areas."

"Some areas" proved to be usually the low income neighborhoods of our urban centers, adding one more obstacle to the reach for a better life where the need is greatest.

Attorney Fees

Almost all states allow consumer credit contracts to contain clauses which provide that, if the creditor has to use an attorney to collect, the debtor will pay the attorney fee, usually 15 to 20 percent of the outstanding balance. This has led to considerable abuse. For example, if collection is handled by an attorney on the payroll of the creditor, it can significantly increase the creditor's profit. If a judgment is obtained, interest must be paid on the increased indebtedness. The ability to cover such collection costs encourages creditors to bring lawsuits indiscriminately, adding severe burdens to our court system. A recent landmark decision by a New York court held that a large commercial bank's practice of using in-house attorneys to collect from consumers attorney those fees based on a percentage formula amounted to illegal, unethical fee-splitting and was fraudulent.

Attorney fees in consumer credit contracts should be prohibited.

Summation

The relationship of consumer credit to the enhancement of the quality of our lives offers three major critical choices:

1. *Credit Discrimination v. Credit Opportunity*. The credit industry should be encouraged to self-regulate out of its practices those credit denials or curtailments which are determined by absolute "traditions" or self-defeating "myths" about the credit-worthiness of any segment of our society—women, blacks, the elderly—all those in any income, residential or employment category where bias exists. The responsibility and willingness of an individual—within a fair determination of ability to pay—should be the single standard of credit availability.

Where the credit industry does not act to achieve this goal, legislation must be written mandating it.

2. *Legal Protection v. Legal Punishment.* Deadbeats should be punished; decent consumers, making a determined effort to meet their obligations, should have the opportunity to exercise their full legal rights as citizens and consumers. Wherever law is a legal right to steal—where consumers have little or no recourse except to pay for shoddy products or services—that law must be changed to bring greater fairness to our marketplace and our communities. Quality of life and equality of law go hand in hand.

3. *Consumer Awareness v. Consumer Apathy.* Involvement is the key to the critical choices which face us today in any area of our society. Our political institutions are stronger to the extent that each of us is a participant—understanding, caring, contributing. Our marketplace is stronger to the extent that each of us as consumers, understands its role in our lives, cares enough to make it work even better, and contributes to its secure future by sharing our own awareness with those who sell to us, in the knowledge that there may be two sides to the sales counter, but only one side to the quality of our lives.

One of the roads ahead can begin in the marketplace—and consumer credit, which is the heart of the marketplace, can also be the heart of the matters which face us as we seek to better our lives.

Massive educational programs, directed at consumers as consumers, must be initiated by the business community, all levels of government, and community groups.

We must develop an individual awareness and familiarity with what the law does for us, and what it does not do for us—because laws work only when people make them work.

We must become as familiar with our individual rights as we are with our individual names—otherwise talk of consumer rights, in credit or anything else, is academic.

Truth, understanding, and cooperation in the marketplace are good foundations for truth, understanding, and cooperation in every facet of our lives.

Business is Business. Every American generation, from the founding generation to the bicentennial generation and beyond, accepts the truth that our marketplace must grow and prosper if our nation is to grow and prosper.

But just as our nation needs a healthy marketplace, our marketplace needs a healthy nation.

In each of our great institutions, including our marketplace, any practices which go counter to the great promise of America are bad for business, bad for all of us who are entrusted with keeping the promise, bad for both the material and moral quality of life we seek to achieve.

Wherever we are going as a nation in the next century, the quality of our journey depends upon how much we trust each other, and how much we lend each other a helping hand over the rough spots.

Our credit system is our marketplace's essential helping hand.

Those who are left outside that system, or who feel abused by it, will tire and drop out on the journey, and the quality of our national life will diminish.

That would be too high a price to pay for the credit discriminations which divide and separate us.

Notes

1. Report, U.S. Commission on Civil Rights, July, 1974.

2. Douglas F. Greer, *Creditors' Remedies and Contract Provisions: An Economic and Legal Analysis of Consumer Credit Collection*, Technical Studies, Volume V, National Commission on Consumer Finance, U.S. Government Printing Office, 1974.

3. See Note 2.

4. David Caplovitz, *The Poor Pay More* (New York: The Free Press, 1963).

5. Philip Schuchman, "Profit on Default: An Archival Study of Automobile Repossession and Resale," *Stanford L. Rev.* 22, 20 November 1969.

6. David Caplovitz, *Consumers in Trouble: A Study of Debtors in Default*, (New York: the Free Press, 1974).

7. See Note 6.

8. See Note 2.

9. See Note 2.

In addition, the following sources were consulted.

1. *Nader Report on the Federal Trade Commission*, by Edward F. Cox, Robert C. Fellmeth, John E. Schulz; (New York: Richard W. Baron Publishing Co., 1969).

2. Arch W. Troelstrup, *The Consumer in American Society: Personal and Family Finance*, 4th ed. (New York: McGraw-Hill, 1971).

3. Credit Complaint Files, New York City Department of Consumer Affairs.

4. Carol Hecht Katz (ed.) *The Law and the Low Income Consumer*, project on Social Welfare Law by New York University School of Law, 1968.

5. Herbert M. Jelly and Robert O. Herrman, *The American Consumer: Issues and Decisions*, (New York: Gregg Division, McGraw-Hill, 1973).

6. David Schoenfeld and Arthur A. Natella, *The Consumer and His Dollars*, (New York: Oceana Press, 1966).

7. Leland J. Gordon and Steward M. Lee, *Economics for Consumers*, (New York: American Book Company, 1967).

8. Philip G. Schrag, *Cases and Materials on Consumer Protection*, 2nd ed. American Casebook Series, (St. Paul, Minnesota: West Publishing Co., 1973).

9. *Consumer Law Handbook*, New York State Consumer Protection Board.

10. George S. Day and William K. Brandt, "Consumer Research and the Evaluation of Information Disclosure Requirements: The Case of Truth In Lending", *Journal of Consumer Research*, 1, (June, 1974,) p. 21-31.

 Mass Media and
the Quality of
Life

Paul H. Weaver

Over the past dozen years—since at least the time of General Eisenhower's famous remark to the 1964 Republican National Convention about "sensation-seeking columnists and commentators"—the mass media have been a subject of growing public interest and controversy. This is not the first time in our history we have witnessed such a trend, nor is it likely to be the last. For mass communications are like every other sort of communication in that they are ultimately incapable of being neutral. It is impossible to depict experience without first making assumptions—and, therefore, assertions—about what is real, important, and desirable. Accordingly, whenever political and cultural divisions have surfaced in American life—as in the 1830s, 1890s, and 1960s—the media, as quintessentially public institutions that cannot avoid taking a stand, have been natural targets for criticism. The fact that the media are so much talked-of today, then, is but an indicator of a deeper truth about modern America, which is that we are deeply divided on many fundamental matters.

Even in the quieter periods of our national experience, attitudes toward the mass media have usually been a telling litmus test of a person's sense of identity and of relationship to American civilization. To such foreign visitors as Dickens and Matthew Arnold, for instance, the American press represented in microcosm everything they believed to be bad or disreputable in the new world. And Americans themselves have been no less accustomed to practicing media criticism as a kind of surrogate for cultural criticism. Those today who argue that American television is too commercial, too materialistic, too crass, violent, and success-oriented are unquestionably sincere, but at bottom what they have in mind is not only the character of TV per se, but also—and more importantly—the quality of American civilization as a whole. In precisely the same way, those who attack the eastern liberal press are expressing a view, not just about a few newspapers and TV networks, but also—and more importantly—about the intellectual and cultural elites whose ethos those media reflect.

This is a natural impulse, and perhaps even a healthy one, but it does suggest an important caveat: when prescribing for the mass media, one must be vigilant about resisting the temptation to engage in subcultural imperialism. Different people have different tastes. In a free and pluralistic society such as our own, it is a central desideratum that different people have different tastes, and that media organizations be free to choose the constituencies and tastes they will serve. The mere fact that one's own tastes are inadequately served, or even offended, by a given media organization or medium cannot be taken as evidence that "the media" are institutionally flawed and in need of reform. In most cases, in fact, it is evidence of nothing less than the vigor of American pluralism, with its inherent tensions between groups, classes and subcultures.

Implicit in the critical habit of treating the media as a surrogate for the society as a whole is the essentially conspiratorial notion of the mass medium as *deus ex machina*—as the inventor and perpetuator of American cultural traits rather than as the creature of them. Although there is little question but that this is a gross exaggeration, in fairness it must be said that the notion is not entirely without substance. Media are *not* simply mirrors which faithfully reflect current events and their constituents' views. They do select, construct, and reconstruct; increasing market concentration permits them to do this in an environment that grows ever less constraining to them; and due to the weakening of the political party and other traditional mediating institutions, how they select seems to have ever more important consequences for politics and society as a whole.

Little is known for sure about the impact of media on opinion, but some things do seem clear. Media create a universe of public discourse and public knowledge. What is contained in this universe defines what "exists" as something for citizens and statesmen to be aware of, think about, and act on. What is excluded from the universe is correspondingly unlikely to become the object of conscious attention, thought, and action. Thus, the media perform a public consciousness-defining and agenda-setting function—and thereby exercise the most elementary, and important, of all political and cultural powers.

But it is also clear that the strictly independent influence of media over public opinion is sharply limited. People, we know, by no means automatically accept everything they are told by the newspapers or through a TV drama. There are many sources of information and attitudes in addition to the mass media, and these often work at cross-purposes, giving the individual room to choose. And there are other countervailing dynamics at work, such as the one we have witnessed over the past decade, whereby the credibility of mass media has declined at the same time as their apparent influence in the political system has grown. Moreover, mass media organizations are not notable as centers of genuinely original thought or research; most of what they disseminate is essentially derivative, having first been formulated and legitimated in such other institutions, as government, universities, foundations, and the like. In short, the notion of the mass medium as *deus ex machina* is a gross overstatement of its real role and power.

Mass communication, in other words, is more or less like every other mode of communication: it is influential but hardly omnipotent, and how influential it is depends on all sorts of circumstances. Where it differs from other modes is precisely in the fact that it is public rather than private, reaching everybody in society as against only a small or select audience. It is this public quality, I think, which accounts for the special intensity of current critical concern over mass media. For as Aristotle pointed out, every act of communication necessarily makes certain assumptions about the audience to which it is directed: assumptions about its interests, emotional makeup, cultural constitution, symbolic identifications, and the like. When mass media speak, they are implicitly describing the American people as a whole—and not only describing them, but also urging them to *assume* the character tacitly imputed to them. The mass media, consequently, are an arena in which the great political and cultural disputes of modern America are acted out. They matter to us for reasons that far transcend the simple accuracy of the images they convey to us, for they are intimately involved in the process by which we collectively define ourselves as a people and polity.

Two conclusions would seem to follow from this. The first is that mass media are usually implicated, in some cases quite massively, in all questions about the quality of life in America. They seem especially noteworthy in the processes that shape the quality of our public life: how we speak to one another, what sorts of persons we admire, whom we elect to office, the kinds of actions we desire and dislike on the part of government, and the like. Mass media also affect the quality of individual life, partly by virtue of their very existence as mass media. The very experience of reading a newspaper or watching a TV program defines each of us as a part of a large and undifferentiated mass rather than as an individual member of one or another distinctive human community. And the specific content of mass communications also affects our daily behavior, from the kind of toothpaste we use to the words with which we greet friends, bosses, or children.

Yet if mass media are too important to escape the scrutiny of the Commission on Critical Choices for Americans—or of any citizen, or of their government—they are also too important to be subjected to the dictates of the political process. For mass media are a central element of the American system of speech and expression. It has always been a basic tenet of American democracy that speech and expression are to determine the shape of public policy and the conduct of government, not vice versa. That is the meaning of the First Amendment: government is not to be in the business of forming opinion or regulating expression. For a quasi-public institution like this Commission, therefore, as for government itself, the mass media are a subject that should be approached, if at all, only with the utmost circumspection. Not only is it illegitimate for government itself to undertake to shape or control mass communication, but recent national experience has reminded us how inappropriate it can be for persons in high public office to address themselves too directly to the issue of how media ought to conduct themselves. In a free society these are questions that are properly left to individual persons and media organizations to grapple with for themselves. In this sense I think one can fairly say that responsible public discussion of mass media is, or should be, torn between two conflicting impulses. On the one hand, one wants everyone to freely scrutinize, criticize, and seek to correct media performance. On the other, one also wants people to observe a rule of respectful noninterference with the content of mass communication and the media consumption preferences of the American people.

Towards a National Communications Policy

In public policy toward the mass media, by contrast, one wants no such ambivalence. Clarity and coherence are not virtues one readily associates with American public policy, and in many areas they may not even be desirable. But in the most sensitive and fundamental areas of national policy—and emphatically in such matters as war and peace, and free expression—clarity and coherence are essential. Unfortunately, both in theory and in practice, the current national posture vis-à-vis mass media and mass communication is confused and contradictory, and there can be little question about its deleterious effect on the quality of American life. There is, in consequence, a large and, I believe, quite urgent national need for a systematic reassessment of public policies in this entire area and for a serious effort to develop a single, integrated, meaningful national communications policy that will reconcile historic American values with current American conditions. If this Commission says nothing else about media, communications, and the quality of American life, it should at least address itself to this central and singular issue.

There are scandals which arise as an unintended consequence of individual action; there are scandals which occur because of government inaction; but the greatest scandals are the ones which are deliberately created by public policy. American communications policy is a scandal of this third variety. The nature of the scandal may be simply stated: it is that of government agencies and elected public officials exercising a systematic power over the content of broadcast communications, in complete contradiction of the letter of the First Amendment ("Congress shall make no law abridging the freedom of . . . the press") and in substantial disharmony with its spirit. Current communications policies incorporate scandals of the lesser varieties as well—as in the inhibition they place on broadcast diversity, for instance, or in the way the current postal rate increases discourage the creation of new vehicles of printed expression. And there is no small amount of simple confusion, contradictoriness, and arbitrariness as well. All in all, this is, in light of its great symbolic and practical importance, one of the most backward and indefensible quagmires in American public law.

The problems afflicting national communications policy are largely an invention of twentieth century politics. Previously, there had been a clear and, in my view, close to ideal policy, firmly grounded in the First Amendment: government would not involve itself in defining or regulating the content of communications. And to this principle it added a second: through development of a postal system (especially rural free delivery) and maintenance of below-cost postage rates for newspapers, books, magazines, and the like, government actively encouraged a proliferation of mass communications and maximization of media diversity and consumer choice. The policy was, in short, the classic liberal policy of a free marketplace of ideas, expression, and media organizations. Where government became directly involved in this marketplace, it did so on an ad hoc basis largely through antitrust prosecution for the purpose of stopping arrangements in restraint of trade and the free flow of information, etc.

As with so much in current public policy, it was the experience of modern war and the introduction of new technology which caused this traditional relationship between government and mass media to be abandoned—and abandoned without there ever having been a clear decision on the principle implicit in the abandonment. The war in question was World War I, during which Americans became accustomed to government censorship and government propaganda; the technology, of course, was broadcast—first radio, and later, television. By the mid-1920s radio signal interference had become so serious that the prospects seemed dim that the broadcast industry would ever get off the ground. There was unanimous agreement that the federal government would have to centrally allocate broadcast frequencies. In 1927 Congress created the Federal Radio Commission, which was supplanted in 1934 by the Federal Communications Commission. The objective of the FCC was to promote the "wider and more efficient use" of broadcasting and to allocate frequencies on a "fair, efficient, and equitable" basis for purposes of maximizing the "public interest, convenience, or necessity." With this act, as applied by the FCC and validated by the courts, government arrogated to itself the power of regulating the content of broadcast communications and conferred upon broadcast media organizations the status of "public trustee"—answerable at least once every three years to the FCC, and at the discretion of federal regulators subject to a range of punishments including the ultimate sanction of being denied the ability to broadcast at all.

In addition to its sweeping powers over the individual broadcaster, the FCC was also given the responsibility of determining the overall structure of the broadcast industry. Would broadcasters serve local, regional, or national markets? Would there be many or just a few broadcasters in each market? What would the division of the broadcast spectrum be as among competing uses—mass broadcasting, civilian radio, police, military, etc.? How many stations of what sort would an individual entity be allowed to own? The answers to all these questions were shaped by the criteria by which the FCC decided to award licenses—and the answers, in turn, powerfully affected the behavior of broadcast media, and thus the quality of life in America. When one speaks of the FCC, then, one has reference to an agency that does more than merely administer standing rules; the agency made the rules in the first place, and the rules shaped the entire nature of the industry as well as the conduct of individual firms within it.

The mere existence of these powers has been extremely important, quite apart from the use the FCC has chosen to make of them. From the beginning it has always been government, rather than individual persons or private institutions, which has possessed the final say-so on all broadcast matters. Given the extremely broad congressional delegation of authority to the FCC and the relatively insulated character of the agency, the exercise of this ultimate say-so has necessarily been arbitrary in character. Faced with such arbitrary power, broadcasters and broadcast organizations have been comparatively cautious; one searches almost in vain, among the members of this dependent industry, for persons of the same crusty independence and forcefulness of character which leaders of print communications have historically exhibited. Moreover, the mere existence of this regulatory power has created a strictly political route for the expression of dissatisfaction with the content of broadcast communications—a route that is effective (or ineffective) quite regardless of the merit and disinterestedness of the complaint alleged. Thus, those who have been unable to persuade broadcasters by the intellectual and moral cogency of their position have always had the option, thanks to government regulation, of trying to bring the content of broadcast media into conformity with their preferences through the exercise of sheer political muscle.

Above all, the existence of this regulatory power has introduced a genuine and perhaps growing confusion about the proper relation between government and mass media. Is the press to be free of government control or isn't it? The Constitution and existing policy toward print media say it is to be free; the existence of the FCC, however, says it is not. And what explains this apparent anomaly? There are many rationales, but no convincing reason. The courts have relied heavily on the quasi-monopoly character of the broadcast industry—and yet the newspaper market, which is vastly more concentrated, remains unregulated. It is also possible to justify regulation on the basis of the inherent power of the broadcast media and the huge size of their audience—yet the Constitution does not limit its protections to media which are weak and unpopular. The more carefully one inspects the arguments for a government presence in broadcast communications, the clearer it becomes that in truth there is no authentic justification. The FCC's powers over the content of electronic expression are a deviation from the spirit of the First Amendment, lacking true philosophic coherence. Is it any wonder, then, that we have witnessed these past several years so many efforts—not all of them associated with the perpetrators of Watergate—to manipulate our media of mass communications? Increasingly it appears that Americans have forgotten the reasons why we have a First Amendment in the first place.

The use of the FCC's regulatory power, of course, has not usually seemed so offensive; indeed the agency is ordinarily accused of being a classic case of the regulator-captured-by-regulatee. To the extent that this is true—and it is a substantial extent—there is only further reason for dismay over the existence of this regulatory power. Perhaps the most importantly objectionable use of FCC authority has been its historic decision to establish local as against regional broadcast markets. Its aim in this was to guarantee for each local population center at least one station, in theory locally owned and operated, that will assume an active role in community affairs. In all but a handful of cases, however, the actual accomplishment of the FCC has been to blanket the nation with a myriad of small local broadcasting monopolies and oligopolies dominated by absentee-owned and operated stations more interested in their "bottom line" than in public affairs and public service. Nor have these stations had to exert themselves so very hard to make money, given their monopolistic advantages: according to one study, they have had an average pre-tax rate of return on tangible investment of between 54 and 74 percent during recent years—and the figure reaches an estimated 200 to 300 percent for the networks' wholly-owned affiliate stations in the largest markets! Another effect of the "local" strategy adopted by the FCC has been to make the television industry one dominated by only three networks—as against the four or more networks which some economists believe would exist if television markets were regional and thus substantially more competitive.

Since opting for the local strategy in the 1940s, the FCC has steered a generally consistent course. It has typically acted to sustain the tightly oligopolistic character of the TV industry. It has done this in part by adopting regulations favorable to maintaining the industry as an oligopoly, as for instance in its unhesitating rejection of proposals for "deintermixture," whereby each local market would be all UHF or all VHF—thereby making it possible to have many more stations in a given local market without creating signal interference problems in neighboring markets. And the FCC has sustained the oligopolistic character of the industry by resisting forces that promise to make television more competitive and more responsive to consumer demand, as for instance in its extremely restrictive regulations on cable TV, pay TV, and other technological and merchandising innovations likely to open the industry up. Instead of encouraging market-type mechanisms for the regulation of television and radio, the FCC has chosen to supply that regulation directly and by itself, thereby intruding itself—and the full powers of government—into the very heart of the communications function. Hence the promulgation of the Fairness Doctrine, which in principle (if not in practice) denies to broadcasters the full First Amendment right to say what they want. Even more important has been the emergence of an informal system of quotas spelling out minimum levels of programming in a range of different program categories—news, public affairs, etc. And the FCC maintains procedures whereby local opinion can express itself as to the adequacies or inadequacies of a station's programming. Though for the most part these procedures are toothless formalities, they are not invariably so; they do provide a way, however tortuous and unreliable, for interest group politics to accomplish the manipulation of the content of broadcast communications.

Apart from its gratuitous affront to the principles of the First Amendment, this regulatory apparatus has had a number of practical effects. On the positive side of the ledger, it has helped television to become a vigorous and flourishing industry, one which has grown extremely rapidly and which now confers many advantages (if possibly also a few disadvantages) on the American people. On the other hand, it has accomplished this at a fairly stiff price. For the regulatory apparatus clearly has restricted entry into the television industry, which in turn has deprived Americans of alternatives they have every right to have and which has also guaranteed the FCC a justification for involving itself in the content of broadcast. And through its informal programming quotas and other such regulations it has managed to insure that the few competing stations and networks will offer the viewer very similar programming menus. A considerable body of evidence indicates that there currently exists a large and unfulfilled excess demand for additional television programming. The fact that it is unfulfilled is largely attributable to the existence of government regulation in its current form—and constitutes powerful evidence for the proposition that current public policy vis-à-vis the broadcast media is confused, often counterproductive, and hard to describe as being in the public interest.

In these circumstances, what is to be done? The beginning of wisdom in this area, I believe, is to stop approaching the matter as a question of devising the right rulings and programs, and to start thinking in much broader terms about how to formulate a coherent policy. We already have all manner of rulings and programs, actual and proposed, and are not discernibly better off as a result; what we only too obviously lack—and need—is a general national policy to give direction and coherence to our more specific undertakings. And it should be a policy, not just toward radio and television, but toward mass media and mass communications as a whole.

One alternative is, of course, to continue with the current arrangement.

National policy would make a sharp distinction between broadcast communications and other forms. The other forms would be unregulated and, through low postal rates, encouraged to flourish. Broadcast media would be regulated by the FCC on the grounds that they are unavoidably a highly concentrated industry in which consumer preferences are comparatively impotent. Regulations would be designed to preserve the oligopolistic character of the industry and to induce various broadcasters to be as much like one another as possible. Great uncertainty would prevail among broadcasters as to the FCC's real intentions and future actions, thereby making the regulating agency a highly influential body and broadcasters highly responsive to its wishes. Most regulations about programming content would thus be made informally, as a result of the threat implicit in a congressional hearing or an FCC proceeding (this is how questions of children's TV are being handled). An occasional arbitrary ruling would occur to the detriment of a broadcaster or the industry—a WHDH license revocation, a "Pensions in America" Fairness Doctrine ruling, a requirement for cigarette counteradvertising, pressure for minority hiring and minority programming—but for the most part the industry would be sustained rather than threatened.

There *is* something to be said for this strategy. It may be that broadcasting cannot be made more diverse and competitive. Television in particular is an extremely powerful medium which is regulated by government in every other society; perhaps it is simply too powerful to be left alone. The medium does have an impact on children which print media cannot have; and it is inherently a more "public" medium. Moreover, we know what can go wrong with our current system—and though things do go wrong, perhaps they are not so serious that they cannot be lived with. Finally, TV may not be perfect, but clearly it is good enough to have achieved, in an extremely short time, an extraordinary degree of market penetration and consumer acceptance. Even in the controversial area of children's TV, a recent poll indicated that more than 80 percent of American parents are satisfied with current children's programming.

To this current system, however, there exists a general alternative which I believe to be much the more desirable. This policy strategy would begin by asserting that, at least in principle, broadcast media are to be treated on the same footing with print media and are to enjoy the same protections of the First Amendment. Government, in other words, would assert that it is none of its business what is said or expressed through any communications medium and would explicitly renounce the proposition that it should have an essentially unlimited general regulatory power over any medium. The FCC in its current form would be abolished.

It would not be abolished (or radically scaled down), however, until certain changes had been made in public policy. The most important of these would be to reshape the frequency allocations so as to maximize the number of channels in a given market; this might include establishing some regional channels. Government should also simply eliminate all the restrictions which currently hamper the entry of new forms of television and radio—cable, pay, cassette and disc, etc. It should allocate new channels by lottery or by auction (or by some combination of the two), and all such channel assignments would then go on the open market, where they could be freely bought and sold (like taxi medallions in New York City). In all probability—if there are enough channels created—there should seldom be any great scarcity of relatively low-cost channels available for a prospective broadcaster to buy. (If one is reluctant to let the market prevail in this area entirely, one could simply have every permit to use a given channel expire after ten or twelve years, after which it would revert to the government for re-auction or reallocation by lottery.)

The central point, however, would be that the government would not pretend to exercise regulatory powers over broadcasters. There would be no Fairness Doctrine, no Equal Time provisions, no informal quotas for categories of programs, no prime time access rule, etc. Broadcasters would be as free as newspapers and magazines to "do their own thing" as their individual lights prompt. The diversity of programming would increase; consumer sovereignty would become something more than a slogan; minority tastes and minority audiences could be served to the extent of their willingness to tune in (and, on pay TV, to pay). The overall welfare of the American people would be greater. Government would not be in the business of reducing broadcast entry and competition and of regulating the content of expression.

If it turned out that, under this system, there were practices and abuses of such harmfulness and such magnitude that they could not be ignored, the hands of government would not be entirely tied. I doubt that we would witness such abuses, and I believe we should be extremely loath to do anything about them through government. But if action did seem absolutely necessary, it could be taken. Instead of acting through the FCC, however, we would act in the traditional manner—through the legislative process with enforcement by the Executive branch. Such a route would make it less likely that there would be much legislation of this sort—which is a good thing—but it would clearly enable a large and persistent majority to eventually take steps to correct some glaring abuse, and to do this in the narrowest and least freedom-eroding manner.

This "escape valve" brings us to another question: What would be the role of public broadcasting in this new system? It would have a useful role, and perhaps a more important one than under the current system. The "television of abundance" envisioned in this deregulatory plan will do many more things, and serve a broader variety of tastes and interests, than TV today; there will be more diversity consistent with audience desires. But there will also be various lacunae in each broadcast market. The purpose of public broadcasting would be to survey the offerings in each market and to develop program menus designed to provide what is lacking. Though not entirely consistent with the spirit of the First Amendment, perhaps, government-supported broadcasting has shown itself to be an independent and trustworthy institution, and it performs—or at least it *should* perform—a crucial role in propagating models of cultural and intellectual excellence. Public TV, under the new system, would represent the public interest in broadcasting in the one way which is truly appropriate to a governmentally-supported entity in a free society: not by requiring nongovernmental broadcasters to conform to this or that rule, but by itself adding to and increasing the variety of viewing and listening options available to the public.

This, I would emphasize, is not a utopian proposal—though I do not guarantee its political acceptability at the moment. Its value does not depend on there being a sudden explosion of brilliant television when the regulations are taken away. Its true objective and justification lies in getting government interventions and rulings out of the process whereby the content of broadcast is determined, and in opening up that process to the free play of market, institutional, and individual forces. We do not say that the First Amendment protections afforded the press, or book publishing, are not valid and should be repealed whenever we encounter a bad newspaper or a disappointing publishing season. The same forbearance should obtain in the case of television and radio.

Government and Media

Quite apart from the issue of public policy toward the mass media—which bears principally on the quality of our private lives—there has emerged, over the past ten or twelve years, a further and much more disputatious question about the working relationship between government and the press, which is important principally for its implications for politics and the quality of American public life.

Once upon a time this relationship seemed reasonably well settled. The business of people in government was to govern and to engage in the traditional variety of political pursuits. The job of the press was to get as much information as it could and to present it as objectively and with as little partisanship as possible. Persuaded of the nonpolitical intentions of the press, people in government afforded newsmen access—not unlimited access, to be sure, but still an access much greater than that which exists in other countries, and substantially greater than could be provided by law even here. Newsmen, for their part, reciprocated by manifesting a certain sympathy and sense of responsibility. The relationship did of course have built-in tensions—government and the press do not have identical interests—but overall it was characterized by cooperation more than by conflict. Everyone derived some benefit from this arrangement. Officials, with good access to the press, had channels for communicating with one another and with the public. Newsmen, with good access to government, had a way to get huge amounts of information and to check its accuracy. And the public enjoyed the greatest benefit of all—an "open" political system, a maximum of information, and a minimum of distortion.

This traditional relationship, however, was neither idyllic nor automatic. Its biggest shortcoming was that it gave public officials the ability to collectively define the terms and limits of public discussion; a related disadvantage was that it made newsmen intellectually dependent. As long as Americans shared a general consensus about the terms and limits of public discussion, and as long as American officials dealt honorably with newsmen, these were not, perhaps, unacceptable costs. But when these two conditions began to erode, as they did during the 1950s and especially the 1960s, the traditional relationship dissolved, to the great detriment of the American political system as a whole.

How things became unstuck is a long and still imperfectly understood story; suffice it to say here that, by the end of the 1960s, the relationship had become demoralized, with each side bearing a growing ill will and hostility toward the other. People in government felt ever less obliged to deal honorably with the press; increasingly they added to their traditional political pursuits a new one—the systematic, and often self-serving, manipulation of public appearances through the press. And the press increasingly saw itself as an adversary of government, as the only force which could expose the dishonest pretense of modern government to the people.

Truth and trust are the cement that holds societies together; relationships of the sort that increasingly obtain between government and the press drive them apart. There is hardly a disorder of modern American public life—from inflation and reform that does not work to Watergate and the crisis of legitimacy surrounding our public institutions—that does not derive, at least in some degree, from the current confrontation between government and press. One of the urgent needs during the 1970s and beyond will be to restore this relationship to some semblance of its earlier state. Failure to do so can poison American public life for decades to come.

Any effort at restoration will have to acknowledge and cope with the worrisome erosion of the American political party system. With each passing year the parties become less effective in performing their traditional functions: selecting candidates, formulating issues, and governing. The result is that public officials are increasingly dependent on publicity—and therefore on the press—to amass the political resources needed to stay in office and to accomplish their public objectives. Their incentive to manipulate the press and to stage publicity-getting extravaganzas is thus greater than it was when the press-government relationship followed the traditional pattern. This suggests that party reform—reform that strengthens the parties rather than weakens them, as most recent "reforms" have done—should be an important part of any effort to restore truth and trust.

As for the restoration itself, two general lines of action would seem to be called for. First and most important, persons in government must relearn and begin to use the arts of honest advocacy. Elaborate, manipulation-oriented "public information" units should be scaled down to the point where they are not capable of doing much more than what they were originally intended to do: release information. Where appropriate, more information should become a matter of public record, available for perusal by journalists and others. There should be ample opportunity for interaction between officials and journalists—particularly in informal settings, which are always more productive than elaborately staged "press conferences" and the like.

Above all, however, officials need to recover the largely lost skills of honest advocacy and begin explaining themselves and their actions. Newsmen will listen—that is their principal job; and if what they hear does not clash violently with reality, makes sense, and reflects a sincere effort to conduct public office responsibly and to explain that conduct to others, they will take it seriously even when they disagree. It is the failure of too many officials to communicate in this way, and their desire to win public support for their actions on the cheap, which underlie much of the current problem. I do not for a minute suggest that this cure is an easy one. It will be difficult and distasteful, and it will require many officials to develop new skills or seek other employment. But it does seem necessary.

The other line of action is to encourage more thoughtful attention to the condition and problems of modern journalism. Though this is something that ought to be done especially by newsmen themselves, this discussion should not be confined to the journalistic community. Everyone should participate, public officials emphatically included. Institutions such as journalism schools, journalism reviews, journalism research centers, and the like can usefully be supported and upgraded. But above all what is needed is attention, thought, and discussion, so that as newsmen define and redefine their role they have full benefit of the information and analysis such discussion can make available. Talk, of course, rarely does away with problems, but it can clarify them—and it can also establish understanding among people who, in the end, may agree to disagree. Achieving agreement of that second order is all that is really required, in a free society, to restore a harmonious relationship between press and government, and by doing so to encourage the recovery of that civility without which public life so easily degenerates into a war of all against all.

There is an institutional aspect to this matter that deserves at least passing mention. To design a coherent national communications policy and to assist in assuring that official communications are in the spirit of honest advocacy rather than of sleazy manipulation, a small but serious policy-making staff of the sort that now exists in the Office of Telecommunications Policy will be necessary. It should be small so that its function really is to monitor rather than to manipulate; and it should give continuing attention to ways in which government's own use of mass media can improve the quality of life, both public and private.

XVI
Art, Architecture, and the Quality of Life

Wolf Von Eckardt

I

It is not enough to protect the environment. We must also make it livable and human. I use the imperative "must" because while clean air and water, as well as thoughtful management of nature, will make life considerably healthier, it will not necessarily make it happier. A more respectful treatment of the earth does not necessarily increase our respect for one another.

Nor does hectic building mean that we are building a civilization. "The machine running wild, the bulldozer on the rampage, the crane swinging aimlessly against the sky—these are signs of a people that is making things over without knowing why, or to what end," August Heckscher wrote. "The physical and cultural environment has meaning only in so far as it bears the marks of what we are and what we aspire to be. Without meaning, this environment must overwhelm the individual and hopelessly blur the beauty of both natural and created things."[1]

An environment without meaning, in other words, is a mean environment. It inspires nothing more than resignation and alienation, a frame of mind hardly conducive to making one's surroundings more attractive.

We acknowledge this vicious circle in the slums. We know that peeling walls in neglected tenements invite vandalism and that their stinking hallways encourage antisocial behavior. We understand that there is little incentive to keep slums clean, let alone to try to make them beautiful.

We are also beginning to see that the same applies to new buildings which

375

have been condescendingly designed to provide what the law calls "decent, safe and sanitary" housing for the poor. When the Pruitt-Igoe project was built in St. Louis in the late 1950s, for instance, it was much praised for the novelty and cost-saving ingenuity of its architectural design. The novelty and ingenuity, however, had no meaning for the residents. Their response to what they considered a demeaning environment made the project so unmanageable in the end that the authorities were forced to abandon it. Many of us watched on television not long ago, as the high-rise slabs were blown up with dynamite in twenty seconds flat. Just think of the similar projects still inhabited.

Some sociologists deny that environment has a profound effect on human behavior. But it does not take elaborate research to observe that an environment which says, in effect, that people do not matter, does not matter much to people. Some people, in fact, will retaliate for the negation of their humanity and assert their individuality with violence.

In a sense, despite private affluence and the luxuries *within* the American home, all of us live in a neglected and misconceived public housing project. There is no need here to mention the absence of sidewalks and playgrounds and the Miltown boredom of suburbia or the frustrating inefficiency and ugliness of our cities. What seems needed is not more exhortation but a more widespread realization that there is a direct relationship between America's current malaise and America's increasingly degraded environment.

Erik Erikson has written about the "reciprocity of identity." If man brings something of his identity to his building, Erikson says, the buildings will return identity to him. A place which we or our fathers and grandfathers have created with pride will give pride to us and to our children.

Today, pride, a sense of identity, and confidence in the American destiny seem to be waning. Nor can they be restored with bicentennial slogans and flag waving. There has been enough spurious patriotism. After Vietnam and Watergate, a concerted, national effort to halt the galloping degradation of our urban regions, and to inspire to a sense of humanism, of beauty and amenity in our metropolitan areas, could go far to restore national self-confidence.

We should recognize, I believe, that careful and loving design, art, and joy in the American habitat are part of the American promise. The public happiness, as Heckscher has called it, is a vital part of the general welfare.

Americans have not traditionally thought so. We have been reluctant to curb private greed and advance public enjoyment. Puritan traditions have inhibited secular pleasure. Rugged individualism holds that the public happiness is none of the public's business.

But along with a growing introspection and reevaluation of our national priorities, there seems to be a new awareness that we deserve to be much richer than we are—richer, not in material abundance, but in the rewards provided by education, art, leisure, and, to cite Heckscher once more, the rewards of an "environment that answers man's needs for order, brightness and variety."

II

Architectural concepts of a rewarding man-made environment are changing drastically. Modern architecture is no longer modern, as it were.

Half a century ago, artists and architects, notably in Europe, greeted the arriving machine age with euphoria. The Italian Futurists, the Russian Constructivists, the German Bauhaus, the Dutch deStijl, and the Swiss-born Frenchman Le Corbusier found one another in the desire to mate art and technology. The marriage, they proclaimed, would give birth to a totally new, totally man-made environment, "everything from the coffee cup to city planning," as Mies van der Rohe put it.

Machine production, glass, steel, concrete, and functionalism would, the modernists said, liberate man from drudgery, squalor, Victorian eclecticism, and the "crime" of ornament. They would bring sunshine and fresh air into the dwelling of every worker. Radiant cities, designed for speed and sanitation, were to scrape the sky with their towers, leaving the verdant ground for play. The technology of mass production, they believed, would lead to mass education and a new mass culture.

The architectural form of this vision was inspired mainly by painters—Picasso (in his Cubist period) and Braque, Malevich and El Lissitsky, Mondrian and van Doesburg. The form-givers of this vision—Gropius, Mies van der Rohe, and, most of all, le Corbusier—intended to create a new social architecture. For the most part, it turned out to be an abstract art.

The marriage of art and technology was never really consummated. Building construction is far from being rationally industrialized. Compared to the mass production of almost everything else, it remains incredibly cumbersome and is increasingly expensive. As a result, there is no hope even of catching up with housing shortages. There never seems to be a shortage of automobiles.

Architects and designers fervently continue to woo the indifferent object of their desire. They use machine-made materials and like to give their glass buildings and steel furniture that machine-made look. It is crafted by hand.

Nor have most people taken to it. The International Style of architecture and design has remained largely an elitist style. Few Americans chose to live in International Style houses and even fewer chose to live with modern furnishings. Abstract architecture and design—that is, design not visibly associated with historic forms and human functions—seems impersonal and cold to people's emotional needs.

The style which was to uplift the masses has failed to please the masses. There is, in fact, a popular rebellion against the icy glass boxes of the International Style and the incomprehensible mystique of the architectural abstract expressionism that followed it. People are ever more loudly protesting the arrogant, inhuman scale and overwhelming monumentality of the ubiquitous "radiant" cityscape with its rhythmically spaced skyscrapers along vast freeways. It seems identical from Alaska to Zanzibar, regardless of the local climate, topography, or culture. The growing clamor for the preservation of historic buildings is as often prompted by an aversion to the new, as by love for the old.

Popular aversion to bare and square modern architecture and city planning is not an aversion to contemporary design as such. It is an aversion to the abrupt, antihistoric disrespect with which brutally large-scale and bland modern structures disrupt the familiar surroundings of pleasantly scaled, old neighborhoods, and a protest against those hallmarks of modern architecture, the high-rise building and the skyscraper.

The Greek architect and city planner, Constantinos A. Doxiadis, whose operations span the globe, publicly confessed to what he called the "crime" of having designed high-rise buildings. They "work against nature," he wrote, "by destroying the scale of the landscape . . . [they] work against man, especially children who lose their direct contacts with nature . . . [and they] work against society, because they prevent the units of social importance—the family, the extended family, and the neighborhood—from functioning as naturally and as normally as before."[2]

Nathaniel Owings, one of the founders of Skidmore, Owings and Merrill, the architectural firm which has designed some of the tallest and most famous skyscrapers of the past two or three decades, "confessed" the high-rise "crime" even more succinctly. "History has proven that skyscrapers tend to dehumanize the area in which they are raised," he said in a recent speech. "They suck the lifeblood of the area around them, drawing up into the air what should be lying closer to the human scale."[3]

High-rise buildings, as recent tragedies at New Orleans and Atlanta have shown, are also firetraps. High-rise apartments, according to a recent study by Oscar Newman conducted under the auspices of New York University, tend to have a crime rate more than twice as high as walk-up apartments inhabited by families who are sociologically and economically identical. Crime, Newman found, tends to increase in relation to the height of the building. Most of the crimes are committed in the elevators, lobbies, corridors, firestairs, and on roofs. People who live in high-rise buildings seldom know one another and therefore do not control strangers.

All this does not mean that we will or should repeal the gains of modern architecture. We could not comfortably build old-fashioned buildings (although some would put "Colonial" or other "period style" veneers even on gas stations).

Nor does it mean that we will or should abolish high concentrations of people. High densities are often desired and desirable. They give intensity to urban life and can help preserve open space. But there are means other than tall towers and enormous slabs to house large numbers of people on small amounts of land. Moshe Safdie's Habitat '67 points in one possible direction.

Instead of stacking people in high-rise apartments, Safdie, an Israeli-born,

Canadian architect, stacked houses at the experimental project he designed for the 1967 World's Fair at Montreal. He gave everyone a garden in the bargain. Safdie's "villas in the sky," as he calls them, vary in size from one bedroom to four bedrooms. They consist of modular concrete boxes which were prefabricated on the ground and lifted by giant crane into a kind of honeycomb, a self-supporting structure shaped like an open pyramid and resembling a mediterranean hilltown.

The roof of the house below forms the terrace garden for the house above. The terrace gardens have views in several directions, measure a respectable seventeen by thirty-eight feet, and are planted with shrubbery and small trees that are centrally watered and fertilized.

Habitat '67 seems to be well liked by its residents. It consists of 158 houses placed alongside or just above or below an open walkway which is reached by elevator. Each house has its own identity and mail delivery. The walkway widens every so often to provide space for play areas. And the houses are loosely stacked to let light and air inside the pyramidical structure.

Safdie originally conceived his Habitat for a thousand houses, which were to straddle community centers, schools, churches, shops and all the other things that make a housing cluster a good neighborhood. The Canadian government, however, had to reduce the project and there is only parking and a park on the ground inside. The reduced scale also increased the unit cost of the houses, leading to charges that Safdie's idea is much too expensive.

Since Habitat, Safdie has worked out several other structural and prefabrication possibilities for his idea, but none of his later Habitat designs have so far been built. His most promising project may be Coldspring New Town in Baltimore where his houses are tightly clustered and, in one instance, stacked down the steep cliff of a quarry. There will be a man-made lake at the bottom.

Other ideas to achieve high densities without elevators and corridors were shown in the summer of 1973 at the New York Museum of Modern Art under the auspices of the New York Urban Development Corporation. The show was entitled: "Another Chance for Housing: Low Rise Alternatives." One of these alternatives, designed by Anthony Pangaro and J. Michael Kirkland, is under construction in the Brownsville section of Brooklyn. It consists of 626 dwellings along with neighborhood stores, daycare centers, playgrounds, stoops for people to sit on and chat, community rooms, and laundries. The dwellings are cleverly tucked into what are basically four-story row houses. Most of them are duplexes of various sizes with efficiency apartments for elderly people mixed in. Every unit has a private entrance on the ground and either a small, private yard or a patio terrace.

Zoning for the Brownsville project, to be sure, permits a thousand units—a third more than are being built. Under conventional wisdom, however, these thousand units would be small apartments arranged in four twenty-story high-rise slabs. The low-rise solution includes three-, four- and five-bedroom apartments for large families and will therefore accommodate just about as many people. High-rise slabs, furthermore, require large open spaces for light and air that are usually taken up by mangy lawns, parking lots, and a few playgrounds, all of which must be publicly maintained. The Pangaro-Kirkland design makes it possible to fit the housing into the existing street pattern and to retain worthy old buildings. More than half of the open space consists of private yards that are kept up and protected by the residents. Although the construction cost for this alternative is about the same as for conventional high-rise apartments, it will cost less in the long run.

Many people suddenly see the damage cars have done to cities and they do not want to see freeways bulldozed across their backyards. But we are not likely to abandon automobiles, or some form of personal transportation, and we will need roads.

The protest against further freeways, urban renewal, modern housing projects and technolgoy is not a protest against the modern age as such. It is not a rebellion against technology, but against the dehumanizing way in which technology is so often applied. People are rebelling with increasing anger against the often needlessly brutal, inanimate and impersonal ways in which the requirements of modern life are accommodated. They are rebelling not against the machine, but against the tyranny of the machine, and the increasing anonymity of their lives.

My neighbors in the Dupont Circle area in Washington, for instance, recently rose in vociferous protest when it was learned that Gino's, a fast food restaurant chain, was about to replace a pleasant, inexpensive Greek restaurant with an outdoor cafe. The protest was by no means confined to homeowners who feared for their property values. It was led by young students who generally welcome inexpensive restaurants, but who voiced their distaste for mass produced food, computerized service, and "plastic" look-alike commercialism. The protest was successful. Gino's withdrew, and this is not an isolated case. In Greenwich Village, for instance, a McDonald hamburger stand also yielded to a similar uproar at just about the same time.

This is not a vegetarian movement, opposed to hamburgers. As with high-rise buildings and freeways, the opposition is to the way it is done. It is a matter of design.

"An environment that answers man's need for order, brightness and variety" needs new approaches to land use, public financing and taxation, as well as political pressures and the cooperation of government. But all this is, in the end, subordinate to what we want our environment to be—to what we want our buildings and neighborhoods, cities and urban regions, our cityscape and our landscape to look like and how we want them to function. It depends on how we envision all this. Artists and architects design that vision for us—or should.

The new urban vision, now slowly coming into focus, is in many respects the opposite of what the modern movement designed for us half a century ago.

Modern architecture set itself defiantly against nature. The new architecture will design *with* nature, in harmony with the ecology and with thrift of energy. Modern architecture glorified technology and machine production. The new architecture will seek to offset their leveling, homogenizing, and dehumanizing effects.

Government on all levels, foundations, and universities can do much to help this trend along. They can encourage experimentation. They can advance interaction between artists and designers and the people for whom they create. They can, most of all, help establish practical examples and models.

America has a large urban research industry. We have ever more urban institutes, centers, departments, and workshops, producing wordy research reports and sociological studies. What we need, it seems to me, is not more to read but more to see and to experience. We need more experimental buildings, more exhibits, inspirations, and demonstrations to advance the environmental arts.

Modern architecture was put on the map, so to speak, when the German Werkbund, an association of artists, architects, industrial designers, and businessmen built the Weissenhof community near Stuttgart, Germany, in 1927. Mies van der Rohe was in charge, and just about every noted architect at the time, including Le Corbusier, Walter Gropius, and Marcel Breuer, showed what he and modern architecture could do. The Weissenhof influence can still be seen all around us.

It is time for another such demonstration of new ideas in design, construction methods, energy-saving heating and cooling, transportation, and other aspects of urban living. The model community should be large enough to be meaningful. It should be built free of the usual crippling restraints of financing, marketing, and legalities that beset even such advanced new towns as Roosevelt Island.

The demonstration should show more than buildings. It should also experiment with ideas in education, public health, law enforcement, fire protection, waste disposal, recreation, and community involvement in the arts. A place to live for all kinds of people, it might also serve as an international conference center and workshop on various aspects of the urban environment.

Our best hopes, Alan Nevins has said, are illustrated hopes.

III

The "city of the future" is a fantasy of the past.

If young people protest even the mild automation of Gino's fast food dispensaries, they will hardly take to the mechanization and regimentation required to sustain life in Paolo Soleri's half-mile-high megastructure cities for 340,000 inhabitants. The models and drawings of Soleri's "archologies" (architecture + ecology = archology) are lovely to look at. But I doubt that people would want to live in super-sized ant hills.

The same is true of Buckminster Fuller's techno-romantic proposal to build bubble-domes two miles in diameter over Manhattan or other cities. Fuller claims that the dome would save money on air conditioning, street cleaning, snow removal, and lost man hours from colds and other respiratory diseases. He never told us, however, how much it would cost to pump out exhausts, to repair and clean the bubble, and whether to keep the birds and the bees inside or out. The dome idea would probably contribute more to our urban anxieties than to the solution of any serious urban problem.

Nor are the popular science fiction fantasies of the British Archigram Group likely to contribute to the public happiness. They suggest that people might live in cable structures which contain spaces enclosed by skins which open and close electronically. The ceilings and floors of these expandable cells are to be transformed from hard to soft by the push of a button or spoken command, and could be inflated in certain areas to make reclining and sleeping comfortable. Light, sound, smells, and films would immerse us in a variety of experiences. The cells form beehives that could be clipped on, plugged into various structures or moved about as desired.

But who desires? There is nothing to indicate that anyone, including their inventors, would want to become passive pawns who surrender the act of living to mechanized archologies, giant bubbles or electronically controlled space capsules. Nor is there any discernible need that might move us in the direction of these utopias. There is no reason to mess up the desert with 340,000 people, most of whom would prefer to live along the seaboard. Airconditioning Central Park does not seem to have a high priority for most people. And there is no reason on earth why we should live in plugged-in or movable beehives. What we need is clean air in the city and efficient garbage collection.

Even sillier than this kind of city-of-the-future talk, is talk that the city has no future. City real estate values keep going up and up, but some planners and architects still insist that the city is doomed, that it should be abandoned. It is never made clear what we should abandon it for. For more "spread city"? For an even wider dispersal and stricter segregation of people and activities? The segregation of people practiced in suburbia is not only by race, but also by income and age, and activities are segregated in residential, commercial, and industrial zones. All this segregation in our habitat threatens the disintegration of our society.

City planners, architects, and officials are beginning to realize this, and there are now efforts to permit and promote integrated developments. They welcome people of different income groups and permit a mixture of uses, such as stores on the ground floor of apartment houses or at the corner of townhouse rows.

The most widely accepted ideal structure for urban order is based on Ebenezer Howard's proposal for "a peaceful path to real reform," first published in 1898. To avert the further growth and overcrowding of London, Howard proposed to surround the city with a ring of satellite towns. He called them "garden cities." They were to be linked to one another and to the center city by railroad. Each of the garden cities was to include industry, so that people could work where they live. Each was to be limited to 30,000 inhabitants and each was to be surrounded by a permanent greenbelt—mostly agricultural land where food for the town would be grown. Times have changed but the intriguing social and ecological benefits of this scheme are still evident. With some modifications, the new town idea has been successfully realized in Great Britain, and many countries have adopted national urban development policies based on the satellite town concept.

In this country, too, there was a flurry of new town talk a few years back. A National Committee on Urban Growth Policy, chaired by Albert Rains, recommended in 1968 that federal assistance be given to build a hundred new communities averaging 100,000 population each, as well as ten new cities of at least one million in population. The recommendation resulted in good legislation but not much construction. Federal appropriations were low and federal action slow. Aside from Reston and Columbia, two privately built new towns which were well on the way before the New Communities Act was passed in 1970, only fifteen new community proposals, not all of them equally promising, have received circumscribed federal loan guarantees. All of them are financially dangerously anemic. Only the New York State Urban Development Corporation is building in the public interest.

If we are to be serious about urban and environmental order and improving the quality of life in America, the new communities program must be put back on the track and moved forward full speed. I do not know if we need a hundred new communities, as the Rains Committee recommended. I do suggest, however, that most of the population growth in our metropolitan areas should be accommodated in comprehensively planned satellite towns. There are two important reasons in their favor. They help arrest urban sprawl and preserve open space for recreation and the regeneration of air and water. And they can and must be economically and racially integrated to help catch up with the shortage of subsidized housing and help people out of the ghettos. Racial and economic integration is easier to achieve in new communities than encrusted suburbs. Properly planned, they provide the relocation housing that alone makes it possible to attack the inner city slums. They must, of course, be part of the metropolitan fabric, strongly linked to the central city by public transit. These purposes are hard, if not impossible, for private developers to meet. It may take the powers of the state, wielded by a nonprofit urban development corporation, to acquire the land where the new town is needed, not where it can readily be assembled. And it will surely take direct governmental funding on tax abatements to provide not only ample housing subsidies but the special quality of educational, social, and recreational services required to make integration successful.

Urban order also demands that the country formulate a national urban growth policy, as required by the 1970 Housing Act, to establish priorities and help balance the need for environmental protection with the need for economic and urban growth. Such a national policy will undoubtedly call for a more intensive use of the land already urbanized rather than increasing costly sprawl. In other words, good planning can accommodate many more people in the three megalopolitan areas in this country—the urban concentrations along the Atlantic and Pacific seaboards and along the Great Lakes—and leave unspoiled country-side unspoiled. (Which is not to say that rural towns should not also be helped to become economically and culturally more attractive, so people will wish to stay there. But it is to say that we can dispense with the Rains Commission's ten new cities of a million inhabitants each out in the wilderness where they have no business.)

Another needed aspect of the urban growth policy is effective, new means of protecting strategically located rural land from urbanization. What kept European cities in bounds and often, in fact, behind walls or up on arid hilltops, was the value of agricultural land. Now it has become more profitable for farmers to harvest cinderblocks and subdivisions rather than edible crops and this is an important factor in our present urban chaos. Perhaps the impending world food shortages will again make agriculture more profitable than real estate speculation.

While city planners worry about urban structure and the form of the city, however, consumers care mostly about its function. People want shelter which suits their needs at a price they can afford. They want good, easily accessible jobs. They want good schools for their children, nearby shopping, security, privacy, community, recreation, and pleasant neighbors and surroundings. They do not much care whether all this is in new towns or old cities or in sprawling suburbia, whether they live in linear cities or nucleated cities, in cities which planners consider too crowded or cities which planners consider too spread out.

People have different needs and tastes, different incomes, different expectations, requirements, and ideas of how they want to live. They are not given much choice. We are all trapped in a series of vicious circles. People drive to work because public transportation is bad. Public transportation is bad, because so many people drive to work. Many middle-income Americans live in suburbia, not because they like mowing lawns and commuting, but because it is the only place where they can find good schools and gardens. Many elderly Americans live in downtown apartments, not because they like elevators or city living, but because there is no way for them to get around in the suburbs, not even sidewalks. Few blacks have volunteered to live in the ghetto.

The problem is not only that there are so few "life-style" choices *available*, but that most people are not aware even that alternative choices are *possible*. There is no realistic fantasy outlet for our urban frustrations. In other words, many dissatisfied people do not even know what to hope for, and that, of course, increases their dissatisfaction. Expectations are raised, as has often been noted. But the expectations are raised only in rigid directions of conventional wisdom, usually directions that would only aggravate our environmental dilemmas. Expectation-raising television advertisements, for instance, lead people to expect more and bigger automobiles, more and bigger unused and unusable front lawns, and vast, uncluttered freeways. It is time to illustrate new hopes.

One hope and desire that is almost universally shared, is that people prefer to live in an active community where neighbors help one another and yet respect one another's privacy, where there is a variety of things to see and to experience, where schools, shopping, recreation, stimulation and essential social and health services are at hand. We want community in the social and physical sense.

The foremost challenge, then, for improving the quality of living in urban America, is to reintegrate our disintegrating society, to make the textbook abstraction of a pluralistic society an experienceable reality in everyday life. The way to meet the challenge is to increase the multiplicity of choices in where and how people can live and to take all possible measures to intensify neighborhood life.

With this in mind, the question of urban form and structure of city versus suburb, new towns versus incremental urban growth, or linear cities versus concentric cities—is of secondary importance. Just how the neighborhood cells are clustered will depend on whatever specific circumstances are most likely to assure their health. The question of urban form can never be answered categorically. As with the question of whether to build roads or railroads, or apartment houses or single-family houses, the answer is never one or the other, but all. It is not a question of "either-or," but of "plus."

The arithmetic is not unlimited, however. We must obviously assign priorities for the public and private energy and money to be expended on the visible (and audible) aspects of the public happiness. I would put both effort and money where I believe people's involvement in art and design may be most needed and effective—in the neighborhood.

It may hardly be necessary in Greenwich Village, Hyde Park, Kenwood, or Georgetown to try and strengthen a sense of neighborhood identity and belonging, but it is vital elsewhere.

Adapting the neighborhood elementary school to use as a community center can often get things started. In some places, a newly-built neighborhood center might be in order and so would special zoning to permit opening a convenience store as a special attraction. The very idea might start a neighborly conversation.

The Postal Service and the Sanitation Department and perhaps even the local newspapers and dairies might help. They all find it increasingly difficult and expensive to provide house-to-house service. A central pickup and delivery point in every block is needed. On nice days, people will probably go to such a Block Pavilion in their bathrobes and slippers to dump trash and pick up their mail, newspaper, milk and perhaps even store deliveries. The pavilion might be furnished with benches, picnic tables and vending machines for coffee and soft drinks and other inducements to easy sociability and spontaneous coffee klatchs.

The place might also include a tot lot and perhaps even a day care center and laundromats and it should, of course, include mail boxes and postage stamp dispensers. All this would, no doubt, enhance the neighborhood spirit and provide the stepping stone, as it were, to the next higher place in the hierarchy of an orderly urban structure—the neighborhood center.

The neighborhood center is where both spectator art and participatory art should be most at home. Spectator art is both permanent and transient. The permanent kind includes sculpture and fountains on playgrounds and in neighborhood parks, murals on fire walls and on and in public buildings, paintings and other creative things wherever they can be displayed. The transient kind includes traveling exhibits of all kinds, as well as dance, theater, film and multimedia performances. The participatory arts include lectures and courses in arts and crafts and such favorites of the young as photography and film-making. Year-round art programs should also include neighborhood group visits to museums, films, theaters, concerts, and dance performances downtown, lectures and discussions about the performances, and architectural tours and appreciation courses. There is no end to the possibilities. And no end to the potentials of creative living.

The neighborhood is also the place for pageantry and ceremony, a much neglected aspect of creative public life. They contain tremendous possibilities for artistic endeavor—music, costumes, banners, and decorations, historic commemoration, ethnic self-awareness, religious experience, and just plain fun.

The activity might lead to a new profession, as Dr. Parker Rossman of New Haven suggested in a letter to me some time ago. "Urban Rangers" would help keep things clean as garbage collectors, janitors, cleaning people, night watchmen, street sweepers, property inspectors, and such. They would staff the Block Pavilions and neighborhood centers, hand out Ping-Pong balls and paints, and keep things in repair. Some would be nursery men and gardeners to take care of the parks and flower displays. And the Urban Ranger Corps would even include skilled building trade craftsmen, architects and landscape architects to help people renovate their houses and repair their houses—a sort of Urban Extension Service.

It may well turn out, as it did under the New Deal, that an economic recession is the time to launch creative environmental programs and to recruit art in the service of the people.

IV

The federal government spends about a billion dollars a year on new buildings—everything from aircraft factories to zoological parks. It owns and occupies over 400,000 buildings across the country, containing more office space than you can put into 1,250 Empire State Buildings.

The federal government, furthermore, holds 780 million acres of land—a third of the continental United States. It builds and owns utility systems, roads, dams, bridges, harbors, and airports. It has, as of the beginning of 1974, amassed some 250,000 city houses and apartments which have been abandoned or repossessed by their owners because of mortgage payment defaults.

With its guidelines and standards, the federal government largely controls the form and function of subsidized housing projects, houses and apartments supported by federal funds and mortgage guarantees, urban renewal projects, schools and colleges, hospitals, historic buildings and places, and a host of other man-made things, to say nothing of the parks under the jurisdiction of the National Park Service, and the environments created by the military.

The federal government is also responsible for the design of the interstate highways which speed us along and kill us and the highway signs that orient or confuse us.

It designs the postage stamps as well as printed instructions that often govern our lives, including those on income tax forms.

If the federal government were to make it a matter of policy to improve federal design and bring more art and livability into our environment, virtually our entire environment would be better designed. The key to the public happiness is in federal hands.

The key was first discovered more than a decade ago by August Heckscher, who was then President Kennedy's special advisor on the arts. The Heckscher report eventually led to the creation by Congress of the National Foundation on the Arts and Humanities. It pointed out that the arts and the man-made environment in this country would make immeasurable strides forward if the federal government, quite without special expenditures, would just do better what it does anyway.

That same year, the President's Ad Hoc Committee on Federal Office Space, chaired by the then secretary of labor, Arthur Goldberg, drafted "Guiding Principles for Federal Architecture." They were issued as an executive order by President Kennedy and instantly ignored. The guidelines set forth a three-point architectural policy for the federal government:

1. The policy shall be to provide requisite and adequate facilities in an architectural style and form which is distinguished and which will reflect the dignity, enterprise, vigor, and stability of the American National Government. Major emphasis should be placed on the choice of designs that embody the finest contemporary American architectural thought. Specific attention should be paid to the possibilities of incorporating into such designs qualities which reflect the regional architectural traditions of that part of the Nation in which buildings are located. Where appropriate, fine art should be incorporated in the designs, with emphasis on the work of living American artists. Designs shall adhere to sound construction practice and utilize materials, methods and equipment of proven dependability. Buildings shall be economical to build, operate and maintain, and should be accessible to the handicapped.

2. The development of an official style must be avoided. Design must flow from the architectural profession to the Government, and not vice versa. The Government should be willing to pay some additional cost to avoid excessive uniformity in design of Federal buildings. Competitions for the design of Federal buildings may be held where appropriate. The advice of distinguished architects ought to, as a rule, be sought prior to the award of important design contracts.

3. The choice and development of the building site should be considered the first step of the design process. This choice should be made in cooperation with local agencies. Special attention should be paid to the general ensemble of streets and public places of which Federal buildings will form a part. Where possible, buildings should be located so as to permit a generous development of landscape.

A decade later, the National Endowment for the Arts, under the direction of Nancy Hanks, took it from there and launched a Federal Design Program. It does not exhaust itself with pious exhortations but seeks to bring leading designers and government officials together to work out practical and realistic guidelines for the design of federal architecture and graphics. It is a continuing program which is beginning to gain momentum and to come to grips with the very tough basic issues. The program's first, interim report, issued as "a framework for debate" is encouraging. It advocates:

1. Increased efforts to attract and keep talented design professionals in public service.
2. Improved patronage-proof methods of hiring architects and engineers for public works.
3. Design competitions for public works to discover talent and to excite public interest.
4. More attention to the siting and landscaping of public buildings as a catalyst of good urban design.
5. Adaptation of historic or architecturally interesting old buildings to new uses.
6. Public works budgets which include provisions for interior design, furnishing, and landscaping.
7. Follow-up evaluations of public buildings.
8. Multiple use of public buildings to make it possible, for instance, to have a cafe and a flower shop on the ground floor of a federal court house.

A most difficult problem is to get the federal government, and, more specifically, the General Services Administration, to hire the best available architects. GSA spends a lot of money on building design—and politicians like to help distribute it. There have been no public scandals involving favoritism and corruption in the selection of architects and engineers for federal buildings, as there have been in some states, notably in Maryland. But it is no secret that GSA administrators do not find it easy to resist suggestions by congressmen or governors as to whom to hire. Until Spiro Agnew's resignation, many architects and engineers had been heavy campaign contributors.

Some people have suggested that designers should be selected on the basis of competitive bids. But that seems a bad idea, simply because it is impossible to measure talent and experience in monetary terms. The lowest bidder may well also be the worst designer.

The Art Endowment's tentative recommendations to improve the way architects are chosen are most helpful and GSA has already changed its rules somewhat since they were published. But for all its advisory committees and elaborate new selection procedures, GSA still picks its architects in the inner recesses of its bureaucracy. What is not in the public light is at least suspected of being shady. Reasonably fool- and corruption-proof selection procedures should be open and written into law.

For their most important buildings, furthermore, federal, state, and local governments should hold design competitions. They are the best way to assure fresh, good design. Most European countries hold competitions as a matter of course. American public administrators generally do not like them because they cost extra effort and are alleged to cost more money for jurors, prizes, and administration although they can also save money. Bureaucrats also fear that competitions may yield designs some senator, governor, or mayor may not like. Established American architectural firms also do not like them because they do not like to risk their prestige, time, and effort on the chance of losing to some upstart. The advantage of competitions, however, is that they arouse much public interest and thereby help raise public awareness; that they force those who hold them to think about their building program and to be precise about their aims and requirements, and because they give young talent an opportunity to be recognized.

Basically, there are three ways government on all levels can and should become more active. It should:

1. prevent bad things from happening,
2. cause good things to happen, and
3. coordinate what it is doing.

Largely because of growing citizen concern, government is increasing its police powers to prevent environmental harm and pollution. Far too little is done to prevent ugliness, bad taste and the needless destruction.

One trouble is that our entire, complex system of building is all but completely indifferent to esthetics. The American "system" makes it generally more difficult and expensive to build something beautiful than to build something ugly. Real estate taxes, for instance, are geared to the appraised value of a property. That means if a man paints his house, he may have to pay higher taxes for the improvement, If he lets his house deteriorate, he will soon pay less because the value of the house has decreased. When the Seagram Building on New York's Park Avenue was completed, the city levied a higher tax on it than on other, less expensive buildings of the same size. Seagram was punished for lavishing money and care on Mies van der Rohe's masterwork.

Local building codes and zoning regulations, too, often inhibit good design, variety, and architectural interest. Their administrators tend to insist on bureaucratically prescribed ways of doing things—on methods rather than desired results. This leaves little room for creativity. Prescribed "minimum" standards for such amenities as open space, greenery, or ceiling height, are in effect the maximum most builders will give us.

It has only recently been discovered that zoning can be used as an instrument to achieve more attractive urban design. Some zoning commissions, for instance, will now give a developer an additional floor or two of rentable space in return for a little plaza. Or, to get more variety and creativity, some zoners now designate certain areas for "unit development." That means that the developer can mix high-rise and low-rise, residential and commercial, in a pleasing, lively arrangement, rather than stick to just one category of building and purpose. The commission approves or disapproves such "planned unit development," as it is called.

Preventing bad things from happening thus means first of all an examination of local tax laws and regulations to see where they help and where they hinder urban livability. This is too important to leave to the bureaucrats and experts alone. Taking advantage of the new interest in the urban environment, a national citizen organization such as the Urban Coalition might try to set up a research center and clearing house on these problems and encourage the formation of local committees of active citizens as well as experts to review and, if necessary, press for the amendment of the regulatory and tax aspects of building.

There is, furthermore, a need for more powerful art commissions and design review boards. By and large, they have worked well where the community wanted them to work well. It may be legally difficult to give review boards police powers. But they can be given sufficient political power to make life difficult for any greedy developer who wants to put up an ugly building that messes up the cityscape.

How does the review board know what is ugly and what is beautiful? Well, it doesn't. The best we can do is apply the same test the Supreme Court has applied to the question of what constitutes pornography. How do we ascertain "prevailing community standards" in architecture and urban design? We let community representatives in on the reviewing. Half of the members of the neighborhood and citywide architectural review boards should be lay citizens. The other half should be design professionals. Review board decisions should be binding. Reviews should include park benches and trash bins, public signs, outdoor advertising, and all the rest of what affects the urban environment.

More than just review is needed to preserve historic buildings and places that are private property. The first essential step is that demolition permits be delayed until public hearings are held, and the community has had time to reflect on the value of the building and find ways to save it. One method is the transfer of development rights, recently proposed by John J. Costonis of the

University of Illinois. The owner of a three-story landmark in a ten-story zone could, under this proposal, sell his rights to develop the unused seven stories to a neighbor. The neighbor would be allowed to build a seventeen-story building. This does not increase the overall density or automobile traffic in the neighborhood, so the planners are happy. It yields the landmark owner money to restore and maintain the old place, so he is happy too. And the neighbor is happy, of course, because a seventeen-story building increases his profits.

The Costonis proposal has worked in several instances. It also shows that good urban design is often as much a matter of administrative and legal ingenuity as of creative design talent.

Some cities, Washington, D.C., for example, now offer tax incentives for the preservation of important old buildings. National legislation to this effect is under consideration in Congress.

A good and increasingly popular way to save worthy old buildings is to "recycle" them for new use. All over the country, old factories are turned into attractive shopping centers, old warehouses into charming offices, and old mansions into elegant apartment houses. This trend to maintain historic continuity in our cityscape is the best thing that has happened to our cities since New York's Central Park was built and set a trend in other cities.

Government's second environmental duty—to cause good things to happen—is more difficult because it requires money. But not much, really. Most European countries and some American jurisdictions have legislation requiring that a small fraction of the construction cost of public works be devoted to their artistic embellishment. Most have settled on 2 percent. The federal government's General Services Administration now allocates one-half percent. Even that is not bad, if you consider that a $10 million construction budget gives us $50,000 for murals, sculpture, paintings, mosaics or other works of art.

The art allocation should be made mandatory for all public works on the part of all public agencies. Why should not army barracks have paintings? Why, more importantly, should not transit authorities put up sculptures in front of their subway stations or murals inside them? Why should not the State Highway Departments, which have wrought so much destruction in the environment, compensate by providing some delight? The beltway around Mexico City is dotted with marvelous sculptures large enough to be appreciated from a speeding car. They were created by some of the world's leading sculptors, such as Henry Moore, as part of Mexico's cultural Olympics in 1970. I could visualize giant sculptures, seen from afar, at important highway intersections. It would be inspiring if our drab and uniform turnpike restaurants and restrooms were turned into artistic oases. Even with a one-half percent art assessment, the highway builders would still have money left over to buy a whole Renaissance in our towns and cities.

The caveat here is to see that the money is actually spent on artistic embellishment, rather than on things the builders ought to be doing anyway.

Some governmental art funds have been spent on sodding front lawns and putting tile in the bathrooms.

Another danger is that too much money is spent on a few, fashionable artists, to buy prestige rather than creativity. Here, too, lay citizens and artists from the community, in addition to officials and experts, ought to make the decisions.

Art allocations are, of course, not the only good thing government can cause to happen. All public works, in fact, can be turned to environmental advantage once Americans decide to make their landscape and cityscape as tidy and attractive as most of them make their homes.

The Tennessee Valley Authority is one government agency which has adopted the premise that "the use of the earth for the good of man," as Gifford Pinchot put it, requires a comprehensive and multiple approach. In the Tennessee Valley, the planning and construction of flood control and hydroelectric power dams has long been combined with conservation, new recreation parks, handsomely designed new towns, and what might be called regional landscaping. Even the "temporary" workers' quarters for some of the power dams were made so attractive back in the 1930s, that they are still in use as popular vacation resorts.

This is not just a matter of huge TVA projects. For instance, TVA decided a few years ago that the grubby little town of Coeburn, Virginia, needed its river tamed because of incessant flood damage. The engineers soon realized that as long as they were building their embankments, they might as well build a walkway along the river opposite Coeburn's major stores. They lined the walkway with trees, shrubs and benches. And, while they were at it, they also built a screened parking lot to keep cars from cluttering up their new little park. Then they discovered that abandoned railroad station across the river. With TVA's help, and funds left over from the flood control program, it is now a community center. Coeburn is no longer a grubby town.

The third point—the need for the coordination of the government's environmental efforts—does not require much elaboration. It is ludicrous, for instance, that one agency of government labors to "revitalize" downtown, while other agencies of government are at great pains to locate their life-giving buildings and employment centers in the suburbs. One part of the government sets up elaborate procedures to save historic buildings, while another sends the federal bulldozers in early on a Sunday morning to destroy them before the procedures can be observed.

With government taking the lead, private enterprise will surely want to compete. In Rotterdam, not long ago, I literally stumbled across a delightful sculpture just standing there on the street. It was sponsored by a local department store, which must surely have figured that this permanent public delight bought more good will than its weight in fleeting television commercials.

It may not be enough to tell those who are worried about spending that a good environment is, in the end, less expensive than a mean one, and that the cost is small in proportion to both accountable and unaccountable benefits.

A better case was made most admirably five hundred years ago by the Florentine architect Antonio di Piero Aeverlino, known as Filarete. Defending his design of a ten-story tower of Vice and Virtue, which was to have a brothel on the ground floor and an astronomical observatory on the top, Filarete said:

I do not say this one can be built without great expense. Some buildings that are to be constructed cannot be produced (without) great expense, but magnanimous and great princes, and republics as well, should not hold back from building great and beautiful buildings because of the expense. No country was ever made poor nor did anyone ever die because of the construction of buildings. . . . In the end, when a large building is completed, there is neither more nor less money in the country, but the building does remain in the country or the city together with its reputation and honor.

Notes

1. August Heckscher, *The Public Happiness* (New York: Atheneum, 1962), pp. 232-33.

2. C.A. Doxiadis, *The Great Urban Crimes We Permit By Law* (Athens: Lycabuttus Press, 1973), pp. 12-15.

3. Cited in the *Washington Post*, December 30, 1972, p. B2. Quoted by permission of the author.

XVII My Philosophy

Charles H. Malik

Whatever the concrete content of what you have called "quality of life," this term certainly must mean that for the sake of which everything else exists. Quality of life then is "the ultimate for-the-sake-of-which." How well and how perfectly Aristotle understood this, and how well and how perfectly Heidegger in our own days understands it! The classical expression of it is of course Christ's meaning about what good the whole world would serve if we lost our soul, and his further injunction to seek first the kingdom of God and his righteousness, and all other things will then be added unto us. There is then something beside which the whole world is worthless, something which we must seek first; and this something is "the ultimate for-the-sake-of-which."

It follows that everything else that this Commission is concerned with—questions of energy and world stability, of food, health, and population, of raw materials, industrial development and world trade, of relatively open and relatively closed societies, and of international peace and security—is for the sake of, is with a view to, is subsidiary and ancillary to, this something. The economy, the environment, social justice, international peace and cooperation, each one of these concerns has its proper domain and validity—each has its own inner structures and laws which can be investigated and ascertained. But without essential reference to the ultimate quality of life which all these laws and conditions must subserve, the ascertaining of them turns into a veritable groping in the dark. One is lost then in the morass of relativity and caprice.

Quality of life is thus prior to everything else. It is in terms of it, it is as conducive to it, that everything else has to be judged and gauged. For the question is always, what you want the clean environment for, what you want health and education for, what you want the prosperous economy for, what you want international peace and security for. And this question traces itself implicitly upon the horizon of every endeavor of the Commission. It is in the presence of a quality of life already known and given that all these other endeavors can gather meaning and purpose.

Fundamentally, human nature has not changed and will never change. This is the rock of offense on which all false humanism in the end founders, I mean the humanism which imagines that man can overcome and master everything—including himself—alone. In fundamental matters Americans are not different from others. This simply means that they are human. The problem therefore is not so much the system or the conditions under which man lives as how to get to the core of his being. Certainly there are good and bad systems, and good and bad conditions, and the bad conditions ought to be changed, and sometimes they can be changed only by revolution. But even under the most perfect system and the ideal economic, social, and political conditions, man—be he American or Russian, Chinese or European, African or Asian—will still gossip and fear, hate and intrigue, fret and worry, covet and lust; he will still rejoice in the misfortunes of others; he will still be tempted by boundless ambition, and now and then he will fail and be frustrated; he will still go through moments of intense anxiety and despair; he will still have to die.

Or, even under relatively imperfect systems and conditions, man can still rise to wonderful heights of personal power and peace; he can still be cleansed and fortified by suffering; he can still repent and feel a sense of shame; he can still be moved to his depths by love and forgiveness; he can still seek the truth and rejoice in the vision of it; he can still be filled with hope, joy, and the inner freedom of the spirit; he can still be noble, magnanimous, unselfish, self-sacrificing; he can still be intensely aware of the mystery of death and wonder how it may be overcome.

In short, man can always, under every system and condition, still do the totally unexpected, whether towards good and being and the building up of others, when touched by God, or towards evil and not-being and the humiliation and destruction of others, when touched by darkness and rebellion.

Quality of life has to do precisely with this unchanging level of human existence. Without minimizing in the slightest the importance and malleability of the level of conditions and systems, it is this constant human nature, which the Bible simply calls the human heart, that must first and last be attacked. Again, what good does it do if you win the whole world, namely, if you make it perfect, and man remains the same?

How to reach the heart of man, how to touch his will and fundamental attitude—that is the question. Until one raises this question in its most radical character, and doggedly refuses to change the subject—and how much we are tempted precisely to change the subject in these matters:—one is still playing with trifles. And this question, under its human aspect, is precisely what religion is all about. For religion is, as Pascal would remark, the painstaking discovery over the ages of the fact that man—every son of man—is essentially capable of total depravity or of incredible holiness, or—and that is the usual mode—of a state somewhere in between. And quality of life means nothing if man's rebelliousness is not attacked at its roots, if there is not hope, trust, love, obedience, satisfaction, brokenness, community, happiness, rest, and peace, in the human heart.

America cannot mean only systems and conditions. Those who reduce the meaning of America only to systems and conditions are not—and I say it with all respect—worthy of America. America must mean something intellectual, moral, spiritual of the profoundest nature. It pains the lover of America to find that this spiritually hungry world, including the children of America itself, look elsewhere than to America for guidance in fundamental ideas. Being heir to 4000 years of cumulative history—and what history!—America has it in itself to mean all this. If it does not mean it now, it must mature this meaning in the future. That is what it must aim at for the year 1985 and the year 2000. And all this, not only in relation to the means and instruments of life, but to inner, personal, human existence.

It is useless to perfect systems and conditions leaving the human spirit to take care of itself. Being left empty, swept, and garnished, far from taking care of itself then, seven evil spirits will rush in to make their abode in it. And the end of that spirit will be far worse than its beginning. The end of perfect conditions in a perfect system, where the human spirit is simply left to take care of itself, stewing as it were in its own juice, will be far worse than the beginning. The spirit then will find itself hollow, idle, meaningless, bored, unhappy, and it will seek outlet in endless unrewarding activity; and if it should have lots of power, it would be tempted to indulge in the pastime of demonic destruction. Destruction will then be enjoyed for its own sake. Contradiction will then be an end in itself. Spite will then be exquisitely delightful. Pleasure will then be all that there is. Hatred will then be the rule of life, or, as the Nazis put it, "in the blood."

Above all, quality of life must mean the considerate man, the loving man, the man who cares, the humble man, the man who is broken in spirit, the man of sorrow and suffering, the forgiving man, the wise man, the free man, the responsible man, the man who acknowledges in his heart his own infirmities, and who, if he cannot master them, and to the extent he cannot master them, at least is always sad about them and always seeks forgiveness for them. And there is absolutely no other way of creating and propagating this type of man except by contagion, namely, by the antecedent presence of such men who will themselves infect others with what they are.

The magical-mechanical impatient itch persists; people will ask, this is all very well, but *how* do you *produce* such men, such spirits, such "quality of life"? It is the "how" of "production" that people are impatient about. And let me at once add that the more people are impatient about this deepest of all questions, the more the real answer to it will escape them. It needs original peace and quiet, it needs original patience and purity of heart, to discover "the how" of "the production" of the deepest quality of life.

Never by magic, never by chance, never mechanically, but always by contagion. And the search for the already existing men who are to effect the contagion becomes the most important search. And there is a deeper search still, the search, namely, of where these already existing men got their own contagion from.

How to cure man of the illusion that he can save himself by himself is the problem. He cannot. I need help from outside—not sentimental help, not psychological help, not help in the sense of material security or reassurance—but help in the form of already existing men and women who will fire my heart and move my will. That is why I take exception to the use of the term self-realization; it smacks too uncomfortably of Indian pantheistic subjectivism. For there are young men and women today who seriously believe that they are the measure of all things, that everything begins with them, that they can begin from scratch, that the lessons of history are all bunk. And once you start sliding on this path, obviously you will end up by allowing only either that which gives you the most intense immediate satisfaction, or that which swells up your pride. And all this without any regard for the consequences. The decay of our times consists in the worship of immediacy and the consequent disregard of consequences. Respect for the past and responsibility for the future—these are the two greatest qualitative lacks of the decadent present.

The quantitative, the material, the elemental can never by themselves mutate into the qualitative, the integral. There is a minimal material standard necessary for life to be called human at all. Above this minimal level everything is practically neutral so far as quality of life is concerned. In fact, the qualitative dangers of affluence far exceed its beneficent effects. The higher one rises in the scale of affluence, the greater the temptations to sloth and softness and degeneracy, the weaker the sharpness of his mind in qualitative discrimination and the determination of his will in decisive action. Decadence then sets in, for decadence is precisely the inability to discriminate and be decisive.

The realm of quality is a realm absolutely apart. It is a realm *sui generis*. It is altogether independent of quantity and matter. In fact, if there is a relationship between the two, it is that it creates quantity and matter, but quantity and matter can never create it. This is one of the half-a-dozen fundamental fallacies of this age—that the more and more by itself creates the better and better, that the parts create the whole. The exact opposite is the truth: the whole is prior to its parts, the whole supervenes independently of its parts, and the better and better comes from outside the more and more altogether. In our unhappy age quality, rank, excellence, order, depth are fighting for their life.

Unless there is goodness and compassion and a sense of truth and justice *to begin with*, these things will never turn up by merely making people healthy, educated, secure, law-abiding, and cooperative, or by enabling them to enjoy lots of leisure. Goodness, compassion, truth, etc., come from existing persons who are themselves already good, compassionate, truthful. The same is true of freedom: unless people were originally free themselves in their traditions and institutions, they would never become free by merely giving them independence and setting them forth on the path of development. Where people got these qualities originally themselves from is of course the great question. But mere piling and compiling will never produce them. David cries: "If the foundations be destroyed, what can the righteous do?" The answer is, Nothing. And the foundations are always of the character of an independently existing spirit.

This extraordinary fountainhead of strength and certainty and wisdom which is the Bible! What question it does not answer concerning the quality of life, what wonderful vista it does not open, and always with a majesty all its own! A few simple passages chosen almost at random will suffice:

O Lord, rebuke me not in thine anger, neither chasten me in thy hot displeasure. Have mercy upon me, O Lord; for I am weak.

If thou, Lord, shouldest mark iniquities, O Lord, who shall stand? But there is forgiveness with thee, that thou mayest be feared.

Seek ye the Lord while he may be found, call ye upon him while he is near.

Knowledge puffeth up, but charity edifieth. And if any man think that he knoweth anything, he knoweth nothing yet as he ought to know.

I can do all things through Christ which strengtheneth me.

And so I say, if there is decay, and whenever there is decay, believe me it is because the Bible has been neglected; and if you seriously want quality of life at its truest and deepest, restore by 1985 or by the year 2000 love and reverence for the Bible into the heart of America; for without the Bible America would never have come into being, neither would it have flourished and endured.

Somebody must find out in the most thorough and authoritative manner what exactly happened in the American institutions of higher learning during the last two generations—what happened in terms of quality of mind, quality of life, quality of spirit, and art of expression; I mean the decay in great ideas, in excellence of character, in norms of beauty, in turning to something real, given and above. Such a study is likely to reveal truths that could spark a revolution of the first order. And it is this revolution about the spiritual state of affairs in the great citadels of learning that America needs in the coming generation above everything else.

For a dark spirit descended upon the universities and seized practically every department in them. I am not referring to the scientific and technical depart- ments—these have made immense advances, and doubtless more and more Nobel Prize winners will come from them. I am thinking rather of the humanities and

the liberal arts, of the social sciences, of the soul- and mind- and character-form-
ing disciplines. I am thinking of literature, history, politics, economics, sociology, psychology, philosophy, theology, and the fine arts. In the nature of
university organization this spirit tends to perpetuate itself.

It is the spirit of skepticism and uncertainty; the spirit of utility and
movement; the spirit of rebellion, denial, and contradiction; the spirit of
subjectivism and human self-sufficiency; the spirit of materialism and atheism;
the spirit of hedonism and moral relativism; the spirit of Freud and linguistic
analysis; the spirit of endless trial and search, as though the fundamental things
were not already known; the spirit of naively or tendentiously interpreting the
past through the prejudices of the present; the spirit of turning against the tested
and tried values; the leveling-down spirit; the spirit which subjectivizes truth and
makes it the outcome of cleverness and the balance of blind forces.

The Americans must ask themselves, is this the best they can do in the realm
of the mind, is this what their greatest men in the 200 years of their independent
existence—their great statesmen, poets, thinkers, saints—would recognize as their
own? Is this what the greatest men in history—David, Socrates, Plato, Aristotle,
Paul, Augustine, Dante, Pascal, Goethe—men who in varying degrees belong to
their own heritage, would applaud and recognize as their own?

The pluralism of American society cannot mean the smothering, the leveling
down, of the distinctive and deep. It can only mean providing the distinctive and
deep, in a climate of freedom, with the opportunity to deepen further and to
flourish, certainly side by side with what is not as distinctive and deep.

For America there is no salvation outside the Greco-Roman-Judaeo-Christian
tradition. With due respect to all other traditions this is unique. It is unique in
the vastness of its diversity, the immensity of its history extending for four or
five thousand years, its continuity, and its unity. Those who seek the salvation
of America outside this tradition have lost their soul. For the quality of life you
are seeking is already given you here in full. It is the passion for beauty, truth
and order; it is faith in the ability of reason to grasp the truth; it is the reign of
law, in the soul through moral discipline, and in society through justice; it is the
affirmation of the ultimacy of the individual human person; it is the proclamation that there is a real God who is one, and whose fear is the beginning of all
knowledge; it is the historical certainty that this very God had compassion on us,
and came and dwelt amongst us, and his name is forgiveness and love.

Nothing is deeper than all this—nothing is as deep. And you have it all at the
base of your being.

XVIII

The Third Generation and the Third Century: Choices Concerning the Quality of American Life

Daniel P. Moynihan

Abstract: There are two critical choices affecting the quality of American life. The first is how much growth we want; the second is how much government we want.

What Do We Mean?

In a letter to his wife Abigail in 1780, John Adams wrote of his duty to study "the science of government . . . more than all other sciences. . . ." In his view, for his time:

Acknowledgments

This essay was written in the spring of 1975. Publication was delayed, and I have accordingly, a year later, made some changes to accommodate recent events, mostly by way of providing more recent statistics. I find the main themes have survived a year of events and nonevents such as combine to set the fashion in public issues. Had they not it were questionable whether the paper should be published at all!

There are some changes, however, which are owing directly to the generous and extensive comments which I have received from a number of my fellow members of the Commission on Critical Choices. I forbear to mention their names, as they might very well not wish to be associated with the result. They know who they are, and I would like in this manner for them to know also of my gratitude to them. As ever, I am indebted to David Riesman and Andrew M. Greeley for indefatigable and invaluable criticism. For them, knowledge has become a form of grace.

Jacqueline Stark was my associate in this study, and it could not have been done without her.

I have tried to follow where facts have led, and perhaps have had some success. I have no great illusions, however. The facts have *proven* little. And there are doubtless other facts, unknown to me. What follows then is not so much research as reflections. The text is filled with judgments which many will question, which makes it all the more important that it be understood that I alone am responsible for them.

The arts of legislation & administration & negotiation ought to take the place of, indeed to exclude, in a manner, all other arts. I must study politics and war, that my sons may have liberty to study mathematics and philosophy. My sons ought to study mathematics & philosophy, geography, natural history & naval architecture, navigation, commerce & agriculture, in order to give their children the right to study painting, poetry, music, architecture, statuary, tapestry & porcelain.[1]

It is a thought worthy of Pareto, and one wonders how much Adams would approve the extraordinary fulfillment of his vision. (Surely he would have hoped for *some* carryover of the disciplines of sterner times: At one point recently the proportion of students at what he called "our University of Cambridge," the proportion of graduates proposing to enter "commerce" dropped to 5.5 percent.) Yet most of us today would acknowledge a movement of politics away from the concerns of the first two generations of Adams, if we may use that image, toward the concerns of the third generation—at least among those Americans who can be thought of as inheriting a measure of substance and tradition from their past.

This appears to be a change in our national life, and poses the challenge to government which any change will do. And on this score it is well to recall a not less prophetic observation of Adams in a letter to Jefferson of 1813: "While all other sciences have advanced, that of government is at a stand; little better understood, little better practiced now than 3 or 4 thousand years ago.[2]

"Quality," said the physicist Ernest Rutherford, "is nothing but poor quantification." Some who speak of the "quality of life" will very likely find in such a statement just those aspects of modern society which concern them: a seemingly pervasive materialism, a philistine denial of spiritual and aesthetic values as evidenced in, well, the quality of things. And yet what spiritual and aesthetic achievement has the modern age witnessed more splendid than that of nuclear physics, an achievement preceded, accompanied, and followed by meticulous, painstaking measurements?

This point acquires further salience when it is recalled that Rutherford was talking about the term quality as applied to physical phenomena. In the early history of modern science the term was much in use—to explain, one fears, that which could not otherwise be explained. In time, of course, more specific—and quantifiable—concepts took over. And yet the term ought not to be discarded. When, for example, we read in William James that "the Alpha and Omega in a university is the tone of it, and . . . this tone is set by human personalities exclusively," we know what he means. And we may reflect that the qualitative term he uses here—tone—is susceptible to exact quantification when applied to music. And why not in other matters? Obviously, we are groping here, but just as obviously we are onto something real.

The question is what is to be measured? To talk of the quality of life is to talk of something. Or many things. Which? One might, not unreasonably, consult that admirable publication *Social Indicators*,[3] recently begun by the United States government, to learn if things now being measured correspond sufficiently to what we think ought to be meant by quality of life such that we move directly to the issue of how matters fare. And yet only one entry appears directly related, "Quality of Employment Life." This, of course, is a venerable social indicator, having first appeared as "job satisfaction," and reflecting a long-established concern of the Bureau of Labor Statistics with working conditions. Here we learn that, in 1973, over 90 percent of American workers would be classified as "very satisfied" with their jobs, or "somewhat satisfied." This appears to be the case for workers of all races, most ages, both sexes, and for the widest range of income and occupation. On a scale of 1 to 4, only youth, workers age sixteen to twenty, show a mean satisfaction score under 3. On the other hand, workers fifty-five years and over have the highest mean score, and, importantly, low status occupations such as "operatives" and "service workers" show scores almost as high as "professional" and "manager." Moreover, these assessments, which are those of the workers themselves, appear quite stable over time. The overall degree of satisfaction recorded in 1969 was virtually the same as that of 1973.

What else can *Social Indicators* tell us? There is a section on "Leisure Time." Americans have a good deal of it, and watch a lot of television. A section "Housing Quality" reports that, in 1940, 48.6 percent of all housing in America was substandard; by 1970, this had declined to 7.4 percent. But here, one feels, a traditional category of measurement has merely been embellished by the new term "quality." There is an entry, "Persons Afraid to Walk Alone at Night," that seems to get at the *kind* of thing persons concerned with quality of life seem to be getting at, and here the data suggest why such concern is said to be rising. In 1965, 49 percent of females said they *were* afraid to walk alone at night. By 1972, this proportion had risen to 61 percent. And yet at this point, with few if any further entries that seem to touch on what we feel we are looking for, we face the probability that whatever quality of life is, it is not something now being systematically measured. We suspect this is what Rutherford was getting at: Quality is what you say when you can not state precisely what you mean.

This is hardly to dismiss the subject. To the contrary, when in the life of individuals, of communities, of nations, a longing appears, an unease, a dissatisfaction with things as they are, it is fair to assume that something may be changing with respect to fundamental orientations. Long settled patterns of motivation may be shifting. People may be changing their minds, an event that does not happen too often, but does nonetheless happen. The strength of democratic government—one reason ours now approaches its Bicentennial—is that when this does happen social arrangements can usually change also, such that after a period of mounting disequilibrium, a new stability emerges.

Something of this order appears to be taking place in the United States, while remarkable resonant developments appear in other industrial democracies, such that the impression grows that cultural rather than merely political forces are abroad. The concept of post-industrial society advanced by Daniel Bell is the most elaborate effort yet made to encompass these changes in a general theory. Predictably, post-industrial society comes to question the preoccupation with economic growth which characterized its predecessor. Or if this was not predictable, it may be said to be logical. There are trade-offs between the acquisition of material goods and the acquisition of other "goods"—leisure as an example—which individuals, once freed from what Engels called "the realm of necessity," deal with all the while, seeking to maximize well being from a "mix" of things, of which produced goods and services is but one component.

As with individuals, so with society. The question of how much *government* growth also arises, albeit answers differ. That the growth of government should be an issue, if not necessarily predictable, certainly *was* predicted. From Aldous Huxley to George Orwell, the spread of government regulation into what de Tocqueville called the "minor details of life" has been part of the prophetic vision of the modern age. But where the first question is much discussed, the second is not. In part, this may arise from the issue of Big Government having been too much discussed at a time when government was anything *but* big. In part, it arises from the seeming tendency of those who would restrict economic growth to turn to government (and hence to government growth) to bring this about. In general, the tendency of those who would change America, for the better, is to seek to do so through an increase in government, even though—such will be an argument of this discussion—it is often the aftermath of previous increases in government which are the conditions it is hoped to change. If this proposition is correct, and to the extent that it is, there is at least a modest hope that social science may help to clarify matters, might even contribute to some resolution.

In 1932, the Committee on Recent Social Trends, submitting its report to President Hoover, remarked that it did "not wish to exaggerate the role of intelligence in social direction," and neither should we.[4] The Committee's assessment of the situation then seems to hold for the present also. "Social action . . . is the resultant of many forces among which in an age of science and education, conscious intelligence may certainly be reckoned as one."[5] One force only, and in no way the most important. Still, it is a defensible belief, based on American experience, that a conscious and hopefully intelligent effort to learn what is bothering us could provide some marginal assistance in what appears to be an incipient revolution of sort, using the term revolution as the founders of the American republic would originally have understood it—that is, as a turning of a circle to a new position, showing forth a different range of principles and preferences in a still joined and harmonious whole. Conscious intelligence may help us to discern what these new principles and preferences may be, and if we do that, we can expect some success with the task of measuring the quality of life as a prelude to improving it.

What Do We Know?

Perhaps we shall have some success. A severe modesty is required as one approaches a subject this large and ill-defined. Moreover, while there has been, within the past generation, a quantum change both in the availability of social data and the means and the methods of analyzing it, it is not so certain that there has been a corresponding increase in the analysis and synthesis of such information as guides for national decision making. Certainly, presidential efforts of this order have shown a formidable decline in quality over the past two generations. During this span of time, three presidents have undertaken systematic enquiries into the state of the nation with respect to large matters of shifting values and judgments, as well as changing conditions. As this is an activity widely and reasonably enough associated with "national planning," it is not without interest that each of the three, President Hoover, President Eisenhower, and President Nixon, was thought by his contemporaries to be more on the conservative side of issues than otherwise—a fact which at least suggests that the correspondence between an interest in centralized economic direction and a comparable interest in comprehensive social assessment is not as strong as is routinely assumed. But more noteworthy is the decline in quality. The first effort, that of President Hoover, resulted in a major scholarly, indeed intellectual achievement, the formidable two-volume report *Recent Social Trends*. It was accompanied by an equally distinguished series of monographs on specific subjects. Almost three decades later, President Eisenhower's Commission on National Goals issued its study *Goals for Americans*, a thoroughly competent, and at points, distinguished study, but if such a comparison may be admitted, a quarter of the size of the earlier effort, and with but little associated scholarship. A decade after that, the first report of President Nixon's National Goals Research Staff, *Toward Balanced Growth: Quantity with Quality*, if not without redeeming features, appeared almost as a fugitive publication in a government setting profoundly suspicious of its essentially undemanding prescriptions.

Too much can be inferred from a sequence of unrelated government reports, and yet one is impressed by the decline in confidence, in the sense of potential mastery, to be sensed in these studies—displayed in them! This is all the more striking in view of the settings in which the successive reports emerged. *Recent Social Trends*, two huge, imposing, authoritative volumes, appeared at the depth of the worst economic depression in American history. The "inarticulate misery of the hundreds of thousands or millions of breadwinners who are deprived of their livelihoods through no fault of their own"[6] is acknowledged throughout the text: But it had not made miserable men or women of the authors.[a] In part this equipoise arose from the laissez-faire assignment they had undertaken. They wrote:

[a]Wesley C. Mitchell of Columbia University was chairman, with Charles E. Merriam, vice-chairman, Shelby M. Harrison, Alice Hamilton, Howard W. Odum and William F. Ogburn. The investigation was made possible by a grant from the Rockefeller Foundation.

We were not commissioned to lead the people into some new land of promise, but to retrace our recent wanderings, to indicate and interpret our ways and rates of change, to provide maps of progress, make observations of danger zones, point out hopeful roads of advance, helpful in finding a more intelligent course in the next phase of our progress.[7]

And they did just that, albeit, they interpreted their charge in a rather more directive manner—"point out hopeful roads of advance"—than their sponsor may have intended. Appointed in the autumn of 1929, they submitted their report three years later. In his Foreword, President Hoover, weeks away from defeat by Franklin D. Roosevelt, noted with laconic indirection: "Since the task assigned to the Committee was to inquire into changing trends, the result is emphasis on elements of instability rather than stability in our social structure."[8]

In truth, the Committee came close to writing the agenda of the New Deal—"a change in the distribution of income," "a solvent unemployment fund," "social insurance," "economic planning." The report pointed to the anomalies of American life: "splendid technical proficiency in some incredible skyscraper and monstrous backwardness in some equally incredible slum." It dealt with just those general subjects which would take up so much of American public life in the generations that followed: "Minority Groups," "Labor in Society," "Women," "Public Welfare and Social Work," "Schools," "Medicine," "Crime," "Growth of Governmental Functions." Some of its concerns would at first recede in interest in the years that followed and then come forward once again: "Ethnic Groups and Immigration Policies," "Rural Trends and Problems," "The Arts," "corruption and ineffectiveness of much of our governmental machinery." Whatever else the Committee's Report achieved, it certainly demonstrated that "conscious intelligence" can make an impressive judgment as to what is going to be bothering a society for a half century to come. "Poverty," the Committee noted, "is by no means vanquished. . . ." Even during the "late period of unexampled prosperity there was much poverty in certain industries and localities, in rural areas as well as in cities which was not of a temporary or accidental nature." In the midst of the depression the task at hand was to "regain our former standards," but the "longer and the greater task to achieve standards socially acceptable, will remain."[9]

Recent Social Trends was remarkable for many things, and not least for the candor and clarity with which the Committee set forth, at the outset, its conviction that science and technology—the work of that second Adams generation—was the primary source of the social trends it was tracing. "The automobile affects the railroads, the family, size of cities, types of crime, manners and morals." It set forth a simple, determinist sequence:

Scientific discoveries and inventions instigate changes first in the economic organization and social habits which are most closely associated with them. Thus factories and cities, corporations and labor organizations have grown up in response to technological developments.

The next great set of changes occurs in organizations one step further removed, namely in institutions such as the family, the government, the schools and the churches. Somewhat later, as a rule, come changes in social philosophies and codes of behavior. . . .[10]

This, of course, is no more than Marx and Engels set forth eighty-four years earlier in the *Manifesto of the Communist Party*. Addressing the "bourgeoisie," they declared:

Your very ideas are but the outgrowth of the conditions of your bourgeois production and bourgeois property, just as your jurisprudence is but the will your class made into law for all, a will whose essential character and direction are determined by the economical conditions of existence of your class.[11]

Recent Social Trends had no doubts about the institutional impact of technology. "Of the great social organizations," the Committee wrote, "two, the economic and the governmental, are growing at a rapid rate, while two other . . . the church and the family, have declined. . . ."[12] Marx and Engels would not have been distressed by this trend, and could fairly claim to have foreseen it. The *Manifesto* speaks of the "bourgeois claptrap about the family," an institution based wholly on "capital, on private gain." It noted "the practical absence of the family among the proletarians" and presumedly looked to the family's general decline, along with the bourgeois decline, which the Great Depression surely adumbrated. And yet there is a profound difference between the two documents. The *Manifesto* looks to technology to bring about a wholesale transformation of the society in a very short order; *Recent Social Trends* has no such apocalyptic view.[b] It assumed that what had been happening would go on happening. If it was in this respect unHegelian, it was nonetheless far more scientific. Compared with Mitchell and Merriam, Marx and Engels come off rather as gifted eccentrics: one could as well imagine them in white robes sitting on top of a middle-western hilltop with other folk of the nineteenth century, waiting for the end of the world.

Mitchell and Merriam's world went on, and so did the trends they forecast. Years later, President Eisenhower's Commission on National Goals met to consider the subject further. It was hardly a less distinguished group, broader in its composition, and even more so, perhaps, in its resources. (Again the Rockefeller Foundation helped, and again the project was based at Columbia

---

[b]Wesley C. Mitchell wrote:

Our best hope for the future lies in the extension to social organization of the methods that we already employ in our most progressive fields of effort. In science and in industry . . . we do not wait for catastrophe to force new ways upon us. . . . We rely, and with success, upon quantitative analysis to point the way; and we advance because we are constantly improving and applying such analysis.

University.) The times, of course, were different. War had come and gone, prosperity had returned. The habit—the condition—of command had come to American life. President Eisenhower, himself not inexperienced in such matters, appointed to his Commission men who had led great armies, governed conquered nations, launched vast scientific enterprises. Much of this is reflected in the Commission's report. It prescribed where its predecessors at most predicted. "We were not commissioned," the earlier committee had written, "to lead the people into some new land of promise, but to retrace our recent wanderings. . . ." Not so this new body of university presidents, board chairmen, former ambassadors, and generals. They had been commissioned to set forth goals, and they did so, although not without awareness that there was a certain preemptive quality to the enterprise. Just what "people" wanted, and what they understood of what they wanted, was not always that clear. In "A Great Age for Science," an essay prepared for the Commission, Warren Weaver took note of a then recent comment in *The New Yorker*:

These are hard times for the layman. He is no longer thought competent to work out his own opinions on many matters, even many that touch him intimately. His very survival has become the property of committees and the subject of learned argument. . . . He has little to say . . . being largely ignorant of the information upon which plans for him are based.[13]

A problem that, but one for which a solution existed. If people did not understand science—teach it to them. The report was everywhere rational, decent, optimistic, and incremental. In almost every area of concern it was judged that more of what then was would get us where we wished to be. Thus after "The Individual," concern for "Equality" was foremost of the social questions examined. The Commission found "Vestiges of religious prejudice, handicaps to women, and, most important, discrimination on the basis of race. . . ."[14] It condemned them and proposed that the 1960s be the decade in which we "sharply lower these last stubborn barriers." Yet it insisted on the reality of progress:

We have ever more closely approached a classless society; there has been a revolution in the status of women; education is more nearly available to all; most citizens have opportunities a century ago were dreamed of by only a handful.[15]

With equal assertion, it set forth a program essentially of government actions, which *could* be carried forward in the 1960s, given the rates of economic growth also proposed, and which *would*—such everywhere was the implication or assertion—bring about palpable and perceived further progress. Good things were ahead: for "The Democratic Process," for "The Quality of American Culture," for "Meeting Human Needs," for "The United States' Role in the World." There would be "A Great Age for Science."

Decades earlier the Committee on Recent Social Trends had cautioned: "there are important elements in human life not easily stated in terms of efficiency, mechanization, institutions, rates of change. . . ."[16] Happiness, the Committee noted, is "one of our most cherished goals" yet "little studied by science." Prudent observations, as the 1960s were to reveal, for in the course of that decade, one after another of the goals set forth by the Eisenhower Commission was reached and surpassed, yet in the end there was the utmost questioning among those elements of the nation concerned with such matters. Whatever the nation was by 1970, it was not happy. Forecasts had come true; goals had been met; there had been abundant success: and yet the quality of life seemed sadly deficient. If science still knew little of the sources of happiness and unhappiness, some advances had been made in measuring it, and recurrently such measures showed decline. Using a scaling technique developed by Hadley Cantril and Lloyd A. Free, a survey taken in January 1971 found Americans quite content with their personal lives, with a sense of their situation having improved and the expectation that it would continue to do so. But the nation was seen as having declined, the rarest phenomenon. By 1971, this measurement technique had been used in nations throughout the world. On only one other occasion, the Philippines in 1959, had citizens reported their nation as having declined in this way. Americans expected things to pick up for the country, but slowly. It would take time just to get back up to where we had been.[17]

Three instances will illustrate the extent to which the goals of the Eisenhower Commission were achieved during the decade for which they were set. The economic advisors to the Commission projected an average annual growth rate of Gross National Product of 3.3 percent.[18] They suggested ways this *could* be increased to 4.0 percent, and clearly hoped it would be. It was. Four percent was precisely the growth rate for the decade. The very considerable increment in income which that small difference in rate implies became available to the society.

The Commission was concerned by the inadequacy of federal government salaries, and the presumed difficulty this caused in obtaining "more public servants equal in competence and imagination to those in private business and the professions." It called for "a drastic increase in their compensation." Under President Kennedy the principle of "comparability" was adopted for federal pay scales, such that the executive salaries rose sharply (at least at first). In 1960, average annual earnings of federal civilian employees were 24 percent higher than those in all private industries; by 1970, they were 41 percent higher.[19] In general, throughout the decade, government pay grew faster than nongovernment pay.[c]

Thus two proposals: one grandly global, the other rather parochial. In between, having both global and parochial qualities, was the Commission's

[c]Neal R. Peirce has calculated that for the period 1955-73, private wages increased 129 percent, federal civilian wages 183 percent, and state-local general government wages 165 percent. (Peirce, "Fiscal Relations," *National Journal Reports* 7, 8 (February 22, 1975):283.)

proposal on education. The Committee on Recent Social Trends had viewed with some pride "the most successful single effort. which government in the United States has ever put forth," to wit, that of those of high school age, about half were then in school. By 1960, far more ambitious standards had been achieved. *Completing* high school, and going on to college had become the measure of achievement. The Commission noted: "In a few states four-fifths of the youth complete four years of high school and one-half enroll in an institution of higher education. This is a majestic accomplishment."[20] But these were after all practical men; they called for a lesser goal for the nation as a whole: "Within the next decade at least two-thirds of the youth in every state should complete twelve years of schooling and at least one-third enter college."[21] Yet by 1972, 56 percent of female high school graduates entered postsecondary education, and 58 percent of males.[22] The Commission proposed that "government expenses at all levels must amount to $33 billion for education by 1970." In the event, the 1970 amount was $57 billion.[d]

And yet we were not happy. Economic growth came to be seen by many more as a problem than as a solution to problems. The very efficiency of government managers, such as it was, came by equally many to be seen as a primary threat to things of far greater value than efficiency. Even where values stayed steadily in place, and few perceptions changed, the 1960s did exceptional damage to the notion that government knows how to obtain the social results it nominally desires.

Education, a near universal public service, and to most minds perhaps the most important one, was hardest hit of all, and will serve to illustrate *this* "unanticipated consequence." Put plainly, in the first half of the decade, all manner of enquiries were launched to demonstrate what everyone knew, which is that in education there is a reasonable and direct relation between expenditure and results. By the end of the decade this belief was in ruins. Indeed, as expenditure increased, it appeared that "results" were actually declining! If there was no cause for actual alarm, it is nonetheless the case that *this* is what had to be explained as the decade wore on. By the mid-1970s, all manner of worrisome trends were appearing in educational achievement. A chart in the 1975 edition of *The Condition of Education*, the annual compendium of the National Center for Education Statistics, states, "Achievement in science measured by National Assessment declined slightly over a 3-year period for all age groups." A headline in the *New York Times* reports "H.E.W. Study Cites a Possible 'Slightly Negative Trend' in Children's Reading Ability."[e] *The Condition of Education* reported that the participation of three and four year olds in prekindergarten programs had almost tripled in the period 1964-1973, and that minority students, with 19.6 percent enrollment in 1973, had the highest proportion of all. Yet the former head of the American Psychological Associ-

[d]$39.2 billion in 1960 dollars.
[e]March 18, 1975.

ation was forced to state "even now we have no compensatory [education] method, reproducible on a large scale, of demonstrated value." In rejoinder, another psychologist came near to asserting that such programs *must* be worthwhile inasmuch as Congress had recently appropriated $1.2 billion to extend one in particular for a three-year period.

Doubts were expressed about the validity and usefulness of tests to measure such matters. But this was in part at least reactive, for there were few social programs of the period which had not come under exceptionally melancholy scrutiny. In 1974, the National Academy of Sciences issued a not uncharacteristic report on the manpower training programs, the first major federal initiative in social policy to follow the report of the Goals Commission.

Manpower training programs have been in existence a little over a decade, yet . . . little is known about the educational or economic effects of manpower training programs. This is troublesome, especially in the light of the fact that about $180 million have been spent in an attempt to evaluate these programs.

It would be an exaggeration to depict the proposals of the Eisenhower Commission as having been uniformly achieved in the decade that followed. Unemployment levels, for example, were below 4 percent, as the Commission proposed, for only *four* years of the decade. But, in the main, the style of American national life in the ensuing period did very much reflect the concepts embodied in the Commission report, and in no one thing more than in the ideal of "strong presidential leadership." This was not explicit in the report (the phrase is from Morton Grodzins' paper on "The Federal System") but it was a precondition, or almost that, of the great bulk of the Commission's proposals, which envisaged a strong, confident, and purposeful United States setting things right at home and, to no small degree, abroad.

At this remove it is difficult for anyone and especially for those who are young, to realize just how general and unquestioning was the support for the policies, especially foreign policies, of the early 1960s which later came to be anathematized in terms that would seemingly preclude any possibility of earlier endorsement.

Hence how very different, the tone of the 1970 report *Toward Balanced Growth: Quantity with Quality*, the work of the National Goals Research Staff, established in the White House by President Nixon in 1969. In keeping with the feeling of the time that "social accounting" ought to be a continuous process (in the final hours of the Johnson administration, a prototype "social report" had been issued), the Goals Staff was directed to issue an annual publication. As a matter of deliberate choice, the Hoover rather than Eisenhower example was to be followed. This annual report was not to be a prescriptive exercise. Rather, its task was merely to be "setting forth some of the key choices open to us [as a nation] and examining the consequences of those choices." The president had written:

It is my hope that this report will then serve as a focus for the kind of lively widespread discussion that deserves to go into decisions affecting our common future. The key point is this: it will make such discussion possible while there still is time to make the *choices* effective. Instead of lamenting too late what might have been, it will help give us, as a people, both the luxury and the responsibility of conscious and timely *choice*. [My emphasis.] [23]

As for the grand undertakings of the past, the Counsellor's Statement, introducing the 1970 report, was perhaps not inappropriately cautionary. "A law of proportionality obtains in the affairs of men. He who would make no little plans must expect to make no small mistakes." [24]

Yet clearly there were choices to be made. The State of the Union Message had forecast a $500 billion increase of GNP in the decade then commencing, an increase greater than the whole of the growth of the American economy from 1790 to 1950. The 1970 report chose to concentrate on four "emerging debates," which manifestly reflected views of considerable ambivalence about this prospect.

Population. The traditional view of population growth as a source of national pride and strength is being re-examined. . . . The merits of sheer size now appear more debatable. . . .

Environment. Historically, our concern over resources focused on whether there would be enough. . . . Today . . . the concern is about the ability of land, air, and water to absorb all the wastes we generate.

Basic Natural Science. To the extent that it was discussed at all in the past, it was generally agreed that science should grow according to its own internal logic. . . . Today . . . many persons, including members of the scientific community, are concerned over the possibility that the knowledge they develop will be used for ends they do not approve. Thus, knowledge is no longer seen as necessarily good. . . . To what extent should basic natural science be permitted to develop in a free unguided manner?

Consumerism. The abundant flow of new consumer goods has been viewed as a clear indication that the economy brings vast direct benefits to the American people. Yet, in the past decade, this virtue has been questioned. [25]

Whatever else, such a list suggests clearly enough that the quality of life, whatever exactly it might be, was becoming an almost political issue in a way that had never occurred before. In 1971, the Institute for Social Research of the University of Michigan conducted a survey of the subject, the first effort of its kind. The results sufficiently confirmed the judgment of the National Goals Research Staff that "emerging debates" about American goals were of a different order from those current at mid-century. By contrast with the more established categories of national goals, where all could agree that conditions improved, and most could desire that they go on doing so, the predominant judgment about the quality of life was that it had deteriorated. If the Committee on Recent Social Trends had maintained its psychological buoyancy in the face of economic collapse, the American public four decades later seemed in almost the opposite circumstance. Half the sample felt that on balance life had not changed, or that where change had occurred the good had about evened out the bad. But of the remaining half, two out of three felt that, "all things considered," things were getting worse. There were some bitter Americans, hating the life America gave them. Nine percent of those interviewed said they would like to "settle down for good in some other country." Another 6 percent could imagine doing so.

These sentiments would not disturb other nations, or at least would come as no surprise to them. In Europe, for example, even the most stable and outwardly successful societies win only moderate approval from their citizens, of whom considerable numbers not only continue to talk of emigrating, but do emigrate. Nor should it be assumed that the findings disturbed Americans in the sense of surprising them. Little is revealed which in some manner we had not been telling one another for some time. An announcement of the survey findings was perhaps slightly oblique:

Some groups are far more critical of the quality of American life than others. Surprisingly, the persons most satisfied generally with life in the United States today are those who have ostensibly gained the least—those with the smallest incomes and the least education.

Forty-five percent of people with a grammar school education are very satisfied compared to 22 percent of the college graduates; 42 percent of those with a family income of less than $3,000 are very satisfied compared to 31 percent of those with an income over $17,000.[26]

This is not exclusively so. In the ISR study and many other surveys, black Americans are shown to be substantially less satisfied with their lives than are whites, but this accords with the common-sense judgment that persons who have been discriminated against and are less well off by many, if not most indicators of economic well being, will reflect this disadvantage in their psychological attitudes. But why should those *better off* feel worse off?

Before adopting too simple a view of this seeming anomaly—which is to say, before assuming that the middle class is somehow rising in revolt against fraudulent values and false-consciousness—it were well to recall James Q. Wilson's dictum that in a liberal society almost all political arguments are arguments *within* the middle classes. (The *Communist Manifesto* was an argument *within* the European bourgeoisie.) A clue to the nature of the argument can be had from Angus Campbell's comment on the responses of the ISR sample of Americans which was interviewed on the quality of life:

Most prominent of their criticisms . . . is the belief that economic conditions have worsened, with inflation and taxation most frequently mentioned. Crime, drug use, declining morality, public protests and disorders, and various aspects of environmental pollution are cited by significant numbers of people as evidence of 'things getting worse'.[27]

An image of W.E.B. DuBois helps clarify these responses. He once compared a people to a vast army on the march, spread out for miles on miles. Those in the van know little of events in the rear, and vice versa. Those in the middle get only confused reports from either. Complete misunderstanding and total ignorance are equally common. And yet one collective event is in process; the group is on the move.

Heading where? Lee J. Cronbach has offered a persuasive hypothesis:

In the first half of this century the American system turned from laissez faire to rationalization, system, and an increasingly managerial government. The world view entrenched before World War II is now under attack, and an alternative scheme that cherishes pluralism, affiliations with local communities, and fulfillment rather than "perfection" is taking shape.[28]

We acquire some sense of this movement from the three presidential reports that have been discussed. The first, arising out of a laissez-faire world but troubled by its failures, proposed the extension to public affairs and to the society at large of just that rationality, system, and management, which in economic activity—in business—had showed both extraordinary potential and performance. The second report was all rationality and systematic management—as the first report would have wished. The third report, however, reflected the disillusion and anxiety which all this system and management had somehow brought about. These were not, then, disconnected events. One flowed from the other.

In just this sense, it is essential that the unhappy citizens whose responses Angus Campbell describes *not* be seen as a uniform group reflecting a common opinion. To the absolute contrary, it should be assumed—there is evidence enough for this—that what we see there is an amalgam of unhappiness, three reasonably distinct groups expressing unhappiness from three reasonably distinct perspectives: that of the "old" and now clearly recessive laissez-faire America; that of the still ascendant rational, managing America; and that of the emergent affective, post-industrial America. This latter group includes many whose concerns are as much religious in nature as secular, persons for whom materialism, be it individualistic or collectivist, is simply not a sufficient view of human nature.

In considering critical choices which Americans face with respect to the quality of life in the society, then, *the first* choice has to do with whether the discussion will go forth with a reasonable respect for the ascertainable facts, and a sufficient tolerance of the unavoidable complexities. We are not unhappy about the same things. In goodly measure, what we are unhappy about is one another. Nothing will come of merely extrapolating the class-bound discontents of any one group into a generalized assertion.[f] Unhappily (if unavoidably) the great simplifiers are much in evidence, although possibly not so much as in a not distant past. But there are, to use David Riesman's term, great complexifiers abroad in the land also. Let us join forces with the latter, and in that spirit offer the reader a simple test. In a general way, is it not the case that concern for the quality of life is seen as rather an advanced view, and not unreasonably associated with a progressive political position? And is it not equally the case that a report that twice as many Americans find the quality of life deteriorating as find it improving has about it a certain penumbral suggestion of progressiveness? And yet examine more closely the specifics Dr. Campbell tells us were complained about:

> inflation
> taxation
> crime
> drug use
> declining morality
> public protests
> disorders
> environmental pollution

Only the last item, "environmental pollution," is a matter which would appear in a wide spectrum of contemporary opinion. Other than that, the complainants present themselves as anything but progressive in their views. Far from desiring change, it is change that evidently persuades them the quality of life has deteriorated. Wherefore, on pain of seeing concern for the quality of life as a positively regressive force in contemporary public affairs, it seems prudent to accept that it is in fact a complex one, mingling various and often contrary views—of which those thought to be the most progressive are scarcely the most evident. What seems reasonable is to suppose that this amalgam of complainants is made up of persons who can be found at almost every point on DuBois' line of march. There will be those for whom change has been unwelcome; those for whom change has been disappointing; and those for whom change has not come fast enough. There is no escaping this complexity. A statement of critical choices has to respond to the concerns of each of these tendencies in opinion.

In 1971, a judgment on the nature of complaints about the quality of life in the United States might have concluded with that caveat—that at least a sizable and possibly predominant element among those dissatisfied were reflecting socially conservative views. Such persons were attached to "old" American standards, were troubled by new standards and new manners. This fits with the

---

[f]Perhaps especially the class-bound discontents of persons likely to read an essay such as this one.

pattern discerned by Cantril and Roll in which individuals found themselves well enough off, but thought the nation in terrible shape. But this conservative group had at least the advantage of thinking the "old" values were right and did work, and with the onset of the 1970s had the psychological reward of a national administration much given to reassuring them on that point. Then came Watergate, a disgrace without equivalent in American history.

There is no satisfactory way to judge just how permanent will be the effect of singular events, nor yet always to know which indeed are singular. First, the 1960s saw a president who had promised peace wage war. Surveys conducted in 1971 and 1972 by William Watts and Lloyd A. Free showed the damage of this and other trauma. The authors wrote,

The people's assessment of the state of the nation in 1971 was unquestionably the most pessimistic recorded since the introduction of public opinion polling . . . in the midst of the great depression. . . .[29]

And then in the 1970s came the shock of a president who had promised probity revealed as having succumbed to sickening, dismaying corruption. These may indeed be idiosyncratic events. Adam Smith's dictum "There is a deal of ruin in a nation" may yet prove the greater wisdom. The evidence seems to be that there is—or has been—a cyclical movement of confidence from peaks to troughs—the 1950s surely were a peak, as the report of President Eisenhower's commission would suggest. Just as surely the 1970s—and the Nixon study—suggest a trough. American leaders have fallen from grace before, and in truth we have lost wars before. It is at least possible—probable?—that we commenced to measure levels of public confidence at a "peak" moment, such that things now look more ominous than they will once a full cycle has been recorded. On the other hand, it is possible that measurement will affect the observation and reinforce the decline. Patterns of war abroad, the subornation of laws and liberties at home, may indeed prove the pattern of civilization changing its character. (See Figure XVIII-1.)

Either way—and it surely will take a generation before anyone could reasonably contend there was sufficient evidence to judge—in the near term we must assume that *every* element of American opinion has been hard hit, and none approaches "the third century" with great confidence. Old standards have been betrayed, new standards have not been accepted, the meliorists and managers in the middle cannot seem to deliver. It must be emphasized that the declining trust in government, a key element surely in assessing the quality of life, commenced well before Watergate. It commenced with the assassination of President Kennedy and has declined with successive shocks to confidence ever since. But there is now no longer much room for further decline. In truth, the case could be made, in Marxist-Leninist terms, that the United States is in a prerevolutionary condition, especially so in the added context of unemploy-

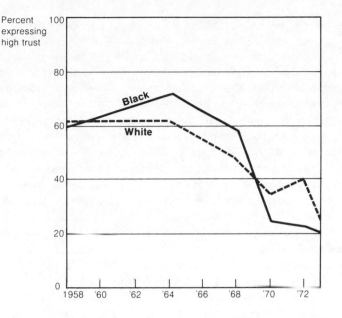

Source: Angus Campbell and Robert L. Kahn, "Measuring the Quality of Life."
Paper prepared for the Commission on Critical Choices for Americans, 1974.

Figure XVIII-1. Trends in Trust in Government.

ment, economic stagnation, and failure in a foreign war (which, if not waged for imperialist purposes, was surely waged in a quintessential imperialist setting). And yet there would be virtually no way to judge which direction a genuine upheaval might take, save to speculate that it would not in the first instance be radical. We dismiss the Marxist-Leninist hypothesis. That doctine has been wrong about almost everything; why should it be right about the United States? We assume there is a "deal of ruin" in a nation, and we note how little damage has been sustained in substantive terms. We do not, however, assume there will be a cyclical return to the buoyancy, say, of the early 1960s. There are choices to be made which lead, in different combinations, to quite different outcomes, and some of these are likely to be anything but buoyant. There are, in any event, deep-set trends in the society which lead us away from the conditions of the past. These need to be worked out, for it is here the critical choices must be made.

Two One-Time Trends

This, then, is a society which, if it be true that men and women have some control over their condition, has critical choices to make—which is nothing

alarming. There is a respectable record of the American democracy having made
such choices in the past, although scarcely in the mode of a research seminar.
Choices will be made in terms of individuals and parties, and not in the abstract.
But this process cannot be much harmed if some effort at abstraction is now
made, based on a preceding effort "... to retrace our recent wanderings, to
indicate and interpret our ways and rates of change...."[30] For wanderings they
have been! In this sense, at least, the image of an army on the march will *not* do.
To the contrary there has been an exceptional amount of vagary, and no small
amount of deception. Most of all there has been a good deal of extrapolating
atypical, one-generation events into long-term trends and conditions.

Two examples will serve. At mid-century a series of one-time events
combined to give the United States an unprecedented economic and military
position in the world. It was readily assumed that American ideology—the
ideology, generally speaking, of the liberal state—was equally influential, and
that this extraordinary hegemony would persist at least through an American
Century. But of course it could not and has not. The world economy soon
enough resumed its long-term pattern of growth—the advent, for example, of
Japan as the second or third most powerful of industrial states—while the Soviet
Union commenced a quick march to military parity with the United States, and
other nations, in other and similar ways, became part of the world military
equation. American influence in such matters hardly disappeared, but it could
not be maintained in the lonely eminence it had briefly enjoyed. As for
ideological hegemony—it had not existed. It had once—but years earlier. At the
close of the *First* World War, the prestige of American institutions reached
extraordinary heights, accompanied by the personal prestige of President Wilson.
It declined precipitously thereafter, as proponents of various and often conflicting forms of collectivism and nationalism everywhere took over the debate. A
quarter century after the American Century commenced, we find ourselves in a
world that might well have been extrapolated from the world of 1925; it was
projections from *1950* that were misleading. The United States remains a nation
of enormous power, and that responsibility which is said to go with power has
scarcely been diminished by the "normalizing" events of the past several years or
more. In this perspective there is little we have lost which we ought to seek to
regain; nor yet have we lost so much as to assume a further decline is now
irreversible.

Similarly, a series of one-time events combined at mid-century to produce an
extraordinary birth cohort: more babies, and from more segments of the
population, than was in any way to be expected save for these one-time events.
Neil J. Smelser has observed to the American Academy of Arts and Sciences,
"Crisis and conflict have accompanied the cohort as each institution has
attempted to quickly accommodate this large mass of people."[31] First came the
problems of children, then of teenagers, then of adults, and all in unprecedent
dimensions. The demographer Norman B. Ryder has likened the coming of age

of successive cohorts of young people to that of a civilization invaded by succeeding waves of barbarians "who must somehow be civilized and turned into contributors to fulfillment of the various functions requisite to societal surviv- al." A key to the outcome is the ratio of defenders to attackers. In the third quarter of the twentieth century in the United States this ratio went down sharply, as the number of attackers went up. From 1890 to 1960, for example, the size of the subgroup in the population aged fourteen to twenty-four increased—slowly—by 13.1 million persons. Then in the single decade of the 1960s it grew by 13.2 million persons. It will grow by 4.6 million in the 1970s, and decline in the 1980s.[32] Defenses crumbled everywhere. There was war abroad, and increasingly the conditions of war at home. James Q. Wilson writes:

American democracy, which seemingly had endured in part because . . . we were a "people of plenty" relieved of the necessity of bitter economic conflict, had in the 1960s brought greater plenty to more people than ever before in its history, and the result was anger, frustration, unrest, and confusion.

True: all true.[g] Yet, as Wilson argues, we must see the almost certain influence of demographic change behind much of this "anger, frustration, unrest, and confusion." Otherwise we will be inclined to assume that this past will persist into the future, even though an essential influence on this past experience has vanished. The number of live births dropped by more than one million from 1960 to 1973.[33]

Live Births

1960	4,257,850
1974	3,159,958

In the 1960s, a new institution of higher education was opened every week for a decade. These same institutions must soon face the 1980s, when the size of the college age population will *drop*, even as the size of the school age population is dropping during the present decade. During this decade, the postwar cohort will have arrived in the job market, and this will not be good for unemployment statistics, nor of course for young people of this troubled generation. But the *long-run* prospect is that the United States will resume the slow, moderate growth in population which was already established a half century ago. Already, the ratio of "defenders" to "attackers," after dropping steadily, turned up in 1969, and will go on rising steadily now. Defined as the ratio of persons 22-64 years old to persons 5-21 years old, this ratio at one point dropped lower (1.46) than three defendants to every two attackers. By 1976, it

[g]Well . . . probably true. Note that levels of *personal* satisfaction among Americans remain quite high.

will be back to the level of 1960 (1.67) and by 1983, will reach the point (2.04) where there are fully two defenders for every attacker, the defense forces having by now been much enhanced by the attackers of 1960s. It may yet prove that the 1960s has left permanent effects, that henceforth higher levels of "anger, frustration, unrest" will in fact be normal. But they will not be associated with the crushing demographic pressures and imbalance of that special period. Issues will continue to produce "anger, frustration, unrest," but they will not be associated with quite that array of youth looking for issues.

Just as there are "one-time trends" which ought to be kept in perspective, so should national experiences which in truth are more in the way of episodes. The Vietnam war was one. It is hard to imagine that particular experience being repeated; legislation precludes it, but more importantly, the calamities which it brought to the presidency must surely influence future presidents. So also of Watergate. It was in any event a failure more of men than of institutions. If Americans were appalled by this breach of standards, it seems fair to say the rest of the world was impressed by what our standards turned out to be, and the relentlessness with which they were pursued to the end so that right was done. American government is not corrupt, save as that term is redefined to suit idiosyncratic or ideological purposes. The comment in *Recent Social Trends* on "the corruption and ineffectiveness of much of our governmental machinery" was far more justified, for at that time state and local government in the United States had indeed been corrupted—by a policy of social betterment, to wit, prohibition, pursued by the Federal government. But even that much more pervasive problem appears in retrospect to have been more an episode than a condition.

Three Main Tendencies

So far, two propositions have been established, or such at least will be the assumptions on which this paper now proceeds. The first proposition, dealt with in the section "What do We Know?" of this chapter, is that with respect to the quality of life—those perceptions to which people apply that term—recent American experience has been troubling. There is a sense of decline or, at very least, of threat. No one set of perceptions dominates, but persons with quite disparate judgments on just *what* is going wrong, seem able to share the general perception that something *is*. Historians tell of such periods, and social analysts do their limited best to explain them. There has been a sustained decline in "trust in government"—unprecedented over the three to four decades that such social measurements have been made—and this probably best summarizes the general malaise, or at all events one malaise of the intellectuals. The second proposition, with which the previously mentioned section was also concerned, holds merely that there are critical choices now to be made. The merely episodic, or the mainly spent vectors of the recent past are not our concern. Let it be clear that this is a judgment for which no conclusive reasons may be adduced. It *may be* the decline in trust in government, for example, was itself episodic and transient. It may be we shall soon be demonstrably less troubled. If this turns out to be the case, well and good. Concern for those matters associated with the quality of life will recede, and there the matter will rest. However, the opposite case seems the stronger, though, to repeat, in no way conclusive. The concerns which, for example, were revealed in the ISR study do not appear to arise from transient phenomena. Moreover, the *elite* concerns— simply defined as the concerns of recent college graduates—do not much appear at all in current surveys, save in the dissatisfaction of educated youth. But these will diffuse in the society. They already have done so in some matters, such as ecology. And here again, these are not concerns that arise from transient phenomena. To the contrary, it will now be argued that powerful and persistent tendencies are at work in the society which make for a sense that the quality of life is somehow diminishing, and will continue to do so barring some fairly decisive choices.

The three main tendencies are the institutionalization of diversity, the growth of government, and the decline of the economy.

To assert there is a symmetry in so large and confusing a set of developments is to invite a salutary skepticism—and yet a certain correspondence between periods and problems does appear. Lee J. Cronbach was previously cited (p. 414) in the movement of the American system from laissez-faire to managerial government to pluralistic affiliations. We have seen the correspondence between these periods and the three presidential efforts at social assessment. Keeping in mind that while a social system may be said to move from one period to another, not *all* opinion moves accordingly. The American public today is made up of groups—age having much significance here—which see things from the quite different perspectives of these three periods. A task of presidential leadership is, and has for some time been, to appeal across these divisions, in the most common form, speaking for one constituency and acting for another, and trusting to each to get the right signal. Each tendency in opinion would at this moment seem almost to be matched by a tendency in events which arises from it—in either a negative or positive relationship—causing difficulties for the polity as a whole. Such is the argument of this essay.

The Institutionalization of Diversity

Following the 1960 tally, the Bureau of the Census devised a "Socioeconomic Status Score" in which data on occupation, educational attainment, and income were combined so as to make it possible to rank ethnic and racial groups by their relative standing. First, "White" was compared to "Nonwhite," revealing the great gap—the primordial wrong of American society—displayed now in unforgiving, unchallengeable statistical terms. Next the "Nonwhite" category was "disaggregated" to show the relative standing of groups within that conventional group. Again primordial wrong—American Indians the lowest ranking group of all. *But* Japanese Americans not only ranked higher by far than other nonwhites, but higher than whites also. When the "White" category is broken down, in this case comparing "Natives of Native Parentage" with first or second generation immigrants, the "Foreign Born" do not do as well as the "Natives of Native Parentage," but second generation immigrants, persons born in the United States of "Foreign or Mixed Parentage," do *better*. Those from Central or Eastern Europe do *far* better—better even than Japanese.[34]

This is one facet of the American experience: great disparities among many groups. Another is that of continued advances for all, or almost all, and ever more access to the "top." In 1973, 26.2 percent of all American families earned from $15,000 to $24,999. For the category "Negro and Other Races," this proportion was 14.4 percent. This is not as large as for the other group, but in constant dollars, *sixteen times* the percentage for 1952. In that year, whites had proportionately six times as many persons in that high income bracket; by 1973, barely twice as many. Furthermore, it was only in 1963 that whites reached the same proportion of persons in this income bracket that nonwhites attained in 1973, and while some nonwhites would have shared more in this prosperity than others, there was no doubt that the upward movement was general.[35] (See Figure XVIII-2.)

Equally, there is no doubt that this upward movement has been accompanied by a rise in the sense of distinctiveness as among the many racial, ethnic, religious and now, perhaps once again, regional populations which make up the nation, and, to a growing degree, of the institutionalization of this diversity. There is an irony here, much commented upon. As one after another group, some which began the twentieth century in what would have seemed irretrievably depressed circumstances, have risen generally, and "spread out" such that a significant proportion of members attain to the highest ranks of achievement and reward—in other words, as ethnic groups have become more like one another—the consciousness of differences has seemingly intensified. This ought not any longer surprise us. What is happening in the United States is happening in *most* nations in the world. Yet it does surprise us, for the onset of ethnic diversity as an organizing principle as well as a social reality of modern society is an event which the principal social philosophies of the modern age have decreed would *not* happen. This has been singularly a problem for Marxist-Leninist doctrine. The *Communist Manifesto* declares:

National differences and antagonisms between peoples are daily more and more vanishing, owing to the development of the bourgeoisie, to freedom of commerce, to the world market, to uniformity in the mode of production and in the conditions of life corresponding thereto.[36]

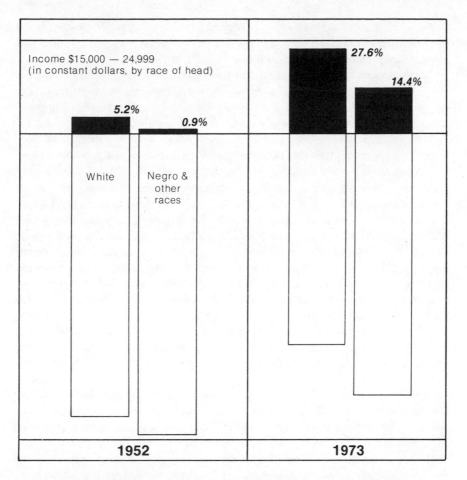

Income $15,000 — 24,999
(in constant dollars, by race of head)

27.6%

14.4%

5.2%

0.9%

White

Negro &
other
races

1952

1973

Source: Unpublished data derived from U.S. Bureau of the Census, *Current Population Reports*, Series P-60, No. 97 (Jan. 1975), Table 11.

Figure XVIII-2. Families with Total Money Income of $15,000-$24,999 in Constant Dollars, by Race of Head

"Universal interdependence," they asserted, was the first fact of the modern world. As the history of ideas proved that "intellectual production changes its character in proportion as material production is changed," it followed—so the *Manifesto* decreed—that the pre-industrial consciousness of being German or Russian, English or French would soon disappear. Well, of course, it did not. What came to pass instead was the First World War, a holocaust of nationalism from which the world has not yet recovered, and from which it may never recover at all. Ethnic tensions and rivalries grow if anything greater in the new Marxist lands, and are the primary threat to social stability there.

Something not dissimilar has occurred in other lands. Great Britain, once the symbol of all that is enduring and stable in national life, faces a genuine prospect of fracture along ethnic lines. By comparison, the United States has relatively muted conflicts at the moment, but its long-range difficulties could be far greater, for they would defy solutions based simply on geographical division. Even so, the *present* level of ethnic consciousness entails philosophic difficulties for Americans. Some assertions attain almost to the condition of heresy concerning what has been seen, and sensibly so, as the civic religion of "Americanism." We are not, after all, alike. We are different. Or so it is argued, and if that it should prove the case, then a fundamental American idea, which Milton Gordon has termed "the liberal expectancy," will have proved wrong. This was the expectation—a laissez-faire expectation—that the "caste" differences in the American population would fairly rapidly disappear. Such epiphenomena would not persist in the fundamentally changed condition of life in the new nation, *not least* because Americans would actively desire that such differences should fade to inconsequence, and would consciously pursue that end. This expectancy was epitomized in the great Civil Rights Act of 1964 which prohibited discrimination, with respect to a variety of matters, based on "race, color, religion, or national origin." (The section on employment included "sex" as well.)

And here is the irony. The legislative triumph of the doctrine that individuals should not be classified in terms of ascribed characteristics led to the onset of wholly unprecedented efforts at classification. Not only was there a revival of identification of persons by race, after years of efforts designed to abolish just that, but all manner of ethnic distinctions, and sex distinctions, came into play in the attempt to sort out the rewards of society equitably—an effort which, despite the best intentions, could only in the end be based on numerical representation. (What else could happen in a democracy, where *numbers* decide?) At the behest of the government in Washington, universities in Texas began asking applicants whether they were "Malay or Aleut." As rewards to ethnicity multiplied, so did ethnic categories and the intensity of ethnic assertions. The liberal expectation, the laissez-faire concept that things work out for the best when everyone is on his own, came to be all but discredited. In part it deserved to be, for certainly it had not brought anything approaching racial equality, defined in terms of the primal categories of black and white. This one huge injustice of American history persisted fully into the twentieth century. Whatever success the American system had had, it had failed with respect to race. No matter that successes in such matters are difficult to find in the world: The United States was not one. The Constitution might be "color blind," but as Woodrow Wilson wrote in *Constitutional Government*, "Every government is a government of men, not of laws . . .''; and it has so far seemingly proved impossible in the American experience for men not to be conscious of race and to act in ascriptive ways.

The impulse to put an end to racial discrimination inevitably was succeeded by a concern to eliminate the consequences of inequality in the lives of those who had been deemed unequal. If laissez-faire arrangements had not accomplished this, and they had not, then it followed that these inequalities would become an object of direct social policy. And if this were to be so, society, in the institution of government, had to begin classifying citizens in precisely those ascriptive terms which it had proscribed for individuals. Thus it became necessary for employers to keep records of race in order to establish that they made no distinction by race. Or, indeed, that they were doing so in order to overcome the effects of negative distinction made in the past. Inevitably government came to be seen in some quarters as doing itself just what it forbade its citizens: classifying persons by race, creed, national origin, even sex.

This practice began in the effort to deal with a fairly uncomplicated type of diversity—that of Anglo-American and Afro-American in the South. Inevitably it brought to light the far more complicated American reality, which is that of a true array of ethnic groups of which no small number can make claims of their own on society, and of which a very considerable number can question just how large are the claims society can make on them. Immigration policy has, from the beginning of our national life, been one of the indisputably critical choices (made or, passively, not made) which has shaped our national experience. In 1924, the critical choice was made to restrict immigration in numbers *and* diversity. Where just prior to the First World War the number of immigrants had reached as high as 1,200,000 per year, it was henceforth to be restricted to 150,000, and through quotas was to reflect the national origins (the term "racial" origins would have been commonly used) of the population of 1920. Forty-one percent of white Americans in that year were judged to be of British and North Irish origin, and another 11 percent from the Irish Free State. Hence, even by 1920, the British Isles accounted for a bare majority of the American "stock," with the specifically English component considerably less even than that. (Of the signers of the Declaration of Independence two were born in England, two in Scotland, one in Wales, and three in Ireland.)

Those who framed the 1924 legislation were making a critical choice about the quality of life in America and intended just that. They desired that the United States not become more diverse than it was. This was a legitimate choice in the sense that an issue of unquestioned importance was involved, and the decision made did no necessary violence to principle. The United States would have been equally entitled, had it wished, to devise a quota system with the object that the American population would come eventually to be a perfect replica of world population. (Nations have no obligations of this order. Most avoid the issue of what kind of immigrants to accept by accepting none.) The

1924 legislation is recalled with embarrassment not because of its objective, but the grounds on which it was based, and the climate of opinion in which it was enacted. It was asserted (and asserted not least in the legislative hearings that preceded enactment) that the "new immigrants," those from Southern and Eastern Europe, were somehow culturally and even biologically inferior to those of the old North European strain. (A process whereby Celts became honorary Aryans, a distinction they assuredly had not been accorded a century earlier!) This *was* offensive: and is. It had no basis in fact, and derogated the status of persons already American of those origins. Precisely the same may be said of the earlier arrangements for excluding or limiting Asian immigration. But the essential fact about the Immigration and Nationality Act of 1924 is that it did not succeed in its purpose. The balance of the American population had moved away from that of Colonial America, and was never to return. America was not ever again to be English. In number, in cultural vitality, new groups—European, African, Asian—began, in effect, to redefine the American experience. Four decades later, in 1965, a new immigration law was enacted. The new provisions had almost the opposite effect of the old. These increase the number of immigrants allowed each year, and provide, or at least make it possible, that this immigration should come disproportionately from precisely those populations which the 1924 legislation had been directed against!

Complexity complicates, but there should be no illusions on this score. The quest for racial equality—which must be the primary obligation of the American society in this age—is unavoidably complicated by ethnic diversity, and complicated further by a curious reluctance to acknowledge that diversity. Thus in Northern and Midwestern cities, black-white encounters are not those of the Old South, the residuum of generations of exploitation of one class by another. In the North, to a significant degree, Black Protestants meet White Catholics—both groups having had their share and more of hard times in their flight from bankrupt and backward rural economies. Both groups overcame the worst of their obstacles, and were not without help in this, for the American creed was, and is, profoundly committed to equality of status. *Recent Social Trends* is sprinkled with encouraging references to the success of "Negro" physicians and "foreign born" scientists. It was duly noted that 8 percent of the entries in *Who's Who in America* were "foreign born"! (This, of course, on the verge of the great migration occasioned by Nazi persecutions, which would bring to the United States a one-time accession of what?—of the most creative minds of the age!)

But inequalities and disadvantages continue to attend the working class and the underclass of these communities, and a separateness also, such that there is a pronounced disinclination to accept the proposition that the one group ought to make sacrifices for the other—or even make room for the other—a disinclination which evidently baffles outsiders. (Increasingly the diversity of the American population is seen not only as normal but normative. This profoundly affects the way we live, and *limits* the kinds of general social decisions that can be made and effectively carried out.) In this situation, government has commenced in effect to allocate justice by assigning certain presumed benefits—housing, jobs, apprenticeships, professorships—to ethnic groups, and also to sexes. This is not entirely a new practice. The "balanced ticket" of northern urban politics was an informal (and much deplored) arrangement of just this sort. Patronage jobs in government were frequently allocated along ethnic lines. But this was the realm of the political. More recently ethnicity has become institutionalized; it has entered the realm of bureaucracy. Expectations are replaced by rights; practices by rules. The bureaucratic dynamic takes hold; what applies in one part of the system must apply in all. Regulation spreads; government grows, both as it seeks to enforce the new rules, and also as it half deliberately seeks to enlarge the domain in which the rules are most readily enforced, which is that of government itself. This process is reinforced by an enlargement in the number of ethnic groups seeking recognition under the new rules owing to the increasingly manifest rewards to those who play by them. This process is obviously difficult to reverse. An example would be the relative ease with which the concept of sex ratios was introduced into all manner of organizational arrangements. It was perceived (and it was certainly the case) that women do not share in the hierarchical rewards of the society, and it was generally accepted as quite reasonable that affirmative action be taken to redress this imbalance.

The present situation is not without its ambiguities. In a period of growing government size (to be discussed in the next section) the greatest growth in government *power* has been in what one observer has termed the "imperial federal judiciary." (Certainly this aspect of the American political system is unique in the world.) This judiciary has been active in support of arrangements designed to redress group imbalances, but it has most commonly done so from the earlier "liberal" perspective that was very much against any institutionalization of diversity. What the courts have evidently done is to assume that in the absence of positive discrimination members of various ascriptive groups will distribute themselves randomly in society. But this is to deny that there is any substance to the ascribed differences, which is to say that everybody is alike even though called by different names. This clearly is at odds with the view that cherishes the *differences* which are asserted to be the source of diversity and the justification for formal accommodation to it. There is not much clarity here, just now, and a rising number of clearly ambiguous issues. (Thus in 1976 a midwestern university went to court to determine which federal pension rules it had to follow. The Equal Employment Opportunity Commission insisted that men and women should draw equal pension benefits upon retirement. The Labor Department held that employers need only equalize contributions. Because women outlive men, they stand to draw *more* benefits if they draw *equal* ones.[37] Obviously, equity is hard to establish in such situations—and there are many such—because in many respects diversity *is* real.)

For all the heightened awareness of diversity in American life, and its increased institutionalization, it does not appear that any critical choices are open to us in this matter. Diversity has always been an American reality. Perception of diversity probably waxes and wanes. (The current vogue of ethnic politics, for example, is surely in part the work of Theodore H. White and Lou Harris who in the early 1960s devised techniques for network television forecasting and reporting of elections which employed "ethnic precincts." The technique has been brilliantly heuristic. But something "newer" could come along!) Indeed the case may be argued that the Civil Rights Act of 1964 was *the* critical choice in this area, and that our present preoccupation with diversity is really only temporary, and somewhat counterintuitive, somewhat ambiguous side effect of the incomparably straightforward and *un*ambiguous decision. Certainly it is a possibility that institutionalizing diversity *could* have the result of increasing uniformity by buffering exposed groups in the society from the shocks to which they have been especially susceptible. Thus in the recession year of 1974, probably for the first time, black Americans did not fare worse than whites. Unemployment was high for blacks, and incredibly high for black teenagers, but black-white ratios did not significantly change. Median family income declined 3 percent for blacks, 4 percent for whites. The annual government compilation of these data reported: "The number of low-income black families in 1974 remained unchanged from the 1973 level; a substantial increase was noted for low-income white families."[38]

In any event, for the moment the subject is too sensitive to admit of anything but indirect preferences with respect to the larger issues involved.

The Growth of Government

Recent Social Trends reported, "The tax bill of all the governments in the country in 1930 was ten and a quarter billion dollars, perhaps 15 percent of the incomes of the people." As a proportion of Gross National Product—a concept that did not then exist—it is now calculated that total government receipts in that year ($10.8 billion) were 11.9 percent of the gross national product, a proportion high or low according to one's impression of the "laissez-faire" world. By 1974, receipts had reached $460.5 billion, 32.9 percent of GNP. The state and local government ratio almost doubled, rising from 8.6 percent to 14.8 percent; the Federal ratio more than quintupled.

In any society this would constitute great change, but especially so in the United States, which was founded in a revolution against the "excesses" of (a rather mild) government and which for the century and one half that followed, professed the limits of government intervention as a distinctive characteristic of American society. Then in four decades government receipts rose from a tenth to a third of national income, loosely defined. Projecting the 1929-74 trend, this

Table XVIII-1
Government as Percentage of Gross National Product (Selected Years, 1929-1974)

Year	GNP (billions of dollars)	Total Government	
		Receipts (billions of dollars)	Receipts as Percent of GNP
1929	$ 103.1	$ 11.3	11.0%
1930	90.4	10.8	11.9
1935	72.2	11.4	15.8
1940	99.7	17.7	17.8
1945	211.9	53.2	25.1
1950	284.8	68.7	24.1
1955	398.0	100.4	25.2
1960	503.7	139.8	27.8
1965	684.9	189.1	27.6
1970	977.1	302.5	31.0
1974*	1,400.1	460.5	32.9

*Average of second and third quarters
Source: U.S. Department of the Treasury, Office of Financial Analysis.

proportion will approach one-half by the turn of the century. Projecting the trend of the twenty years just past, the proportion will reach 50 percent in less than twenty years from now. At *half* of GNP, the quality of life in America will have critically changed, if indeed it has not already done so. A social system in which government (and politics) takes up that much space is different indeed from anything in the American past. (See Table XVIII-1; Figure XVIII-3.)

Rather in the way a formal diversity came upon us all but unawares, so has this seen a change in our national life. It is perhaps too great to try to speculate as to why such things happen as they do, but it can usefully be said that commencing with the depression of the 1930s, there was simultaneously great pressure for and great resistance to increases in government spending. The national administrations of that era displayed this tension. President Hoover seemed to advocate "retrenchment" but in fact spent a good deal of money. President Roosevelt was elected on a platform of stern fiscal conservatism—and spent even more. A generation of political activists was formed which was indelibly impressed with the thought that government ought to spend more on public services than it did, but also that any such attempt would be fraught with legislative obstacle and electoral peril. When this generation came to power, it seemed almost not to notice that these obstacles had all but disappeared, and that the electoral consequences, if not reversed, had at least become far more balanced—which is to say the chances of losing an election by not spending would be seen as at least as great a peril as the other way around. (In the

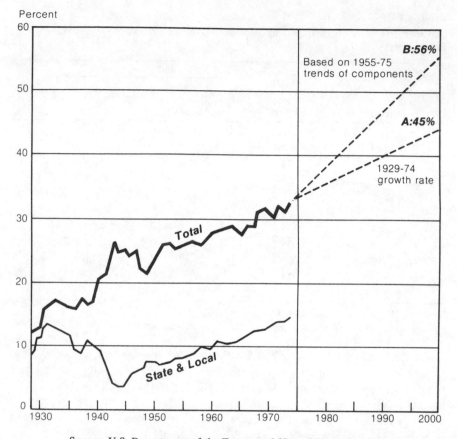

Source: U.S. Department of the Treasury, Office of Financial Analysis.

Figure XVIII-3. Government as a Percentage of GNP.

meantime, of course, yet another generation of political activists was being formed, which might very well, when it comes to power, have quite different perceptions of the Public Propensity to Spend. But this is some time away.)

Samuel Huntington has observed that this transformation—if so strong a term may be used—took place in two phases. First there was the great increase in defense expenditure—the Defense Shift—that took place in the 1950s. Then in the late 1960s and early 1970s came the Welfare Shift—an increase of more than equal magnitude. Somehow, neither of these events seems quite to have registered—at first. Possibly this is because both occurred in an atmosphere of crisis and threat. Whatever was done seemed little enough, or at least did to those who wanted even more done. In both periods the national media very much sided with the advocates of increase, and helped create an atmosphere in which far from being depicted as doing too much, government was seen as doing too little. Politics played a role as candidates and parties discovered an indefinite succession of threats to national security and domestic tranquility. The defense boom ended, however. As will be seen in Figure XVIII-4, government spending on national defense has been somewhat declining, in real dollars, since 1968. Social welfare expenditures (in the wide sense of that term) continue to rise. Whether the time will come when *respectable* voices are raised in opposition to social welfare spending, as for a decade now there has been respectable opposition to defense spending, is a matter for speculation. There is now, of course, and has been much opposition to such spending, but it is not respectable, and has far less influence than it has votes. When an advocate of decreased spending on social welfare can receive an honorary degree from an Ivy League university, this situation will have changed. This did happen to defense spending and could happen to welfare spending, after which government expenditure as a proportion of GNP could well level off. (Barring a third upward movement associated with a movement such as environmentalism.) But it has not changed yet, and it needs at least to be asked whether the style of managerial government which led to the Welfare Shift might not lead to a near indefinite growth in such expenditure. Just as the inability of the laissez-faire regime to eradicate the differences among majority and minority groups led to a wholly unexpected

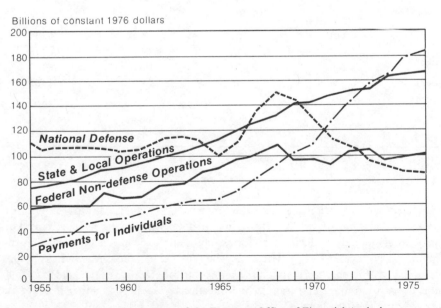

Source: U.S. Department of the Treasury, Office of Financial Analysis.

Figure XVIII-4. Major Categories of Government Spending.

Table XVIII-2
Coordinates for Figure XVIII-4
(in billions of constant 1976 dollars)

Year	Payments for Individuals	National Defense	Federal Non-defense Operations	State & Local Operations
1955	$ 33	$112	$ 60	$ 76
1956	35	107	60	79
1957	38	107	61	81
1958	46	107	60	86
1959	50	108	72	90
1960	51	105	68	91
1961	57	105	69	96
1962	60	114	79	100
1963	63	115	79	104
1964	65	113	88	108
1965	66	110	92	113
1966	73	112	99	120
1967	84	136	103	128
1968	93	151	109	134
1969	103	145	96	142
1970	110	130	97	144
1971	129	114	94	149
1972	143	108	104	152
1973	156	96	105	153
1974	164	91	96	164
1975	180	87	98	165
1976	183	87	103	168

Source: U.S. Department of the Treasury, Office of Financial Analysis.

emphasis on such differences,[h] so the "increasingly managerial government" of recent decades has begun to perform in a manner which *by its standards* must at very least be judged deviant, and possibly pathological. "Managerial government" is presumed to understand what is being managed, and to make reasonably efficient decisions in the allocation of resources. The evidence that this is so grows more uncertain; while questions arise as to whether it *could* be so. (Figure XVIII-5; Table XVIII-3.)

Hopefully these comments will not be read as an indictment of growth in the

[h]*Recent Social Trends* forecast that increased minority consciousness would be associated with a militancy that put emphasis on group differences.

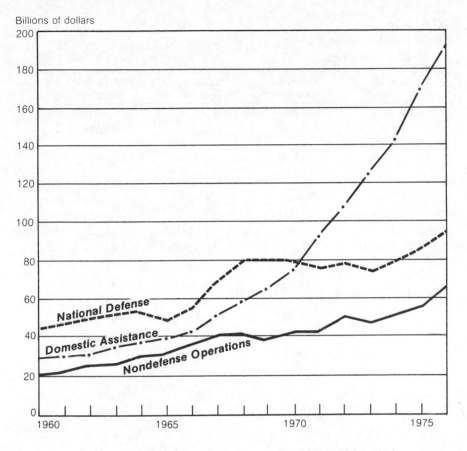

Billions of dollars

Source: U.S. Department of the Treasury, Office of Financial Analysis.

Figure XVIII-5. Major Categories of Federal Spending.

public sector. There is a persuasive case that a modern economy requires an ever larger public sector; that the growth of the private economy *depends* on the growth of the public one. Further, a wealthy society can afford more public amenities just as it can afford more private ones, and accordingly the public sector grows. Finally, a concerned society will do things for individuals and groups which need doing, and are most directly done through government. All of these considerations, however, do not account for the seemingly inexorable growth of the public sector in recent decades. The defense budget no longer accounts for this; to the contrary, there is something troubling about the way in which the growth of the defense budget became a public issue at just about the point when in terms of proportion of the total—and in real terms—it began to decline. Granted there is a lag in public perception of issues, but there has also

Table XVIII-3
Coordinates for Figure XVIII-5
(in billions of current dollars)

Year	Domestic Assistance	National Defense	Non-defense Operations
1960	$ 27,164	$45,219	$19,840
1961	30,055	46,596	21,144
1962	31,688	50,376	24,749
1963	34,164	51,548	25,599
1964	36,354	52,738	29,492
1965	37,580	48,581	32,269
1966	42,721	55,856	36,075
1967	50,435	69,101	38,718
1968	58,103	79,409	41,321
1969	65,612	80,207	38,729
1970	74,879	79,284	42,425
1971	92,027	76,807	42,591
1972	105,905	77,356	48,615
1973	124,559	75,072	46,895
1974	140,291	78,569	49,532
1975	172,558	85,276	55,612
1976	190,210	94,027	65,135

Source: U.S. Department of the Treasury, Office of Financial Analysis.

been a good deal of obfuscation of late on the real source of increased government spending. It comes from domestic assistance of various kinds, largely in the category associated with health, education, and welfare. An important component is social insurance; contributions for this purpose came to 7.3 percent of the GNP in 1974. But other categories of social expenditure grow steadily also, and have become a characteristic of modern American (as of modern industrial) life. Increasingly such expenditures are avowedly concerned with the quality of life, and increasingly they affect it, if only by increasing the role of society in the life of the individual.

In his late nineteenth century study, *The Rise and Growth of American Politics*, Henry Jones Ford states: "It may be laid down as a political maxim that whatever assigns to the people a power which they are naturally incapable of wielding takes it away from them."[39] Woodrow Wilson used this principle to explain the rise of political parties in the United States' system of government. The Constitution, he contended, required the people to fulfill "innumerable elective offices." They could not know enough to do this; they could not find the time to do it. Ineluctably, therefore, the role passed to specialists. In consequence, as Wilson had it, writing in 1908, "the system of election has been transformed into a system of practically irresponsible appointment by private party managers,—irresponsible because our law has not yet been able to devise any means of making it responsible."[40]

Much of American politics before and since has been occupied with this question, to which some answers were found. From the telephone to television, technology has made voters considerably more knowledgeable—so we must believe—and more organizable, as fairly clear evidence will show. Party managers are not what they once were. But, in the meantime, a distinctly similar, if new problem has come along. Today, bureaucracies manage government programs in much the way that party managers were once said to manage government office. They are difficult of access when not actually secretive; they have a tenacious hold on office, such as to outlast "political" superiors who come and go with frivolous regularity; they profess to "know" what others do not "know," such as to add a dimension to their authority that few can challenge. In time, no doubt, countervailing techniques will be worked out, and indeed this is already a principal emergent theme in "post-industrial" politics. Today the FBI is challenged; tomorrow the Environmental Protection Agency. But the point of this discussion—and it will be important to the development of effective checks on the power of these bureaucracies—is to raise the possibility that there has been a corruption of purpose. Professors Jones and Wilson were, in effect, saying that it was a defect in democratic theory that gave rise to the unanticipated evils of political parties, evils primarily associated with the aggrandizement of power by self-selected individuals and the exploitation of public undertakings for private advantage. Similarly, it may be hypothesized—nothing more is intended here—that a like disposition, at bottom nothing more sinister than a certain excess of optimism about the human condition, has led to the assignment of powers to government which it is "naturally incapable of wielding," such that the devolution is mooted, and the undertaking assumes a different nature altogether from that originally intended.

What it comes down to is an excess of expectation which it may be in the nature of democracy to induce. Alfred E. Smith, that most democratic of politicians, laid it down that *his* first principle of government was "Never promise anything you can't deliver." This may account both for the failure of his ultimate political ambitions, *and* the esteem in which he continues to be held. But his was a hard regimen, not much emulated. More suitable, perhaps, to a republic than to a democracy? In any event, the American democracy in recent decades has promised more and more to its people, and clearly is having problems delivering—problems which have begun to compromise the entire effort. In the language of social science, system maintenance, and not results, has become the prime orientation of the institutions that have come into being to deliver on these promises. There is always the problem of evidence for such an assertion, and it is not contended here that the evidence is final, or for that matter even very complete. But the case can nonetheless be made. There is an inductive logic to the argument. And there are some facts. Three examples—from health, from education, and from welfare, narrowly defined—will present, as it were, the deductive case.

All men die. This is accounted by some a defect in the human condition and leads to considerable efforts to prolong life. These efforts never finally succeed. Nonetheless, they are made. And they grow more costly as they become less effective, which is simply to say that maintaining life in a young person is easier and cheaper than maintaining life in an old person. In the end, the latter cannot be achieved. What is true of mortality is true largely of morbidity as well. Whence arises the welfare anomaly. The more resources are applied to a particular problem, the more the problem is likely to be seen as worsening. This arises when the system charged with delivering ever better conditions with respect to a particular aspect of life finds itself pushing wedgelike into an ever-tightening angle of diminishing returns, approaching an asymptotic "ceiling" of possibility. In effect, conditions have improved to the point where there is not much room for further improvement. To accept this thought—to proselytize it—is to accept that the growth of the system is at an end. Organizations typically resist this. Besides it is rarely absolutely the case. Marginal changes always remain possible. Organ transplants are an example in medicine. Compared with the advent of clean water and washable clothes, such new medical techniques are a contribution to health of miniscule consequence. But they are possible, and practically speaking, as much relatively free resources as are made available for them will in fact be used. In any event, the larger public is loathe to be told there is no further hope for improvement in so vital an area. Add in the case of medicine, and similar fields, a kind of technological dynamic which decrees that which can be done will be done, and you have a system relentlessly seeking to accomplish "more." As the evidence increases that not much more is being accomplished, it is common to assert that the system is in "crisis," and requires a further infusion of resources. In Fiscal Year 1950, total national health expenditures accounted for 4.6 percent of GNP. This proportion rose slowly, then rapidly. At 7.7 percent for Fiscal 1973, it had almost doubled.[41] Health had not much changed.

It would appear that Americans have for some time been quite healthy people. Not the healthiest, but ranking high among nations in this category of well being. These rankings are curiously stable. As will be seen from Table XVIII-4, in both Britain and America the life expectancy of males increased by twenty years in the first seven decades of the century. In 1901, American males could expect to live only 0.9896 as long as British males. Seventy years and medical revolutions later, Americans could expect only 0.9825 the life span of Britons. There are differences in health among different groups in America, but let it simply be stated that these differences do not necessarily run in the

Table XVIII-4
Life Expectancy at Birth for Males in the USA, Canada and Great Britain (Selected Years, 1901-1971)

Year	USA	Canada	Great Britain*
1901	47.6	NA	48.1
1931	59.4	60.0	58.4
1961	67.0	68.4	67.9
1971	67.4	NA	68.6

*Excludes Northern Ireland
Source: HEW, National Center for Health Statistics, *Vital Statistics of the U.S., Annual Report 1973*, Volume II, Section 5, Life Table 5-5; Statistics Canada, *Vital Statistics 1973, Preliminary Annual Report* (Table L-1); Central Statistics Office, *Social Trends 1974*, No. 5 (Table 92), London.

expected directions. It is not at all clear, for example, that the poor receive inferior care. The Department of Health, Education and Welfare states, "by 1970, the lower income groups had admission rates [to hospitals] significantly higher than higher income groups." With over 35,000 "health facilities" employing almost four million persons and containing three million beds, there does not seem to be any overall shortage in this area. HEW finds that the number of unoccupied beds over the past decade rose 28 percent.[42] (It is common now for medical literature to refer to a "surplus" of hospital beds, while the question has arisen whether this has had a deleterious effect on health in cases where patients stay in bed *too long*.) But the most striking difference in health among Americans is to be found not in the divisions of class, or race, or ethnicity, or region. It is sex where Two Nations will be encountered. The adjusted death rates for males, at 917 per 100,000 population (in 1971), is almost twice that of females, 526.[i] What medicine per se can do about that is uncertain, but this has hardly dampened the drive for more medicine.

The forces which brought about a great increase in health expenditures in the past decades have been coalescing of late around the issue of a comprehensive health insurance system. Various schemes have been proposed in the executive and legislative branches of the national government. All are expensive, ranging in the $40 billion to $60 billion range, and all appear in the aftermath of a decade in which the costs of health plans have almost invariably proved to have been underestimated. Whatever the costs, what would be the benefits? In 1974, an article in the *New England Journal of Medicine*, based on research sponsored by the Office of Economic Opportunity, concluded they would be few:

---

[i]In 1961, the difference between life expectancy both for males and females and for whites and non-whites was 6.6 years. By 1973, the life expectancy gap between races had closed to 6.3 years, while that between men and women had increased to 7.7 years. (National Center for Health Statistics, *Vital Statistics of the U.S.*)

Realistically, then, policy makers must recognize that even a substantial investment in delivery of more health services is not likely to produce any clearly measurable change in any dimensions of health, whether length of life or physical well-being.[43]

The following year, in the same journal, Dr. Charles C. Edwards, formerly the chief health officer of the United States, while declaring that the nation "must move promptly and effectively toward a rational system of health-care financing," nonetheless saw little prospect of this being done well by the national government. Anticipating "enormous inflationary pressure," he stated:

In fact, I anticipate that we are about to see a failure of leadership whose consequences will be so vast and so pervasive as to dwarf anything that has come before it. I am referring, of course, to the enactment of a scheme of national health insurance.[44]

Health has natural limits; we die. Yet extraordinary changes did take place before those limits were approached, and we have, in a sense, a group memory of those changes. In *Capital*, Marx compares the life of the rich and the life of the poor in nineteenth century Manchester. The upper middle class had a life expectancy of thirty-eight years, "while the average age of death of the laboring classes was 17." Life without smallpox, without cholera, without pellagra, without polio is different and better. To be sure, as fewer and fewer persons themselves actually *experience* any such changes, there will be less sense of improvement. Still, the change did occur, and is recorded. Education presents a more problematic situation. There has been a great expansion of knowledge, but it is not clear how much expansion of learning has accompanied this. It could be this is because some educational equivalent of the Biblical "three score years and ten" of life was reached some time ago, such that education, like health, has for some while been pushing against "natural" limits. Or, it could be that considerable "gains" are still possible. Few would want to pronounce on this point with great confidence. But it can be said that in the aftermath of a contemporary increase in resources allocated to education almost as great as that to health, there are only modest gains to record, and some of these are disputed. This does not refer to actual increases *of* education, as for example the larger number of persons who go to college than once did, but rather to increased returns for a given amount of education associated with increased investment. Corn fields produce more; do school rooms? The answer seems uncertain.

Uncertainty is to be stressed; so, equally, is the perspective in which this uncertainty arises, which is to say the optimistic expectation, so long in place in public rhetoric, that the "limits of schooling" were by no means reached. No one could say this optimism has proved groundless; yet neither are there any very palpable returns to show for what would have to be judged a tolerably increased effort. From 1960 to 1973, expenditure per pupil in average daily attendance in elementary and secondary public schools rose $375 to $1096. Nothing extraordinary happened in the schools: save in districts where reading levels declined. This is not to assert that increased expenditure brings about decreased performance, although one must fear that had the achievement scores gone in the other direction much would have been made of the presumed correlation. It should not even be assumed that increased expenditure actually resulted in any change in the experience of children in the schools, which is to say that they received more "teaching" in the sense that persons may receive more "medical care." More money for education does not necessarily result in more money for teachers, much less more teachers. Indeed the argument can be made that teachers have not benefited from increased school expenditures very much more than have students, that somehow the resources disappear or are dissipated in the organizational structures that surround the school room, the presumed center of the system where teacher and pupils nonetheless struggle on with very little changed.

It is at least possible that optimal returns on education are reached at lower levels of expenditure. The parochial schools of New York City provide a "natural experiment" for approaching this hypothesis. The parochial school system of New York City is as old as the public school system, both having emerged from an earlier system in which education generally was in church-affiliated schools supported in part by public funds. For a century and a half, parochial schools have enrolled about the same proportion of students attending school in the city, and for all of this time the parochial schools have drawn their attendance from working-class and low-income families of the city. In 1973, expenditure per student in the elementary and secondary schools of the Archdiocese of New York was about $430, four times less than that of the public schools. Reading scores for the whole of the Archdiocese have consistently been above grade level, and generally speaking have risen from one grade to another. In Manhattan, reading is below the national norm in the fourth grade, but above it in the eighth. The estimated expenditure per pupil in New York City public schools in 1974 was about $2250. This was a one-year increase of more than the total per pupil expenditure in parochial schools. This pattern will continue, and with it the assertion that there is a crisis in public education.

In these instances drawn from health and education, we see social efforts pushing against certain kinds of limits. These are not limits of resources, in terms of budgetary resources. Rather, they involve inherent limits, as in the case of health, or seeming limits of knowledge, which is probably the case in education. We do not know how to get more than a certain amount of schooling out of the systems we have. We have devoted teachers who are somehow not enabled to do what they clearly desire to do. Nobody seemingly has a better system readily at hand. Efforts are made: sincere and impressive efforts. But not without cost. The cost is twofold: Budgetary in the first instance, but in the second instance—the welfare anomaly again—there seem to be costs in social trust. *Seem to be*: No final evidence is asserted. Whenever greater efforts press against ever more closely approached limits, such that perceptible improvement is slight, citizens can readily get the impression that despite all the huffing and puffing, the effort is not in fact sincere. If it were sincere, there would be more to show. This produces the now familiar charges of bad faith, especially when government services are delivered across class boundaries. For the groups who gain their livelihood from providing such services, an equally "deviant" response is common. Faced with evidence that greater effort is not producing greater results, a common reaction is to assert that the effort has not been great enough. This serves the interest of both producers and consumers, if that term may be used. If the strategy is successful, there is no reduction in the resources allocated to the producers, and there need be no decrease in the expectations of the consumers. But of course this is not a stable solution.

This fix is common to many activities. The record of flood plain management in the United States, for example, is not an inspiring instance of rational programming. The problem of the near term at least is that the budget crises increasingly common to older American cities will lead to reductions in classroom services far sooner than to reforms in flood plain management. A good deal of social mistrust is in the offing as a result of this curious budgetary disorder. Some at least is deserved, for too much was promised by men who thought themselves sophisticated, but were merely ignorant.

Similarly, it could be argued that the behavior of the nation with respect to the problem of poverty has become pathological. For more than a decade now, there has been a formal commitment to end poverty defined in explicit income terms. This commitment has produced a considerable array of social programs. But poverty persists. Worse, the question has arisen as to whether such programs have given rise to *class* interest in the persistence of the social problems which gave rise to the programs in the first instance. (Much as admirals may be said to have an interest in the persistence of opposing fleets.) The matter is not settled, but it may, for example, be hypothesized that most spending on social programs designed to eliminate poverty in fact increases income inequality. Income moves *up* the social hierarchy, from those who pay the taxes to those who receive the payments in return for providing the services. In the spring of 1975, as New York City faced the prospect of bankruptcy, the mayor of New York, on a panel created by the United States Conference of Mayors to deal with welfare problems, told a press conference in Washington that the city has a maze of 160,000 employees working for federal, state, and local agencies handling such income programs as welfare, food stamps, Medicaid, and housing assistance.[45] At four persons to a family, this suggests that two-thirds of a million persons in New York City are supported by the economy of supporting others. In the nation, since 1950, public spending for social welfare purposes went from $23.5 billion to $242.4 billion (1974). Public and private spending went from $35.3

billion to $336.3 billion.[46] Public expenditure rose $29 billion in the decade 1950-60. It rose $190 billion in the fourteen years that followed. (See Table XVIII-5.) And yet poverty persisted. A study by Morgan Reynolds and Eugene Smolensky compared the "post fisc distribution" of income of 1961 and 1970, which is to say the distribution of income before and after public expenditures. This was the decade not only of great increase in expenditure, but of intense commitment to redistribution of income through such expenditure. "Despite all this," Reynolds and Smolensky concluded, "the effect on final income inequality was negligible." Next, a more solemn speculation:

Some might . . . infer that the fisc should be characterized as offsetting the growing inequality in the initial income distribution. It is possible that it was the fisc, however, that was responsible for the widening of the initial distribution.[47]

A simple point may be made here. At any point in the past decade it has been possible for the nation to eliminate poverty—in income terms—by adopting one of a variety of feasible measures of income maintenance. The cost would be trifling, compared with overall expenditure for social welfare purposes—something like 4 percent of the total. (The "poverty gap" or total income deficit of those who are poor came to $12 billion in 1973.) And yet no such program is

Table XVIII-5
Public and Private Expenditures for Social Welfare Purposes (Selected Fiscal Years, 1950-1974)

Type of Expenditure	1950	1960	1974*
	All expenditures (in millions of $)		
Total	$35,337	$78,704	$336,266
Income Maintenance	$10,723	$29,827	$126,035
Health	$12,027	$25,856	$104,240
Education	$10,914	$21,742	$ 90,525
Welfare & Other Services	$ 2,004	$ 2,658	$ 20,265
	All expenditures as percentage of Gross National Product		
Total	13.4%	15.9%	24.9%
Income Maintenance	4.1%	6.0%	9.3%
Health	4.6%	5.2%	7.8%
Education	4.1%	4.4%	6.7%
Welfare & Other Services	.8%	.5%	1.5%

*preliminary data
Source: Social Security Administration, *Social Security Bulletin*, January 1975, p. 19.

enacted. A president proposed one, in 1969, which *almost* was enacted, having twice passed the House of Representatives by emphatic margins. But the legislation was never even voted on in the United States Senate, where it met opposition from all points in the political spectrum. The issue has since all but disappeared from public view. It appears that *no group likely to have any influence in the outcome really wants a guaranteed income.* Some say they do; some say so in the most emphatic terms. But this is not how they behave. They behave so as to prevent any such measure from being enacted. Their behavior has not always been decisive: others who did not want a guaranteed income and said they did not have also had influence. But this only meant that efforts were reinforcing one another. The system does not want it.

What the system will want is federal assumption of all the costs of the existing welfare system, and this will likely happen in five to ten years. If there are undesirable effects in the existing system, this will perpetuate them.[j]

This is pathological behavior. There is much of it. It clearly will not change as a result of internal analysis and effort. A larger—critical—choice will be necessary. In the meantime, it should be understood that American society is not going to deal effectively with many of the problems that it identified in 1960s. It makes no matter that leaders profess to deal with them; nor even that they would like to do. The existing system of incentives effectively blocks action—even where intelligent action seems possible. Of these problems none is more pervasive in its consequences than that of urban social structure. In the early 1960s, it became clear that some combination of forces or other was having a devastating impact on the family structure of the urban poor. It proved impossible to address this problem directly, although indirect approaches were made. They have failed—if by success it is meant that there shall have been some downward movement in the several indices of family stability. To the contrary, there has been a startling increase. There has in any event been an enormous one. This change, however, has been effectively concealed. It is not discussed. This is an aspect of the pathology of "managerial government" of the present time. (See Table XVIII-6.)

In passing it may be noted that this particular pattern of evasion could have an independent effect on the quality of life in America. It seems fair to assume that attitudes of social trust, and of confidence in the future, derive in some measure from the perception that commitments are carried out and progress occurs where it is sought. This is especially true for minorities, to whom binding commitments have been made by American society. However, the disruption of urban social structure has progressed so radically as to make large overall gains unlikely for some time to come. *Within* groups there will be, as there has been, great gains. But these will be lost from view in the overall averages. Inasmuch as the (most likely) nature of the obstacles that retard overall progress will be

---

[j]It should be noted—granted—that a form of guaranteed income, the Supplementary Security Income Program, has been adopted, and provides for the disabled, aged, and blind, with all costs payed by the federal government. This was part of the Family Assistance Plan proposal of 1969.

Table XVIII-6

Population Under Age 18 and Number Receiving Aid to Families with Dependent Children, Money Payments by Status of Father [Selected Years, 1950-1973]

(numbers in thousands)

	1950	1960	1970	1973
Population under age 18*	48,225	65,697	70,905	69,406
Total Children Receiving AFDC				
Number	1,660	2,322	6,093	7,876
Number per 1,000 population under age 18	34	35	86	113
Number of Children Receiving AFDC by Status of Father				
Dead	350	202	NA	315
Absent from home	818	1,493	NA	6,159
Incapacitated	455	569	NA	803
Unemployed	–	–	NA	323
Other**	37	58	NA	268

*Civilian population, including after 1950 Puerto Rico, Guam, and the Virgin Islands.
**Includes children with father in home as caretaker because of death, absence, or incapacity of mother.
Source: Social Rehabilitation Service, *National Center for Social Statistics Report A-4 1969,* page 47, and unpublished data.

denied, other obstacles will have to be invented. Recent experience suggests that this will take the form of general, accusatory indictments of the social system, all of which tend to strengthen the view—in sympathetic circles and *un*sympathetic circles—that ours is a failed society. In the meantime, what Marx and Engels called the "dangerous class," and which they found unfit for revolutionary duties ("conditions of life . . . prepare it far more for the part of a bribed tool of reactionary intrigue") will grow and cities will accordingly decline.[48]

We have dealt with two areas of concern—health and education—which uniquely touch on the quality of life but about which "managerial government" encounters difficulties. In the one case, health, there are natural limits to what can be attained. In the other case, education, there are limits to what is known. In each instance, striving harder to attain more does not, evidently, induce a greater sense of things having got better. The welfare anomaly comes into play: more can seem less. A further class of concerns should also be touched upon, for it is likely to be frequently encountered in a *responsive* society, which seeks to accommodate many goals expressed by diverse groups in the population, and as a result not infrequently finds it is seeking contradictory goals. When, as a result, no one's goals are attained, this can be frustrating. But it is also possible to attain some part of everyone's goals, with a general rise in satisfaction. An instance is the way American society has been dealing with crime.

Crime affects the quality of life. In the present time (1975) only inflation and taxation compete with it among things the American public is "most" worried about. In a not unacceptably loose way, it can be said that for some years now, concern about crime has been rising. Also, for some years, crime has been rising. This might suggest that government has failed. But this would assume that governments have in fact set out to put an end to crime. Governments have not done this. For a complex of reasons, government policy with respect to crime has become one of accommodation—to victims and to criminals. Table XVIII-7 illustrates this. In the 1960s, the number of crimes went up. In the same decade, the number of persons in prison for crimes went down. No amount of explaining will explain away these contrary movements. It is simply the fact that the society was pursuing contrary goals. The society "wanted" to decrease crime. But at the same time the same society "wanted" to increase civil liberties. Two admirable goals. Two perfectly respectable, sane, decent goals. Goals this commentator would unhesitantly endorse. But incompatible. There are many such.

There are unavoidable costs when this kind of situation arises. Much symbolic activity is necessary, and this can be expensive. Under President Johnson the federal government began a "massive" aid program to local law enforcement agencies. Many billions of dollars have been spent, and this, of course, has had no effect on crime, but it has served a symbolic purpose. From the point of view of the political economist, however, there is a problem with such measures, which is that their symbolic value fades fairly rapidly, especially once their original sponsor departs the political scene, but the budget item and the

Table XVIII-7
Crime Rates and Prisoner Rates [1960 and 1970]
(per 100,000 population[1])

Year	Crime[2]			Prisoners			
	Total	Violent	Property	Total	Federal	State	Local
1960	1870	160	1710	183.1	12.9	105.7	64.5
1970	3949	361	3588	157.7	9.8	86.8	61.1

Notes:

1. Crime rates are per 100,000 inhabitants, excluding Armed Forces abroad, based on Census Bureau data. Prisoner rates are per 100,000 estimated civilian population.

2. Violent crime includes murder and nonnegligent manslaughter, forcible rape, robbery and aggravated assault. Property crime includes burglary, larceny-theft, and auto theft.

Source: FBI; *Statistical Abstract of the U.S.* (Tables 2, 242 & 281); Bureau of the Census, *1970 Persons in Institutions and Other Group Quarters* PC 24E (Table 3), *1960 Inmates in Institutions* 8A (Table 4).

bureaucracy goes on indefinitely. An effective managerial government would contrive ways to discontinue activities that have ceased to serve symbolic (or substantive) purposes, but this is not something American government has learned to do, nor is it likely that it soon shall.

The Decline of the Economy

In the spring of 1975, a quiet exchange took place between two United States Senators that encapsulates three themes respecting the future American economy which add up to—decline. Relative decline. This is the third of the three powerful, persistent tendencies mentioned at the outset of Chapter IV, which make for a sense that the quality of life is somehow diminishing. The Senators, both progressive, active, and influential men, were working on a major item of legislation, a bill to mandate categories of energy conservation so as to lessen American dependence on imported oil in the aftermath of the huge price increases of 1973-74. The approach of the proposed legislation was for the national government to set forth a number of areas of possible conservation through limits on heating, cooling, lighting, and similar energy-consuming activities. Each state was to be given a quota of energy to be "saved." Each governor was to be free to fashion his own "mix" of conservation measures from those on the federal list. The first senator wished to include among these measures a heavy, even punitive tax on large automobiles. The second senator contended to his friend that in the United States it is the "poor" who drive large automobiles, which use large amounts of gasoline. The "rich" drive small automobiles which use small amounts of gasoline. He was onto something. The higher the income class in the United States at this point in its development, the more conspicuous is *under* consumption. The proposed tax on large automobiles was dropped; the senators turned to other conservation measures.

And so—three themes.

First, the rise of the "universal inter-dependence of nations" (to use a term from the *Manifesto*) has made the American economy far more dependent than it has ever been before on events elsewhere, and these events are not always favorable to American interests. On occasion they are specifically directed against American interests.

Second, external events, as well as internal ones, lead to increasing management of the economy by the federal government, in circumstances which are frequently, at least, unfavorable.

Third, these events take place against a cultural background in which the "leading" economic class is no longer nearly so committed as it once was to increased economic production and consumption—even for itself.

Not for the first time in this essay, problems of evidence arise. What is it that can be said to be *known* about such trends? Little, perhaps. And yet there is an economic culture comparable in its way to the political culture; general propositions which accord with known facts have some potential usefulness in understanding either. Here we find ourselves once again talking about "quality," and there can be no disputing that mostly this is "poor quantification." And yet for the moment there seems no ready alternative. And so to a grand generalization: the American economy is slowing down. A critical choice has already been made to that effect.

That choice has been in evidence since mid-century. Americans do not save. Our investment rate was low then, with only the United Kingdom, among major industrial nations, having one lower. Nothing changed in the years that followed, save that the rate of investment in Japan came to be more than twice that of the United States, which after a point was surpassed even by the United Kingdom.

This is not a new subject, which is what is most significant about it. In 1960, John F. Kennedy, campaigning for the presidency, stated he was not satisfied with the lowest rate of growth among all industrial nations. To change this situation was a central theme of his campaign, and he won his election. But the American position did not really improve. Edward F. Denison cautions that "the extent to which investment ratios are correlated with growth rates of national income or GNP—regardless of the direction of causation—is a matter of dispute."[49] But whether the two are related or not, both investment rates and growth rates have remained quite low. Not as low as in the period immediately before Kennedy took office, but consistently lower than any major industrial nation save Britain. These rates proved indifferent even to a war. (The period 1965-70 had an annual average GNP growth rate of 3.2 percent. Japan—which also benefited from the Vietnam War—grew at 12.1 percent during this same period.) (See Tables XVIII-8; XVIII-9.) Our lagging position has proved impervious alike to campaign rhetoric and presidential initiative. In President Kennedy's first year in office, the American investment rate declined to 13.8 percent, while the Japanese rose to 40.5 percent. (Japan *doubled* its capital plant in the five years 1965-70. [See Figure XVIII-6])

On the surface, there may seem a contradiction between elite deemphasis on consumption and a simultaneous disinclination to save. In the short run there is more to spend on consumption. But in the not very long run a society that reduces its savings reduces its consumption also, as it will eventually produce less than would otherwise be the case. This can be avoided only by increasing productivity. But this we have not done either. In the period 1950-72, real GNP per employed civilian grew at a slower rate than any major industrial country of the West. The contribution of growth in output per employee to real GNP during this period was also lowest in the United States. An event of symbolic and substantive consequence occurred in the late 1960s when output per man-hour in the Japanese iron and steel industry outstripped that in the United States.[50] In 1966-73, as if in anticipation of the "energy crisis," output per man-hour in coal mining actually decreased.[51] Table XVIII-10 suggests the great

Table XVIII-8
Investment Rates* (Selected Years, 1950-1972)

Country	1950	1960	1970	1971	1972
U.S.A.**	19.0%	14.9%	13.9%	14.5%	15.4%
Canada	25.0	23.1	21.3	22.2	22.1
France	19.6	23.9	28.0	27.1	27.1
Germany	22.3	26.9	28.6	27.3	26.5
Italy	NA	23.9	22.7	20.5	20.2
Netherlands	26.4	26.9	25.5	27.0	25.0
Sweden	18.5	25.3	24.7	22.0	22.0
Spain	NA	19.0	23.2	21.3	22.4
United Kingdom	11.2	18.3	18.6	17.9	17.4
Japan	NA	33.8	39.5	36.7	36.6

*Rate of Investment =

$$\frac{\text{Gross fixed capital formation} + \text{Increase in stocks (i.e. non-fixed investments)}}{\text{GNP}}$$

**Investment Rates for the U.S. =

$$\frac{\text{Private investment (exclusive of government gross fixed capital formation)} + \text{Increase in stocks}}{\text{GNP}}$$

Source: *International Financial Statistics*, 1972 Supplement and June 1974 (IMF, Washington, D.C.).

difference between the changes of output per man-hour in different countries. In the third quarter of the twentieth century, output per man-hour in the United States doubled. It quadrupled in most industrial countries; it increased ten times in Japan. Only the United Kingdom "equalled" the American performance.

This situation ought not to be exaggerated. The American economy is the largest in the world, and hardly the least efficient. John W. Kendrick points out that productivity advanced strongly in the early post-war period, and again in 1960-66. There has been, he notes, a significant deceleration in productivity advance" over the recent period 1966-73. But this is only a *deceleration*. In the main, productivity goes on increasing, but not as fast as other nations.[52] Between 1914 and 1974, real income per capita has almost quadrupled. Even at recent rates it will quadruple again in seventy years. What, then, is to be complained about in the performance of the American economy? The answer, simply, is that it *has never solved the problem of achieving and maintaining full employment*. It will not do so in the foreseeable future. Otherwise we are a "people of plenty," and our economy has done wonders for us. But it has not provided enough jobs. Whatever makes for the quality of life, work is for most

Table XVIII-9
Average Annual Growth Rates of Real GNP, Selected Countries (1950-1974)

Country	Percentage Change in Total GNP							
	1950-55	1955-60	1960-65	1965-70	1970-71	1971-72	1972-73	1973-74
United States	4.3	2.2	4.8	3.2	3.3	6.2	5.9	-2.2
Canada	5.4	3.9	5.6	4.8	5.6	5.8	6.8	3.7
France	4.1	5.0	5.7	5.6	5.3	5.7	6.0	4.0
Germany	9.4	7.9	5.0	4.8	3.0	3.4	5.3	0.4
Italy	5.9	5.6	5.3	5.9	1.6	3.1	5.9	5.0
Belgium	3.5	2.6	5.1	4.9	3.5	5.4	5.7	NA
Netherlands	5.3	3.9	4.9	5.6	3.8	4.5	4.7	NA
Denmark	1.9	4.5	5.2	4.5	3.7	4.9	4.0	NA
Norway	3.5	2.8	5.4	4.6	5.5	4.5	3.7	NA
United Kingdom	2.7	2.6	3.3	2.2	2.2	3.0	6.0	-0.2
Japan	9.0	8.9	10.1	12.1	6.8	8.9	10.5	-3.4

Source: Bureau of Labor Statistics, Office of Productivity and Technology (April 22, 1975).

Table XVIII-10

Indexes of Output Per Man-Hour, All Employees in Manufacturing,* Selected Countries [Selected Years, 1950-1974]

(1967 = 100)

Country	1950	1955	1960	1965	1967	1970	1974p
United States	65.2	74.4	80.5	98.7	100.0	107.9	129.2
Canada	52.3	64.2	75.9	94.5	100.0	115.0	135.0
France	43.9	54.2	68.7	88.5	100.0	121.2	151.9
Germany	36.6	48.9	66.4	90.4	100.0	116.6	142.8
Italy	36.5	51.1	65.1	91.6	100.0	117.8	149.4**
Netherlands	42.7	53.4	67.8	87.8	100.0	132.3	170.6**
Sweden	41.7	47.5	63.3	88.5	100.0	124.5	151.8**
United Kingdom	61.9	66.9	76.8	92.4	100.0	109.1	127.3
Japan	21.4	36.0	52.6	79.1	100.0	146.5	199.8

Notes:

   *The measures of output per man-hour in manufacturing refer to the ratios between real GNP originating in manufacturing industries of the economy, and the corresponding hours of manufacturing employees. Output per man-hour indexes are obtained by dividing an output index by an index of aggregate man-hours.

   Though this index tells us how countries are progressing in relation to one another, it does not indicate their absolute standing. Such level comparisons (except for the steel industry, since 1964) do not now exist and cannot be computed on the basis of available data.

**For 1973.

p. Preliminary estimates—those for 1974 being based on data for the full year for the U.S.; eleven months for Canada, Japan, Germany and the United Kingdom; and three quarters for France.

Source: Source: U.S. Department of Labor, Bureau of Statistics, Office of Productivity and Technology, Division of Foreign Labor Statistics and Trade.

men, many women, and most families an absolute essential. Unemployment is the central social disorder of a capitalist, industrialist economy. It is endemic to the American economy.

   Moreover, official expectations about employment—as of almost no other area of national life—become more pessimistic with time. In the immediate aftermath of the Employment Act of 1946 (originally the *Full* Employment Act), it was thought that 3 percent unemployment was an acceptable level. Given the unemployment rates at that time, it was surely a reasonable one. Then came the 1950s, and a long period of economic doldrums following the Korean War. In the early 1960s, the Council of Economic Advisors wished to set 4 percent as an acceptable unemployment rate, but agreed to define this as an "interim" goal. By the 1970s, official economists were setting targets of 6 percent (admittedly, not on a long-term basis—but when does the short-term end?). Since 1950, only when the United States was at war has unemployment

Percent increase per manhour per year

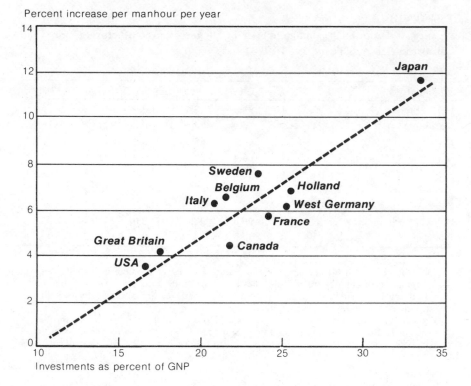

Investments as percent of GNP

Source: Curt Nicolin, "Industry Can Meet the Challenge of the Future," *ASEA International* (Fall 1974), p. 4.

Figure XVIII-6. Production Increases and Investments.

dropped below 4 percent, and only once, in 1953, has it gone below 3 percent. The ratio of unemployment among black and other races to that of whites has been two to one throughout this period. Unemployment rates among teenage minority groups are so outrageous as to suggest an economic system that has collapsed.

To be sure, unemployment in America need not be prolonged. In 1948-73, there were only two years in which more than 2 percent of the work force had been unemployed more than fifteen weeks. Unemployment benefits for workers in some industries can be such as to sustain a long period out of work with no great dislocation, as was shown in 1974-75. Nobody starves. But the impact on the social system and on the quality of life persists. And now the enormous postwar cohort has entered the labor force. The ratio of young workers to older workers—with the young having a disproportionate amount of difficulty—goes up. (Defined as the ratio of workers twenty to thirty-four years old to those thirty-five to fifty-four, the ratio was 0.72 in 1960; by 1972, it had risen to 0.96; by 1980, it is expected to rise to 1.20.[53]) The median age of the labor force declined from forty years to thirty-eight years in the 1960s, and will go down to thirty-five years by 1980. To compound the difficulties of this cohort, it is followed by much smaller cohorts, such that the job opportunities that come from raising young people are necessarily diminished. Present projections see a relatively constant six to seven million persons unemployed from now until 1985. In the 1980s, the number of young persons in the work force will be declining, so that some of the pressure on unemployment rates will ease. Still, the outlook is not good, especially for the unskilled and the inelegant. By 1980, more than half of actual employment will be white collar, only a third blue collar.[54]

Unemployment was the commonplace affliction of industrial democracies everywhere during much of the period preceding the Second World War. Since that time, however, only the United States and Canada have endured high and persistent rates of joblessness. Wars have helped only to bring rates down to levels most industrial nations would regard as unacceptably high. Training programs, job-creating programs have only helped—if at all—to prevent rates from going higher than they would otherwise have done. The problem now is that no one seems to know what to do. In particular economists do not. Those who wish may take exception to this statement, for there is always *somebody* with a plan. But at this point, to seize on any particular proposal or analysis is to court self-deception. Those who thought they knew and in whom confidence was justifiably placed, no longer think they know. Respect is due their judgment now, as in the past.

In the 1968-69 report of the Social Science Research Council, there appeared a general statement of this particular problem:

The difficulty we as a nation face in solving our problems is not will but knowledge. We want to eliminate poverty, crime, drug addiction, and abuse; we want to improve education and strengthen family life, but we do not know how. **** The overwhelming complexity of the nation's social problems and their immediacy . . . should not blind us to our ignorance of ways to solve them.[55]

There is a legitimate sense in which this stalemate has extended beyond social issues, to more general economic issues.

Europeans are accustomed to the idea—some Europeans are—that no social problem is ever solved in the course of a single generation, or even, some say, a single lifetime. But Americans have not been disposed to such passivity, not in any event the managerial Americans who set out to "do" things in postwar America. Amazing things were done. Man landed on the moon. But there were some problems that simply did not yield. It avails but little to say of any particular problem that if *this* were done, and *that* were done, and this *other* measure taken, then all would come right. This and that and the other thing *does not get done*. And seemingly we do not know why.

In 1970, I spoke to this issue, arguing:

The uses of ignorance—acknowledged, understood ignorance—are many, and one can imagine in the decade ahead that social science . . . can help to impose a desperately needed discipline on the way we discuss social issues. . . . If there is a danger that we shall come to think things are too hard, let us be alert for signs thereof. But surely, for the moment, we suffer most from having thought too many things too easy. The result, of course, is the much-heralded crisis in confidence. If you think you know all there is you need to know in order to establish democracy in Southeast Asia, or social stability in the South Bronx, you are likely to make considerably more serious mistakes than would occur if you accept the fact that you don't know very much and aren't going to.[56]

Such counsel is not likely to find wide favor, and has not. Modern man, deprived of the certainty of God, appears to require a great deal of certainty about other, intermediate matters. And so, despite the recent hesitation of economists, the public discourse on the American economy is likely to continue to be a sharp one, as proposals and ideas clash rather than integrate. All the while, unless some welcome deliverance occurs, the situation will appear in one way or another unsatisfactory.

The three tendencies mentioned earlier will almost certainly persist, with the most conspicuous being the third. The American economy was staggered by the quintupled price of oil, and further such blows ought probably to be expected. Certainly there will be other such efforts in other commodities. In any event, the unequal distribution of wealth as among different nations in the world has become politicized. It is now an issue on the basis of which claims can be made by one nation on another, and the heaviest thrust of these claims will be directed against the United States, which for this reason must expect to be a beleaguered and accused society for generations to come. This will expand the role of government. For one thing, merely to cope with the predation of state capitalism abroad—for this is what so many "socialist" economies amount to—will require countervailing measures in the state capitalist mode here at home. The liberal-conservative spectrum gets rather lost in this process, although it will remain a part of the political vocabulary. Leave it that it was a "conservative" administration which first imposed peacetime wage and price controls. But regardless of events abroad, the long-term tendency of political democracies is toward collectivist doctrines of the kind foreseen by Joseph Schumpeter and described by Samuel Beer.

The private sector rarely provides solutions that satisfy everyone, and for those who are dissatisfied it becomes increasingly "respectable" over time to propose that one or another social function be transferred to the public sector. Schumpeter described this in terms of the "conquest" of one sector by another.

Corporate capitalism has few defenses against this. The owners are diffuse, and divided on most issues. The managers have lost the "virtue" of entrepreneurs, and as a class have little access to the intellectuals who create, in Beer's term, the symbols of progress. These symbols are now almost wholly associated with *collective* enterprise. This may be a matter vastly frustrating to those in what might legitimately be called the productive sector of the economy, but little can be done about it; or in any event, about which little is done. Thus Dr. Edwards writes:

... I am convinced that the pluralistic health-care system as we know it in the United States is moving steadily toward its own destruction, not by design, but by default. The failure of the private health sector to accept a leadership responsibility in the allocation of health resources, in controlling the cost and utilization of health services, in making a concerted effort to eliminate care of patently unacceptable quality—all these indicators of a failure of leadership simply nourish the demand for greater federal intervention in and control of the health-care system.[57]

Dr. Edwards is "not at all convinced that the federal government is, or ever will be capable of managing the American health industry," but he sees it coming.

A comparable process led to the regulation of the automobile industry, the largest single sector of the American economy. The issue of design safety was clearly delineated in the 1950s. Had the industry responded on its own, it would have remained unregulated. *It did not.* The system would not work that way: the outcome of federal regulation was ineluctable, and came quickly. Similarly, American capitalism has not been able to create enough jobs to achieve something like full employment. Why this is so is not certain. Somewhere, surely, the interaction between low rates of saving and small changes in productivity, combined with shocks from abroad, does this. It may even be that relative free trade does this. But, whatever the case, free enterprise cannot undo it. The result inevitably—and already much in evidence—is a movement toward job creation by government, a task which it is not likely to do any better than it will do the managing of the health industry. But it is the curious advantage of government in this competition that it can both conceal its inefficiencies and, as an institution, survive them. Dr. Edwards foresees a time when, as a result of government intervention, "the health industry, like the railroads, will have had a glorious past and no future." And yet be clear: even if the railroads eventually shut down, the hospitals will not close. This is the kind of outcome governments *can* avoid.

What is it all about? A pattern, one supposes, of late capitalist development complicated by diversity in the population and a stirring in the world. Institutions seem to mature toward a certain inflexibility; the equivalent of what Veblen called "trained incapacity" in individuals. It must surely arise from the experience of men and women who have for two and three and four generations been removed from what Engels called "the realm of necessity." On the growing edges of society—those occupational groups which increase in size, those educational groups whose number swell—attitudes toward acquisition change. Or in any event, the direction of acquisitiveness changes as a consequence, it may be in part, of what Richard Flacks has termed "the radicalization of educated labor." It is not clear how much basic change has occurred. Alan Marsh has investigated this phenomenon in the United Kingdom. His study, "The 'Silent Revolution,' Value Priorities and the Quality of Life in Britain," comparing "Postbourgeois" (in the main younger and better educated) with "Acquisitives" (those who still see improving their standards of living as a high-order value), found the former to be *more likely* to express dissatisfaction with Material and Security Domains, which is to say their job, their overall standard of living, and their health, than their presumedly more materialistic-minded compatriots. Similarly, the "Postbourgeois" were more likely to express discontent with "Higher-Order" domains, such as leisure, education, and democracy. They were, in sum, rather a discontented lot, and in Marsh's analysis, likely to remain that way, for this discontent was a device of intragenerational aggression.

... Western culture also places a high premium upon worldly intellectualism*** ... A reasonably articulate utterance of radical views can attract to its adherents the desired reputation of intellectualism.*** By appearing to speak against their class interest they may also acquire a reputation for altruism at the same time. These are powerful psychological gains and should not be underestimated. Such gains would certainly ameliorate the sense of power-frustration experienced by many young middle-class Europeans who are excluded from positions of high social respect by what seems to them (probably rightly) to be a mere lack of seniority.[58]

This question is assuredly as yet unresolved in the United States. To repeat, it is not clear how much basic change has occurred. Small automobiles can be means of social aggression as readily as large automobiles if enough "significant others" get the signal. Time tends to settle such issues. The nominally anti-materialist cohorts of the third quarter of the century will come to power in the last quarter—to their share of power. It will be seen what their values turn out to be. Probably they will not prove that different. Yet values have changed before in human history, and the guilt and envy so much abroad in Western culture in recent years may yet bring about profound transformation. The "radicalization of educated labor" may yet leave a permanent impress. (The mixture of the intellectual and the emotional is potent in such groups. In the *Manifesto*, Marx, age thirty, and Engels, twenty-eight, combined the two. In seven paragraphs from a brilliant statement of dialectical materialism, they found room to accuse the bourgeoisie of possessing the wives and daughters of the proletarians, engaging "common prostitutes"—not proletarians they!—and taking "the greatest pleasure in seducing each other's wives.") Society as a theory of crime is not a theme that exhausted itself with Proudhon. And yet it is not clear just how statist the politics of this cohort will eventually turn out to be. But it may very much be doubted that economic growth will be its primary concern.

In any event, concern for the secondary and tertiary effects of economic growth, which has most recently asserted itself as the "environmental movement," will have a sufficient dampening effect on that process. It has, for example, been estimated that the costs of achieving by 1985 the "zero-discharge" standards set by the 1972 Water Pollution Act Amendments will be somewhere between $1 and $2.8 trillion. (Cumulative federal expenditure since 1789 is just over $4 trillion.) These estimates have been challenged, and in the end it is doubtful that zero-discharge standards will ever be fully enforced, if only because of the secondary effects which *environmental* measures have (mainly economic, as when plants close). But a great deal will be spent, and the product will be an enhanced environment—which simply means the nation will have got back to where it once was. Similarly, the enormous investment which will now have to be made in energy production, at most, will only serve—in the coming quarter century—to reestablish the availability of "reasonably" priced energy that existed "naturally" through the first three-quarters of the century. In a word, a good deal of future investment in plant and equipment will do little to increase productive capacity in terms of end products of the economic system. Whatever else that means, it certainly signifies a long period of an economy more than adequate to meet the material needs of the society, but somehow deficient in meeting social needs such as full employment. In part, at least, this will be the result of choices the society has made.

The Critical Choices

This has been an extensive argument: it comes now to a succinct conclusion. There are two critical choices which Americans face concerning the quality of life. These are: How much growth do we want? and How much government do we want?

The reader was forewarned in the abstract which preceded this essay that this would be the conclusion. Many, disappointed, will have stopped at that point. The reader who has persisted is entitled to some explanation as to why so little seeming attention has been paid to subjects that seem far more directly related to those concerns—personal, spiritual—which the term the quality of life clearly seeks to impart. The answer is that such concerns *are* personal and *are* spiritual. They are not of that order of things of which it may be said that collective choices are made. In describing societies, anthropologists, who study man, typically concentrate on sexual practices and religious beliefs. They are studying the quality of lives lived in different civilizations. In a general way it can be said that different peoples in different times and places do make choices. The social anthropologist Joseph Daniel Unwin held, for example, that the levels of energy in a society, and the nature of its religious beliefs also, were largely determined by the degree of sexual opportunity enjoyed by the people. In his view, which he held to be empirical although its theoretical foundations are Freudian, "any limitation or extension of sexual opportunity is seen to have preceded any increase or decrease in the amount of a society's energy."[59] He saw societies as in some way making choices in these matters, which made of the individual, "for the most part, a determined product." (In this sense it may be said that in a democracy the way society chooses leaders and government is something determined for the individual.)

Unwin, whose views would not find wide favor today, would probably judge that American society has made a succession of "choices" to extend sexual opportunities and that in time, now, there should be a pronounced decrease in social energies. Whether he is right or wrong, we see that there is not much on this score that can be usefully put to the nation as a *decision* to be made. Technology, or whatever, has brought on a radical decline in the age of menarche, once in the region of eighteen years, now in the region of twelve. Mores have changed accordingly, the more so as technology has also separated sexual from procreative activity. Even the social decision to legalize abortion (now the second most common operation performed in the United States) probably had only a marginal influence on this large cultural change. Similarly (or conversely!), there are evidences of a certain religious revival among American elites, among which there are those for whom such terms as "reverence for life" have acquired a serious, authentically religious meaning, even as doctrinal restraints in such matters erode in the general populace. But, again, in what sense can the society be called on to choose in such large matters?

The spread of plutonium on the earth, and the prospect that the human species will be destroyed by its own waste is, clearly enough, a choice of large consequence, and will for certain affect the quality of life. So would war. So would various forms of peace. So will the outcome of a truly fateful critical choice which is the decision as to whether we will continue to regard (or, *pace*, commence to regard) political freedom as the principle axis along which our international commitments are made. If we choose otherwise we are almost certain to find ourselves increasingly an isolated and rather singular political society, an outcome which is perhaps not to be avoided in any event. If that should be the outcome, we may be certain that political freedom within the United States will begin to be affected by hostility from without in that regard and the quality of American life will change fundamentally.

Thus the dissociation of domestic and foreign policy which characterized the third quarter of the century will not survive the quarter to come. These are, however, matters beyond the range of this essay. The social choices with which we deal here are both more mundane and more abstract. We may console ourselves for this modesty of objective by the consideration that such matters, if not of the highest seriousness, are serious enough, and that if we choose wisely—if, wisely, we decide to choose—we might somewhat enlarge the opportunities of individuals to make choices for themselves on those highest matters, might somewhat narrow the range in which such individual choices are, in truth, for practical purposes, determined. Hence the issues of growth and government.

Growth is the more critical choice.

It is the singular aspect of the modern condition that growth appears as an option for us. (It may be history's joke that we awoke to the existence of the option at just the moment it was being taken from us, but who can say.) It is clear that for a generation or so Americans have been opting for less growth. We do not save very much. We do not become more efficient at rates other nations maintain. More profoundly, for it says so much more, we have fewer and fewer children, dropping to the point of barely reproducing ourselves. The Census estimates that between now and the year 2000, 27 percent of our population growth will be accounted for by immigration.[60] (There has been an interesting conflict of objectives here. For the longest while "zero population growth" *and* liberalized immigration have coexisted as "progressive" values in the United States.) (See Table XVIII-11.)

However much economic production slows down, we appear likely to add another 60 to 100 million persons to the population in the next half century, and some growth presumedly will be required to care for this not inconsiderable addition. But the real issue of growth involves the provision of employment, and

Table XVIII-11
Estimates and Projections of Total U.S. Population* [Selected Years, 1975-2025]
(numbers in thousands)

Year	Series I (2.7 births per woman)	Series II (2.1 births per woman)	Series III (1.7 births per woman)
1975	213,641	213,450	213,323
1985	241,274	234,068	228,355
2000	287,007	262,494	245,098
2015	342,340	286,960	251,693
2025	382,011	299,713	250,421

*Series I, II and III assume completed cohort fertility rates of 2.7, 2.1 and 1.7 births per woman respectively. The replacement level is 2.1; the 1973 and 1974 level was 1.9.

For all three series, it is assumed that mortality rates will decline slightly until the year 2020 and remain constant thereafter, and that net immigration will total 400,000 per year (which reflects the current level).

Source: U.S. Bureau of the Census, *Current Population Reports,* Series P-25, No. 541 (February 1975).

especially employment for racial and ethnic minorities. This has been a continuing failure of American life, one from which, in this writer's opinion, a myriad range of subsequent failures derives. If we could not provide jobs for black Americans and Hispanic Americans and Appalachian Americans during periods of relatively high growth, what is the evidence that this can be done in a period of prolonged near-stagnation? It may be possible, and yet this is the case that must be proved. For nothing will more pervasively affect the quality of lives of more Americans than prolonged, persistent unemployment. This, unhappily, is not a matter of improving quality nearly so much as preventing a decline.

In the absence of sufficient growth, America's role in the world will be affected, and again for the worse. A nation with a declining economy will have declining influence in the world, not least as it becomes more difficult to provide that bit of surplus in the form of assistance to poor nations which is minimally expected of the rich in the world. And which is little enough. Inequalities of wealth at home and abroad have become politicized: woe to the people who seek to accommodate rising social demands on a declining economic base.

This is a critical choice not least because it is one we are least likely to face. Habits which retard growth are deeply ingrained now, interests which retard growth solidly in place. (When in 1971 the federal government moved to peacetime wage and price controls to get hold of inflation, the new executives found themselves working side by side, in effect, with whole bureaucracies whose federal function was to inflate prices in one economic sector or another.) What is more, knowledge seems for the moment to have run out, or at least confidence in theory has. In such a situation there seems no alternative but to take hold of the issue writ large, and to keep hold, always insisting that a central aspect of the quality of life is at stake here, and that is the issue of providing full employment in an industrial democracy.

The next critical choice is how much government we want.

As with the question of growth, there is obviously a deep-set preference at work which makes for more government. The two choices are related. A polity with a buoyant economy can close defense plants and do without work relief programs. An economy which does not create jobs all but requires that government do so. Similarly, Americans may be said to be ambivalent about growth: wanting it while acting so as not to get as much as they wanted. (All, that is, but a fairly modest-sized echelon of those who truly desire a steady state economy, as J.S. Mills described it. It may be noted that the idea first appears in the high intellectual circles of Victorian Britain.) With government it is rather the opposite, as Lloyd Free long ago demonstrated. Americans will say they do not want an ever-larger government, but for some time have been acting so as to get one. We observed (in my section entitled "What Do We Know?") that the increase in the size of American government has been accompanied by a decline in trust in government. And while this gives us no reason to assume a direct correlation between these contrary movements, neither does it give us any reason to think there is no relation between them at all. Certainly some ambivalence is apparent here as well—forces simultaneously looking to expand government and seeming less than pleased by the consequences of that expansion. This may account for the difficulty we have in acknowledging what has been done: one side of a split political personality does not want it to have been! An element at least in American society finds itself increasingly at odds with government, demanding an end to secrecy, even privacy in government activities, insisting on openness and access. And yet from the same regions of American opinion come demands for more government activity. At almost any point in the political spectrum opinion will be found in favor of cutting some government activities, but increasing others. The natural outcome of democratic bargaining in these situations is more to increase than to decrease.

There is another complication as well. This question of how much government we desire must be posed in a time when we are almost certain to experience further governmental growth. The largest domestic political issue of the last quarter of the twentieth century will be the adequate supply of energy. This problem has been brought about by the actions of governments abroad and will necessarily require a response by government at home. It will present an enormous task of administrative and regulatory organization, and an equally enormous need for government investment or government-directed investment. But the inescapable fact is, that no matter how successful this effort, energy will cost more in the aftermath than it ever did during the period of relatively unregulated, international capitalist control of the market. The more government becomes involved, the scarcer and more expensive energy will become. This has nothing to do with any unique virtues of business or singular disabilities of government—it arises simply from an historical set of conditions and events. But there is no point in not realizing now that the period ahead inevitably invites more discontent with government. It should be made emphatically clear that an increase in government control does not automatically involve an increase in regulation; it just replaces private with public rule making. But it is also clear that the public sector provides a more centralized focus for discontent than does private enterprise in most situations.

As with economic growth, the process of government growth is now so complex and perhaps so little understood as to argue for a fundamentalist's approach. The critical choice in the first instance is how *much* government we want. Until a better indicator is devised, this choice had as well be expressed as a proportion of gross national product. Are we content with a third, or do we wish to go to one-half? Would a quarter be better? Two-thirds? The allocation of activities within these proportions is a secondary question, for all the attention it attracts. If we have learned one thing from the twentieth century, it is that the modern state has surprisingly similar effects on the individual as it moves from minimal concern to total involvement. The critical choice is not what it does, but how much it does. At the one-third mark, it would seem time Americans faced up to the choice.

This necessarily—some will say willfully—speculative final section must conclude on a yet more ruminative note. It is at least possible that a declining rate of growth in the American economy or, at any event, an unsatisfactory and uneven pattern of growth is significantly responsible for the growth of government, while the growth of government is significantly responsible for the declining rate of growth—such that an unstable situation has arisen. The evidence that would prove or disprove this proposition is simply not at hand. It is raised not least in the hope that the thought might spur specific investigation.

Certainly there are nations with lower rates of growth and larger governments; larger rates of growth and lesser governments; lesser and lesser; larger and larger. Few would wish to state that there is an optimal mix. In any event, the American experience at the interface of the government and the economy is unique, or nearly so. It is, by tradition, singularly an adversary relation where business enterprise is concerned, as perhaps nowhere better demonstrated than in the unending accusations of special interests and favoritism. The exceptionally cooperative relations of modern Japan, for example, are rare in the United States. Our situation is ours alone, or nearly so, and it is for us to make the best of it.

The great economist Alfred Marshall laid down the guidelines, as it were, for finding a satisfactory balance.

Government is the most precious of human possessions; and no care can be too great to be spent on enabling it to do its work in the best way: a chief condition to that end is that it should not be set to work for which it is not specially qualified, under the conditions of time and place.

There are those who will view such views as threatening to progressive causes. To them, the most that can be said is that theirs is a minority view today, and would have been at any time in the history of the republic, and at no time more than the years of its founding, and among no group more than the founders themselves. A 1973 Harris survey, commissioned by the Congress, set forth the public view in fairly explicit terms. State and local government was seen in generally favorable terms. But only 23 percent of the population thought that the federal government had improved their lives, while 37 percent thought it had made their lives worse. Only 32 percent wanted to increase the power of the federal government, while 42 percent wished to decrease its power.[61] Here the term "only" may be misleading. The more significant fact is that the public is split as between those who wish for more government and those who desire the opposite, with barely a quarter of the population more or less content with the present situation. This is surely, then, a critical choice, and one must assure it is seen as having implications for the economy as well, and in impossibly complex ways. (Some will want more government controls to prevent the increase of pollution; others more government stimulation to production of whatever kind that produces jobs. Some will want less government so there can be more production that will create jobs that are by definition productive, regardless of secondary consequences—or with the most meticulous concern for them.)

There is less likelihood just now than at almost any time in the past two generations that Americans might tend "to exaggerate the role of intelligence in social direction." The more likely failing is that we should underestimate this role, or possible role, for there are some questions here which can be examined, with an eye to presenting the public with meaningful and feasible choices. This would be pardonable. What would be unpardonable would be to underestimate the intelligence, resilience, and fortitude of the American people in facing up to such choices.

Notes

1. *Familiar Letters of John Adams and His Wife Abigail Adams, During the Revolution. With a Memoir of Mrs. Adams by Charles Francis Adams* (Boston: Houghton Mifflin Co., 1875), p. 381.

2. Richard K. Arnold (ed.), *Adams to Jefferson & Jefferson to Adams, A Dialogue From Their Correspondence* (San Francisco: Arnold & Palmer & Noble, 1975), pp. 3, 8.

3. Executive Office of the President: Office of Management and Budget, *Social Indicators*, 1973 (Washington, D.C.: U.S. Government Printing Office, 1973).

4. Report of the President's Research Committee on Social Trends, *Recent Social Trends*, Vol. 1 (New York: McGraw-Hill Book Company, Inc., 1933), p. lxxiv.

5. Ibid., p. lxxiv.

6. Ibid., p. xxix.

7. Ibid., p. lxxv.

8. Ibid., p. v.

9. Ibid., p. xxxv.

10. Ibid., pp. xiii-xiv.

11. Karl Marx and Frederick Engels, *Manifesto of the Communist Party* (London: Lawrence and Wishart, 1943), p. 24.

12. *Recent Social Trends*, Vol. 1, p. xiv.

13. Copyright 1960, The New Yorker Magazine. Reprinted with permission.

14. The American Assembly, Columbia University, *Goals for Americans* (n.c.: A Spectrum Book, Prentice-Hall, Inc., 1960), p. 3.

15. Ibid., p. 4.

16. *Recent Social Trends*, Vol. 1, p. lxxv.

17. Albert H. Cantril and Charles W. Roll, Jr., *Hopes and Fears of the American People* (New York: Universe Books, 1971).

18. Herbert Stein and Edward F. Denison, "High Employment and Growth in the American Economy," in *Goals for Americans*. The Commission report itself foresaw a growth rate of 3.4 percent.

19. Figures derived from U.S. Department of Commerce, *The National Income and Product Accounts 1929-1965* and *Survey of Current Business*, Vol. 54, No. 7 (July 1974), Table 6.5.

20. *Goals for Americans*, p. 6.

21. Ibid., p. 6.

22. National Center for Education Statistics, *The Condition of Education*, 1975 edition (Washington, D.C., U.S. Government Printing Office, 1975), p. 192, Table 69.

23. Report of the National Goals Research Staff, *Toward Balanced Growth: Quantity with Quality* (Washington, D.C., U.S. Government Printing Office, 1970), p. 221.

24. Ibid., p. 3.

25. Ibid., pp. 26-28.

26. Institute for Social Research, University of Michigan, *ISR Newsletter* 1, 14 (Spring 1972): 3. Reprinted with permission.

27. Ibid., p. 3. Reprinted with permission.

28. Lee J. Cronbach, "Five Decades of Public Controversy Over Mental Testing," *American Psychologist* 3, 1 (January 1975): 12. Copyright 1975 by the American Psychological Association. Reprinted by permission.

29. William Watts and Lloyd A. Free (eds.), *State of the Nation* (New York: Universe Books, 1973), p. 27.

30. *Recent Social Trends*, Vol. 1, p. lxxv.

31. Neil J. Smelser, "The End of Growth in California Higher Education," *Bulletin of the American Academy of Arts and Sciences* 28, 8 (May 1975): 33.

32. Figures derived from U.S. Bureau of the Census, *1970 Census*, "General Population Characteristics: U.S. Summary," PC(1)-B1; *Current Population Reports*, P-25, No. 519 and No. 541.

33. National Center for Health Statistics, *Monthly Vital Statistics Report* 23, 11 (January 30, 1975): 6, Table 1.

34. U.S. Bureau of the Census, *Socioeconomic Status*, 1960 Census, Subject Reports PC(2)-5C, p. 47, Table 3, and p. 60, Table 5.

35. Unpublished data derived from U.S. Bureau of the Census, *Current Population Report*, Series P-60, No. 97 (January 1975), Table 11.

36. *Manifesto of the Communist Party*, p. 26.

37. *Wall Street Journal*, January 20, 1976.

38. Bureau of the Census, *The Social and Economic Status of the Black Population in the United States 1974*, p. 3.

39. Henry Jones Ford, *The Rise and Growth of American Politics* (New York: The Macmillan Company, 1898), p. 299.

40. Woodrow Wilson, *Constitutional Government in the United States* (New York: Columbia University Press, 1921), p. 210. Copyright 1908.

41. Nancy L. Worthington, "National Health Expenditures," *Social Security Bulletin* 38, 2 (February 1975), Table 1.

42. U.S. Department of Health, Education and Welfare, "Executive Summary of the Forward Plan for Health for Fiscal Year 1976-1980" (unpublished), prepared under the direction of Dr. Charles C. Edwards, pp. 2-3.

43. Joseph P. Newhouse, Charles E. Phelps, and William B. Schwartz, "Policy Options and the Impact of National Health Insurance," *New England Journal of Medicine* 290, 24 (June 13, 1974): 1352.

44. Charles C. Edwards, "The Federal Involvement in Health." Reprinted, by permission, from the *New England Journal of Medicine* (Vol. 292; pp. 560-61, 1975).

45. Ernest Holsendolph, "Beame Bids U.S. Operate All Projects to Aid Income," *New York Times* (May 1, 1975), p. 26.

46. Social Security Administration, *Social Security Bulletin* 38 (January 1975): 19.

47. Morgan Reynolds and Eugene Smolensky, "The Post Fisc Distribution: 1961 and 1970 Compared," *National Tax Journal* 27, 4 (December 1974): 519.

48. *Manifesto of the Communist Party*, p. 19.

49. Edward F. Denison, *Why Growth Rates Differ* (Washington, D.C.: The Brookings Institution, 1967), p. 121, footnote 11.

50. U.S. Department of Labor, Bureau of Labor Statistics, *Productivity: An International Perspective*, Bulletin 1811 (1974), p. 15, Chart 7.

51. Bureau of Labor Statistics, *Current Developments in Productivity, 1973-74*, Report 346 (1975), p. 20, Chart 4.

52. John W. Kendrick, "Productivity Issues," *Trade, Inflation & Ethics* (Lexington, Mass.: D.C. Heath and Co., 1976).

53. Denis F. Johnston, "Population and Labor Force Projections," *Monthly Labor Review* 96, 12 (December 1973): 10.

54. Bureau of Labor Statistics, *Occupational Manpower and Training Needs*, Bulletin 1824 (Revised 1974), p. 9, Chart 2.

55. Social Science Research Council, *Annual Report 1968-1969* (New York, no publisher, 1969), p. 15.

56. Daniel P. Moynihan, "Eliteland," *Psychology Today* 4, 4 (September 1970): 68. Reprinted with permission.

57. Edwards, "Federal Involvement in Health." Reprinted, by permission, from the *New England Journal of Medicine* (Vol. 292; pp. 561-62, 1975).

58. Alan Marsh, "The 'Silent Revolution,' Value Priorities, and the Quality of Life in Britain," *The American Political Science Review* 69, 1 (March 1975): 30. Reprinted with permission.

59. Joseph Daniel Unwin, *Sexual Regulations and Cultural Behavior* (Trono, California: Frank M. Darrow, 1969), p. 27. Lecture before the British Psychological Society, 1935.

60. Figures derived from U.S. Bureau of the Census, *Current Population Reports*, Series P-25, No. 541 (February 1975), and unpublished data.

61. Louis Harris and Associates, *Confidence and Concern: Citizens View American Government*, U.S. Senate, Committee on Government Operations, 93rd Congress, 1st Session, December 3, 1973. (Washington, D.C.: U.S. Government Printing Office, 1973), pp. 233 and 299.

Index

Index

Aberle, David, 110

Abortion, 327-329, 456; legislation, 328-329

Accidents, and behavior modification, 322-323

Adams, John, 90, 401-402

Aeverlino, Antonio di Piero, 393

Aid to Dependent Children (ADC). *See* Welfare

Aid to Families with Dependent Children (AFDC). *See* Welfare

Alcoholism, and behavior modification, 321-323

Alienation, 92-93, 129; and "disaffection," 165

American Revolution, and religion, 81-84

Americans, affluence, 153, 159, 163, 177; culture, 102-103, 109-114; family structure, 46-47; morale, 50-51, 143-144, 164-168; on quality of life, 1-2, 69; pluralism, 48-50, 83, 88, 116, 132, 400, 421-428

Anthropology, and quality of life, 99-121

Architects, European, 377

Architecture, and abstract art, 377; International Style, 377-378; community standards, 169, 390-391; federal buildings, 386-388; and human needs, 375-377; and taxes, 389, 390, 391

"Archologies," Paolo Soleri, 381

Arendt, Hannah, 94

Aristotle, 58-72

Art, federal aid, 391-392; and neighborhood identity, 386; and technology, 377

Artificial insemination. *See* Reproductive Engineering

Artists, and architecture, 377

Ashby, Eric, 190, 192, 194, 207

Attitude, public, 412-417; to government services, 178; to housing, 171-172, 384; to occupation, 403. *See also* National morale

Automobile, and transportation policy, 33, 34; credit repossession, 354-355; design safety regulation, 453

Beecher, Lyman, 84

Beer, Samuel, 452

Behavior modification, 322-323, 338-340

Bellah, Robert, 89

Bible, 399

Biomedical ethics, 317-318, 319, 321-322, 332-333; and abortion, 329; and privacy, 341; and prolonging life, 326; of research, 325

About the Authors

EDWARD J. LOGUE is visiting professor at the Department of City and Regional Planning, University of Pennsylvania. He has had a distinguished career in urban affairs, serving as president and chief executive officer of the New York State Urban Development Corporation and development administrator of the Boston Redevelopment Authority and the city of New Haven. He was chairman of the New York City task force that authored the report, "Let There Be Commitment." He was also principal planning consultant to Robert F. Kennedy's Bedford-Stuyvesant Project and the Fort Lincoln New Town.

WERNER J. DANNHAUSER is an associate professor of government at Cornell University and a former editor of *Commentary*. He is the author of *Nietzsche's View of Socrates* and is a contributor to *Commentary, Judaism, American Political Science Review, National Review,* and *American Scholar.*

EDWIN SCOTT GAUSTAD is a professor of history at the University of California at Riverside. His research and writing lies chiefly in the area of America's religious history. His most recent volume is *Dissent in American Religion.*

JAMES P. SPRADLEY is professor of anthropology at Macalester College. An urban anthropologist he has written on bums in *You Owe Yourself a Drunk: An Ethnography of Urban Nomads* and female college students in *The Cocktail Waitress: Woman's Work in a Man's World.* His *Guests Never Leave Hungry: The Autobiography of a James Sewid, a Kwakiutl Indian* reported his research among the Kwakiutl of British Columbia.

PETER L. BERGER is professor of sociology at Rutgers University. He is the author of *Pyramids of Sacrifice: Political Ethics and Social Change*, and coauthor (with Brigitte Berger and Hansfried Kellner) of *The Homeless Mind—Modernization and Consciousness.*

WILLIAM H. OVERHOLT is a political sociologist specializing in political development, Asian politics and foreign policy. He has served on the Hudson Institute research staff since 1971. He is also research associate at Columbia University and editor of *International Change.*

HERMAN KAHN is founding director of the Hudson Institute. A physicist and specialist in public policy analyses, Mr. Kahn is a pioneer and leader in the new field of "futurology" and devotes much of research to long-term cultural, economic, political and technological change. Among his many books and articles are *Thinking About the Unthinkable, The Year 2000, Can We Win in Vietnam, The Emerging Japanese Superstate—Challenge and Response*, and *Things to Come*.

ANGUS CAMPBELL is a director of the Institute for Social Research at the University of Michigan and professor of psychology and sociology. He is a member of the Policy and Planning Board of the American Psychology Association and the Panel on the Significance of Community in the Metropolitan Environment of the National Academy of Science. Among his recent articles and books are *The Human Meaning of Social Change* and *White Attitudes Toward Black People*.

ROBERT L. KAHN is director of the University of Michigan's Survey Research Center and a professor in the University's Department of Psychology. He has been a visiting professor at the University of Cambridge, England, and Massachusetts Institute of Technology. He is a member of the editorial boards of the *Journal of Applied Behavioral Sciences, Journal of Applied Social Psychology*, and *Occupational Mental Health*.

DAVID PIERPONT GARDNER is president of the University of Utah and professor of higher education at the university. He is a former vice president for extended academic and public service programs at the University of California and professor of higher education at the University's Santa Barbara Campus. He is a member of the American Association for Higher Education, the American Association of University Professors, and the Presidents Council of the National Association of State Universities and Land-Grant Colleges. A prolific writer, Dr. Gardner is the author of *The California Oath Controversy*.

WILLIAM E. WEBSTER is deputy superintendent for programs in the California State Department of Education. He has been a teacher and principal at both elementary and secondary levels in California and Massachusetts. His professional experience has also included a research role with the Washington Center for Metropolitan Studies, faculty positions at the Catholic University of America and Harvard, and directorship of Project Redesign in the New York State Education Department. He is the author of numerous articles on education, organizations, and change.

ROBERT DUBIN is professor of sociology and administration at the Graduate School of Administration, University of California at Irvine. He is a former Senior Fulbright Research Fellow, Guggenheim Fellow, and Fellow of the Center for Advanced Study in the Behavioral Sciences. He is the author of eight books, including *Human Relations in Administration, Theory Building,* and *Handbook of Work, Organization and Society.*

RICHARD P. NATHAN is director of the Brookings Institution revenue sharing studies and secretary-treasurer of Manpower Demonstration Research Corporation. He is a former deputy undersecretary of the Department of Health, Education and Welfare and assistant director of the Office of Management and Budget. Dr. Nathan is the author of *The Plot That Failed: Nixon and the Administrative Presidency* and *Monitoring Revenue Sharing* (with Allen D. Manvel and Susannah E. Calkins).

ROBERT M. BALL is a senior scholar at the Institute of Medicine, National Academy of Sciences. He was U.S. Commissioner of Social Security for nearly eleven years. Before that Mr. Ball, as a senior Civil Servant, was active in the planning and administration of social security from 1939 on. During a brief absence from the Executive Branch, he served as director of the Advisory Council on Social Security to the U.S. Senate Finance Committee in 1947-48. He was staff director of a study of pensions in the United States for the National Planning Association in 1952.

GILBERT S. OMENN is associate professor of medicine at the University of Washington. He has been a research fellow at the Woods Hole Oceanographic Institution, the Weizmann Institute of Science in Israel, and the National Institutes of Health. In 1973-74, he was a White House Fellow, working on national and international energy issues. He is the author of over sixty scientific and medical papers and is the editor of two books: *Nature and Nurture in Alcoholism* and *Genetics, Environment and Behavior: Implications for Educational Policy.*

BESS MYERSON is the former Commissioner of the Department of Consumer Affairs of New York City. She is continuing her advocacy for a responsible marketplace as consultant to both consumer and industrial groups. Ms. Myerson is a syndicated newspaper columnist, specializing in consumer and community problems; a contributing editor to *Redbook* magazine, and a commentator for radio and television public service and information programs.

PAUL H. WEAVER is associate editor of *Fortune* magazine. His writings deal with American politics, government, the press, and business. He is a former assistant professor of government at Harvard University and was associate editor of *The Public Interest* magazine.

WOLF VON ECKARDT is the architecture critic and an editorial writer for *The Washington Post*. He has contributed articles on architecture, design, and urban affairs to such magazines as *The New Republic, Harper's, Saturday Review*, and *Horizon*, as well as numerous anthologies. His books include *Bertolt Brecht's Berlin: A Scrapbook of the Twenties* (with Sander L. Gilman), *A Place to Live: The Crisis of the Cities*, and *Eric Mendelsohn* in the Masters of World Architecture series.

CHARLES H. MALIK, educator, philosopher and world citizen is a distinguished professor of philosophy at the American University of Beirut, Lebanon. He was president of the thirteenth session of the United Nations General Assembly and president of the UN Security Council. He has served as minister of foreign affairs and minister of national education and fine arts of Lebanon and as director of the Woodrow Wilson Foundation. He has been decorated by the governments of Lebanon, Italy, Jordan, Syria, Iraq, Cuba, Iran, Brazil, Dominican Republic, Austria, Greece, and Nationalist China.

DANIEL P. MOYNIHAN is the former United States Permanent Representative to the United Nations. He served as assistant secretary of labor from 1963 to 1965, Counselor to the president from 1969 to 1971 and Ambassador to India from 1973 to 1975. He is professor of government at Harvard University. He is coauthor of *Beyond the Melting Pot* and author of *The Politics of a Guaranteed Income* and *Coping: Essays in the Practice of Government*.